Hispanic
NEW YORK

D0735222

Hispanic NEW YORK

A SOURCEBOOK

EDITED BY

CLAUDIO IVÁN REMESEIRA

Columbia University Press *NEW YORK*

Columbia University Press

Publishers Since 1893

New York Chichester, West Sussex

Copyright © 2010 Columbia University Press

"Introduction: New York City and the Emergence of a New Hemispheric Identity,"

"A Splendid Outsider: Archer Milton Huntington and the Hispanic Heritage in the United States,"

and "Carlos Gardel in New York: The Birth of a Hispanic-American Myth"

copyright © 2010 Claudio Iván Remeseira

All rights reserved

Library of Congress Cataloging-in-Publication Data

Hispanic New York: a sourcebook / edited by Claudio Iván Remeseira.

p.   cm.

Includes index.

ISBN 978-0-231-14818-4 (cloth: alk. paper)—ISBN 978-0-231-14819-1 (pbk.: alk. paper)

1. Hispanic Americans—New York (State)—New York—History—Sources.   2. New York

(N.Y.)—History—Sources.   I. Remeseira, Claudio Iván.   II. Title.

F128.9.S75H57   2010

974.7'10468073—dc22

2009043745

Casebound editions of Columbia University Press books

are printed on permanent and durable acid-free paper.

Printed in the United States of America

c 10 9 8 7 6 5 4 3 2 1

p 10 9 8 7 6 5 4 3 2 1

References to Internet Web sites (URLs) were accurate at the time of writing.

Neither the author nor Columbia University Press is responsible for Web sites that may have expired or changed since the book was prepared.

To my mother

CONTENTS

PEOPLE AND COMMUNITIES

HISTORICAL PERSPECTIVES

PERSPECTIVES ON RACE, ETHNICITY, AND RELIGION

Two
CULTURAL HYBRIDIZATIONS

LANGUAGE AND LITERATURE: A BILINGUAL TRADITION

FOREWORD

Sometimes a new anthology can be more than a convenient assemblage of previously scattered documents. I think of *The Puritans* (1938), edited by Perry Miller and Thomas H. Johnson, which permanently changed the way we understand the legacy of early New England to American culture, or *Understanding Poetry* (published in the same year), edited by Cleanth Brooks and Robert Penn Warren, which influenced—even controlled—how poetry was read and taught for decades.

Claudio Iván Remeseira's *Hispanic New York* is such a book. Most—or at least too many—Americans still think of "the Spanish element of our Nationality" (Walt Whitman's phrase) as an alien subculture within a "mainstream" America formed exclusively by English-speaking settlers and their descendants. Sometimes this view entails a candid or covert hostility to putative "newcomers," and, even in the absence of such attitudes, it is a destructively partial view of our history to imagine that America has ever been purely "Anglo"—or, for that matter, purely anything.

Whitman used the phrase in a letter to the people of New Mexico on the occasion of the 333d anniversary of the founding of the city of Santa Fe—a fact that should remind us that the Hispanic presence in some parts of what today is the United States predates the arrival of the first British colonists by a full century.

Before and since Whitman wrote, relations between the United States and the Spanish-speaking nations to its south have, of course, been exploitative, vexed, and sometimes violent. Nearly two centuries ago, the U.S. vastly enlarged its territorial expanse as a result of war with Mexico, and today our relations with such neighbor nations as Cuba and Venezuela, to name only two, remain tense and fraught.

But it is also true that the flow of political, artistic, and literary ideas between North and South America has never been one way, and that their relation has never been purely oppositional. Anyone who reads this book will see with new clarity that the notion of a sharp boundary between "Anglo" and "Hispanic" America is a fantasy that should have been dispensed with long ago.

We are living at a time when that fantasy is finally giving way to a more nuanced appreciation of mutual influence, merging, and transformation. Hispanic Americans—notably the first Hispanic justice to sit on the U.S. Supreme Court, Sonia Sotomayor—have emerged as leading figures in all sectors of American life, while some of our major cities (Miami and Los Angeles are most commonly cited) have become indisputable world centers of Hispanic culture.

In this book—through his introduction as well as in the headnotes and deftly juxtaposed selections—Claudio Remeseira, an Argentine-born writer who now lives in upper Manhattan, makes a passionate case that, of all cities in the United States, none has contributed more to this creative ferment than Whitman's beloved city of New York.

Reading *Hispanic New York* is an experience of instructive delight.

Andrew Delbanco
Director, American Studies
Columbia University
October 2009

NOTE ON THE SELECTIONS

Hispanic New York: A Sourcebook is an anthology of scholarly, autobiographical, journalistic, and literary essays aiming to serve as a reference and course book for college
and high school students, teachers, scholars, librarians, and the general public. Based
on a selection of readings assembled for a seminar that I have cotaught since 2006
with Roosevelt Montás at Columbia University's American Studies Program, the book
is conceived as a companion volume to *Hispanic New York: A Cultural Guide*, a collection of original essays, also to be published by Columbia University Press, that will
highlight the main contributions made by people of Hispanic descent to New York's
multicultural heritage. Although some of the selections are taken from books available in bookstores and others are staples in college and high school course syllabi,
many are either out of print or not easily accessible. By bringing them all together into
one volume, I hope to provide an educational service and help disseminate valuable
works otherwise confined to a more restricted audience.

As is the case with any anthology, there will inevitably be criticism concerning
which texts are included—and, even more, which are *not* included. My first caveat in
this regard is purely physical—limitation of space. The original seminar's reader was
almost twice as large as the present volume, but reasons of publishing feasibility marked
a limit of pages to the printed version. A second caveat, partly derived from the first, is
that except in one case—Bernardo Vega's memoirs—my decision was to present the
selections as they originally appeared, with no abridgments. That meant leaving out
pieces that might have rightly belonged into this sourcebook but that were too long to
be included without crowding out other selections and thus affecting the volume's balance. For the same reason, I decided to leave out works of fiction or poetry—however
relevant the samples chosen might have been, the result would inevitably have been
unfair, with the majority excluded.

One purpose of the further reading list is to counterbalance those unavoidable
omissions. That list follows the same structure of the book's table of contents, and in
conjunction with the works cited at the end of each selection it provides the reader

with a comprehensive bibliographical guide to supplement and update the information covered in this book. We have included many examples of the vast English- and Spanish-language literary corpus produced by people of Hispanic descent who wrote in or about New York as well as a number of important secondary sources on that literature. Similarly, the index of names organizes the wealth of historical information contained in this volume by offering a sort of directory of the city's centuries-long Hispanic culture.

The issues addressed by the selections cut across a huge range of academic areas, including Latino/a, Latin American, and American studies; English, Spanish, and comparative literature; U.S., Latin American, and Caribbean history; studies on race and ethnicity; and an array of disciplines spanning the humanities and social sciences, from anthropology, urban studies, and political science to sociolinguistics, ethnomusicology, and art history. As I mention in my introductory essay, much of today's research is conducted within analytical frameworks developed in the last few decades under the impact of what is broadly termed poststructural, postmodern, and postcolonial theories—a constellation of multidisciplinary approaches to the construction, contestation, and interaction of national, ethnic, gender, and sexual identities and subjectivities, as well as to the dynamics of borders, diasporas, and migrations, all of these in the transnational context created by globalization and by the dissolution of modern Western empires. In the U.S. academy these intellectual endeavors often fall into the omnivorous field of cultural studies, spawning not only new research agendas but also the institutional alliances necessary to foster them. The endeavors of which are reflected in a stream of new publications and research projects that overlap with those traditionally devoted to specific national-origin communities.[1]

This book does not attempt to represent those agendas. Its modest goal is to offer a collection of texts that are required readings for any informed conversation on these issues, and to present other, less well-known texts in the hope that they will call attention to some overlooked historical characters and links. In any case, along with the list of further reading, the index of subjects has been devised to optimize the search for concepts scattered throughout the different selections that are relevant to those academic debates.

Three scholarly initiatives merit special mention. Appearing in the *annus terribilis* 2001 and also published by Columbia University Press, *Mambo Montage: The Latinization of New York* is a major contribution to our subject. Edited by Agustín Laó-Montes and Arlene Dávila, this anthology mustered some of the most thought-provoking and in-depth research done on these topics until that moment. The contributors ranged from well-known authorities such as Juan Flores to up-and-coming authors like Raquel Z. Rivera; many of them, including the editors, would publish important titles of their own in the following years. Laó-Montes's introductory essay—in particular, his analysis of the construction of Latino identities and discourses, and his elaboration on the concepts of landscapes of power and translocation—is an inevitable reference for any serious discussion on this field.

Latinos in New York: Communities in Transition, edited by Gabriel Haslip-Viera and Sherrie L. Baver, was also originally developed for the classroom. Published more than a decade ago, this landmark anthology—of which two essays are included in the pres-ent volume—remains an exemplary case of multidisciplinary empirical-science approach to the demographic, educational, religious, cultural, labor, and political aspects of New York's highly diversified Hispanic population. As in the previous anthology, many of its essays anticipated future books, among them Clara Rodríguez's *Changing Race* and Robert C. Smith's *Mexicans in New York.*

Finally, we must mention the Recovering the U.S. Hispanic Literary Heritage Proj-ect (RUSHLH), a nationwide initiative to locate, preserve and disseminate written tes-timonies of the country's Latino cultures since colonial times. Over the last fifteen years RUSHLH has compiled around seventeen thousand records of books and pam-phlets, a microfilm collection of approximately nine hundred items, and a vast collec-tion of photographs. Through its sister organization, Arte Público Press, RUSHLH has republished many of those original works, including some authored by historic New York figures such as Father Félix Varela or the brothers Jesús and Joaquín Colón as well as nineteenth- and twentieth-century newspaper collections such as *El Laúd del Des-terrado* and *Pueblos Hispanos.* Arte Público Press is also the publisher of *Recovering the U.S. Hispanic Literary Heritage*, a six-volume (and counting) series of critical es-says by the most well-respected specialists, which has been instrumental in rescuing from oblivion the names of Cirilo Villaverde, Luisa Capetillo, and Virginia de Peña de Bordas—to mention just a few of those connected with New York—among the many Hispanics who made part of the history of the United States and the Americas. Hosted by the University of Houston and directed by New York–born Nicolás Kanellos, RUSHLH is in itself an embodiment of the Hispanic national spirit.

Despite all these remarkable efforts, there is still a big gap between the relatively small circle of scholars, cultural activists, and enthusiasts who are familiar with this heritage and the broader national community that remains largely unaware of it. To help bridge that gap is the main purpose of this book.

THE SELECTIONS

Part 1 of this volume, "People and Communities," presents an overview of the historical development of New York's Hispanic population over the past two centuries as well as a discussion of key racial and ethnic issues. Gabriel Haslip-Viera surveys the successive immigration waves from Latin America and the Caribbean to the New York area from the early nineteenth century to the 1990s, describing them in the context of the political and economic relations between the United States and the countries of origin. The census charts in the article demonstrate how, through the incorporation of new constituencies, a core Hispanic community expanded over that period until eventually changing its overall configuration, but without loosing traces of its past.

The next two selections belong to Cuban patriot, journalist, and poet José Martí. To choose what to include in this anthology from his vast output—largely written in New York during his exile from 1880 to 1895—was not an easy decision. One text was mandatory: "Our America," Marti's manifesto of Latin American cultural and political independence. "A Vindication of Cuba," Martí's only piece of journalism published in the English-language press during his lifetime, is a spirited rebuttal of the racist attacks against Cubans published by a Philadelphia newspaper in 1889; the striking similarity between those attacks and the anti-immigrant rants voiced by some media celebrities today proves the relevance of this piece for contemporary readers.

Published posthumously by César Andreu Iglesias and translated into English by Juan Flores, the memoirs of Puerto Rican union activist Bernardo Vega are one of the fundamental sources for the history of the Hispanic communities of New York at the turn of the twentieth century. Vega's firsthand account of the life in Spanish Harlem during those years, the interaction between Puerto Ricans, Cubans, Spaniards, and Sephardic Jews, and the community's social and political struggles constitute an invaluable testimony of that era. Jack Agüeros's autobiographical piece expands Vega's everyday-life depiction of El Barrio into the 1940s, right before the Great Migration that turned Hispanic New York into a distinctively Puerto Rican city.

Roberto Suro's *Strangers Among Us* is another of the most-cited books in Latino studies bibliographies; its chapter titled "New York: Teetering on the Heights" is our next selection. In forceful journalistic prose, Suro celebrates Dominicans' hardworking, entrepreneurial, and life-loving nature, without shying away from describing other conflicting aspects of the history of this Upper Manhattan enclave. Many readers will rightly object to what one critic described as Suro's unquestioned reproduction of the culture-of-poverty argument, the notion that inner-city populations—basically African Americans and Latinos—are doomed to welfare dependence because of some culturally determined inability to prosper in a capitalistic society.[2] That critic notwithstanding, I believe Suro's dynamic narrative will engage the reader and also guarantee a fruitful debate over the contested topics of drug trafficking and poverty in the inner city.

"The Hispanic Impact Upon the United States," by Theodore S. Beardsley, developed from a script written by the author for a TV series on immigration produced in 1973 by CBS and Saint John's University Television Center. Although not exclusively focused on New York, this monographic essay merits inclusion for several reasons. First, it is a fine example of the awareness among many non-Latino scholars like Beardsley (a former director of the Hispanic Society of America) of the nation's Hispanic heritage, an awareness that goes back, as mentioned in the introduction, at least to the Romantic generation. Second, it is a timely reminder that the Hispanic presence in the Western Hemisphere—including North America—predated, by more than a century, the arrival of the first British colonists; reintroducing this essay to the general public will hopefully contribute to place the current immigration debate in a long overdue, larger historical perspective. Third, it highlights the role of cultural hemispheric and transatlantic bridge played for more than a century by the Hispanic Society of America, one of the older New York institutions dedicated to the collection of Spanish art and documentation of Latin America's literary history.

Virginia Sánchez Korrol's selection is a perfect match for Beardsley's. If the Hispanic heritage was ignored for decades by the U.S. cultural establishment, women's place in that heritage endured a double silencing—not just from the mainstream society but from within their own community as well. Sánchez Korrol is one of the scholars who has made the most groundbreaking efforts to correct those gender inequalities. Her essay—a sample of the information collected for *Latinas in the United States: A Historical Encyclopedia*, coedited with Vicki L. Ruiz—reconstructs the historical line that connects women like María Amparo Ruiz de Burton, Emilia Casanova de Villaverde, Luisa Capetillo, and Antonia Pantoja—a two-century-long struggle for social justice, community empowerment, and popular education.

The selection closing the first part of this volume contains what is arguably one of the most compelling arguments ever made in defense of the Hispanic contribution to the American nationality, written by the quintessential American (and New Yorker) poet, Walt Whitman. In just around six hundred words, Whitman laid out what might also be considered the rationale for a hybrid hemispheric identity, the "composite identity" of the future—and established a surprising, vibrant, and unfinished dialogue with José Martí's "Our America."

The next three selections constitute a sort of modulatory transition between the book's main parts; the first two of them, in particular, put Whitman's prediction to the test. Clara Rodríguez's essay is a concise introduction to the racialized status of Hispanics in the United States vis-à-vis Latin American racial classification systems as well as to some classic social science approaches to these issues; the author also elaborates on the impact that Latino immigration will have on the country's predominantly white-black racial self-perception. Milagros Ricourt and Ruby Danta's ethnographical research of the interactions between working-class immigrants from Latin America and Dominican and Puerto Rican long-time residents in Queens—the city's most ethnically diverse borough—provides a model to conceptualize the identity reformulation process that is taking place across the nation. This short but critical section ends with Margarite Fernández Olmos and Lizabeth Paravisini-Gebert's presentation of the Afro-Caribbean religions, a crucial component of the Latino cultural landscape.

The second part of the book, "Cultural Hybridazations," is divided into two sections: the first is dedicated to literature (both in English and Spanish) and other linguistic issues, the second to music and visual arts. Dionisio Cañas's article is the most complete survey of all those disciplines published up till now, and the author's reflections on cultural nomadism and the New York experience are an insightful contribution to Spanish-language literary theory and history. In turn, Carmen Dolores Hernández summarizes the history of Puerto Rican English-language literature, reminding us of the class and racial conflicts underlying the slightly disguised animosity that has marked the relationship between the Puerto Rican cultural elite and the island's "Spanglhishfied" offspring on the mainland. And while heated discussions about the effects of bilingualism and the mixtures of English and Spanish are not likely to recede anytime soon, Ana Celia Zentella's article will provide the conceptual clarity necessary to understand linguistic phenomena such as so-called Spanglish, offering at the same time a guideline to breaking down the polyphony of Spanish accents and dialects described by Antonio Muñoz Molina in his piece.

In the mind and ears of most people, music—specifically, Afro-Caribbean rhythms and musical forms—is probably the epitome of Latino culture. Frank M. Figueroa, a critic and former band leader, gives us an overview of New York's Latino musical scene during the first half of the twentieth century, and Ed Morales completes the picture with a detailed report on the origins of salsa. Another great strain of Latino music, however, does not come from the Caribbean but from Mexico. Paul Berman explores the connections between that music and the tradition of the U.S. ballad, connections made even more significant in the past few decades by the huge immigrant flux from south of the border; in so doing he supplies some of the most important clues for the hemispheric conversation analyzed in the introduction to this volume.

In a powerfully complex, creative, and tragic way, Jean-Michel Basquiat embodied that conversation too. Frances Negrón-Muntaner explains how this artist, the son of a Haitian father and a Puerto Rican mother, came to represent the potentialities and paradoxes derived from the uneasy encounter between the transcultural, multiracial, and multilingual Afro-Caribbean heritage and a market-oriented, white-dominated Western art world—all this in the sexually charged, drug-celebratory New York of the 1970s and 1980s. We are living in the aftermath of that world. In any case, the very attempt to define Latin America and the Caribbean, Luis Pérez-Oramas reminds us, entails an implosion of concepts, the clash between universality and particularity, abstract thought and localized experience, hegemonic power and revolutionary utopias. And the visual and performative arts are a privileged medium to *re*present all this— to reenact identity or the search thereof.

Six of the selections presented in this volume—the essays by Frank M. Figueroa, Antonio Muñoz Molina, Luis Pérez-Oramas, Virginia Sánchez Korrol, and my own two contributions to this volume—have never before appeared in book form. Frances

Negrón-Muntaner especially revised her own essay for this anthology, and minor revisions were introduced to Dionisio Cañas's article in consultation with the author, while Orlando José Hernández expanded his section on literary translation. The story of Archer Milton Huntington and the Hispanic Society of America was my master's project for the Columbia School of Journalism. A first version of my Carlos Gardel article was published in 2005 on occasion of the seventieth anniversary of the singer's death by the Argentine daily *La Nación* (the same newspaper to which José Martí was a correspondent) under the title "Gardel en Nueva York: Donde nació el mito." The editor's footnotes to Cañas's and Ana Celia Zentella's articles update part of the information contained in them, but the articles' content remain untouched. Except for these slight changes, the selections are reproduced as they appeared in their original printed format. The general bibliographical information is as follows:

Jack Agüeros, "Halfway to Dick and Jane: A Puerto Rican Pilgrimage," in Thomas C. Wheeler, ed., *The Immigrant Experience: The Anguish of Becoming American*, pp. 101–9 (New York: Dial, 1971).

Theodore S. Beardsley, "The Hispanic Impact Upon the United States" (New York: Hispanic Society of America, 1990 [1976]). The essay was also published in Frank J. Coppa and Thomas J. Curran, eds., *The Immigrant Experience in America* (Boston: Twayne, 1976).

Paul Berman, "Mariachi Reverie," in Sean Wilentz and Greil Marcus, eds., *The Rose and the Briar: Death, Love and Liberty in the American Ballad*, pp. 201–28 (New York: Norton, 2005).

Dionisio Cañas, "New York City: Center and Transit Point for Hispanic Cultural Nomadism," in Mario J. Valdés and Djelal Kadir, eds., *Literary Cultures of Latin America: A Comparative History*, 2:679–702 (New York: Oxford University Press, 2004).

Margarite Fernández Olmos and Lizabeth Paravisini-Gebert, "Creole Religions of the Caribbean," in *Creole Religions of the Caribbean: An Introduction from Vodou and Santería to Obeah and Espiritismo*, pp. 1–23 (New York: New York University Press, 2003).

Frank M. Figueroa, "New York's Latin Music Landmarks," in *Latin Beat*, 12, no. 10 (2002): 28–31.

Gabriel Haslip-Viera, "The Evolution of the Latino Community in New York City: Early Nineteenth Century to the Present," in *Latinos in New York: Communities in Transition*, pp. 2–23 (Notre Dame, IN: University of Notre Dame Press, 1996).

Carmen Dolores Hernández, "Introduction," in *Puerto Rican Voices in English: Interviews with Writers*, pp. 1–17 (Westport, CT: Greenwood, 1997).

José Martí, "A Vindication of Cuba" and "Our America," in *Selected Writings*, pp. 261–67 and 288–96, ed. and trans. Esther Allen (New York: Penguin, 2002).

Ed Morales, "The Story of Nuyorican Salsa," in *The Latin Beat: The Rhythms and Roots of Latin Music From Bossa Nova to Salsa and Beyond*, pp. 55–93. Cambridge: Da Capo, 2003.

Antonio Muñoz Molina, "Spanish in New York: A Moving Landscape" ("Paisajes del idioma"), *El País*, March 24, 2007.

Frances Negrón-Muntaner, "The Life and Passion of Jean-Michel Basquiat," in *Boricua Pop: Puerto Ricans and American Culture*, pp. 115–44 (New York: New York University Press, 2004).

Luis Pérez-Oramas, "The Art of Babel in the Americas," in Miriam Basilio et al., *Latin American and Caribbean Art: MoMA at El Museo* (New York: El Museo del Barrio and the Museum of Modern Art, 2004).

Milagros Ricourt and Ruby Danta, "Introduction: The Emergence of Latino Panethnicity," in *Hispanas de Queens: Latino Panethnicity in a New York City Neighborhood*, pp. 1–10 (Ithaca: Cornell University Press, 2003).

Clara E. Rodríguez, "Racial Themes in the Literature: Puerto Ricans and Other Latinos," in Gabriel Haslip-Viera and Sherrie L. Baver, eds., *Latinos in New York: Communities in Transition*, pp. 104–22 (Notre Dame, IN: University of Notre Dame Press, 1996).

Roberto Suro, "New York: Teetering on the Heights," in *Strangers Among Us: Latino Lives in a Changing America*, pp. 179–203 (New York: Random House, 2002).

Bernardo Vega, *Memoirs of Bernardo Vega: A Contribution to the History of the Puerto Rican Community in New York*, pp. 3–11, 72–91, 83–91, 101–18, 151–57, and 180–82, ed. César Andréu Iglesias, trans. Juan Flores (New York: Monthly Review Press, 1983).

Walt Whitman, "The Spanish Element in Our Nationality," in *November Boughs* (Philadelphia: David McKay, 1892), rpt. *Walt Whitman: Poetry and Prose*, pp. 1146–47 (New York: Library of America, 1996).

Ana Celia Zentella, "Spanish in New York," in Ofelia García and Joshua A. Fishman, eds., *The Multilingual Apple: Languages in New York City*, pp. 167–96 (New York: de Gruyter, 1997).

NOTES

1. Many of New York's Latino studies academic units grew out of previously established Puerto Rican studies centers. In addition to the pioneering work of Virginia Sánchez Korrol, Edna Acosta-Belén, Gabriel Haslip-Viera, Félix Matos-Rodríguez, Angelo Falcón and Juan Flores, among others, our knowledge of that community owes a great debt of gratitude to El Centro de Estudios Puertorriqueños (Center of Puerto Rican Studies) at Hunter College, City University of New York (CUNY; http://www.centropr.org/mission.html). El Centro, founded in 1973 by sociologist Frank Bonilla and currently directed by Edwin Meléndez, is the leading research institution and archive on the Puerto Rican experience in the U.S. It also publishes the prestigious *Centro Journal*, whose managing editor is Xavier Totti. The equivalent to El Centro for the Dominican community is the CUNY

Dominican Studies Institute (DSI; http://www1.ccny.cuny.edu/ci/dsi/index.cfn, by the City College of New York and directed by sociologist Ramona Hernánde. Hernández, Silvio Torres-Saillant, Daisy Cocco de Filippis, Sarah Aponte, Carlos Dor, Cabral, Jorge Duany, Greta Gilbertson, Pamela Graham, Luis Eduardo Guarnizo, Franklin Gutiérrez, Jesse Hoffnung-Garskof, José Itzigsohn, Nancy Lopez, Patricia Pessar, Milagros Ricourt, Francisco Rivera-Batiz, Audrey Singer, and Anthony Stevens-Acevedo have published some of the most important research on the Dominican diaspora. Arguably, the leading expert in Mexican New York is CUNY'S Baruch College professor Robert C. Smith; other distinguished scholars in this area are Liliana Rivera Sánchez, Jocelyn Solís, and Gabriel Thompson. Kenya C. Dworkin y Méndez, María Cristina García, Rodrigo Lazo, Lisandro Pérez, Gustavo Pérez-Firmat, Oscar Montero, and Araceli Tinajero have produced seminal research on the Cuban diaspora of the nineteenth and twentieth centuries. The list of further reading includes bibliography for the study of other Hispanic New York communities, including Ecuadorians, Colombians, Hondurans, Salvadorans, Peruvians, and Brazilians, among other South and Central American national groups. In addition to the names mentioned in this note and elsewhere in this volume, a very partial list of scholars who have made a significant contribution to different aspects of the New York Latino experience must include Arnaldo Cruz-Malavé, Sybille Fischer, Ramón Grosfoguel, Kirsten Silva Gruesz, Laura Lomas, and Nicole P. Marwell.

2. See Juan Flores, *From Bomba to Hip-Hop: Puerto Rican Culture and Latino Identity* (New York: Columbia University Press, 2000), p. 197. The culture of poverty argument was first suggested by Oscar Lewis in his *Five Families: Mexican Case Studies in the Culture of Poverty* (New York: New American Library, 1959) and further elaborated in his *La Vida: A Puerto Rican Family in the Culture of Poverty, San Juan and New York* (New York: Vintage, 1966). Daniel Patrick Moynihan and Nathan Glazer displayed the same argument in *Beyond the Melting Pot: The Negroes, Puerto Ricans, Jews, Italians, and Irish of New York City* (Cambridge: MIT Press, 1963). The phrase "culture of poverty" entered public discourse in a rather incensing way a couple of years later, when a policy brief written by then Senator Moynihan to give President Lyndon B. Johnson some insight on the social conditions of the inner city ("The Negro Family: The Case for National Action," better known as the Moynihan Report) was leaked to the press. For an assessment of the culture of poverty argument and its effects on research and public policy agendas, see Andrew Cherlin et al., "Welfare Reform in the Mid-2000s: How African American and Hispanic Families in Three Cities Are Faring," in *The Moynihan Report Revisited: Lessons and Reflections After Four Decades*, a special issue of the *Annals of the American Academy of Political and Social Science* 621, no. 1 (2009): 178–201. See also Sudhir Venkatesh, "How To Understand the Culture of Poverty: William Julius Wilson Once Again Defies Both Right and Left," a review of William Julius Wilson's *More Than Race: Being Black and Poor in the Inner City*, *Slate*, March 16, 2009, http://www.slate.com/id/2213618/pagenum/all.

ACKNOWLEDGMENTS

Many people made this book possible. Orlando José Hernández, Nicole P. Marwell, and Lourdes Vázquez reviewed the original proposal; their comments and critiques made me double my efforts to hammer out a theoretical frame strong enough to contain the heterogeneous writings presented in this volume. Those efforts are summarized in my introductory essay, of which different drafts were presented at the Recovery the U.S. Hispanic Literary Heritage Conference held at Houston, Texas, in November 14–15, 2008; the Columbia University Seminar on the City, March 23, 2009; and "A World On the Move: Immigration and Emigration in Europe and the Americas," a conference sponsored by the Herbert H. Lehman Center for American History, the Interuniversity Center for European-American History and Politics (CISPEA), the Italian Academy for Advanced Studies, and the Columbia University Seminar on the City, April 23–25, 2009. I deeply thank Nicolás Kanellos, Kenneth T. Jackson, and Lisa Keller for the opportunity they gave me to participate in those encounters and my fellow panelists and colleagues in the audience for their questions and comments. Thanks specially to Regina Galasso, Kenya C. Dworkin y Méndez, Luisa Kluger, and Juan Pablo Neyret for the long conversations and for their intellectual and personal generosity. Thanks also to Miryam Yataco, sociolinguist at NYU Steinhardt School of Culture, Education, and Human Development's Multilingual Multicultural Studies Program, and to Eduardo Peñaloza, coordinator of cultural affairs at the Consulate General of México in New York, for their information on Amerindian languages from Latin America, an issue that deserves more space than I was able to give it.

As I have noted, this sourcebook was born out of the seminar on Hispanic New York that I cotaught with Roosevelt Montás. From the start, Roosevelt has been absolutely instrumental to the development of what we called the Hispanic New York project, and his masterful intellectual and teaching abilities allowed me to navigate safely through my debut as an instructor at Columbia; for all of that, and for the constancy of his friendship, I am deeply grateful. He also read the manuscript and made important observations. Former seminar students helped me throughout the preparation of the manuscript, mainly fact-checking different sections and alphabetizing the indexes and the additional bibliography. My special thanks to Nathalie Alonso, Constantino Díaz-Durán, Eva Fortes, Giselle Gastell, Lia Hulit, and Gabriel Soto for that collaboration.

I would also like to acknowledge the enormous contribution made by Gregory Horvath, a New York–based copyeditor, translator, researcher, and coauthor of the list of further readings. His dedication, superb research skills, fluency in Spanish and Portuguese, and vast knowledge of Hispanic literature, music, and culture have made him an invaluable collaborator. Gregory's exact revisions and suggestions helped improve the quality of this sourcebook.

The essay on Archer Milton Huntington included in this volume was my first ambitious literary attempt in the English language. My friend and colleague Dan Newland edited that essay as well as most of the things I wrote in the following years. Having been able to write the introduction without consulting Dan is, I believe, the best homage a student could pay to his teacher.

Jennifer Crewe is everything an author would want in an editor. Without her enthusiasm, her support, and her patience, this book would have never happened. Thanks also to her assistant, Afua Adusei Gontarz; her efficiency and affability made my work much easier.

The permissions procedure is probably the most tedious and discouraging part of editing an anthology. I could never have gone through it without the collaboration of Angela Darling, assistant director of the American Studies Program. Her prodigious working capacity, dependability, and steadfastness are legendary among those who know her. Amanda Bueno and Shardenay Palmer, work studies who assisted Angela at different stages of this process, provided additional and welcome aid.

I had the happy chance of interacting closely with some of the contributors too. I want to express my profound gratitude to Dionisio Cañas, Frank L. Figueroa, Carmen Dolores Hernández, Antonio Muñoz Molina, Frances Negrón-Muntaner, Luis Pérez-Oramas, Clara E. Rodríguez, and Virginia Sánchez Korrol for their generosity, their advice, and their support. Special thanks to Paul Berman. It was at a dinner party hosted by Clifford Krauss and his wife Paola in Buenos Aires in the spring of 2001, and after a long and lively conversation on New York, the Puritans, and Rubén Darío–of whom, to my surprise, the Brooklynite Berman knew more poems by heart than I did—that the seed of this book was planted.

A few other names are mandatory. First, Tony Bechara, chairman of the board El Museo del Barrio, who believed in this and other projects of mine and always supported them with unwavering enthusiasm. Knowing him has been one of the great blessings of my New York sojourn.

Estrellita Brodsky was another. Our conversations on Latin American art should be the excuse for another book. Thanks to her, a generous gift of the Daniel J. and Estrellita Family Foundation allowed me to complete the funding for this book.

Main funding, as well as the greatest possible support, was of course provided by Andrew Delbanco, director of the American Studies Program, mentor and inspirational figure. His trust is an honor to me.

Last but not least, thanks goes to my wife Marcia: you made all this possible.

Hispanic
NEW YORK

INTRODUCTION

New York City and the Emergence of
a New Hemispheric Identity

Claudio Iván Remeseira

A CROSSROADS OF THE AMERICAS

People referred to in the United States as Hispanics or Latinos—however they are identified by language, race, ethnicity or national origin—have been part and parcel of New York since the dawn of the city's history. Since those early days, too, their presence has been testament to the diversity that even today confounds attempts to find an all-encompassing definition, a blanket term that would embrace with consistency their multiple and often critically divergent historical, cultural, and sociological traits. Spanish and Portuguese explorers and sailors, a free-African interpreter, Sephardic Jews fleeing religious intolerance, black slaves and Indian servants, all linked primarily by the fact of having been at some point subjects of the Spanish Empire, were active in the Hudson Bay area during the first three centuries of European colonization. At the turn of the nineteenth century, New York became a prime destination for South American revolutionaries and politicos seeking funding and support, first for their struggle for independence from Spain and later for the development of commercial and diplomatic relations between the United States and the new republics. In particular, the city became a safe haven for Cuban exiles fighting the remnants of Spain's colonial rule in the hemisphere and the economic expatriates who followed suit—likely, the first Hispanic immigrant wave to the U.S.—looking for jobs in the tobacco factories and other trade and industry opportunities offered by the nascent global city. Spanish-language workers and investors were originally driven to New York by its significance as financial and manufacturing center for the plantation economy of the U.S. South and the Caribbean, the *Mare Nostrum* of the Manifest Destiny era. As the city's and the nation's economic and political climate changed, so did the immigration thrusts; from the heyday of the slave trade and unabashed expansionism to the Cuban Revolution and beyond, every critical stage of the conflicting relationship between the U.S. and Latin America can be linked with New York. Cubans and Spaniards—the largest group during the first decades of the twentieth century—were eventually surpassed by Puerto Ricans, who in 1917 were granted citizenship to add manpower to the country's effort in WWI and after the Great Migration that followed WWII became synonymous with a Hispanic New York. Dominicans began arriving in large numbers in the 1960s, although they have been around much longer. Throughout that period, migrants from virtually every Latin American country also made their contribution to the city's Latino community, nourishing, through their personal or business networking, the bonds between the city and their homelands. As in the rest of the U.S., this multifaceted heritage is by no means a new phenomenon; the novelty lies, rather, in the growing awareness of the role people of Hispanic descent have played in the nation's life over the past five centuries and into the present.

During the 1990s, however, a radical shift in New York's demographic profile took place. The huge immigration wave that since the early 1980s has been arriving in the U.S. from Latin America turned New York into the city with the largest and most diverse Hispanic population in the whole country.[1] This metamorphosis not only mirrored what was happening in the rest of the nation—it also transformed New York into a microcosm of the Americas, literally turning it, because of the sheer number of nationalities gathered, into the most comprehensive Latin American city of the hemisphere and enhancing its function, already demonstrated since the late eighteenth century thanks to Spanish American exiles and travelers, as cultural hemispheric crossroads.[2] Looking closely into this reality can help us deepen our understanding not just of the Latino experience but also of the American experience in general, both reflected in and transformed by interaction with its Latino component.

NEW YORK CITY AND THE LATINIZATION OF THE U.S.

According to the most recent estimates, New York City is home to 2,259,069 people who define themselves as Hispanics.[3] That figure represents almost one-third of the city's total population (8,008,278 at the time of the 2000 census and an estimated 8,246,310 by 2007) and almost doubles the national average. Roughly 70 percent of New York Hispanics, or 1,576,150 people, were born in Latin America, comprising an outstanding 52 percent of all foreign-born New Yorkers.[4]

The breakdown of these statistics is even more revealing of the transformation undergone by New York City in the past few decades. Unlike Los Angeles, Miami, or Chicago, where one community prevails numerically over the others,[5] New York's largest Latino community, Puerto Ricans, currently accounts for less than thirty-five percent of the entire Hispanic population, followed by Dominicans (24.52), Mexicans (11.78), Ecuadorians (7.50), Colombians (4.47), Central Americans of all nationalities (6.16), and people from every other country in Central and South America (Cubans, the most important Spanish-language community of nineteenth-century New York, nowadays represent less than 2 percent of the city's Latino population). In other words, while still enjoying a predominantly Caribbean flavor, Hispanic New York's demographic mix is seemingly pointing into a broader, pan-Latino direction (see table 0.1).

Enlarging the geographical scope of our analysis sheds more light on the magnitude of this phenomenon. Some 40 percent of the nation's 1.9 million South American–born residents, or 750,000 people, live in the New York metropolitan area.[6] In the neighboring city of Paterson, New Jersey—the only urban concentration outside California, Texas, and Florida where Latinos constitute the majority— some 60 percent of the Hispanic population is made up of Central and South Americans, while only 5.9 percent are Mexicans.[7] These figures reverse the pattern dominant nationwide, where Mexicans account for more than sixty percent of the Latin American–born population.

The full meaning of these figures becomes apparent when we look at them in the larger perspective of the nation's Latinoization. In May 2008 the Census Bureau announced that the U.S. Hispanic population had reached 45.5 million, or 15 percent of the country's estimated total population. Forty-one percent of that group, 14.5 million people—almost half the country's foreign population—were born in Latin America.

As I have noted earlier, this demographic reality is a fairly recent phenomenon: in 1960, only 9 percent of the country's foreign-born population, or 900,000 people, were from Latin America. By 1990 the figure had jumped to 44 percent of the foreign-born population or 8.4 million people. According to projections elaborated by the Pew Hispanic Center, by 2050 the total Latino population will triple in size and make up almost 30 percent of the U.S. population.[8] New York is a harbinger of that future.

Of New York City's Latinos, 1,865,922 people, or 24 percent of the total population over the age of five, speak Spanish.[9] This people represent 51 percent of all New Yorkers who speak a language other than English.[10] As in the rest of the country, the emergence of a sizable bilingual, mostly Latin American–born population has brought the "Latino issue" to the top of the political agenda. Not to mention the anti-immigration backlash in a large part of the public opinion, a twenty-first-century revival of nineteenth-century Know-Nothing nativism, allegedly triggered by concerns about national security, but also nourished by a panoply of racist prejudices of which New York City remained remarkably detached until recently, when a series of harassments against Latinos in different parts of the state culminated in the brutal killings of two men in Suffolk County and Brooklyn.[11] The immediate reaction of community leaders,

TABLE 0.1

Hispanic New York Population, by national origin

As of 2007, New York City's total population of Hispanic or Latino origin was 2,259,069. The breakdown by national origins, with an average margin of error of 5 per cent, is the following:

PUERTO RICANS	785,849 (+/−12,677), or 34,78% of NYC total Hispanic or Latino population
DOMINICANS	553,980 (+/−11,647), or 24,52 %
MEXICANS	266,211 (+/−13,334), or 11,78 %
ECUADORANS	169,622 (+/−8,727), or 7,50 %
COLOMBIANS	101,039 (+/−6,194), or 4,47 %
CUBANS	43,094 (+/−3,271), or 1,90 %
PERUVIANS	38,360 (+/−3,344), or 1,69 %
CENTRAL AMERICANS	139,245 (+/−6,785), or 6,16 %
Honduran	38,899 (+/−3,089)
Salvadoran	35,643 (+/−3,806)
Guatemalan	25,664 (+/−2,659)
Panamanian	19,555 (+/−2,840)
Nicaraguan	9,618 (+/−1,840)
Costa Rican	5,856 (+/−1,177)
Other Central American	4,010 (+/−1,048)
SOUTH AMERICANS	46,480 (+/−9,719), or 2,05 %
(Other than Colombians, Ecuadorans, Peruvians) (*)	
Argentinean	13,788 (+/−1,720)
Venezuelan	10,268 (+/−2,156)
Chilean	6,304 (+/−1,578)
Bolivian	4,184 (+/−1,064)
Paraguayan	4,105 (+/−1,421)
Uruguayan	2,530 (+/−755)
Other South Americans	5,301 (+/−1,025)
OTHER HISPANIC OR LATINO	115,189 (+/−5,274), or 5,09 %
Spanish	18,494 (+/−1,885)
Spaniard	13,285 (+/−1,661)
Spanish American	754 (+/−284)
All other Hispanic or Latino	82,656 (+/−4,456)

*Adding Ecuadorans, Colombians and Peruvians, the total count for South Americans is 356,432, or 15,71 percent of New York City Hispanic population. The overlapping of the categories "Spaniards," "Spanish," and "Spanish-American" misrepresent the population who is originally from Spain, estimated by the ACS foreign-born section in 7,602 (+/– 950) people. According to the same survey, the number or Brazil-born and Portugal-born New Yorkers is 13,438 (+/– 1,807) and 2,509 (+/– 576) respectively. See http://nyc.gov/html/dcp/pdf/census/nyc_boros_05_06_07_place_of_birth.pdf.

Source: U.S. Census Bureau, American Community Survey, 2005–2007, http://factfinder.census.gov/servlet/DTTable?_bm=y&-geo_id=16000US3651000&-ds_name=ACS_2007_3YR_G00_&-mt_name=ACS_2007_3YR_G2000_B03001

public officials, and the general public against those hideous hate crimes was reassuring of New York's awareness as a city of immigrants.

But the reader may wonder whether I am overestimating the importance of New York as an exemplary case. Three-fourths of Hispanics in the state of New York reside within the city's five boroughs, and New York ranks fourth among the states with the largest Hispanic populations in the U.S.[12] However, the state of New York represents just 6.9 percent of the national total, lagging well behind the first two states in the ranking, California (29) and Texas (18.9), which make up half the national Latino population, and is surpassed by Florida (8.2).[13] More than three-quarters of U.S. Latinos live in the West and the Southwest, and almost 60 percent of them are Mexican or Mexican American.[14] What, therefore, is the relevance of a multinational Hispanic New York in the larger landscape of a Hispanic United States?

The answer may lie in what Louis DeSipio described more than a decade ago as one of the key conditions for the development of a pan-ethnic Latino identity: an increasing geographic overlap among the different national-origin communities.[15] Traditionally, Hispanics have toiled and thrived in separate, even distant quarters: Mexican Americans in the Southwest and California, Puerto Ricans in New York and the Northeast, Cubans in Florida or New Jersey. It was not until the 1970s, as Félix Padilla explained in *Latino Ethnic Consciousness: The Case of Mexican Americans and Puerto Ricans in Chicago*, that a substantial interaction between the two largest Latino groups of the twentieth century really came about.[16] In a smaller, though historically significant scale, New York preceded Chicago for almost a century.

Already by the mid 1800s, as Gabriel Haslip-Viera reminds us in the essay that appears in this volume, the city hosted a small sample of Spanish American peoples. By the end of that century, Cubans and Puerto Ricans fighting for the independence of their islands forged what was probably the first pan-Latino alliance in the history of this country, an alliance that cut across racial boundaries—something unthinkable in the segregated mainstream society of those days[17]—and in which women played a momentous role, as Virginia Sánchez Korrol explains in her piece. The political clubs, unions, and community organizations created in New York at that time (and their sister organizations in Boston, Philadelphia, Baltimore, Tampa, and other cities), as well as their local papers, theaters, and other popular entertainment venues, continued, well into the twentieth century, to provide an environment in which Spanish-speaking peoples from all over Latin America, the Caribbean, and Spain, related by language and cultural heritage, engaged in a vibrant social life—extensively portrayed in the excerpts appearing in this volume from Bernardo Vega's memoirs—amidst the English-speaking dominant culture. In so doing, they were able to develop a sense of a shared identity—frequently termed as *Hispanic, Hispano,* or *Hispano-American*—that transcended, without erasing them, the cherished traits of their own national origins.[18]

LANGUAGE AND IDENTITY

Like other first-generation immigrants, the children of those early settlers became English dominant. By the third generation, most could speak just a few words of their heritage language. But uninterrupted communication through family and kinship with the culture of origin as well as the continuous flow of newcomers ensured the survival—and growth—of Spanish. At the same time, the contact between those two languages produced a distinctively *nuyorican* brand of linguistic code-switching or Spanglish, as Ana Celia Zentella explains in her essay in this volume. In just a few decades, a generation of poets, playwrights, and narrators who had grown up in that idiomatic borderland created what Carmen Dolores Hernández describes as a hybrid kind of writing, a literature combining the centuries-old Spanish tradition of oral poetry brought to the Americas by the conquistadors with the spoken-word tradition that, under the influence of the beatniks and William Carlos Williams, harks back to Walt Whitman and the biblical rhythmic patterns of the Puritans.[19]

In addition to Spanish, all the other main languages of the Iberian peninsula—Portuguese, Galician, Catalan, and Basque—and many if not all the lesser-known ones found their way to New York too, as well as many indigenous languages from Mexico, Peru, and the rest of the Latin American countries.[20] But it is undoubtedly Spanish that holds the preeminent position as a collective identity marker. Unlike previous immigrant groups, Latinos from different nationalities, social classes, and racial backgrounds share one common language; in New York, says novelist Antonio Muñoz Molina, the linguistic unity of Spanish manifests itself through the richest variety of accents and dialects. This bond, as the research conducted by Milagros Ricourt and Ruby Danta confirms, enhances in those immigrants the sense of partaking in one overarching Hispanic identity, very much as it happened with Cuban and Puerto Rican immigrants more than a century ago.

That linguistic bond also enhances the connection with the cultural heritage of Spain and Latin America. Dionisio Cañas explains not only how New York became a premier international crossroads of Hispanic culture but also how the *experience* of New York became crucially important for that culture—how the city in itself, especially at a time when no other city in the world could compare to it as a crucible of modern civilization, was assimilated and transformed by poets and artists into a chief component of Spanish-language cultural history. From the seminal figure of José Martí to Juan Ramón Jiménez, Federico García Lorca, Gabriela Mistral, Diego Rivera, Joaquín Torres-García, and many other major literary and artistic personalities of the past to scores of contemporary writers, artists, and intellectuals, a perennial diaspora of Hispanic-American talent has turned New York into one of the undisputable centers of the Spanish-language cultural world.[21] Along with Paris, New York is the only city not belonging to the former Spanish Empire that can make that claim; unlike Paris, it can also be claimed by Latin Americans as their own. Puerto Rican author Luis Rafael Sánchez called it the capital of Hispanic America.[22] In fact, New York is one of the capital nodes of an even larger network—along with Barcelona, Mexico City, Madrid, or Buenos Aires, it is one of the epicenters of the global Spanish-language semiosphere.[23]

This statement applies to the whole range of high and mass culture. Since Irene and Vernon Castle launched the tango rage on Broadway—actually, the first Latino music craze in U.S. history—to the successive "eras" of rumba, mambo, and salsa, as well as the contemporary dominance of hip-hop, rap, and reggaeton, Latino and Latin American popular music have been inextricably linked to each other *through* New York, as the essays by Frank M. Figueroa and Ed Morales make clear.[24] Similar interconnections between U.S. and Latin American culture can be found in classical music and ballet, architecture and visual arts, cinema and sports.

Visual arts provide an exceptional angle to reflect on how New York's prime cultural institutions helped also articulate the hegemonic discourse on the Americas. The very concept of Latin America, the way in which it has been historically perceived in this nation, and the place that U.S. art critics and historians dispense to Latin American artists, are some of the topics addressed by Luis Pérez-Oramas in his essay on the Museum of Modern Art's Latin American collection. To promote the overdue discussion on these issues—just think, for example, of the limited knowledge, even among specialists, of the role played by Marius de Zayas in the reception of modern art in the U.S.—is one of the goals of this anthology.[25]

The decision to focus in this collection on the city's Spanish- and English-language Hispanic heritage forced me to leave out contributions made to the New York Latino experience by the Portuguese and Brazilian communities.[26] Portugal's and Brazil's history is in fact so intertwined with that of Spain and Spanish America that a word was coined to name them as a unit—Iberoamerica. This connection helps us understand

New York's pivotal role in ushering what Immanuel Wallerstein called the capitalist world-system—or, in Fernand Braudel's terms, New York's place in the *longue durée* cycle of Western imperialism and non-Western colonial subjection fostered by the transoceanic voyages of the fifteenth century.[27]

Indeed, the first Hispanics who reached New Amsterdam in 1654 were twenty-three Sephardic Jews escaping the former Dutch colony of Recife, Brazil, after it was bloodily retaken by the Portuguese. Those Sephardic immigrants—the first Jewish settlers of North America—spoke the variety of Spanish known as Ladino and founded the Spanish and Portuguese Synagogue, whose tradition has been continued to this day by Congregation Shearith Israel.[28] Jews and Moors had been expelled from Spain in 1492, the same year that Columbus set sail for the Indies, only to come across a New World; the overlapping of dates is not a coincidence. From the beginning, Hispanic New York has been immersed in the troubled undercurrents of global history, its course propelled by the struggle among Western powers for world dominance and by its counterpart, the diaspora of peoples uprooted by religious or political persecution, by slavery, or by the lack of economic opportunities in their old countries—in short, by the deep forces that shaped the tortuous path of modernity.

GLOBALIZATION, DIASPORAS, HYBRIDITIES

Of those forces, none has been more tragically consequential than the transatlantic slave trade. Initiated in the mid-fifteenth century by the Portuguese and early advocated after the Conquest by Spanish friar Bartolomé de Las Casas to replace Indian forced labor, over the next three centuries it involved all major European nationalities and displaced from Africa an estimated 11 million people, of which around 9.5 million came to the Americas.[29] One of the vertices of the triangular commerce of human bodies that ensued between Europe, Africa, and America was the Caribbean, heart of the middle passage; its connection with the African Diaspora (a term borrowed from the Jewish experience) is relevant to us for a number of reasons.

The first has to do with the emergence of what British scholar Paul Gilroy called the Black Atlantic world, a system of social interactions developed over that trilateral geography during the slave trade period. Among those interactions are the various forms of ethnic, racial, and cultural mixtures that we categorize with the terms *creolization, métissage, mestizaje,* or *hybridity*. These terms, says Gilroy, are rather unsatisfactory ways of naming a process of cultural mutation that exceeds racial discourse, but, at the same time, they prevent us from falling into the essentialist trap of conceiving "immutable, ethnic differences as an absolute break in the histories and experiences of 'black' and 'white' people."[30]

Gilroy's approach provides a key to understanding race in Latin America and the Caribbean vis-à-vis the United States. As Clara E. Rodríguez explains in her article, in most Latin American countries racial identities are largely perceived within a continuum syncopated by fluid internal subdivisions, whereas in the U.S. they are marked by the mutually exclusive dichotomy of white or black, a notion defined in the specialized literature as hypodescent—colloquially put, the one-drop rule.[31] Latin America's racial spectrum has been historically organized as a social hierarchy with whites and light-complexioned people at the top and people of Amerindian or African descent at the bottom—with a huge gamut of skin color and ethnic variances in between—and stultified by Eurocentric racist prejudices that continue to impair the region's economic and political development. But migrating to the U.S. added a new burden: the distressing effects of squeezing such a diverse community into a bipolar racial conception. Although focused on Puerto Ricans, Rodríguez's essay offers further insight into this issue, illustrating the difference between the two classification systems and giving a quick survey of the racial history of Latinos in the U.S. as well as a glimpse of Latinos' own racism.

A second set of reasons, implicit in my previous argument, is that New York's largest Latino communities of the past two centuries had its roots in the Caribbean and its own history, as I have been arguing throughout this introduction, is interweaved with that region. Yet the conceptual and physical boundaries of a Hispanic Caribbean are not as obvious as they appear to be. Again, Gilroy's perspective is to the point: as a transnational creation, the Black Atlantic constitutes a paradigm for the study of a world that is transnational par excellence. The extraordinary complexity of the Caribbean—the intermingling ethnic, linguistic, and national-origin threads of its multicultural makeup, from Chinese, Indian, African to British, Dutch, French, German, Spanish, or Portuguese—challenges any protectionist view of identity that would attempt to fence off a community from alien influences.[32] This point, as we shall see, has major implications in the case of Hispanic New York.

The diversity of the Caribbean—the first true melting pot of modern times—is not only a demographic feature. Silvio Torres-Saillant has noted that the recurrent use by critics of the image of the island as its archetypical representation has somehow obscured the fact that its basin covers also a vast tract of mainland in South, Central, and North America, from Surinam and Guyana to the U.S. coast on the Gulf of Mexico.[33] Regarding New Orleans, for instance, as a Caribbean crossroads of the Americas, adds a new layer of significance to that city's cultural and economic connections with New York and amplifies the scope of the U.S. Latino heritage.[34]

No description of the Caribbean would be complete without a survey of its creolized religions. It was in the Caribbean, as a result of the clash between the spiritual beliefs of masters and slaves, that the current meaning of the word *syncretism* took hold (its definition as "fusion of differing religious creeds" was forged by European humanists during the theological debates sparked by the Reformation, but they applied it exclusively to different forms of Christianity). Although increasingly sharing the limelight with the Virgin of Guadalupe and other symbolic representations of a growing Mexican presence, Afro-Caribbean religions are conspicuously visible in New York's cityscape through the *botánicas*, metaphorical synthesis of the multiple weaves that make up the mixed fabric of Caribbean culture: the amalgamated iconography of Christian saints and animistic deities, the overwhelming poignancy of the senses, the healing power of Nature.[35] Margarite Fernández Olmos and Lizabeth Paravisini-Gebert's selection will introduce the reader to concepts such as transculturation, ritual and performance, which are necessary to decode the tenets of that syncretic spirituality and its ramifications in the general culture. Some of the most significant occur in the visual and performance arts; the work of Ana Mendieta or Jean-Michel Basquiat—the latter subject of Negrón-Muntaner's essay—are a case in point.

Finally, it was a war started in the Caribbean that set the stage for the emergence of the U.S. as a global power. When in 1895 José Martí left New York to lead the invasion of Cuba, his priority was to obtain his country's independence before expansionist politicians at Washington could find an excuse to get involved in the conflict and replace Spain's rule with their own; Martí's death in a skirmish shortly after arriving on the island and the inability of his fellow revolutionaries to win a decisive battle opened the door to U.S. intervention. The Spanish-American War—that "splendid little war," in John Hay's words—allowed the U.S. to take over Spain's last possessions in the Western hemisphere and the Pacific at the same time that it was annexing Hawaii, effectively launching the nation's imperialistic phase. On the other hand, the limitations imposed on Cuba's independence by the Platt Amendment and the irresolution of Puerto Rico's colonial status fueled the antigringo sentiment Spain's defeat had already spread all over Latin America, a sentiment that successive U.S. interventions in the region would only strengthen.

Driven by those historical forces, New York would eventually become the first and foremost metropolis of our time, a title that according to experts remains unchallenged.[36] As we said before, this global city is also a crucial node of Latino international network; one of the main attributes of this condition, as Agustín Laó-Montes and other scholars have shown, is to function as a center for the production and distribution of discourses on *Latinidad*—a global factory of ethnically packaged cultural commodities.[37] This blending of market and popular culture is addressed in the last selection of this book.

The year of Martí's death a new invention made its public debut: cinema. It rapidly moved beyond the stage of arcade curiosity to become a full-fledged artistic, documentary, and propagandistic medium (the Spanish-American War was in fact one of the first major military conflicts recorded *and* manipulated in film), and, along with the gramophone and the radio, the core of early twentieth-century mass media. One of the first artists who took advantage of these technologies was Carlos Gardel, the legendary tango singer. Gardel reached fame around 1914 in Argentina and Uruguay, and in the next two decades established himself as a household name in all Latin America and Spain through his pioneering work in recording, radio broadcasting, and talking pictures; even today his voice and songs are immediately recognized by millions throughout the Spanish-language world. Between 1933 and 1935 he lived in New York, composing, singing under contract for NBC, and, above all, producing and starring in films shot at Paramount's studios in Astoria. This combined multimedia effort transformed Gardel into probably the first transnational Hispanic-American pop celebrity and set a business and artistic model that was followed by other Latin American and Latino performers after him; it is appropriate then that this anthology would close with a brief account of his New York foray.

HISPANIC/LATINO MULTI-IDENTITIES

Up to this point, I have used *Hispanic* and *Latino* as apparently interchangeable terms. This is customary in both scholarly and popular works, although there is also a serious academic and grassroots debate about the meaning and political implications of using one or the other.[38] The debate goes back to the civil rights era, when Chicano and Puerto Rican organizations chose *Latino/a* as a panethnic denomination over the bureaucratically tainted *Hispanic,* the label employed by the government in the census and as a generic category for policy purposes; some even rejected *Hispanic* as ideologically charged with Spain's colonial legacy.[39] Most specialized literature on Hispanics or Latinos in the U.S. use both terms to designate a minority historically defined by experiences of exclusion and discrimination akin to those endured by African Americans; in the case of black Latinos the parallel can be extended to the experience of slavery itself.

In Latin America and Spain, on the other hand, *Hispanic* and *Hispanic-American* have traditionally referred to the cultural heritage of all Spanish-language people (although *Latino,* undoubtedly as an effect of U.S. global influence, increasingly appears there as synonymous in the media and everyday conversation, particularly in connection to popular music and entertainment). In his classic handbook on Latin American literature, the great Dominican humanist Pedro Henríquez Ureña even included Brazil under the Hispanic banner, an inclusion ultimately justified by the original meaning of *Hispania,* a name given by the Romans to the whole Iberian peninsula.[40] Except when mutually substituting them in order to avoid monotony, I employ *Hispanic* in this specific sense, and *Latino/a* to refer to the U.S. descendants of Latin American and Iberian immigrants who tend to speak English as their first language and may or may not identify with their ancestors' cultural heritage.

Why *Hispanic* New York, then, and not *Latino* New York? Because I am not just talking of Latinos or Latinas in the U.S. sense of the word—nor am I talking exclusively from the point of view of U.S. history, but rather from a perspective that considers New York a node in a hemispheric and transoceanic network of cultural exchanges and cross-fertilizations. From this perspective, *Hispanic* is the most comprehensive term, since it allows us, for example, to link New York Spanish-language art and literary traditions with the larger cultural traditions of Latin America and Spain and, at the same time, to broaden the Latino national canon and the self-perception of the U.S. as a bilingual country.[41] Yet my emphasis is set on the city as the material and symbolic space that makes those exchanges and cross-fertilizations possible; therefore the conceptual boundaries established by these definitions should be understood more as permeable membranes than as compartmental divisions. This point is relevant to the discussion of the issue of identity—or, perhaps more appropriately, multi-identities.

When discussing identity, our primary reaction is to stress what makes *us* different from *them*. But what happens when one's own self is made up of the intersection of different, even antagonistic, racial, ethnic, linguistic categories? As I just mentioned, that occurred massively in the Caribbean and Spanish America after the Conquest. The Spanish word that describes that process, *mestizaje,* has no proper equivalent in English; *miscegenation* translates only its racist undertones but falls short of conveying its more positive meaning as a metaphor for cultural fusion.[42] Today it is widely used—sometimes sloppily—as synonymous with hybridity.[43] For more than a century, essayists, poets, and politicians have celebrated mestizaje as the cornerstone of Latin American identity; the cardinal manifesto of that vision, Martí's "Our America," was penned in New York and is included in this anthology. For the United States, perhaps the greatest potential contribution of the idea of mestizaje—and of the demographic changes it represents, what two decades ago critic William A. Henry III called "the browning of America"—is to help the country move beyond the biracial paradigm that has characterized it from its inception, making it more aware of its own history of racial and ethnic mixtures.[44]

Self-reflection, of course, is a two-way street: leaving the home country to start a new life elsewhere is always hard, even at a time when the availibilty of travels and communications makes it possible to develop transnational ties that were unimaginable just a few decades ago. But whereas the traditional assimilation viewpoint sustained that, in order to become full-fledged Americans, newcomers had to cast off their old identities, the latest generation of immigrants from Latin America, as Ricourt and Danta explain in their essay, can naturally share in several identities at the same time.[45] "After almost ten years of living here, I began to feel a part of the United Sates, without that meaning that I had set aside my Bolivian or Latin American or Spanish-American identity," says novelist Edmundo Paz Soldán, summing up the idea.[46]

Far from offering a univocal face, however, Latino identities in the United States resemble a fluid aggregate of shifting tectonic plates, at times overlapping and at times in friction, both among one another and within each community. As Juan Flores reminds us, the "New Nueva York" created by the immigration wave of the past two decades is the result of a centuries-old, multilayered process that cannot be reduced to one simplistic storyline. In order to understand the polyphonic whole, we must first grasp the melodic contour and rhythm of each constitutive theme—each immigrant group's history. These histories are in turn marked by class, racial, and ethnic disso-nances carried along from the country of origin and by the particular relationship that existed between each particular country and the U.S.[47]

New York offers the unique opportunity to observe all the heterogeneous aspects of this complex heritage in motion. No other city in the world provides such a compre-hensive summary of the past and present-day historical experience of the peoples of Hispanic descent, of their diverse and conflicting national, social, racial, and ethnic backgrounds. By bringing together recent immigrants from all over the Spanish-speaking world with long-established Latino communities, New York City offers the possibility of engaging in a personal and collective experience of identity reshaping, an experience through which the legacies of Spain, Latin America, and the United States could eventually coalesce into a new definition of what it means to be an American.

THE HEMISPHERIC TURN

Paul Berman reminds us that the first to ask themselves that question were the poets and writers of the Romantic generation. Similar questions were being asked at the same time in the recently independent Spanish American republics—what does it mean to be a Mexican, a Peruvian, an Argentine? Romanticism, the great cultural and politi-cal movement of the nineteenth century, was an ideology of cultural nationalism, and the creole states of the Americas, as Benedict Anderson dubbed them in his ground-breaking study on nationalism, were precisely the first large-scale experiment in na-tion building.[48]

Searching for the specific qualities that would make someone an American—not in the generic hemispheric sense, but in the restricted sense of the word—some vindi-cated the Indian past (paradoxically, and tragically, at the same time that the actual Indians were being pushed into their long Trail of Tears), while others extolled the Spanish heritage. From Washington Irving to Ernest Hemingway and a big etcetera (Pedro Almodóvar's enthusiasts are a good example) there has always been in this country a vigorous strain of fascination for all things Spanish—fascination, in part, for the exotic otherness of Catholic Spain, the great enemy of Protestant England during the first modern culture wars, but also for its art and history. The extraordinary career of Archer Milton Huntington—collector, amateur archeologist, and poet and founder of the Hispanic Society of America—is an eloquent testimony to the admiration that the U.S. cultural and economic elite had for Spanish civilization even at the height of the Gilded Age, while Uncle Sam's forces were gunning up San Juan Hill or sinking Spain's navy into the depths of the Pacific Ocean. But the Hispanic heritage was indeed much closer and earthier than the morbid abandonment of a Moorish damsel in a foreign, mysterious setting or the folksy vibrance of a Sorolla painting would suggest. As the map sketched in Beardsley's essay shows, just a decade before the Declaration of Independence about two-thirds of present-day continental United States was indeed Spanish territory. Much of that land was scarcely populated, but the annexation of Mexico's northern provinces after the Guadalupe Hidalgo Treaty added approximately eighty thousand Spanish-speaking citizens to the nation's population.[49]

The vast majority of them, about sixty thousand people, lived in the former Mexican province of New Mexico. In 1883 New Mexico's capital, Santa Fe, celebrated its 333rd anniversary, and the city's notables invited Walt Whitman to write and deliver a commemorative poem.[50] By then almost secluded in his final retreat of Camden, Whitman gently declined the invitation but sent the organizers a short letter that was afterwards included in his last collection of prose, *November Boughs*, and titled "The Spanish Element in Our Nationality." As was customary, the letter was reproduced in the papers; the *New York Times* announced it with prophetic tones with the headline "Walt Whitman on America: The Good Gray Poet's View of Our Population and Our Future."[51]

What the Good Gray Poet had to say about the future of America was indeed astounding. The missive starts with Whitman's ultimate answer to the question posed by the Romantic generation—his generation—about national identity. "We Americans have yet to really learn our own antecedents, and sort them, to unify them." Those who believe that the United States is just a second England, a mere Anglo-Saxon country, are wrong; as valuable as it was, the "British and German stock," as he phrases it, "already threaten excess" and needed to be counterbalanced. In a brief jeremiad reminiscent of sections of "Democratic Vistas" and other writings of his latest years, Whitman decries the "seething materialistic and business vortices, in their present, devouring relations, controlling and belittling everything else." But instead of taking refuge in the distorted remembrance of a utopian past, the poet regards the harsh economic and social conditions of the hour as a necessary but transient moment in a larger drama, a stage that ought to be followed by the establishment of more just society.

The vehicle for the establishment of that society is what Whitman calls "the composite American identity of the future." National identity, in his definition, is an inchoate formation, the image of a nation on the move, and is located not in a the past—as the national essence conceived by ethno-nationalisms—but in the future—a dynamic entity in which all the lines of force of the past and present will come together to generate something new. Among those forces, says Whitman, one of the most important, one that will supply some of the most worthy ingredients of the mix, is the "Spanish character"—in today's terms, the Latino or Hispanic heritage.

Whitman was one of those intellectuals who had exalted Spain and its heroic tradition and spiritual values, and it is not surprising that he would exalt them again to counter the excesses of capitalism already chastised. But his view of the Spanish offspring in the Americas and of Native Americans had been more problematic, to say the least. Whitman shared in the racist prejudices of his time and in many ways, particularly in regard to African Americans, he was less open-minded than some of his contemporaries. But here he was, four decades after his first contact with that Hispanic heritage during his stint on a New Orleans newspaper, a sojourn during which he apparently picked up the Spanish words that made him, as Berman likes to say, our first Spanglish poet; the admirer of President Polk, who prompted the war against Mexico; the friend of John L. O'Sullivan, who invented the phrase Manifest Destiny; here he was, at the end of his life, praising before the people of New Mexico—and the whole country—the contribution of "our aboriginal or Indian population" to the composite national identity and placing it, even with his honestly admitted reservations, on the same level of importance as the European immigration.

Another remarkable detail in this remarkable letter is that the Native American group that Whitman mentions first is "the Aztec in the South." It is hard to tell whether he is speaking metaphorically or whether he is indeed referring to the tribes of the U.S. Southwest as Aztecs; in any case, the confusion is indicative of the porosity of the southern borderlands and forces us to reconsider the geographical limits of the United States in a more complex light.

Indeed, Whitman is anticipating a discussion that would have its first major instance half a century after his death, with the correspondence between Herbert Eugene Bolton and Edmundo O'Gorman, and would take another five decades to become a central issue in the academy.[52] It took in fact the civil rights movement of the 1960s, the self-questioning search of the 1970s, the cultural wars of the 1980s, and the impact of structuralism, postmodern and postcolonial theory over the next two decades, along with the political developments in Latin America and the United States, to indict the uncritical handling of the notion of American exceptionalism and to approach the history of U.S. and Latin America from a hemispheric, trans-American perspective. That shift is exemplified by the so-called transnational turn in American studies and by the use of concepts such as *contact zone, cultural geography,* or *Latin American space-in-between* to challenge the idea of a fixed and insular American identity.[53]

The future we now face is quite different from the future contemplated by Whitman's contemporaries. We are not looking at the prospect of an American Century, an era of undisputed U.S. hegemony in the region and the world, but of a century that will likely bring an end to Western dominance in global affairs. Yet Whitman's vision of the American future is more relevant than it was in 1883; it certainly provides a more accurate portrayal of the United States of Barack Obama than of Chester Arthur's United States. His definition of American identity as a "compost" of different "stocks" echoes Martí's notion of mestizaje and constitutes, along with it, a paradigm to rethink national identities in general and to deflate racial and ethnic tensions in an increasingly intermingled world.

The underlying assumption for selecting the pieces gathered in this volume is precisely that New York embodies a hemispheric idea of the Americas, an idea anticipated by nineteenth-century authors such as Whitman and Martí but that only the twentieth-century wave of immigration made possible. In the following selections readers will find the threads of that rich multicultural heritage; by weaving them together I hope to help reconstruct an all-encompassing narrative of the Hispanic New York experience with thought-provoking insight into the past, present, and future of our hemisphere.

NOTES

1. U.S. Census Bureau, "The Hispanic Population," census 2000 brief, table 3, The Largest Places in Total Population and in Hispanic Population. See http://www.census.gov/prod/2001pubs/c2kbr01–3.pdf. See also U.S. Census Bureau, "Overview of Race and Hispanic Origin," census 2000 brief, March 2001, and U.S. Census Bureau Guidance on the Presentation and Comparison of Race and Hispanic Origin Data," June 12, 2003; see http://www.census.gov/population/www/socdemo/compraceho.html.

2. By the end of the 1700s, New York and Philadelphia constituted not only what William Charvat called the "publishing axis" that defined the country's literary standards but also one of the leading Spanish-language print centers of the hemisphere, where exiles and revolutionaries published scores of periodicals and books that helped disseminate the political creed of liberalism and ideals of independence throughout Spanish America. William Charvat, *Literary Publishing in America, 1790–1850* (Philadelphia: University of Pennsylvania Press, 1959), p. 23. See Rodrigo Lazo, "La Famosa Filadelfia: The Hemispheric American City and Constitutional Debates," in Caroline F. Levander and Robert S. Levine, eds., *Hemispheric American Studies* (New Brunswick, NJ: Rutgers University Press, 2008), pp. 57–74. According to Benedict Anderson, the nation-states that sprung to independence in British and Spanish America between 1776 and 1825 are a conspicuous example of the convergence of capitalism, print technologies, and language that "created the possibility of a new form of imagined community, which in its basic morphology set the stage for the modern nation." Benedict Anderson, *Imagined Communities: Reflections on the Origin and Spread of Nationalism* (New York: Verso, 1983), p. 46.

3.   U.S. Census Bureau, *2005–2007 American Community Survey,* March 1, 2009, http://
     factfinder.census.gov/servlet/ACSSAFFFacts?_event=Search&geo_id=&_geoContext=&_
     street=&_county=New+York+City&_cityTown=New+York+City&_state=04000US36&_
     zip=&_lang=en&_sse=on&pctxt=fph&pgsl=010; see also "Statistical Portrait of Hispanics
     in the United States, 2007," Pew Hispanic Center, May 3, 2009, http://pewhispanic.org/
     factsheets/factsheet.php?FactsheetID=46.

     The U.S. Census Bureau conducts: 1. the decennial census, which is a count of every
     person living in the United States. The last census was conducted on April 1, 2010 (see http://
     2101.census.gov/2010census/); by the time this book's manuscript went to print, the census
     results were still unavailable; 2. the Population Estimates Program, which produces annual
     estimates of the total number of inhabitants of states, counties, and cities. In the case of New
     York, those data are also reviewed by the Department of City Planning; and 3. the nation-
     wide American Community Survey (ACS), which aims at filling in the gaps between each
     census and may differ from Population Estimates due to their different statistical proce-
     dures. In 2000, according to that year's census, New York Hispanics were 2,2160,554, or
     one-third of the city's entire population. The last ACS, conducted in 2005–2007 estimated
     the city's total population as 8,246,310 people, of which 5,987,241 (72,45 percent) are classi-
     fied as "Not Hispanic or Latino," and 2,259,069 (27,39 percent) as "Hispanic or Latino." See
     U.S. Census Bureau, *2005–2007 American Community Survey.* See also U.S. Census Bureau,
     "Methodology for the United States Resident Population Estimates by Age, Sex, Race, and
     Hispanic Origin" (Vintage 2008): April 1, 2000 to July 1, 2008, http://www.census.gov/
     popest/topics/methodology/2008-nat-meth.html. The annual Population Estimates are also
     reviewed by NYC Department of City Planning demographers, who through a process af-
     forded by the Census Bureau have successfully challenged the Bureau's 2007 population es-
     timates for each borough. See http://www.census.gov/popest/archives/challenges.html. In
     July 1, 2008, according to NYC Department of City Planning, New York City's population
     reached a historic peak of 8,363,710, largely due to the increase of the Hispanic population,
     "The 'Current' Population of New York City," July 1, 2009, http://home2.nyc.gov/html/dcp/
     html/census/popcur.shtml, and Sam Roberts, "Hispanic Population Growth Pushed New
     York to Census Record," *New York Times,* May 14, 2009, http://www.nytimes.com/2009/05/
     14/nyregion/14nycensus.html.

4.   U.S. Census Bureau, *2005–2007 American Community Survey.* "Place of Birth" and "World
     Region of Birth of Foreign Born," March 1, 2009, http://factfinder.census.gov/servlet/
     ADPTable?_bm=y&-geo_id=16000US3651000&-qr_name=ACS_2007_3YR_G00_DP3YR5
     &-ds_name=ACS_2007_3YR_G00_&-_lang=en&-redoLog=false&-_sse=on.

     Between 2005 and 2007 exactly 3,028,174, or 36.72 percent of NYC's total population, were
     foreign-born; of the 63 percent that was native, 50 percent were born in New York. See ibidem,
     "Population and Housing Narrative Profile" at http://factfinder.census.gov/servlet/NPTable?_
     bm=y&-qr_name=ACS_2007_3YR_G00_NP01&-geo_id=16000US3651000&-gc_url=&-ds_
     name=&-_lang=en.

5. In Miami, the U.S. city that closest resembles New York as a compendium of all Latin American nationalities, Cubans constitute an estimate 48.61 percent of the total Hispanic population, which in turn amounts to around 68.8 percent of the city's entire population. See 2005–2007 ACS at http://factfinder.census.gov/servlet/ADPTable?_bmy&-qr_name= ACS_2007_3YR_G00_DP3YR5&-geo_id=16000US1245000&-gc_url=&-ds_name= ACS_2007_3YR_G00_&-_lang=en&-redoLog=false&-_sse=on, under "Hispanic or Latino and Race." In Los Angeles, Chicago, and Houston, the three cities that follow New York in the ranking of largest places in total population and in Hispanic population, the leading Latino group (Mexicans) represent an estimate 68.85, 73.85, and 75.79 percent, respectively, of the entire Latino population. Source: U.S. Census Bureau, 2005–2007 ACS, for Los Angeles, http://factfinder.census.gov/servlet/ADPTable?_bm=y&-qr_name=ACS_2007_ 3YR_G00_DP3YR5&-geo_id=16000US0644000&-gc_url=&-ds_name=ACS_2007_3YR_ G00_&-_lang=en&-redoLog=false&-_sse=on; for Chicago http://factfinder.census.gov/ servlet/ADPTable?_bm=y&-qr_name=ACS_2007_3YR_G00_DP3YR5&-geo_id= 16000US1714000&-gc_url=&-ds_name=ACS_2007_3YR_G00_&-_lang=en&-redoLog= false&-_sse=on; and for Houston, http://factfinder.census.gov/servlet/ADPTable?_bm=y &-qr_name=ACS_2007_3YR_G00_DP3YR5&-geo_id=16000US4835000&-gc_url=&-ds_ name=ACS_2007_3YR_G00_&-_lang=en&-redoLog=false&-_sse=on. See also U.S. Census Bureau. The Hispanic Population, Census 2000 brief.

6. U.S. Census Bureau, *Coming From the Americas: A Profile of the Nation's Foreign-born Population from Latin America*, Census 2000 brief, January 2002, http:///www.census .gov/prod/2002pubs/cenbr01-2.pdf. See also "Latino Data Project. Census 2000: The Latino Population and the Transformation of Metropolitan New York," Center for Latin American, Caribbean, and Latino Studies and Center for Urban Research, City University of New York's Graduate Center, in conjunction with the MirRam Group and the Global Strategy Group, August 2009, http://web.gc.cuny.edu/lastudies/pages/latinodataprojectreports .html.

7. U.S. Census Bureau, 2005–2007 ACS. See http://factfinder.census.gov/servlet/ADPTable?_ bm=y&-geo_id-16000US3457000&-qr_name=ACS_2007_3YR_G00_DP3YR5&-%20geo_ id=16000US3457000&-ds_name=ACS_2007_3YR_G00_&-_lang=en&-redoLog=false&_ sse=on. The percentage of South and Central Americans results from dividing the number of "Other Hispanic or Latino" (48,127) into the total Hispanic population of any race (78,802), under the assumption that most the former are indeed of South and Central American origin.

8. Pew Hispanic Center, "U.S. Population Projections: 2005–2050, 2.11.2008," http:// pewhispanic.org/reports/report.php?ReportID=85.

9. U.S.Census Bureau, 2005–2007 ACS, "Language Spoken at Home—Population 5 years and Over," http://factfinder.census.gov/servlet/ADPTable?_bm=y&-qr_name=ACS_2007_3YR_ G00_DP3YR2&-geo_id=16000US3651000&-ds_name=ACS_2007_3YR_G00_&-_lang= en&-redoLog=false&-_sse=on.

10. Ibid., "Population and Housing Narrative profile (2005–2997)." See http://factfinder .census.gov/servlet/NPTable?_bm=y&-qr_name=ACS_2007_3YR_G00_NPTable?_bm=y &-qr_name=ACS_2007_3YR_G00_NP01&geo_id=16000US3651000&-gc_url=&-ds_ name=&-_lang=en, under "Nativity and Language."

11. Kirk Semple, "A Killing in a Town Where Latinos Sense Hate," *New York Times*, November 13, 2008, http://www.nytimes.com/2008/11/14/nyregion/14immigrant.html?scp=16&sq=& st–yt. Albor Ruiz, "A Climate of Hate Ends Innocent Life," *Daily News*, December 11, 2008, http://wwwnydailynews.com/ny_local/bronx/2008/12/11/2008–12–11_a_climate_of _hate_ends_innocent_life-10.html.

12. U.S. Census Bureau, Population Division, Press Release: "U.S. Hispanic Population Surpasses 45 Million Now 15 Percent of Total," May 1, 2008, http://www.census.gov/Press -Release/www/releases/archives/population/011910.html. See Table 1: "Estimate of the Population by Race Alone or in Combination and Hispanic Origin for the U.S. and States, July 1, 2007."

13. Ibid.

14. U.S. Census Bureau, *The Hispanic Population*, p. 3.

15. Louis DeSipio, "More Than the Sum of Its Parts: The Building Blocks of a Pan-Ethnic Latino Identity," in Wilbur C. Rich, ed., *The Politics of Minority Coalitions: Race, Ethnicity, and Shared Uncertainties* (New York: Praeger, 1996), p. 186.

16. Félix Padilla, *Latino Ethnic Consciousness: The Case of Mexican Americans and Puerto Ricans in Chicago* (Notre Dame: University of Notre Dame Press, 1985). This book played a crucial role in setting the theoretical framework for the ongoing discussion on pan-Latinidad.

17. Among the active African-Caribbean members of the Antillean independence movement was a very young Arturo Alfonso Schomburg, the future donor of the collection that gave birth to the Schomburg Center for Research in Black Culture, and who had recently migrated to New York from his native Puerto Rico. See infra, Carmen Dolores Hernandez's selection, "Puerto Rican Voices in English," note 3.

18. "Hispanics—that is, Spaniards and Latin Americans." Bernardo Vega, *Memoirs*, ed. César Andréu Iglesias, trans. Juan Flores (New York: Monthly Review Press, 1983), p. 73. The time-long participation of groups from different Latin American countries in nationally defined organizations such as Puerto Rican or Cuban clubs is well documented in the archives of El Centro de Estudios Puertorriqueños (Center for Puerto Rican studies) at Hunter College. For the history of women of Hispanic descent, see Vicki L. Ruiz and Virginia Sánchez Korrol, eds., *Latinas in the United States: A Historical Encyclopedia*, 3 vols. (Bloomington: Indiana University Press: 2006), who are also the project leaders of the educational Web site Latinas in History: An Interactive Project, March 1, 2009, http:// depthome.brooklyn.cuny.edu/latinashistory/lessonplanslatino.html. For a general presentation of the history of the Spanish community during the first half of the twentieth century, see Peter N. Carroll and James D. Fernández, *Facing Fascim: New York and the Spanish*

Civil War (New York: New York University Press, 2007), a catalog of a Museum of the City of New York exhibition.

19. See Miguel Algarín, "The Sidewalk of High Art," in Miguel Algarín and Bob Holman, eds., *Aloud: Voices from the Nuyorican Poets Cafe* (New York: Henry Holt, 1994); and Miguel Piñero, "Introduction: Nuyorican Language," in *Nuyorican Poetry: An Anthology of Puerto Rican Words and Feelings* (New York: William Morrow, 1975).

20. The growth of Latin American indigenous languages in New York is one of the novelties brought by the immigration surge of recent decades. The phenomenon comprises Amerindian languages from: 1. Mexico; 2. the Andean region, Peru, Ecuador, Bolivia, etc.; 3. the rest of Central and South America.

   1. According to Mexico's Instituto Nacional de Lenguas Indígenas (National Institute of Indigenous Languages), there are 364 surviving Ameridian languages and dialects in that country. They are divided into 11 language families, 68 linguistic groups, and their regional forms, which are sometimes mutually unintelligible. The two main linguistic groups of the Mixteco-Poblano region (the states of Puebla, Oaxaca, and Guerrero, where most of New York's Mexican immigrants come from) are Náhua, or Náhuatl, and Mixteco, which includes the variances of Tlapaneco and Zapoteco. As with the rest of Latin American indigenous languages, there is no official information about the number of their local speakers, which varies significantly depending on geographical factors, age, and level of schooling. Younger Mixteco-Poblano immigrants, for instance, tend to be bilingual Spanish and Mixteco or Náhua speakers, for since the 1990s the preservation of pre-Colombian languages has been a federal policy in Mexico. On the other hand, there are also cases of monolingual Mixteco speakers, such as the members (mostly elders, women, and children) of a Staten Island community of immigrants from San Pedro, Oaxaca. A third Mexican linguistic group that is supposedly present in the New York area is Mayan, although this is most likely to be found among Guatemalan and other Central American immigrants. I am deeply thankful to Eduardo Peñaloza, coordinator of Educational Programming of the Department of Cultural Affairs, Consulate General of Mexico in New York, for this information. See Mexico, Instituto Nacional de Lenguas Indígenas, "Catálogo de las lenguas indígenas nacionales: Variantes lingüísticas de México con sus autodenominaciones y referencias geoestadísticas," March 15, 2009, http://www.inali.gob.mx/catalogo2007/.

   2. There are two major Amerindian languages from the South American Andean region: Quechua and Aymara. Quechua (alternative spellings: Quichua, Keshua, also Runa-Simi) was the lingua franca of the Tahuantinsuyo, or Incan Empire; after the Spanish Conquest it continued to be used—in fact, it was expanded—as the local language of government and local administration. As in the cases analyzed before, Quechua is a family of languages and dialectical variances, sometimes very different among themselves. It is found in a vast geographical area ranging from Colombia to Northern Argentina. There are an estimated twelve million bilingual or monolingual

Quechua native speakers, most of them in Peru, Ecuador, and Bolivia; although there are no official statistics, in the New York area it is certainly spoken or understood by most immigrants from those countries. Aymara was the second largest language of the Incan Empire, and today is spoken by approximately two million people in Bolivia, parts of Peru, and Northern Chile. It can be heard mostly in Bolivian communities, which in the Northeast are concentrated in Washington, DC and Virginia. I thank Miryam Yataco for this information. The most comprehensive information about Quechua and Aymara can be found at http://www.quechua.org.uk//Eng/Main/.

3. Although as in the previous cases, there is no official information on the number of speakers, it seems reasonable to expect a repetition of the pattern existing in the home country. For example, it is likely that the four-thousand-odd Paraguayans living in New York City speak Guaraní, Paraguay's official language alongside Spanish, and so on.

21. I have elaborated more extensively on this point in my essay "Is New York the New Center of Latin-American Literary Culture?" *Salmagundi*, vol. no.161–162 (Spring-Summer 2009): 182–191. A previous Spanish-language version, "Nueva York y la literatura hispanoameri-cana," appeared in *El País*, May 17, 2007, http://www.elpais.com/articulo/opinion/Nueva/York/literatura/hispanoamericana/elpepiopi/20070517elpepiopi_5/Tes/.

22. Luis Rafael Sánchez, "El cuarteto nuevayorkés," in *La guagua aérea* (San Juan: Cultural, 1994), pp. 23–34. The complete passage reads: "New York would be the other capital of Puerto Rico if it were not already the capital of all of Spanish America. In New York the capital that Bolivar envisioned, embracing all of the hemisphere's Spanish-speaking na-tionalities, is being established." ["Nueva York sería la otra capital de Puerto Rico si no lo fuera de toda Hispanoamérica. En Nueva York se cimenta la capital ensoñada por Bolivar, la que aloja todas las nacionalidades de la America en español."]

23. See Juri Lotman, *Universe of the Mind: A Semiotic Theory of Culture*, introduction by Umberto Eco (Bloomington: Indiana University Press, 2001). I owe the idea of connecting Lotman's notion of semiosphere with the concept of Border and Latino multi-identities to Donna Kabalen de Bichara, a professor at Instituto Tecnológico de Monterrey, México, who in turn presented it at the Recovering the U.S. Hispanic Literary Heritage Conference held in Houston, Texas, November 14–15, 2008. For the idea of cities as nodes of a network of material and symbolic exchanges, see Saskia Sassen, ed., *Global Networks, Linked Cities* (New York: Routledge, 2002).

24. See also John Storm Roberts, *The Latin Tinge: The Impact of Latin American Music on the United States* (New York: Oxford University Press, 1979); and César Miguel Rondón, *The Book of Salsa: A Chronicle of Caribbean Music from the Caribbean to New York City* (Chapel Hill: University of North Carolina Press, 2008). In the past few years, a number of TV documenta-ries have explored the role of New York in the development of American and Latino music, among them the notable *Latin Music USA;* see http://www.pbs.org/wgbh/latinmusicusa/.

25. See Antonio Saborit, "Marius de Zayas en América," introductory essay to Marius de Zayas, *Crónicas y ensayos: Nueva York y París, 1909–1911*, ed. Antonio Saborit (México,

D.F.: Universidad Autónoma de México/Pértiga), 2008. See also Deborah Cullen, ed., *Nexus New York: Latin/American Artists in the Modern Metropolis* (New York: El Museo del Barrio, with Yale University Press, 2009).

26. In the late nineteenth century, Portuguese sailors and displaced whale-industry workers from the Azores and Cape Verde islands migrated also to the New York area, settling mostly around Newark, New Jersey. It was at the same time that Brazilians began to arrive in New York in significant numbers. For the Portuguese immigration in general, see Manoel da Silveira Cardozo, *The Portuguese in America, 590 B.C.-1974: A Chronology and Fact Book* (Dobbs Ferry, NY: Oceana, 1976). Among the several books on the Brazilian community, see Maxine L. Margolis, *Little Brazil: An Ethnography of Brazilians in New York City* (Princeton: Princeton University Press, 1993); and Bernadete Beserra, *Brazilian Immigrants in the United States: Cultural Imperialism and Social Class* (El Paso, TX: LFB Scholarly, 2003).

27. Immanuel Wallerstein, *World-Systems Analysis: An Introduction* (Durham: Duke University Press, 2004). See also the article coauthored with Aníbal Quijano "Americanity as a Concept, or the Americas in the Modern World-System," *International Social Science Journal* 44, no.4 (1992): 549–57. *Longue durée*, loosely translated "long-term," is a concept derived from the historiographical approach of the Annales school, which gave priority to long-term structures over singular events. It was presented by Fernand Braudel in his groundbreaking *La Méditerranée et le monde méditerranéen à l'époque de Philippe II*, first published in France in 1949; see Fernand Braudel, *The Mediterranean and the Mediterranean World in the Age of Philip II*, 2 vols. (Berkeley: University of California Press, 1995).

28. *Ladino*, also known as *Judezmo*, Judeo-Spanish or *Spaniol*, is essentially fifteenth-century Spanish with lexical borrowing from the different languages (Turkish, Greek, Italian, Portuguese, etc.) spoken in the countries where Sephardic Jews lived after their expulsion from Spain. For a comprehensive analysis of the interrelation between New York, the Sephardic Diaspora, and the Spanish-speaking world, see Kenya C. Dworkin y Méndez, "Caught Between the Cross and the Crescent and Star: Orientalism, Co-Ethnic Recognition Failure, and New York's Sephardic Jews," in Ignacio López-Calvo, ed., *Alternative Orientalisms in Latin America and Beyond* (Newcastle upon Tyne: Cambridge Scholars, 2007). Kahal Zur Israel ("Rock of Israel"), Recife's Sephardic synagogue, was the first synagogue in the New World. See the Museun of the Jewish People online, March 1, 2009, at http://www.bh.org.il/database-article.aspx?48714. For New York's Sephardic history, see "Rabbi Isaac Aboab de Fonseca (1605–1693)," Jewish Virtual Library—A Division of the American-Israeli Cooperative Entrerprise, http://www.jewishvirtuallibrary.org/jsource/biography/Fonseca.html, and the article "New York," http://www.jewishencyclopedia.com/view.jsp?artid=248&letter=N#737. Also see Samuel G. Armistead, *Judeo-Spanish Ballads from New York* (Berkeley: University of California Press, 1981); Aviva Ben-Ur, "We Speak and Write This Language Against Our Will": Jews, Hispanics, and the Dilemma of Ladino-Speaking Sephardim in Early Twentieth-Century New York," *American Jewish Archives* 50, nos. 1–2 (1998): 131–42; Maír José Bernadete, *Hispanic Culture and Character of the Sephardic Jews*

(New York: Foundation for the Advancement of Sephardic Studies and Culture/Sephardic House, 1982); Louis M. Hacker, "The Communal Life of the Sephardic Jews in New York City," *Jewish Social Service Quarterly* 3, no. 2 (December 1926): 32–40. For further documentation of local Sephardic history, visit the archives of Congregation Shearith Israel–The Spanish and Portuguese Synagogue, 8 West 70 Street, New York, NY 10023, http://www.shearithisrael.org/folder/main_frames_new.html.

29. According with the most recent calculations, another 1.5 million people might have died during the middle passage. See Walter C. Rucker, "The African and European Slave Trades," in Alton Hornsby Jr., ed., *A Companion to African American History* (Malden, MA: Blackwell, 2005), pp. 48–66. According to Rucker, the Atlantic expansion of Spain and Portugal during the decades preceding Colombus's voyages was one of the factors that precipitated the formation of modern slavery: "one of the most important events that led to the Atlantic slavetrade was the colonization of the numerous inhabited and uninhabited Atlantic islands by Iberians. By the 1450s, the Portuguese had colonized the previously uninhabited Azores, Madeira, the Cape Verde Islands, and São Tomé and, within a few decades, had transformed each territory into a profitable sugar plantation colony. This pattern was repeated by the Spanish in the Canary Islands with one slight difference—the Canaries were already inhabited by the Guanches. This group, of likely Native American origin, became a slave labor force throughout the Atlantic islands, and both Spain and Portugal quickly became experts in acquiring additional dependent labor. By the early 1500s, all of the Atlantic islands were utilizing a mixture of Guanche, Moor, and Atlantic African slave labor, establishing a pattern that would be replicated on a much a larger scale in the Americas" (p. 56). See also T. Bentley Duncan, *Atlantic Islands: Madeira, the Azores, and the Cape Verdes in Seventeenth-Century Commerce and Navigation* (Chicago: University of Chicago Press, 1972); Herbert S. Klein, *African Slavery in Latin America and the Caribbean* (Oxford: Oxford University Press, 1986); and John Thornton, *Africa and Africans in the Making of the Atlantic World, 1400–1800* (New York: Cambridge University Press, 1998).

30. Paul Gilroy, *The Black Atlantic: Modernity and Double Consciousness* (Cambridge: Harvard University Press, 1993), p. 2. The "rhyzomorphic, fractal" nature of the transcultural and transnational formation that Gilroy calls the Black Atlantic is made up of "structures of feeling, producing, communicating, and remembering" that molded the "stereophonic, bilingual . . . cultural forms originated by, but not longer the exclusive property of blacks." See pp. 3, 4. For a recent elaboration on the concept of African-diasporic identities, see Agustín Laó-Montes, "Decolonial Moves: Translocating African-Diaspora Spaces," *Cultural Studies* 21, nos. 2–3 (March-May 2007): 309–38.

31. See Clara Rodríguez, *Changing Race: Latinos, the Census and the History of Ethnicity in the United States* (New York: New York University Press, 2000), p. 29 and passim.

32. For a brief survey of the new directions in academic research and literary work, see Myrna García-Calderon, "Current Approaches to Hispanic Caribbean Writing: An Overview," *Review: Literature and Arts of the Americas* 74 40, no. 1 (2007): 61–72.

33. Specifically, Torres-Saillant refers to Edouard Glissant's idea of archipelagoization and to Antonio Benítez-Rojo's *The Repeating Island: The Caribbean and the Postmodern Perspective* (Durham: Duke University Press, 1996). See Silvio Torres-Saillant, "New Ways of Imagining the Caribbean," *Review: Literature and Arts of the Americas 74* 40, no. 1 (2007): 6, and his book, *An Intellectual History of the Caribbean* (New York: Palgrave Macmillan, 2005).

34. Probably the most important recent contribution to our understanding of these connections is Kirsten Silva Gruesz's work. See her essays "The Mercurial Space of 'Central' America: New Orleans, Honduras, and the Writing of the Banana Republic," in Levander and Levine, *Hemispheric American Studies*, pp. 140–65; "The Gulf of Mexico System and the 'Latinness' of New Orleans," *American Literary History* 18, no. 3 (Fall 2006): 468–95; and "New Orleans, Capital of the (Other) Nineteenth Century," in her *Ambassadors of Culture: The Transamerican Origins of Latino Writing* (Princeton: Princeton University Press, 2002), pp. 108–120. It was in New Orleans that the first Spanish-language newspaper of the United States, *El Misisipí*, was launched in 1808. Nicolás Kanellos, *Hispanic Periodicals in the United States, Origins to 1960: A Brief History and Comprehensive Bibliography* (Houston: Arte Público, 2000). Another example of the interconnections between New Orleans, the Caribbean Central America, and New York is the history of the Garifuna community; see Sarah England, *Afro Central Americans in New York City: Garifuna Tales of Transnational Movements in Racialized Space* (Gainesville: University Press of Florida, 2006)

35. See Orlando José Hernández, prologue to his translation of Graciany Miranda Archilla, *Hungry Dust/Polvo Hambriento* (Lima: Latino Press, Latin American Writers Institute, Hostos Community College, CUNY/Santo Oficio, 2005), pp. 21–22.

36. See "The 2008 Global Cities Index," *Foreign Policy*, November/December 2008. March 1, 2009, http://www.foreignpolicy.com/story/cms.php?story_id=4509&page=0. The Global Cities Index is developed by *Foreign Affairs*, A. T. Kearney Inc., and the Chicago Council on Global Affairs, in consultation with an advisory team of international experts, including Saskia Sassen, Witold Rybczynski, Janet Abu-Lughod, and Peter Taylor. The ranking is the result of a comprehensive survey of the ways in which the sixty foremost global cities are connected with the rest of the world. The data collected is classified across five different dimensions: business activity, human capital (which includes the size of a city's immigrant population), information exchange (how are news disseminated between that city and the rest of the world), cultural experience (number and quality of attractions offered, from cultural to sport events), and political engagement (the degree to which a city influences global policymaking and dialogue). The two other U.S. Latino cities that made the ranking are Los Angeles (6th) and Miami (32d). There are also seven Iberoamerican cities: Madrid (14th), Mexico City (25th), Sao Paulo (31st), Buenos Aires (33d), Bogotá (43d), Rio de Janeiro (47th), and Caracas (51st). For the notion of global urban spaces, see Saskia Sassen, *The Global City: New York, London, Tokyo* (Princeton: Princeton University Press, 2001); Paul L. Knox and Peter L. Taylor, eds., *World Cities in a World-System* (Cambridge: Cambridge University Press, 1995);

and Joel Kotkin, *The City: A Global History* (New York: Modern Library/Random House, 2005).

37. See Agustin Laó-Montes, his introductory essay to the collection of essays he coedited with Arlene Dávila, *Mambo Montage: The Latinization of New York* (New York: Columbia University Press, 2001), and, in that same collection, his own essay "Niuyol: Urban Regime, Latino Social Movements, Ideologies of Latinidad." See also "Nuebayol y los avatares de lo Latino/Americano: Historias, Discursos y Escenarios Políticos," Arenas de lucha cultural en los Estados Unidos y America Latina: Comparando escenarios y politicas culturales, Diplomado en Gestión de Procesos Culturales y Construcción de lo Público, Bogotá, Colombia, Octubre 28, 2006, http://www.culturarecreacionydeporte.gov.co/cultura_recreacion_y_deporte/sistema_distrital_de_cultura/diplomado/Ponencia%20Agustin%20Lao.pdf.

38. The closest thing to an "official" definition of Hispanics in the U.S. derives from Public Law 94-311 of 1976, which required the collection and publication of data of "Americans of Spanish descent" in censuses and in surveys produced by schools, public health facilities and other government agencies. In compliance to that piece of legislation, in 1977 the Office of Management and Budget developed the "Standards for Maintaining, Collecting, and Presenting Federal Data on Race and Ethnicity," also known as Statistical Policy Directive 15, or Directive 15. Revised in 1997, these standards define Hispanic or Latino as any "person of Cuban, Mexican, Puerto Rican, Central or South American or other Spanish culture or origin, regardless of race"; the term *Spanish origin* can be used in addition to the former two. (Note that this definition includes non-Latin Americans, such as Spaniards, but excludes non-Spanish Latin Americans, such as Brazilians, as well as their European counterparts, Portuguese.) For a history of Directive 15, see Alice Robbin, "Classifying Racial and Ethnic Group Data: The Politics of Negotiation and Accommodation," *Journal of Government Information* 27, no. 2 (2000):129–156. The U.S. Census Bureau, however, does *not* apply Directive 15 to counting Hispanics; instead, it relies entirely on the self-definition provided by the respondents to the census questionnaire. In this regard, a 2006 Pew Hispanic Center survey found that, generally, 48 percent of Latino adults describe themselves first by their country of origin; 26 percent by the terms *Latino* or *Hispanic*; and 24 percent by the term *American*. As for a preference between *Hispanic* and *Latino*, another Pew survey found that 36 percent of respondents prefer the term *Hispanic*, 21 percent prefer *Latino*, and the rest have no preference. See Jeffrey Passel and Paul Taylor, "Who's Hispanic?" Pew Hispanic Center, special report, 5.28.2009, http://pewhispanic.org/files/reports/111.pdf.

The classic scholarly reference on this issue is Suzanne Oboler's *Ethnic Labels, Latino Lives: Identity and the Politics of Representation in the United States* (Minneapolis: University of Minnesota Press, 1995). For some recent academic contributions, see Jorge Duany, "Puerto Rican, Hispanic or Latino? Recent Debates on National and Pan-ethnic Identities," *Centro Journal* 15, no.2 (Fall 2003): 256–67; and Jorge J. E. Gracia, *Hispanic/Latino*

Identity: A Philosophical Perspective (Malden, MA: Blackwell, 2000). For a preliminary bibliography, see also Harvey Choldin, "Statistics and Politics: The 'Hispanic' Issue in the 1980 Census," *Demography* 23, no. 3 (August 1986): 403–18; David E. Hayes-Bautista and Jorge Chapa, "Latino Terminology: Conceptual Basis for Standarized Terminology," *American Journal of Public Health* 77, no. 1 (January 1987): 61–68; Edward Murguia, "On Latino/Hispanic Ethnic Identity," *Latino Studies Journal* 2, no. 3 (September 1991): 8–18; Clara E. Rodríguez, *Changing Race: Latinos, the Census, and the History of Ethnicity in the United States* (New York: New York University Press, 2000); Ilan Stavans, *The Hispanic Condition: Reflections on Culture and Identity in America* (New York: Harper Collins, 1995); Xavier F. Totti, "The Making of a Latino Ethnic Identity," *Dissent* (Fall 1987): 537–43; and Fernando M. Treviño, "Standarized Terminology for Standarized Populations," *American Journal of Public Health* 77 (1987): 89–72. On the issue of panethnic identity, see David López and Yen Espíritu, "Panethnicity in the United States: A Theoretical Framework," *Ethnic and Racial Studies* 13 (1990): 198–224, and the bibliographical references included at the end of Milagros Ricourt and Ruby Danta, "The Emergence of Latino Panethnicity," this volume. See also: "Identity Politics and the Latino vs. Hispanic Debate: A Data-Driven Learning Guide," Ann Arbor, Michigan: Inter-university Consortium for Political and Social Research [distributor], 2009-04-16. Doi:10.3886/identitypol, retrieved August 31, 2009, http://www.icpsr.umich.edu/cocoon/OLC/identitypol.xml.

Last year, the nomination of Judge Sonia Sotomayor to the Supreme Court generated a spirited public discussion on the meaning of the terms *Hispanic* and *Latino* (as well as on Sotomayor's "wise Latina" remark). Some the most relevant contributions in the print media and the blogosphere are Esther J. Cepeda, "Living in Label Land: Are You Hispanic or Latino? May 31, 2009, http://www.600words.com; Michael Jones-Correa Answers About Latino Politics, *New York Times*, June 12, 2009, http://cityroom.blogs.nytimes.com/2009/06/12/answers-about-latino-politics-part-3/; Neil A. Lewis, "Was a Hispanic Justice on the Court in the 1930s?" *New York Times*, May 26, 2009, http://www.nytimes.com/2009/05/27/us/27hispanic.html? r=2; Gregory Rodriguez, "The Generic Latino: What Does the Nomination of Sonia Sotomayor Really Say?" *Los Angeles Times*, June 1, 2009, http://articles.latimes.com/2009/jun/01/opinio/oe-rodriguez; and Passel and Taylor, "Who's Hispanic?"; Zimmerman, "Judge Sotomayor: A Mythic 'Hispanic.'"

39.   See Rachel Dry interview with Grace Flores-Hughes, "She Made Hispanic Official," *Washington Post*, July 26, 2009.

40.   Pedro Henríquez Ureña, trans. Gilbert Chase, *A Concise History of Latin American Culture* (New York: Praeger, 1966). Original Spanish-language version, *Historia de la cultura en la América Hispánica* (México, D.F.: Fondo de Cultura económica, 1947). See also Henríquez Ureña, *Literary Currents in Hispanic America* (Cambridge: Harvard University Press, 1945).

41.   For a brief presentation of the conflicting sides of this issue and a critique of an exclusionary view among Latino scholars, see Edmundo Paz Soldán, "Latino, Latin American, Spanish American, North American, or All at the Same Time?" in Nelsy Echávez-Solano

and K. C. Dworkin y Méndez, eds., *Spanish and Empire* (Nashville: Vanderbilt University Press, 2007), pp. 139–52. See also Debra Castillo, *Redreaming America: Towards a Bilingual American Culture* (Albany: SUNY Press, 2005); and "Los 'nuevos' latinos y la globalización de los estudios literarios," in Boris Muñoz and Silvia Spitta, eds., *Más allá de la ciudad letrada: Crónicas y espacios urbanos* (Pittsburgh: Instituto Internacional de Literatura Iberoamericana, 2003), pp. 439–59.

42. For a critical history of the idea of mestizaje, see Marilyn Grace Miller, *Rise and Fall of the Cosmic Race: The Cult of Mestizaje in Latin America* (Austin: University of Texas Press, 2004). In many ways, the racialized stratification of Spanish American societies, as well as racism in general against mestizos, Indians, blacks, and other people of color, was strengthened after the end of Spain's colonial rule. Indeed, one key factor initially spurring the independence movement in Spanish America—particularly in the plantation economies of the Caribbean and Venezuela—was the fear that the criollo elite (people of European descent born in the Americas) had of slave or Indian revolts; the insurrection that in 1804 led to the establishment of Haiti as the second independent republic in the Americas—and the first independent black republic in the world—was a particularly terrifying prospect for the ruling classes throughout the hemisphere. See Anderson, *Imagined Communities*, pp. 48 and 60 (note 44).

43. For the concept of hybridity in postcolonial theory and cultural studies in general, see Homi K. Bhabha, *The Location of Culture* (New York: Routledge, 2004); Néstor García Canclini, *Hybrid Cultures: Strategies for Entering and Leaving Modernity* (Minneapolis: University of Minnesota Press, 2005); and Robert J.C. Young, *Colonial Desire: Hybridity in Theory, Culture, and Race* (New York: Routledge, 2003). For a general introduction, see Deborah A. Kapchan and Pauline Turner Strong, "Theorizing the Hybrid," *Journal of American Folklore* 112, no. 445 (Summer 1999): 239–53, http://www.jstor.org/pss/541360.

44. William A. Henry III, "Beyond the Melting Pot," *Time*, April 9, 1990, pp. 28–31, http://www.time.com/time/magazine/article/0,9171,969770,00.html. See also Richard Rodriguez, *Brown: The Last Discovery of America* (New York: Penguin, 2002). For a survey of some of the problems involving the use of "brown" as an ethnic-racial category and its delimitation from blackness in the U.S., see Claudia Milian Arias, "Playing with the Dark: Africana and Latino Literary Imaginations," in Lewis R. Gordon and Jane Anna Gordon, eds., *A Companion to African-American Studies* (Malden, MA: Blackwell, 2006), pp. 543–67. At the same time, the self-identification of Hispanics as belonging to "other race" or to "two or more races"in the 1980, 1990, and 2000 census is not equivalent to a definition of mestizaje as a racial category. As Clara E. Rodriguez points out, many Latinos who chose the "other race" box in the census questionnaire most likely regard the term "race" as a substitute for nationality, culture, skin color, ethnicity, or a combination of these. See Rodríguez, *op. cit.* p.152.

45. For an overview of the notion of assimilation from the nineteenth century to the present day, see Richard Alba and Victor Nee, *Remaking the American Mainstream: Assimilation and Contemporary Immigration* (Cambridge: Harvard University Press, 2003). For a New

York perspective, and the disparities among racial and ethnic groups, see also Philip Kasinitz, John H. Mollenkopf, Mary C. Waters, and Jennifer Holdaway, *Inheriting the City: The Children of Immigrants Come of Age* (Cambridge: Harvard University Press, 2008).

46. Paz Soldán, "Latino, Latin American," p. 151. Edmundo Paz Soldán is also coeditor, with Chilean Alberto Fuguet, of a well-known anthology of short stories and chronicles set in the United States, *Se habla español: Voces latinas en USA* (Spanish is spoken here: Latino voices in the U.S.) (Miami: Alfagura, 2000).

47. Juan Flores, *From Bomba to Hip Hop: Puerto Rican Culture and Latino Identity* (New York: Columbia University Press, 2000), p. 144; and "Nueva York, Diaspora City: Latinos Between and Beyond," in Doris Sommer, ed., *Bilingual Games: Some Literary Investigations* (New York: Palgrave Macmillan, 2003), pp. 70–86. Russian literary critic Mikhail M. Bakhtin borrowed the notion of polyphony from music and transformed it into one of the centerpieces of his semiotic theory, along with his concepts of unfinalizability and carnival; see his *Problems of Dostoevsky's Poetics* (Minneapolis: University of Minnesota Press, 1984).

48. Anderson, *Imagined Communities,* chapter 3 and passim.

49. See Richard Lee Nostrand, "Mexican Americans Circa 1850," *Annals of the Association of American Geographers* 65, no. 3 (September 1975): 378–390.

50. The 333 years invoked by the organizers placed Santa Fe's origins in 1550, but that was a real stretch of their imagination—and a nice illustration of Benedict Anderson's notion of national identity as an imaginary construction. In fact, Santa Fe was founded by Pedro de Peralta, third Spanish governor of New Mexico (when it was a province of the viceroyalty of New Spain, present-day Mexico) in 1610, sixty years after the supposed date of settlement. (Still, that makes Santa Fe the nation's oldest state capital). By choosing the date of 1550, the organizers meant to commemorate the Coronado expedition, the first major European incursion in today's U.S. Southwest, which actually took place during 1540–1542. Despite these historical blunders, the celebration was thoughtfully crafted by Governor Bradford Prince and other local authorities and businessmen to promote the territory (New Mexico was not admitted to statehood until 1912) and attract investors for its mining and tourism sectors. The Tertio-Millenial Exposition—such was its rather awkward name—was a forty-five-day fair that showcased regional products alongside horse races, Indian dances, and other amenities. The exposition's centerpiece was a three-day pageant with processions and tableaux vivants that celebrated the territory's "glorious history." The reenactments included the arrival of Coronado's expedition to the area, a mock battle between Pueblo Indians and Spaniards, and General Kearny's occupation of the Santa Fe in 1846. The July 19, 1883, edition of the *New Mexican Review* reported on the first day of the parade under the headline "The Royal Splendor and Barbaric Magnificence of Yesterday's Celebration—The Banner of the Cross Again Planted After a Lapse of Three Centuries." The event was described as "one of the most unique and resplendent parades ever witnessed by an American assembly." The chronicler's enthusiasm reached its climax with the depiction of the Native Americans, which amplified the tone of

Whitman's letter: "Those splendid specimens of physical manhood, the Apache chiefs, warriors and hunters, with their gleaming spears and buckskin robes . . . the Oriental and innocent looking Zunis . . . the sun dried and good hearted San Juan Indians . . . the mild mannered Pecuris . . . aroused the admiration to the highest pitch by the characteristic wildness of their makeup." In his oration during the Coronado parade, Major Jose D. Sena, "attired as a Spanish Chieftain in crimson, black and gold, with high boots, helmet and sword" characterized both the conquistadors and "their descendents here gathered" as "Spaniards." Chris Wilson, *The Myth of Santa Fé: Creating a Modern Regional Tradition* (Albuquerque: University of New Mexico Press, 1997), p.186.

51. *New York Times*, August 7, 1883, http://query.nytimes.com/mem/archive-free/pdf?res= 9A02E5D6123BE033A25754C0A96E9C94629FD7CF.

52. Herbert Eugene Bolton (1870–1953), one of the greatest authorities in Spanish American history, is considered the initiator in the United States of a holistic interpretation of the history of the Americas, summarily known as the Bolton theory. He is also credited with the creation of the concept of the borderland, which is today associated with Gloria Anzaldúa's work. See Herbert Eugene Bolton., *History of the Americas: A Syllabus with Maps* (New York: Ginn, c. 1935) and *Bolton and the Spanish Borderlands*, ed. John Francis Bannon, S.J. (Norman: University of Oklahoma Press, 1964). Edmundo O'Gorman (1906–1995) was a Mexican historian and philosopher, and one of the leading Latin American intellectuals of the twentieth century. See his *The Invention of America: An Inquiry into the Historical Nature of the New World and the Meaning of Its History* (Bloomington: Indiana University Press, 1961). See also Gretchen Murphy, *Hemispheric Imaginings: The Monroe Doctrine and Narratives of U.S. Empire* (Durham: Duke University Press, 2005); Arthur P. Whitaker, *The Western Hemisphere Idea: Its Rise and Decline* (Ithaca: Cornell University Press, 1965); Román de la Campa, "Latin, Latino, American: Split States and Global Imaginaries," *Comparative Literature* 53, no. 4 (Autumn 2001): 373–88; and Felipe Fernández-Armesto, *The Americas: A Hemispheric History* (New York: Modern Library, 2005).

53. For an overview of the so-called hemispheric turn in American studies and the postcolonial and post-national approaches to this field, see Caroline F. Levander and Robert S. Levine's introduction to *Hemispheric American Studies*, a collection of essays by different scholars that cuts across a wide range of disciplinary boundaries; Claire Fox, "The Transnational Turn and the Hemispheric Return," *American Literary Review* 18, no. 3 (2006): 638–47; Claire Fox and Claudia Sadowski-Smith, "Theorizing the Hemisphere: Inter-Americas Work at the Intersection of American, Canadian, and Latin American Studies," *Comparative American Studies* 2, no. 1 (2004): 5–27; and Rachel Adams, "The Worlding of American Studies," *American Quarterly* 53, no. 4 (2001): 720–32. The beginning of this transformation was announced in the early 1990s by a number of books and monographs, such as José David Saldívar, *The Dialectis of Our America: Genealogy, Cultural Critique and Literary History* (Berkeley: University of California Press, 1991); Amy Kaplan and Donald Pease, eds., *Cultures of United States Imperialism* (Durham: Duke University

Press, 1993); and especially Carolyn Porter, "What We Know That We Don't Know: Re-mapping American Literary Studies," *American Literary History* 6, no. 3: 467–526, which came to summarize the concerns floating in the air. In that article, Porter urged her col-leagues to break away from a traditional concept of U.S. nation-state, to reframe their re-search within the broader geographical and analytical territory of hemisphere, and to re-construct the field along "a quadruple set of relations": between Africa and the Americas, Europe and Latin America, Latin America and North America and Europe. Another big impulse took place in 1998 around the centennial of the Spanish-American War, marked by the publication of Jeffrey Belnap and Raúl Fernández, eds., *Jose Marti's "Our America": From National to Hemispheric Cultural Studies* (Durham, NC: Duke University Press, 1998). A large number of individual and collective works soon followed suit, authored or edited among others by Anna Brickhouse, Deborah Cohn, María DeGuzmán, Román de la Campa, Claire Fox, Susan Gillman, Kirsten Silva Gruesz, Michael R. Hames-García, Djelal Kadir, Rodrigo Lazo, George Lipsitz, Laura Lomas, Walter Mignolo, Alberto Moreiras, Paula Moya, Gretchen Murphy, John Carlos Rowe, Vicki L. Ruiz, Claudia Sadowski-Smith, Ramón Saldívar, Silviano Santiago, Sandhya Shuka, Jon Smith, Doris Sommer, Silvia Spitta, Shelley Streeby, and Heidi Tinsman, among others. The notions of "contact zone," "transfrontera contact zone," and "Latin American space-in-between" are respectively associated with the work of Mary Louise Pratt, José David Saldívar, and Sil-viano Santiago. For an update on the discussion on border and diaspora theories, see Claudia Sadowski-Smith, ed., *Globalization on the Line: Culture, Capital, and Citizenship at U.S. Borders* (New York: Palgrave, 2002). For the transnationalization of American studies from a European perspective, see Maruzio Vaudagna, ed., *The Place of Europe in American History: Twentieth-Century Perspectives* (Torino: Otto, 2007). For a brief pre-sentation of transnational theory in immigration studies and the case of New York's Mexican immigrant community, see Robert C. Smith's introduction to his *Mexican New York: Transnational Lives of New Immigrants* (Berkeley: University of California Press, 2006). Another important endeavor is the Trans-Atlantic Project at Brown University, directed by Julio Ortega, which seeks to remap and reconceptualize interhemispheric cultural and literary relations, specifically looking at the triangle formed by Spain, the U.S., and Latin America. For more information, visit http://www.brown.edu/Departments/ Hispanic_Studies/people/facultypage.php?id=10291.

One

PEOPLE AND COMMUNITIES

HISTORICAL PERSPECTIVES

The EVOLUTION of the LATINO COMMUNITY in NEW YORK CITY

Early Nineteenth Century to the 1990s

Gabriel Haslip-Viera

PHASE ONE, 1810–1900

It is perhaps accurate to say that interest in the issues affecting Latinos in New York has intensified steadily in recent years. With greater frequency, journalists, academics, and government policymakers have discussed the growth of a diverse Hispanic population and its impact on employment, education, housing, crime, social services, and politics. In general, the increased scrutiny has focused attention on Latinos as a contemporary phenomenon associated with the "recent wave" of immigrants to the city; however, the origins and the evolution of New York's Hispanic community can actually be traced as far back as the early nineteenth century and possibly even earlier.[1]

Perhaps the first reference to a group that in the twentieth century would be called Latino or Hispanic was made in 1810, when Timothy Dwight, the president of Yale University, compiled a list of inhabitants or "classes" in New York, which he included in a memoir of his travels through the northeastern United States. This list made reference to "a few ... Spaniards and West Indians," who were probably merchants or other persons associated with the small, but growing commerce between New York and Spain's possessions in the Caribbean and Latin America.[2] This was also probably true of most of the "508 persons from Mexico and South America" who were counted during the federal census of 1845; however, it also appears that there might have been a substantial undercount of Latinos in New York by federal census enumerators during this first phase of the migration process that ended around 1900 and that this undercount may have continued in the decades which followed.[3]

For example, the Puerto Rican activist Bernardo Vega refers in his memoirs to the large political gatherings that were frequently organized by advocates of Cuban and Puerto Rican independence. He also makes reference to the 3,000 cigar factories that employed "many Puerto Ricans and Cubans" during the early 1890s. However, it appears that these claims are not confirmed by the official statistics of the period (see table 1.1). According to the census of 1890, the city had a Latino population of just under 6,000, which included 218 Mexicans, 1,421 Spaniards, 907 persons from Central and South America, and only 3,448 persons from Cuba, Puerto Rico, the Dominican Republic and other parts of the Caribbean.[4]

In contrast to what developed later, Latino migration to New York was relatively modest in the years prior to 1900. Hispanic emigration to the United States was generally discouraged by the socioeconomic conditions that were prevalent in Latin America throughout the nineteenth century. Most of the Central and South American republics and colonial possessions were underpopulated or were going through the first stages of economic modernization or industrialization. In Cuba, Puerto Rico,

TABLE 1.1

The Latin American and Caribbean Population of New York City, 1870–1890*

	1870	%	1880	%	1890	%
CENTRAL AMERICA	22	0.6	29	0.5	184	3.1
CUBA & WEST INDIES**	2508	69.6	3480	65.7	3448	57.5
CUBA	1565	43.4	2073	39.1		
MEXICO	86	2.3	170	3.2	218	3.6
SOUTH AMERICA	307	8.5	570	10.7	723	12.1
SPAIN	682	18.9	1048	19.8	1421	23.7
TOTAL	3605	100.0	5294	100.0	5994	100.0

*Total "foreign-born population." Includes Brooklyn, Bronx, and Manhattan for the 1870 and 1880 census. For the 1890 census also includes "Long Island City" (for all countries), Queens County and Staten Island (for Spain, South America, Cuba, and the West Indies only).

**Probably includes many persons of Spanish origin or background who lived in Cuba and Puerto Rico, which were Spanish colonies throughout this period.

SOURCE: U.S. Department of Interior, Census Office, *Compendium of the Ninth Census* (June 1, 1870) (Washington, D.C.: Government Printing Office, 1872), pp. 387–91, 449. *Compendium of the Tenth Census*, Part 1 (June 1, 1880) (Washington, D.C.: Government Printing Office, 1882), pp. 547, 551. *Census of 1890* (Washington, D.C.: Government Printing Office, 1892), pp. 645–47, 670, 672, 674, 676.

and Brazil the importation of African slave labor continued into the 1850s and 1860s because of labor shortages in the expanding plantation sectors. As the economy of the Hispanic Caribbean changed during the late nineteenth century, slave labor was increasingly replaced by Chinese contract labor and by an increased flow of European immigrants who were attracted by the growth of the Caribbean sugar, coffee, and tobacco sectors. In the rest of Latin America, economic modernization and industrialization contributed to a significant increase in European immigration. As was the case in North America during this same period, Argentina, Brazil, Chile, and a number of other countries or regions absorbed large numbers of immigrants from Spain, Italy, France, Germany, Portugal, Great Britain, Ireland, Eastern Europe, and also from Lebanon and Syria in the Middle East.[5]

Most of the immigrants who came to New York from Latin America in the late nineteenth century were business people, professionals, white-collar workers, specialized artisans, and their dependents. It appears that a network of merchants and their subordinates were the predominant group during the early nineteenth century; however, after 1860, the Latino community became much more diversified and included the owners and employees of factories, artisan shops, grocery stores, pharmacies, barbershops, rooming houses, restaurants and other enterprises. Skilled and semi-skilled artisans and laborers came to New York in increased numbers during the final decades of the nineteenth century. The majority of artisans and laborers were employed in tobacco manufacturing which expanded in the years between 1880 and 1920; however, in time, the artisans were also supplemented by a growing number of semi-skilled and unskilled industrial laborers who came to New York in search of employment in factories and in services.[6]

Political exiles also came to New York during the late nineteenth century. They included disaffected liberals, socialists and anarcho-syndicalists from Spain and Latin America. They also included alienated labor leaders, writers, poets, artists, teachers, and intellectuals. In fact, New York became the headquarters for the exiled leaders and supporters of Cuban and Puerto Rican independence during this period. The Cuban patriots, José Martí, Tomás Estrada Palma, and Dr. Julio Henna, an advocate of Puerto Rican independence, became residents of New York during the 1870s and 1880s. For a time, Martí worked for Joseph Pulitzer's *New York World,* which was one of the city's major newspapers, while Henna, a practicing physician, became one of the founders of Flower Fifth Avenue Hospital in upper Manhattan.

The importance of New York as a center for nationalist and revolutionary sentiment was reflected in the successful efforts to raise funds, publish newspapers, and hold political rallies. It was also reflected in the frequent visits by important political and cultural leaders who came to New York to participate in various activities but who were not residents of the city. These persons included Cuban revolutionary leaders such as Antonio Maceo and Máximo Gómez, who was actually a native of the

Dominican Republic. They also included Spaniards, such as the labor leader, Santiago Iglesias; other Dominicans, such as Enrique Trujillo, the author of the epic "El Enriquillo;" and educational and revolutionary leaders from Puerto Rico, such as Eugenio María de Hostos and Ramón Betances.[7]

The political exiles who lived in New York, at least temporarily during the late nineteenth century, became part of a small, vibrant, and growing community. In general, Latinos lived in scattered concentrations throughout Manhattan and downtown Brooklyn. Bernardo Vega suggests that there was relatively little housing discrimination against Hispanics during this period; however, he also acknowledges that the darker or more "African" looking Latinos were compelled to live in neighborhoods where African-Americans predominated. Arturo Alfonso Schomburg, a Puerto Rican activist who later achieved fame as a Black bibliophile in the Harlem community, established his first family residence in an African-American neighborhood called "San Juan Hill," which was located in Manhattan, west of Amsterdam Avenue, between 60th and 70th Streets. Despite this and other instances of racial segregation and discrimination in housing, Hispanics were generally found in most working-class neighborhoods of the city during this period.[8]

Concentrations of working-class Latinos were found in Harlem, Chelsea, Yorkville, the West Side, and the Lower East Side of Manhattan. They were also found in the Columbia Street and "Navy Yard" districts of Brooklyn. In general, most Hispanics lived in the midst of larger immigrant communities, where Germans, Irish, Italians, Jews, Hungarians, and other groups from central and eastern Europe predominated. Bernardo Vega states that affluent Cubans lived in the largely middle-class section of south-central Harlem, north of Cathedral Parkway. He also notes that less affluent Latinos were found in the midst of a working-class Jewish community, along Madison and Park Avenues, between 100th and 110th Streets. These last two concentrations were the nucleus of what later became known as Spanish Harlem or El Barrio.[9]

PHASE TWO, 1900–1945

In the final decades of the nineteenth century, Cubans, Puerto Ricans, and Spaniards were the predominant groups within the Latino population of New York City. This trend continued during the next phase of the migratory process which began in 1900 and ended around 1945. Puerto Ricans, in particular, became the largest Hispanic subgroup by the early 1930s, despite an island population that was very small when compared to Latin America as a whole. According to the estimates that were compiled at that time, the Latino population of New York had reached 22,000 by 1916, 41,094 by 1920, 110,223 by 1930, and 134,000 by 1940.[10] Of the 110,223 Hispanics enumerated by the census bureau in 1930, 44,908 (40.7 percent) were Puerto Ricans, 22,501 (20.4

percent) were Spaniards, 19,774 (17.9 percent) were Cubans and Dominicans, 4,653 (3.5 percent) were Mexicans, and 18,748 (17.0 percent) were persons from Central and South America (see table 1.2).

The Antillean orientation of New York's Latino community between 1900 and 1945 reflected the socioeconomic and political changes that gripped Cuba, Puerto Rico, and the rest of the Caribbean during this period. Cuba and Puerto Rico were annexed by the United States as a result of the military victory over Spain in the War of 1898. Cuba was granted its independence in 1904, but Puerto Rico remained an unincorporated territory of the United States until 1952. Direct political involvement by the United States had an impact on emigration from Cuba and Puerto Rico in the years after

TABLE 1.2

The Latino Population of New York City, 1920–1940*

	1920	%	1930	%	1940	%
CUBA & WEST INDIES	8,722	21.2	19,774	17.9	23,124	17.2
MEXICO	2,572	6.3	4,292	3.9	4,653	3.5
PUERTO RICO	7,364	17.9	44,908	40.7	61,463	45.8
CENTRAL & SOUTH AMERICA	7,777	18.9	18,748	17.0	19,727	14.7
SPAIN	14,659	35.7	22,501	20.4	25,283	18.8
TOTAL	41,094	100.0	110,223	100.0	134,252	100.0

*Includes "foreign-born population" (except for Puerto Ricans) for the 1920 census, the "foreign-born white population" for Cuba and the West Indies in the 1920 census, "foreign-born white" and "native white of foreign or mixed parentage" (except for Mexicans and Puerto Ricans) for the 1930 census, and "foreign-born white" and "nativity and parentage of foreign white stock" (except for Puerto Ricans) for the 1940 census.

SOURCE: U.S. Department of Commerce, Bureau of the Census, *Fourteenth Census of the United States . . . 1920*, vol. 3, table 6, p. 679; table 12, pp. 702 and 704. *Fifteenth Census of the United States: 1930*, vol. 3, part 2, table 17, p. 297; table 18, p. 301; table 19, p. 303. *Sixteenth Census of the United States: 1940*, vol. 2, Characteristics of the Population, part 5, table 24, pp. 63–64; and Special Bulletin, table 7, p. 74. Walter Laidlaw, *Population of the City of New York, 1890–1930* (New York: Cities Census Committee, Inc., 1932), table 40, p. 247; table 51, p. 253. Ira Rosenwaike, *Population History of New York City* (Syracuse: Syracuse University Press, 1972), pp. 101, 121, 203.

1900, but it was the relative geographical proximity to New York and the dramatic infusion of United States investment capital in the economies of both islands that had the greatest impact.

The United States also intervened actively in the internal affairs of the Dominican Republic during this period. The economy of the Dominican Republic experienced substantial growth during the United States military occupation of 1916 to 1924; however, regarding Dominican migration, the impact of U.S.-sponsored modernization was relatively less dramatic because the island economy was less developed than that of Cuba or even Puerto Rico. Economic growth continued with the establishment of the Trujillo dictatorship after 1930, but the movement of Dominicans to the United States or elsewhere was kept to a minimum because of the nature of the development process and the restrictive policies that were placed on emigration from that country from 1930 to 1961.[11]

In Cuba, United States investment capital further strengthened a sugar sector that was already dominant in the late nineteenth century. It also reinforced Cuba's economic dependence on the United States, which was its principle market. The expansion of the Cuban sugar sector created opportunities for some of its citizens, but it also led to economic and social misfortune for other segments of the population. Cubans were increasingly subject to the often dramatic and unpredictable effects of the volatile sugar market. Between 1900 and 1945 the Cuban economy experienced dramatic boom and bust periods that had a detrimental effect on many Cubans at each stage of the economic cycle. The result was increased Cuban emigration to southern Florida and the New York City area in the years after 1900. Cuban emigration to the United States rose because of economic dislocation and monetary inflation during periods of prosperity and growth. It also rose because of high unemployment, decreased wages, a decline in living standards, and increased political instability during periods of economic crisis and decline.[12]

Puerto Rico also experienced the detrimental effects of United States economic investment during the same period, but in contrast to Cuba, the consequences for the island population appear to have been much more devastating. As was the case in Cuba, United States economic investment in Puerto Rico was directed toward the sugar sector. There was also some investment in urban-oriented manufacturing; however, in contrast to Cuba, United States investment in Puerto Rico had a disastrous impact on the traditional, more labor-intensive coffee and tobacco sectors. The coffee industry, in particular, was extremely important to Puerto Rico's economy during this period. In the late nineteenth century it had been the dominant sector, providing most of the wealth and most of the employment for the island's population—especially in the mountainous interior region.[13]

As a result of the dramatic change in the investment climate and the shift in emphasis toward the sugar sector after the United States takeover, the Puerto Rican coffee industry experienced a prolonged and steady decline in the years between 1898 and 1930. The tobacco industry also began to wither away after an initial period of prosperity came to an end in the early 1920s. By the early 1930s, the labor-intensive coffee and tobacco sectors had ceased to be vital or even important components of the Puerto Rican economy. Thousands of rural and working-class Puerto Ricans were compelled to migrate from the coffee and tobacco growing regions of the island's interior to the coastal areas and the cities in search of employment in the sugar, manufacturing, and service sectors of the economy. The migration from the interior regions created enormous hardships for the populations that already lived in the cities and along the coast. Overall, wages fell, living standards deteriorated, and unemployment increased in the years between 1898 and 1930.[14] This was only the beginning of a long and difficult period for the Puerto Rican economy.

Commercial treaties between the United States and Cuba and the effects of the worldwide economic depression of the 1930s initiated a period of crisis and decline for the Puerto Rican sugar industry. By 1935 the Puerto Rican economy had virtually collapsed, largely as a result of the crisis in the sugar sector and the impact that this had on manufacturing, services, and other sectors of the economy.[15] The increased migration of Puerto Ricans to New York in the years between 1900 and 1945 reflected the deepening economic and social crisis that gripped the island throughout this period. It also reflected the ease of travel to New York, the relative prosperity to be found in the United States, and the fact that Puerto Ricans were granted United States citizenship in 1917.[16]

Net migration from Puerto Rico to New York rose rather dramatically during the economic boom years of 1914–1915, 1917–1920, and 1923–1930. After 1930, the pace of migration slowed considerably as a result of the global economic depression and the impact that World War II was to have on both Puerto Rico and the United States. Most of the Puerto Ricans and Latinos who came to New York in the years between 1900 and 1945 were urban-oriented, working-class men and women. In contrast to the late nineteenth century, there were proportionally fewer individuals who were business oriented, well educated or middle class. Most of the newcomers were generally skilled or semiskilled factory operatives, artisans, white-collar workers, and service-sector employees who found similar kinds of work in the New York labor market.[17] A considerable number were skilled and semiskilled working-class women. By the late 1920s, large numbers of Hispanic women were employed in the labor-intensive service and industrial sectors.[18] Many worked in the garment factories or performed piece work for entrepreneurs in that industry. Based on the figures compiled for Spanish Harlem in 1925, which are biased in favor of its mostly working-class population, 62 percent of all Latinos were employed in the industrial sector, 18 percent were employed in services, 16 percent were engaged in commerce, and 4 percent were listed as "owners" and "supervisors."[19]

In the years between 1900 and 1945, the burgeoning Latino population became identified with certain areas or neighborhoods of the city. According to Vega, the "barrio Latino" in East Harlem had already reached a mature stage of development by the late 1920s. Immigrants from Spain and their descendants were associated with the West 14th Street and Chelsea areas of Manhattan. At the same time, other neighborhoods, such as parts of the Lower East Side of Manhattan, South Brooklyn ("Red Hook" and the Columbia Street area), the "Navy Yard" and the Williamsburg section of Brooklyn, also became identified with the Latino community by the late 1920s or early 1930s.

For the most part, Hispanics coexisted with the earlier immigrant populations, or they eventually displaced the earlier groups after a period of time. From 1900 to 1945, the Latino population of South Brooklyn more or less coexisted with the largely Italian-American residents of that neighborhood. In East Harlem, by contrast, the Hispanic population eventually replaced the predominantly Jewish population west of Park Avenue by the Depression years of the early 1930s.[20]

The housing stock that was available to working-class Latinos was among the worst that could be found in New York City during this period. The dwelling spaces were primarily "furnished rooms," "cold-water flats," and "railroad apartments" in the "Old" and "New Law" tenements and row houses that were found in most of the neighborhoods where Latinos lived. Most of this housing stock was already considered substandard soon after it was built between the 1860s and the 1890s. Overcrowding and the lack of maintenance had already turned many of these structures and their neighborhoods into what outsiders called "slums" by the time that they were populated by Hispanics.[21]

Despite the inadequacies of the housing stock and other serious problems, Latinos had a generally optimistic view of life in the city. This appeared to be the case even during the 1930s, when the community was forced to endure the hardships of high unemployment, decreased wages, and the diminished living standards associated with the Great Depression. Latinos worked hard, got married, gave birth to children, attended church, and participated in the rich social and cultural life that they created in their communities. They patronized grocery stores, barbershops, restaurants, tailoring establishments, and other businesses owned by Hispanics and non-Hispanics. They also organized social clubs, self-help groups, and political associations, and the debated the complex social, cultural, and political issues of the day. For the most part, Latino political concerns during this period were largely oriented toward the homelands that most of them still hoped to return to at some point in the future. At this stage in the evolution of the Hispanic community, a real commitment to life in the New York area had not as yet emerged.[22]

PHASE THREE, 1945–1965/1970

The demographic composition and orientation of the Hispanic community underwent a significant change during the next phase of the migration process. In effect, the Puerto Rican community became synonymous with the Latino community in the years between 1945 and 1970. Thousands of Puerto Ricans began to leave the island for New York City during the early part of the postwar period because of economic and social policies that were instituted at this time. After earlier efforts to revive the Puerto Rican economy had failed during the late 1930s and early 1940s, the United States government developed an ambitious program for the industrialization of Puerto Rico in the postwar period. With the cooperation of Puerto Rico's political leaders, the government promoted the establishment of labor-intensive enterprises in an effort to reduce the island's rate of unemployment and underemployment. North American investors received tax benefits, free land, low-interest loans and other incentives in an attempt to expand the number of enterprises, but all of this was considered insufficient to overcome the perceived problem of "overpopulation" and the negative effects of the economic collapse that gripped the traditional agrarian sectors. The result was the implementation of policies designed to encourage the unemployed and the underemployed to leave Puerto Rico for the United States.[23]

Puerto Ricans were advised by government bureaucrats to leave the island for New York, where it was claimed that better employment opportunities could be found. Shipping companies, charter airlines, regular air-travel service and reduced fares were established to facilitate the flow of migrants from Puerto Rico to New York.[24] The result was a dramatic increase in the number of Puerto Ricans in New York City and its environs in the years after 1945 (see tables 1.2 and 1.3). The Puerto Rican population of New York rose from 61,463 in 1940 to 612,574 in 1960, and it continued to increase during the next decade, reaching 811,843 in 1970. There was also a rise in the number of other Latinos who came to New York during this period, but in contrast to the Puerto Ricans, the increase of other Hispanics was proportionally less dramatic. In the years between 1940 and 1970, the Cuban population rose from about 23,000 to 84,179, the Dominican population rose from an unknown figure to at least 66,914, and the population of persons from Central and South America increased from 19,727 to at least 216,120 (see tables 1.2 and 1.3).

Overall, the Latinos who came to New York during this period were overwhelmingly of the working class, and this was especially true of the Puerto Ricans. Most Puerto Ricans found employment in the labor-intensive manufacturing and service sectors of the New York economy. A significant number, mostly from the rural areas, also found employment on potato and vegetable farms in the surrounding suburban and rural areas. These individuals were brought to New York under a special agricultural contract labor program specifically created for this purpose. Normally the Puerto Rican

TABLE 1.3

The Latino Population of New York City, 1960–1990*

	1960	%	1970	%	1980	%	1990	%
CUBA	42,694	5.6	84,179	7.0	63,189	4.5	56,041	3.1
DOM. REP.	13,293	1.7	66,914	5.6	125,380	8.9	332,713	18.7
PUERTO RICO	612,574	80.9	811,843	67.5	860,552	61.2	896,763	50.3
TOTAL SPAN. CARIBBEAN	668,561	88.2	962,936	80.1	1,049,121	74.6	1,285,517	72.1
COSTA RICA	1,761		4,429				6,920	
EL SALVADOR	480		1,022		6,300		23,926	
GUATEMALA	1,019		2,036		6,323		15,873	
HONDURAS	2,516		6,785		14,100		22,167	
MEXICO	8,260		7,893		25,577		61,772	
NICARAGUA	1,300		2,014				9,660	
PANAMA	8,377		15,225		17,700		22,707	
ARGENTINA	7,789		13,327		14,009		13,934	
BOLIVIA	558		1,218				3,465	
CHILE	2,516		3,328				6,721	
COLOMBIA	6,782		27,657		45,160		84,454	
ECUADOR	4.077		20,326		40,320		78,444	
PARAGUAY	127							
PERU	2,297		5,438		11,640		23,257	
URUGUAY	696		1,220				3,233	
VENEZUELA	3,478		3,410				4,752	
"OTHER S. AM."	9,199		13,630		18,974			
SPAIN	27,438		23,225		11,825		20,148	
OTHER HISP.			87,162		144,975		96,561	
TOTAL/NON-CARIB.HISP.	88,670	11.8	239,345	19.9	356,903	25.4	497,994	27.9
GRAND TOTAL	757,231	100	1,202,281	100	1,406,024	100	1,783,511	100

*Figures include the total number of Puerto Ricans and total "foreign-born" and "native of foreign or mixed parentage" for other nationalities in the 1960 census; total number of Cubans, Mexicans, Puerto Ricans, and total number of "foreign-born" and "native of foreign or mixed parentage" for other nationalities in the 1970 census; total number of Cubans, Mexicans, Puerto Ricans and total number of "foreign-born" only for other nationalities in the 1980 census; total number of Cubans, Mexicans, Puerto Ricans, and the total number of persons of "Hispanic origin" by nationality for other groups in the 1990 census.

SOURCE: U.S. Department of Commerce, Bureau of the Census, *Census of Population: 1960*, vol. 1, Characteristics of the Population, New York, part 34, table 99, p. 34/434. *1970 Census of Population*, vol. 1, Characteristics of the Population, New York, part 34, table 119, pp. 34/607–34/611. *1970 Census of Population*, vol. 1, Detailed Characteristics, New York, part 34, table 141, p. 34/720. *1980 Census of Population*, vol. 1, Characteristics of the Population, chapter C, General Social and Economic Characteristics, New York, part 34, table 59, pp. 34/100–34/101. *1980 Census of Population*, vol. 1, Characteristics of the Population, chapter D, Detailed Population Characteristics, New York, part 34, table 195, p. 34/14, *1990 Census of Population*, General Population Characteristics, New York, section 1, table 5, pp. 47, 49–51. *1990 Census of Population*, Social and Economic Characteristics, New York, section 1, table 6, pp. 45, 47–49. John I. Griffin and Jean Namias, eds., *New York Metropolitan Regional Fact Book* (New York: New York Council on Economic Education, 1965), table T2.12. Population Division, New York City Department of City Planning, *Puerto Rican New Yorkers in 1990* (New York: Department of City Planning, 1993), tables A and B, pp. 13–14.

farm workers traveled back and forth from their homes on the island to their jobs in the New York—New Jersey area; however, with the passage of time, many of these individuals settled in the city, where employment in the manufacturing and service sectors of the economy was considered somewhat more lucrative.[25]

The other Latinos who came to New York in the years between 1945 and 1970 were somewhat different in terms of their socioeconomic backgrounds than the Puerto Ricans who came during the same period. For the most part, the other Hispanics were similar to the earlier group of Latinos and Puerto Ricans who came between 1900 and 1945. Many of the other Latinos were unskilled and semi-skilled workers, but in contrast to the Puerto Ricans, they included a much larger group of persons who were well educated, urban oriented, and middle class. Overall, the Puerto Ricans who came between 1945 and 1970 were impoverished, unemployed, or under-employed persons from rural and urban areas of the island, with minimal education and few skills. However, there were also some (but fewer) Puerto Ricans who were better educated, business oriented, and middle class.[26]

A major transformation in the composition of the New York labor force enabled the city's economy to absorb enormous numbers of Puerto Ricans and other Latinos in the years after 1945. Returning veterans of mostly European extraction were able to take advantage of new programs that were established by the federal government to promote upward economic and social mobility in the early years of the postwar period. For example, special education programs enabled returning veterans to leave their jobs in the factories and the low-grade services to become white-collar workers, managers, professionals, and entrepreneurs. At the same time, the federal housing programs of the early postwar period enabled veterans and their families to leave the congested inner city for the greener, more open spaces of the suburbs. The movement of the earlier immigrant groups and their descendants from the city to the suburbs was continuous in the years between 1945 and 1970. It was also reinforced by the exodus of corporations and small businesses and the establishment of new enterprises in the communities that proliferated in the suburbs and in other parts of the country.

The upward mobility of the earlier immigrant groups and the movement of people from New York to the suburbs created a vacuum in the manufacturing and service sectors of the urban economy. In fact, many enterprises in these sectors actually experienced labor shortages in the early postwar period and developed recruitment programs to attract workers from outside the city. The result was the complete transformation of labor in manufacturing and in services in the years after 1950. Persons of European extraction, such as the Irish, Jews, Italians, and Greeks, were increasingly replaced by Puerto Ricans, other Latinos, and by African-Americans who came from the southern states.

Overall, Puerto Ricans and other Latinos worked in the garment industry, in paper box factories, in enterprises that manufactured dolls or plastic products, in restaurants, in grocery stores, in hotels, in office buildings, in residential structures, as cooks, dishwashers, "bus boys," messengers, elevator operators, custodians, and building superintendents. A smaller number were also employed in sales or as white-collar workers or lower-level managers in corporations or in public and private agencies and institutions.[27]

The massive influx of Puerto Ricans and other Latinos and the movement of the earlier immigrant groups and their descendants from the city to the suburbs permitted the growth and expansion of neighborhoods that were associated with the Hispanic population in the years after 1945. "El Barrio" or Spanish Harlem expanded eastward from Park Avenue to the East River between 1948 and 1955. A huge new concentration of mostly Puerto Rican Latinos also emerged in the South Bronx during the same period. In the Lower East Side, Puerto Ricans continued to displace the earlier, mostly Jewish residents, and they also established themselves in new concentrations in the West Side and Upper West Side of Manhattan. The Puerto Rican–Latino neighborhoods of Brooklyn and Queens also experienced growth during this period. The Puerto Rican enclave in the Navy Yard district of Brooklyn expanded northward and eastward into parts of Williamsburg, Greenpoint, and Bushwick. At the same time, the South Brooklyn enclave around Columbia Street expanded southward to include parts of Park Slope and Sunset Park.[28]

To some degree, the quality of the housing stock available to Latinos improved during this period, but overcrowding was a very serious problem, especially in the late 1940s and early 1950s, when severe housing shortages developed. In Spanish Harlem and the Lower East Side of Manhattan, the mostly Puerto Rican Latinos continued to occupy the same cold-water flats, furnished rooms, and railroad apartments that were considered substandard in the 1920s and even earlier. The same was also true of the housing stock in Red Hook, the Columbia Street area, and the Williamsburg section of Brooklyn; however in other neighborhoods, such as the South Bronx, the West Side of Manhattan, and the Sunset Park, Bushwick, Brownsville, and East New York sections of Brooklyn, the housing situation was somewhat more complex. To be sure, tenement buildings were to be found in all of these neighborhoods, but there were also roomier multiple-family dwellings, row houses, brownstones, and the larger apartment buildings that were originally built for middle-class residents. There were also the low- and high-rise housing projects that were built by the city and the state with increased frequency between 1935 and 1970. In general, apartments or accommodations in the privately owned buildings were more spacious, with larger rooms and full-sized kitchens and bathrooms; however, in most cases, the landlords merely collected the rents and allowed their properties to deteriorate soon after they were occupied by Puerto Ricans and other Latinos. By contrast, the publicly owned housing projects were initially established and administered as ideal communities. In time, however, these structures were overwhelmed by the introduction of "problem," "negligent," or "welfare families" and allowed to deteriorate through disinterest or neglect.[29]

PHASE FOUR, 1965–PRESENT

The composition of New York's Latino population and the population of the city as a whole was profoundly transformed during the most recent stage of the migration process which began in the first years of the 1960s. Starting as early as 1959, people from Cuba, the Dominican Republic, Colombia, Ecuador, Peru, and other countries in Central and South America began to arrive in New York in increasing numbers, and many of them came illegally. Cubans fleeing Castro's revolution were the first major group to settle in the New York area during this period, and they were soon followed by the Dominicans, who came in substantial numbers after the 1965 civil war. Most of the Cubans came as political refugees under a special program that was established by the federal government as part of its anti-Castro or anticommunist policies. The influx of Dominicans was made possible by a complex of factors which included the aftereffects of political turmoil and civil war, the never-ending search for cheaper labor in New York, and the relaxation of Trujillo-era restrictions on emigration. Some of these factors as well as other circumstances set the stage for increased immigration from Central and South America during this same period. In the years after 1965, Colombians, Ecuadoreans, Peruvians, Salvadorans, and others arrived in New York in substantial numbers. New York's Latino population increased 135.5 percent from 757,231 in 1960 to 1,783,511 in 1990 (See table 1.3), and non-Puerto Rican Hispanics accounted for a substantial proportion of this increase. Although the Latino population was 80.9 percent Puerto Rican in 1960, Puerto Ricans accounted for only 50.3 percent of the Latino population by 1990.[30]

Economic and social forces were the most powerful contributors to Hispanic migration in the years after 1960. Overall the peoples of Latin America and the Caribbean were profoundly affected by an accelerated process of development that, in most places, had its origins in the early postwar period. Economic modernization, industrialization, rapid population growth, and increased corporate investment from the United States and other industrial countries created economic, social, and political instability in most of the countries of Latin America during this period. As was the case in Cuba and Puerto Rico between 1900 and the 1940s, rapid economic change produced economic and social opportunities for some groups and social dislocation or crisis for other groups. By the late 1950s and early 1960s large numbers of persons in countries such as Mexico, Colombia, Peru, and Ecuador, began to migrate from the rural areas to the urban centers because of unequal regional development or modernization. At the same time the economies of the urban centers in most of these countries were not expanding rapidly enough to accommodate the mass of migrants that came to the cities from the countryside. The result was increased economic, social, and political insecurity for both rural and urban populations. Thousands of persons were uprooted in the countryside by rapid growth, economic reorganization, and monetary inflation. These same forces often had a detrimental effect on significant sectors of the urban populations as well, and this was especially true during periods when development was intense and migration from the countryside was substantial. Economic retrenchment, periods of high unemployment, government austerity programs, and high birthrates also had a negative impact on both rural and urban populations. These same forces were also frequently associated with the rise of political instability, interpersonal violence, rebellions, and civil wars. The result was increased migration to the United States from the increasingly troubled societies of Latin America in the years after 1960.[31]

In contrast to the largely rural and impoverished Puerto Ricans who migrated between 1945 and 1970, the Latinos who came after 1960 were generally urban, better educated, had more skills, and many came from middle-class, professional, or business-oriented backgrounds. In this sense, the new immigrants were comparable to the earlier group of Puerto Ricans and other Hispanics who came to New York in the years between 1900 and 1945. Of course, the proportion of middle-class individuals varied from one Latino sub-group to another. Immigrants from Argentina, Chile, and Uruguay, as well as the Cubans who came in the early 1960s, were more likely to be of the middle class than were the Dominicans, Colombians, Hondurans, or the Mexicans who began to arrive in substantial numbers at the end of the 1980s; however, as was the case in the earlier period, middle-class orientation did not guarantee an easier transition to life in the city. Many of the better-educated persons, including quite a number with middle-class, professional, or semi-professional backgrounds, experienced downward economic and social mobility upon their arrival in New York. Some were fortunate enough to find white-collar employment if they had an adequate command of English. Others started their own businesses in the neighborhoods where they settled, but most were compelled to accept working-class employment in the services and in manufacturing. As a result, Latinos with working-class and middle-class backgrounds were employed in factories, restaurants, hotels, small businesses, and other enterprises, and to a significant degree they replaced the largely Puerto Rican and African-American labor force that was traditionally employed in these sectors.[32]

The neighborhoods traditionally associated with the Latino communities continued to expand rather dramatically in the years after 1960. At the same time new enclaves were established throughout the city and older ones were devastated as a result of increased problems with housing that involved the continued flight of earlier immigrant groups and their descendants, a dramatic slowdown in the construction of residential buildings for lower-income people, and the new phenomena of housing abandonment, vandalism, arson, and rising homelessness.[33]

Certain neighborhoods also became associated with particular Hispanic subgroups or conglomerations of subgroups. For example, the Upper West Side and the Washington Heights section of Manhattan became increasingly associated with the Dominican community. For a time a Cuban community emerged in this area as well; however, most Cubans eventually settled in other places, such as Astoria, the Elmhurst section of Queens, and especially Union City, Jersey City, and West New York, New Jersey. Colombians, Ecuadoreans, Peruvians, Dominicans, and other subgroups became identified with new enclaves that emerged in the Jackson Heights, Woodside, Elmhurst, East Elmhurst, and the Corona sections of Queens. Conversely, it appeared that Mexicans and other persons from Central America were beginning to displace Puerto Ricans and other Latinos from their traditional enclaves in "El Barrio" at the end of the 1980s.[34]

CONCLUSION

This brief historical survey of New York's Latino population begins to reveal the differences that exist among the numerous Hispanic communities that have migrated to the region and to other parts of the United States since the middle of the nineteenth century. In one respect, dissimilarities can be seen in the composition of the Latino communities when these are broken down by national origin. Puerto Ricans, Dominicans, Cubans, Colombians, Ecuadoreans and other persons from South America have been the most important subgroups in the evolution of New York's Latino community, with Puerto Ricans having played the dominant role. In differing combinations these same groups have been important to the evolution of other Hispanic communities throughout the Northeast and Midwest. By contrast, Mexicans and, more recently, Salvadorans and other persons from Central America have been predominant in the Latino communities of Texas, California, and the Southwest. In southern Florida, Cubans and other expatriate groups such as the Nicaraguans have played the most significant role, while in Chicago separate Mexican and Puerto Rican communities have developed in coexistence at different times since the early part of the century. In fact, up until the late 1970s, a line could have been drawn separating the Northeast, the Middle Atlantic states and Florida from the rest of the country. Although there was some overlap in the Middle West, Puerto Ricans, Cubans, Dominicans, and other nationals from South America and the Caribbean were the predominant groups east of the line, while Mexicans and people from Central America were the most important groups in the communities west of the line.[35]

The chronology of Latino migration and settlement also differentiates the various communities that have evolved across the country. Mexicans, "Spanish Americans," and Hispanicized Indians already occupied various parts of Texas, California, and the Southwest prior to the takeover of these areas by the United States between 1836 and 1848. Florida also had a small Spanish-oriented population prior to the United States occupation in 1819, but in the Northeast and the Middle West, most of the Hispanic communities emerged in the late nineteenth or early twentieth centuries and even later. Although the emergence of New York's Latino community can be traced to at least the early 1800s, significant expansion did not begin until the later part of the nineteenth century. The development of Chicago's Hispanic community also began in the late nineteenth century, but it was not until the World War I period that Latinos became a significant factor in the demography of that city. In contrast to what transpired in Chicago and New York, most of the Hispanic communities in the Northeast and Middle West began to evolve in earnest only after the Second World War. This was the case in Philadelphia, Boston, Cleveland, and in Bridgeport and Hartford, Connecticut.

The geographical breakdown of Latino communities can be differentiated in other ways besides chronologically and by country of origin. For example, the Hispanic populations of Texas, California, and the Southwest have been traditionally much more rural in their orientation than the Latino communities of the Northeast, Southeast, or Middle West. At the same time, the communities in southern Florida have attracted or absorbed proportionally larger numbers of the affluent from Latin America than the other Hispanic communities of the United States. At certain times, New

York's Latino community has also been somewhat mixed in terms of its economic and social configuration; however, overwhelming poverty and working-class backgrounds have been the rule in Texas, California, and most parts of the Southwest.

By the mid 1990s it was not clear which direction the Hispanic community would take in the future. Economic, geographic, and social diversification will probably continue, but there also may be a trend toward cultural homogenization within the Latino community as a whole. At this point, assimilation into U.S. society over the long term does not seem very probable because assimilation has failed as a social reality and social policy for most immigrant and minority groups during the past forty years. There has also been a growing acceptance of cultural pluralism and diversity within U.S. society. This is reflected in the promotion of educational programs that emphasize multiculturalism and the positive acceptance of terms such as "African American," "Asian American," "Chicano," "Hispanic," "Latino," and "Native American" in the lexicon of educators, bureaucrats, journalists, politicians, policymakers, and the public as a whole. What seems to be certain is that New York will probably continue to function as a major entry point for Latin Americans, Asians, Africans, and other immigrant and migrant groups in the foreseeable future. At the same time, it also appears that no constitutionally acceptable policy or program will be able to completely stop or even significantly reduce the increased flow of foreigners from other parts of the world in the foreseeable future. Recent calls for a halt to the immigration of "pre-modern," "unskilled people from Third World countries" may have an impact, but if the legislative experience of the 1980s is any guide, compromises will be made.[36] Powerful economic interests, especially in the agricultural and service sectors, are committed to immigration as a means of reducing labor costs. They were successful in their campaigns to weaken the Immigration Reform and Control Act of 1986, and they will probably lobby very hard to stop or weaken any legislation that would significantly reduce the flow of foreigners into this country.

NOTES

1. The terms "Latino" and "Hispanic," used interchangeably in this chapter, refer to all persons living in the United States whose origins can be traced to Spain and the Spanish-speaking countries of Latin America and the Caribbean. Included in this category are all U.S. immigrants who have come from these countries and their descendants who live in the United States, whether they are Spanish-speaking or not.

2. Ira Rosenwaike, *Population History of New York City* (Syracuse, N.Y.: Syracuse University Press, 1972), pp. 22–23. Reference to the trade between the Hispanic Caribbean and New York during the nineteenth century is made in César Andreu Iglesias, ed., *Memoirs of Bernardo Vega: A Contribution to the History of the Puerto Rican Community in New York*, trans. Juan Flores (New York: Monthly Review Press, 1984), p. 46, and Virginia

Sánchez-Korrol, *From Colonia to Community: The History of Puerto Ricans in New York City, 1917–1948* (Berkeley: University of California Press, 1994), pp. 11–12. See also Franklin W. Knight, *The Caribbean: The Genesis of a Fragmented Nationalism*, 2nd ed. (New York: Oxford University Press, 1990), pp. 116–17; Louis Pérez, Jr., *Cuba: Between Reform and Revolution* (New York: Oxford University Press, 1988), pp. 82–85, 107, 138, 149–52.

3. Rosenwaike, *Population History of New York City*, p. 40. Historically, most undercounts in the census have been attributed to the existence of a significant number of poor or working-class people within a given population. It is said that such persons are generally reluctant to enter into any kind of contact with government institutions because of the perception that such contact will lead to obligations or future difficulties with the authorities.

In recent years, the urban census enumerations have become increasingly controversial because of the Census Bureau's inability to accurately count or estimate the urban foreign or impoverished population. This has led to congressional hearings, recounts, lawsuits, and other problems.

For comments regarding the accuracy of the population estimates for New York City for the years prior to 1930 see Sánchez-Korrol, *From Colonia to Community*, pp. 57–58, 59, 62, 107. Also see Iglesias, *Memoirs of Bernardo Vega*, pp. 12, 46, 102, and 146–47 for other estimates on the size of the Latino population during this same period.

4. *Census of 1890* (Washington, D.C.: Government Printing Office, 1892), pp. 645–47, 670, 672, 674, 676, and Iglesias, *Memoirs of Bernardo Vega*, p. 73, also pp. 63–79 and passim.

5. For a general discussion of economic development in Latin America during the nineteenth century see Leslie Bethell, ed., *The Cambridge History of Latin America*, vols. 4 and 5: *1870–1930* (Cambridge: Cambridge University Press, 1985); David Bushnell and Neil Macaulay, *The Emergence of Latin America in the Nineteenth Century* (New York: Oxford University Press, 1988). For case studies that discuss labor shortages and immigration as they relate to economic development in nineteenth-century Latin America see David Rock, *Argentina: 1516–1987: From Spanish Colonization to Alfonsín* (Berkeley: University of California Press, 1987), chapters 4, 5, and passim; Hermanus Hoetink, *The Dominican People, 1850–1900: Notes for a Historical Sociology* (Baltimore: John Hopkins University Press, 1982), chapters 2, 4, and passim; Laird Bergad, *Coffee and the Growth of Agrarian Capitalism in Nineteenth-Century Puerto Rico* (Princeton: Princeton University Press, 1983); Rebecca J. Scott, *Slave Emancipation in Cuba: The Transition to Free Labor, 1860–1899* (Princeton: Princeton University Press, 1985); Manuel Moreno-Fraginals, *The Sugarmill: The Socioeconomic Complex of Sugar in Cuba, 1760–1860*, trans. Cedric Belfage (New York: Monthly Review Press, 1976), pp. 20, 60, 83, 89, 119, 133, 141, and passim; and Pérez, *Cuba*, pp. 114–16, 201–2, and passim.

6. Iglesias, *Memoirs of Bernardo Vega*, pp. 45–46, 53, 57–58, 64, 73, and passim; Sánchez-Korrol, *From Colonia to Community*, pp. 11–17. During the late nineteenth century, the price of sugar produced in Cuba, Puerto Rico, and the Dominican Republic was increasingly

determined by refiners, importers, brokers, and bankers based in New York City. One of the most important brokers of this period was Manuel Rionda, a New York–based Cuban. In the early years of the twentieth century, Rionda merged his successful company with Czarnikow Ltd., a London-based firm, to create the Czarnikow-Rionda Company. Within a few years this company came to dominate the Caribbean sugar market to such an extent that it could act as sole broker for the entire Cuban sugar industry and for some 80 percent of the sugar produced in Puerto Rico and the Dominican Republic. See Manuel Moreno-Fraginals, "Plantations in the Caribbean: Cuba, Puerto Rico and the Dominican Republic in the Late Nineteenth Century" in Manuel Moreno-Fraginals, Frank Moya Pons, and Stanley L. Engerman, eds., *Between Slavery and Free Labor: The Spanish-Speaking Caribbean in the Nineteenth Century* (Baltimore: John Hopkins University Press, 1985), pp. 10–13, 20, and passim.

7. Iglesias, *Memoirs of Bernardo Vega*, pp. 39–79; Sánchez-Korrol, *From Colonia to Community*, pp. 11, 13, 167–72; Angelo Falcón, "A History of Puerto Rican Politics in New York City: 1860s to 1945" in James Jennings and Monte Rivera, eds., *Puerto Rican Politics in Urban America* (Westport, Conn.: Greenwood Press, 1984), pp. 18–20.

8. Iglesias, *Memoirs of Bernardo Vega*, pp. 12, 85–86; Elinor Des Verney Sinnette, *Arthur Alfonso Schomburg: Black Bibliophile and Collector* (New York and Detroit: New York Public Library and Wayne State University Press, 1989), p. 23.

9. Iglesias, *Memoirs of Bernardo Vega*, pp. 7, 9, 12, 16, 33, 46, 74. Also, see Sánchez-Korrol, *From Colonia to Community*, pp. 51–62 and passim, and Lawrence R. Chenault, *The Puerto Rican Migrant in New York City* (New York: Columbia University Press, 1938), pp. 89–109 and passim.

10. Iglesias, Memoirs of Bernardo Vega, p. 12. For the 1920, 1930, and 1940 estimates, see the sources listed in table 1.2.

11. For a discussion of economic development in Cuba, Puerto Rico, and the Dominican Republic during the first half of the twentieth century, see the relevant sections in Knight, *The Caribbean*; Pérez, *Cuba*; Louis Pérez, *Cuba under the Platt Amendment, 1902–1934* (Pittsburgh: University of Pittsburgh Press, 1986); Julio Le Riverend, *Historia económica de Cuba* (Barcelona: Ediciones Ariel, 1972); James L. Dietz, *Economic History of Puerto Rico: Institutional Change and Capitalist Development* (Princeton: Princeton University Press, 1986); Marlin D. Clausner, *Rural Santo Domingo: Settled, Unsettled, and Resettled* (Philadelphia: Temple University Press, 1973); and Frank Moya Pons, *Manual de Historia Dominicana* (Santiago, R.D.: Universidad Católica Madre y Maestra, 1978), pp. 427–525. Also, see Sánchez-Korrol, *From Colonia to Community*, pp. 17–28 for another discussion of Puerto Rican economic development and its relationship to migration during the period 1900 to 1940.

12. Pérez, *Cuba*, pp. 189–288; Le Riverend, *Historia económica de Cuba*, pp. 187–250.

13. The importance of the nineteenth century Puerto Rican coffee and tobacco sectors is discussed in Dietz, *Economic History of Puerto Rico*, pp. 4–78.

14. Dietz, *Economic History of Puerto Rico*, pp. 79–135 and Sánchez-Korrol, *From Colonia to Community*, pp. 17–28.

15. Dietz, *Economic History of Puerto Rico*, pp. 135–81.

16. For a discussion on economic opportunities for Puerto Ricans in New York, the relative ease of travel, and the role played by the 1917 citizenship legislation in the migration process, see Sánchez-Korrol, *From Colonia to Community*, pp. 28–46.

17. Ibid., pp. 28–29, 30, 32–34, 57 and passim.

18. Ibid., pp. 89–96, 107–12, and passim.

19. Ibid., pp. 29, 30.

20. Iglesias, *Memoirs of Bernardo Vega*, pp. 7, 9–12, 16, 28, 85–86, 91, 98, 103, 105, 151, 155; Sánchez-Korrol, *From Colonia to Community*, pp. 53–62.

21. Iglesias, *Memoirs of Bernardo Vega*, pp. 119–20, 155, 184; Sánchez-Korrol, *From Colonia to Community*, p. 57; and Chenault, *The Puerto Rican Migrant*, pp. 97–100, 106–7. Housing conditions in New York between 1900 and 1945 are also discussed in Anthony Jackson, *A Place Called Home: A History of Low-Cost Housing in Manhattan* (Cambridge, Mass.: MIT Press, 1976) and Richard Plunz, *A History of Housing in New York City* (New York: Columbia University Press, 1990).

22. Sánchez-Korrol, *From Colonia to Community*, pp. 135–66, 172–203; Falcón, "A History of Puerto Rican Politics in New York City," pp. 20–42; Rosa Estades, *Patterns of Political Participation of Puerto Ricans in New York City* (San Juan: Editorial Universitaria, Universidad de Puerto Rico, 1978), pp. 29–36. For additional comments, see Iglesias, *Memoirs of Bernardo Vega*, passim.

23. Dietz, *Economic History of Puerto Rico*, pp. 182–310; see especially pp. 206–21, 226–28, 247–55, 282–88. A number of general studies have been written on Puerto Rican migration and the Puerto Rican experience on the United States mainland in the years between 1945 and 1970 or the present. The most current or recent of these include Joseph P. Fitzpatrick, *Puerto Rican Americans: The Meaning of Migration to the Mainland*, 2nd ed. (Englewood Cliffs, N.J.: Prentice Hall, 1987); History Task Force, Centro de Estudios Puertorriqueños, ed. *Labor Migration under Capitalism: The Puerto Rican Experience* (New York: Monthly Review Press, 1979); Adalberto López, ed., *The Puerto Ricans: Their History, Culture and Society* (Cambridge, Mass.: Schenkman Publishing, 1980), pp. 313–466; and Clara E. Rodríguez, *Puerto Ricans: Born in the U.S.A.* (New York: Unwin and Hyman, 1989).

24. Fitzpatrick, *Puerto Rican Americans*, pp. 18–20; Adalberto López, "The Puerto Rican Diaspora: A Survey," in López, *The Puerto Ricans*, pp. 314–19. Rodríguez, *Puerto Ricans*, pp. 6–8 and passim.

25. United States Department of Labor, Bureau of Labor Statistics, *A Socio-Economic Profile of Puerto Rican New Yorkers*, Regional Report # 46 (New York: U.S. Department of Labor, Middle Atlantic Regional Office, 1975); Fitzpatrick, *Puerto Rican Americans*, pp. 24–25; Rodríguez, *Puerto Ricans*, pp. 4–6, 26–48, and passim; and Tom Seidl, Janet Shenk, and

Adrian DeWind, "The San Juan Shuttle: Puerto Ricans on Contract" in López, *The Puerto Ricans*, pp. 417–32.

26. Evidence that demonstrates the differences in socioeconomic background between Puerto Ricans and other Latinos is quite sparse for this period. Two examples of Hispanic subgroups that were clearly more middle-class in their orientation during the period 1958 to 1970 were Cubans and Colombians. See Eleanor Meyer Rogg and Rosemary Santana Cooney, *Adaptation and Adjustment of Cubans: West New York, New Jersey* (New York: Hispanic Research Center, Fordham University, 1980), pp. 35–40 and passim; and Fernando Urrea Ġiraldo, "Life Strategies and the Labor Market: Colombians in New York in the 1970s," *Occasional Papers*, no. 34 (New York: Center for Latin American Studies, New York University, 1982), pp. 8–10 and passim.

27. On the transformation of the New York economy during the period from 1945 to 1970 and the role played by Puerto Ricans in this change, see Fitzpatrick, *Puerto Rican Americans*, pp. 11–13, 92–103, and passim; Rodríguez, *Puerto Ricans*, pp. 31–35, 37–42, 44–45, and passim; Clara E. Rodríguez, "Economic Factors Affecting Puerto Ricans in New York" in History Task Force, *Labor Migration Under Capitalism*, pp. 214–15; U.S. Department of Labor, *A Socio-Economic Profile of Puerto Rican New Yorkers* (1975), pp. 78–104 and passim, and Michael N. Danielson and James W. Doig, *New York: The Politics of Urban Regional Development* (Berkeley: University of California Press, 1982), pp. 50–64 and passim. Also, see the pamphlets and reports that were distributed during this period, such as Commonwealth of Puerto Rico, Department of Labor, Migration Division, "The Jobs We Do," 1953; Joseph Monserrat, "Industry and Community—A Profitable Partnership," 1953; New York City, Department of Commerce, "Puerto Ricans: A Key Source of Labor," 1956; and others.

28. The expansion of Puerto Rican neighborhoods in the period 1945–1970 is discussed in Nathan Kantrowitz, *Negro and Puerto Rican Populations of New York City in the Twentieth Century* (Washington, D.C.: American Geographical Society, 1969); Morris Eagle, "Puerto Ricans in New York City" in Nathan Glazer and David McEntire, eds., *Studies in Housing and Minority Groups* (Berkeley: University of California Press, 1960); and U.S. Department of Labor, *A Socio-Economic Profile of Puerto Rican New Yorkers*, pp. 30–41. Also, see the relevant pages in Jackson, *A Place Called Home* and Plunz, *A History of Housing in New York City*.

29. See Eagle, "Puerto Ricans in New York City," Rodríguez, *Puerto Ricans*, pp. 106–19; and the relevant pages in Jackson, *A Place Called Home* and Plunz, *A History of Housing in New York City*.

30. For a discussion of Cuban and Dominican migration to the United States and New York in the years after 1960, see Richard R. Fagen, Richard A. Brody, and Thomas J. O'Leary, *Cubans in Exile: Disaffection and the Revolution* (Stanford: Stanford University Press, 1968); the relevant sections of Alejandro Portes and Robert L. Bach, *Latin Journey: Cuban and Mexican Immigrants in the United States* (Berkeley: University of California Press, 1985); Rogg and Santana Cooney, *The Adaptation and Adjustment of Cubans*; José del

Castillo and Christopher Mitchell, eds., *La inmigración Dominicana en los Estados Unidos* (Santo Domingo: Editorial CENAPEC, 1987); and Sherrie Grasmuck and Patricia R. Pessar, *Between Two Islands: Dominican International Migration* (Berkeley: University of California Press, 1991).

31. The relationship between investment capital, economic development, social change, and international migration from developing to industrialized societies has been discussed recently in Saskia Sassen, *The Mobility of Labor and Capital: A Study in International Investment and Labor Flow* (New York: Cambridge University Press, 1988). In addition, specific examples from Latin America and elsewhere are found in June Nash and María Patricia Fernández-Kelly, eds., *Women, Men, and the International Division of Labor* (Albany: State University of New York Press, 1983) and Steven E. Sanderson, ed., *The Americas in the New International Division of labor* (New York: Holmes and Meier, 1985).

32. For a discussion of middle-class orientation and downward social mobility among specific Latino subgroups, see Rogg and Cooney, *Adaptation and Adjustment of Cubans*, pp. 35–46, and Urrea Giraldo, "Life Strategies and the Labor Market: Colombians in New York." Discussions or essays dealing with Hispanic immigration to the New York metropolitan area in the years after 1965 are also found in Elizabeth Bogen, *Immigration in New York* (New York: Praeger, 1987); del Castillo and Mitchell, *La inmigración dominicana*; Grasmuck and Pessar, *Between Two Islands*; Evelyn S. Mann and Joseph J. Salvo, *Characteristics of New Hispanic Immigrants to New York City: A Comparison of Puerto Rican and Non-Puerto Rican Hispanics* (New York: Department of City Planning, 1984); Nancy Foner, ed., *New Immigrants in New York* (New York: Columbia University Press, 1987); Constance R. Sutton and Elsa M. Chaney, eds., *Caribbean Life in New York City: Sociocultural Dimensions* (New York: Center for Migration Studies, 1987); Roger D. Waldinger, *Through the Eye of the Needle: Immigrants and Enterprise in New York's Garment Trades* (New York: New York University Press, 1986).

33. Kantrowitz, *Negro and Puerto Rican Populations of New York City*; Jackson, *A Place Called Home*, pp. 254–308, Plunz, *A History of Housing in New York City*, pp. 313–40 and especially pp. 323–24, and *Report of the Mayor's Commission on Hispanic Concerns* (New York: 1986), pp. S15–S18, 54–88; Market Research Department of WADO Radio, *Facts: The New York Hispanic Market Report* (New York, 1988).

34. Market Research Department of WADO Radio, *Facts: The New York Hispanic Market Report*, 1988. Clay F. Richards, "Jobs Top Latinos' List of Concerns," *New York Newsday*, October 13, 1991, p. 28.

35. A number of studies have been written on Latino communities or specific Latino subgroups in various parts of the country outside of New York City or the northeastern part of the United States. These include Fagen, Brody, and O'Leary, *Cubans in Exile*; Portes and Bach, *Latin Journey*; Matt S. Meier and Feliciano Ribera, *Mexican Americans/American Mexicans: From Conquistadors to Chicanos* (New York: Vintage Books/Random House, 1989); Felix M. Padilla, *Puerto Rican Chicago* (Notre Dame, Ind.: University of Notre Dame

Press, 1987); and Julian Samora and Patricia Vandel Simon, *A History of the Mexican-American People* (Notre Dame, Ind.: University of Notre Dame Press, 1976; rev. ed. 1993) among others.

For a general overview of the Latino experience in the United States, see Earl Shorris, *Latinos: A Biography of the People* (New York: W. W. Norton, 1992); Joan Moore and Harry Pachon, *Hispanics in the United States* (Englewood Cliffs, N.J.: Prentice Hall, 1985); and L. H. Gann and Peter J. Duignan, *The Hispanics in the United States: A History* (Boulder, Colo.: Westview Press and the Hoover Institution on War, Peace and Revolution, 1986).

In the opinion of this writer, Duignan and Gann present a distorted, self-serving, and ultraconservative view of the Latino experience which reflects the politics of the Hoover Institute more than it does any attempt at an objective analysis of Latinos and their history.

36. The calls for a halt to immigration by "unskilled," "pre-modern people from Third World countries" have been articulated by Peter Brimelow, among others. See Peter Brimelow, *Alien Nation* (New York: Random House, 1995) and especially Peter Brimelow, "Time to Rethink Immigration?" *National Review* 44, no. 12 (June 22, 1992): 30–46.

A VINDICATION of CUBA

José Martí

To the editor of The Evening Post:

Sir: I beg to be allowed the privilege of referring in your columns to the injurious criticism of the Cubans printed in the *Manufacturer* of Philadelphia, and reproduced in your issue of yesterday.

This is not the occasion to discuss the question of the annexation of Cuba. It is probable that no self-respecting Cuban would like to see his country annexed to a nation where the leaders of opinion share towards him the prejudices excusable only to vulgar jingoism or rampant ignorance. No honest Cuban will stoop to be received as a moral pest for the sake of the usefulness of his land in a community where his ability is denied, his morality insulted, and his character despised. There are some Cubans who, from honorable motives, from an ardent admiration for progress and liberty, from a prescience of their own powers under better political conditions, from an unhappy ignorance of the history and tendency of annexation, would like to see the island annexed to the United States. But those who have fought in war and learned in exile, who have built, by the work of hands and mind, a virtuous home in the heart of an unfriendly community; who, by their successful efforts as scientists and merchants, as railroad builders and engineers, as teachers, artists, lawyers, journalists, orators and poets, as men of alert intelligence and uncommon activity, are honored wherever their powers have been called into action and the people are just enough to understand them; those who have raised, with their less prepared elements, a town of workingmen where the United States had previously a few huts in a barren cliff; those, more numerous than the others, do not desire the annexation of Cuba to the United States. They do not need it. They admire this nation, the greatest ever built by liberty, but they dislike the evil conditions that, like worms in the heart, have begun in this mighty republic their work of destruction. They have made of the

heroes of this country their own heroes, and look to the success of the American commonwealth as the crowning glory of mankind; but they cannot honestly believe that excessive
individualism, reverence for wealth, and the protracted exultation of a terrible victory
are preparing the United States to be the typical nation of liberty, where no opinion is to
be based in greed, and no triumph or acquisition reached against charity and justice. We
love the country of Lincoln as much as we fear the country of Cutting.[1]

We are not the people of destitute vagrants or immoral pigmies that the *Manufacturer* is pleased to picture; nor the country of petty talkers, incapable of action, hostile to
hard work, that, in a mass with the other countries of Spanish America, we are by arrogant travellers and writers represented to be. We have suffered impatiently under tyranny;
we have fought like men, sometimes like giants, to be freemen; we are passing that period
of stormy repose, full of germs of revolt, that naturally follows a period of excessive and
unsuccessful action; we have to fight like conquered men against an oppressor who de-
nies us the means of living, and fosters—in the beautiful capital visited by the tourists, in
the interior of the country, where the prey escapes his grasp—a reign of such corruption
as may poison in our veins the strength to secure freedom; we deserve in our misfortune
the respect of those who did not help us in our need.

But because our Government has systematically allowed after the war the triumph
of criminals, the occupation of the cities by the scum of the people, the ostentation of
ill-gotten riches by a myriad of Spanish office-holders and their Cuban accomplices, the
conversion of the capital into a gambling-den, where the hero and the philosopher walk
hungry by the lordly thief of the metropolis; because the healthier farmer, ruined by a
war seemingly useless, turns in silence to the plough that he knew well how to exchange
for the *machete*; because thousands of exiles, profiting by a period of calm that no
human power can quicken until it is naturally exhausted, are practising in the battle of
life in the free countries the art of governing themselves and of building a nation; because
our half-breeds and city-bred young men are generally of delicate physique, of suave
courtesy and ready words, hiding under the glove that polishes the poem the hand that
fells the foe—are we to be considered, as the *Manufacturer* does consider us, an "effeminate" people? These city-bred young men and poorly built half-breeds knew in one day
how to rise against a cruel government, to pay their passages to the seat of war with the
product of their watches and trinkets, to work their way in exile while their vessels were
being kept from them by the country of the free in the interest of the foes of freedom, to
obey as soldiers, sleep in the mud, eat roots, fight ten years without salary, conquer foes
with the branch of a tree, die—these men of eighteen, these heirs to wealthy estates,
these dusky striplings—a death not to be spoken of without uncovering the head. They
died like those other men of ours who, with a stroke of the *machete*, can send a head
flying, or by a turn of the hands bring a bull to their feet. These "effeminate" Cubans had
once courage enough, in the face of a hostile government, to carry on their left arms for
a week the mourning for Lincoln.

The Cubans have, according to the *Manufacturer*, "a distaste for exertion"; they are "helpless," "idle." These "helpless," "idle" men came here twenty years ago empty-handed, with very few exceptions; fought against the climate; mastered the language; lived by their honest labor, some in affluence, a few in wealth, rarely in misery; they bought or built homes; they raised families and fortunes; they loved luxury and worked for it; they were not frequently seen in the dark roads of life; proud and self-sustaining, they never feared competition as to intelligence or diligence. Thousands have returned to die in their homes; thousands have remained where, during the hardships of life, they have triumphed, unaided by any help of kindred language, sympathy of race, or community of religion. A handful of Cuban toilers built Key West. The Cubans have made their mark in Panama by their ability as mechanics of the higher trades, as clerks, physicians, and contractors. A Cuban, Cisneros, has greatly advanced the development of railways and river navigation in Colombia. Marquez, another Cuban, gained, with many of his countrymen, the respect of the Peruvians as a merchant of eminent capacity. Cubans are found everywhere, working as farmers, surveyors, engineers, mechanics, teachers, journalists. In Philadelphia, the *Manufacturer* has a daily opportunity to see a hundred Cubans, some of them of heroic history and powerful build, who live by their work in easy comfort. In New York, the Cubans are directors of prominent banks, substantial merchants, popular brokers, clerks of recognized ability, physicians with a large practice, engineers of world-wide repute, electricians, journalists, tradesmen, cigarmakers. The poet of Niagara is a Cuban, our Heredia;[2] a Cuban, Menocal, is the projector of the canal of Nicaragua. In Philadelphia itself, as in New York, the college prizes have been more than once awarded to Cubans. The women of these "helpless," "idle" people, with "a distaste for exertion," arrived here from a life of luxury in the heart of the winter; their husbands were in the war, ruined, dead, imprisoned in Spain; the "Señora" went to work; from a slave-owner she became a slave, took a seat behind the counter, sang in the churches, worked button-holes by the hundred, sewed for a living, curled feathers, gave her soul to duty, withered in work her body. This is the people of "defective morals."

We are "unfitted by nature and experience to discharge the obligations of citizenship in a great and free country." This cannot be justly said of a people who possess, besides the energy that built the first railroad in Spanish dominions and established against the opposition of the Government all the agencies of civilization, a truly remarkable knowledge of the body politic, a tried readiness to adapt itself to its higher forms, and the power rare in tropical countries of nerving their thought and pruning their language. Their passion for liberty, the conscientious study of its best teachings, the nursing of individual character in exile and at home, the lessons of ten years of war and its manifold consequences, and the practical exercise of the duties of citizenship in the free countries of the world, have combined, in spite of all antecedents, to develop in the Cuban a capacity for free government so natural to him that he established it, even to the excess of its practices, in the midst of the war, vied with his elders in the effort to respect the laws of liberty, and

snatched the sabre, without fear or consideration, from the hands of every military pretender, however glorious. There seems to be in the Cuban mind a happy faculty of uniting
sense with earnestness and moderation with exuberance. Noble teachers have devoted
themselves since the beginning of the century to explain by their words and exemplify by
their lives the self-restraint and tolerance inseparable from liberty. Those who won the
first seats ten years ago at the European universities by singular merit have been proclaimed, at their appearance in the Spanish Parliament, men of subtle thought and powerful speech. The political knowledge of the average Cuban compares well with that of the
average American citizen. Absolute freedom from religious intolerance, the love of man
for the work he creates by his industry, and theoretical and practical familiarity with the
laws and processes of liberty, will enable the Cuban to rebuild his country from the ruins
in which he will receive it from its oppressors. It is not to be expected, for the honor of
mankind, that the nation that was rocked in freedom, and received for three centuries the
best blood of liberty-loving men, will employ the power thus acquired in depriving a less
fortunate neighbor of his liberty.

It is, finally, said that "our lack of manly force and of self-respect is demonstrated by
the supineness with which we have so long submitted to Spanish oppression, and even
our attempts at rebellion have been so pitifully ineffective that they have risen little
above the dignity of farce." Never was ignorance of history and character more pitifully
displayed than in this wanton assertion. We need to recollect, in order to answer without bitterness, that more than one American bled by our side,[3] in a war that another
American was to call a farce. A farce! the war that has been by foreign observers compared to an epic, the upheaval of a whole country, the voluntary abandonment of wealth,
the abolition of slavery in our first moment of freedom, the burning of our cities by our
own hands, the erection of villages and factories in the wild forests, the dressing of our
ladies of rank in the textures of the woods, the keeping at bay, in ten years of such a life,
a powerful enemy, with a loss to him of 200,000 men, at the hands of a small army of
patriots, with no help but nature! We had no Hessians and no Frenchmen, no Lafayette
or Steuben, no monarchical rivals to help us; we had but one neighbor who confessedly
"stretched the limits of his power, and acted against the will of the people" to help the
foes of those who were fighting for the same Chart of Liberties on which he built his
independence. We fell a victim to the very passions which could have caused the downfall of the thirteen States, had they not been cemented by success, while we were enfeebled by procrastination; a procrastination brought about, not from cowardice, but from
an abhorrence of blood, which allowed the enemy in the first months of the war to acquire
unconquerable advantage, and from a childlike confidence in the certain help of the
United States: "They cannot see us dying for liberty at their own doors without raising a
hand or saying a word to give to the world a new free country!" They "stretched the limits of their powers in deference to Spain." They did not raise the hand. They did not say
the word.

The struggle has not ceased. The exiles do not want to return. The new generation is worthy of its sires. Hundreds of men have died in darkness since the war in the misery of prisons. With life only will this fight for liberty cease among us. And it is the melancholy truth that our efforts would have been, in all probability, successfully renewed, were it not, in some of us, for the unmanly hope of the annexationists of securing liberty without paying its price; and the just fears of others that our dead, our sacred memories, our ruins drenched in blood, would be but the fertilizers of the soil for the benefit of a foreign plant, or the occasion for a sneer from the *Manufacturer* of Philadelphia.

With sincere thanks for the space you have kindly allowed me, I am, sir, yours very respectfully,

José Martí
120 Front Street, New York, March 23

Our AMERICA

The prideful villager thinks his hometown contains the whole world, and as long as he can stay on as mayor or humiliate the rival who stole his sweetheart or watch his nest egg accumulating in its strongbox he believes the universe to be in good order, unaware of the giants in seven-league boots who can crush him underfoot or the battling comets in the heavens that go through the air devouring the sleeping worlds. Whatever is left of that sleepy hometown in America must awaken. These are not times for going to bed in a sleeping cap, but rather, like Juan de Castellanos's men,[4] with our weapons for a pillow, weapons of the mind, which vanquish all others. Trenches of ideas are worth more than trenches of stone.

A cloud of ideas is a thing no armored prow can smash through. A vital idea set ablaze before the world at the right moment can, like the mystic banner of the last judgment, stop a fleet of battleships. Hometowns that are still strangers to one another must hurry to become acquainted, like men who are about to do battle together. Those who shake their fists at each other like jealous brothers quarreling over a piece of land or the owner of a small house who envies the man with a better one must join hands and interlace them until their two hands are as one. Those who, shielded by a criminal tradition, mutilate, with swords smeared in the same blood that flows through their own veins, the land of a conquered brother whose punishment far exceeds his crimes, must return that land to their brother if they do not wish to be known as a nation of plunderers. The honorable man does not collect his debts of honor in money, at so much per slap. We can no longer be a nation of fluttering leaves, spending our lives in the air, our treetop crowned in flowers, humming or creaking, caressed by the caprices of sunlight or thrashed and felled by tempests. The trees must form ranks to block the seven-league giant! It is the hour of reckoning and of marching in unison, and we must move in lines as compact as the veins of silver that lie at the roots of the Andes.

Only runts whose growth was stunted will lack the necessary valor, for those who have no faith in their land are like men born prematurely. Having no valor themselves, they deny that other men do. Their puny arms, with bracelets and painted nails, the arms of Madrid or of Paris, cannot manage the lofty tree and so they say the tree cannot be climbed. We must load up the ships with these termites who gnaw away at the core of the patria that has nurtured them; if they are Parisians or Madrileños then let them stroll to the Prado by lamplight or go to Tortoni's for an ice. These sons of carpenters who are ashamed that their father was a carpenter! These men born in America who are ashamed of the mother that raised them because she wears an Indian apron, these delinquents who disown their sick mother and leave her alone in her sickbed! Which one is truly a man, he who stays with his mother to nurse her through her illness, or he who forces her to work somewhere out of sight, and lives off her sustenance in corrupted lands, with a worm for his insignia, cursing the bosom that bore him, sporting a sign that says "traitor" on the back of his paper dress-coat? These sons of our America, which must save herself through her Indians, and which is going from less to more, who desert her and take up arms in the armies of North America, which drowns its own Indians in blood and is going from more to less! These delicate creatures who are men but do not want to do men's work! Did Washington, who made that land for them, go and live with the English during the years when he saw the English marching against his own land? These *incroyables* who drag their honor across foreign soil, like the *incroyables* of the French Revolution, dancing, smacking their lips, and deliberately slurring their words!

And in what patria can a man take greater pride than in our long-suffering republics of America, erected among mute masses of Indians upon the bloodied arms of no more than a hundred apostles, to the sound of the book doing battle against the monk's tall candle? Never before have such advanced and consolidated nations been created from such disparate factors in less historical time. The haughty man thinks that because he wields a quick pen or a vivid phrase the earth was made to be his pedestal, and accuses his native republic of irredeemable incompetence because its virgin jungles do not continually provide him with the means of going about the world a famous plutocrat, driving Persian ponies and spilling champagne. The incapacity lies not in the emerging country, which demands forms that are appropriate to it and a grandeur that is useful, but in the leaders who try to rule unique nations, of a singular and violent composition, with laws inherited from four centuries of free practice in the United States and nineteen centuries of monarchy in France. A gaucho's pony cannot be stopped in midbolt by one of Alexander Hamilton's laws. The sluggish blood of the Indian race cannot be quickened by a phrase from Sieyès.[5] To govern well, one must attend closely to the reality of the place that is governed. In America, the good ruler does not need to know how the German or Frenchman is governed, but what elements his own country is composed of and how he can marshal them so as to reach, by means and institutions born from the country itself, the desirable state in which every man knows himself and is active, and all men enjoy the abundance that Nature, for the good of all, has bestowed on the country they make fruitful by their labor and defend with their lives. The government must be born from the country. The spirit of the government must be the spirit of the country. The form of the government must be in harmony with the country's natural constitution. The government is no more than an equilibrium among the country's natural elements.

In America the natural man has triumphed over the imported book. Natural men have triumphed over an artificial intelligentsia. The native mestizo has triumphed over the alien, pure-blooded criollo. The battle is not between civilization and barbarity, but between false erudition and nature. The natural man is good, and esteems and rewards a superior intelligence as long as that intelligence does not use his submission against him or offend him by ignoring him—for that the natural man deems unforgivable, and he is prepared to use force to regain the respect of anyone who wounds his sensibilities or harms his interests. The tyrants of America have come to power by acquiescing to these scorned natural elements and have fallen as soon as they betrayed them. The republics have purged the former tyrannies of their inability to know the true elements of the country, derive the form of government from them, and govern along with them. *Governor*, in a new country, means *Creator*.

In countries composed of educated and uneducated sectors, the uneducated will govern by their habit of attacking and resolving their doubts with their fists, unless the educated learn the art of governing. The uneducated masses are lazy and timid about matters of the intellect and want to be well-governed, but if the government injures them they shake it off and govern themselves. How can our governors emerge from the universities when there is not a university in America that teaches the most basic element of the art of governing, which is the analysis of all that is unique to the peoples of America? Our youth go out into the world wearing Yankee- or French-colored glasses and aspire to rule by guesswork a country they do not know. Those unacquainted with the rudiments of politics should not be allowed to embark on a career in politics. The literary prizes must not go to the best ode, but to the best study of the political factors in the student's country. In the newspapers, lecture halls, and academies, the study of the country's real factors must be carried forward. Simply knowing those factors without blindfolds or circumlocutions is enough—for anyone who deliberately or unknowingly sets aside a part of the truth will ultimately fail because of the truth he was lacking, which expands when neglected and brings down whatever is built without it. Solving the problem after knowing its elements is easier than solving it without knowing them. The natural man, strong and indignant, comes and overthrows the authority that is accumulated from books because it is not administered in keeping with the manifest needs of the country. To know is to solve. To know the country and govern it in accordance with that knowledge is the only way of freeing it from tyranny. The European university must yield to the American university. The history of America from the Incas to the present must be taught in its smallest detail, even if the Greek Archons go untaught. Our own Greece is preferable to the Greece that is not ours; we need it more. Statesmen who arise from the nation must replace statesmen who are alien to it. Let the world be grafted onto our republics, but we must be the trunk. And let the vanquished pedant hold his tongue, for there is no patria in which a man can take greater pride than in our long-suffering American republics.

Our feet upon a rosary, our heads white, and our bodies a motley of Indian and criollo, we boldly entered the community of nations. Bearing the standard of the Virgin, we went out to conquer our liberty. A priest,[6] a few lieutenants, and a woman built a republic in Mexico upon the shoulders of the Indians. A Spanish cleric, under cover of his priestly cape, taught French liberty to a handful of magnificent students who chose a Spanish general to lead Central America against Spain. Still accustomed to monarchy, and with the sun on their chests, the Venezuelans in the north and the Argentines in the south set out to construct nations. When the two heroes clashed and the continent was about to be rocked, one of them, and not the lesser one, turned back.[7] But heroism is less glorious in peacetime than in war, and thus rarer, and it is easier for a man to die with honor than to think in an orderly way. Exalted and unanimous sentiments are more readily governed than the diverging, arrogant, alien, and ambitious ideas that emerge when the battle is over. The powers that were swept up in the epic struggle, along with the feline wariness of the species and the sheer weight of reality, undermined the edifice that had raised the flags of nations sustained by wise governance in the continual practice of reason and freedom over the crude and singular regions of our mestizo America with its towns of bare legs and Parisian dress-coats. The colonial hierarchy resisted the republic's democracy, and the capital city, wearing its elegant cravat, left the countryside, in its horsehide boots, waiting at the door; the redeemers born from books did not understand that a revolution that had triumphed when the soul of the earth was unleashed by a savior's voice had to govern with the soul of the earth and not against or without it. And for all these reasons, America began enduring and still endures the weary task of reconciling the discordant and hostile elements it inherited from its perverse, despotic colonizer with the imported forms and ideas that have, in their lack of local reality, delayed the advent of a logical form of government. The continent, deformed by three centuries of a rule that denied man the right to exercise his reason, embarked—overlooking or refusing to listen to the ignorant masses that had helped it redeem itself—upon a government based on reason, the reason of all directed toward the things that are of concern to all, and not the university-taught reason of the few imposed upon the rustic reason of others. The problem of independence was not the change in form, but the change in spirit.

Common cause had to be made with the oppressed in order to consolidate a system that was opposed to the interests and governmental habits of the oppressors. The tiger, frightened away by the flash of gunfire, creeps back in the night to find his prey. He will die with flames shooting from his eyes, his claws unsheathed, but now his step is inaudible for he comes on velvet paws. When the prey awakens, the tiger is upon him. The colony lives on in the republic, but our America is saving itself from its grave blunders—the arrogance of the capital cities, the blind triumph of the scorned campesinos, the excessive importation of foreign ideas and formulas, the wicked and impolitic disdain for the native race—through the superior virtue, confirmed by necessary bloodshed, of the republic that struggles against the colony. The tiger waits behind every tree, crouches in every corner. He will die, his claws unsheathed, flames shooting from his eyes.

But "these countries will be saved," in the words of the Argentine Rivadivia,[8] who erred on the side of urbanity during crude times; the machete is ill-suited to a silken scabbard, nor can the spear be abandoned in a country won by the spear, for it becomes enraged and stands in the doorway of Iturbide's Congress demanding that "the fair-skinned man be made emperor."[9] These countries will be saved because, with the genius of moderation that now seems, by nature's serene harmony, to prevail in the continent of light, and the influence of the critical reading that has, in Europe, replaced the fumbling ideas about phalansteries in which the previous generation was steeped, the real man is being born to America, in these real times.

What a vision we were: the chest of an athlete, the hands of a dandy, and the forehead of a child. We were a whole fancy dress ball, in English trousers, a Parisian waistcoat, a North American overcoat, and a Spanish bullfighter's hat. The Indian circled about us, mute, and went to the mountaintop to christen his children. The black, pursued from afar, alone and unknown, sang his heart's music in the night, between waves and wild beasts. The campesinos, the men of the land, the creators, rose up in blind indignation against the disdainful city, their own creation. We wore epaulets and judge's robes, in countries that came into the world wearing rope sandals and Indian headbands. The wise thing would have been to pair, with charitable hearts and the audacity of our founders, the Indian headband and the judicial robe, to undam the Indian, make a place for the able black, and tailor liberty to the bodies of those who rose up and triumphed in its name. What we had was the judge, the general, the man of letters, and the cleric. Our angelic youth, as if struggling from the arms of an octopus, cast their heads into the heavens and fell back with sterile glory, crowned with clouds. The natural people, driven by instinct, blind with triumph, overwhelmed their gilded rulers. No Yankee or European book could furnish the key to the Hispanoamerican enigma. So the people tried hatred instead, and our countries amounted to less and less each year. Weary of useless hatred, of the struggle of book against sword, reason against the monk's taper, city against countryside, the impossible empire of the quarreling urban castes against the tempestuous or inert natural nation, we are beginning, almost unknowingly, to try love. The nations arise and salute one another. "What are we like?" they ask, and begin telling each other what they are like. When a problem arises in Cojimar they no longer seek the solution in Dantzig. The frock-coats are still French, but the thinking begins to be American. The young men of America are rolling up their sleeves and plunging their hands into the dough, and making it rise with the leavening of their sweat. They understand that there is too much imitation, and that salvation lies in creating. *Create* is this generation's password. Make wine from plantains; it may be sour, but it is our wine! It is now understood that a country's form of government must adapt to its natural elements, that absolute ideas, in order not to collapse over an error of form, must be expressed in relative forms; that liberty, in order to be viable, must be sincere and full, that if the republic does not open its arms to all and include all in its progress, it dies. The tiger inside came in through the gap, and so will the tiger outside. The general holds the cavalry's speed to the pace of the infantry, for if he leaves the infantry far behind, the enemy will surround the cavalry. Politics is strategy. Nations must continually criticize themselves, for criticism is health, but with a single heart and a single mind. Lower yourselves to the unfortunate and raise them up in your arms! Let the heart's fires unfreeze all that is motionless in America, and let the country's natural blood surge and throb through its veins! Standing tall, the workmen's eyes full of joy, the new men of America are saluting each other from one country to another. Natural statesmen are emerging from the direct study of nature; they read in order to apply what they read, not copy it. Economists are studying problems at their origins. Orators are becoming more temperate. Dramatists are putting native characters onstage. Academies are discussing practical subjects. Poetry is snipping off its wild, Zorilla-esque mane and hanging up its gaudy waistcoat on the glorious tree.[10] Prose, polished and gleaming, is replete with ideas. The rulers of Indian republics are learning Indian languages.

America is saving herself from all her dangers. Over some republics the octopus sleeps still, but by the law of equilibrium, other republics are running into the sea to recover the lost centuries with mad and sublime swiftness. Others, forgetting that Juárez traveled in a coach drawn by mules,[11] hitch their coach to the wind and take a soap bubble for coachman—and poisonous luxury, enemy of liberty, corrupts the frivolous and opens the door to foreigners. The virile character of others is being perfected by the epic spirit of a threatened independence. And others, in rapacious wars against their neighbors, are nurturing an unruly soldier caste that may devour them. But our America may also face another danger, which comes not from within but from the differing origins, methods, and interests of the continent's two factions. The hour is near when she will be approached by an enterprising and forceful nation that will demand intimate relations with her, though it does not know her and disdains her. And virile nations self-made by the rifle and the law love other virile nations, and love only them. The hour of unbridled passion and ambition from which North America may escape by the ascendency of the purest element in its blood—or into which its vengeful and sordid masses, its tradition of conquest, and the self-interest of a cunning leader could plunge it—is not yet so close, even to the most apprehensive eye, that there is no time for it to be confronted and averted by the manifestation of a discreet and unswerving pride, for its dignity as a republic, in the eyes of the watchful nations of the Universe, places upon North America a brake that our America must not remove by puerile provocation, ostentatious arrogance, or patricidal discord. Therefore the urgent duty of our America is to show herself as she is, one in soul and intent, rapidly overcoming the crushing weight of her past and stained only by the fertile blood shed by hands that do battle against ruins and by veins that were punctured by our former masters. The disdain of the formidable neighbor who does not know her is our America's greatest danger, and it is urgent—for the day of the visit is near—that her neighbor come to know her, and quickly, so that he will not disdain her. Out of ignorance, he may perhaps begin to covet her. But when he knows her, he will remove his hands from her in respect. One must have faith in the best in man and distrust the worst. One must give the best every opportunity, so that the worst will be laid bare and overcome. If not, the worst will prevail. Nations should have one special pillory for those who incite them to futile hatreds, and another for those who do not tell them the truth until it is too late.

There is no racial hatred, because there are no races. Sickly, lamp-lit minds string together and rewarm the library-shelf races that the honest traveler and the cordial observer seek in vain in the justice of nature, where the universal identity of man leaps forth in victorious love and turbulent appetite. The soul, equal and eternal, emanates from bodies that are diverse in form and color. Anyone who promotes and disseminates opposition or hatred among races is committing a sin against humanity. But within that jumble of peoples which lives in close proximity to our peoples, certain peculiar and dynamic characteristics are condensed—ideas and habits of expansion, acquisition, vanity, and greed—that could, in a period of internal disorder or precipitation of a people's cumulative character, cease to be latent national preoccupations and become a serious threat to the neighboring, isolated and weak lands that the strong country declares to be perishable and inferior. To think is to serve. We must not, out of a villager's antipathy, impute some lethal congenital wickedness to the continent's light-skinned nation simply because it does not speak our language or share our view of what home life should be or resemble us in its political failings, which are different from ours, or because it does not think highly of quick-tempered, swarthy men or look with charity, from its still uncertain eminence, upon those less favored by history who, in heroic stages, are climbing the road that republics travel. But neither should we seek to conceal the obvious facts of the problem, which can, for the peace of the centuries, be resolved by timely study and the urgent, wordless union of the continental soul. For the unanimous hymn is already ringing forth, and the present generation is bearing industrious America along the road sanctioned by our sublime forefathers. From the Rio Bravo to the Straits of Magellan, the Great Cemi,[12] seated on a condor's back, has scattered the seeds of the new America across the romantic nations of the continent and the suffering islands of the sea!

—*El Partido Liberal (Mexico City), January 20, 1891*

TRANSLATION AND NOTES BY ESTHER ALLEN

NOTES

In the late 1880s, the newly elected administration of Benjamin Harrison was bandying about the old idea of purchasing Cuba from Spain. At that point, the purchase was seen as a way of disposing of the surplus in the Treasury and postponing the looming and highly controversial issue of import tariff reduction, since Cuban sugar could be admitted free of tax if Cuba were part of the Union. On Thursday, March 21, 1889, the *New York Evening Post* published a short article titled "A Protectionist View of Cuban Annexation," which noted the surprisingly anti-annexationist stance of the *Philadelphia Manufacturer,* which the *Post* called "the only profess-edly high-tariff organ in the country that is conducted with decent ability." The *Post* cited the following paragraph from an article recently published by the *Manufacturer*: "The people of Cuba are divided into three classes, Spaniards, native Cubans of Spanish descent, and negroes. The men of Spanish birth are probably less fitted than men of any other white race to become American citizens. They have ruled Cuba for centuries. They rule it now upon almost precisely the same methods that they have always employed, methods which combine bigotry with tyranny, and silly pride with fathomless corruption. The less we have of them the better. The native Cubans are not much more desirable: To the faults of the men of the parent race they add effeminacy and a distaste for exertion which amounts really to disease. They are helpless, idle, of defective morals, and unfitted by nature and experience for discharging the obligations of citizenship in a great and free republic. Their lack of manly force and of self-respect is demonstrated by the supineness with which they have so long submitted to Spanish oppression, and even their attempts at rebellion have been so pitifully ineffective that they have risen little above the dignity of farce. To clothe such men with the responsibilities of directing this government, and to give them the same measure of power that is wielded by the freemen of our Northern States, would be to summon them to the performance of functions for which they have not the smallest capacity." The anonymous writer for the *New York Evening Post* then concurred: "All of this we emphatically endorse, and it may be added that if we have now a Southern question which disturbs us more or less, we should have it in a more aggravated form if Cuba were added to the Union, with near a million blacks, much inferior to our own in point of civilization, who must, of course, be armed with the ballot and put on the same level politically with their former masters. If Mr. Chandler and Gov. Foraker can scarcely endure the spectacle which they daily behold in the Southern States, of negroes deprived of the elective franchise, what must their sufferings be when the responsibility of Cuba is put upon them also? Imagine a special Committee of the Senate going to Cuba to take testimony on the disfranchisement of the freedmen. In the first place, the difficulties of language would be insurmountable, for the Spanish tongue as spoken on the plantations would be rather harder to learn than that of the Basque provinces. The report of such a committee would either become a laughing-stock, or would plunge Congress into dire confusion. Probably we shall be spared any such infliction as the annexation of Cuba by the refusal of Spain to sell the island. A Madrid dispatch says that Minister Moret, in reply to a question in the Senate yesterday, declared that Spain would not entertain any offer from the United States for the purchase of the island, and, as if this statement were not sufficiently emphatic, he added that there was not money enough in the whole world to buy the smallest portion of Spanish territory." In response, Martí wrote the following letter, which the *Evening Post* published on March 25, 1889. It appears here exactly as it did there. Martí subsequently published a pamphlet titled "Cuba y los Estados Unidos," which contained Spanish translations of the articles from the *Manufacturer* and the *Post*, and of his response. —Esther Allen, editor and translator, *Selected Writings* by José Martí.

Joseph Benson Foraker (1846–1917): American political leader who served in the Civil War as a young man and went on to become a judge. He strongly supported the McKinley administration in the debates surrounding the Spanish-American War and sponsored the 1900 Foraker Act, under which the United States instituted a civil government in Puerto Rico while retaining control of the island.

1.   Francis Cutting was the leader of the American Annexationist League.

2.   José María Heredia (1803–39): Cuban poet. He is best known for the poems "El Niágara," an impassioned hymn to Niagara Falls, and "En el Teocalli de Cholula," which evokes Mexico's pre-Columbian past.

3.   Joseph Fry is one example of a North American who came to the aid of the Cubans during the Ten Years War. In 1873, as captain of the *Virgilius*, which was fraudulently flying the United States flag, he attempted to carry arms to the Cuban insurgents. He was captured by the Spaniards off the Cuban coast and he and fifty-two of the ship's crew and passengers were put to death.

4.   Juan de Castellanos (1522–1607): Spanish poet and chronicler of the conquest of New Granada (now Colombia) in which he took part.

5.   Emmanuel Joseph Sieyès (1748–1836): Author of the famous tract *The Third Estate* (1789) and leading figure in the French Revolution who subsequently assisted Napoleon in his coup d'état.

6.   Miguel Hidalgo y Costilla (1753–1811), an elderly priest, initiated Mexico's revolution of independence in the town of Dolores at the head of a band of Indians and with the help of the wife of the mayor of nearby Querétaro, Josefa Ortíz de Domínguez (1768–1829).

7.   In South America, revolutions of independence emerged in 1810. Under Simón Bolívar's leadership, independentist forces gradually made their way south from Venezuela, as Jose de San Martín (1778–1850) came north from today's Argentina and Chile. In 1825, a combined patriot force defeated a major royalist army at Ayacucho, Peru, the battle that marked the end of the Spanish Empire in South America.

8.   Bernardino Rivadivia (1780–1845): Argentine politician. Elected as the first president of the United Provinces of Río de la Plata in 1826, he was forced to resign by the caudillo Facundo Quiroga and went into exile. He died in the Spanish city of Cádiz.

9.   Agustín de Iturbide (1783–1824): Mexican general who initially fought against Mexico's independence movement. He later joined forces with insurgent general Guerrero to assure Mexico's independence. But, instead of the liberal state envisioned by the insurgents, Iturbide ushered in a conservative one. When his soldiers proclaimed him emperor, the newly independent Mexican Congress, angry but cowed, ratified the proclamation (1822). A revolution soon broke out against him, and in 1823 he was forced to abdicate.

10.   A reference to José Zorilla (1817–93), a romantic Spanish poet. Martí did not share in the popular enthusiasm for Zorilla's work.

11.   Benito Juárez (1806–72): Widely revered as one of Latin America's greatest nineteenth-century political figures, Juárez was a Zapotec Indian who was president of Mexico from 1857 to 1863 and again from 1867 until his death.

12.   A spirit worshiped by the Taino, an indigenous people of the Caribbean. The *cemi* (or *zemi*) is often represented in the form of a tricornered clay object.

CHAPTER 1. FROM MY HOMETOWN CAYEY TO SAN JUAN, AND HOW I ARRIVED IN NEW YORK WITHOUT A WATCH

Early in the morning of August 2, 1916, I took leave of Cayey. I got on the bus at the Plaza and sat down, squeezed in between passengers and suitcases. Of my traveling companions I remember nothing. I don't think I opened my mouth the whole way. I just stared at the landscape, sunk in deep sorrow. I was leaving a girlfriend in town . . .

But my readers are very much mistaken if they expect a sentimental love story from me. I don't write to pour my heart out—confessions of love bore me to death, especially my own. So, to make a long story short, the girl's parents, brothers, relatives, and well-wishers declared war on me. That's not exactly why I decided to leave, but that small-town drama of Montagues and Capulets did have an influence. Anyway, I left Cayey that hot summer, heavy of heart, but ready to face a new life.

From an early age I had worked as a cigar-roller in a tobacco factory. I had just turned thirty, and although it was not the first time I had left my hometown, never before had I put the shores of Puerto Rico behind me. I had been to the capital a few times. But now it meant going farther, to a strange and distant world. I hadn't the slightest idea what fate awaited me.

In those days I was taller than most Puerto Ricans. I was white, a peasant from the highlands (*a jíbaro*), and there was that waxen pallor to my face so typical of country folk. I had a round face with high cheekbones, a wide, flat nose, and small blue eyes. As for my lips, well, I'd say they were rather sensual, and I had strong, straight teeth. I had a full head of light chestnut hair, and, in contrast to the roundness of my face, I had square jaws. All in all, I suppose I was rather ugly, though there were women around who thought otherwise.

I did not inspire much sympathy at first sight, I'm sure of that. I have never made friends easily. No doubt my physical appearance has a lot to do with it. I hadn't been living in New York for long before I realized how difficult it was for people to guess where I came from. Time and again I was taken for a Polish Jew, or a Tartar, or even a Japanese . . . God forgive my dear parents for my human countenance, which was after all the only thing they had bequeathed me!

I arrived in San Juan at around ten o'clock in the morning. I ordered the driver to take me to El Comercio, a cheap hotel I knew of on Calle Tetuán. I left my suitcase and went out for a walk in the city.

The sun warmed the pavements of the narrow streets. I longed for the morning chill of my native Toa valley. I decided to go for a ride in a trolley car and say goodbye to an old schoolteacher of mine. To her I owed my first stop. Her name was Elisa Rubio and I have fond memories of her to this day. In her little house in Santurce she told me glowing things about the United States and praised my decision to emigrate. I would have a chance to study there. To this day, after all these years, her exaggerated praise echoes in my mind: "You have talent and ambition. You will get ahead, I am sure. And you'll become famous" Heaven forgive my well-meaning teacher.

On my return to the old section of San Juan, I spent the afternoon taking leave of my comrades. There was Manuel F. Rojas, who had been elected secretary general of the Partido Socialista at the constituent assembly recently held in Cayey, my hometown, which I had attended as a delegate. With him were Santiago Iglesias, Prudencio Rivera Martínez, and Rafael Alonso Torres . . . They all were unhappy about my decision to leave because of the loss it would be for our newly organized workers' movement. But they did not try hard to dissuade me. As socialists, we dig our trenches everywhere in the world.

I returned to the little hotel tired and sweaty. Before going up to my room I bought the daily newspapers—*La Correspondencia, El Tiempo, La Democracia*. In shirt-sleeves, I threw myself onto my bed and plunged into the latest events of the day. In those days our newspapers were not as big as they are today—none were over twelve pages. The news, especially about foreign affairs, did not take up much space. But our native writers waxed eloquent in endless polemics—original commentaries, sharp criticism, and plenty of our local humor. They reflected the life of the whole society—or rather, of its ruling class—with uneven success, but in any case they were more truthful than they are today, for sure.

Night fell, and I washed up, dressed, and went back out in the street. I had a long conversation with Benigno Fernández García, the son of a prestigious Cayey family. We talked about the European war, in which the United States was soon to be involved. Then I returned to my hotel, went to bed, and tried to sleep, but it was impossible. My mind was full of memories and my heart ached. Until then I had been acting like a robot, or a man under the influence of drugs. Now, alone in the darkness of my room, I recalled my mother's tears, the sad faces of my little brothers . . . I just couldn't get to sleep.

Once again I went back into the streets. It had rained. A pleasant breeze blew through the city. The bright moon lit up the streets. The damp pavements glistened. And I took to walking, up one street and down another, in an intimate chat with the cobblestones of that city which means so much to Puerto Ricans.

Dawn caught me by surprise, seated on one of the benches in the Plaza de Armas now and then looking up at the big clock. The cheerful rattle of the first trolley car brought me back to sad reality. Within a few minutes the bold tropical sun had taken possession of San Juan, and the streets were crowded with people. Gentlemen in jackets and hats left home to go to work. But the largest crowds were made up of people flocking in from the countryside, dealers in agricultural produce. Cornflakes had not yet replaced corn on the cob, though things were already headed in that direction.

The hours passed quickly. At around two in the afternoon I boarded the boat, the famous *Coamo* which made so many trips from San Juan to New York and back. I took a quick look at my cabin, and went right back up on deck. I did not want to lose a single breath of those final minutes in my country, perhaps the last ones I would ever have.

Soon the boat pushed off from the dock, turned, and began to move slowly toward El Morro castle at the mouth of the harbor. A nun who worked at the women's home was waving *adiós* from high up on the ramparts; I assumed she meant it for me. As soon as we were on the open sea and the boat started to pitch, the passengers went off to their cabins, most of them already half seasick. Not I. I stayed up on deck, lingering there until the island was lost from sight in the first shadows of nightfall.

The days passed peacefully. Sunrise of the first day and the passengers were already acting as though they belonged to one family. It was not long before we came to know each other's life stories. The topic of conversation, of course, was what lay ahead: life in New York. First savings would be for sending for close relatives. Years later the time would come to return home with pots of money. Everyone's mind was on that farm they'd be buying or the business they'd set up in town . . . All of us were building our own little castles in the sky.

When the fourth day dawned even those who had spent the whole trip cooped up in their cabins showed up on deck. We saw the lights of New York even before the morning mist rose. As the boat entered the harbor the sky was clear and clean. The excitement grew the closer we got to the docks. We recognized the Statue of Liberty in the distance. Countless smaller boats were sailing about in the harbor. In front of us rose the imposing sight of skyscrapers—the same skyline we had admired so often on postcards. Many of the passengers had only heard talk of New York, and stood with their mouths open, spellbound. . . . Finally the *Coamo* docked at Hamilton Pier on Staten Island.

First to disembark were the passengers traveling first class—businessmen, well-to-do families, students. In second class, where I was, there were the emigrants, most of us *tabaqueros*, or cigar workers. We all boarded the ferry that crossed from Staten Island to lower Manhattan. We sighed as we set foot on solid ground. There, gaping before us, were the jaws of the iron dragon: the immense New York metropolis.

All of us new arrivals were well dressed. I mean, we had on our Sunday best. I myself was wearing a navy blue woolen suit (or *flus*, as they would say back home), a borsalino hat made of Italian straw, black shoes with pointy toes, a white vest, and a red tie. I would have been sporting a shiny wristwatch too, if a traveling companion hadn't warned me that in New York it was considered effeminate to wear things like that. So as soon as the city was in sight, and the boat was entering the harbor, I tossed my watch into the sea. . . . And to think that it wasn't long before those wristwatches came into fashion and ended up being the rage!

And so I arrived in New York, without a watch.

CHAPTER 2. THE TRIALS AND TRIBULATIONS OF AN EMIGRANT IN THE IRON TOWER OF BABEL ON THE EVE OF WORLD WAR I

The Battery, which as I found out later is what they call the tip of lower Manhattan where our ferry from Staten Island docked, was also a port of call for all the elevated trains. The Second, Third, Sixth, and Ninth Avenue lines all met there. I entered the huge station with Ambrosio Fernández, who had come down to meet me at the dock. The noise of the trains was deafening, and I felt as if I was drowning in the crowd. Funny, but now that I was on land I started to feel seasick. People were rushing about every which way, not seeming to know exactly where they were headed. Now and then one of them would cast a mocking glance at the funny-looking travelers with their suitcases and other baggage. Finally there I was in a subway car, crushed by the mobs of passengers, kept afloat only by the confidence I felt in the presence of my friend.

The train snaked along at breakneck speed. I pretended to take note of everything, my eyes like the golden deuce in a deck of Spanish cards. The further along we moved, and as the dingy buildings filed past my view, all the visions I had of the gorgeous splendor of New York vanished. The skyscrapers seemed like tall gravestones. I wondered why, if the United States was so rich, as surely it was, did its biggest city look so grotesque? At that moment I sensed for the first time that people in New York could not possibly be as happy as we used to think they were back home in Cayey.

Ambrosio rescued me from my brooding. We were at the 23rd Street station. We got off and walked down to 22nd Street. We were on the West Side. At number 228 I took up my first lodgings. It was a boarding house run by Mrs. Arnao, the place where Ambrosio was living.

On my first day in New York I didn't go out at all. There was a lot to talk about, and Ambrosio and I had lengthy conversations. I told him the latest from Puerto Rico, about our families and friends. He talked about the city, what life was like, what the chances were of finding a job . . . To put it mildy, an utterly dismal picture.

Ambrosio himself was out of work, which led me to ask myself, "Now, if Ambrosio is out of a job, and he's been here a while and isn't just a cigarworker but a silversmith and watchmaker to boot, then how am I ever going to find anything?" My mind began to cloud over with doubts; frightening shadows fell over my immediate future. I dreaded the thought of finding myself out in the streets of such a big, inhospitable city. I paid the landlady a few weeks' rent in advance. Then, while continuing my conversation with Ambrosio, I took the further precautionary measure of sewing the money for my return to Puerto Rico into the lining of my jacket. I knew I only had a few months to find work before winter descended on us. If I didn't, I figured I'd send New York to the devil and haul anchor.

Word was that Mrs. Arnao was married to a Puerto Rican dentist, though I never saw hide nor hair of the alleged tooth-puller around the house. She was an industrious woman and her rooming house was furnished in elegant taste. She had a flair for cooking and could prepare a delectable dinner, down to the peapods. At the time I arrived her only other boarder was Ambrosio, which led me to suspect that she wasn't doing too well financially.

But in those days you didn't need much to get by in New York. Potatoes were selling for a fraction of a cent a pound; eggs were fifteen cents a dozen; a pound of salt pork was going for twelve cents, and a prime steak for twenty cents. A nickel would buy a lot of vegetables. You could pick up a good suit for $10.00. With a nickel fare you could get anywhere in the city, and change from one line to another without having to pay more.

The next day I went out with Ambrosio to get to know New York. We headed for Fifth Avenue, where we got on a double-decker bus. It was the first time I had ever been on one of those strange contraptions! The tour was terrific. The bus went uptown, crossed over on 110th Street and made its way up Riverside Drive. At 135th Street we took Broadway up to 168th Street, and then St. Nicholas Avenue to 191st. From our comfortable seats on the upper deck we could soak in all the sights—the shiny store windows, then the mansions, and later on the gray panorama of the Hudson River.

In later years I took the same trip many times. But I was never as impressed as I was then, even though on other occasions I was often in better company. Not to say that Ambrosio wasn't good company, don't get me wrong!

At the end of our tour, where we got off the bus, was a little park. We strolled through it, reading the inscriptions commemorating the War of Independence. We couldn't help noticing the young couples kissing right there in public. At first it upset me to witness such an embarrassing scene. But I quickly realized that our presence didn't matter to them, and Ambrosio confirmed my impression. What a difference between our customs back home and the behavior of Puerto Rican men and women in New York!

We returned by the same route, but got off the bus at 110th Street. We walked up Manhattan Avenue to 116th, which is where the León brothers—Antonio, Pepín, and Abelardo—were living. They owned a small cigar factory. They were part of a family from Cayey that had emigrated to New York back in 1904. The members of that family were some of the first Puerto Ricans to settle in the Latin *barrio* of Harlem. In those days the Nadals, Matienzos, Pietris, Escalonas, and Umpierres lived there too; I also knew of a certain Julio Ortíz. In all, I'd say there were some one hundred and fifty Puerto Ricans living in that part of the city around the turn of the century.

Before our countrymen, there were other Hispanics here. There was a sizable Cuban colony in the last quarter of the nineteenth century, members of the Quesada, Arango, and Mantilla families, as well as Emilia Casanova de Villaverde. They must have been people of some means, since they lived in apartments belonging to Sephardic Jews on 110th Street facing Central Park.

As I was saying, when I took up residence in New York in 1916 the apartment buildings and stores in what came to be known as El Barrio, "our" barrio, or the Barrio Latino, all belonged to Jews. Seventh, St. Nicholas, and Manhattan avenues, and the streets in between, were all inhabited by Jewish people of means, if not great wealth. 110th Street was the professional center of the district. The classy, expensive stores were on Lenox Avenue, while the more modest ones were located east of Fifth Avenue. The ghetto of poor Jews extended along Park Avenue between 110th and 117th and on the streets east of Madison. It was in this lower class Jewish neighborhood that some Puerto Rican and Cuban families, up to about fifty of them, were living at that time. Here, too, was where a good many Puerto Rican cigarworkers, bachelors for the most part, occupied the many furnished rooms in the blocks between Madison and Park.

On Park Avenue was an open-air market where you could buy things at low prices. Early in the morning the vendors would set up their stands on the sidewalk under the elevated train, and in the afternoon they would pack up their goods for the night. The marketplace was dirty and stank to high heaven, and remained that way until the years of Mayor Fiorello La Guardia, who put the market in the condition it is in today.

Many of the Jews who lived there in those days were recent immigrants, which made the whole area seem like a Tower of Babel. There were Sephardic Jews who spoke ancient Spanish or Portuguese; there were those from the Near East and from the Mediterranean, who spoke Italian, French, Provençal, Roumanian, Turkish, Arabic, or Greek. Many of them, in fact, could get along in five or even six languages. On make-shift shelves and display cases, hanging from walls and wire hangers, all kinds of goods were on display. You could buy everything from the simplest darning needle to a complete trousseau. For a quarter you could get a used pair of shoes and for two or three cents a bag of fruit or vegetables.

At the end of our visit to this neighborhood. Ambrosio and I stopped off for dinner at a restaurant called La Luz. We were attracted by the Spanish name, though the owner was actually a Sephardic Jew. The food was not prepared in the style that was familiar to us, but we did notice that the sauces were of Spanish origin. The customers who frequented the place spoke Castilian Spanish. Their heated discussions centered on the war raging in Europe. From what I could gather, most of them thought that the United States would soon be involved in the conflict, and that the Germans would be defeated in the end.

I was impressed by the restaurant because it was so hard to believe that it was located in the United States. There was something exotic about the atmosphere. The furniture and decor gave it the appearance of a café in Spain or Portugal. Even the people who gathered there, their gestures and speech mannerisms, identified them as from Galicia, Andalusia, Aragon, or some other Iberian region. I began to recognize that New York City was really a modern Babylon, the meeting point for peoples from all over the world.

At this time Harlem was a socialist stronghold. The Socialist Party had set up a large number of clubs in the neighborhood. Young working people would get together not only for political purposes but for cultural and sports activities and all kinds of parties. There were two major community centers organized by the party: the Harlem Terrace on 104th Street (a branch of the Rand School), and the Harlem Educational Center on 106th between Madison and Park. Other cultural societies and a large number of workers' cooperatives also worked out of these centers. Meetings and large indoor activities were held at the Park Palace, an auditorium with a large seating capacity. Outdoor public events were held at the corner of 110th Street and Fifth Avenue. All kinds of political, economic, social, and philosophical issues were discussed there; every night speakers aired their views, with the active participation of the public.

Housing in that growing neighborhood was for the most part owned by people who lived there. In many buildings the owners lived in one apartment and rented out the rest. There was still little or no exploitation of tenants by absentee landlords who had nothing to do with the community. The apartments were spacious and quite comfortable. They were well maintained precisely because the owners themselves lived in the buildings. Clearly, the Jewish people who lived in Harlem back then considered it their neighborhood and felt a sentimental attachment to it. Several generations had grown up there; they had their own schools, synagogues, and theaters. . . . But all of this changed rapidly during the war and in the years to follow.

It was late, almost closing time, when we reached the León brothers' little cigar factory. Antonio, the eldest, harbored vivid memories of his little hometown of Cayey, which he had left so many years ago. His younger brothers, Pepín and Abelardo, had emigrated later but felt the same kind of nostalgia. There we were, pining for our distant homeland, when Ambrosio finally brought up the problem at hand: my pressing need for work. "Work, here?" the elder brother exclaimed. "This dump hardly provides for us!" Thus, my dream of rolling cigars in the León brothers' little factory was shattered. My tribulations in the iron Tower of Babel had begun.

CHAPTER 10. THE STRUGGLE TO CARRY THE WAR OVER TO PUERTO RICO AND, FINALLY, THE IMPOSITION OF UNITED STATES MILITARY FORCE

In the United States, 1893 and 1894 were the years of great debate over the silver and gold standards. This controversy was to have a telling effect on the struggle for Antillean liberation.

The bankers and industrialists based in Wall Street regarded silver as too unstable as a standard, and set up a monopoly on gold. Farming and mining interests in the central and western United States, on the other hand, strongly favored silver and pushed for its unlimited coinage. This conflict was the center of political attention, and the two major parties advocated opposing positions—the Democrats upheld silver while the Republicans were the self-proclaimed champions of gold.

Out of this debate there arose the Populist Party, which enjoyed the backing of some sectors of agriculture, of the labor unions, and of socialist groups. This new party came out in support of Democratic presidential candidate William Jennings Bryan. But even with the million and a half votes from the Populists, the Democratic Party was beaten by the Republicans and William McKinley became the new president. The gold standard was imposed, which set United States policy all the more rapidly on the path toward out-and-out expansionism. The Antilles—Cuba and Puerto Rico—were to become the most coveted prey.

The gold standard meant a deepening of the economic crisis that had been begun in the previous year. Cigarmaking was one of the most severely affected industries. Which is why the idea of a strike began to win the approval of more and more *tabaqueros*.

Several Cubans and Puerto Ricans in New York, including Antonio Molina, Pachín Marín, and Jacobo Silvestre Bresman, founded a Comité Populista. This was the first Hispanic political group in the city whose aim was to participate in the electoral debate in the United States. The committee set itself the task of guiding the *tabaqueros'* protest movement so that it would culminate in a general strike in conjunction with other national groups.

When the Spanish agents in the United States caught wind of what they might be up against, they sounded the alarm. They proposed to down the cigar factories in order to strip the Partido Revolucionario Cubano of its solid financial base. But their strategy didn't work. The *tabaqueros* reviewed the situation and decided to call off their strike, and to redirect their attention to the Antillean revolutionary struggle.

The editorial in *Patria* of August 22, 1893, had nothing but praise for the cigarworkers' actions and spirit: "If there are any fools around who still think that just because they're poor the *tabaqueros* have given up their love for freedom, that losing a table in the shop means they no longer love other men like brothers or long to secure the greatest happiness for all, and do not continue to bear vengeance on behalf of their oppressed compatriots and all that is decent and gives dignity to humankind—the *tabaqueros*, though unemployed, will turn around and stand up against anyone who thinks that by losing their jobs they have lost their honor . . ."

As Samuel Gompers reported in a publication put out by the Cigarmakers' Union, by the beginning of 1894 there were already some three thousand cigar factories in New York City. About five hundred there were owned by Hispanics—that is, Spaniards and Latin Americans. The remaining twenty-five hundred had proprietors of other nationalities, but employed many Cubans and Puerto Ricans as cigarmakers and tobacco strippers.

. . . The *New York Herald* came out for prohibiting cigarmaking in the home. One article even described the conditions in which the domestic cigarworker lived back then at the end of the nineteenth century, the days of my Uncle Antonio: "For the most part, families live in three-room apartments. One room—12×15 feet with a window facing the street—is used as the bedroom and work area. The next room is smaller, 10×12 feet, and serves as both a second bedroom and a kitchen. And the third room, which is smaller still (7×9 feet) and usually without any light, is for the children and for storing tobacco. Between these quarters and the identical apartment next door there is a hallway hardly big enough for two people. There are no fewer than 3,750 people working in those domestic cigar factories. Earnings are about $2.00 lower per thousand cigars than the prevailing rate for the larger businesses. In addition, the family has to strip the tobacco for nothing. The rent for these apartments is $7.50 to $12.00 a month."

Very often these tiny factories, especially those that were run by Cubans and Puerto Ricans, sold their cigars to tobacco stands and stores, or else directly to individual customers. But the majority operated on contract for the larger concerns. In both cases, the work was shared by the head of the family and his wife and children.

. . . In every factory there was a committee in charge of raising funds for the Antillean revolution. There were even some Spanish cigarmakers who made contributions. Each factory also had its press representative who would distribute the workers' newspapers—*Yara* and *El Proletario* from Key West, *Verdad* (Truth) from New Orleans and, of course, *Patria* from New York.

Single *tabaqueros*, and even some married ones, lived in boarding houses or with friendly families. They would pay anywhere from $3.00 to $5.00 a week for room and board. In those days Puerto Rican *tabaqueros* were concentrated in the area around 100th Street and Third Avenue, though there were some scattered in other places, such as along Morris Street. And by 1894 many of the families who were arriving from Puerto Rico were settling on Jefferson, Johnson, and Adams streets in Brooklyn.

The Partido Revolucionario Cubano was at the height of its activity. In the cigar factories and wherever else the emigrants got together, that was the topic of conversation. Even the wealthy Cubans living in New York, although they didn't contribute much, were impressed by the likes of José Martí. That frail and sickly man managed to organize fifty thousand people in support of the Antillean revolution. Martí's influence among the *tabaqueros* was so strong that on Christmas Eve 1893 they had a marvelous present for him. In the cigar factories everyone agreed to donate one day's pay. They called it El Día de la Patria (The Day of the Homeland) and the $12,000 they collected was donated to the party.

On January 15, 1894, at a meeting held at Hardman Hall, Martí gave a detailed report on the prospects for the Cuban revolution. He especially cautioned the emigrant audience about the latest moves by the autonomists. A few months later, in March, he moved to Central Valley, where Tomás Estrada Palma lived and had his school. There he met with General Emilio Núñez, who managed to make frequent trips to Cuba under the pretense of buying tobacco. The news he brought back was inspiring.

General Máximo Gómez made a trip to New York in April of that year, which was the occasion for a variety of public events and gave added impetus to the fund-raising drive. That was the time when preparations were being made for the expedition aboard *La Gonda* and *El Amadis*, in which practically the entire party treasury— some $60,000—was invested. The government in Washington seized the ships even before they left port.

Once again Spanish espionage had won out. When Martí heard about this loss of arms, he fell into a deep depression. A suit was brought against the government demanding the return of the confiscated materiel. There followed months of agony, but the work of the revolution went on without interruption.

On January 29, 1895, in New York, José Martí issued the command to rise up and take arms. His orders were conveyed to Key West by Gonzalo de Quesada. There they were passed on to Juan de Dios Berríos, who slipped the document between some large tobacco leaves and rolled a cigar, which was sent on to Juan Gualberto Gómez in Havana. In the same way, wrapped in a cigar, Martí received confirmation of the plan in New York. And a few days later he left to join Máximo Gómez in Santo Domingo . . .

[After Martí's death] the Partido Revolucionario Cubano carried on under the leadership of Benjamín Guerra, a cigar manufacturer. On July 10, 1895, Tomás Estrada Palma was chosen to succeed José Martí as the party's representative. Support for the revolution came from Ramón Emeterio Betances in Paris and Eugenio María de

Hostos in Santiago, Chile. And, from his home in La Ceiba, Honduras, Juan Rius Rivera put his military expertise at the service of the revolution.

Until that moment the better-off Puerto Rican professionals and intellectuals, with the exception of Betances and Hostos, had shown little or no support for the Antillean revolution. There is no evidence that they ever offered financial assistance to the revolutionary clubs, the Partido Revolucionario Cubano, or its newspaper *Patria*. But with the death of Martí, upper-class Puerto Ricans began to play a visible role in the struggle against Spain. Thus on August 8, 1895, the Puerto Rican section of the Partido Revolucionario Cubano was founded in the home of Dr. Julio J. Henna.

Leadership of the group, headed by Dr. Henna, was made up of prestigious figures from the upper class. Representation from the artisan and working classes was conspicuously absent. Men who were well known in the struggle, like Pachín Marín, Antonio Vélez Alvarado, Rosendo Rodríguez, Rafael Delgado, Angelito García, Flor Baerga, Isidoro Apodaca, I. Ferrer, José Rivera, Jesús Rodríguez, Nicasio García, Sandalio Parrilla, Arturo Schomburg, Eusebio Márquez, and Domingo Collazo—to mention some names from the registry of the Borinquen, Dos Antillas, Mercedes Varona, and Martí clubs—were nowhere to be found among the leaders of the Puerto Rican section. The reasons for this omission? Aside from their not having been invited to the meeting, readers will draw their own conclusions from what follows.

The founding of the Puerto Rican section had an icy reception among the working class, particularly the *tabaqueros*. When he became aware of this, Sotero Figueroa—who had been named to a leadership position—tried to remedy the situation. At his urging the governing body called a general meeting on December 22, four months after the section's founding. It was on that occasion, in fact, that the flag with one star was adopted as a symbol of the Puerto Rican revolution.

According to the account given me in Harlem by José Rivera, a Puerto Rican who was at that historic gathering, when Dr. Henna had finished delivering his address, Antonio Molina León asked for the floor. His name isn't even listed as being among those who attended, at least not in the records published, years later, by Roberto H. Todd. Those records do note, though, that "Molina made demands which the audience deemed to be out of order."

According to Rivera's report, which has been confirmed by Jesús Rodríguez, Sandalio Parrilla, and Flor Baerga, Molina objected to the actions of the governing body, claiming that it should only be provisional in nature and proposing that its membership be submitted to a general election. The leadership rejected the suggestion, at which point the majority of the cigarworkers got up and walked out. But the meeting went on without them.

Despite such divisions, the new wave of revolutionary activity in New York worried the autonomists in Puerto Rico. Wary that the proposed armed invasion would upset his negotiations in Spain, Luis Muñoz Rivera sent his emissary Pedro J. Fournier to confer with Dr. Henna. Fournier landed in New York in August 1895, spoke with leaders of the section, and asked for a postponement of all revolutionary action pending Madrid's response to the demand for autonomy. But the request was not granted. On the contrary, it was agreed to carry on with plans to send a revolutionary expedition to Puerto Rico.

The most important Cuban and Puerto Rican clubs affiliated with the Partido Revolucionario Cubano in New York that were active around that time were the following:

—Los Independientes: Juan Fraga, president, and Genaro Báez, secretary; 839 Fulton Street, Brooklyn

—Rifleros de La Habana: Antonio G. Camero, president, and Adelaido Marín, secretary; 2141 Pacific Street, Brooklyn

—Borinquen: I. M. Torreforte, president, and Domingo Collazo, secretary; 129 McDougal Street, Brooklyn

—José Martí: B. H. Portuondo, president, and Sotero Figueroa

—Martín del Castillo: Felipe Rodríguez, president, and Eusebio Molina, secretary; 1642 Park Avenue, Manhattan

—Dos Antillas: Rosendo Rodríguez, president, and Arturo Alfonso Schomburg, secretary; 1758 Third Avenue, Manhattan

—América: J. R. Alvarez, president, and E. M. Amorós, secretary; 231 East 61st Street, Manhattan

—Guerrilla de Maceo: Juan B. Beato, president, and Juan Fernández, secretary; 146 West 24th Street, Manhattan

—Hijas de Cuba: Angelina R. de Quesada, president, and Carmen Mantilla, secretary; 116 West 64th Street, Manhattan

—Hijas de la Libertad: Natividad R. de Gallo, president, and Gertrudis Casano, secretary; 1115 Herkimer Street, Brooklyn

—Mercedes Varona: Inocencia M. de Figueroa, president, and Emma Betancourt, secretary; 235 East 75th Street, Manhattan

—Céspedes y Martí: Petrona Calderón, president, and Juana Rosario, secretary; 2012 Fulton Street, Brooklyn

There were similar societies and clubs in many other cities, including Boston, Philadelphia, and Chicago, as well as broad-based organizations in Key West, Tampa, and New Orleans. Most of the members were *tabaqueros* and their wives and families, and artisans in other trades.

Such a vast range of organized support for the Antillean revolution was the legacy that José Martí left in the United States. His successor as representative of the Partido Revolucionario Cubano, Tomás Estrada Palma, did not have a shadow of his personal influence in the Cuban and Puerto Rican communities. Dissension between the two sectors began to grow. The establishment of the Puerto Rican section, led by Dr. Julio J. Henna, did nothing to improve these relations.

. . . The bombing and sinking of the *Maine* in Havana harbor on February 15, 1898, gave an unexpected turn to the revolutionary battle in the Antilles. Henna, who had all along shown annexationist tendencies, immediately set off for Washington and offered Theodore Roosevelt and Henry Cabot Lodge the support of the Puerto Rican emigrants in the plan to invade Puerto Rico. On March 21 Henna had a personal audience with President McKinley. A few days later he met with General Miles, the man who was to order the landing of troops on Guánica on July 25, 1898.

The United States army made full use of all the information provided by Henna and Roberto H. Todd—president and secretary, respectively, of the delegation. But not the slightest recognition was granted to a single Puerto Rican. As those very leaders were to state, soon thereafter, in a pamphlet in English entitled *The Case of Puerto Rico:* "The voice of Puerto Rico has not been heard. Not even by way of formality were its inhabitants consulted as to whether they wanted to ask for, object to, or suggest any conditions bearing on their present or future political status. . . . The island and all its people were simply transferred from one sovereign power to another, just as a farm with all its equipment, houses, and animals is passed from one landlord to another."

From Paris came words of warning from Ramón Emeterio Betances: "I do not want us to be a colony, neither a colony of Spain nor a colony of the United States." Eugenio María de Hostos set off from Chile for the United States. On August 2, 1898, he took part in the final meeting of the Puerto Rican section of the Partido Revolucionario Cubano held in Chimney Hall, New York. On that day it was agreed to dissolve the group, and an era in the history of the Puerto Rican community in New York came to an end.

CHAPTER 11. HOW THE CENTURY BEGAN FOR THE PUERTO RICAN COMMUNITY, AND RELATED INCIDENTS

Once the thunder of revolutionary struggle against Spain had subsided in the Antilles, the Cuban and Puerto Rican emigrant community in New York fell silent. The only groups to show any signs of activity were a few of the mutual benefit societies, and, of course, the cigarworkers' unions. There were two of them—the International Cigarmakers' Union, affiliated with the A.F. of L., and the one known as La Resistencia. Most of the Spanish-speaking *tabaqueros* belonged to the latter.

The International Cigarmakers' Union followed the basic tenets of United States trade unionism. It was opposed to the formation of a workers' party, not to mention the idea of social revolution. La Resistencia, on the other hand, regarded itself as revolutionary and advocated the principles of anarchosyndicalism. Its members did not accept the notion of a "home country." For them, *patria* only exists for capitalists. The workers have no country or, to put it another way, the workers' homeland is the planet Earth.

As anarchosyndicalists, the *tabaqueros* in La Resistencia repudiated any and all political parties, even if they called themselves socialist. But that didn't mean that they did not help the patriotic movements. In practice, though, it would seem contrary to their principles, they supported the struggle for the independence of Cuba and Puerto Rico. They justified this position in the name of human rights. They also argued that such popular upheavals provided a good opportunity to preach the idea of "one huge fatherland without borders."

In mid-1899 the socialists in New York split into two factions, the Daniel De Leon and Morris Hillquit factions. This division had its repercussions among the *tabaqueros*. The end result was that De Leon remained at the head of the Socialist Labor Party and Hillquit and his followers founded the American Socialist Party. The Socialist Labor Party began to take on more and more narrowly doctrinaire positions, whereas Hillquit's group steered in the direction of mass politics, and quickly swelled its ranks.

Toward the end of 1899 Santiago Iglesias and Eduardo Conde came to New York as delegates from Puerto Rico to the American Socialist Party Convention, to be held in January 1900 in Rochester. For the first time in history, representatives chosen by Puerto Rican workers took part in a convention outside of the country. At that convention in Rochester Puerto Rico's cry for justice fell on sympathetic ears, and a resolution of solidarity won easy approval.

On their return from the convention, the delegates from Puerto Rico were royally welcomed by the workers' unions, which held a series of events that received a great deal of publicity. At one of those activities, organized by La Resistencia in Brooklyn, a lengthy manifesto was approved that was then widely circulated, both in New York and Puerto Rico. It proclaimed:

> The Spanish-language organizations of this city, at a meeting held on February 20, 1900, on the occasion of the presence among us of the Puerto Rican delegation, agree unanimously and enthusiastically to give to the work of that delegation all possible support within the limits of our power and intelligence . . .
>
> In the face of the close collaboration between the governments and bourgeoisies of all nations in order to oppress and exploit the workers, the working class cannot remain disunited. . . . Seeing the capitalists join hands in stealing from and tyrannizing the working masses, let us unite in the common task of attaining a better lot in the present and our total emancipation in the future.
>
> Working and living under the conditions that you do, it is of little importance to Puerto Ricans whether they are governed by Muñoz or Muñiz, the Republicanos or the

Federales . . .[1] What is urgent is that you join the Federación Regional de Trabajadores, that you struggle unceasingly and indefatigably to improve your moral, material, and intellectual conditions, and that you strive to secure higher wages, adequate food, and decent clothing . . .

The manifesto was signed by S. Monagas and Miguel Rivera for the Cigarmakers' Union, Cándido Ladrero and José López for the Escogedores, Benjamín Miranda and José R. Fernández for the Rezagadores, and Juan García and G. Quintana for the Círculo de Trabajadores of Brooklyn.[2]

In March 1900 Uncle Antonio and his family moved to a spacious apartment in a new building on 88th Street off Lexington Avenue. Their new home had seven rooms and cost $25.00 a month. It had steam heat and a tile bathroom. The family was in heaven, except that . . . when they were living down on 13th Street they used to buy their food in the Spanish shops along 14th Street. But their new neighborhood was mostly German and Irish, and in the Jewish stores on Second and Third avenues everything was more expensive.

One Sunday afternoon they heard a knock on the door. One of Uncle Antonio's daughters went to answer it and invited the visitors in. To their surprise, not one or two but nine people stepped into the living room, all of them looking serious. They refused to sit down and didn't even bother taking off their hats. Uncle Antonio broke the ice: "To what, might I ask, do we owe the honor of this friendly visit?"

"We come on behalf of the tenants of this building," one of them finally volunteered. "We bear no ill feeling toward anybody, but this is a white neighborhood. We have noticed that you frequently have Negroes coming to your house. People around here don't like that. We do hope that in the future you will be more careful about who you invite to your house."

The members of Uncle Antonio's family were aghast; their jaws literally dropped. "Are you saying that these people, because of the color of their skin . . ." began my uncle . . .

"See here," broke in the same spokesman, "we have not come to discuss the matter. If you wish to keep up such friendships, then you should just move out!" Uncle Antonio tried to get another word in, but the visitors promptly turned on their heels and were gone. And from that day on, not a word was exchanged with the neighbors.

Then came the first incident. Someone picked up a baby carriage that Antonio's wife had left in the hall and threw it into the street. Next a bunch of kids broke it in pieces, with all the neighbors watching. And the next day the wheels of the broken carriage were at the front door of the apartment. The day after that someone threw a rock through their front window, and a few days later they found the hallway in front of their door covered with feces. As if that was not enough, the family's mail was stolen and their gas was shut off.

Life in that house began to be unbearable. At first nobody paid any attention, but as the incidents became more and more perverse, the family, especially the women, began to get nervous.

Calling the police was useless. When they lodged a formal complaint about the disappearance of their mail, the authorities promised to investigate but never even took the trouble to visit the building. The superintendent was part of the scheme, as was the agent who managed the building. Pressure built up all around them to move out!

But Vasylisa, one of Antonio's daughters, insisted that they not submit to discrimination. One night she hid, waiting to catch by surprise whoever it was that was throwing filth on their doorstep. It was a woman; she jumped up, grabbed her by the hair, and smeared the feces in her face. The scuffle woke up all the tenants, who were outraged.

The superintendent called the police and the entire family was arrested. Morris Hillquit, the socialist leader, bailed them out of jail and went on to serve as the attorney for their defense. The trial was an uphill battle: the prosecution called no fewer than fifty witnesses, neighbors, of course. Some members of the family were exonerated, but Vasylisa was sentenced. Not only that—she was also forced to give up her job with the Board of Education because of "improper conduct." The family had no choice but to move, a few months later, over to 72nd Street and First Avenue.

At around that time Puerto Rico was passing through a very turbulent period in its history. Two political parties vied for control—the Partido Republicano, led by José Celso Barbosa, and the Partido Federal, under Luis Muñoz Rivera. With the backing of the first United States—appointed governors, Barbosa won the upper hand and Muñoz Rivera's party went into opposition. Irreconcilable enemies since the days of Spanish rule, the followers of both leaders were at each other's throats. Where the Barbosa wing held sway, supporters of Muñoz Rivera could hardly survive, and vice versa. San Juan was an example of the first case and Caguas of the second.

The so-called Republican mobs destroyed the offices of *La Democracia*, Muñoz Rivera's paper in San Juan. This attack, along with the pressing economic situation, forced the leader of the Federales—later to become the Unionistas—to flee to New York. There, on July 13, 1901, Luis Muñoz Rivera began publication of the *Puerto Rico Herald*, a weekly written in Spanish and English. Its offices were located at 156 Fifth Avenue.

... The manifesto of the Partido Federal appeared in the October 1901 issues of the *Puerto Rico Herald*. There the goal of the party was declared to be "that Puerto Rico become a state of the American Union, and that it be so without restrictions, just as the other states of the Federation."

It was in Muñoz Rivera's paper—in the November 2, 1901, edition—that Santiago Iglesias published an article that was to provoke serious criticism among the socialists and *tabaqueros*. Iglesias attempted to defend the A.F. of L. against the accusation that was being raised in New York and in Puerto Rico that its member unions discriminated against black workers. "The Federation," he said, "has declared openly that there can be no fraternity or solidarity among the working people if they fail to organize without regard to color or creed. . . . But, have workers of color responded, as is their duty, to this call pronounced by their fellow workers?"

"We must not confuse," he went on, "colored workers in Cuba and Puerto Rico with those in the United States. In Puerto Rico the majority are responding to the call to organize. But such is not the case in the United States, where most colored workers are the unwitting enemies of their unionized American coworkers . . ."

In the view of his critics, this position smacked of racism. Why, they asked, didn't Iglesias make the same accusation against the millions of German, Irish, and Italian workers with blond hair and fair skin who also didn't belong to the A.F. of L.? And why didn't he have anything to say about the thousands of whites of all nationalities who had served as strikebreakers on so many occasions? Is it true, they said, that the A.F. of L. declares itself, in theory, for fraternity among all workers, but no one can deny that there are unions that do not admit black workers.

A statement to that effect, signed by Schomburg, Rosseau, Apodaca, and Baerga, was soon made public.

Meanwhile, the economic situation in Puerto Rico worsened every day. The Island was still suffering from the effects of the San Ciriaco hurricane. Coffee production was reduced to a minimum. Tobacco could not even break into the United States market, and the sugar industry was only beginning.

. . . At the end of 1901 a Latin American boarding house, Puerto Rico in New York, was established under the supervision of José D. Sulsona. Young people from various countries, including Puerto Rico, came there to live while they studied in New York. Most of them were attending St. Joseph's, a Catholic academy in Brooklyn. Among the many young Puerto Ricans, Agustín Fernández, Miguel Angel Muñoz, José Juan Monge, and Gustavo Amil studied at that school.

. . . More such recognition came when the Puerto Rican tenor Antonio Paoli, already acclaimed in Europe, held a recital in New York. Opening night was on April 22, 1902, in Mendelssohn Hall. He sang arias from *Tosca, Lohengrin, Othello*, and *William Tell*. There were many Puerto Ricans there, including quite a few *tabaqueros*. No one in the entire community appreciated Paoli—already known as the "tenor of kings and the king of tenors"—more than the *tabaqueros*, who had known of him from articles by Luis Bonafoux, Anatole France, and Guido de Varona, which were read in the cigar factories.

The *tabaqueros* were the boisterous claque in the uppermost tier of the Metropolitan Opera House. Everyone knows that wealthy audiences who go to the opera usually do so just to show off their fancy clothes and jewelry. It was a different story with the artisans who so admired Caruso, Tita Ruffo, Chaliapin, Frances Alda, and Mardones. The "claque," which was admitted to performances free of charge, was made up of Alfonso di Salvo, Leon Kortisky, Luigi Sabella, Tony Gualtieri, Alfonso Dieppa, and others with a whole range of national origins. Many of them knew the most outstanding opera scores by heart and had a sharp eye for the major artists. The bleachers at the Met were filled with impeccable judges. So it was not surprising that the members of the claque went to the cigar factories and to the cafés and restaurants at which the Bohemians of the time congregated.

Around the same time, too, a well-known Puerto Rican painter, Adolfo María Molina, had an exhibition on 12th Street and Second Avenue. But unlike Paoli's recitals, this event did not attract the slightest attention in artistic circles in the city.

The year 1902 also saw the establishment of Nuestra Señora de la Guadalupe, the first Catholic church in New York City to hold services in Spanish. It was located in what was at that time the heart of the Latin community, at 229 West 14th Street.

But neither this gesture by the traditional church of the Puerto Rican people, nor the sporadic visits by a few famous artists, nor the efforts of Muñoz Rivera with his newspaper, could alter the lowly opinion in which the sons of Puerto Rico were held by the Anglo-Saxon population of New York. For the majority of Yankees, Puerto Ricans were an expendable species—an ignorant, juvenile, and uncultured people . . . Many of them think no more of us today!

CHAPTER 13. DAY-TO-DAY LIFE IN NEW YORK AND OTHER DETAILS

In about 1918 entertainment for Puerto Ricans in New York was confined to the apartments they lived in. They celebrated birthdays and weddings and, of course, Christmas Eve, New Year's Day, and the Feast of the Epiphany. But always at home, with friends and neighbors.

There would be dancing, and between numbers somebody would recite poetry or hold forth about our distant homeland. At some of the parties there were *charangas*, lively groups of Puerto Rican musicians. But most of the time we played records. By that time Columbia Records was recording *danzas, aguinaldos,* and other kinds of music from back home.

Almost every family owned a victrola, and many even had a pianola. The fact is that once this music gained in popularity, Puerto Ricans were exploited mercilessly. Pianolas cost about $500.00, on credit. Many was the worker who wound up losing what little he earned by falling behind on his payments. Not to mention the times a family would move and have to leave their pianola behind . . . Just getting it from one place to another cost more than moving the rest of their belongings!

Those boisterous Puerto Rican parties would often disturb neighbors of other nationalities, which led to some serious conflicts and unpleasant quarrels.

. . . By then there were over ten thousand Puerto Ricans living in El Barrio. The first stores and restaurants that were like those back home were opening up. Every week a new shipload of emigrants would arrive in the city. The landlords up in Harlem were making good money by charging the Puerto Ricans high rents—relative, that is, to what they were getting for their money. I remember a building on 113th Street off Fifth Avenue where, back when the Jews were still living there, apartments were renting for only $17.00. . . . When the Puerto Ricans moved in, the rents went up to $35.00.

In the winter of 1918, Manuel Noriega's theater company made its debut at the Amsterdam Opera House. Thanks to Noriega the Puerto Rican community in New York was able to see Spanish theater for the first time. One night more than two hundred Puerto Ricans attended, many of them theater-loving *tabaqueros.*

. . . All this time the Brooklyn Círculo de Trabajadores, which I mentioned earlier, remained active. To give you an idea of how the Círculo got started; it was founded in the previous century and was largely made up of *tabaqueros.* They were all progressive in their thinking—anarchists, socialists, or at the very least left-wing republicans. Back then most of them were getting on in years, but their minds were young and alert, their hearts filled with optimism.

I went to the Círculo often. On any given night, in wintertime, they would get together at tables to play dominoes, checkers, or chess, or just to talk. I went from one group to another. The venerable old man Castañeda would be sitting in a corner. I can still hear him saying, "It was a shame that Martí took that rumor-mongering by Trujillo and Collazo so much to heart, and that his own pride brought him to his end in Dos Ríos. If he had only stayed on to direct and guide the revolution, Cuba today would be the freest and most democratic republic in the world . . ."

I then went to another group, where Miguel Rivera, a native of Cayey, was enthusiastically reporting the resolutions submitted by the Mexican delegation to the Congress of Laredo. "Even though the A.F. of L. accepted them," he commented, "the Yankees are sure to go on holding the Mexicans down, the same as before . . ."[3]

From another group I heard cheerful laughter. I went over and found them enjoying the latest story by "El Malojero"—the "Corn Seller," as he was called—an anecdote passed on to him by Luis Bonafoux.

Making the rounds, I met up with Pepín and Anastasio Fueyo over by the Círculo's little office. They were discussing the events scheduled for that winter. I found out about a production of Guimera's *Tierra Baja* and Gorky's *The Vagabonds.* They were also thinking of staging Chekhov's *Uncle Vanya*, the Spanish version by the Puerto Rican worker Alfonso Dieppa.

Going over to the canteen for a cup of coffee, I overheard a discussion between the Spaniard José López, an *escogedor*, and the anarchist Rojas. "The Bolsheviks," Rojas was saying, "have betrayed the Russian workers. They should have set up free communities and not those iron-clad Soviets." To which López responded: "All of you anarchists have a screw loose. Only yesterday man left his wild, untamed state and already you're talking about showing them a new world, free of all restraint, and all in one fell swoop? If we are ever to arrive at a just society, you have to force men to be good and not animals."

That's what it was like in those days.

Years later I got to know a Puerto Rican cigarworker named Pedro Juan Bonit, who had been living in New York since 1913. Here is a conversation I had with him, which fills out my picture of the emigrants' life in those times.

"When did you arrive here?"

"On December 22, 1913."

"What town do you come from?"

"I was born and raised in San Juan."

"Why did you leave Puerto Rico?"

"To get to know the world. And, of course, because I thought I would be better off economically."

"Where did you live when you arrived here?"

"In a roominghouse run by Ramón Galíndez. The address was 2049 Second Avenue, between 105th and 106th."

"Was it easy to find work?"

"Immediately. There were a lot of jobs for cigarmakers back then. Besides, the cigar manufacturers had agents who would find them workers, and for every cigarworker they delivered they'd get $5.00. I still remember one of those agents; his name was Damián Ferrer, alias 'Batata,' or 'Sweet Potato'."

"Where was that first job?"

"In a little factory. Later I worked at Samuel I. Davis's factory on 81st Street and First Avenue. Over a hundred Puerto Rican *tabaqueros* were working there."

"Were there any other places that hired so many Puerto Ricans?"

"Many."

"And did those factories have readers like the ones in Puerto Rico?"

"Practically all of them did. In the Davis factory there were two—Fernando García, who would read us the newspapers in the morning, and Benito Ochart, who read novels in the afternoon."

"Was there any difference between the works they read here and the ones they read back in Puerto Rico?"

"Well, I think the quality of the readings here was somewhat higher. They would read books of greater educational value."

"Do you remember any of them?"

"There was *Le Feu* by Barbusse and *La Hyène enragée* by Pierre Loti . . ."

"Who paid the readers?"

"We did. Each of us donated 25 cents a week."

"Were any other collections taken?"

"Yes. Every week we also contributed to the working-class press. And then they were always raising money to support some strike movement or another."

"Were there already Puerto Rican businesses in El Barrio?"

"No. No *bodegas* or restaurants had been established yet. There were only boarding houses and a few barber shops."

"Then where did people buy plantains and other vegetables?"

"There was a Latin grocery on 136th Street near Lenox Avenue, in the middle of the black community. And as for Spanish products, you could get them at Victoria's down on the corner of Pearl and John."

"Did you know of any authentic Puerto Rican businesses?"

"None that I am aware of. But yes, come to think of it, there was a drugstore owned by a certain Loubriel on 22nd Street and Seventh Avenue."

"Do you remember any Puerto Ricans who lived near you?"

"Sure. There was Andrés Araujo, Juan Nieto, Antonio Díaz, Agustín García, Felipe Montalbán, and many more. I think that by then there were already a good hundred and fifty Puerto Rican families living on 105th and 106th off of Second Avenue."

"How about in what we now know as El Barrio?"

"No. For the most part that was where the Jewish people lived. There were only a handful of Hispanic families. In those times the Puerto Ricans were scattered in other areas—in Chelsea, and over in Brooklyn around the Armory and Boro Hall. There were also Puerto Rican neighborhoods on the East Side, in the 20's and along Second and Third avenues from 64th Street up to 85th. And the professionals and better-off families were over on the West Side, on the other side of Central Park. That's where people like Dr. Henna and Dr. Marxuach lived . . ."

"How did people get along in the community?"

"Well, each class had its own way of associating. The *tabaqueros* were the only ones who were organized collectively. There were no exclusively Puerto Rican organizations. But we *tabaqueros* did have mutual aid societies like La Aurora (Dawn), La Razón (Reason), and El Ejemplo (The Example) . . . The educational circles were almost all anarchist except for the Brooklyn Círculo de Trabajadores, which admitted workers of different ideological leanings. The trade unions were the International Cigarmakers' Union and La Resistencia . . . Where I lived there was a club called El Tropical, which had dances and where meetings were held from time to time. It was presided over by Gonzalo Torres. Over on the West Side I remember that Dr. Henna was president of the Ibero-American Club."

"What were the Spanish-language papers published here in those days?"

"*Las Novedades*, a Spanish publication put out by a man by the name of García, whom we nicknamed 'Little Priest.' And there was the anarchist weekly *Cultura Proletaria*, and *La Prensa*, which also came out weekly back then."

"Where did you buy clothes for the first time when you got to New York?"

"I got them from Markowsky, a Jew who had a store downstairs in the building where I lived. A lot of *tabaqueros* bought things there on credit."

"Were there any notable racial differences among the Puerto Ricans?"

"Not among the *tabaqueros;* for us there were no problems of race or religion. But when it came to the so-called better-off people, some of them were even more prejudiced than the Americans."

"How much were your earnings back then?"

"At Davis's I was averaging about $30.00 a week."

"And what were your expenses like?"

"For a room, food, and clean clothes I paid about $10.00 a week."

"Did anyone play *bolita*, or lottery?"

"Yes. I've been told that game started back in 1870."

"What about problems between Puerto Ricans?"

"There would be a fight now and then, but never anything serious."

"What kind of parties did you have?"

"We celebrated Christmas, New Year's, and the Feast of the Epiphany in people's homes."

"Was there much concern over the situation in Puerto Rico?"

"Of course."

"Would you like to go back?"

"Don't make me sad. I've been back twice and if I could I'd be off again tomorrow."

News from Puerto Rico at the end of 1918 and the beginning of 1919 told of widespread misery and of strikes that crippled the country. Thousands of agricultural workers went out on strike, and many were persecuted and beaten. The *tabaqueros* also had frequent work stoppages. And on top of that there were the victims of the earthquakes . . . *La Prensa* called for donations from the public to help those struck by the catastrophe. Angered at the lukewarm response of its readers, it published an editorial complaining of the lack of charity in the Hispanic community. A lively debate ensued, involving Luisa Capetillo, Gabriel Blanco, and other writers of note.

The most widely discussed position was the one Luisa held. She openly blamed the people in power for the miserable living conditions in Puerto Rico. She called for making progressive people in the United States aware of this situation, and ended by saying that "Tyranny, like freedom, has no country, any more than do exploiters or workers."

I should say something about that great Puerto Rican woman. At that time Luisa Capetillo was employed as a reader in a cigar factory. She belonged to the leadership of the Federación Libre de Trabajadores and took part in meetings and strikes all over Puerto Rico. She could rightly be called the first woman suffragist in the Antilles. Aggressive and dynamic by temperament, she was devoted body and soul to defending the rights of workers and the cause of woman's liberation. She came to New York from Havana, where she had created a scandal by showing up in the streets dressed in culottes, which only the most advanced women at that time dared to wear.

The last time I spoke with Luisa was at a boarding house she ran on 22nd Street and Eighth Avenue. She worked interminable hours and always looked tired. But that didn't stop her from using every chance she had to propound her revolutionary and strongly anarchistic ideas to her boarders. Nor did that prevent anyone from eating very well at her place, because aside from her enthusiasm for the revolution, Luisa had a great love for cooking. And as that noble woman from Puerto Rico never cared very much about money, everyone who came there hungry got something to eat, whether he could pay for it or not. Needless to say, her "business" was in a constant crisis, and she was often hard put even to pay her rent.

. . . Meanwhile, thousands of Puerto Rican workers continued to land in New York. The apartments of those already here filled up with family, friends, and just anyone who was down and out. The number of Puerto Ricans climbed to 35,000. According to statistics kept by the International Cigarmakers' Union, there were over 4,500 Puerto Ricans enrolled in its various locals around the city. But the majority of the workers lacked a skilled trade, and made a large labor supply willing to take on the lowest paying jobs in New York.

No serious effort was made to organize the community and fight for its civil rights. The groups that did exist, as I have pointed out, had no other purpose than to organize dances. The only exception was the Club La Luz, located on the corner of Lenox and 120th Street, which in addition to dances would hold occasional cultural evenings.

In early 1919 the first issue of *El Norteamericano* circulated among us. Published by the South American Publishing Co. at 310 Fifth Avenue, that weekly became very popular in Hispanic homes. But it did not last long.

Around the same time the great Spanish novelist Vicente Blasco Ibáñez visited New York. He gave three lectures at Columbia, the first and most controversial on the subject of "How Europeans View America."

But the only event really worth remembering, the one that had a lasting impact on the Puerto Rican community, was the Floral Games sponsored by *La Prensa*.[4] This was, in fact, the most outstanding event in the Spanish-speaking community in New York since the turn of the century. The nominating judges were Federico de Onís, Orestes Ferrara, Pedro Henríquez Ureña, and the North American Hispanist Thomas Walsh.

Prizes were awarded on May 5 at an event held in Carnegie Hall. All of the Spanish-American peoples were represented. At no other event did I ever see so many beautiful women—Mexican, Spanish, Dominican, Cuban, and Puerto Rican. First prize went to José Méndez Rivera, a Colombian poet who received the Flor Natural prize. The Dominican writer M. F. Cesteros won another prize. And as for the Puerto Ricans in the audience, all of us left happy. A young Puerto Rican poet had been given Honorable Mention for his poem, "Yo soy tu flauta." His name: Luis Muñoz Marín.

CHAPTER 14. POLITICAL CAMPAIGNS, THE DECLINE OF TOBACCO, AND THE GREAT DEPRESSION

The first political campaign in New York in which Puerto Ricans participated was the Alfred Smith campaign of 1918. Around seven thousand Puerto Ricans registered to vote, the majority in the first and third electoral districts in Brooklyn. A major force behind the drive was the Club Democrático Puertorriqueño, the first organization of its kind inside the Democratic Party of the United States. It was founded and directed by two Puerto Ricans, J. V. Alonso and Joaquín Colón.

During that election campaign other Hispanic groups were established in Harlem. They were set up not as independent clubs, but in affiliation with the local Democratic Club. There the outstanding Puerto Rican leaders were J. C. Cebollero and Domingo Collazo—the latter was recognized by Tammany Hall as the representative of the Puerto Rican community.

But the vast majority of Puerto Ricans in New York did not exercise their right to vote. It was no easy matter to go down to the Board of Elections and register. The officials would question the applicant in order to intimidate him. That kept a lot of Puerto Ricans away from the ballot box. Besides, most Puerto Ricans felt they had "nothing to get out of American politics," that "it didn't concern them." And that was the general attitude for many years thereafter, until Fiorello La Guardia and Vito Marcantonio entered the city's political life.

Neither of the political parties, Republican or Democrat, showed any real interest in winning the support of the Puerto Rican people. While their campaigns were in high gear, of course, some of their propaganda reached the Puerto Rican neighborhoods, but they did nothing to register voters. To this very day, so many years later, those parties have nearly the same attitude.

The drive to unionize Puerto Rican workers was facing similar problems. For the most part Puerto Ricans worked in nonunion shops. Sewing shops and restaurants, in particular, were filled with Puerto Ricans. But the unions in those lines of work didn't do a thing to recruit them. Furthermore, carpenters, bricklayers, tailors, and barbers who came from Puerto Rico were not admitted as members of the A.F. of L. unions.

In fact, not until the cigarmakers began to wage their union battles did unions in other trades show any interest in Puerto Rican workers. And that didn't happen until into the 1920s. Shortly before that, the first union to break through that barrier within labor, after the International Cigarmakers' Union, was the Furriers' Union.

The first committee of the Socialist Party to be made up of Puerto Ricans—and it enjoyed a long and active life—was formed in 1918 by Lupercio Arroyo, Jesús Colón, Eduvigis Cabán, Valentín Flores, and myself. Further on there will be ample opportunity to say more about those comrades.

Around that time there were a few Puerto Ricans in New York with nationalist ideas, but they were not grouped together in any one organization. Only somewhat later, under the spiritual leadership of Vicente Balbás Capó, did they go on to found the Asociación Nacionalista.

The heated political campaign gave rise to rivalries among some of the Puerto Ricans who were leaders in the Democratic Party. A battle followed over "leadership of the colony," as it was called back then. While there can be no doubt that those people were struggling for the good of their fellow countrymen, envy and divisiveness doomed every collective effort to failure. As a result, pessimism and frustration were everywhere.

In 1919 a trying period for the Puerto Ricans began. When the Great War in Europe ended, the war industries in the United States were shut down. With the conversion back to a peacetime economy, Puerto Ricans were among the first to find themselves out of work. And while incomes fell, rents and the cost of living in general were on the rise.

That year also saw the political persecution of socialists and any one else suspected of sympathizing with the Russian Revolution. Anyone and everyone who voiced the slightest criticism of the system was labeled "Bolshevik." Many notable figures found themselves in prison for their pacifist and anti-imperialist ideas. Such was the case with Victor Berger, the U.S. Congressman elected on the Socialist Party ticket who was sentenced to ten years in prison. Eugene V. Debs, the party's outstanding leader, was also found guilty, and hundreds of other labor leaders from all over the country met the same fate.

The wave of repression was extended to Puerto Rico. Striking *tabaqueros* in San Juan sent two of their leaders, Ramón Barrios and Alfonso Negrín, to Cuba in search of assistance and support. Both were arrested upon landing and charged with being "anarchists." The International Cigarmakers' Union and the Socialist Party appealed to Washington, and through the intervention of the United States embassy in Havana they were set free.

On February 23 the New York dailies published a story that had an immediate effect on the Hispanic communities of the city. The headlines in one paper announced, "Uncover Plot to Assassinate President Wilson, 14 Hispanic Anarchists Held."

Among the various anarchist circles in New York there was one that went by the name of Los Corsarios (The Corsairs). Its membership included some *tabaqueros*, but the majority were dockworkers and sailors, some of them Puerto Rican. The group published a newspaper, *El Corsario;* contributors included Marcelo Salinas, Pedro Estuve, J. de Borrán, Maximiliano Olay, Ventura Mijón, and other Spanish, Cuban, and Puerto Rican writers. The paper circulated widely among Spanish-speaking sailors, dockworkers, and miners in several industrial centers across the United States.

The "muchachos" ("boys") of El Corsario, as their friends called them, would meet at 1722 Lexington Avenue near 107th Street. That was the newspaper's editorial office. One Sunday afternoon, when the group's entire membership came together to begin distributing the papers, they realized they were surrounded by about fifty policemen and federal agents. The paper was confiscated and they were all arrested on charges of conspiring to assassinate President Wilson, who was due to return from Europe at about that time. Only one Puerto Rican, Rafael Acosta, was among those detained.

There were vehement protests against the arrests, and a prisoners' defense committee was set up. But this time the struggle did not last long. After a few preliminary hearings, the defense lawyers succeeded in getting the charges dropped. Even that did not prevent the Spaniards involved—and they were the majority—from being deported back to Spain.

Puerto Rican political activity picked up in the course of that year. The *tabaqueros* initiated several demonstrations against the imprisonment of Eugene V. Debs, who started serving his ten-year sentence on May 13. In July a massive strike brought cigar production in New York to a standstill, and the strike soon spread across the United States.

That strike had a special meaning for Puerto Rican workers. An indirect result of that struggle was that many other unions came to recognize the important role that Puerto Ricans can play as workers. It was then that they began to organize Puerto Rican confectioners, bakers, hotel and restaurant employees, and workers in the needle trades. We finally began to enjoy wages and hours equal to those of workers of other nationalities.

Another significant outcome of the cigarmakers' strike was that for the first time Puerto Rican delegates to union meetings participated on an equal footing with representatives and leaders of other nationalities. Several of our countrymen, whose intelligence and militancy had earned them the respect of the leaders of the major national unions, served on the strike committee. Some of the many who played distinguished roles were Santiago Rodríguez, Angel María Dieppa, Rafael Acosta, Lupercio Arroyo, Eduvigis Cabán, Enrique Plaza, Rafael Correa, Ceferino Lugo, Domingo García, A. Villanueva, Tomás and Valentín Flores, and Angel Cancél.

It was in those days that the Puerto Rican nationalist movement first emerged in New York. What sparked it off, indirectly, was a statement by Antonio R. Barceló, who had replaced Luis Muñoz Rivera as leader of the Partido Unionista. He declared to the press: "We are aware that the United States needs Puerto Rico for strategic reasons, because of the position our Island occupies at the entry point to the Caribbean and opposite the Panama Canal. . . . What we are asking for is a government that will allow us to manage our own affairs. Give to our people the right to elect their own governor by popular vote, and allow all government officials to be elected or appointed in Puerto Rico . . ."

Such pronouncements from the man who was supposed to represent the cause of independence and who led the party that included independence in its program were regarded as signs of "humiliation and surrender" by those who had begun to call themselves nationalists. They came together to organize a protest demonstration, and they have remained together ever since.

The economic depression hit hard in 1920. Traditionally, the *tabaqueros* had been the highest paid workers in the Puerto Rican community. But now their relative prosperity came to an end. Handmade cigar production was the sector most severely affected by the crisis. There was only a demand for cheap cigars, and the tobacco companies began to mechanize production and lay off the workers they no longer needed.

Inevitably this transformation of the industrial process led to head-on clashes between workers and bosses. Manufacturers in New York began to move their factories over to New Jersey and Pennsylvania. There they taught the trade to women, thus dropping the price of labor still further. In spite of all this, over two hundred independent factories producing choice cigars remained in New York.

Spanish-speaking workers, along with Jews and Italians, organized a new union which we called the Trabajadores Amalgamados de la Industria del Tabaco. Local chapters were established in several cities, and we started *The Tobacco Worker*, a newspaper published in Spanish and English. The editorial staff was made up of the Cuban W. Rico, the Jew Sam Sussman, the Italian Cayetano Loria, the North American J. Brandon, and me, who served as the representative of the Puerto Rican *tabaqueros*.

Our organizing activity, of course, brought us into conflict with the International Cigarmakers' Union of the A. F. of L., which was attempting to hold back the mechanization of the industry by offering concessions to the small factories. The *amalgamados*, as we called ourselves, condemned this policy and advocated the organization of the workers in the newly mechanized factories.

The fact is, though, that the age in which the *tabaqueros* were an important factor in the economic life and trade union movement in the United States was drawing to a close. Mechanization left many Puerto Rican *tabaqueros* no choice but to set up little workshops, known as *chinchalitos*. Unemployment also dispersed them. Even so, as we shall see, the *tabaqueros* still contributed to the betterment of the Puerto Rican community in New York.

In 1920, at the beginning of the harvest season, workers in the sugar industry in Puerto Rico staged a widespread general strike. Serious confrontations between workers and police occurred at several points on the Island. In the U.S. newspapers, the

North American corporations, especially the Aguirre Refinery, roundly denounced the workers as "revolutionaries" and "bandits" and called on Washington to intervene with repressive force.

In New York, the *tabaqueros* organized numerous acts of solidarity with the strikers. To counteract the sugar corporations' propaganda, they issued reports to the press, news agencies, and the U.S. Congress, giving the real story. This task was undertaken by Lupercio Arroyo, Pedro San Miguel, Jesús Colón, the socialist leaders Algernon Lee and August Claessens, and Luis Muñoz Marín. . . . This was the first time Luis Muñoz Marín took an active part in the workers' struggle.

In August 1920, at the behest of the Puerto Rican legislature, Alfonso Lastra Chárriez stopped over in New York on his way from France with the remains of Ramón Emeterio Betances. At the request of Dr. José J. Henna, the ashes of our illustrious patriot were placed in City Hall so as to give the Puerto Rican community an opportunity to pay their final tribute. Representatives from Mexico, Cuba, the Dominican Republic, and Haiti paid their respects, and countless workers filed past the urn with deep veneration. Finally, Betances' remains were returned to Puerto Rico.

Back then there were many Hispanic actors and singers around the city—Eduardo Fort, Pilar Arcos, and Carlos Blanc, to name a few—who had great difficulty getting public performances. In many ways, the times simply weren't right.

I should mention that the times were no better for me personally than they were for most other *tabaqueros*. When the Trabajadores Amalgamados de la Industria del Tabaco was founded, I accepted a job in the leadership, with pay. Aside from being editor-in-chief of the paper, the *Tobacco Worker*, I also served as mediator between the bosses and the workers. This latter task was extremely difficult because of the changes taking place in production. It meant, on the one hand, defending the interests of the workers, without at the same time forcing the factories to move to other cities. Many of my problems were with well-meaning comrades who failed to understand the magnitude of the changes taking place in industry. In time I was exhausted by the endless debates and the fruitless battle—totally illogical, in fact, from the socialist point of view—against the machines that a handful of people were trying to impose. So I resigned, and joined the huge army of unemployed. . . .

CHAPTER 19. THE CONSOLIDATION OF EL BARRIO, AND NEW PAGES IN ITS HISTORY

By now the Puerto Rican neighborhood extended from Lexington Avenue between 96th and 107th streets over to the beginning of the Italian section on First Avenue. Through this entire area, life was very much like what it was back home. Following the example set by the *tabaqueros*, whites and blacks lived together in harmony. There were many Hispanic *bodegas*, barbershops, and butchers. Branches of green plaintains hung in the store windows, and the sidewalks were lined with food and vegetable stands. In the stores and in the streets, all you heard was Spanish.

But the other national groups living in the area resented the constantly growing Puerto Rican population. For them the way of life of the *boricuas* was scandalous, and relations among the different nationalities were fraught with tension. Women would often clash while shopping, and at times the fights in the neighborhood bars would become serious. After the disturbances up in Harlem, this situation got even worse.

Hardly a day went by that a Puerto Rican child didn't come home from school with a black eye. Mothers lived in constant fear. The schoolchildren, of course, fought back. And it would have remained a squabble among children had racism not reared its ugly head. But it was not long before the adults began to step into the fray. One day—June 14, 1927, to be exact—on the corner of 96th Street and Third Avenue, a grown man kicked a young boy named Luis Berríos. An on-duty policeman who was standing nearby laughed it off, as though it were a joke. But at that moment a fellow Puerto Rican, Juan Sabater, happened to be passing. Ignoring everyone else, he jumped on the aggressor as though he were stomping out a raging fire, and he didn't stop until the man was carted off to the hospital. Only then did the cop step in: he arrested the Puerto Rican on charges of felonious assault!

In a matter of minutes the news spread through the neighborhood. Whole groups of irate *jíbaros* poured into the streets to stand up for their kin, and this prevented the conflict from becoming even more serious than it was.

The many groups in the Puerto Rican community immediately met and agreed to mount a vocal protest against the city authorities. Another well-attended meeting was held at the Harlem Terrace. Some of the speakers were J. V. Alonso, J. N. Ocasio, Rafael Rivera, Luis Torres Colón, Alfonso Lastra Chárriez, and Blas Oliveras. There was an appeal for peace and tolerance, but everyone agreed that any further aggression had to be met in like manner.

This firm but calm approach had a positive effect in the neighborhood. Those who had shown ill will toward Puerto Ricans quieted down, or simply moved out. Our countrymen made it clear that we were in charge in that part of town.

The Puerto Rican community had its bad types, of course, like any other community. The fact is, though, that so many lowlifes of other nationalities—many stowaways from the Latin American countries—had wound up in El Barrio that there had been a considerable increase in crime and vandalism. And the sad thing is that these people were usually taken for Puerto Ricans.

Which is not to say that our countrymen never engaged in illegal activities. But there is evidence that we were accused of more crimes than we actually committed. I exposed this injustice in *Gráfico* after studying all the police reports filed between 1930 and 1933 having to do with hold-ups and robberies.

... Washington had stepped up its campaign of aggression against Nicaragua. The press was filled with horror stories about the "gang of bandits" down there, and about their ringleader, César Augusto Sandino. Socrates Sandino, the leader's brother, was in New York at the time and met the slander campaign head-on. North American liberals, progressives, socialists, and communists made common cause with the Nicaraguan people.

One of the many protests against the invasion was a large rally held on February 19, 1928, at the Labor Temple on 14th Street and Second Avenue. The principal speakers were Scott Nearing, the well-known author of *Dollar Diplomacy;* Leon Ganett, editor of the *Nation;* John Brophy, president of the International Mineworkers' Union; Juan De Jesús, president of the Philippine Club; Ricardo Martínez of the Unión Obrera Venezolana; H. C. Wu of the Chinese Writers' Society; and the author of these memoirs in his capacity as editor of *Gráfico*. After this event the struggle against the invasion of Nicaragua took on a new dimension.

Shortly afterward, while visiting New York, Santiago Iglesias spoke at an event held by the Liga Puertorriqueña without once mentioning that act of United States imperialist aggression. Not only that, he even praised Washington's policies toward Latin America. The socialist labor leader's attitude was bitterly and widely censured by leaders of the Puerto Rican community in New York.

... That year the Republican Party won the election and Herbert Hoover moved into the White House. At a time when Nicaragua was being invaded by the Marines, Haiti was under military occupation, exports from the Dominican Republic were rigidly controlled, Cuba was being dominated through the Platt Amendment, Puerto Rico was being subjected to a process of assimilation, and Colombia was bleeding from the wound of Panama—at such a time the newly elected president chose to pay a goodwill visit to the countries of Latin America. This served to heighten anti-imperialist sentiment in progressive circles throughout the hemisphere, and especially in New York.

In the large hall of the Park Palace, right in the heart of Harlem, a public debate was held between students from the Universidad de Puerto Rico and Columbia University on the subject of United States intervention in the Caribbean. Our team was made up of Antonio J. Colorado, Gabriel Guerra, and Vicente Roura. The jury was composed of Columbia professors Fernando de los Ríos, William Shepherd, and José Padín, and the president of the Hispanic Chamber of Commerce, Eduardo López.

The young men from the United States made an able showing, but the jury, with the support of the audience, decided in favor of the Puerto Ricans. Our team proved superior both by virtue of the position it took and the brilliance of the arguments it put forth. "Unless it declares war," we held, "the United States has no right to intervene in the Caribbean."

At around the same time the case of a Puerto Rican sentenced to die in the electric chair gripped the community. It concerned Félix Ostolaza, who had been convicted of murder in the first degree. Had it not been for the intervention of several organizations, especially the Federación Puertorriqueña de Clubs Demócratas, Ostolaza would have suffered the death penalty. But thanks to the work of some good lawyers, it was proved that the accused man had acted in self-defense. And so we saved our compatriot from the electric chair.

When the news reached New York of the destruction caused by the San Felipe hurricane in Puerto Rico, a relief campaign began immediately. Aid was sent to the victims through the Red Cross. To raise funds we held an artists' festival at the Star Casino. Fiorello La Guardia offered us his wholehearted cooperation. I still remember when Pedro San Miguel, Alberto Hernández, and I went down to visit him in his offices.

. . . Fiorello La Guardia enjoyed great support in the Puerto Rican community. As soon as he was named Republican Party candidate for mayor, the Puerto Rican Republican organization pledged its support. The leaders of that group were R. Villar, Juan B. Matos, Fernando Torres, Frank Torres, Francisco M. Rivera, and Felipe Gómez.

As time went by the main areas where Puerto Ricans lived changed, both in location and social composition. By 1929 the old neighborhood on the East Side, made up mostly of *tabaqueros*, had moved up toward Harlem, and El Barrio was finally consolidated as the heart of the Puerto Rican community in New York.

Living conditions, far from improving, grew worse and worse. Once a building was occupied by our countrymen, no more maintenance was done on it. Garbage collection also became inadequate, and the whole neighborhood gave the impression of being totally neglected. Living quarters, which included cellars and basements, were packed with people. Men, women, and children shared what little room they had with rats, cockroaches, and garbage.

El Barrio took on its own distinctive features. There arose a culture typical of that common experience of people fighting for survival in the face of hostile surroundings. In the long run, that culture was to bear fruit in its own right.

Small pharmacies and *botánicas* sprang up throughout the neighborhood. There wasn't much difference between one and the other—*boticas* and *botánicas*. Both dealt in herbs like lemon verbena, sage, and rue, and they even carried pieces of the devil's claw . . . Doctors, witches, druggists, mind readers, dentists, spiritualists, palm readers, all shared the same clientele. Misery always seems to breed superstition, and when there is no hope of getting out of a life of poverty, dreams are the only consolation left. This helps explain the role of religion, in all its popular forms. It also helps explain why there was so much gambling, as is always true of destitute communities. And, of course, there was dancing.

Scores of groups competed in organizing dances, and personality and beauty contests. Young women, especially, were drawn to that kind of flashy show. But the worst thing about these activities wasn't that they were all so frivolous; it was that many of them were really just a front used by a whole range of good-for-nothings to win favors and make profits. Some of those hustlers would set themselves up as president or secretary-treasurer of some nonexistent organization whose only service was to line the pockets of its founders. A few such groups were, no doubt, on the level. But there were a lot of "coronations," with some naive little backwoods girl as "queen," that were organized by operators who would "clean up," as they would say, a few hundred dollars in the process.

At those festivities there were often little skits, supposedly funny, in which the characters were always *jíbaros* from Puerto Rico. The skits would consist of a few ridiculous scenes where some fool would think he was a comic actor just because he had a peasant's hat on his head and came on stage in patched-up pants playing *maracas*. There was always someone in the audience who would protest. But that's what people wanted. And I should also point to one notable exception: Erasmo Vando, a versatile actor, who with his group "Los Jíbaros" staged performances that did capture the genuine flavor of Puerto Rican peasant life.

The events sponsored by the Centro Obrero Español, which had become a focal point for many social concerns, were quite different. Many groups were organized at the center, including the Liga Anti-imperialista Puertorriqueña, which was headed by Domingo García, Antonio Rivas, Sandalio Marcial, Concepción Gómez, Angel María Dieppa, and José Santiago.

That group put out the paper *Vida Obrera* (Workers' Life) as part of its union organizing drive. One fruit of its effort was the organization of a Hispanic branch of the Amalgamated Restaurant and Cafeteria Workers' Union; its founding director was Pablo Martínez.

As for the arts, I must point especially to the founding of Puerto Rico Literario. Some of our fellow countrymen, who in the course of their lives achieved things of some note, set up this society in June 1929. It defined its aim as "cultivating Spanish letters, promoting an interest in study, and upholding the faith of Puerto Rican youth in the cause of independence."

We met at the public library branch on 115th Street, in a little office graciously put at our disposal by our compatriot Pura Belpré, who was a librarian. Registered members of the group were soon to excel in many different areas of Puerto Rican life and letters. Francisco Acevedo was a pioneer in radio broadcasting in San Juan. Lorenzo Piñeiro, also a journalist, later became a lawyer and an outstanding leader of the Partido Independentista Puertorriqueño, which he represented in the U.S. Senate. Max Vázquez was an outstanding journalist and writer; Bartolo Malavé, a lawyer; Rafael Mariotta, another journalist; René Jiménez Malaret, an essayist; Juan Bautista Pagán, a journalist and author; Luis Hernández Aquino, one of the foremost poets of his generation; Erasmo Vando, an actor . . . That was the group, then, with whom I had the honor of sharing some of my fondest hopes and dreams.

At around that time Rafael Hernández was making the rounds in New York. These were his bohemian days, when he was hard at work. His song "Lamento borincano" began to fill the air in El Barrio . . . We were on the eve of the most serious economic depression ever to hit the United States of America.

On March 21, 1935, Harlem was hit by a major riot. It was sparked off by the arrest of León Rivera, a young boy accused of stealing from the Kress store on 125th Street off Lenox Avenue. Several women who witnessed the event thought Rivera was a black American, although he was of course Puerto Rican, and rushed out into the street to protest the abusive manner in which the private guards (whites, of course) made the arrest. Hundreds of people gathered around the women, anger flared, and rocks started sailing through the store's windows. Violence spread throughout the neighborhood and lasted for several hours. When order was finally restored, Harlem looked like a city in ruins and was in a state of siege.

The roughing-up of the young boy by the guards and the women's outburst was like pulling a cork, and all of the pain and suffering of the black people rose to the surface. There were thousands of business in the area, all of them run by whites. In none of them—from the largest to the smallest—was there a single Afro-American person working. Discrimination was rampant, and was all the more abusive and humiliating because Harlem had the greatest concentration of blacks in New York City. The refusal to hire Negroes, even in businesses largely patronized by them, and at a time when the most severe unemployment was among black people—who, on top of all that, also had to pay higher rents than whites—made racial discrimination all the more disgusting.

Fortunately, Fiorello La Guardia was mayor of New York at the time. As soon as he heard about the riot, he went up to Harlem himself, restrained the police—who thought they could solve the problem with billy clubs—and stated publicly that black people were victims of a grave injustice. He called a meeting right there on the spot, spoke in conciliatory tones, and pledged the resources of the city government to alleviate the most pressing problems afflicting the Negro population—immediate assistance, jobs, and so forth. His quick action prevented a repetition of the violence.

That riot of March 21 seemed to strike panic into the managers of companies operating in Harlem. From then on, nearly all the stores began to hire blacks for menial work. The recently established "relief agencies" recruited blacks to conduct some of their investigations, and employment became available at the Board of Education and in the Police Department. These were some of Fiorello La Guardia's achievements during his first term in City Hall.

If anything taught the Puerto Ricans—including white Puerto Ricans—what life is like in the United States, it was the awareness of discrimination. As we have come to see, racial prejudice takes on many different faces. One form it took, around that time, was exemplified by the New York City Chamber of Commerce. Claiming that it needed to determine the "intelligence quotient" of Puerto Rican children, it sponsored a series of experimental tests. After administering the exam to 240 students, the Chamber announced in the papers that Puerto Rican children were "deficient" and lacked "intellectual development."

That "experiment" provoked a protest from groups representing the Puerto Rican community. In a message to the Chamber of Commerce, we proposed that they name a committee of teachers, to include representatives of our community, that would draw up an examination to be administered to an equal number of Puerto Rican and North American children. We were certain that our children would not come out any worse as far as natural intelligence is concerned. But the Chamber of Commerce showed little or no interest, and turned to other matters. Our suggestion was never followed up.

By that time the Puerto Rican community had spread out considerably. In addition to El Barrio in Harlem, thickly populated neighborhoods had sprung up in the Bronx, Washington Heights, and on parts of Long Island. The owners and managers of apartment buildings actively resisted this Puerto Rican expansion. In many cases, especially up in Washington Heights, they refused to rent to families who had come from Puerto Rico, which is what gave rise to the Comité de Defensa de Derechos de los Hispanos. Its membership included such prominent figures as Drs. E. Verges Casals, Max Ríos, and Vando de León, and attorneys Enrique Sarabals and Carlos Rodríguez.

. . . In the elections of 1934 a new man, of Italian background—a young lawyer named Vito Marcantonio—defeated J. J. Lanzetta, who had snatched the Congressional seat from Fiorello La Guardia. As he was now in City Hall, La Guardia's former post in Washington—which included representation of El Barrio—was filled by Marcantonio. It is no exaggeration to say that with that event a new age began for the Puerto Rican community in New York.

TRANSLATION BY JUAN FLORES

NOTES

1. The reference is to the new names for the Island's political parties after the U.S. occupation in 1898. Thus on July 1, 1899, the Partido Autonomista Ortodoxo became the Partido Republicano Puertorriqueño; on October 1, the Partido Liberal Puertorriqueño was renamed the Partido Federal Americano. The Partido Republicano was led by Dr. José Celso Barbosa, while Luis Muñoz Rivera headed the Partido Liberal. Both parties advocated statehood for Puerto Rico.

2. In a cigar factory, the *escogedores* were those who selected and classified the cigars according to their color and quality; the *rezagadores* classified the tobacco leaves in terms of color, elasticity, and size. *Escogedores* and *rezagadores* belonged to separate units within the union.

3. The Congress of Laredo was held on November 13, 1918, to set conditions for the founding of the Federación Pan-Americana de Trabajo (Pan-American Federation of Labor), later referred to as the Confederación Pan-Americana (COPA). The meeting, attended by representatives from the United States, Mexico, Guatemala, El Salvador, Costa Rica, and Colombia, was convened by the A.F. of L. for the purpose of stemming the revolutionary tide of the Latin American workers' movement and bringing it under the control of organized labor in the United States.

4. The Juegos Florales, or Floral Games, are a long-standing tradition in the Spanish-speaking world, going back to the late Middle Ages. The Juegos Florales generally included a beauty contest and a poetry contest; the prize flower often went to the best poem in praise of that year's beauty queen.

HALFWAY *to* DICK *and* JANE

A Puerto Rican Pilgrimage

Jack Agüeros

My father arrived in America in 1920, a stowaway on a steamer that shuttled between San Juan and New York. At sixteen, he was through with school and had been since thirteen or fourteen when he left the eighth grade. Between dropout and migrant, the picture is not totally clear, but three themes dominate: baseball, cock-fighting, and cars. At sixteen, my father had lived in every town of Puerto Rico, had driven every road there in Ford Models A and T, had played basketball, baseball, studied English and American History, hustled tourists, and had heard the popular and classical music of two cultures.

With a superficial knowledge of America, wholly aware that the streets were not paved in gold, interested specifically in neither employment nor education, my father visited New York in the same spirit in which a family might drive out in the country on a Sunday afternoon. But it was winter 1920, and my father's romantic picture of snow was shattered. His clothes were inadequate for cold weather, and he himself was not prepared either physically or emotionally for cold. The light English patter he had charmed the tourists with was no match for the rapid-fire slurred English of New York's streets. His school English, with its carefully pronounced "water" and "squirrel," seemed like another language compared to "wudder" and "squaral."

It was a three-day winter for my father. In seventy-two hours, he thought he understood New York: the flatness of its geography and humanity, the extreme cold of climate and character, the toe to toe aloneness. On the fourth day, Joaquin Agueros went back to San Juan.

He came back "north" again in his early twenties, but again there is an unclear time span. There appears to have been a short hitch in the Puerto Rican National Guard, and during this time, there was an upheaval in island and mainland politics. Governors of Puerto Rico were appointed by the White House and had considerable powers over the island's economy and politics. The new governor began a thorough shake-up of the civil service, and as a result, my father left the National Guard and my grandfather, Ramon Agueros, was relieved of his title and duties of police captain. My father's family, composed of my grandparents, three brothers, a sister, and one or two *hermanos de crianza* (literally, "brothers of upbringing," or children brought up as if brothers), was plunged into total poverty. My grandfather was not and had never been a landowner. His policeman's pay was the only source of income. Joaquin was the oldest son, and unemployed. The family was spared starvation by the Order of the Masons, which delivered trucks full of food once or twice a month (Grandpa was a master).

The tyranny of the new gringo governor was causing serious repercussions on the island. Puerto Rico was an extraordinarily underdeveloped country, very poor and depressed, without a unanimity of affection for America. There was a massacre of civilians at Ponce by the police. This was blamed on the new governor, as were all the island's problems. My father has told me that talk and rumors of assassination were common. Many people expected to hear of the governor's death. Nevertheless, the governor was not assassinated, and there were no more Ponce massacres. Capitan Ramon Agueros was readmitted to the force but not reinstated in rank. Soon thereafter, his eldest son Joaquin also became a policeman.

In my youth, I loved to look at the pictures of Father and Grandfather in their police uniforms. Of Ramon, bald and clean shaven in his *capitan*'s jacket, I remember a large chest, a strong jaw, and tough eyes. Set in a gilded oval frame with an American eagle at the top, it hung under glass in my parents' bedroom. Of my father, I remember a patched-up photo, probably torn up by my mother after a spat. In it a tall, very handsome young man was standing full length with hat and riding boots. Face not stern like Ramon's, but with a look of forced seriousness. Joaquin bore a resemblance to Rudolf Valentino and to Carlos Gardel, the Argentinian singer and film star.

"Are you still a policeman?"

"No," my father says. He is sitting in a rocking chair, stroking his mustache idly, enjoying the nightingale in the cage hanging between rooms. "No, I am not a cop." He pauses, strokes, rocks, gives a big smile as if enjoying some inside joke, and says, "I had a bad revolver. Used to chew up the bullets, chack, chack, chack; finally, bang." Then he stops smiling.

"Why did you have such funny shoes?"

"Your father was a mounted police," my mother tells me from the kitchen. (One day I told a cop on a horse in Central Park, "My father was a mounted policeman." "So what?" shot back the cop.) "He was very skinny, but very tall in the saddle, and a good rider."

"Those are riding boots. I had a big red, sixteen hands, so alive he couldn't walk." (Furious rocking.) "I'd take him down to the beach and let him go. It was illegal, but we both loved it, and we'd wash down in the ocean . . ."

My father, once animated, would and does go on telling stories. Most of high adventure, with chase-escape climaxes, and every one peppered with mischief.

I was told that my father left the police force because he had shot and wounded a moonshiner in a raid on a still. (Not very unlikely, for such raids were common: there is a photo, sepiaed by time, Grandpa and Father, guns pointing at a group of desperados with hands held high up against a wall of vats, jugs, and plumbing.) The wounded moonshiner turned out to be a member of high society, and my father was accused of misconduct and promiscuous use of a firearm—the chack chack story had its undivulged point.

Joaquin, like many Puerto Ricans, has always been proud to a fault. Standing departmental hearings, he was exonerated of the charges. But the exoneration was meaningless; outraged that his integrity had been questioned at all, he resigned from the force.

This pride and value of integrity is ancient. You can find it in *El Cid*, in the plays of Lope de Vega, in *Don Quixote*. And you find it among the Puerto Ricans today. In America it debilitates them, it keeps them from filing complaints of violation of human and civil rights, from contesting employers' decisions before state referees, and it keeps them from insisting upon full service from city and state agencies.

That's what I know about my old man's early life—he was a picaresque character from a Spanish novel. It is a collage of information, some of it concrete and verifiable, most of it gathered haphazardly and connected by conjecture. Does it matter what the governor's name is? Does it matter whether any or all of it is fact or fiction? What matters is that I thought my old man enjoyed life, let no grass grow under his feet, and it also matters that he came back to New York.

I was born in Harlem in 1934. We lived on 111th Street off Fifth Avenue. It was a block of mainly three-story buildings—with brick fronts, or brownstone, or limestone imitations of brownstone. Our apartment was a three-room first-floor walk-up. It faced north and had three windows on the street, none in back. There was a master bedroom, a living room, a kitchen-dining room, a foyer with a short hall, and a bathroom. In the kitchen there was an air shaft to evacuate cooking odors and grease—we converted it to a chimney for Santa Claus.

The kitchen was dominated by a large Victorian china closet, and the built-in wall shelves were lined with oilcloth, trimmed with ruffle, both decorated by brilliant and miniature fruits. Prominent on a wall of the kitchen was a large reproduction of a still life, a harvest table full of produce, framed and under glass. From it, I learned to identify apples, pumpkins, bananas, pears, grapes, and melons, and "peaches without worms." A joke between my mother and me. (A peach we had bought in the city market, under the New Haven's elevated tracks, bore, like the trains above, passengers.)

On one shelf of the kitchen, over the stove, there was a lineup of ceramic cannisters that carried words like "nutmeg," "ginger," and "basil." I did not know what those words meant and I don't know if my mother did either. "Spices," she would say, and that was that. They were of a yellow color that was not unlike the yellow of the stove. The kitchen was itself painted yellow, I think, very pale. But I am sure of one thing, it was not "Mickey Moused." "Mickey Mousing" was a technique used by house painters to decorate the areas of the walls that were contained by wood molding. Outside the molding they might paint a solid green. Inside the wood mold, the same solid green. Then with a twisted-up rag dipped in a lighter green they would trace random patterns.

We never used wallpaper or rugs. Our floors were covered with linoleum in every room. My father painted the apartment every year before Christmas, and in addition, he did all the maintenance, doing his own plastering and plumbing. No sooner would we move into an apartment than my father would repair holes or cracks, and if there were bulges in the plaster, he would break them open and redo the area—sometimes a whole wall. He would immediately modify the bathrooms to add a shower with separate valves, and usually as a routine matter, he cleaned out all the elbow traps, and changed all the washers on faucets. This was true of the other families in the buildings where I lived. Not a December came without a painting of the apartment.

We had Louis XIV furniture in the living room, reflected in the curved glass door and curved glass sides of the china closet. On the walls of the living room hung two prints that I loved. I would spend hours playing games with my mother based on the pictures, making up stories, etc. One day at Brooklyn College, a slide projector slammed, and I awoke after having dozed off during a dull lecture to see Van Gogh's "The Gleaners" on the screen. I almost cried. Another time I came across the other print in a book. A scene of Venice by Canaletto.

The important pieces of the living room, for me, were a Detrola radio with magic-eye tuning and the nightingale, Keero. The nightingale and the radio went back before my recollection. The bird could not stop singing, and people listened on the sidewalk below and came upstairs offering to buy Keero.

The Detrola, shaped like a Gothic arch with inlaid woodwork, was a great source of entertainment for the family. I memorized all the hit songs sung by Libertad Lamarque and Carlos Gardel. Sundays I listened to the Canary Hour presented by Hartz Mountain Seed Company. Puppy, a white Spitz, was my constant companion. Puppy slept at the foot of my bed from the first day he came to our house till the day he died, when I was eleven or twelve and he was seven or eight.

My *madrina* lived on the third floor of our building, and for all practical purposes, her apartment and ours formed a duplex. My godmother really was my second mother. Rocking me to sleep, playing her guitar, and singing me little songs, she used to say, "I'm your real mother, 'cause I love you more." But I knew that wasn't so.

Carmen Diaz, my mother, came to New York in 1931. Her brother, a career soldier, had sent for her with the intention of taking her up to Plattsburg, where he was stationed. Like my father, she arrived in New York on a steamer. My uncle had planned to show his kid sister the big city before leaving for Plattsburg, but during a week in New York my mother was convinced to stay. More opportunities, and other Spanish-speaking people, were the reasons that changed her mind.

Carmen had had a tough time all her life in Puerto Rico. Her mother had died when she was only two. Her father, a wealthy farmer and veterinarian, remarried and began paying less and less attention to his business affairs. The stepmother was not very fond of the children. Thus, when her older sister married a policeman, Carmen accepted the invitation to live with the newlyweds, acting as a sort of housekeeper-governess. After many years in this role, which my mother describes as "rewarding, but not a life for a young girl," came the offer to "go north."

On the island, my mother had had two serious suitors. One was a schoolteacher who had an ailing mother and could not afford to marry on his salary. The other was a rookie cop who had arrested her brother-in-law for carrying a concealed weapon. The brother-in-law took the arrest in good humor, and after proving that he was an off-duty cop, invited the rookie home for dinner. The rookie became a frequent visitor, twirling apples for Carmen's delight, but one day he came to visit and said he was going north, to find a good job. He said he would write, but no letter ever came from Joaquin.

Carmen had big plans for her life in America, intending to go to school and study interior decorating. But the Puerto Ricans who came to New York at that time found life in the city tough. It was the Depression, and work was hard to come by. My mother went from job to job for about six months and finally landed a job in the garment district as a seamstress. Twenty years later, she retired from the ILGWU, her dream of becoming a decorator waylaid by bumping into my father on a Manhattan street and reviving the old romance. My father had been back in America since the mid-twenties. In America he remembers working a long day to earn $1.25. After a time, he found a job in a restaurant that paid nine dollars a week and provided two meals a day. That was a good deal, even at a six-day week, twelve to fifteen hours a day.

I am an only child. My parents and I always talked about my becoming a doctor. The law and politics were not highly regarded in my house. Lawyers, my mother would explain, had to defend people whether they were guilty or not, while politicians, my father would say, were all crooks. A doctor helped everybody, rich and poor, white and black. If I became a doctor, I could study hay fever and find a cure for it, my godmother would say. Also, I could take care of my parents when they were old. I liked the idea of helping, and for nineteen years my sole ambition was to study medicine.

My house had books, not many, but my parents encouraged me to read. As I became a good reader they bought books for me and never refused me money for their purchase. My father once built a bookcase for me. It was an important moment, for I had always believed that my father was not too happy about my being a bookworm.

The atmosphere at home was always warm. We seemed to be a popular family. We entertained frequently, with two standing parties a year—at Christmas and for my birthday. Parties were always large. My father would dismantle the beds and move all the furniture so that the full two rooms could be used for dancing. My mother would cook up a storm, particularly at Christmas. *Pasteles, lechon asado, arroz con gandules*, and a lot of *coquito* to drink (meat-stuffed plantain, roast pork, rice with pigeon peas, and coconut nog). My father always brought in a band. They played without compensation and were guests at the party. They ate and drank and danced while a victrola covered the intermissions. One year my father brought home a whole pig and hung it in the foyer doorway. He and my mother prepared it by rubbing it down with oil, oregano, and garlic. After preparation, the pig was taken down and carried over to a local bakery where it was cooked and returned home. Parties always went on till daybreak, and in addition to the band, there were always volunteers to sing and declaim poetry.

My mother kept an immaculate household. Bedspreads (chenille seemed to be very in) and lace curtains, washed at home like everything else, were hung up on huge racks with rows of tight nails. The racks were assembled in the living room, and the moisture from the wet bedspreads would fill the apartment. In a sense, that seems to be the lasting image of that period of my life. The house was clean. The neighbors were clean. The streets, with few cars, were clean. The buildings were clean and uncluttered with people on the stoops. The park was clean. The visitors to my house were clean, and the relationships that my family had with other Puerto Rican families, and the Italian families that my father had met through baseball and my mother through the garment center, were clean. Second Avenue was clean and most of the apartment windows had awnings. There was always music, there seemed to be no rain, and snow did not become slush. School was fun, we wrote essays about how grand America was, we put up hunchbacked cats at Halloween, we believed Santa Claus visited everyone. I believed everyone was Catholic. I grew up with dogs, nightingales, my godmother's guitar, rocking chair, cat, guppies, my father's occasional roosters, kept in a cage on the fire escape. Laundry delivered and collected by horse and wagon, fruits and vegetables sold the same way, windowsill refrigeration in winter, iceman and box in summer. The police my friends, likewise the teachers.

In short, the first seven or so years of my life were not too great a variation on Dick and Jane, the school book figures who, if my memory serves me correctly, were blond Anglo-Saxons, not immigrants, not migrants like the Puerto Ricans, and not the children of either immigrants or migrants.

My family moved in 1941 to Lexington Avenue into a larger apartment where I could have my own room. It was a light, sunny, railroad flat on the top floor of a well-kept building. I transferred to a new school, and whereas before my classmates had been mostly black, the new school had few blacks. The classes were made up of Italians,

Irish, Jews, and a sprinkling of Puerto Ricans. My block was populated by Jews, Italians, and Puerto Ricans.

And then a whole series of different events began. I went to junior high school. We played in the backyards, where we tore down fences to build fires to cook stolen potatoes. We tore up whole hedges, because the green tender limbs would not burn when they were peeled, and thus made perfect skewers for our stolen "mickies." We played tag in the abandoned buildings, tearing the plaster off the walls, tearing the wire lath off the wooden slats, tearing the wooden slats themselves, good for fires, for kites, for sword fighting. We ran up and down the fire escapes playing tag and over and across many rooftops. The war ended and the heavy Puerto Rican migration began. The Irish and the Jews disappeared from the neighborhood. The Italians tried to consolidate east of Third Avenue.

What caused the clean and open world to end? Many things. Into an ancient neighborhood came pouring four to five times more people than it had been designed to hold. Men who came running at the promise of jobs were jobless as the war ended. They were confused. They could not see the economic forces that ruled their lives as they drank beer on the corners, reassuring themselves of good times to come while they were hell-bent toward alcoholism. The sudden surge in numbers caused new resentments, and prejudice was intensified. Some were forced to live in cellars, and were then characterized as cave dwellers. Kids came who were confused by the new surroundings; their Puerto Ricanness forced us against a mirror asking, "If they are Puerto Ricans, what are we?" and thus they confused us. In our confusion we were sometimes pathetically reaching out, sometimes pathologically striking out. Gangs. Drugs. Wine. Smoking. Girls. Dances and slow-drag music. Mambo. Spics, Spooks, and Wops. Territories, brother gangs, and war councils establishing rules for right of way on blocks and avenues and for seating in the local theater. Pegged pants and zip guns. Slang.

Dick and Jane were dead, man. Education collapsed. Every classroom had ten kids who spoke no English. Black, Italian, Puerto Rican relations in the classroom were good, but we all knew we couldn't visit one another's neighborhoods. Sometimes we could not move too freely within our own blocks. On 109th, from the lamp post west, the Latin Aces, and from the lamp post east, the Senecas, the "club" I belonged to. The kids who spoke no English became known as Marine Tigers, picked up from a popular Spanish song. (The *Marine Tiger* and the *Marine Shark* were two ships that sailed from San Juan to New York and brought over many, many migrants from the island.)

The neighborhood had its boundaries. Third Avenue and east, Italian. Fifth Avenue and west, black. South, there was a hill on 103rd Street known locally as Cooney's Hill. When you got to the top of the hill, something strange happened: America began, because from the hill south was where the "Americans" lived. Dick and Jane were not dead; they were alive and well in a better neighborhood.

When, as a group of Puerto Rican kids, we decided to go swimming to Jefferson Park Pool, we knew we risked a fight and a beating from the Italians. And when we went to La Milagrosa Church in Harlem, we knew we risked a fight and a beating from the blacks. But when we went over Cooney's Hill, we risked dirty looks, disapproving looks, and questions from the police like, "What are you doing in this neighborhood?" and "Why don't you kids go back where you belong?"

Where we belonged! Man, I had written compositions about America. Didn't I belong on the Central Park tennis courts, even if I didn't know how to play? Couldn't I watch Dick play? Weren't these policemen working for me too?

Junior high school was a waste. I can say with 90 per cent accuracy that I learned nothing. The woodshop was used to manufacture stocks for "homemades" after Macy's stopped selling zip-guns. We went from classroom to classroom answering "here," and trying to be "good." The math class was generally permitted to go to the gym after roll call. English was still a good class. Partly because of a damn good, tough teacher named Miss Beck, and partly because of the grade-number system (7–1 the smartest seventh grade and 7–12, the dumbest). Books were left in school, there was little or no homework, and the whole thing seemed to be a holding operation until high school. Somehow or other, I passed the entrance exam to Brooklyn Technical High School. But I couldn't cut the mustard, either academically or with the "American" kids. After one semester, I came back to PS 83, waited a semester, and went on to Benjamin Franklin High School.

I still wanted to study medicine and excelled in biology. English was always an interesting subject, and I still enjoyed writing compositions and reading. In the neighborhood it was becoming a problem being categorized as a bookworm and as one who used "Sunday words," or "big words." I dug school, but I wanted to be one of the boys more. I think the boys respected my intelligence, despite their ribbing. Besides which, I belonged to a club with a number of members who were interested in going to college, and so I wasn't so far out.

My introduction to marijuana was in junior high school in 1948. A kid named Dixie from 124th Street brought a pack of joints to school and taught about twelve guys to smoke. He told us we could buy joints at a quarter each or five for a dollar. Bombers, or thicker cigarettes, were thirty-five cents each or three for a dollar. There were a lot of experimenters, but not too many buyers. Actually, among the boys there was a strong taboo on drugs, and the Spanish word *motto* was a term of disparagement. Many clubs would kick out members who were known to use drugs. Heroin was easily available, and in those days came packaged in capsules or "caps" which sold for fifty cents each. Method of use was inhalation through the nose, or "sniffing," or "snorting."

I still remember vividly the first kid I ever saw who was mainlining. Prior to this encounter, I had known of "skin-popping," or subcutaneous injection, but not of mainlining. Most of the sniffers were afraid of skin-popping because they knew of the danger of addiction. They seemed to think that you could not become addicted by sniffing.

I went over to 108th Street and Madison where we played softball on an empty lot. This kid came over who was maybe sixteen or seventeen and asked us if we wanted to buy Horse. He started telling us about shooting up and showed me his arms. He had tracks, big black marks on the inside of his arm from the inner joint of the elbow down to his wrist and then over onto the back of his hand. I was stunned. Then he said, "That's nothing, man. I ain't hooked, and I ain't no junky. I can stop anytime I want to." I believe that he believed what he was saying. Invariably the kids talking about their drug experiences would say over and over, "I ain't hooked. I can stop anytime."

But they didn't stop; and the drug traffic grew greater and more open. Kids were smoking on the corners and on the stoops. Deals were made on the street, and you knew fifteen places within a block radius where you could buy anything you wanted. Cocaine never seemed to catch on although it was readily available. In the beginning, the kids seemed to be able to get the money for stuff easily. As the number of shooters grew and the prices went up, the kids got more desperate and apartment robbing became a real problem.

More of the boys began to leave school. We didn't use the term drop out; rather, a guy would say one day, after forty-three truancies, "I'm quitting school." And so he would. It was an irony, for what was really happening was that after many years of being rejected, ignored, and shuffled around by the school, the kid wanted to quit. Only you can't quit something you were never a part of, nor can you drop out if you were never in.

Some kids lied about their age and joined the army. Most just hung around. Not drifting to drugs or crime or to work either. They used to talk about going back at night and getting the diploma. I believe that they did not believe they could get their diplomas. They knew that the schools had abandoned them a long time ago—that to get the diploma meant starting all over again and that was impossible. Besides, day or night, it was the same school, the same staff, the same shit. But what do you say when you are powerless to get what you want, and what do you say when the other side has all the cards and writes all the rules? You say, "Tennis is for fags," and "School is for fags."

My mother leads me by the hand and carries a plain brown shopping bag. We enter an immense airplane hangar. Structural steel crisscrosses on the ceiling and walls: large round and square rivets look like buttons or bubbles of air trapped in the girders. There are long metallic counters with people bustling behind them. It smells of C.N. disinfectant. Many people stand on many lines up to these counters; there are many conversations going on simultaneously. The huge space plays tricks with voices and a very eerie combination of sounds results. A white cabbage is rolled down a counter at us. We retaliate by throwing down stamps.

For years I thought that sequence happened in a dream. The rolling cabbage rolled in my head, and little unrelated incidents seemed to bring it to the surface of my mind. I could not understand why I remembered a once-dreamt dream so vividly. I was sixteen when I picked up and read Freud's *The Interpretation of Dreams.* One part I understood immediately and well, sex and symbolism. In no time, I had hung my shingle: Streetcorner Analyst. My friends would tell me their dreams and with the most outrageous sexual explanations we laughed whole evenings away. But the rolling cabbage could not be stopped and neither quack analysis nor serious thought could explain it away. One day I asked my mother if she knew anything about it.

"That was home relief, 1937 or 1938. You were no more than four years old then. Your father had been working at a restaurant and I had a job downtown. I used to take you every morning to Dona Eduvije who cared for you all day. She loved you very much, and she was very clean and neat, but I used to cry on my way to work, wishing I could stay home with my son and bring him up like a proper mother would. But I guess I was fated to be a workhorse. When I was pregnant, I would get on the crowded subway and go to work. I would get on a crowded elevator up. Then down. Then back on the subway. Every day I was afraid that the crowd would hurt me, that I would lose my baby. But I had to work. I worked for the WPA right into my ninth month."

My mother was telling it "like it was," and I sat stupefied, for I could not believe that what she said applied to the time I thought of as open and clean. I had been existing in my life like a small plant in a bell jar, my parents defining my awareness. There were things all around me I could not see.

"When you were born we had been living as boarders. It was hard to find an apartment, even in Harlem. You saw signs that said 'No Renting to Colored or Spanish.' That meant Puerto Ricans. We used to say, 'This is supposed to be such a great country?' But with a new baby we were determined not to be boarders and we took an apartment on 111th Street. Soon after we moved, I lost my job because my factory closed down. Your father was making seven or eight dollars a week in a terrible job in a carpet factory. They used to clean rugs, and your father's hands were always in strong chemicals. You know how funny some of his fingernails are? It was from that factory. He came home one night and he was looking at his fingers, and he started saying that he didn't come to this country to lose his hands. He wanted to hold a bat and play ball and he wanted to work—but he didn't want to lose his hands. So he quit the job and went to a restaurant for less pay. With me out of work, a new apartment and therefore higher rent, we couldn't manage. Your father was furious when I mentioned home relief. He said he would rather starve than go on relief. But I went and filled out the papers and answered all the questions and swallowed my pride when they treated me like an intruder. I used to say to them, 'Find me a job—get my husband a better job—we don't want home relief.' But we had to take it. And all that mess with the stamps in exchange for food. And they used to have weekly 'specials' sort of—but a lot of things were useless—because they were American food. I don't remember if we went once a week or once every two weeks. You were so small I don't know how you remember that place and the long lines. It didn't last long because your father had everybody trying to find him a better job and finally somebody did. Pretty soon I went into the WPA and thank God, we never had to deal with those people again. I don't know how you remember that place, but I wish you didn't. I wish I could forget that home relief thing myself. It was the worst time for your father and me. He still hates it."

(He still hates it and so do many people. The expression, "I'd rather starve than go on welfare" is common in the Puerto Rican community. This characteristic pride is well chronicled throughout Spanish literature. For example, one episode of *Lazarillo del Tormes*, the sixteenth-century picaresque novel, tells of a squire who struts around all day with his shiny sword and pressed cape. At night the squire takes food from the boy, Lazarillo—who has begged or stolen it—explaining that it is not proper for a squire to beg or steal, or even to work! Without Lazarillo to feed him, the squire would probably starve.)

"You don't know how hard it was being married to your father then. He was young and very strong and very active and he wanted to work. Welfare deeply disturbed him, and I was afraid that he would actually get very violent if an investigator came to the house. They had a terrible way with people, like throwing that cabbage, that was the way they gave you everything, the way we used to throw the kitchen slop to the pigs in Puerto Rico. Some giving! Your father was, is, *muy macho*, and I used to worry if anybody says anything or gives him that why-do-you-people-come-here-to-ruin-things look he'll be in jail for thirty years. He almost got arrested once when you were just a baby. We went to a hospital clinic—I don't remember now if it was Sydenham or Harlem Hospital—you had a swelling around your throat—and the doctor told me, 'Put on cold compresses.' I said I did that and it didn't help. The doctor said, 'Then put hot compresses.' Your father blew up. In his broken English, he asked the doctor to do that to his mother, and then invited him to transfer over to the stable on 104th Street. 'You do better with horses—maybe they don't care what kind of compresses they get.'

"One morning your father tells me, 'I got a new job. I start today driving a truck delivering soft drinks.' That night I ask him about the job—he says, 'I quit—bunch of Mafia—I went to the first four places on my list and each storeowner said, "I didn't order any soda." So I got the idea real fast. The Mafia was going to leave soda in each place and then make the guys buy from them only. As soon as I figured it out, I took the truck back, left it parked where I got it, and didn't even say good-bye.' The restaurant took him back. They liked him. The chef used to give him eggs and meats; it was very important to us. Your father never could keep still (still can't), so he was loved wherever he worked. I feel sorry for people on welfare—forget about the cabbage—I never should have taken you there."

Pity was not a universal emotion provoked by welfare recipients in Harlem—East Harlem—residents. One old man on whom I used to gingerly test my developing notions despised welfare and people on it. Don Pedro had pure white hair, his back was rounded into a slight hump, and he was not very tall—at sixteen I was taller than he. He had come to America looking for something he did not find. He was bitter about people who did not work, and he did not work. He was for me the local wise man, historian of Harlem and American commentator, willing to discuss anything with me—so long as I remembered my place—*los niños hablan cuando las gallinas mean* (the Puerto Rican version of children should be seen and not heard, literally, "children speak when chickens urinate"). That small saw quickly ended conversations, for it indicated annoyance— and I was taught never to be disrespectful in any way to an elder.

Don Pedro never said whether he had been on welfare, but everything about it was mind-bending for him. His pride would have prohibited him from accepting welfare, and if life had been cruel enough to force him to it, his pride would have kept him from such an admission. He was the contemporary starving squire. And the racist and conservative arguments that I came to hear as an adult from White America, I first heard as a teenager from Don Pedro. "Lazy bastards. I see them every day playing dominoes, drinking beer. Late in the afternoons going off to buy parts for their cars. Healthy as me. Have two or three women pregnant, children running around like savages, no discipline, no education [meaning in Spanish not school, but manners and morals]. And the other ones, you think they like to answer so many questions? You think they like to buy on credit, wait for checks? Why shouldn't they have a TV? What government has the right to tell me I can't give a person a TV as a gift? [Welfare families were not allowed to buy or receive as gifts TV sets. On the day the investigator was due, the tenements were like a scene from a Beatles movie—many doors open—out come people with TVs, carrying them all into one door. End of day back go people with their TV sets.] And what about those investigators? Where do they find people who take such jobs? They don't ask so many questions if you work out an 'agreement.' A few bucks from your miserable check to them every month and they won't look under the bed. Bastards! But they all deserve what they get. You know what—I have more respect for a thief than any of them. A thief has—well I don't mean I would be a thief—I mean if it came to welfare or stealing—I'd steal. I'd steal before I would become an investigator, let alone a client."

And welfare was not the only thing Don Pedro was turned off on. He didn't believe in voting. "Fixed, the whole thing is fixed. First they decide who they want for anything. Take the judges. All of a sudden you have a bunch of names for a judge. Their names on all the parties. Well hell, if the guy is both a Republican and a Democrat, what's the sense of voting? He is an automatic winner! Then, I've seen them take the machines and turn them around. Or else somebody conveniently forgets to turn the little key, so no votes register. Or else they get you on technicalities. You changed your address. You gotta take the literacy test again. You can't vote—you got two last names. [In Puerto Rico, children assume the father's surname followed by a hyphen and then the mother's maiden name, but this causes so much confusion in New York that most Puerto Ricans eventually drop the usage.] Then they get you the other way. You sit and read about the candidates and what they stand for. You go down and vote for what you think is right. Meanwhile they take a truck up to the Bowery and pick up fifteen or twenty guys, tell them how to vote, and then give 'em a pint of whiskey for their troubles. I've seen them buy a whole family with a bag of groceries, and I've seen dead men vote, if you know what I mean."

If there was one thing that Don Pedro believed about America, it was that it was a thoroughly corrupt nation. There was not one bureaucracy, not one establishment that he dealt with, that didn't have somebody on the make. The problem for the poor, he said, "is that they didn't have any money to bribe people."

"You know how many jobs, how many apartments I lost because I couldn't fix somebody? Some goddamned Irish could go to a super and give him twenty-five dollars for an apartment, but if you were Puerto Rican you had to give fifty dollars for the same apartment."

Why shouldn't I believe him? By sixteen I had my own collection of anecdotes supporting discrimination. Police telling me to "move on" for no reason, to get off the stoop of the building where I lived, being called fag and spic, stopped and searched on the streets, in hallways, in candy stores, and anywhere that we congregated. Called fag because in a time of crew cuts the Puerto Rican male took pride in his long hair. With the postwar movies of American heroes in Germany, Gestapo and Nazi were familiar figures, and for me they were our police. Who could you complain to about police? Hitler?

In school, Mr. Miller, goddamn him to hell forever, took a Puerto Rican boy named Luis and kept him under the teacher's desk during class periods. When Luis would moan, Miller would kick him. Between periods, Miller walked Luis around the school, keeping him in a painful armlock. Mr. Flax, the principal, laughed. And Diamond, the algebra teacher, either sent us to play basketball or asked us to lay our heads on our desks while he checked the stock market reports in the *New York Times*. To whom did you complain about a teacher—a laughing principal?

But in the process of discrimination, different attitudes are produced. Don Pedro, prejudged in housing, employment, and health services, hated the Puerto Ricans who made slums, the Puerto Ricans who would not work, the Puerto Ricans who did not respect the Gestapo. And he hated Luis under the desk as much as Mr. Miller. And when I tried to tell Don Pedro, "Baby, who you really hate is you," he would say, "When chickens urinate."

My father and I are walking through East Harlem, south down Lexington from 112th toward 110th, in 1952. Saturday in late spring, I am eighteen years old, sun brilliant on the streets, people running back and forth on household errands. My father is telling me a story about how back in nineteen thirty something, we were very poor and Con Ed light meters were in every apartment. "The Puerto Ricans, maybe everybody else, would hook up a shunt wire around the meter, specially in the evenings when the use was heavy—that way you didn't pay for all the electric you used. We called it '*pillo*' (thief)."

We arrive at 110th Street and all the cart vendors are there peddling plantains, avocados, yams, various subtropical roots. I make a casual remark about how foolish it all seemed, and my father catches that I am looking down on them. "Are they stealing?" he asks. "Are they selling people colored water? Aren't they working honestly? Are they any different from a bank president? Aren't they hung like you and me? They are *machos*, and to be respected. Don't let college go to your head. You think a Ph.D. is automatically better than a peddler? Remember where you come from—poor people. I mopped floors for people and I wasn't ashamed, but I never let them look down on me. Don't you look down on anybody."

We walk for a way in silence, I am mortified, but he is not angry. "One day I decide to play a joke on your mother. I come home a little early and knock. When she says 'Who?' I say 'Edison man.' Well, there is this long silence and then a scream. I open the door and run in. Your mother's on a chair, in tears, her right arm black from pinky to elbow. She ran to take the *pillo* out, but in her nervousness she got a very slight shock, the black from the spark. She never has forgiven me. After that, I always thought through my jokes."

We walk some more and he says, "I'll tell you another story. This one on me. I was twenty-five years old and was married to your mother. I took her down to Puerto Rico to meet Papa and Mama. We were sitting in the living room, and I remember it like it happened this morning. The room had rattan furniture very popular in that time. Papa had climbed in rank back to captain and had a new house. The living room had double doors which opened onto a large *balcon*. At the other end of the room you could see the dining table with a beautiful white handmade needlework cloth. We were sitting and talking and I took out a cigarette. I was smoking Chesterfields then. No sooner had I lit up than Papa got up, came over, and smacked me in the face. 'You haven't received my permission to smoke,' he said. Can you imagine how I felt?" So my father dealt with his love for me through lateral actions: building bookcases, and through tales of how he got his wounds, he anointed mine.

What is a migration? What does it happen to? Why are the Eskimos still dark after living in that snow all these centuries? Why don't they have a word for snow?

What things are around me with such high saturation that I have not named them? What is a migration? If you rob my purse, are you really a fool? Can a poor boy really be president? In America? Of anything? If he is not white? Should one man's achieve-ment fulfill one million people? Will you let us come near your new machine: after all, there is no more ditch digging? What is a migration? What does it happen to?

The most closely watched migrants of this world are birds. Birds migrate because they get bored singing in the same place to the same people. And they see that the environment gets hostile. Men move for the same reasons. When a Puerto Rican comes to America, he comes looking for a job. He takes the cold as one of a negative series of givens. The mad hustle, the filthy city, filthy air, filthy housing, sardine transportation, are in the series. He knows life will be tough and dangerous. But he thinks he can make a buck. And in his mind, there is only one tableau: himself retired, owner of his home in Puerto Rico, chickens cackling in the back yard.

It startles me still, though it has been five years since my parents went back to the island. I never believed them. My father, driving around New York for the Housing Authority, knowing more streets in more boroughs than I do, and my mother, curious in her later years about museums and theaters, and reading my books as fast as I would put them down, then giving me cryptic reviews. Salinger is really silly (*Catcher in the Rye*), but entertaining. That evil man deserved to die (*Moby Dick*). He's too much (Dostoevski in *Crime and Punishment*). I read this when I was a little girl in school (*Hamlet* and *Macbeth*). It's too sad for me (*Cry, the Beloved Country*).

My father, intrigued by the thought of passing the foreman's exam, sitting down with a couple of arithmetic books, and teaching himself at age fifty-five to do work problems and mixture problems and fractions and decimals, and going into the civil service exam and scoring a seventy-four and waiting up one night for me to show me three poems he had written. These two cosmopolities, gladiators without skills or lan-guage, battling hostile environments and prejudiced people and systems, had graduated from Harlem to the Bronx, had risen into America's dream-cherished lower middle class, and then put it down for Puerto Rico after thirty plus years.

What is a migration, when is it not just a long visit?

I was born in Harlem, and I live downtown. And I am a migrant, for if a migration is anything, it is a state of mind. I have known those Eskimos who lived in America twenty and thirty years and never voted, never attended a community meeting, never filed a complaint against a landlord, never informed the police when they were robbed or swindled, or when their daughters were molested. Never appeared at the State or City Commission on Human Rights, never reported a business fraud, never, in other words, saw the snow.

And I am very much a migrant because I am still not quite at home in America. Always there are hills; on the other side—people inclined to throwing cabbages. I can-not "earn and return"—there is no position for me in my father's tableau.

However, I approach the future with optimism. Fewer Puerto Ricans like Eskimos, a larger number of leaders like myself, trained in the university, tempered in the ghetto, and with a vision of America moving from its unexecuted policy to a society open and clean, accessible to anyone.

Dick and Jane? They, too, were tripped by the society, and in our several ways, we are all still migrating.

Up on Manhattan's high ground, nearly 250,000 immigrants from the Dominican Republic are taking a stand. In the 1970s and 1980s, they built an enclave that once seemed as cohesive and as vibrant as any the city had ever produced. Their neighborhood, Washington Heights, at the northern neck of the island, was a world apart. While other parts of New York decayed and were abandoned, this hilltop remained crowded and pulsating with life. When the Dominicans could not find jobs, they invented new ones. When others would not hire them, they opened businesses of their own. Undaunted by the ethnic jockeying of New York City politics, they organized themselves and gained influence.

For a while, it seemed as if Washington Heights might serve the Dominicans as a point of transition into the American mainstream, but instead the barrio became a trap. Too many Dominicans came north thinking they would go back. Convinced they were just in New York for a sojourn, they neglected what the city was doing to their young. By the time they began to suffer regrets, their community had been corrupted and they had been painted as outsiders.

One Sunday afternoon when the sun came out after a long, cold spring rain, the towers of midtown a hundred blocks to the south glowed in the yellow light. In between and below, Harlem was lost in a mist. As soon as the weather broke, the Dominicans were in motion, like bees building a hive in crowded chaos.

A shopkeeper unfurled an awning on Broadway. He hauled out boxes of sweatshirts and blue jeans. Plastic trees holding baseball caps filled the vertical space. Then came balloons and a display of cheap toys packaged in bright primary colors. The storefront became an avalanche of merchandise cascading onto the sidewalk. As a final touch, the shopkeeper fired up a stereo, and a loudspeaker hanging over the doorway blared the sound of trumpets and conga drums.

On side streets lined with fine brownstones, little clusters of young men assumed their posts, eyeballing anyone who turned into their territory. Even as they kept watch, they took time for mock slap fights among themselves and to mutter unsubtle suggestions to a few girls who walked by in tight miniskirts. As a stranger, I attracted a different kind of attention. My steps would be accompanied by odd shouts, like *"Bajando"* ("Coming down") or *"Pajarito"* ("Little bird"). The guys on the corners would start it as soon as I entered one of these short, narrow crosstown blocks, and other young men sitting on stoops relayed the alert until all the lookouts were certain that it had been heard all up and down the block. Cocaine dealers don't like surprises, and they rule their streets like sovereign territory.

On Broadway and the other commercial avenues, people with overloaded shopping carts plied the sidewalks and accosted passersby. Anywhere else in Manhattan, they would have shouted the beggar's chant—"Spare change? Spare change?" In Washington Heights, the street people are peddlers and they cried, *"¿A peso! ¿A peso!"* ("For a dollar! For a dollar!") They were selling, rather than soliciting. Their wares included fruit drinks, sandwiches, baked goods, batteries, pinwheels, and other cheap toys, even underwear. Women sold cookies and sweet cakes from trays. Some men stood on corners with nothing but a big bag full of oranges and still they tried to get the attention of every passing car. Washington Heights is a barrio. People are poor, but they all work.

On a sidewalk in front of a bodega, two men set up a little table and a pair of folding chairs so they could play dominoes. Four boys began a basketball game beneath a milk crate tied onto a lamppost. Before the streets were even dry, there was a crush on the sidewalks of Broadway. Elsewhere in New York, the streets might be quiet on a rainy Sunday afternoon and people might fear being alone, but in Washington Heights, no one is ever alone and the streets are always crowded.

Since it was Sunday, there were meetings, because the Dominicans are organizers above all else. Sports leagues were meeting to plan the baseball season for their youth teams. A social club for immigrants from the city of Santiago gathered to plan a dinner dance that would raise money for the schools there. I chose to attend a gathering of gypsy-cab drivers who met in a little community center on Amsterdam Avenue. About twenty of them sat on metal folding chairs and talked about their problems. Soon I began hearing tales of how the fate of the whole neighborhood had always depended on the bold men who drove the streets of Manhattan.

The Dominicans first came to New York in the mid-1960s as whites were leaving, and that created opportunities. In neighborhoods like Washington Heights, apartments became vacant and rents dropped. The city was changing in other ways, as well. Crime became more fearsome than before. The yellow cabs, the only ones permitted to operate then, stopped driving anywhere but in the nice parts of Manhattan. Blacks, Puerto Ricans, and Dominicans started unlicensed car services where the yellows would not venture. It was often dangerous work, but for young immigrants, particularly if they were illegal or did not speak English, it was inviting. Eventually, there were so many unregulated cars that the city enacted new ordinances in the 1980s to bring the gypsy cabs under its control.

Dominicans came to dominate the business in northern Manhattan. With Washington Heights and other barrios growing wildly and with the city regaining some of its lost economic glitter, driving a gypsy cab got to be good business. The cars operated out of dispatch services often set up as cooperatives by the drivers. As they prospered, the cooperatives invested in restaurants, car-repair shops, and bodegas, sometimes operating enterprises both in New York and in the Dominican Republic. Men would go back and forth, driving a few months at a time in Manhattan to raise capital and then returning home to tend to family farms and businesses.

The drivers had gathered this Sunday afternoon because several of their colleagues had been shot in a spate of robberies. But the Dominicans did not just bemoan hard times in the city; they had plans to join forces so they could bargain with insurance companies for lower rates and lobby the city for better police protection. It seemed a fine example of a mature immigrant community organizing itself to deal constructively with American institutions. After a few minutes, the discussion turned away from the agenda and developed into an abstract debate on such issues as the differences between individual and corporate ownership of taxi dispatches and the proper role for independent drivers in collective arrangements. Speaking in earnest, bombastic tones, the men took turns addressing such questions in an almost-parliamentary fashion. After an hour, the meeting concluded, with no signs of progress on any practical matters.

Listening to their arguments, I was mystified and not a little bored. These men and the entire community had a lot at stake in the future of the gypsy cabs, and yet they had spent a Sunday afternoon wrangling like a bunch of college freshmen who had just read Marx for the first time.

When it was over, I went to one of the organizers of the event to get an explanation. Nelson Díaz, a veteran driver and dispatch manager, said ruefully, "It seems everything is frozen and nothing can be done until after the elections." In response to even greater puzzlement on my part, he explained that he was talking about upcoming elections in the Dominican Republic, not any in the United States. Díaz explained that each of the major speakers represented a Dominican political party or labor federation. Their ideological debate was a way of saying that no consensus ventures were possible until after the upcoming electoral campaign.

Díaz explained that his taxi cooperative was associated with the Partido Revolucionario Dominicano, the Dominican Revolutionary party, known, like all Dominican political parties, by its initials, PRD. He himself was best known around the barrio as "Camacho," the nom de guerre he had adopted as a young activist in the rough-and-tumble of Dominican politics. When I asked Camacho what role, if any, American political parties played in Washington Heights, he smiled under a graying thin mustache.

"The Republicans don't exist here," Camacho said, "and as for the Democrats, they are important, but almost every Dominican party is stronger. My party alone is much better organized in this community than any American party." Camacho proudly reported that in Washington Heights the PRD had fourteen precinct organizations, each of which collected dues and held monthly meetings. He personally headed the Frente de Taxistas–PRD, the taxi drivers' front of the PRD, which raised money, covered cars with campaign placards, and held rallies. Getting Dominicans to volunteer their time and open their wallets for a presidential campaign back home was easy, he said. A lifelong activist, he was proud of that. But he was more than a little perturbed that the partisanship was so intense that taxi drivers of different parties would refuse to work together even though their lives were at stake.

Active participation in home-country politics is a common trait in immigrant communities, and the involvement can continue for several generations. Some Americans send contributions to parties in the Northern Ireland conflict even though their ancestors crossed the Atlantic more than a century ago. Such a preoccupation becomes a problem only when communities remain so completely tied to the home country that it impedes engagement with the realities of life in the United States.

"Maybe one of the mental errors we have made is always keeping our minds focused on home," Camacho told me after his failure to organize the taxi drivers in New York. "That's because we are always thinking about going back. The first thing everybody does as soon as they make some money here is to buy a house back home and then a car. Dominicans don't buy houses here because they don't think they live here. In fact, they don't care if they live in a cheap little apartment here as long as they are building a nice big house back home. So when problems start developing here, even problems that affect their children or their own safety, they don't always pay attention, because they think, I'll be gone in another year. But then a year passes and they are still here and they have serious problems."

Among the Miami Cubans, an obsession with Castro undoubtedly isolated them even as it drove them to excel in their new land. Among the Dominicans in Washington Heights, preoccupations with the home country also provided the means and the motives for material success. But, unlike the Cubans, the Dominicans constantly traveled back home, so their links were real, not symbolic. The Dominican Republic was not their past, but very much part of their present, and they thought of their enclave as a transit zone where they could make quick profits and be gone. This proved to be a dangerous distraction when the United States treated them much more harshly than it did the Cubans. By the time the Dominicans realized that their future lay in Washington Heights, they were on the brink of losing all they had built.

Driving down Broadway, St. Nicholas Avenue, or one of the other shopping streets in Washington Heights, it looks like the Dominicans have done everything right.

There are restaurants, travel agencies, and bodegas on every block. Glittery little shops with phone booths lined up against the wall offer cut-rate calls to the Dominican Republic. This is a neighborhood with a lot of poverty and a high crime rate, but it still has movie theaters, florists, and toy stores. Here the only storefronts not open for business are the ones undergoing remodeling. People are out on the commercial streets late into the evening. On weekends, the restaurants are crowded. Most significant, the patrons, the personnel, and the owners of these establishments are all Dominicans and they are all neighbors.

By any measure, Washington Heights has avoided the economic losses and communal frustration that develops when the local retail sector is in the hands of outsiders. In New York, many African-American and Puerto Rican communities have felt drained and exploited by absentee merchants, first European ethnics and later Asians. Local residents turn wages and welfare checks over to the businessmen, and the merchants spend and invest the profits elsewhere.

Washington Heights represents a textbook example of how a successful enclave economy is built. The key is that money remains in the neighborhood and changes hands several times among residents. Even small businesses can develop an economic momentum of their own when the merchants live among their customers and form part of a coherent community. Money spent to buy food at one shop then gets spent to buy shoes at the store down the street, and then it goes to the travel agent and then back to the food store. Once this dynamic is under way, it draws new immigrants to the enclave because it creates job opportunities, and in turn the stream of new arrivals ensures that the enclave is an expanding market. That's the way it worked for many of the European ethnics when they established themselves in American cities, and that's the way it worked in Washington Heights until the early 1990s. The barrio built on itself.

Like Koreans and other Asians, the Dominicans effectively pooled resources among friends and family to create seed capital for new businesses. The same kinship networks provided a source of trusted employees. Newly arrived Dominicans would work in a relative's bodega for a while, learn the business, and eventually open one of their own. The bodega economy even took advantage of the community's deep and active links to the Dominican Republic. Having created a market for Dominican specialty goods in New York, the *bodegueros* established strong commercial relationships with suppliers back home.

The same system operated for more sophisticated businesses, such as travel agencies and money exchanges, as well as simpler ones, such as clothing stores, beauty salons, and laundries. Tightly knit networks of fellow immigrants operated in each sector of the retail trade, exchanging information, loaning one another capital, and forming clubs or associations that brought people together for social or political events. People relied on one another and could count on help. They fueled one another's success and magnified their overall accomplishments. The barrio developed institutions and a social structure of its own that gave the community a sense of permanence and texture even as it became more efficient as a port of entry for new arrivals. The Dominicans had seemed to become self-sufficient.

The barrio built on itself, but it also fed on itself. All the bright storefronts on Broadway were a sign of weaknesses as well as strength. All that entrepreneurship made for an efficient enclave, but it did not create a community.

"The business of the bodegas was to buy them cheap, get them going, and sell them in a year or so," said José Delio Martin, a prominent businessman and head of a merchants' association in Washington Heights. "One family would manage the place, two or three others would provide the capital, and with luck you could divide fifty thousand dollars when you sold it."

A dapper fellow sporting a brown fedora on a winter day, Delio Martin draws respectful greetings from most of the customers who enter the restaurant where he sits many mornings drinking thick black coffee from little cups. Rattling off addresses machine gun–style, Delio Martin lists all the bodegas he has owned in part or in whole since he came to New York in 1968, and then he pauses to remember a few more. He describes a fast-moving, quick-profit, high-turnover kind of business. By the early 1980s, the Dominicans had saturated Washington Heights with bodegas and had begun branching out to other Latino neighborhoods around the city. According to the most reliable estimates, a decade later the Dominicans owned more than twenty thousand small businesses in New York, including about 70 percent of the city's bodegas.

As he recounts the fabled growth of the Dominican business empire, there is a note of nostalgia in Delio Martin's voice. He is clearly talking about the past. "The problem is that it all comes to a stop when no one has the money to buy, and that's what's happening now," he said.

The Dominicans' vaunted economic enclave turned out to have been a highly speculative enterprise. Like stocks traded on Wall Street, the value of bodegas was based on what someone would pay to own them more than on the inherent profitability of the business. The *bodegueros* were brokers managing the capital funds accumulated by family networks. The restaurant tables became trading pits where shops were bought and sold for prices set by the market. It all depended on a steady influx of immigrants who would work in a relative's shop for a while, get to know the business, and then quickly become anxious to get a shop of their own. These newcomers created the demand that kept the price rising. The turnover was generated by people looking for short-term capital gains. This had a number of drawbacks.

Banks had little interest in financing this kind of activity, especially in a highly mobile immigrant community. So when family funds no longer sufficed, *bodegueros* often relied on loan sharks, and the hefty interest rates increased the pressure for quick profits. Some businessmen turned to neighborhood drug dealers, who had large supplies of ready money and needed ways to launder their cash.

In addition, the Dominicans overmilked the cow. Business owners cashed in their profits as soon as possible rather than making long-term investments in Washington Heights. Most sent the money back to the Dominican Republic, while those more committed to life in the United States bought homes in the suburbs and became absentee owners in their own community. By continually drawing money out of the enclave, they ensured that it would never make the quantum leap into real prosperity, even in good times. And because so much of the bodega economy was built on speculation, the bad times hit extra hard.

The 1990s brought a recession, the ongoing effects of economic restructuring, competition from other immigrant groups, and a near saturation of markets that had once offered easy pickings. As a result, the trade in bodegas came to a standstill, and the thousands of Dominicans who owned them struggled to protect their investments in an increasingly difficult environment.

Like the Puerto Ricans before them, many Dominicans lacked the skills to find work anywhere but in the low end of the manufacturing sector. They competed with the Puerto Ricans and took over certain job categories, such as garment pleaters. This proved to be just as much a dead end for the Dominicans, except they reached it faster. In 1980, about half of the New York City Dominican work-force held factory jobs, but after a decade of rapid decline in manufacturing, that was down to only a quarter. The result was unemployment rates higher than for any other major component of the city's population and average earnings that rose more slowly than anyone else's. For the *bodegueros* and all the other business owners in Washington Heights, that meant their main pool of clients had less and less spending power.

As New York again became a great port of entry for immigrants from all over the world, the Dominicans found themselves squeezed from all sides. Skilled newcomers from East Asia, Europe, Africa, India, and the West Indies competed for the better jobs sought by Dominicans. Meanwhile, an influx of low-skilled immigrants from China and Latin America made it harder to get entry-level jobs and kept wages down. Wherever Dominicans looked for new retail opportunities in the New York area, they encountered Koreans, Jamaicans, and other rivals who had set up effective self-help networks of their own.

The Dominicans had persevered on the economic front almost as model immigrants, embracing the American virtues of entrepreneurship, competition, and self-reliance, even as they were building a barrio with a multitude of civic organizations and self-help networks. By the late 1980s, twenty years after they had first landed in Washington Heights, the Dominicans were the largest immigrant group in the city and they should have been taking the first steps toward acceptance by the Anglo mainstream. But instead, the Dominicans got exclusion. The name Washington Heights became synonymous with cocaine. Dominicans became typecast as criminals. The NYPD became the chief representative of American society in the neighborhood, and conflict with the police came to signify the way the whole community related to the outside world.

"I can't compete anymore," said Angel, a tall, dark-skinned forty-year-old man standing beside an almost-empty refrigerated meat case in his bodega on St. Nicholas Avenue. "I used to get a whole tray of chicken parts and another of meat and sell them both every day, and now there is just this." He pointed to a single chicken that looked a bit too yellow and a coil of sausage sitting undesirably alone.

Angel's bodega is only about twelve feet wide and it is packed to the ceiling with dry goods, canned foods, and bins of yucca and plantains. Pots and pans hang from the rafters. Twenty-pound sacks of rice are stacked in the corner. The shelves behind the counter are loaded with fancy bottles of Florida Water, bay rum, and other toiletries favored by Dominicans.

Sales slips with names scrawled on them are taped up all over the back of a display case by the cash register, forming a ticker-tape cascade of IOUs. "My customers are very loyal, mostly from the apartment building next door, but I can't give anyone more than three dollars' credit anymore because I need the money to buy merchandise. I used to order from the wholesalers week by week, but now I have to buy almost day by day."

From his front door, Angel can see three other bodegas, along with a meat market and a small supermarket. "There are a lot of people in this neighborhood, more every day, it seems, but there are too many bodegas, too much competition, and so now more and more *bodegueros* are taking the easy way."

Supplementing grocery store sales by participating in the numbers game has been a way of life in New York since long before the Dominicans showed up, but now there is another easy way that is much more profitable. Police officials and community residents have long contended that some bodegas operate primarily as a means to launder drug money. No one, not even the neighborhood's most ardent defenders, disputes this fact. People simply disagree over how many are in on the game.

"When a *bodeguero* takes the easy way, he can also sell for less. He doesn't worry about his profit because the main thing is to keep money moving through the place. One guy like that, if he is close by, can ruin you."

A young man wearing a silk shirt walked into the bodega, looked around, bought a pack of cigarettes, and made a phone call. Angel stopped talking and ignored me the whole time the young man was in the store. He gave me a kind of "coast is clear" signal as soon as the visitor was gone. Looking toward the door and shaking his head contemptuously, he returned to our conversation.

"The worst thing here is that the authorities do not take control. The police know who is here and who is doing what. Do they think these guys can dress in silk and gold because they work for a living? Everybody sees them every day, and the police just drive by. When they do stop, it is just to bother ordinary people. So what are we supposed to think? That the police are stupid? Or are they *vendido* [sold out] to the drug traffickers?" Angel grew worried about what he had just said and pleaded that he not be identified in any way that could lead the dealers or the police to him. But then he continued.

"What we Dominicans are trying to build here in Washington Heights could be a very beautiful thing, but we could lose it all because, like in any family, there are some bad characters here. The way to save this community is to do what you would do in your own family—come in with *la mano dura* [the hard hand] and sweep all the evil away. They should come in here with soldiers, if the police will not do it, and say to these guys, 'You, you, and you—we know what you are doing with the *coca* and we are taking you away and you will never come back.'"

"If the Americans do not do this, it is because they do not want to, because they are perfectly happy to let people sell drugs right here on the streets of Manhattan."

Angel never mentioned the possibility that the Dominicans themselves might have been a little too happy to let the drug dealers thrive, and he certainly never suggested that they could do anything about cleaning up their own neighborhood. Most Latino immigrants, like many European immigrants of an earlier time, have come from countries where governments are powerful but arbitrary and where police agencies in particular are rightfully feared and yet assumed to be corrupt. In the United States, those attitudes can translate into a presumptive suspicion of American authorities. Combined with the nationalistic loyalties common to an immigrant enclave, the result is an inherent tolerance for misbehavior by fellow immigrants. To the newcomers, it might seem innocent at first; they see themselves as poor people surviving by getting around somebody else's rules, but the enclave breeds an acquiescence in the sins of fellow immigrants so dangerous that the newcomers do not realize what they have done to themselves until it is too late. Aside from the direct costs of living with criminality, an entire immigrant community can be stigmatized by the criminal behavior of a few. It happened to the Italians and the Irish. The twin perils of corruption and stigmatization are particularly grave for Latinos today because most illegal narcotics come to the United States from their countries and because the drug trade now spawns exceptional levels of violence, profits, and addiction.

To the casual observer, Jerry Giorgio would appear no more than a graying sixty-something businessman in a department store suit, maybe an accountant or an insurance adjuster, no doubt a harmless kind of guy. That would be a mistake. Giorgio has investigated homicides for the New York Police Department since 1972, mostly in upper Manhattan. He is also well known throughout the force for his skill as an interrogator, and he is legendary for his doggedness. He has repeatedly broken cases long given up as unsolvable by other detectives. He spent thirteen years piecing together clues in one murder before he finally made an arrest.

Giorgio is a proud man who is approaching the end of a long career. He is proud of his reputation, of the young detectives who have learned their craft by working with him, and of the satisfaction he has given victims' families. Nothing has frustrated him more than working among the Dominicans of Washington Heights.

"You get cases where a respectable, hardworking family man gets shot dead on a busy street in broad daylight, and when you go looking for witnesses, no one has seen anything, nada, zero. Here's a dead guy on the sidewalk, who was not involved in narcotics or anything criminal, and a dozen people must have seen what happened to him, but no one talks."

"You ask his family to put out the word. You ask them to tell people that they can make anonymous calls and that all they have to say is that the shooter was tall or short or anything. You wait for the calls, but nobody calls."

Giorgio insists that no other community is quite so hard to work in.

"I'll break ninety-eight percent of Harlem cases. You give me a Harlem case and I promise I'll get some people to give me something. It's not me. Any detective worth his salt can get some cooperation in Harlem. Up here, we get fifty percent of our cases, and I'll tell you, we sweat blood—we sweat blood to get them."

Giorgio has many explanations for this.

"There is a lot of distrust and I think a lot of it is based on their cultural background. There's a lot of corruption down there where they come from. When you tell these people you are a cop, they immediately think you are looking for money. These people feel or believe that cops sell cases, that they go after people who have got money, and it's very hard to talk them out of this because that is what they are used to back home."

Some of the problem, he says, is caused by the drug trade.

"There're a lot of people making money out there from cocaine, even if it is just kids working as lookouts. The money goes to families and lots of it gets shipped back to the Dominican Republic. You see all the money that is going around this community, and—come on—this is not being earned by the mechanic and the bodega owner. It doesn't take a genius to see that you got a lot of people up here with a stake in what's going on."

He concedes there is another side to it, as well.

"The other side is that our credibility stinks. We don't have a positive image out there, and who do I blame? I put the majority of the blame on the media. The media would much rather run with the story that a police officer brutalized a youngster than a positive story about how the police have done a good job for the community."

Giorgio returned to the terrible suspicion that the Dominicans harbor of the police.

"There's this impression that we allow the drug trade to flourish. Well, the public doesn't know the restrictions we operate under. We can't go up to anyone and search him. We can, but it will be a bad search, and it will leave you open to lawsuits. And these people have learned about that already. God forbid you make one false step out there, even half a false step; they will sue the jock off you. The frustration level is unreal up here, unbelievable."

Amid all the indecipherable scrawls, all the goofy, loopy script spray-painted on walls, doorways, and even sidewalks, there is a kind of graffiti in Washington Heights that struggles to convey real human feelings. An eerily rendered outline of a sprawled body is neatly painted on the sidewalk outside the entranceway to a charcoal gray apartment building on Amsterdam. Alongside it in block letters is the inscription RIP—WASTED I LOVE YOU. The side of a building just off Broadway is decorated with a painting of a huge mauve tombstone remembering a man named Pepe. All around it, overblown signatures form a giant sympathy card. These are memorials to victims of a crossfire that bloodied the streets of every major American city when two distinct and unrelated events overlapped in the 1980s: the arrival of Latino immigrants and the arrival of crack.

During the worst years of the crack epidemic—1985 to 1990—the number of murders in New York rose by a horrifying 63 percent, but in the northern Manhattan precinct that encompasses Washington Heights, there was an increase of 115 percent. And, similarly, the number of felonious assaults and total arrests rose more than twice as fast in the Dominican enclave as in the city overall.

Because they came from the south, because they kept up a heavy regular traffic of people, goods, and money to the Caribbean, because they speak Spanish, because they came from a clannish society streaked with corruption, because they are foreigners, a very specific and very lucrative niche in New York's vast drug trade opened up to Dominican criminals. Washington Heights became a major wholesale distribution point for raw cocaine. Geography played a major role, according to the police. The George Washington Bridge soars up from the very heart of the neighborhood and crosses the Hudson River to New Jersey. That means it is just minutes from an apartment house on 157th Street to Interstate 95, the main north-south highway artery on the East Coast. The riverside highways that run along the east and the west sides of Manhattan end up in Washington Heights. And bridges spanning the East River connect the neighborhood to the Bronx and from there to other boroughs.

"It is a crossroads community," said Sgt. John McDonnell, who was assigned to an antidrug task force working upper Manhattan. "No matter who lived up there, it would be a logical place to set up this kind of operation. Buyers from all over can just pop across a bridge, get the stuff, and be gone in minutes."

While Colombian organizations handled the importing, Dominican gangs acted as the wholesale vendors, selling several ounces of cocaine at a time to retailers who then cooked it into rocks of crack. A handful of successful prosecutions showed that Dominicans were no less entrepreneurial about the drug trade than they were with grocery stores. Rather than create a few large criminal organizations as Italian immigrants had done a generation earlier, the Dominican drug dealers in Washington Heights formed many small partnerships that usually operated out of several apartments in a single building. Each operation had a platoon of lookouts, others who guarded the cash and the coke, and still other young men who acted as intermediaries between the buyers and the person who actually held the coke. An abundance of foot soldiers thoroughly insulated the dealers from rip-offs and from the police.

With their big payrolls, the dealers could also hope to win some loyalty on the streets. They certainly made little effort to disguise their presence. Dom Pérignon champagne became a much requested item in restaurants where the usual specialties were curried goat and chicken with rice. Young men streaked around the traffic in shiny new European sedans or big four-wheel-drive sport utility vehicles while the rest of the neighborhood plodded along in rusty clunkers.

Members of one cocaine operation became so brazen that they all got the same kind of hair treatment and became known as the Jheri-Curl Gang. The fact that their permanents made them easier for the police to spot did not seem to worry them. With their black hair still in tight, shiny ringlets, five young men accused of being the top members of the gang were sentenced in April 1993 to jail terms ranging from sixteen years to life. Along with these five, who were convicted of running the cocaine operation, several dozen other Dominicans drew jail terms for working as salesmen, lookouts, and couriers.

Eventually, the Dominican dealers became somewhat more discreet. Once they established their hegemony, the level of violence associated with the drug trade dropped precipitously, as reflected in New York's declining murder rates in the mid-1990s. The Dominican drug dealers and their Colombian suppliers then branched out to a new product: highly potent, smokable heroin, which appealed not only to crack addicts and users of injectable heroin but also to white middle-class kids who found it fit their grungy sense of fashion. In 1996, the Drug Enforcement Administration declared that the same Dominican-Colombian connection that controlled the New York crack market also dominated heroin sales in the city and had successfully branched out to New England. The product changed, the market evolved, and the jails filled, but the steady flow of new arrivals meant that the same basic dynamic was always at work within the immigrant enclave.

"There are just a lot of kids who come up here with the idea that they are going to get jobs and make money, and the easiest work to find, often the only work they can find, is to sign up with the dealers," said Sergeant McDonnell. "You pick these kids up, and they don't know what's going on with the law. It's not like with black and Puerto Rican kids who know the street and who know what kind of risks they're taking. These Dominican kids are just set up to do the grunt work, and they are told not to worry about the law."

There is a broad, flat wall near the corner of 162nd Street and Amsterdam Avenue that lends itself to expansive graffiti expressions. For several years, it bore a crudely painted triptych. Hands folded in prayer filled one side and a heart topped with flames decorated the other side panel. In the center lay an open book, like a Bible, with the name Kiko emblazoned across it. And above in large faux-Gothic script was the legend TE RECORDAMOS (We remember you).

Dominicans and the police alike do indeed remember Jose "Kiko" Garcia, but they have very different recollections of who he was and how he died the night of July 3, 1992. Everyone does agree, however, that the events that followed proved a turning point for Washington Heights and for New York City. The Dominicans of Washington Heights found a new way to assert their identity as immigrants, then discovered how little that would get them.

According to the police version of the events that rainy July night, Officer Michael O'Keefe was on a plainclothes anticrime patrol when he saw a bulge in Kiko's jacket, which suggested to the officer that the twenty-three-year-old man was carrying a gun. O'Keefe approached him. There was a scuffle. Kiko fled into the lobby of an apartment building, where he pulled a gun, later found on his body. The cop shot him twice in self-defense. Accepting this account, a grand jury declined to bring any charges against O'Keefe.

According to the Dominican version, O'Keefe was a marauding cop who, like many other policemen in Washington Heights, spent more time hassling people on the street than he did busting drug cases. Witnesses claimed that O'Keefe beat Kiko and shot him needlessly. Alleging that the gun had been planted on Kiko, they noted that no fingerprints were found on the weapon.

For the police and much of the news media, Kiko was a "low-level drug dealer." He had come to the United States illegally at the age of nineteen and within a year had been caught with a small quantity of cocaine. That encounter with the law led to nothing more than a guilty plea on a charge of personal possession and a five-year suspended sentence. No effort was made to deport him.

For many Dominicans, he was another young man who had come to the United States with few prospects and had done what was necessary to get along. If he had an association with drug dealers, it could not have been too lucrative, they said, because he lived in a run-down one-bedroom apartment with his mother and at least four other relatives.

These conflicting realities provided the spark for five days of violent disturbances in which one man was killed and dozens were injured. Although the crowds that rushed into the street after Kiko's death set several cars and at least one building on fire, the looting, burning, and gunfire were quite limited compared with riots elsewhere. In one sense, it was just another spontaneous urban riot sparked by a police shooting. But it was also a moment of collective protest that involved many different sorts of people in an organized effort to express their anger and frustration.

Unlike almost any other riot, community leaders were out in the streets from the beginning, trying to direct the crowds into peaceful protests against the police. People from the Dominican political parties, prominent figures from the amateur baseball leagues and fraternal organizations, social workers, and ministers all put on yellow ribbons and went into the street as umpires, often positioning themselves between angry crowds and police in riot gear. They had walkie-talkies, command centers, and endless meetings. The goal was to let people, especially the young people, vent their frustration without losing control of the streets. While the effort did not entirely prevent violence, the neighborhood never fully exploded into all-out rioting.

Foreigners together in a strange land seek one another out on the basis of kinship, business interests, home-country political allegiances, and much else. That is the nature of the immigrant experience. At their best, barrios develop these connections into a rich civil society that provides structure and leadership. Washington Heights was highly organized, and so it did not blow up when all the ingredients for an explosion were present. In this regard, the disturbances following Kiko's death are a measure of how much the Dominicans had accomplished during their time in Washington Heights. However, all these relationships pointed inward, and the real test of an immigrant community lies in whether these internal structures allow it to gain a positive relationship with American institutions and with society as a whole. The Dominicans never got a chance to find out.

Instinctively defensive when faced with accusations of brutality, the police drew sharp battle lines. They insisted that anyone who criticized them was endorsing the criminality of crack dealers. When Mayor David Dinkins tried to avert further violence by visiting Kiko's grieving family, the Patrolmen's Benevolent Association took out a full-page newspaper advertisement saying the mayor had "callously ignored the traumatic plight of the police officer involved and managed to transform a drug villain into a martyr." The Dominican leaders who tried to contain the violence were even easier marks. The PBA said their efforts merely "served to exacerbate the rioting, looting and burning, as misguided individuals and street punks rallied around a convoluted cause."

The Democratic National Convention was about to open at Madison Square Garden that July when the disturbances provided a fresh peg for the obligatory "rotten apple" stories about New York's dark side. Both the local and national media rolled out vivid accounts of the drug trade in Washington Heights, making it seem that everyone in the neighborhood had sold out to the "Dominican drug cartels." The Dominicans, who had attracted little notice in all the years they had been building their enclave, instantly became larger-than-life tabloid fiends.

And yet the Dominicans acted as accomplices in their own demonization. No one could dispute the fact that drug money had penetrated legitimate businesses in the neighborhood, just as it does everywhere there is a drug trade. The Treasury

Department announced a crackdown on wire transfers of cash to the Dominican Republic in 1997 after looking at just fifteen money transfer companies in the New York area and discovering that they were sending more than half a billion dollars a year to the Dominican Republic. More than a fifth of the cash came from the proceeds of drug sales, the Treasury said. As blatant as the dealers had become, most of the prominent Dominican spokesmen refused to condemn them explicitly. The whole barrio turned out to march in protest against alleged brutality by the NYPD, but there had never been that kind of public outrage expressed against the drug dealers, whose brutality was indisputable and undisguised. For the people of the barrio, the police were outsiders. The dealers were not.

Proving themselves just as defensive as the police, prominent Dominicans argued that American realities were at fault for fomenting drug usage and permitting large-scale trafficking. It was the same gambit for disavowing responsibility used often by government leaders in Latin America: Get your own people to stop using the stuff before you come bothering us. The Dominicans insisted on collective innocence despite the evidence of guilt all around the neighborhood.

"This is not a Dominican phenomenon. You could put the Irish here and the same thing would happen," said Moises Perez, the head of the largest community service organization in Washington Heights, the Alianza Dominicana.

Defense of the enclave became a patriotic matter, as if defense of the homeland was at stake. For example, Delio Martin, the head of the merchants' association and no rabble-rouser, said, "We did not go to the streets in defense of Kiko, one boy that no one knew. We did it in defense of our homes. We did it not just because of that one act of aggression but to stop all the abuses against our community by all sectors of power."

As in many African-American communities subdued by caravans of squad cars and long lines of mounted officers, the police were seen as an invading power. In Washington Heights, this took on a peculiarly Dominican flavor when the immigrants, like generations of their forefathers at home, protested that they had fallen victim to *yanqui* intervention once more. And the perception of an external threat solidified and energized the Dominicans' identity as a people detached from the American mainstream, just as it did for the L.A. barrio kids marching to protest Proposition 187 under Mexican flags.

Utilizing imported habits of mind and inherited rhetoric, the Dominicans stood up for the barrio they had constructed here. They defended a territorial reality, not an abstract demand for equal justice. Even though a strong element of national pride permeated their rhetoric, they did not pursue grievances on behalf of all Dominicans, just for the Dominicans of Washington Heights.

When some of New York's activist gadflies showed up in the neighborhood and tried to tell the Dominicans that they were "oppressed people" and that they should struggle in solidarity with other "people of color," they were told to go home. The Dominicans never tried to make some broader ethnic claim. They never alleged that they had been victimized because they were Latinos. Indeed, they did not seek and did not receive notable support from the Puerto Ricans or from other Latinos. The people of Washington Heights did not behave like an American minority group. When the Dominicans complained of police abuses, they did not cite events two hundred years old and they did not claim to be victims of some larger evil that infected the whole of the United States. They spoke only about what had happened to them since they had come to New York. They strutted around proud and defensive but not on behalf of an ethnic or political cause. They had built a barrio with considerable enterprise, and they wanted it respected.

But Washington Heights, like many other barrios, was not built as a place where newcomers could start the process of becoming Americans. Instead, the purpose was to allow its inhabitants to become transnationals or simply to remain Dominicans. Both the immigrants and the nation that hosted them seemed happy to let things go that way, and the easy travel home that characterizes Latino immigration prolonged the condition. The Dominicans of Washington Heights, perpetual in-betweens, left themselves vulnerable to the worst of two nations.

Kiko Garcia's death and the Washington Heights disturbances added to tensions that had been developing between the police force and Mayor Dinkins almost since the start of his administration. The cops had berated him for not allowing them to carry semiautomatic pistols. They had complained about his appointment of a commission to investigate police corruption, and they had vehemently rejected his plan to create a civilian review board that would investigate charges of police brutality and other forms of misconduct. Then Dinkins's expressions of sympathy for Kiko's family and his other efforts to calm the Dominicans in Washington Heights were taken as acts of outright hostility by the police rank and file.

Six weeks after Kiko's death and a few days after Officer O'Keefe was exonerated in the slaying, the Patrolmen's Benevolent Association organized a protest rally and march at City Hall. Rudolph Giuliani gladly agreed to appear as a featured speaker. He had never really stopped running against Dinkins following his narrow defeat in 1989 and now as he prepared to challenge Dinkins in 1993, the former prosecutor was taking every opportunity to decry the mayor as weak on crime.

Less than half an hour after the rally began on the morning of September 16, 1992, thousands of cops swarmed across barricades and took over the steps of City Hall. Giuliani made his way to the chaotic rally, found a soapbox, and whipped up the crowd, estimated to number ten thousand police officers and supporters. He sarcastically derided Dinkins's police policies as "bullshit," setting a tone that then reverberated for hours. The crowd repeatedly referred to the mayor as a "nigger." There were chants of "The mayor's on crack" and "Dump the Dink." A senior uniformed police officer was booed down when he appealed for order. Police officers poured into nearby bars and drank openly on the street during the speeches.

According to a *New York Times* account of the event, "The greatest applause was reserved for Officer O'Keefe, who called the aftermath of the Washington Heights disturbance 'a personal attack on you.' Facing his protesting colleagues, he said, 'We are a force. We will be a force for good.'" Eventually, more than a thousand of the police protesters moved to the entrance and exit ramps of the Brooklyn Bridge and blocked all traffic in a raucous act of civil disobedience, which on-duty police officers did little to impede. Acting Police Commissioner Raymond W. Kelly issued an interim report on the incident twelve days later, describing the actions of the police officers as "unruly, mean-spirited and perhaps criminal."

It did not really matter that the official inquiries found the police at fault. At a time when uncompromising toughness with criminals was becoming a hallmark of American politics, the Dominicans had decidedly ended up on the wrong side of that issue. Having winked at the drug traffic when it was taking over their streets, and having brawled with the NYPD, they were extremely vulnerable. Just how much so was evident during a small but bloody episode shortly before the 1993 mayoral elections.

For years, the police had run regular tow-truck raids on Washington Heights to clear narrow streets that often became parking lots, especially around gypsy cab dispatch offices. One such sweep was under way when a man tried to stop a tow truck from hauling a gypsy cab off 175th Street. A crowd gathered. Police swarmed in. A melee erupted, and in the midst of it, Officer John Williamson was struck in the head by a bucket half-filled with hardened spackling compound that had been thrown off a rooftop. As he crumpled, blood pouring from his fatally smashed skull, some people cheered, according to press accounts.

Dinkins suspended the towing operation the next day to let both the police and the Dominicans cool off. Giuliani issued a statement with a very telling use of buzzwords: "This sends a message that the city has given in to urban terrorists and that if you want to get your way, kill a police officer and cheer about it."

A few weeks later, Giuliani narrowly defeated Dinkins and was elected mayor of New York. In a close, hard-fought campaign, he resorted to one of the very oldest gambits in American politics by demonizing recently arrived immigrants as a threat to public safety. The difference is that when Latinos are made scapegoats now in harsh media-driven campaigns like the one in New York in 1993 or in California a year later, the stigma is darker and deeper than when the French were the victims in the 1790s or the Irish in the 1890s. In American cities at the end of the twentieth century, a community that is marked for exclusion once has a hard time ever winning acceptance again. As mayor, Giuliani extolled the benefits immigration brought to New York, but the taint he had helped apply remained indelible. When Abner Louima, a Haitian immigrant, was allegedly beaten by New York police officers inside a Brooklyn station house in August 1997, he initially claimed to have heard something that stuck in his mind. As a toilet plunger handle was rammed into his rectum, causing critical injuries,

Louima recalled, one of his assailants saying, "This is Giuliani time, not Dinkins time." Although it was immediately disputed, the statement acquired a notoriety that revealed widespread fears and biases.

Census data shows that during the 1980s the Dominican population of New York rose 165 percent, to nearly 333,000 people, making Dominicans the fastest-growing major ethnic group in the city; estimates show the growth rate accelerating in the 1990s due to a baby boom among the Dominicans in New York. As a result of this population explosion, every public facility in Washington Heights, from the subway stations to the kindergartens, was overcrowded. Parks, clinics, and police precinct houses operated far beyond their capacities because the Dominicans had crammed more people, especially young people, into the neighborhood than any previous residents. A school district designed for 14,000 students was trying to handle 25,000. George Washington High School had so many students that they had to arrive in three shifts.

Immigration has touched off many different kinds of fears among Americans in this decade, and the backlash has generated many new forms of exclusion. The kind of exclusion the Dominicans experienced was not racial or ethnic, as it was with blacks or the Mexican-Americans of South Texas. Rather, it was derived from a series of specific markers. The Dominicans of Washington Heights were dark-skinned people, poor but entrepreneurial. They were immigrants. They were people who flouted the law and American ways by entering the country illegally. They were corrupt foreigners who fed the American appetite for narcotics. The accumulation of these traits constituted an identity much narrower than broad categories derived from skin color or economic class. At a time of increased immigration, exclusion can be targeted to specific people in a specific place. To have been Irish from South Boston or Polish from the northwest side of Chicago carried a very particular meaning that did not extend to others of the same national origins even in the same city. The demonizing that occurred in New York applied only to the Dominicans of Washington Heights, not to all Dominicans, and certainly not to all Latinos.

Because the ostracism was circumscribed, it could be escaped. A sizable number of successful business owners and professionals left the neighborhood for multinational barrios in Queens, where they could be Dominicans without the cocaine stigma of Washington Heights. Others left for the suburbs, where they could be anything they wanted. The smart kids who went away to college never came back. Once they left Washington Heights, no one called them urban terrorists.

When exclusion can be escaped so readily by those who are resourceful, it becomes powerfully self-reinforcing. As the upwardly mobile depart to negotiate their own private arrangements with the white mainstream, a barrio is left to serve as a port of entry for new arrivals and as a warehouse for those who are too poor, too corrupt, or too old to move on. Many, perhaps most, Dominicans will escape stigma by moving out of Washington Heights and becoming productive, law-abiding members of the middle class, and their residual ethnic identity will fade with each successive generation. But up on that hill in Manhattan, there will be other Dominicans who will remain perpetually poor and who will be perceived as darkly foreign. Over time, their isolation and their numbers are likely to grow. The benefits that American society draws from the success stories may outweigh the costs associated with the poor, but it is the urban hot spots that will grab all the attention, generate anxiety, and perpetuate prejudice. That is the case with blacks now and there is no reason for it to be different with Latinos.

The Dominicans failed to build institutions that could effectively advance their interests here. They bear a good deal of blame for what happened to them, and many of them have accepted that. So it came as very little solace to them when many of their worst suspicions about the United States were proved right.

On July 6, 1994, two years after Kiko Garcia's death, a special investigative commission issued a final report, concluding that corruption was rampant in the NYPD. The Mollen Commission found that police officers were deeply implicated in the cocaine trade throughout the city. They practiced traditional corruption by protecting dealers in exchange for bribes, but also a large number of cops were found extorting drug dealers, stealing from them, and often reselling the drugs themselves. Some officers had become so involved with Washington Heights cocaine dealers that they had made several trips to the Dominican Republic.

A series of dramatic arrests occurred at the station house of the 30th Precinct, which covers the southern part of Washington Heights, including the territory that the Jheri-Curl Gang used to work. Crowds formed to cheer as police officers, five or six at a time, were led away from the station house in handcuffs. Eventually, so many cops were busted for taking part in the upper Manhattan cocaine trade that the precinct earned the nickname "the dirty Thirty."

Some of the Dominicans and some of their American neighbors had connected after all, but it was the dark angels on both sides who found one another. It was the classic process of assimilation, but in a downward cycle. The immigrant culture had combined with something it had found in the new land to create a new identity. The danger is that the same corrupting process, though on a less dramatic scale, could befall many in the second generation. They could learn to be poor and to be outcasts in America.

Despite all the difficulties encountered by the Dominicans of Washington Heights and all the troubles they have brought on themselves, their fate is hardly certain. During their first thirty years in the United States, they learned a great deal and they built a barrio with its own rich web of connections and institutions. If they ever take it upon themselves to combat the drug traffickers, if economic trends work in their favor, if the city halts the deterioration of services and infrastructure, if any or all of these things happen, the Dominicans of Washington Heights might yet find a way to incorporate themselves into the nation around them.

But for the most recently arrived immigrants, as we are about to see, there is less potential for a happy ending because they were struck by the political and economic whirlwinds of the 1990s before they had gotten their feet on the ground, before they had marked off a barrio or made any connections at all.

The HISPANIC IMPACT Upon the UNITED STATES

Theodore S. Beardsley Jr.

We often forget that the earliest European settlers in what is now the continental United States were not English but Spanish. As early as 1513 Florida was discovered and explored by Ponce de León, and in 1527 the first colony of Europeans was established by Panfilo de Narváez near present-day Pensacola. The colony failed, but a half-century later, in 1565, a permanent colony under Pedro Menéndez de Avilés founded our oldest American city, Saint Augustine, Florida. By this time various expeditions had been conducted by the Spaniards in the Southwest so that when the Pilgrims reached Plymouth Rock such Spanish centers as Saint Augustine in Florida or Santa Fé in New Mexico were already flourishing.

Today, Spanish is the second language of the United States, and it is estimated that as many as 20 million people in this country, almost ten percent of the population, speak primarily Spanish. At most, only half of that number can be considered immigrants of the first or second generation. Before one can discuss Hispanic immigration to the United States, the patterns of Hispanic colonization prior to the annexation of Spanish territories must be established.

The accompanying map shows the ultimate reaches of Spanish domain which peaked in 1762 with the acquisition of the Louisiana territory. Almost immediately thereafter, Spanish territory began to recede—in 1763 the Florida territory was ceded to the British. In 1800 the Louisiana territory was returned to the French who in 1803 agreed to one of the great real estate purchases in modern history by selling the entire territory to the United States. Had Spain been able to maintain that brief consolidation of land from Florida to California the history of this country would have been very different. In 1783 Spain regained control of part of the Florida territory but lost it again, and forever, in 1821. Little remains today in modern Florida of the days of Spanish rule except for the Castillo San Marcos and other monuments carefully preserved and restored in Saint Augustine. In New Orleans, the famous main square in the old French quarter is not really French at all. It was constructed by the Spaniards. However, the stronghold of the old Spanish traditions is the Southwest rather than the Southeast.

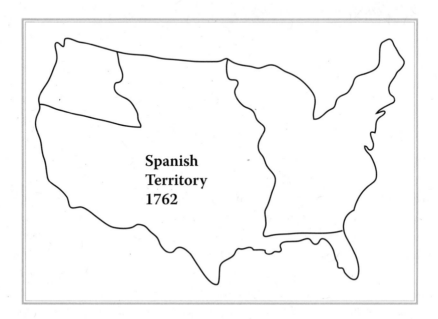

Spanish colonization of the Southwest spilled north from Mexico first in the arc of land extending from near present-day Tucson, Arizona, northeast to Santa Fé, New Mexico, and then southwest to San Antonio, Texas. Major settlements were usually located on rivers like the Río Grande, the Pecos, or the San Antonio. Colonial Spanish life centered around military presidios, missions, or major churches. The missions, it must be remembered, constituted far more than a church or a purely religious missionary effort, but rather an entire Christian community in which the Indians were taught farming and other related skills in an attempt to create an ideal society providing for the well-being of mind, body, and soul. The founding dates of the first Spanish communities in the Southwest are very early, for example: Santa Fé, New Mexico, 1610; San Bernardino Mission, Arizona, 1629; Nuestra Señora de Guadalupe de El Paso, Texas, 1659; Albuquerque, New Mexico, 1706; San Antonio, Texas with four separate missions, 1718.

The settlement of California came somewhat later. Monterey, the first capital, was founded in 1769 as a military presidio and only lost its role of supremacy when Sacramento became the capital of the California territory in 1854. The initial Spanish colonization of California is due primarily to the efforts of one extraordinary man, Fray

Junípero Serra, who became head of the missionary effort in California for the Franciscan order at the age of 56. During the following thirteen years, from 1769 to 1782, Serra personally founded nine of the major California missions starting with San Diego and including San Gabriel, San Luis Obispo, San Francisco, and San Juan Capistrano. In 1781, the Spanish governor of California established what was to become the state's largest city, now third in the entire nation: El Pueblo de Nuestra Señora la Reina de los Angeles.

Spanish Colorado, the southwestern part of the state, is a later extension by Santa Fé and Taos colonists who migrated north in the later eighteenth century in search of new farmlands. The Spanish cities of the area were not created until the mid-nineteenth century: Pueblo in 1842, San Luis in 1851, and Trinidad in 1877.

The Spanish history of Texas is perhaps the most colorful. The church community of Nuestra Señora de Guadalupe de El Paso had been founded in 1659. Throughout the rest of the century numerous missions were constructed throughout the state and in the area of San Antonio, founded in 1718, four major missions were in operation. The entire Southwest remained a part of colonial Spain as a dependency of the Mexican vice-royalty until 1821 when Mexican independence from Spain became certain. Texas was notably torn by intrigues and counter-intrigues, including the illegal entry of numbers of Anglos from the north. Finally in 1836 the Republic of Texas was born with Sam Houston elected as its first president in spite of the overwhelmingly Spanish population in the new nation. After nine years of continuing Mexican attacks, which have become famous in legend and film, Texas voted in 1845 to accept statehood in the union. The northern part of the state was rather quickly anglicized with the south remaining to this day heavily Spanish-speaking. The other areas, ceded to the United States by Mexico in 1846 and 1848, were increasingly slower in gaining statehood: California in 1850, Colorado in 1875, and Arizona and New Mexico in 1912. Those dates tend to reflect the concentration of Spanish-speaking inhabitants, who were naturally reluctant to come under the total control of a culturally different, foreign nation.

The most recently published estimates for the Spanish-speaking population of the United States indicate half of that population concentrated in five states: California (over 3 million), New York (2½ million), Texas (2½ million), Illinois (over 1 million), and Florida (almost 1 million).

It is not quite the same list, however, as that of the five most Hispanic states in terms of proportion: New Mexico (38.4%), Texas (22.3%), Arizona (21.2%), California (15.0%), and Colorado (12.5%).

For various reasons the official census figures for Spanish-speaking persons in the United States are notably imperfect. In the Southwest where almost half of the Spanish-speaking population is concentrated (perhaps as many as 10 million people), large numbers have never been included in the immigration statistics for the simple reason that their ancestors automatically became citizens upon the cession of the Spanish Southwest to the United States. Illegal entry from Mexico is also a fact of life in the Southwest. Such entries are naturally encouraged and facilitated by the cultural unity of the Hispanic Southwest and northern Mexico, for the Mexican border is a political division that artificially bisects a single cultural unit.

The composition of the hispano society of the Southwest is in the Western European tradition. Maximum prestige is acquired only after some generations of relative wealth, education, and community status. Bilingualism is common among the best hispano families of the Southwest, except in a few isolated areas, and for the most part there is little social disadvantage deriving from their non-anglo heritage. For the poorer, uneducated, monolingual hispano classes, the picture is different, and it would appear that especially in the urban areas the social and economic status of the hispano citizen is little better than that of the recent immigrant, legal or illegal. Color is also frequently an important factor—in Mexico as well as in the Southwest. Social prestige tends to be linked to Spanish family origins as opposed to Indian origins, and thus by definition the poorer classes are strongly mestizo or even pure Indian. The nomadic existence of the migrant workers, *braceros*, is often detrimental to the social adjustment and to the education of the children so that, unwittingly, a disadvantaged ambient is passed on from one generation to the next. The immigration patterns, as well as we can judge, from Mexico to the Southwest, legal and illegal, tend to respond primarily to the need for unskilled, low-paid workers on the ranches and in the cities of the Southwest.

In more recent years a rather curious form of internal immigration has occurred. Substantial numbers of more or less unskilled Hispanos from the Southwest have gone to work for industry in such northern cities as Chicago and Detroit, creating Spanish-speaking neighborhoods. The social problems encountered there differ little from those of the true immigrant. At this point we must define the two major terms used to designate the representatives of our two cultures, the one Hispanic and the other Anglo-Saxon, originally English. The term *Hispano* designates primarily a person of Hispanic tradition and language, regardless of national origin, as opposed to the *Anglo*, an English-speaking American of nordic heritage, primarily Anglo-Saxon. The two terms, based on cultural heritage, are often used for racial distinctions as well.

At the moment the most popular word for the poorer, *mestizo* classes of the Southwest is the term *chicano* which apparently derives from the usage *patas chicas* ("small feet") used to distinguish persons with Indian blood from the Spaniards, *patas grandes* ("large feet"). If we define *Anglo* in its strictest terms (Nordic Caucasian, English-speaking, and Protestant), then we are quite a distance from the *Hispano* (Mediterranean Caucasian, perhaps with a mixture of Indian or Negro, Spanish-speaking, and Roman Catholic) in three crucial ways: racially, linguistically, and theologically. These are considerable cultural barriers just as strong for Hispanos as they are for Anglos. And in the Southwest we must add for the Hispanos the ever-present consideration that we have invaded *their* territory.

After the Southwest, the greatest area of Hispanic concentration in the United States is the greater New York City area. Again, statistics lack precision primarily because the Puerto Ricans (the largest national group of Hispanos in the area) are already United States citizens. It is believed that only four cities in the world have more Spanish-speaking residents than New York: Madrid, Mexico City, Barcelona, and Buenos Aires. The two major Spanish-language newspapers, *El Diario-La Prensa* and *El Tiempo-Mirador*, circulate daily to over one million readers. The internationally renowned Madrid newspaper, *ABC*, has recently found it profitable to publish a weekly New York edition.

A private study conducted in the latter sixties gives the following percentages for the Hispanic population in the New York City area: Puerto Rico (45%); Cuba (20%); Dominican Republic (8%); Colombia, Argentina, Spain, and Venezuela (4% each); Ecuador and Peru (3% each); Bolivia, Chile, and Mexico (1% each); Honduras, Nicaragua, Costa Rica, Guatemala, Panamá, El Salvador, Paraguay, and Uruguay (2% for all). New York presents, then, an almost total panorama of the hispano immigrant in the United States including representatives from almost all of the Spanish-speaking countries of the world as well as complete distribution of social levels. Beyond the usual problems of the immigrant (a person from a different culture with a different language and different customs) the Hispanos of New York also must deal with the problems of multiracial background. We can estimate the black or mulatto hispano population of New York at almost 60% and Indian or mestizo at 10%. Certainly it is a fact that the Caucasians of Cuba, Spain, Argentina, and Chile (the remaining 30%) have integrated far more successfully into the mainstream of American life.

Another large center of hispano immigration in the United States is southern Florida, with almost one million Cubans concentrated primarily in the Miami area. Apart from smaller colonies in Key West and Tampa, the majority of the Florida Cubans were overwhelmingly Caucasian and had better-than-average educations. After initial periods of difficult adjustment, this professional class has managed to reestablish itself in a satisfactory manner in a new nation in spite of the cultural and linguistic barriers. The success in the adjustment and Americanization of the Cuban immigrants has been spectacular and would appear to be a consequence of social class, race, and education as well as of personal industry—the will to succeed.

Another large center of Hispanos is the Chicago area with about the same hispano population as Florida but, on the other hand, a national-origin distribution far more similar to that of New York.

Let us take a broad look at the educational and economic facts of hispano life in the United States. The U.S. Department of Commerce in a report published in 1971 finds that persons of hispanic origin have a notably lower level of educational attainment than other Americans especially among those 25 years old or older. In that group Hispanos average 12 years of schooling (a high school education).

Those statistics are reflected in the employment and income figures. Three-fifths of the hispano population is reported in the American labor force, about the same proportion as for other Americans. However, unemployment averages 6 percent as opposed to 3.5 percent for all Americans, and the category *white-collar job* which embraces 41 percent of the American male population only includes 25 percent of the hispano male population. In late 1969, the median income for the American family was slightly over $8,000 a year. For the hispano family in the United States, the median was only $5,600. The median income for a Puerto Rican family was slightly under $5,000, for a Mexican-American family, $5,400. Yet for the recent Cuban immigrants it was already close to $6,500.

It is clear that the interrelationship of language, schooling, racial considerations, and employment opportunity create for many Hispanos a culture of poverty. The major task of the anglo and the hispano communities, working in unison, is to break the cycle without destroying the values of hispano culture.

The Southwest of the United States has a distinct Hispanic flavor. Our folklorists, our history books, and our guidebooks are eager to tell us about it. Indeed in southern Texas one is closer to Mexico than to the United States. But curiously enough, that Hispanic tradition has two faces: it reflects the romantic characteristics of bygone days, the survival of old love songs and Spanish lace shawls—but it also represents the wrong side of the tracks, a way of life that is squalid and repugnant. In the rest of the nation the existence of hispano culture in the Southwest was largely ignored until quite recently. One Mexican-American was quoted by a national magazine as follows: "We are the best-kept secret in America."

You will recall from our previous remarks that the Southwest has the largest number of Hispanos in the United States, roughly half our entire hispano population. The official estimated distribution there is as follows: California, 3,001,830 (15% of the total population); Texas, 2,500,000 (22.3%); New Mexico, 390,000 (38.4%); Arizona, 375,000 (21.2%); Colorado, 275,000 (12.5%); Nevada, 60,000 (12.3%); Louisiana, 55,000 (1.5%); and Oklahoma, 50,000 (.2%).

Other estimates state the figures as considerably higher. It is thought, for example, that there may be as many as 6 million persons of Mexican origin in the United States. The majority of that number reside in the Southwest but at most would appear to constitute half of the hispano population of that region. In other words even without counting Indians of the Southwest, the area is characterized by a tripartite cultural division consisting of Anglos, recent immigrants primarily from Mexico, and American-born Hispanos. Such areas as Los Angeles or New Orleans also have colonies from Cuba and Puerto Rico as well as from other Spanish-speaking countries.

Perhaps the best place in the Southwest to study the different shadings of the American hispano social structure is the state of New Mexico. The oldest settlement, Santa Fé, is located in the northern hill country, considerably removed from what was to become the Mexican border. Santa Fé and the surrounding villages apparently remained in relative isolation from the other Spanish settlements in the southern part of the state and in northern Mexico and southwestern Texas. The Santa Fé trail brought exposure to anglo culture in the northern area in the earlier nineteenth century. The aristocracy, without losing their Hispanic traditions, adjusted to the process of Americanization with relative ease and success, thus remaining firmly established in the new social structure. The great influx of Anglos into New Mexico, however, came in the southern part of the state and served as a rather definitive buffer between the north and Mexico. As a consequence, the Hispanic traditions, and notably the Spanish language in northern New Mexico, have remained in nearly pristine condition, affected by anglo traditions but not by modern Mexico. The descendants of that early aristocracy felt little or no affinity at all for the recent Mexican immigrant and indeed saw their social position somewhat threatened by the very existence of *wetbacks, braceros*, and *chicanos*. This rather curious but understandable human reaction is to be found throughout the hispano culture in the United States. It has been more readily observed in New Mexico because of geographical circumstances, but it functions universally in such diverse places as Los Angeles, New York, or Florida. Thus, the older, upper-class hispano families tend to have at least adjusted to anglo culture, and throughout the nation in numerous instances their descendants have been completely absorbed to the extent of having lost Hispanic traditions and even the ability to speak Spanish. Within the older hispano communities which have Americanized without being absorbed, the recent immigrant may well find far greater hostility and discrimination than in a more enlightened anglo community.

What generally characterized the hispano communities in the southern parts of the Southwestern states is the constant contact with Mexico, including frequent visits back and forth across the border. That fact, on the one hand, stimulates immigration into the U.S. because the immigrant can adjust with relative ease into the hispano community. On the other hand, that contact works against Americanization and thus serves to maintain the gap between Anglos and Hispanos.

Various sociologists and historians have pointed to the origins of the hispano-anglo gap as being perhaps more the consequence of differences in social class rather than of different cultures and languages, the latter factors being of considerable weight in maintaining the gap. The Anglos who invaded the Southwest in the later part of the nineteenth century and who now account for the larger proportions of residents were, or have become, of the middle class. They had no counterparts in Hispanic culture, still almost feudal then, and therefore reacted negatively to the uneducated, unskilled vast majority.

Statehood brought with it, slowly, a public school system in which the language of instruction was English. Parochial schools did exist in some areas where for many years instruction was given in Spanish, and in the rural areas schooling could be avoided by resistant farmers. But increasingly the hispano children of the Southwest have been thrust into an English-speaking environment for the first time at the tender age of five or six and expected to learn to read and write in a totally foreign language. The results, as might be expected, are often disastrous, with the ever-present danger of total alienation on the part of the young.

During the Second World War the first large-scale expression of such alienation exploded briefly into national awareness. The causes of the explosion were for the most part misunderstood, and all too soon the incident was forgotten. The word *pachuco*, apparently formed on the name for the Mexican city Pachuca, became at some point around World War I the slang term in Spanish for El Paso, Texas—a city right on the Mexican border with a large Mexican-American population. Originally founded as Nuestra Señora de Guadalupe de El Paso in 1659, the settlement was a haven for the refugees of Santa Fé at the time of the Indian uprisings. One of the very oldest hispano settlements north of the Río Grande, the city today has a population of some 350,000. As a new style of dress evolved in the late 1930's, the duck-style hair and a Hispanic variant of the zoot suit, the term *pachuco* came to mean an adolescent hispano male from El Paso who dressed in that style and who behaved in a certain manner.

Some sociologists have regarded the *pachuco* as a hard-core criminal linked with border-traffic drugs. In its extreme degrees, the *pachuco* could be exactly that. But more often he was simply an alienated Mexican-American, rather ill-educated with an imperfect knowledge of English, who did bear some resentment toward anglo culture. His behavior generally did not go beyond an occasional outrageous prank, and he was far more interested in girls, the jitterbug, and beer than he was in social reform. The *pachuco* style swept across the Southwest in the late thirties, especially to urban areas like San Antonio, Albuquerque, Tucson, and Los Angeles. Along with dress, coiffure, and general demeanor, the *pachuco* life-style created something unique in the history of hispano culture in the United States. A new dialect or lingo was created, also called *pachuco*, which may well have influenced the anglo counterpart of that period, known as jive-talk. *Pachuco* is far more radical and hermetic than jive-talk, however, for it does not rely on the creation of new meanings for old words. Rather *pachuco* consists almost entirely of brand new terms whose origins are largely unknown. Again, some are definitely associated with illegal drug traffic over the border. It would appear, however, that *pachuco* was developed by adolescents as a means of excluding all outsiders, parents included, who often represented a more traditional outlook.

Except for the criminal element, which formed only a small minority, *pachuco* culture was at first looked on with the same disdain shown their anglo counterparts, the zoot suiters. But in the summer of 1943 an unfortunate skirmish between sailors on leave and *pachucos* in Los Angeles resulted in bitter attacks against not just the *pachucos* but against many Mexican-Americans in the Los Angeles area. The battle raged for days. It appears that the zoot-suit riots that subsequently broke out all over the country in such diverse places as Philadelphia, Chicago, Detroit, and Harlem were the results of the anti-*pachuco* war in Los Angeles. The Mexican Ambassador finally intervened with an inquiry to the State Department and then, almost as suddenly as the trouble began, it faded into oblivion, along with the interest in the Hispanos of the Southwest.

The original *pachucos* are now parents of the present adolescent population. Styles have changed over the years and the *pachuco* dialect has also evolved, but the basic subculture continues to thrive. In many areas they are simply referred to as *chicanos*. But in El Paso, Texas, where it all seems to have begun, the term *tirilones* has emerged to designate the delinquent and criminal adolescent element of South El Paso, a district so proverbially tough that its mores and language are imitated by the hardened criminals of San Antonio and even Mexico City. A recent study of the area reveals that as many as fourteen people live in a two-room apartment which may rent for as low as $9 a month. Drug traffic and prostitution are major industries, and although some 5% of the population is officially enrolled in the schools in the area, the absentee and drop-out rate is exceedingly high. The language of the schools is, of course, English; whereas the speech of the area is border-Spanish and neo-*pachuco*. Contact with Anglos is minimal or nonexistent.

Just before the First World War Mexicans and Mexican-Americans from the Southwest began to immigrate to northern cities in the Midwest where they could obtain employment in industry. The largest colonies were established in the Chicago area and in Detroit where the war industry encouraged such migration. By 1930, the Chicago colony was estimated at about 20,000. These colonies existed, and to some extent still do, in relative isolation from the mainstream of American life.

The effect of the Mexican-American migration to the North seems even more drab in the smaller locations. In some instances in the Midwest as early as 1918, Mexican-American villages in barracks style were expressly created at some distance from the town for the new labor force. Children were taught, if at all, in Spanish by whoever had time or inclination to do so. Thus it was possible for several generations to live in almost complete isolation, the men going to and from industrial chores which required little use of English.

Tightened immigration quotas reduced the number of Mexicans going directly to the Midwest by 1930, but those quotas did not affect internal migration from the Southwest. The Spanish-speaking population of Illinois alone now totals well over one million and that of Michigan, primarily the Detroit area, near 200,000. In all there are perhaps 3 million Hispanos in the American Midwest, traditionally an anglo stronghold.

There are indications that the quality of life for some Mexican-Americans may be rising slowly. World War II brought young men of service age into much closer contact with anglo culture. For the first time in many cases, close social relationships between Hispanos and Anglos could be formed. Hispanos of necessity learned to communicate in English. And when the war was over they had the privileges of the G.I. Bill, with the opportunity to obtain further education. These circumstances appear to be reflected in various statistics. For example, the highest percentage of Mexican-Americans in 1969 who were fluent in both Spanish and English is precisely males between the ages of 35 and 55. It is also this age group which has the highest annual income. Their children, unfortunately, seem to be losing the use of Spanish. For example, the age group 16 to 24, shows only 52% fluency in both English and Spanish as opposed to over 62% for their parents' generation. This second generation also evidences a higher level of schooling, again in English, so that their economic situation will undoubtedly improve but at the cost of gradual alienation from their own culture. Many Hispanos consider the cost too high.

We have talked around hispano life but perhaps not specifically about it. What are, indeed, its characteristics that some hispano parents jealously guard and wish to see perpetuated? Perhaps old-fashioned Southwestern hispano life can best be compared to rural life in mid-America before World War II. The family is the basic social unit embracing grandparents, parents, and children with all collateral relatives included. The unit itself is institutionalized by the church, although attendance is primarily the responsibility of women and children. Social life centers around the traditional church festivals, with birthdays celebrated on one's saint's day. The important social events center around religious holidays, as well as weddings, christenings, and even funerals. A *fiesta* is by definition a family affair attended by babes-in-arms, young people, the middle-aged, and those with canes or in wheelchairs. A man's social life may also include a friendly glass or a game of chance at a local café where he visits with his male friends. Family ties are strong and override all other considerations. Marriages are contracted only with the full approval of the families of both parties. Formerly a man would not consider an opportunity for professional advancement, no matter how enticing, if it entailed separation from the larger family unit. The comportment and movements of an unmarried girl were vigilantly regulated by parents and brothers. World War II and the spread of *pachuquismo* began, of course, to dissipate that style of life which now seems confining to the younger generation. At the same time the specter of anglo life as a frightening antithesis, exaggerated by film and press, is hardly an attraction to the hispano parent. Divorce, wife-swapping, baby-sitters, nightclubs, legalized abortion, families separated by the distance of an entire continent, lack of church attendance and orientation—these are all anathema to conservative hispano families, who in consequence fear that contact with Anglos, including education in their schools or even use of their language, will contaminate.

By contrast, conservative Anglos may find that Hispanos make too much noise, laugh or anger too easily and too intensely, and do not seem sufficiently work-oriented. Beyond this generalization, actual contact is usually so limited that the Anglo is far more aware of the criminal element dramatized by the press. And thus, the *pachuco* who switch-blades a colleague in a drunken brawl over a drugged prostitute stands as a typical representative of hispano culture.

The passivity of the Mexican-American community for more than a century began slowly to end with the Second World War. Almost half a million Mexican-Americans served in that war, many heroically, and it has been pointed out that their numerical service record is proportionately higher than that of the anglo community. In any event, the generation of Mexican-Americans who went into military service received a liberal education in sociology. Increasingly in the 1950's and finally with some explosions in the 1960's the Mexican-American community has asked or demanded to be heard. The Second World War also witnessed the birth of the Good Neighbor Policy which, among other consequences, made Spanish the most widely taught foreign language in the American school system. Today, the American Association of Teachers of Spanish and Portuguese numbers well over 15,000, and it is estimated that over 20 million Anglos have studied some Spanish.

The past decade has been stormy, but we are perhaps closer to a *rapprochement* between anglo and hispano culture than ever before. Bilingual education is beginning to be accepted in areas where its very mention a few years ago would have created dissent. Such spectacular events as the grape boycott of 1965 attracted adherents throughout the land and served to dramatize eloquently the plight of the migrant Mexican-American workers. Perhaps even more significant is the publication of successful novels like *Chicano* by Richard Vasquez in 1970 which probes the universally human aspects of an admirable Mexican-American family striving to adjust to life in the United States. Congressmen from New Mexico, California, or Texas now have names like Montoya, Roybal, González, or de la Garza. The former mayor of El Paso, Raymond Telles, was appointed ambassador to Costa Rica. Distinguished scholars from Texas with names like Sánchez teach in such traditionally anglo areas as Wisconsin.

Indeed our universities are now discovering, many for the first time, the existence of a hispano culture in the United States. The latest annual list of new doctoral dissertations in the Hispanic field includes four concerning the Spanish of New Mexico, Texas, Arizona, and Chicago. In the entire past century only a dozen or so dissertations were devoted to the Spanish of the United States.

A great deal has already been achieved by the press in the past few years. A supposedly exhaustive study on the foreign-language press in the United States, published a few years ago, stated that the German language press was the most widespread in our country. However, a concise listing of the Spanish-language periodicals published in the United States, now in preparation, may require more than one volume in view of the thousands of titles already collected. The vast majority are local newspapers or general news magazines, but in 1967 in Berkeley, California, there was created a more serious quarterly periodical *El Grito*, "A Journal of Contemporary Mexican-American Thought," This journal has given a unified, if sometimes shrill, voice to the Spanish Southwest which the fragmented, local publications could not by definition achieve. A comprehensive bibliography on Mexican-American studies appearing in *El Grito* in 1972 lists almost 500 works, the vast majority of which were published after 1960.

Although the thought that the hispano flavor of New York City is primarily Puerto Rican is an oversimplified *cliché*, the heavy migration of Puerto Ricans to New York City is historically a very recent development. Indeed, one of the earliest distinguished European visitors to New York was Francisco de Miranda, who was to become one of the founding fathers of the Republic of Venezuela and to serve briefly as head of that nation from 1811 to 1812. In 1783, while still a colonel in the Spanish colonial army, he started a tour of the United States and stayed in New York in early 1784. His description of Brooklyn may well be one of the first: "a small place," he says, "one of some 150 little houses, inhabited in the main by poor people."

Before the middle of the nineteenth century, almost 150 years ago, the city was beginning to acquire a Hispanic flavor. Trouble was brewing in the island of Cuba. By 1843 various political conflicts in Cuba had produced in Key West, Florida, the establishment of a revolutionary force under the leadership of General Narciso López. He was to make various landings and expeditions against the colonial Spanish government in Cuba, and as the revolutionary movement became more widespread, with the colonial government taking even stricter measures, the partisans of a liberated Cuba were forced to leave.

The successive waves of political upheaval in Cuba sent intellectuals and politicians as well as numerous middle- and upper-class professionals to New York City, where an exile class could most conveniently conduct their activities without harassment and with the advantages found in a large center. It must be remembered that Cuba is our closest hispano neighbor in the East, Havana being only some eighty miles from the Florida Keys. The increasing immigration of literate Cubans to New York City is eloquently reflected by the establishment of Cuban, Spanish-language newspapers and magazines in the city. A total of 34 different periodicals appeared between 1848 and 1872. As those figures suggest, the Cuban immigrants of this period constitute a highly literate group. Indeed several Cuban literary masterpieces of the nineteenth century were first published in New York City, written in part or entirely in New York. Cirilo Villaverde, one of Cuba's most distinguished novelists, was by 1850 editor-in-chief of the popular paper, *La Verdad*, in New York.

We have arbitrarily cut the story at 1872 only to emphasize the fact that just over a century ago New York City was already acquiring a Hispanic flavor, primarily Cuban.

But Cuba's troubles were only beginning, and the establishment of 42 new Spanish periodicals, almost entirely Cuban, continued throughout the nineteenth century. Some of these journals were, of course, short-lived. But their number and their caliber are formidable. In all, Cirilo Villaverde founded two journals and served as editor for two others. In 1882 his greatest novel, *Cecilia Valdés*, was published in New York; he died there in 1892. By this time Cuba's most famous statesman and one of her most outstanding writers was also associated with New York. After 1885, José Martí founded one periodical in New York, served as editor for another, and wrote for six more up to his death in 1895.

This constant Cuban immigration to New York City created a whole spectrum of hispano social life in the city including an active Cuban theater in Spanish. In 1891 a magazine was founded to cover Spanish-language theater in New York. One view of Cuban life in the city at this time is interestingly described by Carlos Loveira in his novel *Generales y doctores* published later in Havana, in 1920. This chapter in our immigration history has gone largely unmentioned for two reasons. Firstly, the Cubans do not seem to have formed Cuban neighborhoods or ghettos; secondly, they were generally Caucasian, well educated, and professionally trained and quickly integrated into the economic life of the city. Progressively their children, educated in English, simply Americanized and passed into the mainstream of American life. The metropolitan complex and the need to earn a livelihood worked against the kind of extended family existence possible in more rural areas like the Southwest or in some areas of Florida. It is doubtful, for example, that a very large proportion of the descendants of that nineteenth-century Cuban immigration have even retained any substantial memory of the Spanish language.

Cuba finally obtained independence from Spain in 1898. The fact is immediately reflected in the history of Spanish-language periodicals in New York. In the first 25 years of the twentieth century, only 19 new periodicals were founded—most of them by American commercial firms for distribution elsewhere. A small number reflect a slowly increasing immigration from Spain and the better Cuban literary journals survive in ever decreasing numbers as the older Cuban immigrants die off or return home.

As political difficulties and dissent grew in Spain, the number of immigrants, primarily to New York City, grew throughout the 1920's. After almost a century, the torch of hispano cultural life in the city passed from the Cubans to the Spanish who by 1928 supported an active theater and a new magazine devoted to it.

Indeed, Spanish cultural and intellectual life in New York became increasingly brilliant just after the turn of the century. In 1904 the American philanthropist and scholar, Archer M. Huntington, founded in upper Manhattan The Hispanic Society of America, a research institution devoted to the arts and the humanities with one of the world's finest museums and libraries specializing in the culture of Spain. Under the

Society's auspices Spain's great literary critic, Ramón Menéndez Pidal, lectured in New York in 1909. In 1915 Latin America's greatest poet, Rubén Darío, read his new antiwar poem *Pax!*, commissioned by the Society. In 1916, the world premiere of Granados' opera *Goyesca* was given at the Metropolitan Opera. In the same year occurred the marriage of Juan Ramón Jiménez, future recipient of the Nobel Prize, to Zenobia Camprubí—a girl of Spanish, Puerto Rican, and American parentage, sister of the editor of New York's outstanding Spanish newspaper, *La prensa*. In 1916, with Huntington's backing, the distinguished Spanish scholar Federico de Onís was brought to Columbia University, and in 1920 the *Casa hispánica*, Spanish House, was inaugurated there and quickly became one of the major centers of Spanish cultural and intellectual life in the city. Lectures, concerts, plays, and receptions were held frequently and included performances by such outstanding figures as Lucrezia Bori, Andrés Segovia, and La Argentinita as well as readings and lectures by Salvador Dalí, Diego Rivera, Gabriela Mistral (another Nobel Prize recipient), and the poet Federico García Lorca, whose stay in New York in the late twenties was to produce his well-known collection *Poet in New York*.

It is not surprising, then, that the tragic Civil War in Spain in the thirties should have sent to New York an outstandingly large proportion of its major professional figures. Numerically that immigration figure seems almost inconsequential, but the exceptional caliber of these immigrants, combined with the already established Spanish cultural centers, caused the Spaniards to completely dominate hispano life in the city.

The establishment of New York City as the major world center of Spanish exile life occurred prior to the explosion of Puerto Rican immigration to the city. The estimated Puerto Rican population of the United States is as follows: 1910: 1,513; 1920: 11,811; 1930: 52,774; 1940: 69,967; 1950: 301,375; 1960: 887,662; 1969: 1,600,000. The greatest upsurge in Puerto Rican immigration occurred between 1910 and 1920. This corresponds to the demand for labor, primarily in New York City, during the World War I boom. The postwar period continued to show a notable increase, although only half that of the war period. The depression of the 1930's is quite visible in the strong decline in immigration.

The figures are misleading, however, unless we compare them to the total population of New York City where the vast majority of Puerto Ricans reside. Thus, although the percentage increase of Puerto Rican immigration to the continental United States is the highest between 1910 and 1920 (almost eight times that of the preceding decade), the total number of some 12,000 persons was quickly absorbed by a city of 5½ million. Even by 1945, the Puerto Rican figure of some 75,000 only constituted about one percent of the city's total. The postwar boom in the United States created a vast need for unskilled labor, and the initiation of low-cost air transportation in 1946 from San Juan to New York resulted in a new landmark in immigration: the transportation of huge numbers of people within a brief span of time. In 1946 alone almost 40,000

Puerto Ricans came to New York, thus in one year increasing the Puerto Rican population of the city by over 50%. In the five years from 1945 to 1950, the number of Puerto Ricans in the city had grown from one percent to over four percent, and in the ensuing decade, from 1950 to 1960, came to surpass ten percent of the city's total population.

The Puerto Rican immigration to New York City is in many ways similar to the Mexican immigration in the Southwest. Both consist primarily of unskilled, relatively uneducated laborers impelled by a low standard of living at home to go elsewhere. In New York as in the Southwest, they meet with some hostility both as foreigners—that is, of a different language and culture—and usually as members of a minority racial group, Indian or Negro, mestizo or mulatto. Although their new standard of living may represent an improvement over the old, they find themselves in the same relative economic and social corner that they had left. This is true even within the hispano environment of the new locale, in New York as well as in the Southwest or even Florida. Thus betterment for these immigrants is primarily in terms of those they left behind. As their ties with home diminish, they increasingly find themselves quite understandably as unhappy and restless over their new lot as they had been with the old.

Statistics indicate a rising educational level and corresponding economic and professional improvement for the earlier Puerto Rican immigration. In 1960 the educational gap between second generation Puerto Ricans and all Americans had been reduced to a fraction, with income lagging by only $675 annually and top employment classification by only two percent. However, these figures for the second generation concern primarily those born well before the massive airlift beginning in 1946. For this earlier group of people it is evident that a climate of rising expectations was created which in all probability was a major factor in that massive airlift. However, those rising expectations seem to have peaked in the earlier generations with a tendency to diminish with the younger generation, those born in the United States. Comparable figures for the group of Puerto Rican males between the age of 25 and 34 in the year 1960 show that the two-year gap in education has widened to almost four at this age level. This younger generation of Puerto Ricans had slightly *less* schooling at this age than the entire Puerto Rican group. And in spite of the rise in job classification to over 11 percent in the category "Professional and Technical," the discrepancy in salary for this younger generation of Puerto Ricans as opposed to the national level was up to $700 annually. That trend seems to have been readily noticed in Puerto Rico. After the peak year of 1953, the immigration figure begins to slowly diminish until 1960 when it drops to almost half the figure for 1959.

We are still in the middle of the story of Puerto Rican immigration to the United States. There has been a growing proportion of Puerto Ricans who leave the New York City area. In 1940, 93% of the immigrants remained in the Northeast (primarily in the New York area but with some colonies in Boston and Philadelphia). By 1950 the proportion declined to 88.7%, and by 1960 to 84.2%. A shift to the northern central section of the country, mostly the Chicago area, has occurred. Thus, that portion of the country accounted for 1.3% of Puerto Rican immigration in 1940 but 7.6% in 1960.

For the moment the Puerto Rican population of the United States seems to have leveled off with the number of new immigrants fairly well balanced by the number of emigrants back to the island. Nonetheless some estimates of the Puerto Rican population in the United States run to 3 million. The vast majority have come here since 1946 and the oldest of their children are only now reaching the age of 27. It will be another ten to fifteen years before we can evaluate their progress and adjustment. Society at large, and more specifically our schools and then our employers, will determine the fate of the new generation of Puerto Ricans born here. Sociologists, historians, and educators all seem to agree on one point—the urgent need for successful bilingual school programs.

You will recall, of course, that the Hispanos of the Southwest are not immigrants but rather the first settlers of that area. The oldest Spanish-speaking immigrant group in the United States is that of the island of Key West which is the last of the Florida keys. It lies in the Caribbean, at the entrance to the Gulf of Mexico, only 80 miles north of Havana, Cuba, but almost 160 miles south of Miami, and contains the southernmost city of the continental United States.

Its past is especially romantic, for during the seventeenth and eighteenth centuries the island served as a base for the pirates of the Caribbean beginning with the expeditions of Sir Walter Raleigh and ending, just after 1800, with Jean Lafitte. By this time small groups of Cuban fishermen had gradually established small communities on the island. In 1823, Key West came under the flag of the United States as part of the Florida territory. The first English-speaking colonists began to arrive from the Bahamas about 1830. The closest city to Key West is Havana. Thus, when in 1843 the Cuban revolutionary movement began, it was natural that Key West should have served as a base for the Cuban revolutionaries. By 1868 Cuban immigration to the island had grown considerably, and in that year two of the major cigar manufacturing companies of Havana transferred their entire operations to Key West: lock, stock, and employees. Before the end of the century Key West was to become the world's major manufacturer of Havana cigars as well as the wealthiest and largest city in Florida. Officially, of course, the language of Key West was English after 1823. In practice the city was primarily Spanish-speaking. Indeed the mayor of Key West in 1876 was Carlos de Céspedes, one of the chief figures in the Cuban revolutionary movement and originator of the slogan "Cuba libre" ("Free Cuba"), which now survives to designate the drink also known as rum and Coca Cola.

In 1871 Céspedes founded a cultural institution unique in the hispano areas of the United States. The Instituto San Carlos, in addition to an active program of prestigious cultural and social events, inaugurated a private grade school where all instruction was given in Spanish. In an extraordinarily wise move for such early and supposedly unenlightened times, the state of Florida at the turn of the century supplied the Institute with a teacher of English so that the graduates of the Institute in the twentieth century indeed received a bilingual education. The Institute also maintains a summer program in Spanish for students of the public schools wherein English is the language of instruction.

Contact with the Florida mainland was minimal until the twentieth century. There was no overland connection with the Florida mainland until 1912 when the railroad from Miami reached Key West over an extensive series of bridges. But the distance to Miami, only a small town of 5,000 then, was a long ride of one hundred sixty miles. By contrast, the exciting city of Havana was only eighty pleasant sea miles away. The railroad was in serious economic difficulty when the disastrous hurricane of 1935 destroyed miles of rail bridges and, thus, the twenty-three-year-old rail connection with the peninsula of Florida ended forever.

By this time the American Naval Base and the fishing industry had brought anglo-Americans to the island in some number, but we are not certain at what point the Spanish-speaking population ceased to be a majority. What is more important is the unexpectedly pleasant fact that it does not seem to have mattered.

Toward the close of the century labor troubles resulted in a new transfer of the cigar industry to Tampa. By 1910 the village of Tampa had grown to twice the size of Key West, and new migration from Cuba, lessened now because of Cuban independence, was mainly to Tampa. Key West's hopes for a new revival as a tourist center did not materialize with the railroad. Finally in 1943 a highway was completed over the old railroad bed. By the late 1940's Key West did begin to attract more adventurous tourists resulting in general expansion in the city during the 1950's. Today the population of the island is about 30,000 with approximately one-third Spanish-speaking, that is some 10,000 persons. Until the Castro revolution in 1959, contact with Havana remained close; however, we must remember that substantial immigration ceased about 1900. For a century and a half the hispano residents of the island, with the help of their institutions like San Carlos and with the goodwill of the resident Anglos, have managed to preserve their hispano identity, language, and customs. At present the mayor of the city is Anglo and the chief of police Hispano. Such combinations in government as well as in private enterprise reflect the harmony of two cultures in Key West. The daily newspaper, in English, regularly includes articles in Spanish. The Spanish-language weekly regularly includes a few articles in English.

Various factors explain this exemplary situation. The original expansion of population in the earlier nineteenth century included both Anglos and Hispanos arriving more or less simultaneously. The Anglos themselves consisted of both continental Americans and colonial British from the Caribbean. No one group seems to have claimed or felt supremacy, although we must remember that as of 1823 the island was officially part of the United States. In the case of the non-Anglos, the Cubans, we must also remember that the immigration consisted almost exclusively of hard-working, literate Caucasians. Such distinguished personalities as Carlos de Céspedes or José Martí, Cuba's hero, were familiar figures in the island. Indeed cigar manufacturing was a skilled and relatively prestigious occupation in Cuba, and the workers had extraordinarily literate tastes reflected in a unique custom, the factory reader. Throughout the work day he performed for the worker audience reading novels, plays, poetry, or sometimes special accounts from newspapers and magazines. His high salary was paid by the workers themselves. Usually trained actors, the factory readers were highly respected, prosperous members of the community.

The absence of a priest or a Roman Catholic Church in Key West throughout most of the nineteenth century resulted in the conversion of large numbers of the Cuban immigrants to Protestantism.

The immigrant Cubans were industrious, educated, and culturally inclined. By the same token, the pace of life even for Anglos in this scenic, tropical island is not the same as that of Boston or New York. Cultural shock, then, between the original anglo and hispano settlers of Key West seems to have been minimal. Indeed, there still exists a charming ballad of the nineteenth century, *Una ledi de Naso*, which recounts in a delightful mixture of English and Spanish the courting of the Lady from Nassau by a Cuban cigar maker. Intermarriage is quite common in the island so that names like Mary Valdés or Ramón Smith are typical. The old Cuban families are fiercely loyal to their Key West heritage. They are Americans not Cubans. The Anglos of the island as well as Floridians in general are in turn proud of the Hispanic flavor of the state.

We have looked at many of the sordid, unhappy realities of Hispanic life in the United States like social and economic discrimination and even mistreatment. There is, however, a happy side of the coin. In looking at Hispanic achievements in our country, we shall now concentrate mainly on the twentieth century, reminding the reader that we are skipping over a rather formidable history of exploits: the discovery of the New World by Cristóbal Colón, that of Florida and the North American continent by Ponce de León, the expeditions of Coronado and DeSoto, or the founding of the missions by Serra and many others.

We can begin with an atmosphere—the sound and the sight of the colonial Spanish Southwest. Its style of architecture has been reproduced in millions of dwellings, private and public, throughout the nation. In the 1930's a major revolution in American music was achieved. In the 1920's Caribbean music, with its heavy reliance on percussive instruments and rhythms new to our ears, came slowly to be heard occasionally in the repertoire of American dance bands. In 1932, George Gershwin gave us a more serious work, *Cuban Overture*. In 1933, the Waldorf-Astoria hotel in New York, the epitome of chic in the nation, hired a young bandleader to appear with his group in the "Starlight Roof." This young musician born in Barcelona, and raised in Havana, came with excellent credentials. He had played first violin with the National Theater Symphony in Havana and after classical concerts in New York and Europe had formed a popular Cuban dance band in California. As an ambassador of music, Xavier Cugat was a major factor in bringing to the American consciousness on a nationwide scale the existence of Hispanic music. The words *rhumba* and *conga* and, later *mambo* and *cha-cha-cha*, were to become part of American English. And their sounds were to change American music. By 1935, Cole Porter wrote "Begin the Beguine" in the Caribbean mode. The song "Ojos verdes" by Cugat's pianist, Nilo Menéndez, first became a best seller as an instrumental and then swept the nation with English lyrics as "Green Eyes."

The Cuban atmosphere invaded classical music. In 1941, Morton Gould's *Latin American Symphonette* appeared and in 1942 the distinguished composer, Aaron Copland, wrote his *Danzón Cubano*. Inspired by the Puerto Rican "problem" in New York City and cast in a modernized version of Romeo and Juliet, Bernstein created in 1957 one of America's masterpieces for the musical stage, *West Side Story*, using the sounds of Caribbean, Hispanic music now a part of national folklore. The modern American orchestra, popular or classical, includes as a matter of course *bongó* and *maracas* and uses freely the rhythms and phrasing of Cuban music.

In view of the numbers and the kinds of immigration that have occurred, as well as the attitude of Americans toward the immigrants, we should expect the greatest and most spectacular achievements in the United States to come from the Spaniards and the Cubans. Let us look first, however, at the groups theoretically far less well prepared or educated to achieve Nobel Prizes or national recognition.

Just off the press at the University of Texas is a new book entitled *Mexican-American Artists*. The author, Jacinto Quirarte, born in Arizona of hispano parentage, is an internationally recognized expert in the field of Latin American art. After treating the early architecture and church sculpture of the Southwest, Professor Quirarte first describes and illustrates the work of two outstanding Mexican artists achieved in the United States during relatively brief residence here: José Clemente Orozco's works including the outstanding murals for the New School for Social Research in New York and the extensive series at Dartmouth College. Rufino Tamayo spent ten years as Professor of Art at the Dalton School in New York and during that time completed a massive mural for Smith College now housed in their new museum. The author then proceeds to treat the work of twenty-seven notable Mexican-American artists, all of the twentieth century. As we might expect, the vast majority are from the Southwest. The rather high representation from Texas and New Mexico seems to be in part the consequence of the active art colonies in San Antonio and Albuquerque. The list is too long to enumerate, and we need only point out that these artists are nationally and even internationally known. In addition to their art, seven are also professors at American colleges and universities, and another three teach in secondary schools. One is director of the Museo del Barrio in New York City, and several others are also employed in such various enterprises as commercial art, newspaper cartoons, and military technology. About half are already supported entirely by their art. Their specializations range from oil painting through drawings, sculpture, collage, and multimedia work; their works have been exhibited as far away as China or London and displayed in distinguished permanent collections, both public and private.

The contributions of the Hispanic Southwest to American music have been primarily folkloric, especially the cowboy ballad which derived from earlier hispano ballads. These have been collected by various scholars and a representative number have been recorded by local singers. The adolescent *pachuco* subculture has produced a small body of rather fascinating popular songs which we might classify as hispano pre-rock. Outstanding figures from Spain in American music include the late Lucrezia Bori, Victoria de los Angeles, and Montserrat Caballé in opera; the conductor and pianist José Iturbi, and the composers Carlos Suriñach and Leonardo Balada. From Puerto Rico comes the noted pianist José María Sanromá as do the Metropolitan Opera's Justino Díaz and the popular and concert singer Emilia Conde. The two Spanish-language television stations in New York City regularly feature popular singers like Myrta Silva from Puerto Rico or Miguelito Valdés from Cuba. In the past few years various outstanding hispano concerts have been presented in New York City including the premiere at Carnegie Hall of Leonardo Balada's opera *María Sabina*, portrayed by María Soledad Romero of Puerto Rico. In New Orleans, Balada's *Ponce de León* for orchestra with narrator José Ferrer from Puerto Rico was recently premiered. Cuba's outstanding composer, Julián Orbón, now resides and creates in New York City. For many years his countryman, José Echániz, was professor of music at the Eastman School of Music in Rochester.

In addition to the extraordinary collections of hispano art in the nation's museums, especially in New York, we should also note such outstanding works as the old Sert Room at the Waldorf-Astoria Hotel in New York. For some forty years this elegant meeting place was lined with murals painted especially for the room by Spain's José María Sert. A frequent resident of the city is Salvador Dalí whose portraits grace a number of this country's best drawing rooms. In Cleveland, there is a new museum exclusively devoted to his works. In Key West, Florida, the artist Mario Sánchez combines the primitive art of woodcarving with the medieval technique of polychromed wood sculpture to provide panels that give the initial appearance of oil paintings.

These notable figures and their work have given in our own time a Hispanic flavor to the culture of the United States which makes it unique and quite different from its origins, the *anglo* culture of the British Isles. The Hispanic sights and sounds that are part of our daily life, including music and even words, immediately set us apart from our anglo brothers in Europe or Australia and even to some degree in Canada.

Professor Stanley T. Williams of Yale University first published in 1955 two substantial volumes entitled *The Spanish Background of American Literature*. The wealth and depth of Hispanic influence on American letters was increasingly pervasive after 1800, beginning with such notable figures as Washington Irving, Prescott, and Henry Wadsworth Longfellow who, it is often forgotten, earned his livelihood as a professor of Spanish literature at Harvard. Twentieth-century American literature is notably subject to Hispanic influences: Maxwell Anderson's *Night over Taos* dramatizes the emotional conflicts between Anglos and Hispanos in mid-nineteenth-century New Mexico, and Willa Cather's masterpiece *Death Comes for the Archbishop* views through the clergy, early hispano life in New Mexico. Eugene O'Neill in *The Fountain* treats the exploits of Ponce de León, and in his novel *The Bridge of San Luis Rey* Thornton Wilder re-creates colonial Perú. The influence of Spain was especially pervasive in the works of the "Lost Generation," notably Gertrude Stein and Ernest Hemingway, and predominately in the latter's novel *For Whom the Bell Tolls*, in his study on bullfighting, *Death in the Afternoon*, and in his play *The Fifth Column*.

But the history of Spanish-language letters in America is still waiting to be written. It appears, for example, that the first performance of a play in the United States occurred in 1595 in New Mexico. Captain Farfán, the author, and his company presented a new play to the recently arrived Spanish colonists on the bank of the Río Grande. Religious drama flourished in the Southwest in the seventeenth century, and various of these early plays are not only preserved but continue to be performed today. A secular literature, independent from that of Spain or Mexico, did not flourish in the Southwest until the nineteenth century, most of it published in local periodicals. This body of substantial literature awaits collecting and study.

Another especially notable and substantial body of literature in Spanish is that produced in the United States by the immigrants of the Spanish Civil War. You will recall that this immigrant group was of exceptionally high caliber, a large number cordially received by American universities. Thus a proportion of the work of two of the most outstanding Spanish poets of the twentieth century was produced in the United States. They are Jorge Guillén of Wellesley College and Pedro Salinas, professor of literature at Johns Hopkins University up to his death in 1951. Two other major figures spent briefer periods in the United States, although sufficient to cause an impact on some of their works: Luis Cernuda, and especially, Federico García Lorca in his work *Poet in New York*. The novelist Ramón Sender has resided in the Southwest for a quarter of a century.

The total number of Spanish intellectuals in our universities is considerable. In the field of Spanish literature alone it is estimated that over one hundred distinguished immigrants from Spain presently teach in major American universities. Estimates are not available for other disciplines, but it is perhaps sufficient to point out a few notable examples. The Nobel Prize in Medicine for 1959 was awarded to Severo Ochoa, professor of biochemistry at New York University, primarily for his work in the United States after 1941. One of the outstanding philosophers of the twentieth century is George Santayana, born in Madrid and for many years professor of philosophy at Harvard University. One of the outstanding mathematicians for the Apollo Space Program is Pedro Ramón Escobal, nephew of the famous eye surgeon Ramón Castroviejo who perfected in New York the technique for cornea transplant. The dean of Harvard University's School of Architecture is José Luis Sert, born in Barcelona. In little more than a quarter of a century the contributions of the Spanish immigrants have been obviously substantial.

In barely a decade the Cuban immigrants have begun to distinguish themselves in similar fashion. By the mid-sixties over forty Cuban professors were teaching in the Spanish departments of major American universities. These included, for example, the former Dean of the Graduate School of the University of Havana, also a distinguished playwright. Well over two thousand Cuban physicians have been certified to practice in the United States through one center in Miami, including the Nobel Prize Nominee Augustín Castellanos, a pediatric cardiologist.

Puerto Rican achievement has by no means been negligible. A substantial number of Puerto Ricans teach in American universities. In literature, the poets Juan de Avilés and Pablo Figueroa, and the short story writer Pura Belpré, specializing in children's folkloric tales, are permanent residents of New York City, as are painters like René Guzmán or Ralph Ortiz. Luis Quero Chiesa, writer and artist, has had a distinguished career in commercial art as well as in cultural leadership in the Puerto Rican community. The distinguished actor and director, José Ferrer, was born in Puerto Rico, as were the actresses Miriam Colón and Rita Moreno. In city government the highest office held by a woman is Commissioner of Youth Services, Amelia Betanzos. In New York City one of the outstanding figures in politics is Herman Badillo. Various Puerto Rican cultural organizations in New York have in recent years stimulated an increased awareness of Puerto Rico's cultural heritage. These include the *Asociación Pro Cultura Hispánica-Puertorriqueña* which in addition to a program of cultural events maintains a museum and library soon to be moved to larger quarters. Founded in 1969, the Museo del Barrio maintains exhibitions of Puerto Rican art from pre-Colombian days to the present, as well as a lively program of cultural events and workshops for both children and adults. Puerto Rican theater under the leadership of outstanding performers like Miriam Colón has blossomed in New York.

Who's Who in America and *Who's Who in the East* are fairly reliable lists of distinguished persons in our society. The latest editions include ninety names in the New York City area of Hispanic origin. *Who's Who* for the South and Southwest also includes notable figures in Mexico as well, thus tacitly acknowledging the cultural unity of the American Southwest and our neighbor to the south. The distribution of birthplaces for the hispanos resident in the South and Southwest has a far more cosmopolitan profile than we might expect, quite similar to that of the greater New York City area. In spite of difficulties, which we have only been able to outline briefly, Hispanic achievement in the United States has been considerable. As educational opportunities increase for Mexican and Puerto Rican–Americans and as the second generation of Spanish and Cuban-Americans emerges, we can expect such achievement to be even more marked.

As a final consideration, it is well to emphasize again the Hispanic influences on American English. Eight of our states have Spanish names. Florida was baptized for its flowering groves as well as for the occasion of its discovery by Ponce de León at Eastertide, *Pascua Florida*. The remaining seven, as is to be expected, are states of the Southwest: California (a legendary island of plenty in Spanish folklore and literature), Nevada (land of snow), Colorado (red land), New Mexico (from *Nuevo Méjico*), Arizona (arid zone, desert), Texas (*Tejas*, land of tile roofs), and Montana (land of mountains). Over forty years ago a full fledged separate *Dictionary of Spanish Terms in English* by Harold W. Bentley was published at Columbia University. Such words originated primarily in the Southwest where Spanish flows over the borders and into the United States. Given the fact that the Spanish-speaking people of the Southwest were the first European settlers there and had established a rather fixed way of life long before the coming of the Anglos, it is not surprising that the newcomers should have adopted a great many local terms. A large nucleus of these words concerns the way of life of the cowboy. Our term, cowboy, itself is only a translation of Southwestern Spanish *vaquero*. A language tends to borrow words from another language in two major ways. If possible it translates the word, as from *vaquero* to *cowboy*. Often, however, there is no possible translation and the foreign word is simply accommodated to English phonetics. *Vaquero* also came into American English in that fashion, giving us *buckaroo*. The translations, of course, are much more difficult to spot and have lost, in any event, their Spanish flavor. Thousands of accommodated words from Spanish have been adopted: tough *hombre* from *hombre*, barbecue from *barbacoa*, *hoosegow* from *juzgado*, *lasso* from *lazo*, rodeo from *rodeo*, and on and on. The cowboy terms have, of course, been given extremely wide use first by the dime novel and then by the movie western. Unfortunately they have also contributed to a distorted picture of the Southwest and, thereby, of the Hispanos. Another lexical invasion occurred with the Good Neighbor Policy and the sudden popularity in the United States of Hispano-American, and especially Cuban, music. Thus *rumba, conga, mambo, cha-cha-cha*, and *pachanga* have all become part of American English, again to some degree distorting the image of the Hispano. One of the latest terms to gain currency is *machismo*, he-man or tough guy-ism, used as the synonym, *par excellence*, for male chauvinism.

As we indicated earlier, the sights and the sounds of the United States incorporate a multitude of Hispanic flavors which set us apart from our anglo cousins either in

Canada, England. or Australia. Our language itself is impregnated with Spanish words thus confirming our national heritage which includes a hispano population of over ten percent.

SELECTED BIBLIOGRAPHY

Beardsley, Theodore S., Jr. "El estreno mundial de *María Sabina*: Apuntes bibliográficos." *Papeles de Son Armadans*, no. 170 (March 1971): 321–36.

——. "El hispanismo universitario en los Estados Unidos." *La estafeta literaria*, nos. 480–85 (November 15, 1971–February 1, 1972).

——. "Influencias angloamericanas en el español de Cayo Hueso." *Revista Exilio* 7 (1973): 87–100.

Bentley, Harold W. *A Dictionary of Spanish Terms in English*. New York: Octagon, 1932.

Blanco S., Antonio. *La lengua española en la historia de California*. Madrid: Cultura Hispánica, 1971.

Bloch, Peter. *La-Le-Lo-Lai: Puerto Rican Music and Its Performers*. New York: Plus Ultra, 1973.

Bolton, Herbert E., ed. *Spanish Exploration in the Southwest, 1542–1706*. New York: Scribner's, 1916.

Carenas, Francisco. *Poetas españoles en U.S.A.* Madrid: Rialp, 1972.

Clark Moreno, Joseph A. "A Bibliography of Bibliographies Relating to Studies of Mexican Americans." *El Grito* 5, no. 2 (1972): 47–79.

Cue Cánovas, Agustín. *Los Estados Unidos y el México olvidado*. México: Costa-Amic, 1970.

Cugat, Xavier. *Rhumba Is My Life*. New York: Didier, 1948.

Espinosa, Aurelio Macedonió. *Romancero de Nuevo Méjico*. Madrid: Revista Filología Española, 1953.

Fernández-Florez, Darío. *The Spanish Heritage in the United* States. Madrid: Cultura Hispánica, 1971.

Fernández-Shaw, Carlos M. *Presencia española en los Estados Unidos*. Madrid: Cultura Hispánica, 1972.

Fishman, Joshua A., Robert L. Cooper, and Roxana Ma. *Bilingualism in the Barrio*. Vol. 7. Bloomington: Language Science Monographs, 1971.

Fody, Michael, III. "The Spanish of the American Southwest and Louisiana: A Bibliographical Survey for 1954–1969," *Orbis* 19 (1970): 529–40.

Gamio, Manuel. *El inmigrante mexicano*. Mexico: Universidad Nacional Autónoma de México, 1969.

Gómez Gil, Alfredo. *Cerebros españoles en U.S.A.* Barcelona: Plaza y Janés, 1971.

González, Nancie L. *The Spanish-Americans of New Mexico*. Albuquerque: University of New Mexico Press, 1969.

Helm, June, ed. *Spanish-Speaking People in the United States*. Seattle: University of Washington Press, 1970.

"The Hispanic Society of America." *Apollo Magazine* 95 (April 1972).

A History of The Hispanic Society of America, Museum and Library (1904–1954). New York, 1954.

Isern, J. *Pioneros cubanos en U.S. A.* [Miami]: Cenit, 1971.

Jato Macías, Manuel. *La enseñanza del español en los Estados Unidos de América*. Madrid: Cultura Hispánica, 1961.

Leavitt, Sturgis E. "The American Association of Teachers of Spanish and Portuguese." *La estafeta literaria*, no. 487 (March 1, 1972): 30–34.

Lewis, Oscar. *La vida*. New York: Random House, 1966.

Linehan, Edward J. "Cuba's Exiles Bring New Life to Miami." *National Geographic* 144, no. 1 (July 1973), 68–95.

Longland, Jean R. "Granados y la ópera *Goyesca*," *Papeles de Son Armadans* No. 128 (November 1966): 229–55.

McWilliams, Carey. *North from Mexico: The Spanish-Speaking People of the United States*. New York: Greenwood, 1968.

Major, Mabel and T. M. Pearce. *Southwest Heritage, A Literary History with Bibliographies*. Albuquerque: University of New Mexico Press, 1972.

Manuel, Herschel T. *The Spanish-Speaking Children of the Southwest*. Austin, Texas: University of Texas Press, 1965.

Norquest, Carrol. *Rio Grande Wetbacks. Mexican Migrant Workers*. Albuquerque: University of New Mexico Press, 1972.

Orozco, José Clemente. *El artista en Nueva York*, ed. Luis Cardoza y Aragón. México: Siglo XXI, 1971.

Padilla, Ray. "Apuntes para la documentación de la cultura chicana," *El Grito*, V, no. 2 (1972), 3–46.

Peón, Máximo. *Cómo viven los mexicanos en los Estados Unidos*. México: Costa-Amic, 1966.

Pizzo, Anthony P. *Tampa Town*. Miami: Trend House, 1969.

Quirarte, Jacinto. *Mexican American Artists*. Austin, Texas, University of Texas Press, 1973.

Reynolds, John J. and Thomas D. Houchin. *A Directory for Spanish-Speaking New York*. New York: Quadrangle, 1971.

Ribes Tovar, Federico. *El libro puertorriqueño de Nueva York*. New York: Plus Ultra, 1970.

"Spanish-Speaking Population in the United States," *Hispania* 55 (1972): 353.

State of California, Department of Industrial Relations. *Californians of Spanish Surname*. San Francisco: State of California, 1969.

"Teaching Spanish in School and College to Native Speakers of Spanish." *Hispania* 55 (1972): 619–31.

Tully, Marjorie and JUAN B. RAEL. *An Annotated Bibliography of Spanish Folklore in New Mexico and Southern Colorado.* Albuquerque: University of New Mexico Press, 1950.

Ucelay, Margarita. "The Hispanic Institute in the United States," *La estafeta literaria,* Núms. 488–92 (March 15, 1972–May 15, 1972).

U.S. Department of Commerce, Bureau of the Census. *Persons of Spanish Origin in the United States: November, 1969 (Current Population Reports,* Series P-20, No. 213). Washington, D.C., 1971.

Vasquez, Richard. *Chicano.* New York: Doubleday, 1970.

White, Louise V. and Nora K. Smiley. *History of Key West.* St. Petersburg, FL: Great Outdoors, 1959.

Williams, Stanley T. *The Spanish Background of American Literature.* 2 vols. Hamden, Conn.: Shoestring, 1968.

In SEARCH *of* LATINAS *in* U.S. HISTORY, 1540–1970s

Virginia Sánchez Korrol

> One must be a student before one can be a teacher
> —*Chinese proverb*

The history of Latinas—women of Mexican, Latin American, or Hispanic Caribbean heritage in the United States—has varied over time and region but they have left their imprints on the historical landscape and enable us to appreciate their roles in building American communities. The growing scholarship on Latina history begins to surface as stories told at the kitchen table or over backyard fences, passed down from generation to generation, and sheds light on their experiences as actors or witnesses to major historical events. It is found in the written record, official government and church documents, land grants, memoirs, diaries, and in creative expression. It is teased out from children's games, songs, oral traditions and cultural practices, and the arts. And it is increasingly documented as we strive to uncover a hidden past, long marginalized from conventional accounts of the American saga.

Beginning in 1540 the first northward migrations took place when the Spanish crown sanctioned explorations of present-day California, Kansas, Arizona, Texas, New Mexico, and Oklahoma; the Coronado Expedition induced women to participate in the enterprise with promises of stockings and petticoats. In spite of the lavish offers, only three women accompanied Coronado: María Maldonado, expedition nurse, Francisca de Hozes, wife of a shoemaker, and the wife of Lope Caballero. Subsequent northbound expeditions to Santa Fe, San Antonio, and Los Angeles included military wives and daughters and a few counted widows and orphans among the settlers. Historian Vicki L. Ruiz points out that while the majority of settlers would claim "Spanish" blood, most were *mestizo* (Indian/Spanish) and many were of African ancestry.[1]

In colonizing what is today the southeastern coast of the United States, women brought stability to the founding and settlement of St. Augustine in 1565, an uninviting outpost subject to frequent attacks by foreign interlopers. For almost two hundred years until 1763 when the colony passed from Spanish sovereignty into British hands,

St. Augustine women participated in every aspect of colonial life, becoming landowners and investors in their own right. An account of the settlement following the British occupation revealed that, of a population of 3,096 inhabitants, there were 544 families. While a small number of elite women enjoyed privileges accruing from their upper-class status, the majority of women belonged to the lower classes where they toiled besides other settlers to live relatively safe and productive lives in the crosshairs of political and economic instability.[2]

Undeniably, Latinas tamed the frontiers of the Spanish empire in the Americas as they continued to do in northern Mexico before 1848 and throughout the American Southwest thereafter. In numerous ways women sought to leave their mark for future generations. The home front became the school for transmitting cultural values and work ethics; the place where girls became women handling all aspects of life regardless of gender roles. They experienced the pressures of colonialism, racism, class, and gender discrimination, compounded by economic hardships, but consistently strove to improve conditions and convey their personal and collective convictions to future generations. In life journeys often strewn with harshness and disadvantages, they surmounted daily challenges through the support of community, activism, organizing, the strength of family bonds, and religious beliefs, defying and redefining the forces that shaped their existences.

For Mexican settlers in the Southwest, life was drastically altered following the U.S.-Mexico War (1848). The Treaty of Guadalupe Hidalgo, which ended hostilities between Mexico and the United States, ushered in a period of appropriation of almost half the Mexican patrimony and the marginalization of the conquered peoples who lived on those lands. The landed elite comprised a small percentage of the population but wielded inordinate political, social, and economic power in both the rural and urban sectors. Many became powerless, rapidly reduced to wage laborers, suffering a devastating actual and psychological reversal of fortune. Coinciding with the discovery of gold in California, the region was ripe for a vast invasion of Americans seeking to make their fortunes. Evoking static interpretations of mission and hacienda life, the colonial past was relegated to a quaint, romantic interlude.

María Amparo Ruiz de Burton (1832–1895), a resident of Monterey, California, chronicled her experiences during this period in *The Squatter and the Don* (1885).[3] The novel tells the story of a Californio family who lost their immense landholdings to taxes and litigation in efforts to reclaim their property from American squatters. Based on Ruiz de Burton's own familiarity with the loss of property, the book offers a scathing indictment of the American government, industrialists, and their complicity in the displacement and destruction of a centuries-old Mexican way of life.

María Amparo Ruiz married Lieutenant Colonel Henry S. Burton in 1849. Within five years the couple owned Rancho Jamul, an estate of five hundred thousand acres. Ownership of the ranch came into question on Burton's death in 1869. A series of court hearings over seven years resulted in an award to Ruiz de Burton of a mere 8,926 acres. Perhaps the first novelist to describe the bitter resentment of the declining landed class in California, Ruiz de Burton also wrote a second novel, *Who Would Have Thought It*, an account of hypocrisy and racism leveled against Mexicans in the nineteenth century.[4] Along with a collection of her letters, Ruiz de Burton's invaluable work offers insights into her own complicated life as well as to understanding a critical period in Latina history termed in conventional textbooks only as the westward movement.[5]

A contemporary of Ruiz de Burton, Loreta Janeta Velázquez (1842–?), and the Florida Sánchez sisters, attest not only to the importance of transnational connections in mid-nineteenth-century America but also point to a seldom acknowledged factor, the role of Latinas and Latinos in the American Civil War. Velázquez's claim to fame was that she fought in several major battles of the conflict, including the first Bull Run and Shiloh, disguised as a young lieutenant named Harry T. Buford. While scholarly estimates indicate that some four hundred women engaged in similar circumstances, only two have written about their experiences, and only one, Velázquez, was a Latina. *The Woman in Battle (A Narrative of the Exploits, Adventures and Travels of Madame Loreta Janeta Velázquez Otherwise Known as Lieutenant Harry T. Buford, Confederate States of America)* was published in 1867.

Velázquez was born into a landed elite family in Cuba in 1842. As a child she fantasized about a life of adventure, acknowledging early on that traditional gender roles privileged males over females in such pursuits. Grounded in a social ambience that elevated wealth, whiteness, heritage, and male authority, Velázquez adhered to a strict hierarchical order girded by class and race, but devoured literature where daring female protagonists, such as Joan of Arc, or Catalina de Eraso, the Basque nun-lieutenant who, disguised as a man, joined an expedition to the New World, flaunted tradition.

Entrusted into the custody of an aunt at the tender age of eight, Velázquez moved to New Orleans to embark on an appropriate convent education, indispensable preparation for a suitable marriage. While her propensity toward the romantic remained intact, her interests in the domestic arts appeared to take another direction. At fifteen Velázquez eloped with an American officer, formerly affianced to a classmate. Before her twentieth birthday, she had raised the Arkansas Grays, her own militia of 246 men, and presented them to her flabbergasted husband in Pensacola, Florida, shortly before his own death on the battlefield.

Like hundreds of other Latinos living in the United States at the time, Velázquez articulated a firm commitment to the Confederate cause that essentially echoed the ideology of the Cuban *hacendado* class whose wealth derived from the labor of enslaved workers. To a great degree, Cuba and the American South were linked by common political concerns over abolition, commercial interests, and imperialism. A center for trade and transportation, the city of Havana frequently disrupted the Union blockade. Among Latino expatriates, some fought for the South but others aligned themselves with the North. Wounded in battle, her masquerade unveiled, Velázquez herself engaged in espionage following her ouster from the army. She also joined a group of ex-Confederate officers who hoped to establish a colony in Venezuela following their defeat at the hands of the Union army.

Similarly, the Sánchez sisters, Lola, Panchita, and Eugenia, daughters of a Cuban family that returned to St. Augustine long before the war between the states, served as spies for the Confederate cause. Union army officers appropriated their home, incarcerating their father in the fortress of San Marco on suspicion of spying. Resentful yet fearful of Yankee reprisals, the sisters sought imaginative ways to extract troop movement and battle information that could be fed to the Confederates. According to the records of the Los Floridanos Society, Yankee officers enjoyed spending their evenings at the Sánchez hacienda where the sisters were expected to prepare their meals and offer entertainment.

> On one momentous Saturday evening. . . . The sisters withdrew to prepare a Spanish supper for them. . . . As Lola Sánchez flitted from pantry to dining room she overheard earnest conversation between the officers about two activities to be carried out the next day. She bade her sister, Panchita, to entertain the Yankee officers with song and laughter while . . . Eugenia prepared the supper. A mile and a half lay between her and Camp Davis, which consisted of dense tropical Florida woods and the strong currents of the St. John's River. She sped first by horse, thru the woods and then by skiff, over the water. She . . . relayed the information to Captain Dickerson. . . . The next morning in the gray mist of dawn; the Confederate battery lay in wait of the Yankee transport and gunboat. The transport was captured, the gunboat disabled and the troops captured.

Stories like that of Lola Sánchez's ride are traditionally treated as legends, handed down by word of mouth, but the Sánchez saga ignited public awareness in 1909 when the State Convention of the United Daughters of the Confederacy was held in St. Augustine. At this event the two daughters of Panchita and Lola acted as ceremonial pages in honor of their mothers' service to the Southern cause. The story adds another layer on the road to recovering the obscured past depicting a Cuban American incident that addresses their longevity on these shores. Spurred in many respects by the civil rights struggles for self-definition and determination of the 1960s, the search for heritage, witness, and agency is clearly ongoing.

Continuing our narrative from the mid to late nineteenth century, about the time that Velázquez was living out her fantasies and writing her memoirs, another Cuban woman hoisted the banner for Cuban independence from the fledgling Spanish barrios of New York City. Cuban activist and club organizer Emilia Casanova de Villaverde (1832–1897) merits recognition for unwavering patriotism and staunch support of the Antillean movement for independence during the last half of the nineteenth century. Often left out of the historical accounts, the efforts to liberate Cuba and Puerto Rico over thirty years spawned cadres of women in the U.S. vigorously involved in revolutionary activities.

Since girlhood, Casanova nurtured liberation and abolitionist sentiments very much in opposition to her conservative upbringing. A life-altering visit to Philadelphia in 1854 resulted in her marriage to exiled Cuban patriot and writer Cirilo Villaverde (1812–1894), author of the island's seminal novel on slavery and society, *Cecilia Valdés*, excerpts of which first appeared in print in 1833. Twenty years her senior, Villaverde published a second version of his novel in 1882, taking into account the effects of the Ten Years' War, the aftermath of the American Civil War and Reconstruction, events that further buttressed the couples' commitment to liberation.

A resident of New York City since her marriage, Casanova de Villaverde's political orientation intensified with the outbreak of the Ten Years' War (1868–1878), an event she wholeheartedly supported with her writings in the local community presses, particularly the newspaper *América Latina*, which, from 1869 until 1897, regularly published her essays. Stateside, she engaged in zealous organizational activity, establishing one of the earliest women's political clubs dedicated to the independence movement, La Liga de las Hijas de Cuba. Founded on February 6, 1869, at the Hotel St. Julien under Casanova de Villaverde's presidency, this patriotic society boasted a membership of fourteen women and set forth an agenda that denounced the annexationist tendencies of other expatriate organizations active during this period.

Intent on internationalizing Cuba's cause for independence throughout Europe and Latin America, Casanova de Villaverde penned innumerable epistles to influential figures, many of them leading political progressives of her day, imploring them for moral support. We have little indication if Victor Hugo, one recipient of Casanova de Villaverde's correspondence, ever responded, but we do know that Giuseppe Garibaldi sent a generic message of encouragement that probably failed to please the feisty activist. "He would always be on the side of the oppressed," he wrote, "'whether the oppressors are kings or nations,' and he wished that "beautiful Cuba would gain independence." As the first Latina ever to address the United States Congress and a woman who raised impressive resources by selling her household furnishings and jewelry, Garibaldi's response must have seemed halfhearted.

Casanova de Villaverde was part of a small Cuban and Puerto Rican immigrant community that encompassed working-class men and women, professionals, artisans, students, and political exiles. Forming the earliest Spanish-speaking unions, sociocultural, and political organizations, the most progressive among those in the skilled trades were the cigar workers, whose socialist sympathies aligned them with other ethnic groups in the city. Concerned with the plight of the working class, these individuals laid the foundations for future migrant flows.[6]

Overlapping Casanova de Villaverde's activism in New York City, Luisa Capetillo (1876–1922) provides another view, that of the Puerto Rican women who inhabited the early New York *colonia*. She was born into a politically progressive family in Puerto Rico. Capetillo shared Casanova de Villaverde's rebellious nature and Velázquez's fondness for male attire. A well-known feminist fighter for workers' and women's rights, Capetillo was home educated by enlightened parents who supported her radical ideas and lifestyle and encouraged her to read Victor Hugo, Leo Tolstoy, and Emile Zola. Committed to social reform, improving the plight of the working class, and promoting gender equality, she became a labor organizer for the Puerto Rican Federación Libre de Trabajadores. Known as a charismatic speaker and performer, Capetillo penned plays and essays that carried her message of liberation to a wider public and was a reader in the island's cigar factories. Famous for her progressive views throughout the Hispanic Caribbean, but also infamous for conduct unbecoming a lady (she was often thrown into jail for wearing men's clothes), Capetillo spent several years in south Florida, Cuba, and New York, enclaves conducive to her socialist and anarchosyndicalist leanings.

In 1912, probably as a result of the island's government repression of anarchists, Capetillo settled in New York City in the bosom of a thriving community of political exiles and émigrés where she ran a boardinghouse. Collaborating on working-class issues with cigar workers in Ybor City and Tampa, Capetillo embarked on a period of international labor organizing. In 1913 she moved to Tampa. During this period Tampa, Ybor City, and the Spanish-speaking colonias of New York were hotbeds of radical politics. Drawn by the bustling cigar-making centers, Cubans, Puerto Ricans, African Americans, Spaniards, and Italians comprised the bulk of the working-class population.

In particular, readers, or *lectores*, in the cigar factories drew suspicion for instigating strikes and radical movements because they were in a position to present new ideas and international views on labor issues. Capetillo was one of two women *lectoras*, situating her in the crux of conflict. With regard to her thoughts on feminism, a manifesto in support of an industrywide strike in Tampa in 1910 indicates that Capetillo was not alone; some twenty-eight women's signatures attest to a flourishing feminist ideology that recognized the international legacies of Louise Michel, Belén de Ságarra, Teresa Claramunt, and Soledad Gustavo. In addition to the liberation of women, and the exploitation of the workers, in her writings Capetillo "proclaimed the benefits of vegetarianism and cold water baths; the dangers of religious orthodoxy; (and) the transformative power of progressive education." While living in Florida, Capetillo completed the second edition of her classic, *Mi opinión obre las libertades, derechos y deberes de la mujer como compañera, madre, y ser independiente.* In recent years Capetillo's biography and her writings have been translated into English, bringing new transnational facets to feminist studies, demonstrating a Puerto Rican/Caribbean perspective seldom accredited in the literature, and documenting the radical roots of diasporic communities in the United States.[7]

Tobacco workers and feminist leaders offer important insights into women's work outside the home, but other experiences reveal as well an abiding concern for the education of children that cuts across regions and ethnicity during the same period. As Capetillo completed the writing of major treatises in south Florida, another woman, Amelia Margarita Maldonado, was graduating from the University of Arizona in 1919, destined to become a pioneer in bilingual education. Born into a poor family that considered education a "sacred honor," Maldonado became a teacher and taught the primary grades at Drachman Elementary for over forty years. She was one of the first Latinas to validate the use of Spanish in the classroom as students transitioned into English-language skills. Known as a caring teacher sensitive to her students' daily needs, especially evident during the Depression and the years of the Second World War, Maldonado dispensed a breakfast of hearty corn muffins and hot chocolate, along with high academic standards, on the premise that hungry children could not be expected to learn. While she never developed pedagogical theories about bilingual education, she lived them.

Maldonado's story invites further exploration into the Latino struggle for equity on a national scale such as the legal court cases like *Méndez v. Westminster* (1946) a "cornerstone case in school desegregation," which prohibited the separation of Mexican American students from white students in California and influenced *Brown v. Board of Education*.[8] Judge Paul McCormick ruled in favor of the plaintiffs, citing the segregation of Mexican American youngsters as a clear denial of the equal protection clause of the Fourteenth Amendment. The U.S. Ninth Circuit Court upheld the ruling on appeal and Orange County school districts moved toward desegregation.

Méndez received support from then frontline attorneys of the NAACP Thurgood Marshall and John Carter and was probably the first case to use expert witnesses in the social sciences, a strategy that would become invaluable for the *Brown* decision. It may have set the stage for contracts like the Aspira Consent Decree on the East Coast in 1974, which supported the claim by 182,000 Puerto Rican school students and their parents that the New York City Board of Education denied them equal educational opportunity. These and other court cases affecting the education of Latino students attest to both an overarching concern for education and the role of Latino activism on national, state, and local levels that brought about changes in American educational policies.

Antonia Pantoja (1921–2002) came to live in New York City as the Second World War was coming to an end and the Great Migration began, with Puerto Ricans leaving the island in record numbers in search of better economic opportunities. Attracted by the abundance of work in a peacetime economy, they fled from an island undergoing industrialization with a limited supply of jobs and a declining agricultural sector.[9] Antonia Pantoja would come to exemplify the type of leader who transcended formidable challenges to bring about social and educational changes in the United States and personified as well a teacher/activist who through profound dedication to the progress of New York's Puerto Rican community became a national treasure; a builder of institutions.

Pantoja was born into a poor mulatto family in 1921 in Barrio Obrero, Puerto Rico, and struggled to gain an education in a family steeped in union activism, but one that desperately needed her earning power. These experiences are described in her chronicle, *Memoir of a Visionary*.[10] After a short but successful teaching career in the rural mountains of Puerto Rico, she arrived in New York City in 1944. Here she entered a racialized world of exploitation in the workplace, lack of educational opportunity, substandard housing, and poor health care. Her first jobs were in factories where she witnessed sexual harassment and exploitation firsthand. Almost immediately she began to organize the workers and probably would have followed a career as a union organizer or politician. But her innate leadership abilities and thirst for knowledge took her in other directions.

In the mid-1950s Pantoja enrolled at Hunter College. Concerned with the issues and problems facing the Puerto Rican community, she sought explanations for the group's lack of education, low-paying jobs, poor health conditions and discrimination. Along with a cadre of like-minded individuals, she organized the Hispanic Young Adult Association, a group of youthful rebels dedicated to developing an analytical framework for understanding the Puerto Rican presence in the United States. Within this communal leadership, Pantoja soon emerged as a "first among equals," a visionary, and a risk taker prepared to create the institutions that would prove instrumental in bringing about social change.

Among the many organizations she is associated with, Pantoja is credited with the founding of three key self-sustaining groups, the HYAA, the Puerto Rican Forum, and the Puerto Rican Association for Community Affairs. Along with a visible presence in the city's political structure, she would go on to establish a graduate school for community development, a research center, a bilingual college, and two island-based, economically focused organizations. But perhaps, as Pantoja herself came to realize, her greatest contribution was the creation of ASPIRA in 1961.

ASPIRA forged a new concept by creating community leadership based on educating city youngsters, which prompted active intervention in the schooling of Puerto Rican youth. The conduit for the plan's implementation was the formation of ASPIRA club chapters in the schools. Chapters became nurturing and empowering enclaves where students received tutoring in their core subjects and the opportunity to learn about their own Puerto Rican history and culture. The result was the inculcation of knowledge, pride, and confidence that prepared students to *aspire* to higher education. Sessions designed for parents and students investigated college opportunities, admissions, and financial aid.

ASPIRA offices appeared in five states, Washington, D.C., and Puerto Rico. Between 1963 and 1999, the organization served some thirty-six thousand Puerto Rican and Latino youth. Graduates of the earliest clubs enrolled in college and formed the core of student movement that demanded the establishment of Puerto Rican studies departments at their universities. Today thousands of *aspirantes* hold influential positions in community service, government, universities, hospitals, schools, the performing arts, and other sectors of American society. Among them are academics like Dr. Milga Morales, dean of students at Brooklyn College, Isaura Santiago, first Latina president of Hostos College, Aida Alvarez, former head of the Small Business Administration, Jimmy Smits, acclaimed film and television actor, and Fernando Ferrer, the former Bronx borough president and mayoral candidate.

Pantoja's story illustrates community activism at its finest. On the heels of the civil rights movement, the belief in solidarity, the power of the collective, self-empowerment, definition, and self-determination could, and *did*, move mountains. The formation of departments and programs in ethnic studies, women's studies, Puerto Rican, Chicano, Mexican American, and Cuban studies, born of the fervor of collective mobilization like Pantoja's, stands as an important example of social change. Their foundational principles called for bringing the community to the university and the university to the community. Their objectives included creating a cadre of college graduates to study and find solutions to the problems of their communities. And their scholarly mission was to set the record straight, to recover and reinterpret the histories of their communities, to redefine research methods, and to transmit this legacy to future generations.

The women cited in this overview are representative of thousands over five hundred years of Latina history throughout the United States. They are *simply* the tips of the proverbial icebergs. Each has left a legacy not only to her discrete ethnic community but to the American people. It is said that "stories are the spirit threads passed from generation to generation." As the *cuentos* of Latinas and Latinos continue to emerge through concerted intellectual efforts and community and family histories, these collective threads will bind together a stronger, more diverse, and multifaceted nation.

NOTES

1. Vicki L. Ruiz, "From Out of the Shadows: Mexican Women in the United States." *OAH Magazine of History*, 10 (Winter 1996) ISSN 0882–228x. (Organization of American Historians, 2000), pp. 15–18.
2. See Susan L. Pickman, "Women in St Augustine," in Vicki L. Ruiz and Virginia Sánchez Korrol, eds., *Latinas in the United United States: A Historical Encyclopedia* (Bloomington: Indiana University Press, 2006), pp. 714–716.

3. María Amparo Ruiz de Burton [pseud. C. Loyal], *The Squatter and the Don: A Novel Descriptive of Contemporary Occurrences in California* (San Francisco: Samuel Carson, 1885; rpt., with an introduction and notes by Rosaura Sánchez and Beatrice Pita, 2d ed., Houston: Arte Público, 1997).

4. María Amparo Ruiz de Burton [pseud. C. Loyal], *Who Would Have Thought It?* (Philadelphia: Lippincott, 1872; rpt., with an introduction and notes by Rosaura Sánchez and Beatrice Pita, Houston: Arte Público, 1995).

5. Beatrice Pita, "Ruiz de Burton, María Amparo," in Vicki L. Ruiz and Virginia Sánchez Korrol, eds., *Latinas in the United States: A Historical Encyclopedia* (Bloomington: Indiana University Press, 2006), pp. 650–651.

6. See Bernardo Vega, *Memoirs of Bernard Vega* (New York: Monthly Review Press, 1984); and Jesús Colón, *The Way It Was and Other Stories,* ed. Edna Acosta-Belén and Virginia Sánchez Korrol (Houston: Arte Público, 1993).

7. The English language translation of Capetillo's work is Luisa Capetillo, Felix V. Matos Rodríguez, and Alan West-Duran, *A Nation of Women: An Early Feminist Speaks Out/Mi opinión sobre las libertades, derechos y deberes de la mujer* (Houston: Arte Público, 2005).

8. Vicki L. Ruiz, *"Méndez v. Westminster,"* in Vicki L. Ruiz and Virginia Sánchez Korrol, eds., *Latinas in the United States: A Historical Encyclopedia* (Bloomington: Indiana University Press, 2006), pp. 445–447.

9. Gabriel Haslip-Viera, Angelo Falcón, and Félix Matos Rodríguez, eds., *Boricuas in Gotham: Puerto Ricans in the Making of Modern New York City* (Princeton: Wiener, 2004). For an early history of Puerto Ricans in New York City, see Virginia Sánchez Korrol, *From Colonia to Community: The History of Puerto Ricans in New York City,* 2d ed. (Berkeley: University of California Press, 1994); and Carmen Teresa Whalen and Victor Vázquez-Hernández, eds., *The Puerto Rican Diaspora: Historical Perspectives* (Philadelphia: Temple University Press, 2005).

10. Antonia Pantoja, *Memoir of a Visionary* (Houston: Arte Público, 2002). See also "Antonia Pantoja and the Power of Community Action," in Vicki L. Ruiz and Virginia Sánchez Korrol, eds., *Latina Legacies: Identity, Biography and Community* (New York: Oxford University Press, 2005).

The SPANISH ELEMENT in Our NATIONALITY

Walt Whitman

[Our friends at Santa Fé, New Mexico, have just finish'd their long drawn out anniversary of the 333d year of the settlement of their city by the Spanish. The good, gray Walt Whitman was asked to write them a poem in commemoration. Instead he wrote them a letter as follows: —*Philadelphia Press*, August 5, 1883.] CAMDEN, NEW JERSEY, *July 20, 1883*

To Messrs. Griffin, Martinez, Prince, and other Gentlemen at Santa Fé:

DEAR SIRS:—Your kind invitation to visit you and deliver a poem for the 333d Anniversary of founding Santa Fé has reach'd me so late that I have to decline, with sincere regret. But I will say a few words off hand.

We Americans have yet to really learn our own antecedents, and sort them, to unify them. They will be found ampler than has been supposed, and in widely different sources. Thus far, impress'd by New England writers and schoolmasters, we tacitly abandon ourselves to the notion that our United States have been fashion'd from the British Islands only, and essentially form a second England only—which is a very great mistake. Many leading traits for our future national personality, and some of the best ones, will certainly prove to have originated from other than British stock. As it is, the British and German, valuable as they are in the concrete, already threaten excess. Or rather, I should say, they have certainly reach'd that excess. To-day, something outside of them, and to counterbalance them, is seriously needed.

The seething materialistic and business vortices of the United States, in their present devouring relations, controlling and belittling everything else, are, in my opinion, but a vast and indispensable stage in the new world's development, and are certainly to be follow'd by something entirely different—at least by immense modifications. Character, literature, a society worthy the name, are yet to be establish'd, through a nationality of noblest spiritual, heroic and democratic attributes—not one of which at present definitely exists—entirely different from the past, though unerringly founded on it, and to justify it.

To that composite American identity of the future, Spanish character will supply some of the most needed parts. No stock shows a grander historic retrospect—grander in religiousness and loyalty, or for patriotism, courage, decorum, gravity and honor. (It is time to dismiss utterly the illusion-compound, half raw-head-and-bloody-bones and half Mysteries-of-Udolpho, inherited from the English writers of the past 200 years. It is time to realize—for it is certainly true—that there will not be found any more cruelty, tyranny, superstition, &c., in the *résumé* of past Spanish history than in the corresponding *résumé* of Anglo-Norman history. Nay, I think there will not be found so much.

Then another point, relating to American ethnology, past and to come, I will here touch upon at a venture. As to our aboriginal or Indian population—the Aztec in the South, and many a tribe in the North and West—I know it seems to be agreed that they must gradually dwindle as time rolls on, and in a few generations more leave only a reminiscence, a blank. But I am not at all clear about that. As America, from its many far-back sources and current supplies, develops, adapts, entwines, faithfully identifies its own— are we to see it cheerfully accepting and using all the contributions of foreign lands from the whole outside globe—and then rejecting the only ones distinctively its own—the autochthonic ones?

As to the Spanish stock of our Southwest, it is certain to me that we do not begin to appreciate the splendor and sterling value of its race element. Who knows but that element, like the course of some subterranean river, dipping invisibly for a hundred or two years, is now to emerge in broadest flow and permanent action?

If I might assume to do so, I would like to send you the most cordial, heartfelt congratulations of your American fellow-countrymen here. You have more friends in the Northern and Atlantic regions than you suppose, and they are deeply interested in the development of the great Southwestern interior, and in what your festival would arouse to public attention.

Very respectfully, &c.,

PERSPECTIVES ON RACE, ETHNICITY, AND RELIGION

RACIAL THEMES *in the* LITERATURE

Puerto Ricans and Other Latinos

Clara E. Rodríguez

As we examine the experiences of recent Caribbean and Latin American immigrants to the United States, we see that they—like many previous immigrants—bring in their own perspectives on race and ethnicity. These perspectives may sometimes be at variance with the perspectives which prevail in the United States. We also see that there is an interest in issues of race and ethnicity that continues, indeed sometimes surfaces, well beyond the first generation. As more recent immigrants begin to contend with the racial structure and dynamics of the United States, the earlier experiences of Puerto Ricans with regard to race hold important lessons for other and/or newer immigrant groups. Of particular relevance are the views of scholars who early examined the experiences of Puerto Ricans. For it is this type of academic writing that often forges the broader lens through which groups come to be understood in the United States—and through which groups come to understand or reinterpret themselves. It is these writings that often give impetus to revisionist, oppositional, or more integrative works by others.

I will begin by examining the difference between the Latin American and the North American racial classification systems and the anomalous and/or fluctuating racial position that Latinos have held in the United States. I then proceed to a discussion of the racial themes in the literature on Puerto Ricans. The methodology of the major works reviewed is analyzed and six themes in this literature are discussed. These are: (1) the question of whether Puerto Ricans are a race or not; (2) the continuum of racial types among Puerto Ricans and a corresponding nomenclature for these types; (3) the generally more "benign" quality of race relations in Puerto Rico; (4) the harsher racial climate in the United States; (5) the hypersensitivity to color of Puerto Ricans; and (6) the theme of "mistaken identity."

The last section reviews the perspectives taken by the authors in the major works and highlights three areas that are also germane to the issue of race. One is the authors' expectations or predictions about Puerto Rican assimilation in the U.S.; another is their preoccupation with the relationship between African Americans and Puerto Ricans; and, the third is the focus on racial "intermediates" within the Puerto Rican community. I conclude by suggesting that the presence of Puerto Ricans and the increasing numbers of other similar multiracial groups challenge the black/white notion of race in the United States.

THE CLASH OF RACE ORDERS

The Puerto Rican racial experience in the U.S. illuminates many of the difficulties experienced when a group migrates from one racial environment to another. Puerto Ricans arrived in the United States with different perceptions of race, and different racial mixtures. They entered a U.S. society that had a biologically based, biracial structure and that had tended to accommodate multiracial cultural groups into this structure. The U.S. racial structure assumed a white-notwhite division of the world. Euroamerican whites were at one end of this polarity and African blacks were at the other. Groups, such as Asians and Native-American Indians, who had also been in the U.S. since its earliest beginnings, occupied ambiguous "grey" positions within this dichotomy. They were not white, they were not black. Historical events and the geographic distribution and isolation of these groups made their racial position less salient in the public mind than the basic white-black dichotomy.

Similarly, the racial status of Latinos, as a group, was not prominent. In many regards it was ambiguous,[1] as is reflected in the changing racial classifications used for Hispanics in the U.S. census. According to Omi and Winant (1983:56), in 1930 Hispanics (more specifically, Mexicans) were included in the census as a racial category. In 1950 and 1960 they surfaced as "Persons of Spanish Mother Tongue." In 1970 they were "Persons of Both Spanish Surname and Spanish Mother Tongue." Finally, by 1980 a specific Hispanic identifier was added.[2] Identification of race was asked in a separate question. In planning for the 1990 census, the suggestion that perhaps Latinos should be counted as a separate racial group was defeated through strenuous community opposition.[3] In essence, Latinos rejected the idea that they should be counted as a separate race group. Thus, historically, it appears that in terms of categorizations Latinos have straddled the white–notwhite race order in the U.S.

RACE IN LATIN AMERICA

There is another dimension to be taken into account in analyzing the question of race among Latinos in the U.S. This is that the racial perceptions and ambiences of Latin

America differ from those which evolved in the United States. Although each country in Latin America has evolved its own racial context because of its unique history, a number of authors argue that Latinos, as a whole, have a different conception of race. Ginorio (1986:20) articulates the distinction well:

> As a result of all the extensive racial mixture and the fluidity of racial definitions, the conception of race in Latin America is one of a continuum with no clear demarcation between categories. In contrast to this racial system, in the U.S. race is seen as a dichotomous variable of white or black. Not only does the U.S. racial system differ from the Latin American one in recognizing discrete as opposed to continuous groups, it also limits racial distinctions to a very small number of categories—four or perhaps five, if in addition to white, black and yellow, red and "brown" are seen as distinct racial categories. The basis for such distinctions in the U.S. is genealogical. If an arbitrary set amount of black blood can be determined to exist, the individual is classified as black. Thus, an individual is racially defined at birth and can change that identity only by "passing."

Thus, race in Latin America is often seen as a continuum of "social races" (Wagley 1965) or a "black-white" continuum (Ginorio 1979; Wade 1985).

Others argue that race for Latinos is as much cultural or social as it is racial (Ginorio 1979; Pitt-Rivers 1975; Wagley 1965; Petrullo, 1947:16; Padilla 1958:75; Wade 1985; Harris 1970). For example, Pitt-Rivers (1975:90) argues that race in Latin America "refers to a group of people who are felt to be somehow similar in their essential nature." This more "ambiguous" concept of race has been a strong theme in Latin American literature and political thought (Muñoz 1982; Vazconcelos 1966). Yet it is not often alluded to in North American discussions of Latin America. This conception of race may have had its antecedents in Spain, been redefined in the colonial context, and may now again be in the process of redefinition in the United States.

The fact that race may be seen differently in Latin America, or that it may be less discussed, does not mean it is an issue that has been effectively resolved (Wade 1985; Betances 1972; Rodríguez 1989: ch. 3). Race has always been an important, not always commendable part, of the evolution and development of Latin America. The enslavement of both Africans and indigenous peoples was widespread, and it was often accompanied by cruelty and harsh treatment. Neither Puerto Rico nor other parts of Latin America have been racial paradises. The emphasis on the racial superiority of white Europeans during Spain's colonization period became an inherent part of Spain's legacy to Latin America. Moreover, traces of these earlier historical antecedents can be found in the present-day cultures of Latin America. This legacy is evident today and is often subtlety manifested, e.g., in common parlance, kinky hair is referred to as *pelo malo* (bad hair) and standards of beauty seldom deviate from the European model—as a glance at the models in popular Latin American publications will attest.

Nonetheless, the race orders are different in the north and in the south. The Puerto Rican racial experience points up these differences and the difficulties that result when a multiracial cultural group migrates to an essentially biracial country. The literature to be reviewed reflects the conflict of racial classification systems and the problems that flow from this conflict. For purposes of clarity, the review will emphasize major works on Puerto Ricans written during the early period of the migration, when Puerto Ricans were relative newcomers and when issues of race were not yet affected by the subsequent and substantial changes introduced by the Black Power movement.[4] But first a word on the studies examined and their methodologies.

METHODOLOGY OF THE MAJOR WORKS

With the exception of Padilla's (1958) and Gosnell's (1945) community studies, most of the works reviewed were done by North American social scientists using a variety of descriptive, ethnographic, and survey research methods. For example, Mills et al. (1950) and Tumin and Feldman (1961) used a fairly structured survey approach, with Mills emphasizing participant observation as well. Both of these survey studies involved over 1,000 respondents. Padilla (1958) and Gosnell (1945) also used structured interviews, participant observation, and had considerable numbers in their samples. But they appear to have also investigated more qualitative sources than Mills et al. (1950) and Tumin and Feldman (1961). Padilla (1958), for example, included the diaries and personal experiences of the interviewers and workers; and Gosnell (1945) made many references to the literature and popular culture of Puerto Ricans. Chenault (1970), the earliest recorder of the Puerto Rican community cited here, used a mixture of secondary sources, e.g., census reports, data from the Puerto Rico Department of Labor, the Emergency Relief Bureau of New York City, the New York City Housing Authority, the Department of Health, and newspapers. He also interviewed social workers and those in close contact with the group; finally he indicates he also had "experiences of life" in Puerto Rico and in New York. Handlin (1959) also approached his study of Puerto Ricans (and African Americans) in a similar multifaceted manner.

Petrullo (1947) and Rand (1958), on the other hand, present rather journalistic accounts. Indeed, Petrullo says, "To make it readable I have avoided full documentation and detailed discussion of minutiae" (preface, p. v). While Rand calls his study a "sociologist's objective view," he cites no methodology or other significant documentation. A working journalist, his narrative weaves in and out of what he's heard or read about Puerto Ricans from others. There are a number of works that stand somewhere between these two extremes. They combine a variety of sources and make reference to information derived from surveys and questionnaires that others have gathered (e.g.,

Senior 1961; Glazer and Moynihan 1970), or they present logically thought-out essays (e.g., G. Lewis 1963; López 1973). Lastly, there are the fieldwork and community studies, which were mainly done in Puerto Rico and which also range from the life history approaches taken by O. Lewis (1966) and Mintz (1960) to the more extensive fieldwork studies of La Ruffa (1971), Landy (1959) and Steward et al. (1956).

RACIAL THEMES IN THE LITERATURE

A reading of these works yields a series of common themes that speak to the issue of race among Puerto Ricans. (1) One theme has been the question of whether Puerto Ricans are a race or a multiracial society. Although this has been a constant question, it has not yielded a definitive answer. There are other themes that have elicited more general agreement. These are: (2) that there exists a continuum of racial types and corresponding nomenclature for these types among Puerto Ricans; (3) that there is a generally more "benign" quality of race relations in Puerto Rico; and (4) that darker Puerto Ricans experience negative social and economic consequences upon migrating to the U.S. There are also areas and themes where there has been disagreement. For example, (5) despite the general consensus on the insignificance of race in institutional treatment in Puerto Rico, there has been some disagreement on how salient or significant race is on other more personal levels, while one author has asked whether Puerto Ricans have a hypersensitivity to color. (6) The last theme, found most often in the fictional literature, is that of "mistaken identity," i.e., being identified racially instead of culturally. Each of these themes is discussed below.

The Puerto Rican Race?

Although some of the themes speak to the situation of race in Puerto Rico and others are relevant to race in New York or the U.S., one theme that has spanned both the island and the States has been the debate about whether Puerto Ricans are a race or a multiracial society. Gosnell (1945:180 ff.) in her early study of Puerto Ricans in New York noted the persistent (and by then historical) debate that existed in Puerto Rico concerning the racial composition of Puerto Ricans in Puerto Rico. Petrullo (1947) in his study of Puerto Rico devotes a chapter to the question of "The Puerto Rican 'Race.'" He concludes, "There is no Puerto Rican race, but there are white and black Puerto Ricans and all sorts of mixtures in between" (p. 14). This issue of the percentage distribution of whites and blacks among Puerto Ricans has also been touched upon by most social scientists researching Puerto Ricans. This debate continues today. It is fueled by the tendency to view Puerto Rico and Puerto Ricans from the North American racial perspective—where one is white or notwhite—and not from the Latin American racial classification system.

Continuum of Racial Types

The racial classification system in Puerto Rico has more in common with the Latin American conception of race than with the U.S. conception. Thus, in Puerto Rico there is a continuum of racial types. On this, i.e., the continuum of racial types and corresponding nomenclature for them, there has been general agreement (Gosnell 1945; Padilla 1958; Steward et al. 1956; Landy 1959; La Ruffa 1971; Mills et al. 1950; Fitzpatrick 1971; Glazer and Moynihan 1970; Mintz 1960). The general categories noted in Puerto Rico are "blanca/o" (white), "india/o" (similar to the U.S. conception of Asian Indians, i.e., dark-skinned and straight-haired), "morena/o" (dark-skinned with a variety of Negroid or Caucasian features), "negra/o" (equivalent to very black, black Americans in the U.S.) and "trigueña/o," a term that can be applied to each of the foregoing groups except very blond, European-type blancos. The term "negra/o" is also commonly used as a term of endearment without any racial connotation. Where each of these categories ends and another begins is vague and there is not always complete agreement on this (Ginorio and Berry, 1972).[5]

The Quality of Race Relations in Puerto Rico

In the literature, there has also been general agreement that the quality of race relations in Puerto Rico is superior to that in the United States. The majority of North American social scientists who have studied the island have found race relations within the body politick to be rather "benign" and somewhat unimportant (Chenault 1970; Glazer and Moynihan 1970; Petrullo 1947; Mintz 1960; Steward et al. 1956 and Giles et al 1979). Some authors have argued that color is also less important to Puerto Ricans in social and family relations than is the case in the United States (Chenault 1070; Glazer and Moynihan 1970:142). Despite this general consensus on the *insignificance* of race in institutional treatment, there has been some disagreement on how salient or significant race is on other more personal levels. Steward et al. (1956:291), Landy (1959), G. Lewis (1963:424), and Tumin and Feldman (1961:228) argue that Puerto Ricans in Puerto Rico are very conscious of race, especially skin color, while La Ruffa (1971) argues there is covert racism on the island especially toward "Africanisms," and Padilla (1958:74) states that it is to your advantage to look white in Puerto Rico. Thus, there is agreement on the relatively more benign nature of race relations in Puerto Rico as compared with the U.S. There is less agreement on whether race for Puerto Ricans is important or unimportant on more personal levels.

Prejudice in Puerto Rico

Given what has been generally agreed to be a more benign racial climate in Puerto Rico, the issue of whether prejudice exists has been greatly debated. Some authors have argued that "Puerto Ricans seem to have developed a Creole ethos tolerant of the mulatto group . . . but scornful of the black sector . . ." (Duany 1985:30, see also Zenon

Cruz 1975; and Longres 1974:68 ff.), while Betances (1972) has argued that there is a "prejudice of no prejudice" in Puerto Rico and that this in itself constitutes a prejudicial act. Zenon Cruz (1975) has argued that there are specific prejudices against Africanisms in Puerto Rico and that there is a depreciation of negritude.

Other rather complex and still debated questions have been raised concerning the question of prejudice in Puerto Rico. For example: Have Indian and African elements been destroyed or integrated into Puerto Rican society? Is the race issue in Puerto Rico dealt with by ignoring it, or is it really not an issue? Is it necessary for harmonious "race" relations that all Puerto Ricans have some African ancestry? Are the prejudices against Africanisms in Puerto Rico an American import (Movimiento Pro Independencia, 1963)? Is there an unrecognized color gradient as one moves up the income scale in Puerto Rico (Picó de Hernández, 1975)? If so, is this due to Puerto Rican preferential policies for light Puerto Ricans, discriminatory policies against blacks, inequalities inherited from slavery days, or the result of American imperialism? Is the whole debate over whether there is prejudice in Puerto Rico the result of a colonialized mentality? These questions indicate the complexity of the race issue in Puerto Rico, but they are questions that can also be asked of other Latin American countries.

Hypersensitivity to Color

An interesting perspective is presented by G. Lewis (1963), who sees the racial mixture as having produced a massive complex of color psychology "with serious results both for the quality of self-esteem and of social life" (p. 225). He agrees there is no overt racism but says there is a very real sense of color snobbishness based on the awareness of "shades." The whitening or bleaching phenomena that some attributed to racial transformation in Latin America is seen by Lewis as a problem, for it implies that self appraisal revolves around whether or not individuals are able to garner the recognition necessary to be whitened. If this is the case, then migrants to New York may be bringing (or may have brought) a heightened sensitivity to color and race that became all the more acute with the sharp, biologically based segregation existent in the States and with the significant changes wrought by the Black Power movement. Fitzpatrick (1971) alluded to this when he said that the Puerto Rican's problem with color in New York was a concern which was already present but in a much different context in Puerto Rico.

Racial Consequences in the United States

What happened when Puerto Ricans came to the States? The literature of Puerto Ricans in the United States takes note of the many difficulties that resulted because of race. Chenault (1970:92), speaking of the pre-World War II community said that instances of difficulty on account of color were so frequent that numerous examples could be given. While Steward et al. (1956:127) said "An outsider cannot easily tell how the color line works in Puerto Rico but there seems no doubt that dark skin is a worse handicap in New York than there, and that realization of this can shock the dark-skinned migrant." The negative *economic* consequences for dark Puerto Ricans in New York were noted by a number of authors. Mills (1950:72–74) found that in the late 1940s "colored" or intermediate men, i.e., those who would be defined as "indios" and "grifos" in Puerto Rico, earned less than white men and experienced less mobility.[6] Senior (1961) also found somewhat later that in New York the "colored" Puerto Ricans had a problem getting jobs. While Katzman (1968), using 1950 census data, found Negro Puerto Ricans to be more underemployed and underpaid than white Puerto Ricans but to have few differences with regard to white-collar employment.[7]

According to the literature, early on there seemed to be an awareness of the harshness of the U.S. race order particularly on darker Puerto Ricans. A number of authors make reference to what they perceive to be selective migration patterns—that is to say, a tendency for more white Puerto Ricans to migrate to New York than dark Puerto Ricans (Chenault 1970:60–61; Senior 1961:28; Petrullo 1947:23). They also took note of a tendency among the "colored," i.e., the intermediate and Negro Puerto Ricans, to want to return to Puerto Rico and to be more cautious about staying in New York (Mills et al. 1950:48; Senior 1961:28). Chenault (1970:24) observed early on that "the colored" find less discrimination on the island than in the U.S.

In the housing area, there was also note made of the difficulties experienced because of race. As Senior (1961:28) observed: "When he comes to the States, the Puerto Rican newcomer who is colored may experience his first difficulty getting a job or finding a place to live because of his color." He became, according to Senior (1961), a minority within a minority. Earlier indications of residential patterning according to race had also been noted by Chenault (1970:127), who observed a tendency in the pre–World War II period for "colored Puerto Ricans" to live in East Harlem and for color to be an important determinant of whether they could move into the more white area of Washington Heights (p. 92). Similarly, in the 1940s Gosnell (1945:313) noted some residential patterning according to the race of Puerto Ricans and a tendency for some Puerto Ricans to "pass for white" in white areas. Thus, residence early on was significantly affected by "race."

Less visible but, nonetheless, just as significant were the social and psychological changes experienced as a result of race. These too were duly noted in the early literature on the Puerto Rican community in the U.S. Gosnell (1945:310–11), for example, noted that in New York City the "traditional pride in white descent" was intensified. Padilla (1958:75 ff.)—looking at the Puerto Rican in New York a decade later and through a similar ethnographic study—found that while in Puerto Rico social race was subordinate to social class, in New York, social race was central to Hispanic life and important in mobility. She also noted the use of whiteness for upward mobility in New York. Mills et al. (1950:7) also noted the concern of the migrants with proving that they were white, while López (1973) was to argue later that Puerto Ricans had internalized race prejudice toward others and themselves.

Psychological Impact

Some speculation about the impact of race on mental health is also to be found in the literature. For example, Berle (1958) noted that black Puerto Ricans seemed to predominate among Puerto Rican drug addicts. Malzberg (1967) noted that more Puerto Rican blacks were admitted to New York state psychiatric hospitals than non-black Puerto Ricans. Teichner and Berry (1981:281) made reference to the need to address the racial problems of Puerto Ricans in the treatment of psychiatric illness, while Longres (1974:67) said, "Psychologically, the most damaging experience encountered by a Puerto Rican continental is an encounter with racist attitudes." He argued that this undermined "the sense of autonomy and initiative brought by the migrating Puerto Rican" and left "a residue of self-doubt and inadequacy" (p. 67). He saw this as a collective problem affecting all Puerto Ricans, a problem that was detrimental to individual mental health as well as to social cohesion. At the base of the problem was the experience of being forced to identify according to the socially defined racial standards of the U.S. and thereby confronting and questioning their own racial identity.

Being classified according to U.S. racial standards has meant being identified racially instead of culturally; this has meant for many being reclassified into a different culture. This reclassification experience and its consequences have been a persistent theme in the literature. It is an experience that has affected Puerto Ricans of all colors. It is found in the memoirs and literary works of the Puerto Rican migration, e.g., in the *Memorias de Bernardo Vega*, Colón's *A Puerto Rican in New York*, and Thomas's *Down These Mean Streets* and Rivera's *Family Installments*. The experience most often cited in the works is that of the darker Puerto Rican who is taken to be Negro, colored, or black.

However, the perplexing situation of the Puerto Rican who is viewed as white similarly yields confusion, anger, and a clear awareness of group divisions. For example, there are the stories retold by Colón (1961), where the white-looking daughter cannot meet her darker mother at her work place because the people she works for don't like colored people; or when only the white Puerto Ricans in an extended family will be served at a segregated restaurant in the pre-sixties period; or the case in which an apartment is rented to a white-looking member of the family, and when the others arrive, they all become the object of discrimination (Iglesias 1984).

If such reclassifications did not have real consequences, they might be seen as trivial aberrations in the stream of life. However, this has not been the case; identification as African American or even as Hispanic/Puerto Rican or Latino has had economic, residential, social, and even political consequences. Although the political consequences of race have been less well documented, it is clear that gerrymandering and voting prohibitions have been used to suppress racial minorities. On an individual level, political consequences are also often a consequence of other forms of discrimination, e.g., housing, income. The real consequences to such classifications in the U.S.—regardless of phenotype—were made quite explicit by a respondent in Oscar Lewis's *La Vida*; he said: "I'm so white that they've even taken me for a Jew, but when they see my Spanish name, they back right off" (1966:180–81).

The respondent in the Oscar Lewis study was faced with the historical choice that many ethnic Americans met, i.e., whether to change their name and pass for non-ethnic or whether to keep their ethnic name and pay the consequences. For Puerto Ricans the process was more complicated. Another choice had to be made, i.e., whether to be of the "white" race or of the "black" race. It appears that when Puerto Ricans first came they perceived that there were two paths, to the white world and to the not-white world. Two realities seemed to be evident: choice of path was dependent on racial classification according to U.S. standards, and race influenced the rewards to be gained from the system (i.e., housing, jobs, income). It seems that use of these standards would divide the group, negate the cultural existence of Puerto Ricans, and ignore their expectation that they be treated, irrespective of race, as a culturally intact group (Rodríguez 1989c, 1991).

RESEARCHER'S PERSPECTIVES

That the literature provides evidence of greater racial discrimination in the U.S. does not come as a great surprise, although it is always of interest to see such patterns documented. What is more curious are the perspectives or the assessments of social scientists with regard to race and Puerto Ricans. For example, there are: (a) the scholars' expectations about Puerto Rican assimilation in the U.S.; (b) the preoccupation with the relationship between African Americans and Puerto Ricans; and (c) the focus on racial "intermediates" within the Puerto Rican community. Each of these will be discussed in turn.

Anticipated Assimilation Paths

The assumption or conclusion of many of the authors reviewed was that with greater time in the U.S., Puerto Rican racial attitudes would become more like those in the U.S. This point had early been made by Chenault (1970:151), who noted that "the attitude of Puerto Ricans with regard to color seems to be affected by the length of residence in this country. It is the opinion of those who have studied the group for many years that the white Puerto Rican, after he has lived in New York for several years, takes up what is described as the 'American attitude' on the question of color." Fitzpatrick (1971) also speculated about whether Puerto Rican openness on race would change in the U.S. and make for a division of the community into white and black. In other words, whether the race order in the U.S. would make for separate assimilation paths. The expectation was that this would eventually happen and that those who could not assimilate into the white communities and who would not assimilate into the black communities would remain as the standard bearers of the Puerto Rican community.

Handlin (1959:60 ff.) also articulated this possibility but added that another possibility existed. This was that there would be a decline in color-consciousness and that white and "colored" Puerto Ricans might "develop a coherent community to which newcomers would be added" through immigration. However, he pointed out that this possibility would depend not just on a decline in color-consciousness but "in some part on the reactions of the larger community.... As far as the Puerto Ricans were concerned, there seems to be a growing consciousness of, and pride in, their group identity. That may reflect their preference for the second alternative, if the penalties of following it do not become too great." Thus, it was anticipated that Puerto Ricans would become white or black with greater time in the U.S. Alternatively, if Puerto Ricans were to retain a "coherent," i.e., an integrated, community they would have to pay a price and it would ultimately depend on the reactions of the larger community and on a decline in color-consciousness. Whether this has occurred is discussed elsewhere (see Rodríguez 1990).

Blacks and Puerto Ricans

There are various references in the early literature on the desire of Puerto Ricans to distinguish themselves from African Americans. Chenault (1970:150) says, for example, "Probably the outstanding fact about the racial attitude of the Puerto Rican in Harlem is that he insists upon being distinguished from the American Negro." Making general reference to other studies (on West Indians in Harlem), he suggests that there appears to be an interesting correlation between color and the desire to be distinguished from the American Negro. It seems that the darker the person is, "the more intense is his desire to speak only Spanish and to do so in a louder voice" (p. 150). Similar observations are also noted by Glazer and Moynihan (1970:11), Handlin (1962:60, 114) and Rand (1958). Indeed, Rand (1958:128–29) notes, "When the dark migrants learn about the color line, they react by differentiating themselves from the Negroes as much as they can. If they go to one of the city's hospitals, for instance, they object if the attendants write them down as 'Negro' on the admission forms.... They cling to their Spanish as a badge of distinction, and often they speak it with loud voices in public places, like subway trains.... I have heard from various sources that some Negroes in Harlem are learning Spanish too, as a way of ceasing to be Negroes."

What is puzzling about these observations is that the observers should be so surprised that any group would be reluctant to identify with a group that was not just culturally and linguistically quite different, but that was also a stigmatized group within the society. It raises the question of why they would expect darker Puerto Ricans to identify with blacks.[8] It appears that the surprise is the result of applying the North American racial classification standards; thus, because you look black, you must be black and to be black is to be just like American blacks, not to have a different culture or language. Although it is possible and easy to distinguish between Italians, Greeks, and Germans, it is not possible, or perhaps desirable, to distinguish between African blacks, West Indian blacks and American blacks. Culture becomes subordinate to race, and perhaps in the case of blacks, it ceases to exist altogether in this conception.

Intermediates

The focus on intermediates is also in some ways curious. Given the biracial nature of the U.S., one would expect that Puerto Ricans would be seen as just white or black. This more traditional classification has been evident in some studies (see, for example, Katzman 1968) and in the earlier census treatment of Puerto Ricans. In the decennial censuses of 1950, 1960, and 1970 Puerto Ricans were classified as white or Negro/black. However, other studies have focused on intermediates. Mills et al. (1950:152 ff.), for example, defined intermediates as those who in Puerto Rico might be seen as "indios" or "grifos."[9] In this study, intermediates were found to be the least adapted as compared with white and Negro Puerto Ricans. The authors state: "The facts of migration present problems to them that the whites or Negroes do not have to face so crucially. About three times as many of the men in the intermediate racial group score low on adaptation as do the white or Negro men." The study argued that intermediates were lacking a model of adaptation within the city; thus, it was "harder for the intermediate groups" because there were no "standards with which to conform."

Mills et al. (1950) argued that intermediates were not accepted by American whites and that they were reluctant to enter the American Negro community. This same study also found intermediate (and Negro) migrants to be "more cautious than the whites about planning unreservedly to stay in N.Y." (p. 48) and perceived themselves as less liked, inferior, and less adapted to the New York situation. The conception of an intermediate category is noted in other studies. Padilla (1958), for example, noted the difficulty of intermediates, their ambiguous feelings, and their tendency to heighten Puerto Rican identification for fear of being taken as anything else. Glazer and Moynihan (1970:134), citing the earlier Mills et al. (1950) work, echoed the same theme that intermediates were the least assimilated and the most passionately attached to whatever identified them as Puerto Rican. However, they added that the anxiety of the intermediates with regard to their color was greater than any objective differences in treatment would warrant.

What is curious about the use of the intermediate category is why it exists within a country with an essentially biracial, genetically based racial classification system. It is possible that the conception of the intermediate group had its roots in the Puerto Rican racial context and that this was transported via respondents or researchers to the research done in the U.S. However, it is also possible that the existence of a multiracial group, a group that is neither clearly white nor black, yields (within a biracial context) the conception of a third alternative. Thus, we see the brown category for Chicanos or Mexican Americans, or the general reference to Latinos as tan, Spanish, or Spanish white. The racial implications that some attribute to the terms "Hispanic" or "Latino"—as when the police describe a suspect as a "young Hispanic male"— might also be seen as examples of this phenomenon.

A REFLECTION ON THE RESEARCHERS' PERSPECTIVES

In the literature, a common perception of the researchers is that this intermediate group was afraid of being seen as black and of not being accepted as white. The comments on intermediates also imply the existence of a polarized racial structure wherein individuals and groups have to be accommodated. The last inference that can be made from the literature is that individuals who did not accommodate to the biracial structure would have to pay a price. The assumption was that you must be white or black— there could be no in-betweens. The assumption was also made that Puerto Ricans chose the intermediate categories as (1) a way of avoiding being seen as black and because (2) they would not be accepted as white.

However, other possibilities must be calculated when considering why individuals would use intermediate classifications. It may have been that some who would not be classified as racial intermediates might nonetheless have chosen to see themselves as intermediates, even though phenotypically they were white. It may also have been that intermediates "preferred" to be intermediates and this might have had little to do with *not* wanting to be black or *not* being able to be white. For example, they might have found that an intermediate classification was more representative of who they were physically or racially. Or, it might have allowed or affirmed a cultural identity that was subsumed or lost in the identification as white or black American. Others might have felt that such a classification was also a more accurate reflection of who they weren't, i.e., they were not white Americans and they were not black Americans and they did not care to be either. They may have opted to be intermediates because they had a personal attraction for intermediates, found greater personal or political identification with intermediates, or perceived greater freedom of class movement as intermediates.

This is not to say that there were not some who typified the pattern described in the literature. The power structure of the society cannot be denied, and identifying with whites was identifying with the more powerful, while identifying with blacks was identifying with the less powerful. However, to assume that this was the only pattern or preference is a large assumption. The assumption also implies that people accepted and wanted to be a part of a biracial structure. But, these assumptions are perhaps better understood in hindsight. Writers of the time had not yet experienced the racial transformations that were to follow in the late sixties and seventies. The perspective encompassed in the "Black is beautiful" movement had a major impact on the racial and cultural identities of many who were of African, European, Asian, and Latin American heritage. Consequently, alternatives to traditional modes were more readily understood and expected. Recent census data also confirms Latinos' tendency to respond to race in ways that differ from those expected in the U.S. In 1990, when asked what their race was, 43.5 percent of all Latinos in the country responded they were "other" and wrote in a Spanish descriptor; 52.1 percent said they were "white"; and 3.0 percent said they were "black" (U.S. Bureau of the Census, 1990).

CONCLUSION

In analyzing both the fictional and nonfictional literature on Puerto Ricans we have found a number of racial themes and perspectives that illustrate the difficulty that North Americans have had in coming to terms with Puerto Ricans as a multiracial group. These difficulties have undoubtedly also been experienced by other earlier groups that were, or became, multiracial cultural groups, e.g., Native-American Indians, and Cape Verdeans. The research suggests that Puerto Ricans and other similar groups present a challenge—by their mere presence—to the demise of the biracial system in the United States.

NOTES

The author gratefully acknowledges the assistance of Karen Carrillo and Janet Guerrero as research assistants.

1. Race is in many ways similar to gender. It is socially constructed and it is basic to identity and therefore to society. Ambiguity about one's "race" is in many societies like ambiguity about one's gender. It leads to confusion, sometimes rejection, anger, and intolerance. The fully androgynous individual must be very consciously or purposely androgynous or they will not be able to deal with the societal consequence, i.e., the often negative or ambivalent reactions their androgyny elicits among others in the society who are more clearly gender defined and who seek to define others according to strict gender definitions.

2. The 1980 Census question asked if the person was "Hispanic" or of Spanish origin and allowed individuals to indicate whether they were Mexican, Puerto Rican, Cuban, or to

write in something in the "other" category. A separate item was asked to determine race for the total U.S. population.

3. The proposal was strongly opposed "through the most aggressive campaign ever seen by the Bureau of the Census." The census agency officials decided to abandon the proposal, fearing it would cause a withdrawal of much-needed community support. Quote from N. McKenney, Census Bureau official, cited in *Hispanic Link Weekly Report*, vol 4, no. 21 (May 26, 1986).

4. See Omi and Winant (1983) for an excellent analysis of how social relations were transformed through political struggle over racial meanings.

5. An interesting conception of this continuum was advanced early on by Padilla (1958:74), who argued that in Puerto Rico there was a biracial continuum, with the two poles being white and black. Although her premise was that there was an overarching biracial structure, she maintained that, contrary to the situation in the United States, the categories in the middle of the continuum were not castelike and that one could experience mobility within one's lifetime from one group to the next.

6. Mills et al. (1950:72–74) also found white men to experience greater upward and downward mobility than the intermediate group, who tended to stay in semiskilled and unskilled jobs both in New York and in Puerto Rico.

7. Katzman (1968:373) also found black Puerto Ricans to be "more successful in obtaining white-collar jobs" than black Anglos.

8. Would the comments have been made of Italians, Greeks, or Germans who insisted on being identified as Greeks, etc., or on speaking their language?

9. However, in the text, intermediates and Negroes are often lumped together and this combined group is referred to as "the colored."

BIBLIOGRAPHY

Berle, B. 1958. *Eighty Puerto Rican families in New York City*. New York: Columbia University Press.

Betances, Samuel. 1972. "The prejudice of having no prejudice." *The Rican* 1:41–54.

Chenault, L. 1938c, 1970. *The Puerto Rican migrant in New York City*. New York: Columbia University Press.

Colón, J. 1982. *A Puerto Rican in New York and other sketches*. New York: International Publishers.

Duany, Jorge. 1985. "Ethnicity in the Spanish Caribbean: Notes on the consolidation of Creole identity in Cuba and Puerto Rico, 1762–1868." *Ethnic Groups* 6:99–123.

Fitzpatrick, J. P., Rev. 1971. *Puerto Rican Americans*. Englewood Cliffs, N.J.: Prentice-Hall.

Ginorio, Angela. 1979. "A comparison of Puerto Ricans in New York with native Puerto Ricans and Native Americans on two measures of acculturation:

Gender role and racial identification." Ph.D. diss., Fordham University, New York City.

———. 1986. "Puerto Ricans and interethnic conflict." In *International Perspectives on Ethnic Conflict: Antecedents and Dynamics*, ed. Jerry O. Boucher, Dan Landis, and Karen Arnold. Sage Press.

——— and Paul C. Berry. 1972. "Measuring Puerto Ricans' perceptions of racial characteristics." (Summary.) Proceedings of the 80th Annual Convention of the American Psychological Association, 7:287–88.

Glazer, N., and D. P. Moynihan. 1970. *Beyond the melting pot.* 2nd ed. Cambridge, Mass.: MIT Press.

Gosnell Aran, Patria. 1945. "The Puerto Ricans in New York City." Ph.D. diss., New York University.

Handlin, O. 1959. *The newcomers: Negroes and Puerto Ricans in a changing metropolis.* Cambridge, Mass.: Harvard University Press.

Harris, Marvin. 1970. "Referential ambiguity in the calculus of Brazilian racial identity." In *Afro-American Anthology*, eds. Norman Whitten, Jr., and John F. Szwed. New York: The Free Press.

Iglesias, C. A., ed. 1984. *Memoirs of Bernardo Vega.* New York: Monthly Review Press.

Katzman, Martin. 1968. "Discrimination, subculture and the economic performance of Negroes, Puerto Ricans and Mexican-Americans." *American Journal of Economics and Society* 27, no. 4: 371–75.

Landy, D. 1959. *Tropical childhood.* Chapel Hill. University of North Carolina.

La Ruffa, A. 1971. *San Cipriano: Life in a Puerto Rican community.* New York: Gordon and Breach Science Publishers.

Lewis, G. K. 1963. *Puerto Rico: Freedom and power in the Caribbean.* New York: Monthly Review Press.

Lewis, O. 1966. *La Vida: A Puerto Rican family in the culture of poverty—San Juan and New York.* New York: Random House.

Longres, John F. 1974. "Racism and its effects on Puerto Rican continentals." *Social Casework*, February, pp.67–99.

López, A. 1973. *The Puerto Rican papers.* New York: Bobbs-Merrill.

Malzberg, B. 1956. "Mental disease among the Puerto Ricans in New York City, 1949–1951." *Journal of Nervous and Mental Disease*, 123, no. 3: 262–69.

———. 1965. *Mental disease among the Puerto Ricans in New York City, 1960–1961.* Albany, N.Y.: Research Foundation for Mental Hygiene, Inc.

———. 1967. "Internal migration and mental disease among the white population in New York State, 1960–61." *International Journal of Social Psychiatry* 13, no. 3: 184–91.

Mills, C. W., C. Senior, and R. Goldsen. 1950. *The Puerto Rican journey: New York's newest migrants.* New York: Harper & Bros.

Mintz, S. W. 1960. *Worker in the cane: a Puerto Rican life history.* New Haven, Conn.: Yale University Press.

Movimiento Pro Independencia. 1963. *Tesis Política: La hora de la independencia*. San Juan, P.R.: Movimiento Pro Independencia.

Muñoz, Braulio. 1982. *Sons of the wind: The search for identity in Spanish American Indian literature*. New Brunswick, N.J.: Rutgers University Press.

Omi, M., and H. Winant. 1983. "By the rivers of Babylon: Race in the United States." Parts 1 and 2. *Socialist Review* 71:31–66 and 72:35–68.

Padilla, E. 1958. *Up from Puerto Rico*. New York: Columbia University Press.

Petrullo, V. 1947. *Puerto Rican paradox*. Philadelphia: University of Pennsylvania Press.

Picó de Hernández, I. 1975. "The quest for race, sex, and ethnic equality in Puerto Rico." *Caribbean Studies* 14: no. 4: 127–41.

Pitt-Rivers, J. 1975. "Race, color and class in Central America and the Andes." In N. R. Yetman, and C. H. Steele, eds., *Majority and minority*, Boston: Allyn and Bacon.

Rand, C. 1958. *The Puerto Ricans*. New York: Oxford University Press.

Rivera, E. 1983. *Family installments: Memories of growing up Hispanic*. New York: Penguin.

Rodríguez, C. E. 1989. *Puerto Ricans: Born in the USA*. Boston: Unwin & Hyman. (Reissued by Westview Press in Boulder, Colo., in 1991.)

———. 1990. "Racial classification among Puerto Rican men and women in New York." *Hispanic Journal of Behavioral Sciences* 12, no. 4: (November): 366–79.

Senior, C. 1961. *The Puerto Ricans: Strangers—Then Neighbors*. New York: Freedom Books.

Steward, J. H., R. A. Manners, E. R. Wolff, E. Padilla Seda, S. W. Mintz, R. L. Scheele. 1956. *The people of Puerto Rico: A study in social anthropology*. Chicago-Urbana: University of Illinois Press.

Teichner, V. J., and F. W. Berry. 1981. "The Puerto Rican patient: Some historical and psychological aspects." *Journal of the American Academy of Psychoanalysis* 9, no. 2: 277–89.

Thomas, P. 1967. *Down these mean streets*. New York: A. Knopf.

Tumin, M., and A. Feldman. 1961. *Social class and social change in Puerto Rico*. 2nd ed. Princeton, N.J.: Princeton University Press.

U.S. Bureau of the Census. 1990. Public Use Microdata tapes (1 percent sample of the population).

Vazconcelos, J. 1966. *La raza cósmica*. 3rd ed. Mexico: Espasa-Calpe.

Wade, P. 1985. "Race and class: The case of South American Blacks." *Ethnic and Racial Studies* 8, no. 2: 233–49.

Wagley, C. 1965. "On the concept of social race in the Americas." In *Contemporary cultures and societies of Latin America and the Caribbean*, ed. D. B. Heath and R. N. Adams. New York: Random House.

Zenon Cruz, I. 1975. *Narciso descubre su trasero*. Humancao, P.R.: Editorial Furidi.

The EMERGENCE of LATINO PANETHNICITY

Milagros Ricourt and Ruby Danta

What happens when persons of several Latin American national groups reside in the same neighborhood? Our research in Corona, and more widely in the borough of Queens in New York City, suggests that a new overarching identity may emerge— one termed *hispano* or *latinoamericano* in Spanish, and *Hispanic* or *Latino* in English. This new identity does not simply replace one's identification as an immigrant from a particular country. Instead, repeated interactions between individuals of various Latino ethnic groups may foster cultural exchange and create an additional identity, one that can be mobilized by Latino panethnic leaders and organizations. This book analyzes the social forces that structure this process in both the everyday interactions and the organizational and institutional life of immigrants of diverse Latin American nationalities residing in Corona and elsewhere in Queens. Four factors are critical, and we devote attention to each: language, geographic concentration, class, and gender.

Unlike past European or contemporary Asian immigrants to the United States, Latinos from different countries all share a language, and thus the potential for shared experience and self-perceptions. Our research supports Ana Celia Zentella's assertion that among the diverse Latinos living in contemporary New York City, "the Spanish language ... is their most powerful unifier" (1997, 168). This use of Spanish involves more than ease of communication, for, as Geoffrey Fox explains, "Spanish speakers and their descendants from places as widely separated as Chile and Mexico often feel a *simpatía*, a recognition of themselves in the other, that they do not have with non-Hispanics" (1996, 6). Latin Americans of all national backgrounds living in English-dominant North America also discover that "language-based discrimination is a part of the Latino experience in the United States," even for "native-born, non-Spanish-dominant Latinos" (DeSipio 1996, 179).

Geographic concentration can enhance the unifying effect of language (DeSipio 1996, 186–187). In earlier European immigrant neighborhoods, such concentration not only contributed to the formation of ethnic identity among different groups (Gans 1962; Whyte 1955; Yancey, Erickson, and Juliani 1976) but also helped forge solidarity across ethnic lines among their English-speaking second- and third-generation descendants (Kornblum 1974; Sanjek 1998). Corona is a neighborhood where a diverse Hispanic population is concentrated: by 1990 more than 38,000 Latino residents accounted for 60 percent of Corona's population—whites, blacks, and Asians accounted for the rest—with a score of Latin American nationalities represented. As people of color in the United States, Latinos also face housing discrimination, which limits residential choices and reinforces geographic concentration (Denton and Massey 1988; Massey 1981; Massey and Denton 1993). This circumstance distinguishes them from earlier European immigrants, whose children were able to escape residential segregation, and resembles the plight of the Africans Americans and other people of color who settled in the same urban settings contemporaneously (Lieberson 1980; Suttles 1968).

The fact that Corona's Latinos are mainly working-class inhabitants of a working-class neighborhood further reinforces Latino panethnic interaction and identification. Living in small, often overcrowded apartment buildings and private homes, Corona's Spanish-speaking residents meet at the street level in stores, coin-operated laundries, hospital waiting rooms, buses and subways, parks, churches, and schoolyards, where they share information about housing, store prices and sales, babysitters, jobs, and one another's cultures. They also meet in workplaces—for many, typically the "low-wage service and manufacturing industries [that] depend almost completely on immigrant labor working at minimum wage," and which nationwide employ concentrations of Latino immigrants (Moore and Pinderhughes 1993, xxvi). Here working conditions differ from those encountered by European working-class immigrants and their offspring in the 1940s, 1950s, and 1960s (Gans 1962; Kornblum 1974), reflecting the economic transformations affecting New York and other cities in the decades since the 1970s (Sassen 1992; Sassen-Koob 1981, 1983, 1985; Tabb 1982; Waldinger 1985). As Roger Sanjek (1998, 119–139) conceptualizes it, there are three economies in contemporary New York: the "speculative-electronic" financial sector, the "real economy," and the informal "underground economy." Most Latinos in Corona are employed in the real economy in low-wage, dead-end jobs and also use informal, off-the-books labor opportunities to survive. And their children attend working-class Corona's severely overcrowded and under-funded neighborhood schools.

Gender also shapes Latino panethnic experience. Through the daily-life experiences we term *convivencia diaria*, women more than men interact in neighborhood residential, health- and child-care, commercial, religious, and other settings, as well as in immigrant workplaces, such as the sewing shops in which most Corona Latinas find their initial employment. This experiential Latino panethnicity, together with the categorical panethnicity manifested in referring to one another as hispanos and latinoamericanos, is the base upon which institutional Latino panethnicity is created in Roman Catholic and Protestant Hispanic congregations and in Latino panethnic social service programs, cultural events and organizations, and political activism. Although some working-class Corona women are involved in organizing these activities, so are middle-class and professionally employed Queens Latinas. Indeed, women play a larger role than men in terms of initial organizing efforts and leadership tasks. Both female and male organization founders and leaders display a more purposeful, or ideological, panethnic consciousness.

CHANGING LATINO RESIDENCE PATTERNS

In 1980 more than half the nation's Hispanic population lived in two states— California and Texas—and an additional 17 percent in New York and Florida (Bean and Tienda 1987, 78). More recent data (del Pinal and Singer 1997, 10) show that although Latinos live in every state, their population remains concentrated in just nine, with some 85 percent residing in California, Arizona, New Mexico, Colorado, Texas, Illinois, Florida, New Jersey, and New York. However, as Louis DeSipio points out, "Traditionally, Latino populations had very little contact with each other. Mexican Americans resided primarily in the Southwest; Cuban Americans in Florida; and Puerto Ricans in New York and the Northeast" (1996, 186). All these groups grew dramatically in the two decades after World War II. Under the 1942–1964 Bracero Program, more than 4.6 million Mexicans entered the United States; between 1940 and 1960, the number of Puerto Ricans residing in the continental United States increased from roughly 70,000 to 893,000; and after the 1959 Cuban Revolution, more than half a million Cubans entered the United States by 1970 (Bean and Tienda 1987, 24, 28; DeSipio 1997, 317).

In 1965 changes in the U.S. immigration statutes opened doors to Latinos from other nations in South and Central America and the Caribbean (Kraly 1987; Sanjek 1998, 62–64). In New York, Dominicans joined the longer-established Puerto Rican and smaller Cuban populations, soon becoming the second-largest Latino group. Significant numbers of Colombians, Ecuadorans, and other South Americans, as well as Central Americans of diverse nationalities, arrived in the 1960s, 1970s, and later decades. In the 1980s the flow of Mexicans to New York also accelerated. According to estimates by New York's Department of City Planning, in 2000 the city's 850,000

Puerto Ricans accounted for 38 percent of the total Hispanic population, 615,000 Dominicans for 27 percent, 200,000 Mexicans for 9 percent, 125,000 Colombians and 125,000 Ecuadorans for 6 percent each, and other Latin Americans for about 14 percent (Gonzalez 2000). Joining the newer Hispanic immigrants after 1965 were substantial numbers of Asians of many nationalities, English-speaking West Indians, Haitians, diverse Europeans, and Africans.

As a consequence of this "new immigration," by 1990 many parts of New York City had become multiminority neighborhoods (Alba et al. 1995; Denton and Massey 1991). New York City's immigrants settled everywhere, but central Brooklyn (the destination of many West Indians and Haitians), Chinatown, northern Manhattan (a target for Dominicans), and northwest Queens (a highly diverse area that contains Corona) absorbed the largest numbers (Salvo, Ortiz, and Vardy 1992, 89–91). The historically Puerto Rican areas in Manhattan, the south Bronx, and Brooklyn remained heavily Puerto Rican, but Washington Heights in Manhattan became a strongly Dominican neighborhood (Ricourt 1998). In Queens, however, there was no majority group among the borough's diverse Latin American residents. By 1990 the 381,120 Latinos living in Queens included 100,410 Puerto Ricans (26 percent of Queens Latinos), 63,224 Colombians (17 percent), 52,309 Dominicans (14 percent), 35,412 Ecuadorans (9 percent), 18,771 Cubans (5 percent), 14,875 Peruvians (4 percent), 13,342 Mexicans (4 percent), 10,893 Salvadorans (3 percent), 4,050 Panamanians (1 percent), and 3,607 Hondurans (1 percent) (Department of City Planning 1992, 32; 1993, 24).

Neighborhoods in Queens, and Corona in particular, were in fact as much multi-Latino as they were multiminority. But by 1990 diverse Latino populations were becoming more common in other New York City boroughs as well. In Williamsburg–Greenpoint, a strongly Puerto Rican Brooklyn neighborhood, the Puerto Rican share of the Hispanic population fell from 76 percent to 63 percent between 1980 and 1990, with other Latinos (Dominicans, Ecuadorans, Mexicans, and Colombians in largest numbers) increasing from 24 percent to 37 percent (Department of City Planning 1992, 90; 1993, 126). In Washington Heights–Inwood, Dominicans accounted for 65 percent of Latino residents in 1990, with Puerto Ricans, Cubans, Ecuadorans, Colombians, Mexicans, and others constituting 35 percent (Department of City Planning 1992, 210; 1993, 304). Even in longtime Puerto Rican East Harlem, "Mexicans and other persons from Central America were beginning to displace Puerto Ricans and other Latinos from their traditional enclaves in 'El Barrio' at the end of the 1980s" (Haslip-Viera 1996, 20).

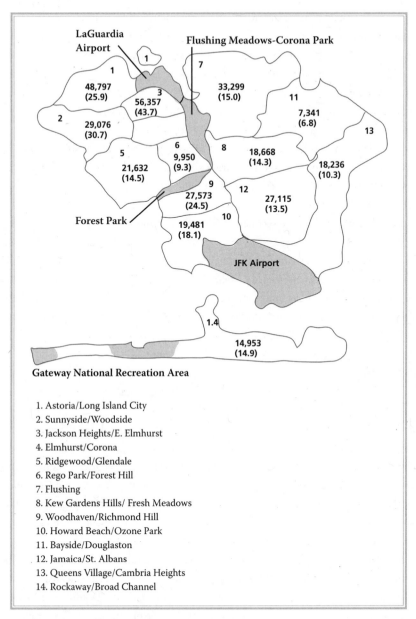

Queens Latino population by community district

1. Astoria/Long Island City
2. Sunnyside/Woodside
3. Jackson Heights/E. Elmhurst
4. Elmhurst/Corona
5. Ridgewood/Glendale
6. Rego Park/Forest Hill
7. Flushing
8. Kew Gardens Hills/ Fresh Meadows
9. Woodhaven/Richmond Hill
10. Howard Beach/Ozone Park
11. Bayside/Douglaston
12. Jamaica/St. Albans
13. Queens Village/Cambria Heights
14. Rockaway/Broad Channel

LATINO STUDIES IN NEW YORK CITY

Research on Latin American New Yorkers to date has concentrated on particular national groups—primarily Puerto Ricans, Dominicans, Colombians, and Mexicans— or on comparative studies of two or more groups. Although a few studies have focused on the social interaction of different Latino groups in residential, religious, or work-place settings (see Jones-Correa 1998, on Latino political attitudes in Queens; Mahler 1995, on diverse Latino service workers on Long Island; and Zentella 1997, on the Spanish language in New York City), none has addressed panethnic activity along several dimensions.

A rich literature on Puerto Ricans in New York City dates from the 1930s. (For overviews, see Haslip-Viera 1996; Rodriguez 1989; Rodriguez, Sánchez Korrol, and Alers 1980.) Several studies have examined labor-force participation, politics, commu-nity formation, religion, race, and cultural expression (Diaz-Stevens 1993, Falcón 1985; Flores 1987, 1994, 1996; Garrison 1974; Rodriguez 1996; Sánchez Korrol 1983; Stevens-Arroyo 1980; Torres 1995).

Dominicans are now the second most-studied Latino group. (See Hernandez and Torres-Saillant 1996; Pessar 1995; Ricourt 1998; and Torres-Saillant and Hernandez 1998 for overviews.) Research has concentrated on migration, labor-force participa-tion, small-business ownership, households, poverty, and ethnic persistence (Bray 1984; Duany 1994; Georges 1990; Grasmuck and Pessar 1991; Hernández, Rivera-Batiz, and Agodini 1995; Pessar 1987; Portes and Guarnizo 1991). Two early neighborhood studies by anthropologists also concerned community politics in Washington Heights (Georges 1984) and immigrants from the Dominican Cibao region in Corona (Hen-dricks 1974).

The few published studies of Colombians in New York City have focused on Queens, where most Colombian immigrants reside, and offer a rounded overview of the Jackson Heights community in the 1970s (Chaney 1976, 1980, 1983) and a portrait of women workers (Castro 1982, 1986). In addition, several quantitative analyses com-pare the employment patterns and household structures of Colombian and Domini-can immigrants (Gilbertson 1995; Gilbertson and Gurak 1993; Gurak and Kritz 1982). For the rapidly growing Mexican population, Robert C. Smith's ethnographic research (1996, 1998) on immigrants from a Puebla town covers settlement and employment patterns in New York City.

Smith's work also carefully documents the transnational linkages to their home community of this particular Mexican population; as Peggy Levitt phrases it, on the basis of similar fieldwork on transnational connections between Dominicans living in Boston, Massachusetts, and their relatives in the village of Miraflores, "Both migrants and nonmigrants expressed a sense of consciously belonging to a group that spanned two settings" (1998, 929). Jorge Duany, however, sees transnationalism among Domini-cans in Washington Heights as producing "ambivalent attitudes toward the host soci-ety," with immigrants "torn between the desire for material progress in the United States and persistent emotional attachment to the Dominican Republic" (1994, 43). Advocating a multifaceted and comparative approach to transnationalism, Michael Peter Smith and Luis Guarnizo (1998, 11) insist: "Transnational practices, while connecting collectivities located in more than one national territory, are embodied in specific social relations established between specific people, situated in unequivocal localities, at historically determined times. The 'locality' thus needs to be further conceptualized."

One "unequivocal" reality in Corona certainly is the existence of transnational ties that individual Latino immigrants maintain with kin and communities in their homelands. Several examples of these relationships, both for newly arrived immigrants and for those contemplating an eventual return to the home country (compare Jones-Correa 1998, 98–100), are described in later chapters. However, in conceptualizing Corona as a locality, we cannot portray the "specific social relations established between specific people" among its Latino residents as limited to transnational considerations. Rather, we agree with Arjun Appadurai (1996, 185) that "as local subjects carry on the continuing task of reproducing their neighborhood, the contingencies of history, environment, and imagination contain the potential for new contexts," and in particular new Latino panethnic ones. Moreover, transnational behaviors do not form an obstacle to the emergence of Latino panethnic experience, categories, organization, or ideology. Both processes can, and do, occur simultaneously. Nonetheless, we argue that a continuing research focus on individual Latino national groups, one by one, in neighborhoods now containing mixes of Puerto Ricans, Dominicans, Colombians, Mexicans, and other Latinos, is more likely to uncover transnationalism than panethnicity. If we wish to heed the "contingencies of history, environment, and imagination" in neighborhoods where diverse Latinos are geographically concentrated, we must ask: Is it still possible to study each group separately, without looking at their interaction?

CONCEPTUALIZING LATINO PANETHNICITY

As "residents of the United States who can trace their ancestry to the Spanish-speaking regions of Latin American and the Caribbean" (DeSipio 1996, 178), Latinos in Corona and Queens vary individually and situationally in how they identify themselves. Most attach the strongest cultural meanings and values to their own national identities as Dominicans, Colombians, Nicaraguans, and so forth, and prefer that others acknowledge these national—or, in the United States, "ethnic"—identities (compare Hardy-Fanta 1993; Oboler 1995). However, people also use *hispano* and *latinoamericano* in Spanish, and *Hispanic* and *Latino* in English, to refer to the larger Spanish-speaking, multinationality group.

Martha, for example, is a working-class Guatemalan who immigrated to the United States in 1980. During an interview Martha stated, "I am from Guatemala," and then invited Ricourt to taste the *taquitos* she was preparing, remarking that her Guatemalan national food had many similarities to Mexican and other Central American cuisines. When asked about her Corona neighborhood, she said that her street was "Hispana." "Hay gentes de todas partes—dominicanos, colombianos, ecuatorianos. Mi vecina de arriba es ecuatoriana y la del piso de mas arriba es colombiana." ("There are people from everywhere—Dominicans, Colombians, Ecuadorans. My neighbor upstairs is from Ecuador, and the other is Colombian.") When she recalled an incident at the factory where she worked in Long Island City, Queens, she referred to her coworkers as "nosotros hispanos," or "we Hispanos."

In another interview, Aida Gonzalez, a middle-class Ecuadoran who arrived in the United States in the early 1960s and worked as director of cultural affairs at Queens Borough Hall, responded she was "Ecuadoran American" to a question about her ethnic identity. As she then pointed to an Ecuadoran clay pot with an American flag in it, she added, "I am working and serving a Latin American community. I am also *latinoamericana*. Here in Queens we are of many nationalities, and numbers are almost equal. In order to gain political recognition we need to have a united voice."

A massive scholarly literature discusses the uses, meanings, and nuances of *Latino, Hispanic*, and other terms referring to this diverse population (Anzaldúa 1987; Anzaldúa and Moraga 1983; Bean and Tienda 1987; Calderón 1992; de la Garza et al. 1992; Moore and Pachon 1985; Murguia and Martinelli 1991; Nelson and Tienda 1985; Oboler 1995; Portes and Truelove 1987; Sullivan 1985; Totti 1987; Zinn 1981). These authors all acknowledge the complex and diverse nature of the Latino population in the United States. Alejandro Portes and Cynthia Truelove (1987, 360) point to socioeconomic, racial, historical, cultural, and immigration-status differences, as well as to varying patterns of entry and settlement. Frank Bean and Marta Tienda (1987, 56) conclude that Mexicans, Puerto Ricans, and Cubans have different socioeconomic and demographic characteristics, and Rodolfo de la Garza and colleagues (1992) contrast the political behavior of these three groups, asserting that few individuals consider themselves part of a Latino or Hispanic collectivity. Gloria Anzaldúa and Cherríe Moraga (1983), Suzanne Oboler (1995, 1), and Maxine Baca Zinn (1981, 18–24) stress internal differentiation by gender and sexual orientation, as well as by race, class, and language use.

Some authors, however, conclude that diverse Latinos may be able to find unity through common political action. Portes and Truelove (1987) mention shared problems around job discrimination or affirmative action, but they admit that this circumstance does not automatically produce a strong collective self-identity. Michael Jones-Correa argues that "state-offered incentives" to "Hispanics" can lead to "self-interested mobilization of various Latin American origin groups," and that "Latino identity" is thus "partly a construction of the state" (1998, 111). DeSipio usefully summarizes five interconnected factors facilitating the development of Latino panethnicity: "common cultural characteristics," "increasing contact between Latino populations with various ancestries," "common public policy needs and concerns," "statutory recognition of Latino rather than national-origin based ethnicity," and "the role of . . . elites in shaping a common identity" (1996, 177). These factors are consistent with the data and argument of our book.

The first fieldwork-based examination of Latino panethnicity was Felix Padilla's 1985 study of Mexican Americans and Puerto Ricans in Chicago. Although the Spanish language provided the medium for the formation of "Latinism," as Padilla termed the political ties formed between these two groups, each group resided separately in different Chicago neighborhoods. Concerns over inequalities in education and employment united them, but a shared base of convivencia diaria in neighborhood, churches, and public space was absent. Padilla stressed situational and collective political action in producing a Latino panethnicity, but not cultural or interpersonal factors. Carol Hardy-Fanta's 1993 study, *Latina Politics, Latino Politics: Gender, Culture, and Political Participation in Boston*, like Padilla's work, focused on political action and leaders, and usefully pointed to women as significant shapers of Latino panethnic activism. Again, however, the textures of daily life and neighborhood realities in the lives of these leaders' constituents remained out of the picture. Still other researchers have studied situations in which Latino panethnic interaction has become fragmented in daily life. Greta Gilbertson and Douglas Gurak (1993), for example, see "ethnic enclave" employment among Dominican and Colombian men as limiting contact with other Latinos; and Sarah Mahler (1995) documents how competition and jealously among casually employed Latino male laborers on Long Island hampers ethnic as well as any panethnic unity.

For the Queens case, we need to extend this insight along four dimensions to account for Latino panethnicity at both the organizational level and the level of convivencia diaria. First, we document *experiential panethnicity* in the daily-life settings of residence, neighborhood, and workplace; here diverse Latinos in Corona interact with each other using the medium of Spanish and establish a variety of new crossnationality ties. *Categorical panethnicity* emerges in these settings as people view and speak of one another as hispanos or latinoamericanos. Martha, the Guatemalan factory worker, exemplifies these two dimensions.

Third, *institutional panethnicity* emerges when religious congregations, senior citizen centers, social service programs, cultural organizations, and political groups are created by leaders to attract and serve all Latinos in Corona or Queens. Fourth, *ideological panethnicity* is voiced by these leaders of what they usually identify as Latino or Hispanic social service, cultural, and political organizations. Aida Gonzalez, the Ecuadoran director of cultural affairs at Queens Borough Hall, expressed this ideological version of Latino panethnicity, and her various activities in Queens Latino panethnic organizations, as we shall see, exemplified her involvement along the third, or institutional, dimension.

Latino panethnicity is something created in the United States. It combines old customs and relationships brought from countries of origin with new forms of interaction generated in the receiving country. Latino panethnicity arises at the grassroots community level through daily-life activities, most particularly those of working-class women. Some of them are joined by middle-class Latinas to develop a variety of organizations that serve their diverse Spanish-speaking community. All these women interact together through their common identification as Hispanas or Latinas.

REFERENCES

Alba, Richard, Nancy Denton, Shu-Yin J. Leung, and John Logan. 1995. "Neighborhood Change under Conditions of Mass Migration: The New York City Region, 1970–1990." *International Migration Review* 24(3): 625–632.

Anzaldúa, Gloria. 1987. *Borderlands/La Frontera*: The New Mestiza. San Francisco Spinsters/Aunt Lute.

Anzaldúa, Gloria and Cherríe Moraga, eds. 1983. *This Bridge Called My Back: Writing by Radical Women of Color.* New York: Kitchen Table Press.

Appadurai, Arjun. 1996. *Modernity at Large: Cultural Dimensions of Globalization.* Minneapolis: University of Minnesota Press.

Bean, Frank D., and Marta Tienda. 1987. *The Hispanic Population of the United States.* New York: Russell Sage Foundation.

Bray, David. 1984. "The Economic Development: The Middle Class and International Migration in the Dominican Republic." *International Migration Review* 18(2): 217–236.

Calderón, Jose. 1992. "'Hispanic' and 'Latino': The Viability of Categories for Panethnic Studies." *Latin American Perspectives* 19(4): 37–44.

Castro, Mary Garcia. 1982. "Women in Migration: Colombian Voices in the Big Apple." *Migration Today* 10(3/4):22–32.

——— 1986. "Work versus Life: Colombian Women in New York". In June Nash et al., *Women and Change in Latin America*, 231–259. South Hadley, Mass.: Bergin and Garvey.

Chaney, Elsa. 1976. "Colombian Migration to the United States". In *The Dynamics of Migration*, 87–141. Washington, D.C.: Interdisciplinary Communications Program, Smithsonian Institution.

———1980. "Colombians in New York City: Theoretical and Policy Issues." In *Sourcebook on the New Immigration*, ed. Roy Simon Bryce-Laporte, 285–294. New Brunswick, N.J.: Transaction.

———1983. "Colombian Output in New York City". In *Awakening Minorities: Continuity and Change,* ed. John Howard, 67–76. New Brunswick, N.J.: Transaction.

de la Garza, Rodolfo, Louis DeSipio, F. Chris Garcia, and Angelo Falcón. 1992. *Latino Voices: Mexican, Puerto Rican, and Cuban Perspectives on American Politics.* Boulder: Westview.

Del Pinal Jorge, and Audrey Singer. 1997. *Generations of Diversity: Latinos in the United States.* Washington, D.C.: Population Reference Bureau.

Denton, Nancy, and Douglass Massey. 1988. "Racial Identity among Caribbean Hispanics: The Effect of Double Minority Status on Racial Segregation." *American Sociological Review* 54: 790–808.

—— 1991. "Patterns of Neighborhood Transition in a Multiethnic World: U.S. Metropolitan Areas, 1970–1980." *Demography* 28:41–63.

Department of New York City Planning, City of New York. 1992. *Demographic Profiles.* New York.

DeSipio, Louis. 1996. "More than the Sum of Its Parts: The Building Blocks of a Pan-Ethnic Latino Identity." In *The Politics of Minority Coalitions: Race, Ethnicity, and Shared Uncertainties*, ed. Wilbur Rich, 177–189. Westport, Conn.: Praeger.

—— 1997. "The Engine of Latino Growth: Latin American Immigration and Settlement in the United States." In *Pursuing Power: Latinos and the Political System*, ed. F. Chris Garcia, 314–342. Notre Dame, Ind.: University of Notre Dame Press.

Diaz-Stevens, Ana Maria. 1993. *Oxcart Catholicism on Fifth Avenue: The Impact of the Puerto Rican Migration upon the Archdiocese of New York.* Notre Dame, Ind.: University of Notre Dame Press.

Duany, Jorge. 1994. *Quisqueya on the Hudson: The Transnational Identity of Dominicans in Washington Heights.* New York: City University of New York, Dominican Studies Institute.

Falcón, Angelo. 1985. *Black and Puerto Rican Politics in New York City: Race and Ethnicity in a Changing Urban Context.* New York: Institute for Puerto Rican Policy.

Flores, Juan. 1987. "Rappin', Writin', and Breakin': Black and Puerto Rican Street Culture in New York." *Dissent* 34(4): 580–584.

—— 1994. "Puerto Rican and Proud, Boyee!: Rap, Roots, and Amnesia." In *Microphone Fiends: Youth Music and Youth Culture*, ed. Andrew Ross and Tricia Rose, 89–98. New York: Routledge.

—— 1996. "Puerto Rican Culture at the Crossroads." In *Latinos in New York: Communities in Transition*, ed. Gabriel Haslip-Viera and Sherrie L. Baver, 331–338. Notre Dame, Ind.: University of Notre Dame Press.

Fox, Geoffrey. 1996. *Hispanic Nation: Culture, Politics, and the Constructing of Identity.* Secaucus, N.J.: Birch Lane.

Gans, Herbert. 1962. *The Urban Villagers: Group and Class in the Life of Italian-Americans.* New York: Free Press.

Garrison, Vivian. 1974. "Sectarianism and Psychosocial Adjustment: A Controlled Comparison of Puerto Rican Pentecostals and Catholics." In *Religious Movements in Contemporary America*, ed. Irving Zaretsky and Mark Leone, 298–329. Princeton: Princeton University Press.

Georges, Eugenia. 1984. *New Immigrants and the Political Process: Dominicans in New York.* New York: Center for Latin American and Caribbean Studies, New York University.

——— 1990. *The Making of a Transnational Community: Migration, Development and Cultural Change in the Dominican Republic.* New York: Columbia University Press.

Gilbertson, Greta. 1995. "Women's Labor and Enclave Employment: The Case of Dominican and Colombian Women in New York City." *International Migration Review* 29: 657–671.

Gilbertson, Greta, and Douglas Gurak. 1993. "Broadening the Enclave Debate: The Labor Market Experiences of Dominican and Colombian Men in New York City." *Sociological Forum* 8(2): 205–220.

Gonzalez, Carolina. 2000. "The Changing Face of New York." *New York Daily News,* 27 June.

Grasmuck, Sherri, and Patricia Pessar. 1991. *Between Two Islands: Dominican International Migration.* Berkeley: University of California Press.

Gurak, Douglas, and Mary Kritz. 1982. "Dominican and Colombian Women in New York." *Migration Today.* 10(3/4): 15–21.

Hardy-Fanta, Carol. 1993. *Latina Politics, Latino Politics: Gender, Culture, and Political Participation in Boston.* Philadelphia: Temple University Press.

Haslip-Viera, Gabriel. 1996. "The Evolution of the Latino Community in New York City: Early Nineteenth Century to the Present." In *Latinos in New York: Communities in Transition*, ed. Haslip-Viera and Sherrie L. Baver, 3–29. Notre Dame, Ind.: University of Notre Dame.

Hendricks, Glenn. 1974. *The Dominican Diaspora: From the Dominican Republic to New York City- Villagers in Transition.* New York: Teachers College Press.

Hernandez, Ramona, Francisco Rivera-Batiz, and Roberto Agodini. 1995. *Dominican New Yorkers: A Socioeconomic Profile.* New York: City University of New York, Dominican Studies Institute.

Hernandez, Ramona, and Silvio Torres-Saillant. 1996. "Dominicans in New York: Men, Women, and Prospects." In *Latinos in New York: Communities in Transition*, ed. Haslip-Viera and Sherrie L. Baver, 30–56. Notre Dame, Ind.: University of Notre Dame.

Jones-Correa, Michael. 1998. *Between Two Nations: The Political Predicament of Latinos in New York City.* Ithaca: Cornell University Press.

Kornblum, William. 1974. *Blue Collar Community.* Chicago: University of Chicago Press.

Levitt, Peggy 1998. "Social Remittances: Migration Driven Local-Level Forms of Cultural Diffusion." *International Migration Review* 32: 926–948.

Lieberson, Stanley. 1980. *A Piece of the Pie: Blacks and White Immigrants since 1880.* Berkeley: University of California Press.

Mahler, Sarah. 1995. *American Dreaming: Immigrant Life on the Margins.* Princeton: Princeton University Press.

Massey, Douglas. 1981. "Hispanic Residential Segregation: A Comparison of Mexicans, Cubans, and Puerto Ricans." *Sociology and Social Research* 65: 311–322.

Massey, Douglas and Nancy Denton. 1993. *American Apartheid: Segregation and the Making of the Underclass.* Cambridge, Mass.: Harvard University Press.

Moore, Joan, and Harry Pachon. 1985. *Hispanics in the United States.* Englewood Cliffs, N.J.: Prentice-Hall.

Moore, Joan, and Raquel Pinderhughes. 1993. "Introduction." In *In the Barrios: Latinos and the Underclass Debate*, ed. Joan Moore and Raquel Pinderhughes, xi–xxxix. New York: Russell Sage Foundation.

Murguia, Edward, and Phylis Cancilla Martinelli, eds. 1991. "A Special Issue on Latino/ Hispanic Ethnic Identity. *Latino Studies Journal* 2(3): 5–83.

Nelson, Candace, and Marta Tienda. 1985. "The Structuring of Hispanic Ethnicity: Historical and Contemporary Perspectives." *Ethnic and Racial Studies* 8:49–74.

Oboler, Suzanne. 1995. *Ethnic Labels, Latino Lives: Identity and the Politics of (Re)Presentation in the United States.* Minneapolis. University of Minnesota Press.

Padilla, Felix. 1985. *Latino Ethnic Consciousness: The Case of Mexican Americans and Puerto Ricans in Chicago.* Notre Dame, Ind.: University of Notre Dame.

Pessar, Patricia. 1987. "The Dominicans: Women in the Household and the Garment Industry." In *New Immigrants in New York*, ed. Nancy Foner, 103–129. New York: Columbia University Press.

—— 1995. *A Visa for a Dream: Dominicans in the United States.* Needham Heights, Mass.: Allyn and Bacon.

Portes, Alejandro, and Luis Guarnizo. 1991. *Capitalistas del Trópico: La Inmigración en los Estados Unidos y el desarrollo de la pequeña empresa en República Dominicana.* Santo Domingo: Facultad Latinoamericana de Ciencias Sociales, Proyecto República Dominicana.

Portes, Alejandro, and Cynthia Truelove. 1987. "Making Sense of Diversity: Recent Research on Hispanic Minorities in the United States." *Annual Review of Sociology* 13:359–385.

Ricourt, Milagros. 1998. "Patterns of Dominican Demography and Community Development in New York City." *Latino Studies Journal* 9(3): 11–38.

Rodriguez, Clara. 1989. *Puerto Ricans: Born in the U.S.A.* Boston: Unwin Hyman.

—— 1996. "Racial Themes in the Literature: Puerto Ricans and Other Latinos." In *Latinos in New York: Communities in Transition*, ed. Haslip-Viera and Sherrie L. Baver, 104–125. Notre Dame, Ind.: University of Notre Dame.

Rodriguez, Clara, Virginia Sánchez Korrol, and José Oscar Alers, eds. 1980. *The Puerto Rican Struggle: Essays on Survival*. Maplewood: N.J.: Waterfront.

Salvo, Joseph, Ronald Ortiz, and Francis Vardy. 1992. *The Newest New Yorkers: An Analysis of Immigration into New York City during the 1980s*. New York: Department of City Planning, City of New York.

Sánchez Korrol, Virginia. 1983. *From Colonia to Community: The History of Puerto Ricans in New York City, 1917–1948*. Westport, Conn.: Greenwood.

Sanjek, Roger. 1992. "The Organization of Festivals and Ceremonies among Americans and Immigrants in Queens, New York." In *To Make the World Safe for Diversity: Towards an Understanding of Multicultural Societies*, ed. Ake Daun, Billy Ehn, and Barbro Klein, 123–143. Stockholm: Ethnology Institute, Stockholm University.

—— 1998. *The Future of us All: Race and Neighborhood Politics in New York City*. Ithaca: Cornell Univeristy Press.

Sassen, Saskia. 1992. "Why Migration?" *NACLA Report on the Americas* 26(1): 14–19.

Sassen-Koob, Saskia. 1981. "Exporting Capital and Importing Labor: The Role of Women." In *Female Immigrants to the United States: Caribbean, Latin American and African Experiences*, eds. Delores Mortimer and Roy Simon Bryce-Laporte, 203–234. Washington, D.C.: Research Institute on Immigration and Ethnic Studies, Smithsonian Institute.

—— 1983. "Formal and Informal Associations: Dominicans and Colombians in New York." In *Caribbean Life in New York City: Sociocultural Dimensions*, ed. Constance Sutton and Elsa Chaney, 278–296. New York: Center for Migration Studies.

—— 1985. "The Changing Composition and Labor Market Location of Hispanic Immigrants in New York City, 1960–1980." In *Hispanics in the U.S. Economy*, ed. George Borjas and Marta Tienda, 299–320. Orlando, Fla.: Academic.

Smith, Michael Peter, and Luis Guarnizo, eds. 1998. *Transnationalism from Below*. New Brunswick, N.J.: Transaction.

Smith, Robert C. 1996. "Mexicans in New York: Memberships and Incorporation in a New Immigrant Community." In *Latinos in New York: Communities in Transition*, ed. Haslip-Viera and Sherrie L. Baver, 57–103. Notre Dame, Ind.: University of Notre Dame.

—— 1998. "Transnational Localities: Community, Technology and the Politics of Membership within the Context of Mexico and U.S. Migration." In *Transnationalism from Below*, ed. Peter Michael Smith and Luis Guarnizo, 196–238. New Brunswick: Transaction.

Stevens-Arroya, Antonio. 1980. "Puerto Rican Struggles in the Catholic Church." In *The Puerto Rican Struggle: Essays on Survival*, ed. Clara Rodriguez, Virginia Sánchez Korrol, and Jose Oscar Alers, 129–139. Maplewood, N.J.: Waterfront.

Sullivan, Teresa. 1985. "A Demographic Portrait." In *Hispanics in the United States: A New Social Agenda*, ed. Pastora San Juan Cafferty and William C. MacCready, 7–32. New Brunswick, N.J.: Transaction.

Suttles, Gerald. 1968. *The Social Order of the Slum: Ethnicity and Territory in the Inner City*. Chicago: University of Chicago Press.

Tabb, William. 1982. *The Long Default: New York City and the Urban Fiscal Crisis*. New York: Monthly Review Press.

Torres, Andres. 1995. *Between Melting Pot and Mosaic: African Americans and Puerto Ricans in the New York Political Economy*. Philadelphia: Temple University Press.

Torres, Saillant, Silvio, and Ramona Hernandez. 1998. *The Dominican Americans*. Westport, Conn,: Greenwood.

Totti, Xavier. 1987. "The Making of a Latino Identity." *Dissent* 34(4): 537–542.

Waldinger, Roger. 1985. "Immigration and Industrial Change in the Apparel Industry." In *Hispanics and the U.S. Economy*, ed. George Borjas and Marta Tienda. 323–349. Orlando, Fla.: Academic.

Whyte, William Foote. 1955. *Street Corner Society: The Social Structure of an Italian Slum*. Chicago: University of Chicago Press.

Yancy, William, Eugene Erickson, and Richard Juliani. 1976. "Emergent Ethnicity: A Review and Reformulation." *American Sociological Review*. 41: 391–403.

Zentella, Ana Celia. 1997. "Spanish in New York." In *The Multilingual Apple: Languages in New York City*, ed. Ofelia Garcia and Joshua Fishman, 167–201. Berlin: Mouton de Gruyter.

Zinn, Maxine Baca. 1981. "Gender and Ethnic Identity among Chicanas." *Frontiers* 5(2): 18–24.

—— 1998. *The Future of us All: Race and Neighborhood Politics in New York City*. Ithaca: Cornell Univeristy Press.

CREOLE RELIGIONS *of the* CARIBBEAN

Margarite Fernández Olmos and Lizabeth Paravisini-Gebert

> What piece of our soil was not saturated with secret African influences?
> —*Lydia Cabrera, Yemayá y Ochún*

INTRODUCTION

Luis is a young man who works in the stockroom of a tourist café in Havana. An inventory reveals five boxes of missing supplies and, despite his claims of innocence, the police consider him a suspect. In his distress, he seeks Marín, his spiritual godfather or padrino, a lifelong friend whose spiritual work in Santería, Regla de Palo, and Espiritismo follows the practices of his African ancestors. Marín summons the spirit of Ma Pancha, an African slave with whom he has communicated on previous occasions. Marín sits before a home altar that contains, among other things, the statues of the Catholic saints San Juan Bosco and Santa Bárbara, and a glass of water. Uncorking a bottle of strong cane liquor, he pours a drink into a dry gourd, lights a homemade cigar, and chants a verse, calling upon her spirit to respond "in the name of Jesus Christ and of Papá Changó." At this point Ma Pancha greets them in broken Spanish through Marín's voice with "Good morning, how are my children here on this earth?" and is informed of the problem. Stating that Luis's boss is responsible for the theft, Ma Pancha counsels the men to gather the bark of certain types of trees "to open the eyes of the police" and suggests that Marín prepare a macuto or magical pouch, and dedicate it to Ochosi, the deity of forests and herbs, patron of those with problems involving the law, to protect Luis and convince the authorities of his innocence. The macuto is assembled with the name of the guilty party placed inside and set at the base of a *nganga* or spiritual cauldron.

Paulette, a middle-aged Haitian woman living in Coral Gables, Miami, has been married to a lawyer and former politician for many years. When she discovers that her husband is having an affair with his young secretary, a friend suggests she speak with Denizé, a *houngan*, or Vodou priest who does spiritual readings using cards for divination. During the reading Paulette discovers that her tutelary *loa* is Erzulie, spirit of femininity and sensuality, and Denizé advises her to make efforts to become more attractive to her husband. He recommends a purifying bath of white flowers, powdered egg shells, and perfume, during which Paulette would be released from all negativity. Afterwards, she is to leave the flowers at a crossroads. He instructs Paulette to cleanse her house with water composed of the same ingredients as the bath, adding a bit of honey. She is to make an offering to Erzulie of sweet fruit and honey to be placed on her home altar. After the reading, Denizé prepares a small bottle of perfume for Paulette to bring her *chans*, or luck. In it he had inserted a small plant believed to have the power to open paths for the achievement of goals.

Desmond and Earl, young Jamaicans living in Toronto, have engaged in a series of robberies involving small suburban banks. They are assiduous clients of an Obeahman, from whom they seek the ritual cleansings and massages they believe will protect them from arrest and punishment. When they kill a young woman during a robbery, their Obeahman alerts the police to their possible involvement. Surveillance equipment is installed in his consultation room, and when his clients return—this time seeking protection that will allow them to return to Jamaica, where the woman's *duppy* or spirit will not follow them to do them harm—their sessions are recorded and the evidence leads to their arrest. The case against them centers on the admissibility of the evidence, an issue that itself revolves around the confidentiality—or sacredness—of the communications, or "confessions," between the Obeahman and his client. The sanctity of their interactions is rejected by the courts on the basis of Obeah being a healing practice and not a religion, and the two are convicted of robbery and murder.

These tales—based on the actual experiences of people living in the Caribbean and its Diaspora—speak to the continuing power of the Afro-Caribbean spiritual traditions that have sustained the peoples of the region for centuries. *Creole Religions of the Caribbean* is intended as a comprehensive introduction to the creolized, African-based religions that developed in the Caribbean in the wake of European colonization. It seeks to show how Caribbean peoples fashioned a heterogeneous system of belief out of the cacophony of practices and traditions that came forcibly together in colonial society: the various religious and healing traditions represented by the extensive slave population brought to the New World through the Middle Passage; Spanish, French, and Portuguese variants of Catholicism; the myriad strands of Protestantism brought to the English and Dutch colonies; and remnants of Amerindian animistic practices.

These creolized religious systems, developed in secrecy, were frequently outlawed by the colonizers because they posed a challenge to official Christian practices and were believed to be associated with magic and sorcery. They nonetheless allowed the most oppressed sectors of colonial Caribbean societies to manifest their spirituality, express cultural and political practices suppressed by colonial force, and protect the health of the community. These complex systems developed in symbiotic relationships to the social, linguistic, religious, and natural environments of the various islands of the Caribbean, taking their form and characteristics from the subtle blends and clashes between different cultural, political, and spiritual practices. This book traces the historical-cultural origins of the major Creole religions and spiritual practices of the region—Vodou, Santería, Obeah, Espiritismo—and describes their current-day expression in the Caribbean and its Diaspora.[1]

Caribbean Creole religions developed as the result of cultural contact. The complex dynamics of encounters, adaptations, assimilation, and syncretism that we call *creolization* are emblematic of the vibrant nature of Diaspora cultures. They led to the development of a complex system of religious and healing practices that allowed enslaved African communities that had already suffered devastating cultural loss to preserve a sense of group and personal identity. Having lost the connection between the spirits and Africa during the Middle Passage, they strove to adapt their spiritual environment to suit their new Caribbean space. The flexibility, eclecticism, and malleability of African religions allowed practitioners to adapt to their new environments, drawing spiritual power from wherever it originated. More than simply a strategy for survival, this active, conscious, syncretic process demonstrates an appreciation for the intrinsic value of creativity, growth, and change as well as for the spiritual potential of other belief systems.

Transculturation, a term coined by Cuban anthropologist Fernando Ortiz to describe the ceaseless creation of new cultures, was intended to counterbalance the notion of *acculturation*, the term in vogue among anthropologists during the 1940s. Ortiz understood the notion of acculturation as one that interpreted the development of Caribbean cultures as the one-way imposition of the culture of the dominant or conquering nation on the conquered societies, an imposition that devalued and eventually supplanted the conquered cultures. Believing that colonization had initiated instead a creative, ongoing process of appropriation, revision, and survival leading to the mutual transformation of two or more pre-existing cultures into a new one, Ortiz posited the notion of transculturation as a more accurate rendering of the processes that produced contemporary Caribbean cultures.

Religious practices were at the very center of the processes of transculturation. "Throughout the diaspora, African religions provided important cultural resources for not only reconstructing ethnic ties and social relations that had been disrupted by slavery, but also for forging new collective identities, institutions and belief systems which partook of the cultures of diverse African peoples to meet the daunting challenges of new and oppressive social contexts" (Gregory 1999: 12). The metaphor for the process of transculturation used by Fernando Ortiz is the *ajiaco*, a delicious soup made with very diverse ingredients, in which the broth that stays at the bottom represents an integrated nationality, the product of synthesis. This metaphor has found an echo throughout the Caribbean region, finding its counterpart in the Dominican *sancocho* and the West Indian *callaloo*. However, although rich in metaphoric power, neither the ajiaco nor the callaloo are ideal formulas. They have been challenged by Caribbean scholars and critics for failing to do full justice to the "undissolved ingredients" represented by the magical, life-affirming elements of Afro-Caribbean religions. Cuban art critic Gerardo Mosquera, for example, has argued that "beside the broth of synthesis, there are bones, gristle, and hard seeds that never fully dissolve, even after they have contributed their substance to the broth. These undissolved ingredients are the survivals and recreations of African traditions within religious-cultural complexes" (1992: 30).

Creolization

Creolization—that is, the malleability and mutability of various beliefs and practices as they adapt to new understandings of class, race, gender, power, labor, and sexuality— is one of the most significant phenomena in Caribbean religious history. Given the subtle negotiations necessary for the survival of the cultural practices of the enslaved and colonized in the highly hierarchical colonial societies of the Caribbean, the resulting religious systems are fundamentally complex, pluralistic, and integrationist. In our approach to the creolized religious systems that developed in the region in the wake of colonization, we seek to avoid essentialist definitions of religious experience, opting instead for a practice- or experience-based presentation and analysis, rooted in particular historical circumstances. Although the Creole religions vary in their origins, beliefs, and rituals, all of them demonstrate the complexities and the creative resourcefulness of the creolization process.

The term *creole* was first used in the Americas to refer to native-born persons of European ancestry. It was later extended to other "transplanted" categories of interchange: from linguistic (*Créole* refers to the national language of Haiti, developed as a result of Old and New World contact) and literary to a wide range of cultural contexts—religious, musical, curative, and culinary (Mintz and Price 1985: 6–7). "There is, then, a vast range of examples of the Creolizing process, even without taking into account such areas of human activity as art, law, material culture, military organization, politics, or social structures" (Buisseret, "Introduction" 2000: 12). The term eventually evolved from a geographical to an ethnic label: New World enslaved Africans were distinguished from African-born contemporaries by the label *criollos*. Hoetink notes the multiple contemporary nuances of the term:

> I take the word *creole* to mean the opposite of foreign. Thus *creole culture* refers to those aspects of culture that evolved or were adapted in the Western Hemisphere and became part of a New World society's distinctive heritage. In Latin America, the term *criollo*, when used in reference to people, was originally reserved for native whites. In the Hispanic Caribbean nowadays, it often includes all those born and bred in a particular society. Elsewhere, as in Suriname, the term may be used to denote long-established population groups, such as the Afro-Americans, as opposed to more recent immigration groups.
>
> (1985: 82)

For anthropologists and historians the concept of creolization has contested and now supplanted assumptions regarding the "assimilation" and "acculturation" of subordinate peoples into a dominant "donor" European culture. Much has changed since Melville Herskovits challenged prevailing assumptions regarding the survival of African influences in the New World in his *The Myth of the Negro Past* (1941), proving in great detail that African culture has survived and indeed thrived. Today scholars recognize what Herskovits and others only inferred: that the process was not unidirectional but, as Fernando Ortiz has argued, *transcultural*. "Creolization" thus describes the ongoing and ever-changing process (not the static result) of new forms born or developed from the interaction of peoples and forces due to "adaptive pressures omnipresent and irresistible" in the Americas (Buisseret, "Introduction" 2000: 7).[2]

Among the first to recognize the process of creolization as a better way of understanding the development of Caribbean cultures was Edward Kamau Brathwaite, who in his essay "The African Presence in Caribbean Literature" and in *Folk Cultures of the Slaves in Jamaica*, written in the 1970s, claims that the Middle Passage "was not, as is popularly assumed, a traumatic, destructive experience, separating the blacks from Africa, disconnecting their sense of history and tradition, but a pathway or channel between this tradition and what is being evolved, on new soil, in the Caribbean" (E. Brathwaite 1974: 5). Likewise, Antonio Benítez Rojo has examined the notion of creolization through three fundamental principles: plantation, rhythm, and performance.

> [C]reolization is not merely a process (a word that implies forward movement) but a discontinuous series of recurrences, of happenings, whose sole law is change. Where does this instability come from? It is the product of the plantation (the big bang of the Caribbean universe), whose slow explosion throughout modern history threw out billions and billions of cultural fragments in all directions—fragments of diverse kinds that, in their endless voyage, come together in an instant to form a dance step, a linguistic trope, the line of a poem, and afterward repel each other to reform and pull apart once more, and so on.
>
> (1998: 55)

The view of creolization has expanded in recent years to become synonymous with "hybridity" and "syncretism," transforming and challenging the static and binary Western rhetorical oppositions of white-black, center-periphery, civilized-primitive, and the like. In an age of mass migrations and globalization, the concept is even more crucial to reframe notions of past and present transnational and Diasporan cultures and communities. Edouard Glissant has spoken of the "archipelagoization" of the Caribbean in its interaction with Africa and the United States, and indeed of the "cultural creolization" of the world:

Europe is being "archipelagoized" in its turn and is splitting into regions. Florida is in the process of changing completely in response to its Cuban and Caribbean populations. It seems to me that these new dimensions of existence escape national realities which are trying to resist the forces of archipelagoization.... We must accustom our minds to these new world structures, in which the relationship between the center and the periphery will be completely different. Everything will be central and everything will be peripheral.

(2000)

Syncretism

The strategies of religious syncretism—the active transformation through renegotiation, reorganization, and redefinition of clashing belief systems—are consistent with the creolization process. In *African Civilizations in the New World*, Roger Bastide differentiated between various categories of religious syncretism in the Caribbean, among them morphological or mosaic syncretism based on the juxtaposition and coexistence of African-derived elements and Catholic symbols—the Vodou *pé*, or altars, with stones, wax candles, crosses, the statues of saints, and pots containing souls of the dead, for example—and institutional syncretism, which combines prescribed religious observances by reconciling Christian and African liturgical calendars (1971: 154–156). The most common, however, is syncretism by correspondence, or what Leslie Desmangles calls a "symbiosis by identity," through which an African deity and a Catholic saint became one on the basis of mythical or symbolic similarities.[3]

Syncretism has been a polemical term for centuries. In the seventeenth century it was used to defend "true" religion against heresy and referred to the "illegitimate reconciliation of opposing theological views" (Droogers 1989: 9). The term was later applied by scholars to the early forms of Christianity that were perceived to be syncretic as well, and was later broadened to apply to all religions when a review of religious history revealed syncretic elements at the foundation of all major religions. However, syncretism is not a value-free concept. The identification of Creole religions as "syncretic" is problematical and disparaging: there is a Eurocentric bias in limiting the definition to non-European religions, negating their full legitimacy. Creole religions are frequently identified with and "legitimized" by accentuating their Roman Catholic elements, for example, but are not always afforded an equivalent status.

It is significant to note that the term "syncretism" first appeared in Plutarch's *Moralia* in reference to the behavior of the Cretan peoples who "mixed together," came to accord, or closed ranks when confronted by a mutual enemy. The term was later used to describe an integration of two or more separate beliefs into a new religion. Thus, from its origins, the term presupposes encounter and confrontation between systems: "Syncretism is in the first place *contested* religious interpenetration" (Droogers 1989: 20).[4] Though all definitions of syncretism are thorny, Michael Pye recognizes the term's dynamism when he describes it as "the temporary ambiguous coexistence of elements from diverse religions and other contexts within a coherent religious pattern" and considers that the process should be understood as "a natural moving aspect of major religious traditions . . . a part of the dynamics of religion which works its way along in the ongoing transplantation of these religious traditions from one cultural context to another whether geographically or in time" (1971: 92). However, despite the existence of historical interactions, borrowings, and modifications based on contact and context that have occurred among all the major religions, the rhetorical division between "pure" faiths and illicit or "contaminated" syncretic belief systems persists.

Syncretism, particularly in the Creole context, is not therefore the description of a static condition or result but of a dynamic process. Roman Catholic missionaries adopted a policy of "guided syncretism" during the conquest of the Americas and the colonial period, tolerating the existence of a polytheistic idolatry that could be identified with Catholic saints and considering it a necessary evil—a transitional state that would eventually lead the conquered peoples to the "true" faith and the elimination of such beliefs. However, the policy never fully realized its goals. The old gods refused to disappear (and still do). Whether to avoid further oppression or to gain legitimacy, the conquered peoples embraced Christian forms but with new meanings they themselves had refashioned, at times appropriating them as tools of resistance.[5] According to Mosquera, syncretism should designate "something that corresponds more to the concept of 'appropriation,' in the sense of taking over for one's own use and on one's own initiative the diverse and even the hegemonic or imposed elements, in contrast to assuming an attitude of passive eclecticism or synthesis," strategies that he claims are clearer now thanks to the evolution of a "post-modern" contemporary consciousness (1996: 227). The stress on syncretism and such terms as "syncretic cults" emphasizes the "accessory syncretic elements to the detriment of the essence: the truly effective evolutions of African religions in America" (Mosquera 1992: 30).[6] For Andrew Apter, religious syncretism is yet another form of empowerment, another modality of revision and popular resistance:

> The syncretic revision of dominant discourses sought to transform the authority that these discourses upheld . . . the power and violence mobilized by slave revolts and revolution were built into the logic of New World syncretism itself. The Catholicism of Vodou, Candomblé and Santería was not an ecumenical screen, hiding the worship of African deities from official persecution. It was the religion of the masters, revised, transformed, and appropriated by slaves to harness its power within their universes of discourse. In this way the slaves took possession of Catholicism and thereby repossessed themselves as active spiritual subjects.
>
> (1991: 254)

Shared Characteristics of Creole Religions

Despite notable differences among African-based Caribbean Creole practices, a general overview of the Creole religions reveals that they share a number of fundamental features.[7]

1. The first of these is their characteristic combination of monotheism and polytheism. At the center of all Afro-Caribbean religions is a belief in a unique Supreme Being—creator of the universe. This belief is complemented by belief in a pantheon of deities (*orishas*, *loas*, and the like) who are emanations of the Creator and who serve as intermediaries between mankind and the supreme god.

2. These religious practices are also linked by a cult of dead ancestors and/or deceased members of the religious community who watch over and influence events from beyond.

3. In addition, Creole religions share a belief in an active, supernatural, mysterious power that can be invested in objects (mineral, vegetable, animals, humans); this force is not intrinsic to the objects themselves.

4. This belief is in turn linked to animistic beliefs in other spirits (often found in nature), beyond the divinities and the ancestors, who can also be contacted and who can exert a positive or negative influence over a person's life. Plants and trees, for example, have a will and a soul, as do all things under the sun.

5. Afro-Caribbean religions are centered on the principle of contact, or mediation between humans and the spirit world, which is achieved through such numerous and complex rituals as divinatory practices, initiation, sacrifice, spiritual possession, and healings.[8]

6. These contacts are mediated by a central symbol or focus, a fundament or philosophical foundation that serves as the dynamic organizing principle of spiritual worship: the sacred stones (*otanes*) of the Afro-Cuban Regla de Ocha and the *nganga* cauldron and sign tracings of Regla de Palo, the sacred Ekué drum of the Abakuá Secret Society, and the *potomitan* of the Vodou ritual space (the *hounfort*). These and other consecrated objects are not merely the symbols of the gods but are the material receptacles of divine power. The image of Catholic saints and the crucifix may appear to dominate altars or shrines, but, as Bascom has noted regarding the Afro-Cuban religions, the stones, blood, and herbs of ritual offerings and sacrifice contain the "secrets" and are the real focus of religious power (1950, 1972).

7. The practice of magic in the form of spells, conjurations, and ethnomagical medicine-healing following the principles described by Sir James Frazer in

his classic text *The Golden Bough*, is central to Creole religious practices in the Caribbean: "homeopathic" or "imitative" magic following the law of similarity in which like produces like and an effect resembles its cause so that one can produce any effect by imitating it; and "contagious" magic which follows the law of contact, namely, that things which have once been in contact continue to act upon each other at a distance, a "magical sympathy" that exists between a person and any severed portion of his or her person. Anyone gaining possession of human hair, nails, or other portions of the body may work his or her will upon the person from whom they were obtained, at any distance.[9]

8. For Bastide, magic is a syncretistic variant that must be taken into account in order to understand the framework in which Afro-American religions operate (1971). He notes that the Europeans brought their own varieties of medieval magic with them to the New World, often in the form of witches and magicians who were no longer burned at the stake but rather deported to the new Western territories. European magic retained the advantage of representing the practices of the ruling class and was perceived to be superior in one major aspect: it guaranteed European hegemony, while African magic had not prevented enslavement. "This is why, though they never rejected any of their own African practices which proved effective, the black population would reinforce the unsuccessful one with some European formula" (1971: 16) in a process referred to as "magical accumulation" which serves to strengthen the operative force of a given spell or remedy.[10]

9. Central to this "magical accumulation" in religious ceremonies is music and dance: sound has the power to transmit action. Consecrated drums and the polyrhythmic percussion they produce, along with clapping, the spoken or sung word in repeated chants and dance (rhythms and dance are coded to the identities of the gods that are summoned in ceremonies and rituals), produce an altered focus of consciousness that beckons the supernatural entities and communicates between worlds.[11]

10. Music and dance are also instrumental in strengthening the conscious sense of community and an institutionalized regrouping of Africans and their descendants, and a transference of African "space" into houses, temples, or rooms. More than simply religious groups, ritual communities re-create the type of family ties and obligations to the deities and to each other that would have existed in Africa.

11. Central to this re-creation are the religious leaders responsible for the care of the religious space, sacred objects, and ritual implements and the general spiritual care of the community, who represent "the depository of

maximum mystical and initiatory powers and liturgical knowledge. The cult priest [priestess] distributes or 'plants' power by initiating novices and infusing them with the power of which he is the depository" (Dos Santos and Dos Santos 1984: 77). There is no central authority in Creole religions, however; worship is individualized and community-based. Devotees are members of a religion, but not of a specific institutionalized church.

12. In Caribbean Creole religions, spiritual power is internalized and mobilized in human beings who become, through the experience of possession, "a real live altar in which the presence of the supernatural beings can be invoked."[12] In possession, the deities—orishas, loas—manifest themselves through the bodies of the initiated.[13] "During the experience of possession, the entire religious system, its theogony and mythology, are relived. Each participant is the protagonist of a ritualistic activity, in which Black historic, psychological, ethnic, and cosmic life is renewed" (Dos Santos and Dos Santos 1984: 78). Ritual dramatizes myth and promotes the magic that responds to life's problems.[14]

The chapters that follow will trace how these various elements manifest themselves in the specific systems of belief and practice of the major Creole religions of the Caribbean. As we trace their histories and characteristic elements we will seek to illustrate how, although at times severely restricted, controlled, penalized, ostracized, and devalued by the dominant cultures of the respective countries, they constitute practices of resistance which devotees have succeeded in maintaining for centuries, contesting the racialized inequalities in their societies, defining and shaping the everyday lives of individuals and communities. As such the Creole religions are at the very center of the process of transculturation that has defined Creole societies.

HISTORICAL BACKGROUND

> *L'histoire d'un morceau de sucre est toute une leçon d'economie politique, de politique et aussi de morale.* (The history of a cube of sugar is an entire lesson in economy, politics, and also in morality.)
> —*Agustin Cochin (1823–72)*

The Sugar Islands and the Plantation (1492–1900)

The islands of the Caribbean—the focus of this book—were Europe's first colonies in the New World, and as such, the site of the first multicultural experiment, the cradle of ethnic and cultural syncretism. Spain, the nation responsible for Columbus's momentous "discovery" of these new lands in 1492, ruled unchallenged over the region for a century, but by the final decades of the sixteenth century other aspiring European maritime powers—England, France, Portugal, the Netherlands, and Denmark—had begun to contest its hegemony over the area that would become known as the West Indies.

The diversity of the metropolitan powers vying for hegemony in the Caribbean led to the fragmentation of cultural and linguistic patterns characteristic of the present-day West Indies. However, their collective focus on the development of a plantation economy centered on the production of sugarcane by African slaves provided a common link between the various islands. During the early decades of the seventeenth century, the ever-threatened enclaves of European-style farming communities that had struggled to flourish throughout the Caribbean during the previous century were gradually replaced by large-scale plantations. The consolidation of sugar production through the plantations was the foundation of the Caribbean colonial economy. By the middle of the seventeenth century, the sugar industry had become so pervasive throughout the archipelago that Adam Smith, in his *Wealth of Nations*, would refer to the entire area as "our sugar islands."

As the plantations of the Caribbean became the centerpiece of an international trade subordinated to the needs of the European markets and often financed from abroad, the region became the destination for thousands of African slaves, themselves a valuable commodity central to the triangular trade that fed upon the plantation system for centuries. According to Franklin Knight, African slaves became as a result "the most important single ingredient in the economic success of plantation society."[15] While it is true that millions of human beings of diverse racial, geographic, and cultural origins would be pressed into service in the sugar system, the brunt of the enterprise was undoubtedly borne by enslaved Africans, making the Caribbean archipelago "the historical and geographical core of Afro-America" (Hoetink 1985: 55).

The first African slaves arrived in the Caribbean at the very beginning of the "discovery" and conquest, and the region was among the last areas in which slavery was abolished in the Americas (Cuba in 1886, two years prior to its abolition in Brazil in 1888). Lasting nearly four centuries, African slavery would span nearly all of postcontact Caribbean history. Consequently it has been described as "the most massive acculturational event in human history" (Mintz 1974: 9). Upon arriving in the Americas, Africans experienced multiple levels of acculturation: an initial adaptation to new languages and customs in an interchange with slaves of other cultures, and later with the culture of their masters. The strategies of accommodation, transformation, and resistance of African peoples are exemplified in the syncretic religions described in the following chapters, practices that evolved from the experiences in which Africans were obliged to re-create their cultures and systems of belief within a very restrictive social structure in a new and unfamiliar environment.

Of the roughly five million Africans transported to the Americas, more than half were intended for the sugar plantations of the Caribbean. The plantations, which first proved their potential as producers of "white gold" in the English-held territories of Barbados, Antigua, and Surinam in the middle decades of the seventeenth century, consumed their greatest number of African slaves during the eighteenth. By 1750 Jamaica had superseded Barbados and Antigua as the region's leading producer of sugar, only to lose its dominance to the French colony of Saint Domingue by 1780. Cuba would surpass them all in the nineteenth century, but only after the Haitian Revolution brought an abrupt end to sugar production in Saint Domingue, and those planters who survived the violence fled the newly independent island to start anew in Cuba.

The importation of slaves and their ultimate destination within the Caribbean followed the uncertainties of these changing patterns of sugar production, with the highest concentrations of slaves to be found wherever production was highest and most technologically advanced. The shifting patterns of these concentrations are central to our discussion, as they were responsible for the intensity of cultural exchange that would bring about the development of the African-based religious practices commonly known today as Creole religions. The practice of Obeah, for example—the set of "hybrid" or "creolized" Caribbean beliefs "which includes such practices as ritual incantation and the use of fetishes or charms"[16]—was perceived to be widespread throughout the late seventeenth and early to mid-eighteenth centuries in Barbados, Antigua, and Jamaica, then at their highest level of sugar production. Even at that early stage in the history of slavery in the New World, Obeah could be traced to the concentrations of Ashanti and kindred tribes from the Gold Coast of Africa, heavily represented in the slave population of the British colonies of the Caribbean.

The practice of Obeah, seen by British colonial authorities as a threat to the stability of the plantation and the health of colonial institutions, had been outlawed in most British Caribbean islands early in the eighteenth century, after being perceived as one of the few means of retaliation open to the slave population. Moreover, Obeahmen were seen as potential leaders who could use their influence over the slaves to incite them to rebellion, as had been the case in the Jamaican rebellion of 1760. "The influence of the Professors of that art," wrote the authors of the *Report of the Lord of the Committee* . . . (1789) at the time, "was such as to induce many to enter into that rebellion on the assurance that they were invulnerable, and to render them so, the Obeah man gave them a powder with which to rub themselves." As Alan Richardson underscores, Edward Long had discussed the role of a "famous obeiah man or priest in the Tacky Rebellion in his *History of Jamaica* (1774), a work notorious for its virulent racism, and stated that among the 'Coromantyns' (slaves shipped from the Gold Coast) the *'obeiah-men'* were the 'chief oracles' behind conspiracies and would bind the conspirators with the 'fetish or oath.'"[17]

Likewise, the practice of Haitian Vodou—the array of practices that Michel Laguerre has called "the collective memory of the [African] slaves brought to the sugar plantations of Haiti"—grew in intensity as the colony's accelerated rate of production during the mid-to-late eighteenth century redoubled the massive migration of thousands of men and women to a new and unfamiliar world marked by their brutal exploitation and early deaths in the plantations of Saint Domingue. The French colony of Haiti, on the western half of the island of Hispaniola, the site of Spain's first colony in the new world, had achieved an unprecedented degree of economic prosperity during the eighteenth century, becoming the world's leading producer of sugar. French pirates, taking advantage of Spain's neglect of its Caribbean colonies after the discovery of the gold-rich territories of South America, had established sugar plantations on the western end of the island following the foundation of Port-de-Paix in 1664 and the establishment of the French West India Company. Haiti's aboriginal Arawak population having disappeared early in the colony's history as a result of conquest, warfare, excessive work, or disease, the island's sugar-based prosperity was built on a violent and systematic exploitation of labor unlike any known in early modern history. It represented the "epitome of the successful exploitation of slave society in tropical America" (Knight 1978: 149).

In 1791, the Haitian slaves—a population estimated at 452,000 in 1789—rebelled against the brutal conditions of the plantation and the denial of the most basic civil liberties, beginning the long process that became known as the Haitian Revolution, which would eventually lead to the establishment of the first independent republic in the Caribbean. Like the Obeah-inspired rebellions in the British West Indies, the Haitian Revolution was rooted in the commonality of religious and cultural practices centered on Vodou, and its beginnings were marked by a pact between the revolutionary leaders and the Vodou loas or spirits at a ceremony held at Bois-Caïman (described by a captured slave during legal proceedings against him at Cap-Français). The links between religion and the uprising were established early through the slaves' belief in the powers of their legendary leader Makandal to predict the future and transform himself into various animals, attributes that served him well in his clandestine war against the French colonists. Makandal's chief strategy was sabotage by means of poison, but his reputation as a houngan or Vodou priest grew in proportion to the fear he instilled in the French settlers that his knowledge of the poisons, spells, and other subtle weapons he deployed against the white population had its source in magical powers linked to mysterious African practices.

The implications of the Haitian Revolution for the entire Caribbean were enormous, as the former slaves laid the country to waste, destroying its economic structure and severing their connection to international markets, to which they had been the leading supplier of sugar, coffee, and cacao. The vacuum opened a golden opportunity for Cuban sugar producers who had met with only limited success in their ability to compete against Saint Domingue's enormous production capacity. Thousands of

French émigrés from Saint Domingue resettled in Cuba, bringing with them capital, slaves, and, most importantly, considerable skill and experience in sugar and coffee production. A surge in the price of sugar, new trading possibilities with the United States after the American Revolution, an industrial revolution that mechanized and greatly facilitated sugar production, and the successful independence movements of Spain's mainland colonies that eliminated Cuba's former strategic role set new priorities for Cuban growers, who dominated the industry throughout the nineteenth and twentieth centuries. As the burden of sugar production shifted to Cuba, so did the concentration of slaves, making of Cuba the crucible of syncretism in the nineteenth-century Caribbean.

The nineteenth century was a period of transition for the region. After the consolidation of the new Haitian Republic, the island's political leaders were hard-pressed to establish and maintain a stable regime. As a result, the country's history since independence has been marked by social turmoil, economic instability, frequent political coups, and the use of political assassination as an instrument of terror. Dessalines, who emerged from the Revolution as Emperor Jacques I, was killed in 1806 while trying to put down a mulatto revolt. Henri Christophe, heir to his kingdom, forced the newly freed slaves to return to the plantations in order to improve the country's economy, and committed suicide in 1820 at his citadel of Laferrière, with rebelling soldiers storming his gates. His successor, President Jean Pierre Boyer, invaded the Spanish half of the island, which had just declared its own independence from Spain, and was overthrown in 1842, a year before the Haitian army was expelled from the Dominican Republic. Between then and 1915 a succession of twenty heads of state tried to govern Haiti, sixteen of whom were overthrown by revolution or were assassinated. The resulting political instability, greed, and corruption, coupled with a systematic depletion of the country's resources, contributed to Haiti's becoming the poorest nation in the Western hemisphere. At the dawn of the twentieth century, the once-promising young republic was poised for a lengthy American occupation and a tortuous struggle against poverty, corruption, and despair.

Prior to the nineteenth century, the Spanish-held territories of Cuba, Puerto Rico, and Santo Domingo—on the eastern half of the island of Hispaniola—had failed to fulfill their early promise as major sources of colonial wealth. For the greater part of their histories they had been severely neglected by Spain, particularly following the discovery of the more valuable territories of Mexico and Peru. Unlike Cuba, whose main port of Havana had played a major role as a supply depot for the Spanish fleet on its way to and from Latin America, Puerto Rico and Santo Domingo had failed to establish themselves as important posts in the line of defense against Spain's European enemies—the French, British, and Dutch pirates intent on interdicting the gold and silver pouring out of the Americas and interrupting the empire's supply systems. Largely characterized by under-populated small towns, tobacco farms, cattle ranches, coffee plantations, and a small number of sugar plantations whose production was geared to internal consumption, and few African slaves, the population of Santo Domingo (today the Dominican Republic) and Puerto Rico—mostly Creoles of mixed European, Amerindian, and African stock—had expanded slowly. Until the Haitian Revolution gave them an increased role in sugar production, they had found themselves subordinated to a peripheral role as way-stations for the Spanish *flota* transporting the wealth of South America to Spain. Their social and political lives had revolved around fortified garrisons for the armies protecting the naval routes between the new center of the empire and the metropolis, their economies dependent on the *situado*, a subsidy collected from the Mexican treasury. Their fates would be significantly altered by events in Saint Domingue, although they would remain in Cuba's considerable shadow.

The Haitian Revolution truly transformed Cuba, turning it into the greatest of the Spanish "Sugar Islands." Among the numerous changes caused by the resulting economic upheaval was the concomitant increase in Cuba's general population and the tremendous new demand for African slave labor. Between 1512 and 1761 about sixty thousand slaves were imported into Cuba; from 1762 to 1838 the figure rose to four hundred thousand (an increase from two hundred and fifty per year to nearly five thousand).[18] Although one quarter of the slave population (mostly Creoles, or native-born) lived in urban centers, the majority of Africans toiled on the sugar plantations or in the coffee and tobacco fields where they worked under the most wretched of conditions, not unlike those the slave population of Haiti had known during the heyday of that country's sugar production. The mortality rate was so high that new acquisitions were constantly required to replenish the population.[19] The response to such oppression, as in Jamaica and Haiti, was very often *marronage* (flight), suicide, or rebellion. Controlling the slave population soon became a dominant social and political issue in Cuba.[20] Slave revolts were frequent, ranging from spontaneous eruptions of violence on individual estates to large organized uprisings that included free persons of color and whites. Perceived as a serious threat to central authority, these organized revolts were brutally crushed, among them the famous conspiracy referred to as La Escalera (The Ladder, 1844), one of the best organized and most severely repressed. Thousands were tried in military tribunals and hundreds were condemned to death, imprisoned, or deported.

Within Cuba's restrictive colonial social and economic structure, the free population of African descent, which during certain periods represented a dominant percentage of the population, maneuvered a space for themselves in many occupations and trades, due in part to the policy of *coartación* (manumission), through which a number of Cuban slaves were permitted to purchase their freedom from their masters in installments. The system favored Creole or native-born over newly arrived slaves from Africa, and urban over rural slaves who generally lacked similar opportunities to save money to purchase their freedom. In rural agricultural areas, where conditions were harsher and emancipation more elusive, many disregarded the brutal punishments reserved for recaptured runaways and fled to the isolated interiors of the south and central-eastern Cuba's mountain range to establish fortified maroons settlements, the *palenques*,[21] where they fashioned their own unique cultural traditions. The experience of culture building that took place in maroon societies is considered emblematic of the process that resulted in the syncretic African-based traditions (including religions) shaped by enslaved Africans in the Americas. The difficulties of creating and maintaining maroon societies in the colonial slave systems of the Americas required the full range of the collective experiences of Africans from a variety of cultures who had to adapt themselves not only to a challenging environment but also to a new social community that could range from newly arrived Africans to highly acculturated Creoles.[22] "What the majority of these people did share was a recently forged Afro-American culture and a strong ideological (or at least rhetorical) commitment to things 'African'" (Price 1973: 26).

Cuba remained a slave society until the abolition of slavery in 1886, and the tensions and alliances created during a long history of racialized labor exploitation featured prominently in the coalitions brought together to fight the Cuban War of Independence in 1895. Black and mulatto soldiers fought side by side with the most liberal sectors of Cuban Creole society, hoping to establish a new nation on democratic principles and greater class and race representation. The victory over Spanish forces—coming in the wake of the United States joining Cuban forces in what would be known as the Spanish-American War—would disappoint the broader social aspirations of the black and mulatto sectors of the Cuban population. Independence, when it finally came in 1903, came under restricted neo-colonial conditions, with American sugar corporations taking over sugar plantations, and the United States throwing its considerable support behind the most conservative military-backed dictatorships. Renewed hopes would wait until the 1959 Cuban Revolution, which opened a new chapter in Afro-Cuban history.

Cuba's Spanish-speaking Caribbean neighbors—Puerto Rico and the Dominican Republic—followed significantly different paths during the nineteenth century. Both intensified their production of sugar in response to the opening of markets following the Haitian Revolution. Neither would rival Cuban production, although both would see their economies transformed by sugar production. The colony of Santo Domingo opened the decade by joining Haiti, the United States, and Spain's Latin American colonies in wars of independence against continued colonial rule. As the Dominican Republic, it gained its independence from Spain in 1821, only to be invaded by the Haitian army in 1822, in Haiti's bid for annexation of Santo Domingo and consolidation of the island's territory under one flag. The struggle against Haiti, and the humiliation of an almost twenty-two-year occupation, left deep emotional scars on the young

Dominican nation, and frequent boundary disputes only consolidated the already existing animosity between the two nations. As a result, the consolidation of national independence was the salient political and economic intellectual focus of Dominican leaders throughout the nineteenth century.

The Dominican Republic, bound as the country had been throughout the century in a seemingly ceaseless struggle to solidify its independence, entered the twentieth century solidly in the orbit of the new neocolonial power in the region, the United States. Like Cuba, its sugar production, long neglected because of the internecine war against Haiti, and plagued by inefficiency and limited access to new technologies, fell into the hands of American sugar corporations. Its governments, corrupt and greedy for the most part, subordinated the country's independent economic development to serving American interests. As in Haiti, American occupation loomed ahead in the opening decades of the new century; like Cuba, it would see its full share of American-backed dictatorships and would have to defer dreams of racial justice and greater class equality.

Puerto Rico followed a different path during the nineteenth century. Although it intensified sugar production in the wake of the Haitian Revolution, it maintained a steady production of coffee throughout the century, with coffee surpassing sugar after 1850. As a result, it never reached the high percentages of slave population of other Caribbean islands. At the height of its slave-centered sugar production, only 11 percent of its total population was enslaved. The only one of Spain's possessions in the Caribbean and Latin America not to wage a war of independence against Spain, Puerto Rico, despite a strong separatist movement responsible for at least one serious attempt at rebellion—the 1868 Grito de Lares—would close the century having obtained an Autonomous Charter from Spain. Only months later it was ceded to the United States as a new American territory, following Spain's loss of the Spanish-American War in 1898. As a result of its idiosyncratic path—the result, perhaps, of having been the refuge of conservative Latin American Creoles fleeing the continent's wars of independence as well as the main garrison for the deployment of armies to fight the rebels of South America—Puerto Rico had the heaviest influx of European immigrants of any Caribbean island in the nineteenth century. The 1815 Decree of Thanks—granted by Spain in recognition of the island's loyalty during the Latin American wars of independence—ironically opened the island's doors to Catholic immigrants from all parts of Europe, bringing an influx of French, Corsican, German, Irish, and Scottish immigrants who would transform the island culture, opening it to a flow of new ideas. Chief among these was European *espiritisme* (Spiritism), a major ingredient in the creolized Afro-Hispanic Espiritismo widely practiced on the island today.

The British islands of the Caribbean—Jamaica, Trinidad, and the various islands of the Lesser Antilles, such as Barbados, Antigua, and St. Kitts—had experienced the heyday of their sugar production in the eighteenth century. Some of them, like Dominica, had never been efficient producers of sugar, and their economies had been sustained by smaller cash crops such as coffee, indigo, ginger, and lemons. By the dawn of the nineteenth century, West Indian sugar production was becoming increasingly uncompetitive both on the international market and within the empire itself. As a result, planters were philosophical about the cessation of the slave trade and the declaration of Emancipation that followed in 1838. The remaining French colonies in the archipelago, Martinique and Guadeloupe, faced similar declining returns from the production of sugar by slave labor, and Emancipation was declared in the French colonies in 1848.

The second half of the nineteenth century, in both the British and French-Caribbean islands, would be characterized by the dynamic growth of a free colored peasantry that followed Emancipation and the breakdown of the large formerly slave-run estates. Land became inexpensive, or readily available for occupation by squatters. A local economy based on the plot system of agriculture, independent from the remaining large sugar estates, began to impact the social, political, and cultural development of the various islands. Those estates which continued the large-scale production of sugar, had to rely on imported Asian laborers, mostly Chinese and Indian, who arrived in the Antilles in large numbers in the second half of the nineteenth century and brought new languages, cultures, and religious beliefs and practices to the amalgam of the region's Creole religions.

In both the British and French Caribbean islands, the social pressures brought about by a free colored peasantry pushing for greater participation in the political and economic processes led to strong attempts at controlling the peasant population through the prohibition of certain religious and cultural practices. As a result, many of the activities associated with Obeah and the related Quimbois practices of the Francophone Caribbean became illegal or were discouraged and persecuted. Throughout the nineteenth century—perhaps as a backlash against the renewed power given to the former slave population by freedom and access to land—there was widespread discrimination against believers and practitioners of Afro-Caribbean religious and healing practices, as well as relentless campaigns on the part of mainstream religions and civic organizations to eradicate all Obeah and Quimbois practices, deemed superstitious and pernicious by many. These efforts seriously limited Obeah and Quimbois practices from regaining their ancestral religious roots and reestablishing community-based rituals and priestly duties, although their healing aspects actually gained strength during this period. When syncretized with newly arrived Asian practices, already endowed with strong healing components, they would develop into a significant element of Afro-Caribbean cultures in the lesser Antilles.

As the postslavery Caribbean looked ahead to the twentieth century, it faced a transformed social and political reality. The plantation, although not a thing of the past, had bowed to the pressures of the international markets and had lost its hegemony. Although the lives of many Caribbean laborers would continue to revolve around the cultivation of sugar, the diversification of the agricultural sector and the introduction of new industries—among them the growing tourist industry—would change forever the nature of work in the region. As the new century dawned, the seeds of the labor and independence movements that would control political development in the first half of the twentieth century had been planted. With the affirmation of the workers' power to define the terms of their relationships with the metropolis would come independent nations whose national identities would be bound with the affirmation of cultures rooted in African-derived cultures. Among the deepest of those roots would be those of the Afro-Caribbean religions that had sustained the Caribbean slave populations through the dark years of plantation America.

NOTES

1. The spelling of Vodou (also Voodoo, Vodoun, and Vaudon) is, like many other terms of African origin used to describe various practices and beliefs, a constant source of debate among scholars and believers. The text reflects our preferences; citations naturally maintain the individual preference of those cited.

2. "Such is the case of the 'Caribbean,' a term that in practice goes beyond the purely geographic and refers to areas farther south and as far as the Pacific Ocean as a way of noting the internal presence in various cultures of distinctive features of African origin.... Anthropology has recently begun to use the adjective 'Caribbean' to categorize an experience contrary to the monocultural narrative" (Mosquera 1992: 30).

3. Desmangles (1992: 172). In "Trans-Caribbean Identity and the Fictional World of Mayra Montero," Fernández Olmos argues for yet another category of religious syncretism, exemplified by the *Gagá* cult in the Dominican Republic. Gagá is a Vodou-derived practice brought by emigrating Haitian sugarcane workers to the Dominican Republic, where it was transformed and reinterpreted by local folk practices and beliefs. It is "an interesting example of nontraditional Caribbean syncretism: instead of a hybridity between the European and the colonized, Gagá exemplifies a secondary type of syncretism, one between (ex)colonized peoples" (1997: 273).

4. [T]he concept of syncretism has been used in many different ways since Plutarch wrote the history of the Cretans. During the period of expansion of European colonialism, for instance, when ethnography was deployed to describe colonized peoples, syncretism defined a stage of evolution (progress), serving to explain the ways "uncivilized" societies "assimilated" more "advanced" cultures.... [W]e propose a reinscription of the contact between, for example, European and African symbolic systems in syncretic articulations, not as contradictory but as *antagonistic*, i.e., in

relations which are animated by the partial presence of the other within the self, such that the differential identity of each term is at once enabled and prevented from full constitution. These relations, which, depending on the configurations of power in contingent historical conditions, may or may not crystallize into oppositionalities, exist both horizontally (in equivalential alignments among diverse groups united in struggle, as in the Cretan example) as well as vertically (in dominant/subaltern confrontations, as in colonialism). Antagonistic relations, then, indicate the limits of absolutist conceptions of culture based upon a closed system of unalloyed, hetero-topic differences, and thereby expand the logics of struggle.

(Becquer and Gatti 1991: 70–72)

5. For a discussion of legitimacy and religious syncretism in Latin America, as well as power and empowerment via the articulation of syncretic elements, see Benavides (1995).

6. A movement to eliminate any vestiges of European religions from Santería and other Creole religions, led by the so-called "African revisionists," and return to a more "pure" and "authentic" African-centered religion has led to African-centered movements in the United States and in Cuba where some advocate for a "religión Yoruba" to replace Regla de Ocha/Santería.

7. Based primarily on Castellanos and Castellanos, *Cultura afrocubana* (1992, 3: 16–18). Just as the insights regarding the creolization process described above have crossed the boundaries of the geographic region—Brazil and other Latin American countries, and even such U.S. cities as New York and Miami reveal the type of cultural amalgamation characteristic of the region—it should be noted that Creole religious beliefs have gone beyond geographic, racial, and class boundaries as well. Their devotees are found throughout South America—including areas of Brazil with Italian, Polish, and German immigrants and in countries like Uruguay and Argentina with an insignificant number of persons of African descent—and in the United States outside the Cuban and Latino communities (Barnes 1989: 10).

8. See Cros Sandoval (1995), and Fernández Olmos and Paravisini-Gebert (2001).

9. See Frazer (1966: chapter 1). According to Eugene Genovese,

Magic, in the widest sense of the word, as Frazer, Tylor, and other pioneer anthropologists taught, is a false science with an erroneous idea of cause and effect, but it is akin to science nonetheless in its appeal to human devices for control of the world. . . . For peasantries magic, however petty many of its applications, has served the vital social function of providing some defense, no matter how futile in the end, against the natural disasters and forces beyond their control.

(1976: 230–231)

10. "It remains to be said that, while Negroes may borrow European magic to strengthen their own spells, the reverse is also true. Europeans tend to regard Negro magic as more effective, because of its 'weird' character and the old colonial terrors which it inspired" (Bastide 1971: 161).

11. Dos Santos and Dos Santos (1984: 78).

12. African-derived practices are often described in the scholarly literature as "spiritist" religions due to the element of possession of followers by the spirits. In this book only Espiritismo is referred to as "Spiritism" or spiritist, as identified in the Caribbean. Of course, to some degree all religions that believe in the spirits can be identified as spiritist; the Christian Pentecostal rituals that attempt to achieve a direct experience of possession by the Holy Ghost are one example of a Christian spiritist practice, albeit one with a more "mainstream" spirit.

13. Spirit possession exists throughout the world in one form or another and can be defined as an "altered state of consciousness indigenously interpreted in terms of the influence of an alien spirit" (Crapanzano and Garrison 1977: Introduction, 7).

14. Joan D. Koss has written of the creativity of Caribbean cult rituals and the "transformation of the mundane through the use of possession-trance" (1979: 376). When ritual participants are possessed by the *dramatis personae* of a particular belief system, rather than follow the limited stereotypical patterns associated with the supernatural character incarnated, numerous variations (the multiple avatars of the *orisha* and the *loa*, for example, and the portrayal of the more typical spirit guides in *Espiritismo*) allow for individual variation of their characterization in possession. A successful cult leader, she claims, must be flexible and creative in combining meaning and aesthetics to the cult ritual "performance." Koss cites Métraux (1972: 64), who describes the ideal *hungan* as "at one and the same time priest, healer, soothsayer, exorcizer, organizer of public entertainment and choirmaster."

   Ritual as a creative forum is most clearly seen, in my opinion, in these cult cases. Two important attributes of cult activity provide for this condition: first, cult rituals, as distinct from those of most established religions, attract their participants through the offer of direct contact with supernatural beings. Even though this contact may be achieved initially only through a third party, the cult adept, priest, or spirit medium, there is a process of democratization of the "power" to communicate with the supernatural world which is both ideal and actual—that is, that any believer can become an adept, even though not all develop sufficient powers to do so. Second, cult ideologies in the Caribbean are, in terms of their basic patterns, deceptively simple. They consist of good and bad *loa, orisha*, spirits or powers who "work" according to the dictates of their human communicants but can as often manifest their own characterological attributes to disturb the behavior of those who lack the knowledge and power to deal with them. Those who become adepts and can organize their own groups acquire their leadership status by successfully dealing with the multiple, variable expressions of the personal disturbances of their followers. Their manipulative techniques of divining, healing, and advice-giving cannot possibly respond to set and detailed formulas, pedantically derived by arduous interpretation over years of discussion. To be a successful cult leader or adept, creative ability is requisite (376–377).

15. Knight (1978: 83).

16. Richardson (1997: 173).

17. Long (1774, 2: 451–452, 473). Quoted by Alan Richardson in "Romantic Voodoo."

18. Figures from Knight (1970: 10) based on Aimes (1907) and von Humboldt (1969). See also Curtin (1969). The slave trade continued illegally in Cuba until the mid-1860s. Abolition was formally decreed in 1880 with an eight-year "apprenticeship" of freed slaves which ended in 1886. On abolition, see Knight (1970: chapters 7–8).

19. For a description of the conditions of life in the sugar mill, see Moreno Fraginals (1976: 142–153). On Cuban slavery, see Thomas (1971: chapter 13).

20. Estimates on the number of slaves imported to Cuba vary. Curtin (1969) describes the difficulty of arriving at an accurate number and offers the following estimates: to 1773 (based on Aimes 1907) 13,100; 1774–1807, 119,000; 1808–1865, 568,500 (Curtin 1969: 44); for the entire period of the slave trade in Spanish America, 702,000 (Curtin 1969: 46). Manuel Moreno Fraginals (1976) places the number at over one million but many agree that Curtin's figures underestimate the count (Castellanos and Castellanos 1988, 1: 25).

21. For defense and concealment purposes, maroon communities took advantage of the harshness of their natural environment. Many of their villages were surrounded by palisades or, in Spanish, *palenques*; hence the generic name.

22. For a more general discussion of maroon societies in the Americas, see Price (1973), especially the Introduction, 1–30.

BIBLIOGRAPHY

Aimes, Hubert H. S. *A History of Slavery in Cuba, 1511–1868*. New York: Putnam, 1907.

Apter, Andrew. "Herskovits's Heritage: Rethinking Syncretism in the African Diaspora." *Diaspora: A Journal of Transnational Studies* 1.3 (1991): 235–260.

Barnes, Sandra T., ed. *Africa's Ogun: Old World and New*. Bloomington: Indiana University Press, 1989.

Bascom, William R. "The Focus of Cuban Santeria." *Southwest Journal of Anthropology* 6.1 (1950): 64–68.

Bastide, Roger. *African Civilizations in the New World*. Trans. Peter Green. London: C. Hurst and Company, 1971.

——— *The African Religions of Brazil*. Baltimore: Johns Hopkins U. Press, 1978.

Becquer, Marcos, and José Gatti. "Elements of Vogue." *Third Text* 16–17 (winter 1991): 65–81.

Benavides, Gustavo. "Syncretism and Legitimacy in Latin American Religion." In *Enigmatic Powers: Syncretism with African and Indigenous Peoples' Religions among Latinos*. Anthony M. Stevens and Andrés I. Pérez y Mena, eds. New York: Bildner Center for Western Hemisphere Studies, 1995, 19–46.

Benítez Rojo, Antonio. *The Repeating Island: The Caribbean and the Postmodern Perspective*. Trans. James E. Maraniss. Durham: Duke U. Press, 1996.

—— "Three Words toward Creolization." In *Caribbean Creolization: Reflections on the Cultural Dynamics of Language, Literature and Identity*. Kathleen M. Balutansky and Marie-Agnès Sourieau, eds. Gainesville: University Press of Florida, 1998, 53–61.

Brathwaite, Edward. *Folk Cultures of the Slaves in Jamaica*. London: New Beacon Books, 1970. Reprint 1974.

Buisseret, David, and Steven G. Reinhardt, eds. *Creolization in the Americas*. "Introduction" by D. Buisseret. College Station, Tex: U. of Texas Press, 2000.

Castellanos, Jorge and Isabel Castellanos. *Cultura afrocubana 1 (El negro en Cuba, 1492–1944)*. Miami: Ediciones Universal, 1987.

Crapanzano, Vincent, and Vivian Garrison, eds. *Case Studies in Spirit Possession*. New York: John Wiley, 1977.

Cros Sandoval, Mercedes. "Afro-Cuban Religion in Perspective." In *Enigmatic Powers: Syncretism with African and Indigenous Peoples' Religions among Latinos*.

Curtin, Philip D. *The Atlantic Slave Trade: A Census*. Madison: University of Wisconsin Press, 1969.

Desmangles, Leslie G. *The Faces of the Gods: Vodou and Roman Catholicism in Haiti*. Chapel Hill: University of North Carolina Press, 1992.

Dos Santos, Juana Elbein, and Deoscoredes M. Dos Santos. "Religion and Black Culture." Trans. Leonor Blum. In *Africa in Latin America: Essays on History, Culture and Socialization*. Manuel Moreno Fraginals, ed. New York: Holmes and Meier, 1984, 61–82.

Droogers, André. "Syncretism: The Problem of Definition, the Definition of a Problem." In *Dialogue and Syncretism: An Interdisciplinary Approach*. Jerald Gort et al., eds., Grand Rapids, Mich.:William B. Eerdmans, 1889, 7–25.

Fernández Olmos, Margarite. "Trans-Caribbean Identity and the Fictional World of Mayra Montero." In *Sacred Possessions: Vodou, Santería, Obeah, and the Caribbean*. New Brunswick: Rutgers University Press, 1997, 267–282.

Fernández Olmos, Margarite, and Lizabeth Paravisini-Gebert, eds. *Sacred Possessions: Vodou, Santería, Obeah, and the Caribbean*. New Brunswick: Rutgers University Press, 1997.

Frazer, Sir James George. *The Golden Bough*. Abridged ed. New York: St. Martin's Press, 1966. (Unabridged edition published 1936).

Genovese, Eugene D. *Roll, Jordan, Roll: The World the Slaves Made*. New York: Vintage Books, 1976.

Gilroy, Paul. *The Black Atlantic: Modernity and Double Consciousness*. Cambridge, Massachusetts: Harvard University Press, 1993.

Glissant, Edouard. *Caribbean Discourse: Selected Essays*. Trans. J. Michael Dash. Charlottesville: University Press of Virginia, 1989.

—— "The Cultural 'Creolization' of the World: Interview with E. Glissant." *Label France* 38 (January 2000). http://www.france.diplomatic.fr/label_france/ENGLISH/DOSSIER/2000/ 15creolisation.html.

Gregory, Steven. *Santería in New York City: A Study in Cultural Resistance*. New York: Gardland, 1999.

Hoetink, H. "'Race' and Color in the Caribbean." In *Caribbean Contours*. Sidney W. Mintz and Sally Price, eds. Baltimore: Johns Hopkins U. Press, 1985, 55–84.

Knight, Franklin W. *Slave Society in Cuba during the Nineteenth Century*. Madison: University of Wisconsin Press, 1970.

—— *The Caribbean: The Genesis of a Fragmented Nationalism*. New York: Oxford University Press, 1978.

Koss, Joan D. "Artistic Expression and Creative Process in Caribbean Possession Cult Rituals." In *The Visual Arts: Graphic and Plastic*. Justine M. Cordwell, ed. The Hague: Mouton, 1979.

Long, Edward. *The History of Jamaica*, 3 vols. London: T. Lowndes, 1774.

Métraux, Alfred. *Voodoo in Haiti*. Trans. Hugo Charteris. New York: Schocken, 1972.

Mintz, Sidney W. *Caribbean Transformations*. Baltimore: Johns Hopkins U. Press, 1974.

Mintz, Sidney W., and Sally Price, eds. Baltimore: Johns Hopkins U. Press, 1985.

Moreno Fraginals, Manuel. *The Sugarmill: The Socioeconomic Complex of Sugar in Cuba 1760–1860*. Trans. Cedric Belfrage. New York: Monthly Review Press, 1976.

Mosquera, Gerardo. "Africa in the Art of Latin America." *Art Journal* 5.4 (winter 1992): 30–38.

—— "Elegguá at the (Post?) Modern Crossroads: The Presence of Africa in the Visual Art of Cuba." In *Santería Aesthetics in Contemporary Latin American Art*. Arturo Lindsay, ed. Washington, D.C.: Smithsonian Institution Press, 1996, 225–258.

Paravisini-Gebert, Lizabeth. "Women Possessed: Eroticism and Exoticism in the Representation of Women as Zombie". In *Sacred Possessions: Vodou, Santería, Obeah, and the Caribbean*. New Brunswick: Rutgers U. Press, 1997, 37–58.

Patterson, Orlando. *The Sociology of Slavery: An Analysis of the Origins, Development and Structure of Negro Slave Society in Jamaica*. London: Macgibon and Kee, 1967.

Price, Richard, ed. *Maroon Societies: Rebel Slave Communities in the Americas*. Garden City: Anchor Press/ Doubleday, 1973.

Richardson, Alan. "Romantic Voodoo: Obeah and British Culture, 1797–1807." In *Sacred Possessions: Vodou, Santería, Obeah, and the Caribbean*. Margarite Fernández Olmos and Lizabeth Paravisini-Gebert, eds. New Brunswick: Rutgers University Press, 1997, 171–194.

Stevens, Anthony M., and Andrés I. Pérez y Mena, eds. TK title TK New York: Bildner Center for Western Hemisphere Studies, 1995, 81–98.

Thomas, Hugh. *Cuba: The Pursuit of Freedom*. New York: Harper and Row, 1971.

von Humboldt, Alexander. *The Island of Cuba*. Translated into English with notes and preliminary essay by J. S. Thrasher. New York: Derby and Jackson, 1856. Reprint, New York: Negro Universities Press, 1969.

CULTURAL HYBRIDIZATIONS

LANGUAGE AND LITERATURE: A BILINGUAL TRADITION

NEW YORK CITY

Center and Transit Point for Hispanic Cultural Nomadism

Dionisio Cañas

This essay will explore from a historical point of view the coordinates legitimating the contention that New York City is an important Hispanic cultural center. To this end we have explored the following themes: first, the trajectory of Hispanic immigration, the use of the Spanish language, and the establishment and evolution of the principal Hispanic sociocultural institutions in the city, and second, the production of Hispanic culture in the New York City region. Within this second theme, we will examine publications and the media, many of the genres of literature, popular music, graffiti, and the arts. For reasons of space, we will not explore Hispanic classical music, opera, ballet, dance, and other performance arts, or the manifestations of religious culture, architecture, or academic scholarship. A number of factors ought to be borne in mind by the reader. First, in this study of New York City as a Hispanic cultural center and as a point of transit for the same, we have given equal consideration to Hispano-American and peninsular Spanish figures, institutions, and publications. Second, because in the United States these people have been designated, generally and statistically, as Spanish people—Latin Americans, Hispanics and, finally (whether or not they speak Spanish), Latinos—we have, therefore (regardless of whether the name or label "Latino" is the preferred term today) indiscriminately employed all of these terms. Third, the important literary and humanistic production made by this Hispanic or Latino population in English will only be considered here as a point of reference and not to the full extent it deserves. And, finally, nomadism and cultural cross-fertilization (*mestizaje*) appear to have taken hold in the twentieth century, and as a consequence the cultural products under discussion here are marked by the co-existence of different traditions—for Hispanics or Latinos—Spanish, Latin American, English, Anglo-American, Native American, African, Jewish, Arabic, Chinese, and many other cultures.

On the basis of these considerations, we can state that New York City is, at the same time, both a fixed and nomadic Hispanic or Latino cultural center. These terms have been carefully chosen: *center*, because the city is a geographic and cultural space that has attracted and has accommodated, temporarily or permanently, persons of Hispanic origin; *cultural*, in this site where cultural products and expressions are generated by these same people; *nomadic*, because the protagonists of this cultural travel (in reality or in their minds) move between different localities and traditions; and *Hispanic* or *Latino* because, for better or for worse, this is how people of a Hispano-American background are known in the United States, even though a part of this community was born in the United States.

POPULATION, LANGUAGE, AND SOCIOCULTURAL INSTITUTIONS

Ever since 1527, when Diego Ribero sketched the outlines of "The Bay," in which present-day New York City is located, the Hispanic imagination has been constantly entranced with the space and the city that would become not only the cultural capital of the world in the second half of the twentieth century, but one of the most important and vital Latino cultural centers in existence. In those early days the present-day Hudson was known as the San Antonio River because a Spanish ship captained by the black Portuguese navigator Esteban Gómez explored the mouth of this river on 17 January (the feast of St. Anthony) 1526, one year after its sighting by the first European explorer, the Italian Giovanni da Verrazano.

In 1612, Dutch merchants constructed the first trading post in Manhattes (present-day Manhattan); their interpreter was a free African, Jan Rodríguez, who would eventually settle on the island. Visiting New Amsterdam in 1643, the French Jesuit missionary Isaac Jogues noted that eighteen different languages were spoken in the town, including Spanish. The historical documents show that the origins of the use of Spanish in New York are tied to three marginalized groups of Iberian extraction: Spanish-Portuguese Jews; Spanish sailors, locally known as "Spanish negroes"; and a group of slaves identified as the "Spanish Indians," although it is not known if these latter actually spoke Spanish (Goodfriend 114). The first historically important reference to a Spanish presence in New York is dated August 1654. In that month a group of twenty-three Jews of Spanish-Portuguese origin arrived in the city from Recife, Brazil. In the same month the Spanish and Portuguese Synagogue was founded in secret, the first Jewish congregation in what was to become the United States. Since then (and until today), a part of the Spanish-Jewish community in the city has continued to use the Ladino dialect of Spanish, not only in daily life, but also in literary expression, as a vehicle for the transmission of the Sephardic oral tradition.

In 1741, the population of New York numbered 10,000 people, two thousand of which were slaves, many of these being "Spanish negroes." The term "Spanish negroes" refers to the formerly free crewmen of Spanish ships captured in the Caribbean by the English, who were brought to New York and there traded as slaves. Documents show that some, but not all, of these Africans spoke Spanish, although at a very rudimentary level. Five "Spanish negroes" were accused of arson in 1741. This accusation was, in part, thanks to the fact that a witness is said to have overheard someone say in Spanish, "*Ven aquí, señor*" (Come here, sir), at the beginning of the fire (Davis 81). While four of the accused were pardoned, the fifth, pleading his innocence, was sentenced to death; at the moment of execution he broke into prayer in Spanish (Davis 226; Ellis 129–37).

The same year (1741) saw the publication in New York of the first Spanish grammar for use in the Thirteen Colonies. In 1835 Francis Lieber (1800–1872) stated that Spanish, among other languages, could be heard on a daily basis on the principal street of the city, Broadway. Already by this date New York had three Spanish newspapers (García 22), and it is known that a Spanish guide to the city was published in 1876.

In this register of the dates related to New York's Hispanic population and their culture, the floating, vague, and nomadic aspect of their existence as well as the more stable side, their anchorage at the heart of U.S. society, ought to be kept in mind. For this reason we wish to stress two fundamental perspectives that have informed our research: the official view, based on census data and historical documents, and the extra-official view, based on sources which are less scientific but form part of an empirical and oral history of the very same facts and events. In this sense the memoirs written by the Puerto Rican Bernardo Vega (1885–1965) have been indispensable for a better understanding of the Latino ambience of the Big Apple during the first half of the twentieth century. The novel *Windmills in Brooklyn* (1960), written in English by the Spaniard Prudencio de Pereda (b. 1912), has also been an interesting source of information on the Latino community in the same time period.

The various censuses taken in New York in the nineteenth century can only be considered approximations and not entirely trustworthy. Nevertheless, there are documents showing that between 5 May 1847 and 31 December 1860, 4,537 "Spanish," 1,376 "South American," and 324 "Mexican" immigrants arrived at the port of New York City, for a total of 6,237 Hispanics in less than two decades (Ernst 188). Over the course of the nineteenth century and up until the 1920s, the Spanish community would be the largest among all immigrant communities in New York. Toward the end of the nineteenth century Spanish sailors began to take up residence in the Chelsea district of Manhattan also known as "Little Spain" (La pequeña España), between West 14th and 23rd streets. However, Spaniards also lived in other sections of the city: in lower Manhattan, at the foot of the present day Brooklyn Bridge, resided some 25,000–30,000 Spaniards; in Brooklyn, 5,000–6,000; and in Astoria, Queens, a sizable number also resided (Rueda 85–92). Starting from 1920, political refugees, in the majority socialists and anarchists, came to live in New York, fleeing the Spanish dictatorship of Primo de Rivera; during the Spanish Civil War (1936–1939) a new wave of Spanish refugees arrived, and it would not be until the end of the Franco dictatorship in 1975 that this flow of immigrants from Spain would begin to fall off. By and large the Spaniards who came to New York in these waves were artists and intellectuals, and, as we shall see, very few would make the city their permanent place of residence; in fact, today there are less than 25,000 New Yorkers who were born in Spain.

Toward the middle of the nineteenth century a wave of Cuban refugees began to make itself felt. In general, these Cubans had a high level of education and were mostly white; thus, many of them and their children integrated into U.S. society, despite their initial plan to return to their homeland once Spanish colonial rule had been ended. Later, in the 1860s and 1870s, Cuban tobacco workers began to show up in New York. In the twentieth century, another wave of exiles was seen at the time of the Batista dictatorship—in 1959 more than fifteen thousand Cubans lived on the Upper West Side. During the 1970s, fleeing yet another regime, that of Fidel Castro, Cubans continued to arrive in New York. It is to be noted that among this last wave were significant numbers of a very particular group, the Cuban-Chinese, a group speaking not only English, but Chinese and Spanish as well, and who have kept alive the traditions linked to these two languages (Leeds 375–79).

What is today known as Spanish Harlem, or *el barrio*, began taking shape during the last quarter of the nineteenth century, in the Upper East Side of Manhattan, from 96th Street to 124th Street. According to Bernardo Vega, this area already contained at that time a considerable Cuban community. In 1904 the first Puerto Rican families, approximately 150 people, established themselves there, with a similar number being scattered around other parts of the city. Spanish Harlem in those days was an area where the Sephardic Jews had established many businesses, shops, and restaurants, and while they spoke Ladino among themselves, their clientele were mostly Latin Americans and peninsular Spaniards. Vega notes that already by 1913, even though the Hispanics were not concentrated in any specific district and were to be found scattered here and there throughout the city, "there was a community of professionals and affluent families living in the West on the other side of Central Park" and that by 1916 "the Spanish-speaking population of the city was reckoned to be 16,000 people"). (Vega 132, 30)

About this time, Juan Flores, one of the intellectuals whose works are indispensable for learning about the Puerto Rican community of New York, wrote: "Years ago, back in the 1920s and 1930s, you used to be able to tell where the Puerto Rican families lived by the green plants and colored flowers on their windowsills. Of all the immigrant nationalities settling in New York in those times, it was the Puerto Ricans who would freshen up their humble tenement walls with splashes of nature and provide themselves, neighbors, and passers-by some relief from the dreary grays and browns of the big-city streets" (331). In effect, already by the 1920s and 1930s, "the Puerto Ricans had extended themselves from Lexington Avenue, between 96th and 107th Street, up to the border of the Italian neighborhood at First Avenue. All throughout this district the *criollo* way of life was lived. . . . In shops and on the streets the only language you would hear was Spanish" (Vega 183). Around the beginning of 1929, "the old neighborhood on the East Side of Manhattan, composed of largely Cuban tobacco workers, moved to Harlem. From this moment, Spanish Harlem was definitively constituted as the heart of the New York Puerto Rican community" (Vega 187). Vega goes on to point out, citing census figures, that Puerto Rican immigration grew from 2,000 in 1904 to 26,000 in 1947, and that during the 1940s 60,000 Puerto Rican children were born in New York City (267). This phenomenal growth in the immigration and population of the Puerto Rican community also brought with it some pernicious consequences that, despite the quasi-poetic description that Flores paints today of the Puerto Ricans, began to create a much more negative image of them in the eyes of other New Yorkers. This unfair simplification of how the Puerto Ricans in New York live unfortunately has obscured the important contributions they have made. In the final account, the fact that Spanish language and culture enjoys a well-deserved privileged status in the city today is largely due to them.

The first and still the best study about immigrants from the Dominican Republic to New York City is "Dominicans in New York: Men, Women and Prospects" by Ramona Hernandez and Silvio Torres-Saillant. The first to arrive in the city from what is now the Dominican Republic were the relatively small number of whites and mulattos who fled a slave revolt in the capital, Santo Domingo, at the end of the eighteenth century (Leeds 368). However, in the 1970s, Dominican immigration would become massive: "The largest numbers of post-1970 immigrants came from the Caribbean. After the 1960s, Puerto Rican migrants declined, but the figures for other Caribbean newcomers increased. Whereas in the 1950s about 90 percent of the city's Hispanics were Puerto Ricans, by 1990 only about 50 percent were" (Binder and Reimers 227). Dominican immigrants and their children, born in the city, would take up residence in the Washington Heights area of the city at the northern end of the island of Manhattan, and in certain areas of Queens. While in 1967 there were only 125,000 Dominicans in the city (Hendricks 153), by 1990 the Dominican community would be estimated at 300,000—evidence of an extremely rapid rate of immigration. Although the Trujillo dictatorship had prohibited emigration to the United States from its beginnings in 1930, after the assassination of Trujillo in 1961, Dominicans began arriving in the Big Apple in considerable numbers (Leeds 369; Ugalde and Larson 98). Despite their large numbers the Dominicans "have yet to produce solid institutions with the power of transmitting social values, practices, and norms aimed at ensuring the protection and preservation of the community" (Leeds 46). In 1998 Hernández and Torres-Saillant published *The Dominican Americans* and Francisco Rodriguez de León published *El furioso merengue del Norte. Una historia de la comunidad dominicana en los Estados Unidos* [The Furious Merengue of the North: A History of the Dominican Community in the United States]. The establishment of an Institute of Dominican Studies at the City University of New York in 1992 in part demonstrates that the community is in the process of legitimating, with resolution and rigor, its own cultural values.

Colombian and Mexican immigrants are two other groups who have added to the numbers of New York's Hispanic community. It is difficult to ascertain the exact number of Mexicans and Colombians in the city since a large number of them, especially the Mexicans, are illegal immigrants and thus do not appear in census figures. However, the Colombians, principally living in the Jackson Heights area of Queens, began arriving at the beginning of the 1990s and now number around three hundred thousand. Anneris Goris and José Hernández, in their *Latin Communities in New York City*, offer a panoramic overview of these two communities as well as other groups that we will not deal with here.

In 1990 the Hispanic population of the city was 1,783,511. This number is of course approximate, for the already mentioned reason that the census does not include those Latinos who reside in New York illegally. As well, many Hispanics who do figure in the census classify themselves as belonging to other ethnic groups—African-American, for example—or do not identify with the official census denominations. It is thought that in reality there are about 2 million Latinos living in the city, more than a quarter of the total population, and that by the year 2010 that figure will rise to 35 percent.[1]

New York Spanish has a decidedly Caribbean flavor, not only because the largest group of Spanish speakers come from that region, but also because, in marriages between Latin Americans in New York, one of the two is frequently of Caribbean origin. The tendency of New York Spanish is to adapt to the vocabulary established principally by the Puerto Ricans. At the same time, however, the general phonology in use by the majority of the Spanish speakers in the city demonstrates a desire to employ and learn a standardized Spanish, or better put, an idiom in which Americanisms and Anglicisms do not hinder its comprehension at a national or international level.

In the Spanish media, especially television and periodicals, there is a tendency toward the use of a Spanish that can be comprehended without difficulty by all Spanish-speaking groups in the city and the nation in general. In addition to the variations in pronunciation, intonation, lexicon, and grammar, Spanish as it is spoken in New York City is significantly marked, to varying degrees and depending on the country of origin of the speaker, by the influence or interference of English. However, the influence of English on New York Spanish, while subject to much criticism from linguistic purists, is not that different from the English influence felt by the various Spanish idioms spoken in

Latin America and Spain. Nevertheless, the Spanish spoken in the city, and the Spanish used by American Hispanics in general, possesses its own characteristic features.

"Spanglish" is one of the most extreme and interesting modalities of the Spanish spoken in New York and in the U.S. Spanglish is composed of the following constituents: First, a number of English loan-words have been Hispanicized (e.g., "to have lunch" has become "*lonchar*"); second, those Spanish words bearing a phonetic similarity to English words are used with their English signification (e.g., *librería* means "library" instead of "bookstore," because of its resemblance to the English word); third, words and phrases are translated literally from English into Spanish (e.g., "I'll call you back" is in New York Spanish *te llamo pa tras*). In a similar manner, while conversing in English, for example, it is not uncommon for New York Hispanics to introduce fragments of Spanish speech, and vice versa. However, as numerous linguists have demonstrated, these changes or substitutions of codes are not arbitrary or chaotic but rather possess certain very concrete and coherent guidelines, with specific reasons and intentions. Those who employ this mix of English and Spanish assume that their interlocutors understand the two languages perfectly and, in general, when the other speaks only one language (whether it be Spanish or English), the bilingual speakers do everything possible to sustain the dialogue within the parameters of that language (Zentella 179–81).

According to a report by the Modern Language Association of America, in 1998 Spanish continued to be the foreign language most studied in U.S. universities: A total of 656,590 students were registered in Spanish courses in that year (Brod and Welles 23). This interest on the part of U.S. students to make Spanish their second language is due, in part, to the Hispanic presence in the United States, as well as to the geographic proximity of Latin America and the fact that many institutions, in addition to the Hispanics and the Latino media, have kept Hispanic language and culture alive.

Although evidence of a significant Anglo-Saxon culture was already present in the 1730s (theatrical performances and periodical publication), 1750 is the date traditionally assigned to the initiation of an autonomous New York City cultural life. In 1754, for example, the first New York Society Library was established. In the following decade children's books and Latin and Spanish school texts began to be published (Kammen 243–48). Given that toward the beginning of the nineteenth century the first Spanish periodicals edited in New York began to appear and during these same years a number of Hispanic sociocultural associations were founded, it can be seen that the formation of New York as a Hispanic cultural center is tied, from a chronological point of view (with a half-century lag), to the birth of an autonomous U.S. cultural life in the metropolis. Nineteenth-century Hispanic sociocultural enclaves were of an almost exclusively political, nationalist, and regional character (at times there were cultural centers representing people from a single Spanish or Caribbean town), although there was no lack of cultural activity of a more general nature. Over time these centers have become more "specialized." Today many of them make every possible effort to integrate their programs with the community and its popular cultural expressions.

It is possible at the start of the twenty-first century to view the concept of "culture," however inclusive and vague, as no longer having an inherent meaning and, therefore, to deem any selection of cultural points of focus arbitrary. This is to say that, while we mention El Museo del Barrio, we could just as easily have studied the culture of *botánicas*, barber shops, and the mini-marts known as *colmados* and *bodegas*, respectively. However, in a certain sense a large part of the cultural identity of New York Hispanics survives, at least institutionally, thanks to the continual use of the Spanish language and the activities of certain cultural centers. Thus, Gustavo Bueno, in his *El mito de la cultura* [1996; The Myth of Culture], writes: "To invoke cultural identity as a means of justifying a conservationist politics vis-à-vis the language or the institutions of a people is nothing but a vacant, ideological, and propagandistic gesture, because cultural identity is ultimately the product of the persistence of the language and institutions, and not the other way around" (176). In this sense, we can state that if it is legitimate to speak of a Hispanic communal identity in New York City, it is because people have continued to use the Spanish language in an active and dynamic form, not only as a vehicle of communication and creation, but also as a principal point of reference for a Latino sensibility, however latent, in those Hispanics who speak only English. On the other hand, clearly a number of institutions have taken up the task of actively reminding Hispanic New Yorkers not only that they form part of a very rich tradition, but also that Latin American, Spanish, and U.S. Latino cultural expression is just as much a living force in the United States as it is in the other nations of the Hispanic world.

With respect to the peninsular Spanish cultural institutions of the city, Germán Rueda has noted, "New York saw the integration of the majority of the regional cultural centers into national centers toward the end of the 1930s and throughout the 1940s. Thus, one of the Galician centers, the Casa Galicia, united with the Centro Español in 1939, and the same happened to the Centro Montañés (Santander region) and the Centro Aragonés (Aragón). The Centro Asturiano (Asturias) was integrated to La Nacional in 1947" (221). The Casa de España was created later, and in the 1990s came the Instituto Cervantes de Nueva York. The dynamic of transformation from regional to national or international groupings was also seen in many other cases in the Latin American community of the Big Apple. Later, we will examine what form the institutional infrastructure of Hispanic culture in the city takes today.

Reviewing the chronological evolution of the Hispanic population of New York, it can be seen that the most important Hispanic cultural institutions have been directly related, in terms of their resources and the frequency of their activities, to the origin of the majority group resident in the city. In the final decade of the twentieth century this pattern was partially broken because Spain had transformed itself into a developed and economically powerful nation. Spain's new-found cultural maternalism, her desire for an international cultural prestige, and, for some Spaniards, the most antiquated imperialist nostalgia have all combined to mean that the degree of Spain's cultural presence in New York is not related to the number of Spanish citizens in the city but rather to its economic muscle. The names of the most significant and well-funded Spanish cultural institutions in the city speak volumes: Instituto Cervantes (1991) and the Centro Rey Juan Carlos I at the University of New York (1997). During the first four decades of the twentieth century, when the majority of the Spanish-speaking community was of Spanish origin, the Instituto de las Españas (1920, now known as the Hispanic Institute and la Casa de España) and the Hispanic Society of America (1904) were the most relevant Spanish cultural centers. In the 1930s there also existed a Spanish and American Alliance, publisher of the bilingual review, *Alhambra*. Later, the Spanish Institute (1954) would add its weight to those prestigious institutions. However, despite the fact that these institutions are today still in operation, Spanish cultural leadership resides with the Instituto Cervantes and the Centro Rey Juan Carlos I at New York University.

In the 1960s, with the Puerto Ricans and other Latin Americans forming the majority of Spanish speakers in the city, two new centers were created: The Americas Society (1968) and the Centro de Estudios Puertorriqueños, as part of the Department of Black and Puerto Rican Studies at Hunter College, City University of New York (1969). Starting in these years, the New York public university system began creating on every one of its campuses centers similar to the one at Hunter College, the most recent and significant of these being the already mentioned Instituto de Estudios Dominicanos (1992) at City College, City University of New York. In tandem with these centers, other institutions were created, some of whose efforts and activities we will highlight in each section of this text. The most important of these still active today are: EL Museo del Barrio, the Ollantay Center for the Arts, the Instituto de Escritores Latinoamericanos (The Institute of Latin American Writers), the Mexican Cultural Institute, the INTAR Hispanic American Arts Center, the Centro Cultural Eugenio María de Hostos, and the Caribbean Cultural Center.

It is to be noted that throughout the entire twentieth century, museums, cultural centers, and galleries have consolidated the image of New York as a platform for the introduction and launching of Spanish and Latin American artists into the cultural marketplace. Hispanic art maintains a presence in New York through expositions of Spanish and Latin American art, the temporary or permanent residence in the city of Latino artists, and through the galleries and institutions that mount and promote this art. These factors notwithstanding, for the enormous number of New York Latinos, Hispanic art is only relatively known. Much more fertile for the knowledge of Hispanic art has been a phenomenon that moves in the opposite direction: the general and popular use of images, symbols, subjects, figures, and materials of a Latin American origin. Beginning in the 1960s, New York became not only a center of attraction and a stopover for Hispanic artists, but was also transformed into an important center of artistic production for the Latinos temporarily or permanently resident in the city, as well as for those born or raised there. At the end of this essay we will concisely trace the trajectory of the presence of Hispanic art in the city.

The First Latin American Congress of New York Visual Arts, a point of reunion for a discussion of various aspects of the Latino art situation in the United States, was held at the Ollantay Center for the Arts on 26 May 1990. According to photographer Charles Biasiny-Rivera, U.S. "mainstream institutions come to us now more than they ever have" (Monge-Rafuls 17); and we can second this opinion by pointing to, for example, the "Emerging Latino Artists in New York" exposition, sponsored by AT&T, that was held in July and August 1997 in the Art Gallery at the Queens Theater in the Park.

With the minimal parameters established, it is important for us to ask, "What are the most important institutions for the legitimation of New York as an important center of Latino art?" Lucy R. Lippard, in 1990, laid down a number of coordinates for an approach to the U.S. artistic scene, coordinates representing the situation in which U.S. Latino art found itself at the end of the twentieth century. According to Lippard, we must take into account the fact that "we now look at art within the context of disorder—a far more difficult task than following institutional regulations" (7). However, in order to arrive at this point of disorder, there must necessarily have been a pre-existing order. Let us consider, then, the institutions that, until today, have given us an organized picture of Hispanic art.

El Museo del Barrio, founded by the Puerto Rican artist Rafael Montañez Ortiz in 1969, is perhaps the most significant cultural center in the United States exclusively devoted to Latin American art. Within Manhattan itself, other centers such as the Americas Society and the Spanish Institute have institutionally backed the contemporary art of Spain and Spanish America. Various cultural centers contain galleries that regularly mount shows by Latino and Latin American artists. Among this group, INTAR, Hostos, the Ollantay Center, El Taller Latinoamericano, El Taller Boricua, GALA, the Mexican Cultural Institute, and the Colombia Center have been the most prominent. Some other museums, by virtue of their multicultural character, have promoted expositions of Latino artists: the Studio Museum in Harlem, the Bronx Museum of Arts, and the Caribbean Cultural Centre, in particular. In addition to these institutions, almost all of New York's art museums have at one time or another, and some with great frequency, put on exhibitions of Spanish or Latin American art because it falls within their general mandate for holding art exhibits. The cultural bulletins and journals put out by the consulates of various Spanish-speaking nations have published monthly notices of the Latino art to be seen in the city. More than any other publication, *¡AHA! Hispanic Art News* has kept the Hispanic community abreast of the most important exhibits.

PERIODICALS, JOURNALS, AND OTHER MEDIA

Around the middle of the eighteenth century, as already mentioned, one can identify the beginnings of an autonomous Anglo-Saxon culture in New York City. Although all evidence indicates a plurality of ethnic groups, languages, and religions within the urban center, little is known about the participation of the Spaniards and Latin Americans in the cultural activity of the city (Kammen 243–45). The first important English-language periodical published in New York, *The Independent Reflector* (1752), was primarily of a political and social character; similarly, the beginnings of the Spanish-language periodical press in the city in the nineteenth century is also tied to Independence movements, those of Cuba and Puerto Rico. "A clear differentiation between *reviews* and *periodicals* during this epoch is very often impossible to make, or at least very difficult to maintain, whether on the grounds of form, content, or frequency, and there is no advantage that we can see in attempting to do so. However, there clearly were newspapers, and plenty, in more or less the modern sense of the term, since these publications came out on a daily basis, were principally occupied with furnishing information and editorial opinions, thus servicing a Spanish speaking public, and carrying out the traditional and fundamental role of the periodical" (Shearer 50). Thus, when we use the term *newspaper*, it is not to be confused with the modern connotation of the word (i.e., a daily newspaper); similarly, when we refer to reviews or journals, neither should this be associated exclusively with the contemporary notion of literary, or specialized, journals.

The launching of New York Spanish-language periodical publication really began in the 1820s: *El Habanero* (Philadelphia-New York, 1824–1826), edited by Father Félix Varela; *El Redactor* (1826?–1831?) concerned itself with literary subjects, information on Latin America, and commercial affairs; *El Mensajero Semanal* (1828–1831); *Espejo Macénico* (sic), a Freemason publication; *Noticioso de Ambos Mundos* (1836–1859?); *El Continental* (1861), mostly dedicated to business but also containing political and cultural information; *El Porvenir* (1863); *La Voz de la América* (1865?); *La Voz de Puerto Rico* (1874, only one issue published); *El Espejo* (1869–1894); *El Comercio* (1875–1930); and *La Crónica* (1848–1853 and afterward as *El Cronista*, possibly as late as 1877):

> None of these papers was as successful as the *La crónica* which survived their competition and lived beyond the period of the Civil War. From the start, *La crónica* appealed to Latin American merchants and carried many advertisements of Havana businessmen; its

news columns dealt chiefly with events in Spain and Latin America; but after the middle of the century it printed more news of the United States and, as did most of the foreign press, supported the Democratic party and opposed nativism and abolitionism. It was at once the medium of expression of the Hispanic community, the leading political and commercial paper in the Spanish language during the fifties, and the chief source of information for Latin American immigrants.

(Ernst 157)

As well as these full-fledged publications, a number of more modest informational broadsides appeared in these years: *La Verdad* (1848–1860, after 1855 published in New Orleans), a free multi-page circular subsidized by the newspaper *The Sun*; *El Mulato* (1854); *El Pueblo* (1855); and *Delta* (1882–1885, bilingual).

However, one of the best known periodicals of the era was *Patria* (14 March 1892–31 December 1898), founded and edited by the Cuban writer and revolutionary José Martí (1853–1895). From its first issue to its last, *Patria* adopted a position laid out in its first editorial: "Founded by the will and the means of the independent Cubans and Puerto Ricans of New York City, this periodical is devoted, without haste and without rest, to the organization of the free society of Cuba and Puerto Rico" (in Ripoll 18–19).

It can be said, then, that beginning with *El Redactor* and *La Crónica*, Latino journalism in New York began to shape its own identity within the Hispanic world. With the end of Spanish colonial rule in Cuba and Puerto Rico (1898), revolutionary matters disappeared from the Hispanic press, and local problems, in addition to Latin American subjects, constituted the bulk of the coverage in the New York Spanish-language press. Parallel to Spanish-language journalism was the translation into Spanish of certain U.S. publications: *América Científica* (1890–1909), a literal version of *Scientific American*, and *La Gaceta de Policía* (1894–1896), a translation of *The Police Gazette*, are two examples. In addition, there were a number of very specialized publications also published in Spanish that we will not consider here, such as *La Moda Ilustrada* (1896–1897), *El Círculo del Joyero* (1876–1877), *La Gaceta de Bomberos* (1884–1885), *Gaceta de Ferrocarriles* (1892), *El Museo de las Familias* (1872–1873?), and *El Ateneo* (1874–1877) (Shearer 47–48).

Although the twentieth century opened in 1901 with the publication of the *Puerto Rico Herald*, founded by Luis Muñoz Rivera (1859–1916), the most outstanding Latino daily of the entire century, *La Prensa*, would begin publishing in the following decade. According to Bernardo Vega:

La prensa, the longest running Spanish-language daily in the history of New York City, began publication on June 4, 1918, although it had been in circulation [as a weekly] since October 12, 1913. It was founded by Rafael Viera, who established his editorial office at 87 Broad Street. For a time the celebrated Colombian writer José María Vargas Vila

(1860–1933) was the editor, later, the post passed to V.H. Collao, who transformed the paper into a daily; and shortly after that, the Spaniard José Camprubí took the reins. Under the tenacious leadership of Camprubí, and with the backing of the Unión Benéfica Española (The Spanish Benevolent League), *La prensa* achieved financial stability.

(125)

In 1948 *El Diario de Nueva York* arrived on the scene and began competing with *La Prensa* until the two were amalgamated in 1962 under the banner *El Diario La Prensa*. Still publishing today, the paper has a print run of 321,000 and some sixty thousand readers in the New York City region. New York's second present-day Spanish-language daily, *Noticias del Mundo*, (founded in 1980) has a readership of 28,000. In 1954, John H. Burma, in his *Spanish-Speaking Groups in the United States*, passed a death sentence on the Spanish press: "The Spanish-language press is on the decline . . . it is probable that in fifteen years the Spanish-language press will virtually die out" (99). Despite Burma's prognostication, precisely the opposite has transpired: The National Association of Hispanic Publications, founded in 1982, represents forty-two Hispanic periodicals (some of which are written in English), with a total circulation in 1986 of 1,340,000 copies (Veciana-Suárez, v).

Throughout the entire twentieth century Spanish-language periodicals were published in New York, but their history has been only partially documented. In his memoirs, Bernardo Vega mentions *Las Novedades, Cultura Proletaria, El Norteamericano, El Corsario, The Tobacco Worker* (bilingual), *El Machete Criollo, Metrópolis, Liberación, Pueblos Hispanos*, and the weekly *Gráfico*, which was bought and run by Vega himself in 1927. Collaborating with Vega were the distinguished Puerto Rican intellectuals Cayetano Coll y Toste (1850–1930) and Jesús Colón (1901–1974).

In addition to the local papers, the major Latin American and Spanish periodicals can be bought in New York; with a circulation of 25,000, the Santo Domingan *El Nacional* is the most read. Also to be found are a number of weeklies, some of them distributed gratis; among these are *El Especial, Resumen* (founded in 1971), *Impacto* (founded in 1975), *El Tiempo, El Continental, Visión Hispana, Eco Latino*, and *Noticiero Colombiano e Hispano* (founded in 1983), *El Sol de México y Latinoamérica*, and *El Sol de Colombia*, now known as simply *El Sol*, and others such as *Nosotros los Latinos* (founded in 1995), and *El Puente Latino* (founded in 1997), a free newspaper with a circulation of 100,000 (Zentella 182–83).

Although, as we have noted, in the nineteenth century it is difficult to distinguish between what was a periodical and what was a review, a number of these publications do draw close to what we mean by a review: *La América* (1871), reappearing the following year as *La América Ilustrada* (1872–1874), and later amalgamated with *El Mundo Nuevo* (1871–1876) under the editorship of Enrique Piñeyro; *Ambos Mundos* (1865?); *La América* (1882–1889?), a journal (different from the previously mentioned review with the same name) dedicated to agricultural and industrial subjects, but which included information about literature, edited and managed for a time by José Martí; and *Cuba y América* (1897–1898, New York; 1899–1917, Havana). Two of the reviews in this category deserve special mention for being literary journals of some significance and longevity: *Las Novedades. España y los Pueblos Hispano-Americanos* (1877–1905; Shearer gives other dates: 1876–1918), where, among others, Leopoldo Alas 'Clarín' and Emilia Pardo Bazán were published; and *La Revista Ilustrada de Nueva York* (1886–1893; Shearer's dates: 1882–1894). (For a fuller study of the history and import of these two journals, see the book by Vernon A. Chamberlin and Ivan A. Schulman [Sotelo 11]). Other important journals are *Las Tres Américas* (1896–1899; Shearer: 1893–1896), founded by the Venezuelan poet Nicanor Bolet Peraza (d. 1906 in New York), as well as the *La Revista Lustrada*, in which many of the famous Latin American *modernistas* were published: Rubén Darío (1867–1916), Manuel Gutiérrez Nájera (1859–1895), José Martí, Salvador Díaz Mirón (1853–1928), Salvador Rueda (1857–1933), and Enrique José Varona (1849–1933). Some journals followed a complex publishing path, such as *Literatura Americana*, which was founded in Curaçao (1849) by the Guatemalan poet Antonio José Irisarri (1786–1868) and later began publishing in New York in January 1850, the year in which it ceased operations (Shearer 47).

In the first half of the twentieth century, a number of publications with a political character came out in New York, such as *España Libre* and *Ibérica*, but the most comprehensive and rigorous literary journal of the epoch was the *Revista Hispánica Moderna*, founded in 1934 by Federico de Onís (1885–1966) as the *"Boletín del Instituto de las Españas"* (Casa de las Españas, Columbia University). The objective of this latter publication was to "study and disseminate Hispanic culture"; it contained articles, book reviews, and information on contemporary literature, a Spanish-American bibliographic section, and another section devoted to students of Spanish. Today it is almost exclusively a journal of academic scholarship (Sobejano 222).

Other reviews in these first decades worth mentioning are *El Liberal* (1935–?), New York/Havana, a mostly political journal; *Norte* (1940–1950?), with numerous articles on the painters of Cuba, and among whose collaborators were intellectuals and writers such as Ernest Hemingway—with an article on the Cuban painter Gattorno (February, 1941, n. 32)—Américo Castro, and Ciro Alegría (1909–1967), and in the February 1946 issue several interesting pages devoted to "El Nueva York que vio García Lorca" (New York Through the Eyes of García Lorca) (Esquenazi 43–44, 50–51). Among the more specialized publications were *Cine Mundial* (1916–1935), *Ecos* (1946–?) and, in the 1970s, *Furia*, a journal of politics and current events which, according to its editors, "recoge todas las pasiones que se registran en los distintos sectores: amor, teatro, cine, deportes, televisión, en general" ("gathers together all the passions to be found in distinct sectors: love, theater, cinema, sports, television"); we have only been able to find three issues published in 1974.

In the last half of the twentieth century, New York has seen a large number of Latino reviews and magazines, both in Spanish and English, an account of which must here be limited to a selection. Among those no longer in circulation are: *Exilio* (1966–1973); *Lugar sin Límite* and *Caronte*, both created by the Puerto Rican writer Iván Silén (b. 1944); *Románica*, founded by Rafael Catalá, and *Lyra*, both edited by the Cubans Lourdes Gil (b. 1951) and Iraida Iturralde (b. 1954); *Escandalar*, created by the Cuban poet Octavio Armand (b. 1946); *Emen-Ya*; *Enlace*; *De Azur*, edited by the Dominican poet Leandro Morales; *Transimagen; Punto 7*, edited by the Dominican Silvio Torres-Saillant; *Alcance; AREITO; Ollantay Theater Magazine*, founded by Pedro R. Monge-Rafuls; *Centro de Estudios Puertorriqueños, Extremos Líricos: del Caribe a la Araucania*, a poetry journal published simultaneously in San Juan, Puerto Rico, Stony Brook, NY, and Concepción, Chile; *Encuentros*, a bilingual journal published by Columbia University students; *Al Aire Libre*; *Boletín del CEPI (Círculo de Escritores y Poetas Iberoamericanos de Nueva York)*; and *Espacio de Escritores*. Among the journals most active today are *Review: Latin American Literature and Arts*, published by the Americas Society; *Brújula/Compass*, edited by the Peruvian writer Isaac Goldemberg (b. 1945); *Tercer Milenio*, edited by the Puerto Rican poet Pedro López Adorno (b. 1954); *La nuez*, founded by the Cuban poet Rafael Bordao (b. 1951); *Realidad Aparte*, edited by the Colombian poet Gabriel Jaime Caro (b. 1949); and the most recent, *Ñ*, created in 1995 by the Colombian Ricardo Léon Peña-Villa (b. 1962).

In addition to the press, among the other most influential communications media in the Spanish-speaking community of New York are Latino television and radio.[2] The history of these two forms has been recounted in practically every book dedicated to the U.S. Hispanic community. Geoffrey Fox's chapter, "The Image Machine," in his book *Hispanic Nation* (1996), is perhaps the best, in the sense of most informative, of the accounts to date (40–66). The New York television channels 41, 44, 47, MH, ACQ, and BQ offer a total of 557 hours of weekly programming in Spanish (García 34). Serious doubts have been raised about the deplorable state of Hispanic television programming, specifically its propensity to foment a brutalization and alienation of the Latino community rather than promoting the development of greater Latino self-esteem. However, despite these reservations, it is unquestionable that a sentiment of unity, and therefore of mass identity, emerges from these programs—not only because they are realized in a Spanish that is at the same time local and standard, but because the focus that they place on Latino and Latin American subjects is a priority with all these channels. Ana Celia Zentella, in an excellent essay entitled "Spanish in New York," has taken up this subject (181–86) and with respect to radio programming (of the four stations, La Mega and Radio Wado deserve special merit), Zentella has come to the following conclusions: "Overall, Spanish radio is much more reflective of life in New York than Spanish television in programming, advertisements, and in the type of Spanish that is spoken, because most radio programs are produced locally and many people call in" (185).

LITERATURE

Although many of the authors to whom we will refer form an integral part of the literary history of their country of origin, we have deemed it necessary to limit our discussion here to those books that have made significant use of New York City as a theme
within Hispanic literature. It can be said that the experience of New York in these
works and for these authors has varied: Some have only passed through the city; others stayed for either a short time or a considerable number of years; still others have
made the city their permanent place of residence; and finally there are those who arrived as children or were born here, the majority of whom write in English. Although
this latter group must be considered an integral part of a history of Latino literature in
New York, we treat them here only briefly, largely because this text centers on Hispanic cultural manifestations that have employed Spanish as their principal means
of expression. The situation of the Puerto Rican writers of New York—forming part of
two histories, that of Puerto Rico and that of the United States—is a fine example
of the extent to which circumstances of unrest, uncertainty, crisis, and affirmation of
identity can give rise to works that, beyond their historical significance, have in themselves an aesthetic importance. These works are important because they throw light
on the conflict (in the sense of collision and separation, identification and alienation)
of the human being with his or her surroundings, society, and institutions, with the
historical moment in which it has been their fate to live, with their imposed identity
and their inherited identity, and ultimately, with the desire to be oneself, an individual
and part of a collective identity within the history of humanity and far beyond a solely
national history.

Finally, we wish to alert the reader that we have not arranged the writers by literary
genre, but have rather followed a chronological order, grouping these figures into those
of a Latin American origin and those who come from Spain. While many of the writers we will mention are much better known within a specific genre (José Martí, for
example, in poetry and journalism), some have also been practitioners of other genres
and have at times been translators, editors of journals, professors, cultural animators,
and so forth. A separate section is devoted to theater, and a number of the names already mentioned will appear there again. In *El poeta y la ciudad: Nueva York y los escritores hispanos* [1994; *The Poet and the City: Hispanic Writers and New York*] the
author of this chapter studied numerous authors and works that will be discussed
much more briefly in these pages. In addition, the bibliography lists a series of articles
and essays that followed that book and in which the author traced in a historical fashion the relation between Hispanic poetry and New York City. Thus, although the
pages that follow amount to no more than a very abridged approximation of certain
authors and works that, because of their importance, really deserve a much fuller
study, what is important here is to give a more panoramic picture of the intellectual

and creative activity of New York's Hispanics; this is not, then, an analysis of these works.

The emergence of Latino literature in New York can be dated from the era during which the city saw the publication of the first ever anthology of Hispanic literature in exile, *El laúd del desterrado* [1858; The Outcast Lute] (see Kanellos 1997), and in which José Martí's magnificent book, *Versos libres* [Free Poems] (1882; published much later) and his literary and political journalism were written (1882–1891). The influence of New York City on the works of other nineteenth-century Spanish-American writers resident in the city was a relative one; this is the case with, for example, José María Heredia (1803–1839) (who published the first book of Spanish-language verse in the city in 1825) and Juan Clemente Zenea (1832–1871) (also from Cuba), both of whom were included in the aforementioned anthology, as well as with Juan A. Pérez Bonalde (1846–1892) (Venezuelan) and Lola Rodríguez de Tió (1843–1924) (Puerto Rican). On the other hand, the impress of the city was in the works of the Nicaraguan Rubén Darío (1867–1916) and the Mexican José Juan Tablada (1871–1945), two of whose most important books were published in the city: *El Jarro de Flores* [1922; The Flower Jug] and *La feria* [1928; The Fair, or The Market]. Other works that were first published in New York are the book by the Nicaraguan Salomón de la Selva (1893–1959), written in English, *Tropical Town and Other Poems* (1918), and *Desolación* [1922; Distress] by Gabriela Mistral (1889–1957), who died in Hempstead, New York. Later, the Chileans Humberto Díaz-Casanueva (1907–1992), Rosamel del Valle (1900–1965), and Nicanor Parra (b. 1914), and the Puerto Ricans Clemente Soto Vélez (1905–1993) and Graciany Miranda Archilla (1908–1993), founders of the avant-garde group Atalaya, would come to New York.

Arriving in 1855 and remaining until 1872 (with a brief return to Colombia in 1856–1857), Rafael Pombo (1833–1912) resided in New York, first as a diplomat and later as a writer. He translated, created, and adapted a number of children's fables that would be published by the New York house Appleton. Pombo knew Ralph Waldo Emerson and counted among his intimates Henry Wadsworth Longfellow, with whom he corresponded for more than nine years, and whose poem "The Psalm of Life" he translated into Spanish. A number of Pombo's most important works were written here, including a *Diary* [1855; *Diario*] recounting his experiences in the United States, "Hora de tinieblas" ["The Twilight Hour"], his most representative philosophical poem, and his famous "En el Niágara" ["In the Niagara"]. In addition, Pombo published a sonnet written in English in the U.S. review *Post* (Orjuela 69–79, 142–49).

As a literary curiosity, the works of the Mexican politician and poet Guillermo Prieto, pseud. Fidel (1818–1897), can also be mentioned; his *Viaje a los Estados Unidos* [1877; Voyage to the United States] includes some poems composed in the United States. A number of Prieto's journalistic pieces written in New York are of interest because they contain some information about the Hispanic literary ambience of the city. For example, in his diary (123–4) he writes: "Señor Pérez Bonalde is a man of commerce, but his leisure time is devoted to literature, which he cultivates with great success in his poetry. He speaks a number of languages, among them German, with remarkable perfection. His most outstanding gift, however, is his admiration for the merits of others. Exempt from every pretension, sincerely ignorant of his own great talents, he makes a worship of his affection for Heine, and that great poet has found in him a faithful interpreter of his unique images. The translation of the "German Voltaire's" verse made by Señor Pérez Bonalde has just been published in New York to the most enthusiastic praise in the local press."

The residence in the city of the Cuban writer Cirilo Villaverde (1812–1894) (from 1849 to 23 October, 1894, although with a number of trips of both long and short duration to other places in the United States as well as to Cuba) is very significant because it was in New York that Villaverde wrote his most important novel, a denunciation of slavery, *Cecilia Valdés, o la loma del ángel* [Cecilia Valdés, or Angel's Hill], published in New York in 1882. Villaverde not only edited the separatist periodical *La verdad*, but was the editor of a number of other reviews and periodicals, including *La América*, *Frank Leslie's Magazine*, *La ilustración americana*, and *El Espejo*, as well as a contributor to the journals *La familia*, *El avisador hispanoamericano*, *El Fígaro*, and *Revista cubana*. In addition to these journalistic activities, Villaverde was also a translator of a number of writers, including Charles Dickens.

The Cuban writer José Martí towers over the historical panorama of Hispanic literature in New York City as a kind of foundational figure, a literary patriarch. Both in his poetry and in his prose works, Martí established a horizon that will forever be a point of necessary reference. His sharp observations on U.S. society and culture in the 1880s constitute an enormous literary corpus that demonstrates in large measure his modernity. Arriving in the city in the flower of his youth on 3 January 1880, on the cusp of his 27th birthday, Martí would wear many hats during his years in New York: professor, journalist, children's writer, consul, clerk, translator, and political ideologue of Cuban Independence. He would also edit the journal *La América*, found the revolutionary periodical *Patria*, publish two books of verse, *Ismaelillo* (1882) and *Versos sencillos* [1891; Unaffected Verses], leave behind after his departure two unpublished verse collections, "Versos libres" and "Flores del destierro" ["Flowers of Exile"], as well as write and publish in the city one of his first *modernista* novels, *Amistad funesta: Lucía Jerez* [1885; Ill-fated Friendship]. Martí remained in New York (with visits to and periods of residence in other U.S. cities and other countries) until 1895.

Among the Latin American intellectuals who resided in New York during the nineteenth century there are a number of others who should be mentioned: the Puerto Rican Eugenio María de Hostos (1839–1903); the Argentinean Domingo Faustino Sarmiento (1811–1888), who arrived in New York in 1865 and remained in the United States until 1868, and who took a great interest in the institutions and literary life of the nation (his diary *Diario de un viaje de Nueva York a Buenos Aires* [1944; Diary of a Voyage from New York to Buenos Aires] is based on these experiences); the Venezuelan Nicanor Bolet Peraza (1838–1906), whose cultural mentorship and enthusiasm were important and whose house was the headquarters of the Sociedad Literaria Hispanoamericana de Nueva York (Shearer 49–50); and Arturo Alfonso Schomburg (1874–1938), the Puerto Rican writer and bibliophile (whose English works form part of the African-American intellectual history of the United States).

Rubén Darío visited New York on a number of occasions—in 1893, 1907, and for several months between the end of 1914 and the beginning of 1915—and wrote there a number of poems, some of them taking up the theme of the city. In 1893, Darío was received into New York's Cuban community led by José Martí. In his *El viaje a Nicaragua* [Voyage to Nicaragua], Darío wrote: "I passed through the Yankee metropolis when it was in the full boil of a financial crisis. I experienced the full force of the Stock Market hurricane. I witnessed the omnipotence of the multi-millionaire and admired the mammonic madness of the immense capital of the checkbook" (1919a, 2). Darío, despite being endowed with a cosmopolitan outlook, was basically a poet of Parisian sensibility and genuinely Spanish-American sensitivities. Thus, despite all his attempts, Manhattan ultimately remained a lusterless city for Darío; in his essay on Poe written in New York he stated: "One thinks one hears the voice of New York, the echo of an immense soliloquy of ciphers. How distinct from the voice of Paris...!" (1918, 19). On his last trip to the city, Darío published a number of pieces in the New York daily *La Prensa*. However, despite having partially integrated into New York cultural life, his poem "La gran cosmópolis" ["The Great Cosmopolis"] well illustrates his discomfort with the city (1919b, 35–39).

In the twentieth century, writers from every country in Latin America took up residence in or passed through New York. Among numerous possible examples, the Dominican Pedro Henríquez Ureña (1884–1946) comes to mind. Editor of the New York periodical *Las novedades*, Ureña published his book *El nacimiento de Dionisos* [The Birth of Dionysus] in the city in 1916. Another important writer, for whom the experience of the great metropolis appears to have been quite different from that of Darío, was the Mexican José Juan Tablada. First arriving in flight from the dictator General Victoriano Huerta, he stayed in New York four years (1914–1918); later, he came back for an extended residence between 1920 and 1935, and finally returned, for reasons of health, in 1944, the year before his death (in New York). Tablada not only published his most significant work in New York, but was also an active Hispanist, re-creating in the city, through various U.S. and Spanish-American journals, a Mexican artistic panorama and opening the bookstore known as Libros Latinos on East 28th Street. In 1945, a month after his death, Octavio Paz delivered a homage to Tablada in Manhattan, highlighting the fascination the poet had for travel and flight, in the sense of continual exile: "fuga de sí mismo y fuga de México" ("flight from himself, flight from Mexico"),

Paz wrote. As he describes in his travel diary "Nueva York de día y de noche (313–25) [New York by Day and Night], New York signified for Tablada this condition of flight because it was a permanent jack-in-the-box where nothing was static or definitive. We may see in him the first Latin American literary nomad of the twentieth century, a writer who made the U.S. metropolis his most frequent place of transit.

Within the Spanish American context, the three most important and influential points of reference for the literature written in New York are Puerto Rican, Cuban, and Dominican writers. Arriving in New York by and large because of economic reasons, the Puerto Ricans have had an attitude to the English language that has been one of both resistance and assimilation. For their part, the Cubans, in the majority of cases, came to the Big Apple for political reasons, and although there would be no lack of frustration with the condition of exile, including a critical attitude toward the big city, as refugees they have been much more acquiescent to the host country. If we recall that half of the present-day population of Puerto Rico resides in New York, it can be understood that for these writers the fundamental condition is not that of exile, as it is for the Cubans, but rather that of a "doubling" of the spiritual and intellectual field, divided between Puerto Rico and New York. The Dominicans, for their part, constitute a group whose presence and influence (both in Spanish and in English) is becoming more important day by day.

The figure of Julia de Burgos can be taken as representative of the historical tensions experienced by the Puerto Ricans in New York. On the one hand, in her work we encounter a multi-leveled search for an identity: personal, as a woman; literary, as a poet; and political, as a partisan of Independence. The tempestuous biographical trajectory of her life (1914–1953) is directly tied to her poetic production. Born into a family of modest means in a working-class part of the town of Carolina, she studied at normal school in San Juan, Puerto Rico, where she discovered what would be a lifelong social and political commitment to the people of Puerto Rico. She went through a number of stormy love affairs and ended tragically dying of alcoholism in New York before she was thirty-six. Burgos's long residence in New York (eleven and a half years, first in 1940, and later between 1942 and 1953) is principally reflected in the fourteen poems she wrote in the city and in her correspondence. Margarite Fernández Olmos, in her *Sobre la literatura puertorriqueña de aquí y de allá: aproximaciones feministas* [1989; On the Puerto Rican Literature of Here and There: A Feminist Approach], situates Julia de Burgos at the point of transition between those poets who resided in Puerto Rico and wrote in Spanish, and those poets who lived in New York and who sometimes wrote in English or in a mix of the two languages. This question of a divided Puerto Rican literature has been much debated, and José Luis González (1926–1997), for example, in his *El país de cuatro pisos y otros ensayos* [1980; *Puerto Rico: The Four-Storeyed Country, and Other Essays* (1990)], has demystified the various views of a Puerto Rican cultural homogeneity. Julia de Burgos played a very important role in

Puerto Rican literature: Without losing her sense of being completely Puerto Rican, she opened up the possibility for other Puerto Rican writers to compose poetry in English, as she herself had done at the end of her life in her poem "Farewell in Welfare Island." Arcadio Díaz Quiñones, commenting on *Puerto Rican Voices in English: Interviews with Writers* (published in 1997), has remarked: "the vigor of these voices has made it possible to reconceive the rigid construction of a fixed cultural legitimacy, formulated exclusively in terms of the possession of an insular space, and transplant it into the Spanish language and Puerto Rican citizenry in the United States" (10).

The New York poetry of the Cuban writer Eugenio Florit (born in Madrid in 1903, moved to Cuba in 1918, later to New York in 1940, and finally in the 1980s to Miami, where he died in 1999) has grown out of a conversational style evocative of a sharp Catholic-existential consciousness entirely free from any rhetorical tendencies. In his *Antología penúltima* [1970; Penultimate Anthology], in a section entitled "Intermedio de Manhattan" ["Manhattan Interlude"], we can find one of Florit's most important and emblematic poems of the 1960s, "Los poetas solos de Manhattan" ["The Solitary Poets of Manhattan"], in which he portrays the essential solitude of the human condition within the metropolitan multitude. Similarly, in the poem "En la ciudad grande" ["In the Big City"], a poetic response to José Martí's "Amor de ciudad grande" ["Metropolitan Passion"], Florit reflects on the human condition from a position of serenity, solitude, and Christian stoicism that he opposes to the rat-race life—contaminating everything, including love—of New York City. Florit also played an important role in New York cultural life as a translator of U.S. poetry and as a cultural animator from his professorship at Columbia University; his final New York book was *De tiempo y agonía—Versos del hombre solo* [1974; *Of Time and Anguish—Poems of a Solitary Man*].

Following in the footsteps of Rafael Pombo, one of the first Colombian writers to come to New York, many other Colombian authors would pass through or take up residence in the city. Eduardo Márceles Daconte (b. 1942), in his book *Narradores colombianos en U.S.A.* [1993; *Colombian Writers in the U.S.*], has pointed out that José Eusebio Caro (1817–1853) also spent a time in New York, that José María Vargas Vila (1860–1933) founded there the journal *Hispanoamérica*, published until 1905, and that the poet Porfirio Barba Jacob (1883–1942) made New York his home between 1919 and 1921. Other important Colombian writers to be mentioned in this context are José Eustasio Rivera (1888–1928), author of *La vorágine* [1924; *The Vortex*], who died in the city, and the *Nadaísta* poets Amílkar U (Osorio) (1940–1985) and Elmo Valencia, both of whom lived the life of the Beat generation. Valencia would write an important prose poem on his New York experiences entitled "Extraña visión" ["Strange Vision"].

The position taken by social poetry with New York City as a theme is, at times, overly simplistic and has continually fallen back on the use of platitudes in poems that certainly contain an expected political-social message (as is the case with the Spanish poet Rafael Alberti, although the same can be said of the sporadic allusions to the city in the works of Pablo Neruda [1904–1973]). However, the use of such clichés does little to communicate the real complexity of the U.S. metropolis. In 1971 Nicolás Guillén (1902–1989) composed a sonnet entitled "A las ruinas de Nueva York" ["To the Ruins of New York"], in which he summons up a tradition of meditations on the ruins of great cities, following, in particular, in a genealogy stemming from Rodrigo Caro's (1573–1647) "Canción a las ruinas de Itálica" ["Lyric on the Italic Ruins"]. However, there is little, if anything at all, in the works of these three great writers bearing upon Spanish-language cultural activity in the city of New York.

The Nicaraguan poet Ernesto Cardenal's (b. 1925) poetic chronicle, "Viaje a Nueva York" ["Voyage to New York"], however, is a different case. In this work Cardenal employs a poetic narrative tradition in which the personal, the social, and the religious are intertwined, producing a vision of New York as the diabolical center of capitalism. A number of the topical themes worked into this poem by Cardenal had already been mined by García Lorca in his "Poet in New York" and would continue to be reproduced in a multitude of books on the city. The significance of this text, perhaps, lies in its documentary value: The poem reflects with a certain fidelity the ambience of 1970s New York, describing Cardenal's experience in the Nixon era and in the Gay Liberation movement; it is addressed to another Spanish American poet and novelist, the Chilean Enrique Lihn (1929–1988), who frequently visited New York and published in 1979 a book entitled *A partir de Manhattan* [*From Manhattan*]. The theme of the subway is Lihn's most constant preoccupation, and already in these texts Lihn signals the arrival of those who would in the 1980s become a multitude: the homeless.

In 1989 it was calculated that some 160 Hispanic writers lived in the New York City area; ten years later this number had likely doubled.[3] In addition to countless poetry, short story, or novel-excerpt readings, as well as innumerable performances, conferences, and book launchings, every year New York holds a Spanish-language book fair. A number of U.S. publishers have begun issuing Spanish-language literary collections, including Penguin U.S.A., Ballantine, and Vintage (the latter in collaboration with Santillana), in which Latino, Latin American, and to a lesser extent Spanish authors are published in their original languages. Small Hispanic editorial houses and bookstores have existed in New York since the nineteenth century; in the twentieth century this situation continued, and two of these, Las Américas and Eliseo Torres (both are publishers and booksellers) have taken up important roles in the Latino cultural life of the city. Today, many would agree that Librería Lectorum and Macondo (both on East 14th Street in Manhattan) are the most important bookstores, although not the only ones. (As for the other Spanish-language editorial houses, given their limited size and publishing efforts, we will pass them by here.) In an article on the changing conditions of New York Hispanic poetic production, Jaime Giordano has written that if the Hispanic presence in New York in the 1970s drew attention to itself in the "street fights" of social and political protest groups like the *Young Lords* or the *Real Great Society*, the 1980s has been marked by the invasion of an elite that does not consider itself to be a wave of immigrants and that maintains strong ties to its countries of origin, returning there once or twice a year. This phenomenon is absolutely new in the history of immigration to the United States, and is due not only to the enormous differences between Hispanic and U.S. culture, but also to the great development that has been seen in the means of transportation and communication, as well as to the fact that it has been political conditions (dictatorship, dependency) and academic conditions (unpleasant material working conditions) that have motivated their move, conditions not considered to be irreversible and, thus, conditions favoring an outlook that is much more that of exiles than that of immigrants. The vigor with which these elites defend and cultivate the Spanish language is, in part, a result of the cohesive existence of this community of *foreigners* rooted in the U.S. and their stubborn defence of the cultural oases of the universities.

(83)

Although Giordano refers in this article to the Hispanic writers who live in the "area" of New York, this notion of the New York area is somewhat difficult to define, as its coordinates are much more poetic than geographic. What can be said is that some of these writers, even though they do not live in New York City, do orbit around it, its Hispanic cultural centers, its journals, and its universities, and these institutions have, as Giordano points out, from the beginning of the twentieth century until the present day, played a fundamental role in the development of Hispanic literature written in New York.

From a historical point of view, 1977 was extremely significant for the Latino writers of New York, because it was in that year that the Centro para las artes Ollantay was founded. From its inception, the center was dedicated to the promotion of Hispanic artists residing in the New York City area, as its mission statement-manifesto published in March of that year underlines:

We believe that there exists in New York City a poetry unlike the poetry of our countries of origin, a poetry in which the currents of Hispanic verse are transformed into something original and independent. For this reason we seek to uncover the roots of this fugitive and fleeting Tradition of Flight! This tradition perhaps lies buried in the recesses of the poetry of Heredia, Martí, Tablada, García Lorca, Florit, and many more unknown to us. For to create in a linguistic environment and in circumstances that are foreign to us transforms our poetry, and it is in this transformation that it is distinguished from the poetry that is produced in our countries of origin; it is for this reason that we make this announcement. We seek to discover and give a name to the characteristics of a poetry that can be written in the Spanish language in New York.

(qtd. in Cañas 1994, 169–70)

Since 1977 Ollantay has sponsored a wide variety of meetings, lectures, theatrical presentations, and exhibitions and has published a number of books. This moment in the 1970s signified a particular coming to consciousness for many of the Hispanic writers residing in New York City. This new awareness was tied to the double recognition that they had to reopen the question of their own relation to the poetic tradition of their country of origin, and at the same time that their living in New York made them participants in a tradition that, as a coherent ensemble—and not as a series of isolated works or as works seen from within the poetic perspective of their respective countries—was, let us say, marginalized and forgotten: the tradition of Spanish-language poetry written in New York City. While recognizing that the authentication of place is a necessary and supplementary theme of their work, these writers of Spanish-language U.S. literature have yet to formulate the parameters in which that authentication might be accomplished.

The contingent of New York Puerto Rican, Cuban, and Dominican writers, from three of the city's most important Hispanic groups, calls for an extensive and particularized study of its own. Nevertheless, a number of these poets and prose writers have already appeared in numerous anthologies (some of them published in Spain), and critical attention, both inside and outside the United States, has recently begun to be paid to their works. The account that follows will deal with writers from other Spanish-American countries resident in New York. Before that task can be begun, however, a number of essential writers, and beginning with the Puerto Ricans of this group, must at least be mentioned: Iván Silén (b. 1944), Manuel Ramos Otero (1948–1990), Giannina Braschi (b. 1954), Marithelma Costa (b. 1955), Pedro López Adorno (b. 1954), among others. In 1994 the Ollantay Press of New York published a collection of essays entitled *Lo que no se ha dicho* [That Which Has Been Left Unsaid], in which a significant portion of the Cuban literary production in exile was studied. Of the New York Cubans, Octavio Armand (b. 1946) and José Kozer (b. 1940) were singled out for special attention.

It needs to be stressed that in both the Cuban and the Puerto Rican literature of today, the poetic work of women constitutes one of the most significant and interesting creative forces. The anthology *Poetas cubanas en Nueva York* [*Cuban Women Poets in New York*] was published in Spain in 1991; included in it were the five excellent writers Magali Alabau (b. 1945), Alina Galliano (b. 1950), Lourdes Gil (b. 1951), Maya Islas (b. 1947), and Iraida Iturralde (b. 1954). Among Dominican poets, Alexis Gómez Rosa (b. 1950), resident in New York since 1985, is the best known. In the last few years he has published *Contra la pluma la espuma. Poemas 1980–1986* [1990;

Foam Against the Feather: Collected Poems 1980–1986], *Tiza & Tinta (Antología poética)* [1991; Chalk & Ink: An Anthology], *New York City en tránsito de pie quebrado* [1990; Crossing New York City on Broken Feet ("feet" in a metrical sense)], and *Si Dios quiere y otros poemas* [1992; God Willing, and Other Poems]. Rosa's poetry is a continual meditation on the poetic phenomenon, writing, language, self-identity, and time. Among the group of Spanish-language Dominican writers, Angel Rafael Lamarche (1900–1962) (who published his first stories in New York in the 1950s), Viriato Sención (b. 1941), Tomás Modesto (b. 1951), Juan Rivero (b. 1940), Daisy Cocco de Filippis (b. 1949), José Carvajal (b. 1961), Juan Torres (b. 1955), and León Félix Batista (b. 1964) are particularly interesting. The New York journal *Brújula-Compass* dedicated a special issue in the winter of 1998 to Dominican writers living in the United States.

With regard to other parts of Latin America, let us consider the Peruvian novelist and poet Isaac Goldemberg (b. 1945), who took up residence in the city in 1965. Goldemberg's double origin, as a Jew and a Peruvian Amerindian, placed him in the precarious position of being an *Hombre de Paso* (Man of Passage), the title he gave to a book he published in the United States in 1981. With a language that is at once direct and mythic, Goldemberg's work is endowed with the psalmodic power of the Bible and the simple and profound wisdom of the Amerindian oral tradition of the natives of Peru. In 1992, he published another book of poems, *La vida al contado* [Life: Cash on Delivery]. A similar response to the big city life, although at a much more intellectual and hermetic level, has been that of Roberto Echavarren (b. 1944), resident in New York since the middle of the 1970s and a writer who, in recent years, lives with one foot in Uruguay and one in the United States. During the years he lived in New York, Echavarren published two books of verse, *La planicie mojada* [1981; The Moist Plain] and *Animalaccio* [1985; Beast]. The works of Raúl Barrientos (Puerto Montt, Chile, 1942) offer us a more referential world, although one charged with imagination. He published his first book of poetry in the United States in 1981, *Ese mismo sol* [That Sun Itself], and since the fall of Allende in 1973 has wandered throughout various locales of the United States. Closely connected to a group of Spanish American poets writing in New York, where he himself now resides, Barrientos published *Libro de las imágenes* [Image Book], a collection of his most significant work to date, in 1989. Two more books have appeared, *Monarca* [1997; Monarch] and *Llave de néon* [1998; The Key of Neon]. The Colombian writer Jaime Manrique (b. 1949) came to the United States when he was eighteen and has lived in New York since 1982. A number of his novels have been published there, the most recent of which is *Twilight at the Equator* (1997). Although Manrique wrote his latest two novels in English, when it comes to poetry he writes in Spanish; *My Night with Federico García Lorca/Mi noche con Federico García Lorca* (bilingual edition, 1997) is his most recent book of verse. It is also necessary to take note of two more writers from Ecuador who have recently made important contributions to the cultural life of New York City: Jaime Montesinos (b. 1938) and Petrorio Rafael Cevallos (b. 1953). In addition to those writers from other countries we have already mentioned, or will soon mention, the Argentinean Manuel Puig (1932–1990), a large number of whose works were written in New York, and the Cuban Reinaldo Arenas, born in 1943, who took his life in the city in 1990, are among the prominent writers because consideration of their *oeuvres* cannot be reduced solely to a discussion of poetry and prose but must also include an account of their works in other genres such as theater.

One of the most important literary phenomena of the last decades has been the poetry and literature of the "Nuyorican" group. Nuyorican poetry had its origin at the end of the 1960s and the beginning of the 1970s, and culminated in 1975 with the publication of the anthology *Nuyorican Poetry: An Anthology of Puerto Rican Words and Feelings.* On the Lower East Side of Manhattan one can still find the Nuyorican Poet's Café, the former meeting place for these writers. *Aloud: Voices from the Nuyorican Poet's Café* (1994) was the final anthology of works that came out of the scene at this already mythic meeting place.

LITERARY TRANSLATION

In the field of literary translation, Caribbean exiled intellectuals who lived in New York City during the latter part of the nineteenth century made significant contributions to the emerging Hispanic cultural presence in the United States. Translation was an important intellectual and literary tradition in Cuba that also flourished abroad. A good number of exiled Cuban writers and educators translated as a means to supplement their income, and many of them did so as a literary undertaking. In the numerous Spanish-language periodicals that the Cubans founded in exile, these writers published translations that helped to disseminate major 19th-century European and American writers in Spanish, among them: Byron, Tennyson, Longfellow, Emerson, Poe, William Cullen Bryant, Hugo, Lamartine, Musset, Schiller, Heine.

In this regard, the contributions by novelist Cirilo Villaverde, the brothers Antonio and Francisco Sellén, and José Martí deserve mention. Villaverde translated Dickens's *David Copperfield*, as well as other works of fiction and non-fiction, including Victor Hugo's *Les Miserables* (attributed to him). The Sellén brothers were particularly active in disseminating German lyric poetry. Francisco published in 1875, in New York, the first complete Spanish version of Heine's *Intermezzo lírico*, and in 1881 he published an anthology of German Romantic verse, *Ecos del Rin*, that included 38 German poets, on which his brother Antonio collaborated. In 1875, also in New York, a Spanish version of Heine's *El cancionero* [*Buchj der Leider*] appeared, translated by the Venezuelan poet

José Antonio Pérez Bonalde. In the 1890's Francisco Sellén translated narrative fiction: Willkie Collins' *A Rogue's Life* and Hawthorne's *The Scarlet Letter*. For his part, Martí rendered into Spanish poems by Horatio, Emerson, Thomas Moore, Longfellow and Poe, as well as the novels *Mystery*, by Hugh Conway, *My Children*, by Hugo, and *Ramona*, by Helen Hunt Jackson.

This was also a time of expansion for the publishing houses. The New York–based Appleton Publishing Company engaged exiled Hispanic authors, most notably Puerto Rican educator Eugenio María de Hostos and Martí, as translators of technical and pedagogic texts and as collaborators in the preparation of dictionaries.

Several decades later, two translations helped to shape Federico García Lorca's influential book *Poeta en Nueva York* (published posthumously in 1940), during his stay in New York City in 1929–30: León Felipe's unpublished version of Walt Whitman's *Leaves of Grass*, and T. S. Eliot's *The Waste Land* [*La tierra baldía*], translated by Puerto Rican critic Ángel Flores. In 1946 Flores's English language version of Neruda's *Residencia en la tierra* [*Residence on Earth and Other Poems*] was published and stirred American interest in the Chilean author, who would be awarded the Nobel Prize in 1971.

In the 1940's and 1950's, two landmark anthologies were instrumental in disseminating modern poetry: The *Anthology of Contemporary Latin American Poetry* (1942) and *Antología de la poesía norteamericana contemporánea* (1954), edited and translated by Dudley Fitts and by the Cuban poet and critic Eugenio Florit, respectively. During this same period, Harriet de Onís's translations contributed to make known the narrative work and essays of major authors: Alejo Carpentier, Jorge Luis Borges, Alfonso Reyes, Jorge Amado and Teresa de la Parra. Interest in Latin American letters would deepen in the following decades, both in academic circles and in the book market.

Beginning in the 1960's, an increasing number of Latin American and Spanish works were translated into English. The excitement generated by the Boom in the Latin American Novel and by the excellent works that were being published in every genre had a huge impact. The important book industry in New York supported the publication and promotion of Latin American literature in translation. This created a demand for translators that resulted in the professionalization of the trade. Many of the versions that followed were well received and several of them became best sellers.

During this phase, the outstanding work of Gregory Rabassa and of Helen Lane gained them critical acclaim, as they brought into English the most celebrated novels of the Latin American Boom, as well as other contemporary and 19th-century Spanish and Brazilian narrators. Rabassa has been noted for his renditions of Julio Cortázar, Gabriel García Márquez, Jorge Amado, Mario Vargas Llosa, Juan Benet, José Lezama Lima, Clarice Lispector, Machado de Assis and Luis Rafael Sánchez. Lane was successful in her versions of Juan Rulfo, Juan Carlos Onetti, Octavio Paz, Juan Goytisolo, Elena Poniatowska, Augusto Roa Bastos, Luisa Valenzuela, Nélida Piñon, Ernesto Sabato, Tomás Eloy Martínez and Fray Servando Teresa de Mier. In the meantime, Scottish poet Alastair Reid attained recognition for producing some of the finest versions of Borges's and Neruda's poetry.

Post-boom translators have already made their mark felt. Esther Allen's edition and translation of José Martí's *Selected Writings* and Edith Grossman's new rendering of *Don Quixote* are both noteworthy. Allen and Grossman have also translated the Spanish novelist Antonio Muñoz Molina: *In Her Absence* and *A Manuscript of Ashes*, respectively. Natasha Wimmer has translated recent works by Mario Vargas Llosa: *Letters to a Young Novelist* and *The Way to Paradise*, and by Roberto Bolaño: *The Savage Detectives* and *2666*. Katherine Silver's versions include Antonio Skármeta's *The Postman*, Elena Poniatowska's *Tinísima*, Horacio Castellanos Moya's *Senselessness*, and José Emilio Pacheco's *Battles in the Desert and Other Stories*. The novelist Kristina Cordero has translated Carlos Fuentes' *The Eagle's Throne* and Gioconda Belli's *The Country Under My Skin: A Memoir of Love and War*. New York poet Elizabeth Macklin has rendered Basque poet Kirmen Uribe's *Meanwhile Take My Hand* into English.

Contemporary Spanish-language Puerto Rican literature has been made available to American readers through a host of books. In terms of poetry, these include the following: *Puerto Rican Poetry: An Anthology*, edited and translated by Roberto Márquez; *Inventing a Word: An Anthology of Twentieth-Century Puerto Rican Poetry*, edited and translated by Julio Marzán; *Song of the Simple Truth: The Complete Poems of Julia de Burgos*, translated by Jack Agüeros; Clemente Soto Vélez's *The Blood that Keeps Singing*, translated by Martín Espada and Camilo Pérez Bustillo; and Lourdes Vázquez's *Bestiary*, translated by Rosa Alcalá. Concerning fiction and testimonial literature, several books are of interest: Kal Waggenheim's version of Manuel Zeno Gandía's novel *La Charca*, and Juan Flores's translation of *Memoirs of Bernardo Vega*, and of *Cortijo's Wake*, by Edgardo Rodríguez Juliá.

My own contributions to the field have focused on poetry and include my Spanish versions of Elizabeth Bishop in *Antología poética*, the translation of Graciany Miranda Archilla's book of poems *Hungry Dust/Polvo hambriento*, selections from Elizabeth Macklin's and John Ashbery's work, and my English rendition of poems by Dionisio Cañas and by José Lezama Lima.

New York City, where Caribbean political emigrés engaged in the art of translation over a century ago, has promoted in its universities and cultural institutions a deep interest in Hispanic cultures. The publishing industry and the work of translators have helped to validate the reputation that Latino literature has gained throughout the world during the last few decades.

—Orlando José Hernández

Latino literature written in English is an area of letters that is being assimilated into the U.S. book publishing industry, and it can be said that it has very recently become something of a vogue. Names like Oscar Hijuelos (b. 1951), Julia Álvarez (b. 1950), Ed Vega (b. 1938), Piri Thomas (b. 1928), Cristina García (b. 1958), Sandra Cisneros (b. 1954), and Junot Díaz (b. 1968) are already familiar to U.S. readers. The phenomenon of writers whose background is Hispanic but who either were born or grew up in the United States is so complex that neither the historians nor the literary critics yet have been able to come to a consensus on how to "classify" such figures. Are they U.S. writers whose themes are related to their Hispanic roots, or are they simply writers whose narratives may be in English but whose cultural ambit is Latin American? Arcadio Díaz Quiñones, referring to Puerto Rican English language writers, has advanced a possible answer to this question:

> Here, literature moves between diverse times and spaces. There is here another social and cultural topography that questions the old modes of thinking the *national*, and de-hierarchizes the traditional legitimations of the literary. The existence of the U.S. Puerto Rican communities implies, on the one hand, the difficulty of imagining a self sufficient culture situated in a unique place within a linear historical continuum. On the other hand, it also implies a new spatialization of memory that belies every illusion of a facile *integration* into the U.S. culture.
>
> (10)

The precursors of this wave of English language novels by U.S. Hispanics were figures like the nineteenth-century María Amparo Ruiz de Burton (1832–1895), with *Who Would Have Thought It?* (1872), and, in the next century, George Santayana (1863–1952) with his novel *The Last Puritan: A Memoir in the Form of a Novel* (1935) (see Kanellos 1997). With the publication in 1989 of *The Mambo Kings Play Songs of Love*, and its garnering the Pulitzer prize that same year, Oscar Hijuelos (b. 1951) raised this strong Latin-flavored tradition to the highest level of respect it has ever seen. There are over a hundred important Hispanic fiction writers, writing in Spanish or English, spread out over the vastness of the continental United States; many of them can be indexed in the *Biographical Dictionary of Hispanic Literature in the United States/Diccionario Biográfico de la Literatura Hispana en los Estados Unidos.*

The peninsular Spanish writers who passed through or remained for a longer time in New York did so for a wide array of reasons, but almost every one of them, sooner or later, has written an account of his/her New York experience. Similarly, the impact of New York has become, within our imagination, a literary commonplace (whether or not the city has been visited), and thus poets such as Rafael Alberti (1902–2002); the novelist Camilo José Cela (1916–2002), with his unfortunate book of poems *Viaje a U.S.A.* [1967; Voyage to the U.S.A.]; José Hierro (b. 1922), in his last book *Cuaderno de*

Nueva York [1998; New York Notebook]; and, among others, Luis García Montero
(b. 1958) have all written texts whose central theme is some aspect of Manhattan. In
the field of prose, also, many books have been written about New York by Spanish
writers: Joaquín Belda's (1883–1935) *En el país del bluff, veinte días en Nueva York* [1926;
The Land of the Bluff: 20 Days in New York], Julio Camba's (1882–1962) *Un año en el
otro mundo* [1947; A Year in the Other World], Diego Hidalgo's (b. 1888) *Nueva York:
impresiones de un español del siglo XIX que no sabe inglés* [1947; New York: Impres-
sions of a Nineteenth-Century Spaniard Who Speaks No English], Josep Pla's (1897–
1981) *Viaje a América* [1960; Voyage to America] (the poet lived in New York in 1954
and published in 1987 *Weekend (d'estiu) a Nova York* [Weekend in Nova York]), José
María Carrascal's (b. 1930) *Groovy* (1973), Carmen Martín Gaite's (1925–2000) *Caperucita en Manhattan* [1990; The Adventures of Little Red Riding Hood in Manhattan],
Carlos Perellón's (b. 1957) *La ciudad doble* [1995; The Double City], and a book by one
of the most important cultural promoters of the last decade, José María Conget's (b.
1948) *Cincuenta y tres y Octava* [1997; 53rd and 8th]. The extremely interesting case of
the Spaniard Felipe Alfau (1902–1999), who lived in New York from 1916 on and published two novels in English, *Locos* (1936) and *Chromos* (1948), also deserves mention.
In the last few years these works have been reissued to considerable critical acclaim.
However, while it is difficult to place this author within the U.S. narrative tradition,
the same can be said vis-à-vis the Spanish tradition.

Although the two best-known Spanish poets to have written pieces on New York
are García Lorca and Juan Ramón Jiménez, a number of other Spanish poets have
passed through the city, including Dámaso Alonso (1898–1952), León Felipe (1884–1968),
Jorge Guillén (1893–1984), Concha Espina (1869–1955), Pedro Salinas (1892–1951), and
José Moreno Villa (1887–1955). Moreno Villa, who was in New York on a couple of occasions in 1927 and 1937, published two New York-related books, one in prose, *Pruebas de Nueva York* [1927; New York Proofs], and one in verse, *Jacinta la pelirroja*
[1929; Jacinta the Red-Haired Woman]; this latter inaugurated the use of conversational turns of phrase in Spanish poetry. In the last few years a couple of other books
of verse have been published: J. M. Fonollosa's (1922–1991) *Ciudad del hombre: New
York* [1990; City of Man: New York] and a bilingual book by the previously mentioned
Catalan novelist, Felipe Alfau: *Sentimental Songs: La poesía cursi* [1992]. Juan Ramón
Jiménez (1881–1958) came to New York on 12 February, 1916, and remained for almost
six months. The book he partially wrote during his stay in Manhattan, *Diario de un
poeta recién casado* [Diary of a Recently Married Poet], made a significant contribution to the Spanish poetry of the time and became a point of reference for the fundamental shift in Jiménez's work that dates from this moment in his career. Jiménez
bequeathed to the Spanish-language poetic tradition of the city, a much less moralis-
tic and less negative vision than that of José Martí (1853–1895) and Rubén Darío
(1867–1916), and later García Lorca (1898–1939). Distancing himself from ideological

preoccupations, Jiménez traced the outward face of the city with a great deal more freedom than his predecessors. The advertising landscape and illuminated "sign-scape" of New York produced in Jiménez a sensation of unreality, in which the city was doubled by the mutual reflection of the actuality of the streets and the graphic world of advertising that mocked it, writing its parody in neon signs traced against the nighttime sky. It is hardly surprising, then, that Jiménez writes in his farewell to the city: "New York, a reality unseen or an unreal vision" ("Despedida sin adios" [Farewell without Goodbye"]). What is more surprising is the characterization in the poem "De Boston a New York" ["From Boston to New York"]: "New York, marvelous New York! Presence of your own, complete oblivion!" Contradictions of this sort can also be found in Lorca's *Poet in New York*, poetry between a negative and shattered vision of the city and a positive, childlike exaltation. As Octavio Paz has pointed out, Jiménez's "Espacio" ["Space"] is one of the most important texts of twentieth-century Spanish writing. In 1941, twenty-five years after his visit to the city, Jiménez began his finalization of "Espacio," bringing to completion, in the second fragment of the poem, his vision of the great city.

During his nine-month residence in New York, between 1929 and 1930, Federico García Lorca wrote the poems that would become a fundamental and emblematic work for twentieth-century Hispanic poetry: *Poeta en Nueva York* [*Poet in New York*]. This is a book whose echoes can still be heard today in much of the city's Latino poetry. In 1997 the New York journal *ñ* inaugurated a new award, the Premio Internacional de Poesía—"Poeta en Nueva York" (there already being a Federico García Lorca Prize in the city)—and we can read in this an index of the influence that García Lorca's book has had and continues to have on the Latino writers of the city. García Lorca knew how to capture, better than any other, the commercial violence, the social in-justice, the racial discrimination, and the lack of consoling spirituality that charac-terizes life in New York. On the other hand, both in the letters written from New York and in the lectures he gave introducing his New York poems to the Spanish au-dience, there is a clearly marked double tension between admiration and contempt animating García Lorca's feelings about New York and New York society in general. This famous book is the subject of many critical studies, including a section of my own *El poeta y la ciudad* [The Poet and the City], and this is not the place to delve deeper into its problematics. What should be underlined, however, is that if José Martí is the founding father of Hispanic literature in New York, García Lorca is the modern poet who best embodies the Hispanic spirit of New York throughout the twentieth century.

In 1956 Odón Palacios Betanzos (1926–2007) arrived in New York, publishing there his first book of verse, *Santidad y Guerrería* [1969; *Sanctity and Belligerence*], and the majority of the rest of his works. Betanzos was the director of the Academia Norteamericana de la Lengua Española (founded in 1973), and played an important role as a cultural promoter. Beginning in the 1970s a new generation of Spanish writers began establishing themselves in New York. The author of this article, Dionisio Cañas (b. Tomelloso, 1949), has resided in the city since 1972 and written all his critical and literary work here. Octavio Zaya (b. Las Palmas, 1954) has resided in the city since 1978; his first book of verse, *Aproximación de la manera más abrupta* [1982; *The Most Abrupt Approach*] was written in collaboration with his twin brother. While in the last few years Zaya has dedicated himself almost exclusively to art criticism and journalism, a number of his poems (some of them in English) have appeared in exhibition catalogues and art journals.

The abundant tradition of Spanish-language poetry written in or about New York City was enriched in the 1980s with two new books: *Balada de la misericordia* [1989; The Ballad of Mercy] by Luis Moliner (b. Lumpiaque, 1949) and *Puer Profeta* [Boy Prophet] (winner of the Adonais Prize, 1989) by Juan Carlos Marset (b. Albacete, 1963). These two collections have moved their respective authors to the front ranks of new Spanish poetry, both for their maturity and finesse and for the independent aesthetic they each embody, distancing their works from the known schools, groups, and literary coteries of peninsular Spanish verse. At the same time, however, they form part of the trajectory of Spanish voices that, for very diverse reasons, have found in the subject of the urban space of Manhattan a stimulating challenge, both from a poetic and from a social and personal perspective. The prize-winning collection, *Aquel mar de esta orilla* [That Sea of This Shore] (Premio de Poesía Hiperión, 1990) by Francisco Javier Ávila (b. Madrid/Chozas de Canales, 1961), marked the debut of one of the most interesting poetic voices of the new decade. This book is the product of an artist who, facing his experience of New York City, has opened up the question not only of his own identity as a Spaniard between two worlds (alluded to in the title of the collection, a free paraphrase from Juan Ramón Jiménez), but also of this moment and this place in history. Avila's response is alternately critical, ironic, tender, and melancholic, but always endowed with a poetic surety and suggestiveness. In 1997 the Catalan poet Gabriel Planella published *New York, obert tota la nit*, and in 1998 the *Premio*. Moliner, Marset, and Ávila were all pursuing doctoral studies in New York when the aforementioned books were written, and have since returned to Spain to continue their careers. In 1998 the Premio Internacional de Poesía Gastón Baquero was awarded to Hilario Barrero (b. 1948), a Toledean poet who resides in New York, for his collection *In tempori belli*.

The subject of literary translations, both from English to Spanish and Spanish to English, is an extremely interesting one and important to an understanding of the role that New York has had and continues to have in the cultural relations between Latin America and the United States.

THEATER

Theatrical works began to be published in New York in the 1820s. Although the 1855 Census counted 231 actors in the city, three of whom were Spanish and one Latin American (Ernst 216), the first notice of a Hispanic theatrical production would appear in José Martí's periodical *Patria* in 1892. In general, the theater productions advertising in this paper were being staged, often by the Cuban actor Luis Baralt, in order to collect funds for the Cuban Independence movement. As the groups mounting these plays did not have a theater of their own, they were staged in places frequented by Spanish-speaking, and principally Cuban, immigrants: el Club Lírico Dramático Cubano and the Carnegie Lyceum Theater, for example. The last known performance of this kind in the nineteenth century took place in the Central Opera House on 16 January 1899, with the aim of raising funds for the purchase of a tombstone for José Martí (see Kanellos 1990; 1993).

Latino theater was not seen again in New York until 1916. The promoter of this new wave of performances was the Spanish actor and *zarzuela* singer Manuel Noriega. In this year he founded the first Hispanic theatrical troop in the city, the Compañía Dramática Española, whose repertoire consisted of Spanish *comedias*, farces, and *zarzuelas*. In 1919 Noriega opened New York's first regular Hispanic theater, the Park Theater, which later changed its name to El Teatro Español (see Kanellos 1990; 1993; Miller).

During the 1920s and 1930s the number and frequency of Hispanic theatrical productions grew. A number of companies had their own theaters or signed contracts with theaters that gave them a measure of stability; this was the case with the Dalys, Apollo, San José/Variedades, and Campoamor theaters, as well as with the longest running of them all, El Teatro Hispano. The majority of the works staged, either by local companies such as La Compañía del Teatro Español, Compañía de Bufos Cubanos, Compañía Narcisín, or the Compañía Hispana de Nueva York, or by visiting groups from Cuba, Spain, Mexico, or the U.S. Southwest, continued to be melodramas, *comedias*, farces, and *zarzuelas* (again, see Kanellos 1990; 1993; Miller).

As John V. Antush has pointed out, "[t]he golden age of New York's Hispanic theater came during the 1920s and 1930s when it was predominantly Spanish and a vital part of the international cultural life of the city. The Spanish Civil War dissipated much of that cultural impact, and the Second World War almost snuffed out any cultural exchange between Spain and the United States for a time" (ix). Although the first Puerto Rican play written in New York, Gonzalo O'Neill's *Borinquen o bajo una sola bandera* [Puerto Rico: Under a Single Flag], was staged in 1929, local companies were not that interested in serious works written locally. From time to time works directly related to the local community were mounted, though these were almost always comedies, such as the Cuban farce *En la calle 116* [On 116th Street], by René Borgia. The

Apollo Theater, located in the heart of Harlem on 125th Street, was the place where numerous Cuban opera *bufas* on New York Latino daily life were staged: *Mientras Nueva York duerme* [While New York Slumbers], *Bronca entre latinos* [The Quarrel Between Latinos], *Terremoto en Harlem* [The Harlem Earthquake], *Cuadro en el precinto* [Precinct Scenes], *Lo que hace el Black Bottom* [What Black Bottom Does], *Cosas de policías* [Police Business], *Kid Chocolate* (see Kanellos 1990). Despite the ephemeral nature of these productions, they were enjoyed by the working population of the immigrant community, and in their "local content" they did impart a certain unity to the Spanish-speaking community. Plays of this kind were also produced at the Teatro Variedades, works with titles like *Mosaico hispano* [Hispanic Mosaic], *Locuras de Nueva York* [New York Follies], and *Ecos de Harlem* [Harlem Echoes]. Nicolás Kanellos cites a review originally appearing in *La Prensa* (26 September 1933) that gives us a sense of this identification: "*Harlem Arrabalero* [The Other Side of the Tracks in Harlem] paints a picture of a typical night in the Latino quarter of Harlem—a farrago of marijuana, rumbles and stabbings, women, men and misery, cops and whistles, gunfire and blood. Very rarely has there ever been amassed and successfully presented in a single spectacle a more vivid description of what one imagines the Latino quarter of Harlem to be like" (1990, 129). In these theatrical shows and musical reviews (and many others like them: *De Puerto Rico a Nueva York* [From Puerto Rico to New York], *De México vengo* [I Came from Mexico], *Nueva York de noche* [New York Nights], and *Sucedió en Harlem* [It Happened in Harlem]), a tradition of addressing the themes of New York immigrant life began, a tradition that continues in the theatrical and literary works of today.

Although the general keynote struck in Latino theatrical representations of this era was fundamentally one of entertainment, they were not lacking in nationalist elements, in the form of political vindications and grievances over the cause of Puerto Rican Independence, or in social commentary, in general, and on the subject of racism, in particular. This "popular" tendency notwithstanding, local and visiting companies did produce, although without attracting large audiences, plays of a more serious character by authors such as Alejandro Casona (1903–1965) or Miguel de Unamuno (1864–1936). On the other hand, although Cuban and Spanish plays predominated in these decades, during the same years a Puerto Rican theater more committed to social and political causes also emerged, whose principal authors were Franca de Armiño (almost certainly a pseudonym), José Enamorado Cuesta, and Gonzalo O'Neill. In a similar manner, the Spaniard María (or Marita, Merita, or Mariita) Reid Masalla, whose bilingual upbringing (English father, Spanish mother) allowed her to alternate between the English- and Spanish-language theater scenes, played a fundamental role in the development of Hispanic theater in New York. Owing to her efforts, New York's Spanish-speaking audience was exposed to sophisticated theater; during the mid-1930s these performances were frequently in support of the Spanish Republican cause.

Other, smaller groups such as Cultura Proletaria and Cuadro Artístico Proletario were, as their names suggest, also producing works inspired by political and social themes. In general, the intention behind the staging of many of these works was not only to entertain the public, but also to expose them, either before or after the performance, to political speeches. Important artists such as David Alfaro Siqueiros (1896–1974), for example, were involved in these events; at the Ateneo Hispano in May 1933, Siqueiros gave a lecture prior to the performance on "Art for the Masses" (see Kanellos 1990). According to the theater historian Pablo Figueroa:

> [t]here are two figures whose contributions to the first two decades of Spanish-speaking theater in New York stand out: the Spaniard Manuel Aparicio and the Cuban Edelmiro Borrás, both of whom continued working as actors into the 1960s and '70s. They were the ones to light the creative spark in the new generations of theatrical artists. Until his death in 1976 Borrás was known in the community as the Father of New York Hispanic theatre.
>
> (13)

In the 1940s musical revues continued their dominance of the Latino theater scene. Only a few centers, such as Barnard College (at Columbia University), under the leadership of Ángel del Río, Amelia Agostini, and the Cuban Luis Baralt, produced Spanish works. There was, nonetheless, no shortage of short-lived theater companies, such as the one started by the Dominican Rolando Barrera, Gala, and the Futurist Company. One interesting development in this period was the influence of the San Juan theatrical scene on New York: "During the 1940s one of the most sophisticated national theaters in all Latin America was developing in Puerto Rico. When large numbers of Puerto Ricans migrated to the mainland in the 1940s and 1950s, they brought with them the seeds for a theater that would blossom in the 1960s and 1970s" (Antush ix). This movement was already in evidence in 1954 when one of the fundamental works on the issue of Puerto Rican immigration to New York was staged, La carreta [The Wheelbarrow], by René Marqués, a writer who had been a theater student at Columbia University and at Piscator's Dramatic Workshop in 1940. In 1956 Roberto Rodríguez and Miriam Colón formed El Círculo Dramático, one of the few groups of this epoch having its own theater. In this same year the first play in English on a Latino theme, Walter Anderson's Innocent Me, was staged (see Miller).

In the 1960s Hispanic theater maintained its high level of activity. John C. Miller has described the scene:

> The first half of the 1960s saw many theatrical companies and productions appear and disappear in a weekend. New playwrights appeared—Alvarado, Arriví [in Puerto Rico], Anteló, and Rodríguez, among them—as well as a cadre of professional actors and

actresses: Miriam Colón, Raúl Juliá, and Carla Pinza. The year 1964 in which the New York Shakespeare Festival initiated plays in Spanish, and 1965 in which *La carreta* was produced off-Broadway and in which Chelsea Theater presented *Las ventanas* [*The Windows*] of Roberto Rodríguez, music re-entered the theater, not as in the review, but integrated into *La jíbara* [The Peasant], music by Bobbie Collazo.

(25)

From 1965 on, three broad tendencies that are still in existence began to distinguish themselves: (1) a series of companies frequently related to European and Latin American theater groups and styles (INTAR, Puerto Rican Traveling Theater, Teatro Repertorio Español, Nuestro Teatro, Centro Cultural Cubano, Duo, Instituto Arte Teatral INTI, Latin American Theater Ensemble [LATE], Thalía (in Queens), the Tremont Art Group (in the Bronx), the Theater of Latin America, Inc. [TOLA]); (2) a group of popular and political street-theater companies (Teatro 4, Teatro Orilla, Teatro Jurutungo, Teatro Guazábara, and El Nuevo Teatro Pobre de América); and (3) a group of companies composing the Nuyorican theater movement (Aquarius, Latin Insomniacs, El Teatro Ambulante de Bimbo Rivas, Puerto Rican Organization for Self Advancement, Teatro Otra Cosa, The Family, and the Nuyorican Poet's Café), whose principal characteristic is the use of English, Spanish, or a mix of the two languages and whose greatest achievement has been Miguel Piñero's play *Short Eyes*. One significant aspect of some of these groups is their link to various poets; for example, Magali Alabau and Teatro Duo, Pedro Pietri and Latin Insomniacs, and all the poets of the Nuyorican Poet's Café (Miller).

In its entirety, and especially for those troupes with their own theaters, the range of Latino Spanish- or English-language theatrical productions in these years was very diverse, running the gamut from traditional and modern Spanish peninsular classics (*La Celestina*, Calderón de la Barca, Lope de Vega, Federico García Lorca, Fernando Arrabal) to Latin American plays and works more related to the Latino community of New York, such as *Carmencita, Swallows, Rice and Beans, El super* [The Superintendent], *Canciones de la vellonera* [Jukebox Hits], *Simpson Street, Tiempo de amor y guerra* [The Time of Love and War]. Miller sums up the panorama of recent Hispanic theater in New York thus: "since 1977 the following conclusions can be made. Young, creative playwrights exist and are occasionally produced—for example, Gallardo's *Simpson Street*—but too often their works are limited to staged readings" (32). Miller's conclusions notwithstanding, many of these new playwrights are today in full creative stride and have been produced with success: Randy Barceló (b. 1951), Migdalia Cruz (b. 1958), Moisés Kaufman (b. 1954), Edwin Sánchez (b. 1955), and Pedro R. Monge Rafuls (b. 1943) among them. The last of this group is the editor of the only Hispanic journal in New York dedicated to the theater, *Ollantay: Theater Magazine* (first published in January 1993).

In the last two decades of this century there have been a number of developments. Of the previously mentioned companies that got off the ground in the 1960s several are still going strong, including: INTAR (on 42nd Street), Puerto Rican Traveling Theater and the Repertorio Español (on 27th Street), the Thalia Spanish Theater and Ollantay (in Queens), the Nuyorican Poet's Café (3rd Street), and a number of cultural centers such as CHARAS (in lower Manhattan), the Centro para las artes y la cultura del Colegio Comunal Eugenio María de Hostos, the African Caribbean Theater, and Pregones Touring Puerto Rican Collective (all in the Bronx), and the Amistad World Theater. In 1988, New York counted thirty-four Hispanic theatrical organizations (Pottlitzer 35). Starting with the La Mama Theater in the 1970s, various organizations have opened their doors to productions realized by Spanish, Latin American, and local Latino theater groups. The support of Joseph Papp made possible the Latin American Popular Theater Festival and El Festival Latino held annually under the umbrella of the New York Shakespeare Festival's Public Theater. In addition, Ollantay sponsored the first Festival de Dramaturgia Española in New York in September 1997.

Two new phenomena that characterize the present-day state of Spanish-language theater in the city are the existence of theatrical workshops, held in many of the previously mentioned cultural centers, and the emergence of the genre of "performance" as a medium for the presentation of local Latino works. The Gas Station (now closed), led by the Spaniard Javier Domingo, was a meeting place for experimental productions and "performances" in the final years of the 1980s. A number of alternative spaces in the Tribeca and Soho neighborhoods, as well as the Mabou-Mines-Suite on 9th Street, still offer these kinds of theatrical experiences. In addition to the critics we have already cited in this section, the works of Mario Peña, Pablo Figueroa, José Monleón, Moisés Pérez Coterillo, and Manuel Martín have taken up the task of documenting the history of Spanish-language theater in New York; Martín, in the article (1997) cited in the bibliography to this chapter, lists a large number of the theater groups active today (11–37).

In pace with the rapidity of urban life, new Latino theater groups and organizations appear and disappear, virtually overnight. The strongest institutions, like the Repertorio Español, maintain their base by a combination of high-quality work and shrewd business instincts. Hispanic theater in New York, whether in Spanish, English, or Spanglish, possesses an indisputable vitality. The cosmopolitan and multicultural climate of New York has ensured that the range of Spanish-language theater to be seen in the city is much more varied than what is offered in Miami or Los Angeles. In 1998 the Repertorio Español mounted productions of the Cuban Senel Paz's (b. 1950) *Fresa y chocolate* [Strawberry and Chocolate] and García Lorca's *El público* [The Public], one more indication of the diversity we have referred to and also of a political and aesthetic openness in New York's Hispanic theater scene. In spite of the spectacular flop of Paul Simon's *Cape Man*, 1998 was a particularly rich year for Hispanic theater. Two works in particular, *Forever Tango* by Luis Bravo and the Colombian John Leguizamo's monologue *Freak*, have received kudos in the English-language mainstream press.

At the beginning of this essay it was mentioned that the Spanish Jews were the first group to establish the presence of the Spanish language in New York, in the seventeenth century. The Ladino-speaking Sephardic community has kept its musical and oral traditions alive, and in February 1998 the Sephardic Home of Brooklyn produced the play *Hank Halio's Ladino Reveries*, interpreted by "The Ladino Players," in the synagogue on West 70th Street in Manhattan. In spite of being a costume drama recounting the experience of the Turkish and Greek Sephardic immigrants to New York in the first half of the twentieth century, the sound of that peculiar mix of fifteenth-century Spanish and English, sprinkled with Turkish and Greek words—something we might call "Ladinoenglish"—did not fail to move all those in attendance. In the final analysis, this modest New York Judeo-Hispanic theatrical event—and the various Judeo-Spanish songs that accompanied the performance, songs (or songs like them) that have been sung in the Sephardic community since their arrival in New York in the seventeenth century—forms part of the Latino theatrical panorama that we have attempted to sketch in these last few pages.

MUSIC AND GRAFFITI

In the first three decades of the twentieth century New York was a veritable laboratory of popular music. At the same time that jazz was invading the night clubs, Hispanic-Caribbean music was making its appearance in Manhattan. This musical movement, which would become common practice by the 1920s, was not viewed sympathetically by those who felt that the commercialization of Afro-Caribbean music undermined its national roots and spirit. Thus, in the 1940s, Alejo Carpentier in his *La música en Cuba* [1946; Music in Cuba] would claim that "by a peculiar paradox, the world's vogue for certain genres of Cuban dance music would, after 1928, do immense damage to the island's popular music. When the publishers of New York and Paris faced a constant demand for *sones*, congas, and rumbas—designating no matter what under this latter rubric—they foisted their laws on the creators of a light music, until then full of grace and agility. They demanded simplicity in the notation, a less complex matrix of rhythms, a *more commercial* style." (360) Even Rafael Cortijo Verdejo (1928–1982), the prince of Puerto Rican music, appears to have later "disowned salsa" forever, the ultimate consequence of the metamorphosis of Caribbean music into a decidedly New York style (Rodríguez Juliá 71). Despite this opposition to the commercialization of Caribbean rhythms, today it can be said that, thanks in large part to the commercial market and, it goes without saying, popular taste, the music of preference for New York's Latinos is the salsa. Let us examine in more detail how this musical form evolved in the city.

Because New York has been a platform for the international launching of salsa and rap, it has also been responsible for the partial image of the Spanish-speaking community that exists in the wider world. In Spain, in Europe in general, and in countries as remote as Japan, salsa is listened to, danced to, and musically recycled. The beginnings of this fusion of Afro-Caribbean music were toward the end of the 1960s. This epoch also saw the rise to consciousness of a Latino self-awareness that no longer desired to be the "other" (neither Anglo- nor African-American), but rather sought to assert Latino identity as an integral constituent of the U.S. mix. In this sense, salsa from the very beginning played an important role in the movement for social revindication (Manuel 72–79). These former sociopolitical currents have all but disappeared from salsa today, but rap music has taken up the cause and has become the musical witness to many of the problems experienced on a daily basis by the New York Latino community.

SOUNDS AND RHYTHMS

In the early phase of its development, New York Latino music remained confined to the ghetto. Latino musicians played for a Hispanic audience at private parties and at dances sponsored by community organizations. Economic factors, the high degree of technical and creative artistry of these musicians, and the ancestral affinity between Caribbean and African-American musical styles and forms meant that Caribbean musicians made sorties out of the Latin quarter in order to join American combos and orchestras, principally jazz groups. It should be recalled that, before the advent of jazz, in the nineteenth century Cuban rhythms formed part of the sound-scape of New Orleans and that among the pioneers of early jazz at least twenty four had Hispanic family names (Storm Roberts 36–37). These relations between different musicians and different music resulted in what came to be known in the twentieth century as Latin jazz, a style that continues to be played not only by Latinos but also by Anglo-American musicians to this day. The Latin-quarter musicians were participants in the Harlem jazz club scene as well as playing at hotels, parties, and concerts for a select white New York audience.

However, popular recognition of the music of the Latino immigrants began with its "dance" forms. Theatrical and cinematic spectacles have contributed to this popularity. A notable development was the inclusion of Latino themes in movie musicals depicting a Hollywood vision of the universe "south of the border." Carmen Miranda, Xavier Cugat, and Desi Amaz, among others, became North American re-creations and personifications of the Latino world. Already in the 1920s, from Buenos Aires via Paris, Argentine tangos were making a splash on Broadway. The popularity of ballroom dancing in North America opened the door for the easy acceptance throughout the entire twentieth century of the tango, the rumba, the conga, and the samba (in the 1930s) and of the mambo, the cha-cha, and calypso (from the end of the 1940s). The 1950s phenomenon of mambo mania contributed, perhaps, more than any other event to the recognition of a distinct "Latin" sound. What is interesting is that the mambo that was popularized in the Manhattan night club the Palladium, was already a syncretization of Afro-Cuban rhythmic structures and the "big band" sound (Storm Roberts 123), and that the mambo as a dance form integrated steps from the lindy and other North American dances. In the 1960s the bossa nova arrived from Brazil and left its melodic and rhythmic impression on jazz music. Also in this decade there appeared for a short time the rhythmic form of the "boogaloo," an attempt to combine rhythm and blues with jazz and Latin sounds.

The recording industry, interested in the commercial possibilities, took measures to popularize these musical forms, simplifying and altering the musical structures in order to make Hispanic music a more salable commodity. The result was the "invention" of "Latin music": an exotic musical commodity denoting color and sensuality that corresponded to the stereotype of the Latino as a "natural" musician (just as had been the case with African-American music and musicians). The repertoire of Latin music was commercialized and assimilated in order to attract a North American audience. Songs with Latin names and rhythms ("Papa Loves Mambo," "Italian Mambo"), and English versions of "international" boleros ("Qué será, será," "Quiéreme mucho," "Aquellos ojos verdes," etc.), sung by North American balladeers, began to appear. The complex rhythmic structure of Latin music was converted, thus, into background raw material for pop arrangements. Meanwhile, in Spanish Harlem and in other Latino ghettos in the city, the immigrants of many countries and from different generations continued singing and dancing to the sound of a diverse array of rhythms: some were traditional and folkloric; some recently brought to the city by new immigrants; and others marked by a combination of styles. Toward the end of the 1960s, a new sound arose in the Latino musical community, a new manifestation reflecting the ethno-cultural syncretization of New York's Latin quarter: salsa. This was the synthesis and logical result, the unfolding and re-solution of New York's Hispanic urban immigrant stew. Although originally cooked up in the ghettos of New York, salsa has spread throughout all the Americas, and thanks to its open form and improvisational and experimental spirit, it has developed a number of novel combinatory forms and been enriched by new local materials, stylistic variations, and rhythmic ingredients. The New York ghetto has also been the breeding ground for Latino rap (some of the first rap singers were Nuyoricans) and Jamaican reggae, forms that have had strong repercussions for rock music in recent decades. The most recent movement of immigrants from the Caribbean basin to New York has brought with it other rhythms: Dominican *merengue*, Colombian *cumbia* and *vallenato*, Haitian *konpa direk* (*konbit*), Lesser Antillean *zouk*, Jamaican *ska*, and many other forms.

We must ask what impact, if any, this music has had in the non-Latino world. Internationally speaking, these works are known, assimilated, embellished, and studied. The music consortia record, promote, export, and import Latino musical ideas for a Latino public. In both the United States and Latin America there is a captive audience for the commodities purveyed by the recording companies.

However, in the North American context, for the New Yorker who encounters this music at his or her local record shop under the rubric of "Third World" or "World" music, Latin music continues to be something exotic, something other, something foreign. Clearly there is a kind of assimilation within the mass music industry in the use, for example, of congas as rhythmic backdrop, in which stylistic echoes of Latino music form a popular subtrack to pop songs. However, this assimilation is unconscious on the part of the consumer—the ethnic equivalent of Muzak—and as a result salsa, bolero, and all the other Latino musical forms have returned to the ghetto.

—Doris Schnabel

TRANSLATED BY COLMAN HOGAN

It is important to underline the leadership role that Puerto Rican immigrant musicians have played in the origins of salsa and rap music in New York City, without, however, glossing over the Cuban roots of the former. A number of studies have attempted to trace the historical development of salsa, although often from a Cubanocentric point of view. Among these are the works of John Storm Roberts (1979), Miguel César Rondón (1980), Argeliers León (1984), Isabelle Leymarie (1985), Charley Gerard and Marty Sheller (1989), Peter Manuel (1990, and 1995), Vernon Boggs (1992), Ruth Glasser (1995), and Ángel G. Quintero Rivera's (*Salsa, sabor y control! Sociología de la música "tropical"* [Salsa, Taste and Control!: Sociology of "Tropical" Music] (Casa de las Américas Award, 1998). In addition, an important study of Latino rap by Mayra Santos Febres has been completed. Whatever the future holds for salsa (and, in part, for rap), this is the emblematic music of the New York Latino community and, in one way or another, salsa and rap are the two distinguishing marks of the nomadic identity of the city's Hispanics.

It is in this context that we need to consider another form of artistic expression, graffiti, in which the use of language, and particularly the Spanish language, has (as was the case with salsa and rap) both acquired an artistic value and become a means of affirming Hispanic identity.

Graffiti have been another popular artistic form in which New York Latinos have played and continue to play an important role. According to Martha Cooper and Henry Chalfant, "[t]he history of subway graffiti in New York is a brief one, and the phenomenon differs from all other kinds of graffiti, both past and present. In the 1960s, teenagers in New York began to write their names on neighborhood walls" (14). In the 1970s and the 1980s, however, the graffiti craze would reach its apogee. In 1972 Hugo Martínez brought to the City College Department of Art a group of graffiti artists, and at that moment the art world profile of graffiti was born. The "United Graffiti Artists" exhibition at the Artists Space in 1975 was the first attempt to introduce graffiti art into New York galleries. This was followed by the creation of Fashion Moda in the Bronx in 1978, and the open spaces of the collectives Group Material and ABC No Rio, two years later. CUD (Contemporary Urbicultural Documentation) and PADD (Political Art Documentation-Distribution) were other organizations promoting projects related to graffiti in these years. In the 1980s the graffiti movement saw a resurgence, this time in more commercial galleries, and, in one way or another, influenced artists such as Jean Michel Basquiat and Julian Schnabel. Similarly, graffiti artist Keith Haring made the transit from the streets to the galleries and from there to international fame. The phenomenon of graffiti opened up possibilities for collaborations between Latino and non-Latino artists, although the Latinos have frequently been forgotten once these collaborations became the subject of attention. This has been the case in the collaborations between Jenny Holzer and Lady Pink (the Colombian Sandra Fabara, and one of the few female graffiti artists), between Tim Rollins and KOS (Kids of Survival), and that between John Ahearn and Rigoberto Torres (Lippard 158–69). Graffiti continue to be a living phenomenon in New York in the 1990s, but subject to controls. The majority of today's graffiti works are done on commission, at times to adorn some wall or other in the poorest quarters of the city, and especially as a form of street commemoration of the death of someone:

> Latino artists play a predominant role in the development of the New York memorial tradition. . . . The strong Latino presence reveals a historic precedent for the memorial tradition. The walls are updated versions of the simple roadside crosses often erected at the site of an automobile accident in predominantly Catholic countries.
>
> (Cooper and Sciorra 10)

The municipal government of New York City has erased all the graffiti in the city's subway system and has the intention of doing the same with the graffiti still found on walls. Former Mayor Rudolph Giuliani created in 1995 an Anti Graffiti Unit to pursue the practitioners of graffiti as if they were common delinquents.

ART

In the introduction to this essay it was mentioned that throughout the twentieth century New York has played an important role as both a launching platform and a center of attraction for many Hispanic visual artists. We should now examine this historical trajectory in more detail. One artist who was of fundamental importance to the launching of the avant-garde art movement in New York was Marius de Zayas

(1880–1961), the Mexican caricaturist and promoter of aesthetic modernity, who arrived in the city in 1906. Friend and artistic confidant of Alfred Stieglitz, Zayas was instrumental in bringing African and pre-Columbian arts to the attention of the New York art world, particularly through his various galleries, including the Modern Gallery (1915–1918) and the De Zayas Gallery (1918–1921); he was a point of contact through which New York artists established relations with Tristan Tzara and the Zurich Dadaists. In addition, he was a writer and collaborated in the launching of Stieglitz's avant-garde journal, *291*, where his article "African Negro Art: Its Influence on Modern Art" was published (Sims 153–54). Furthermore, Zayas opened the door in the New York scene for the introduction of Mexican art, a phenomenon that would become important from the 1930s. In 1928 The Art Center gallery presented the first exhibition of Mexican artists in the city; twenty-two painters were represented, among them Orozco, Siqueiros, and Tamayo. Shortly thereafter, The Metropolitan Museum organized a large exposition entitled "Mexican Arts" (October 1930), in which a number of important contemporary Mexican painters again appeared; in the same year Orozco and Thomas Hart Benton painted the mural in the New School for Social Research. In 1931 a retrospective of the works of Diego Rivera was held at the Museum of Modern Art (MOMA); and in 1933 the Mexican artist completed the famous mural in Rockefeller Center. Another important event of these years was the participation of Orozco and Siqueiros in the Congress of American Artists in February 1936. Frida Kahlo had her first New York show at the Julien Levy Gallery in 1938 and also appeared two years later at the MoMA's "Twenty Centuries of Mexican Art" exposition. A further couple of exhibitions of Mexican contemporary art were held in 1945 (in various New York galleries) and in 1946 at the Grand Central Galleries. *A Vital Dialogue: Mexican Artists in New York* (November 2000 to January 2001, Gallery of the Mexican Institute of New York) provides a brief, selective look at art produced by fourteen Mexican artists living in New York in the late years of the twentieth century. But the greatest achievement of the century with respect to Mexican art in New York City was without a doubt the 1991 exhibition *Mexico: Splendors of Thirty Centuries* at the Metropolitan Museum of Art (April to August 1991).

Among the peninsular Spanish artists who enjoyed the most influence with young U.S. painters were Pablo Picasso, Joan Miró, and Salvador Dalí. Miró's work was already to be seen in a large exhibition held at the Brooklyn Museum in 1926; fine examples of Picasso's cubist works formed part of the Gallatin Collection at New York University from 1927 to 1942; and in 1933 the famous Julien Levy Gallery mounted an exhibition of the works of Miró and Dalí, with Dalí giving a very important lecture the following year at MoMA against "logical" art. From the beginning of the Spanish Civil War in 1936, New York artists and intellectuals turned their attention to Spain, and this interest in the Spanish situation culminated in 1939 with the exhibition of Picasso's famous "Guernica" at the Valentine Gallery and the large retrospective of his work at MoMA in the same year, attracting thousands of visitors, including of course almost all artists of New York (see Ashton). From the 1940s, a number of Spanish painters including Esteban Vicente and José Guerrero took up residence in the city and collaborated with their U.S. colleagues in the systematic shift of the center of the international art movement from Paris to New York.

Besides Picasso, Miró, and Dalí, the most germane artist to an understanding of the development of twentieth-century U.S. art (without forgetting, of course, the Mexicans José Clemente Orozco [1883–1949], Alfaro Siqueiros [1896–1974], and Diego Rivera [1886–1957]) was the Chilean Roberto Matta (1911–2002), who arrived in New York in 1939 and remained there until 1947. Together with the surrealist writers and artists who spent much of the decade of the 1940s in New York (e.g., Breton, André Masson, and Max Ernst, among others), Matta had an enormous influence on the group of painters that would later be known as the New York School. Critics have recognized Matta's influence on the work of artists like Arshile Gorky, Jackson Pollock, and Robert Motherwell, and on U.S. abstract expressionism in general; in 1957 MoMA organized a selective exhibition of his work (Sims 162–63). The Cuban Wifredo Lam (1902–1982) was another Hispanic presence in the New York art scene in these years. He first visited the city in 1946, and later came on frequent visits, especially in the 1950s. Lam, Matta, and Frida Kahlo (1907–1954) were the three artists linked to Latin American surrealism whose works received the most attention on the New York scene. Among the other Latin American artists whose contributions enriched the artistic panorama of the city in these years were the Cubans Mario Carreño, Daniel Serra-Badué, and Agustín Fernández, the Brazilian Maria Martins, and the Chilean Nemesio Antúnez.

From the beginning of the 1960s a new generation of Latin American artists established themselves in New York. The 1964 exhibition at the Bonino Gallery, "Magnet: New York," provoked the New York Times critic John Canady to say: "It is not exactly an invasion but there is at least a strong Latin American infiltration into the international strongholds so largely cornered by New York galleries" (Stellweg 284). Canady was referring to the twenty-eight Hispanic artists in the exhibition, most of whom were resident, and some of them are still, in New York. One of these artists was Mathias Goeritz (born in Germany, founder of the Spanish Escuela de Altamira, moved to Mexico) who, during his time in New York, provoked considerable interest with his conceptual art interventions. A student of Goeritz in Mexico City, the Argentinean Liliana Porter, also established herself in New York in the 1960s and, together with the Uruguayan Luis Camnitzer, was able to create a certain community of Latin American sensibility in New York. Jaime Davidovich, also an Argentinean, was another artist associated with the conceptual art movement in these years; in 1970 he created in Soho the "Artists Television Network."

Marta Minujín, another Argentinean, was considered to be the creator of a Hispanicized, or hot-blooded, Pop Art in New York. According to Stellweg, "[a]lthough her media-oriented ideas were already crystallizing in Argentina, her reaction to the U.S. technological society, to the possibility of global communication, allowed her to become very quickly an American technological creation. By choosing the most debated issues of the times and presenting these in media spectacles, Marta Minujín became, more than any other Latin American artist, a media celebrity not unlike Andy Warhol. She adapted to U.S. culture and became an outright proponent of the American dream" (290). Rafael Montañez Ortiz (Ralph Ortiz), born in New York of Puerto Rican and Mexican parents, was the leader behind the Destruction in Art movement, and one of the first Latino (by birth and by education) artists to win an international reputation. Beginning in 1963, with his destruction of a piano and a mattress, Ortiz began to acquire a name for himself. However, despite his Hispanic origins, Ortiz has defined his late 1950s and 1960s stance as one that is "not just the result of my own roots but rather based on questioning diverse historical and aesthetic contexts" (in Stellweg 290–91).

The "kinetic" artist Julio Le Parc, born in Argentina, held his first New York exhibition in 1962 as a part of the Parisian collective Groupe de Recherche d'Art Visuel (GRAV). Since then he has been creating pieces that attempt to enter into dialogue with the community, as a way of overcoming the barriers between the elitist arts and the average citizen. The Chilean Enrique Castro-Cid, who arrived in the city in 1962, exhibited his first robots at the Richard Feigen Gallery in 1965. Another Chilean, Juan Downey, has expressed his reasons for coming to New York: "There wasn't any specific reason for leaving Chile other than I knew that to make art I had to move to a cultural center, one where art is marketed" (Stellweg 291). In 1966 Downey would enter into contact with the circle of artists that had founded the E.A.T. (Experiments in Art and Technology), Billy Klüver and Robert Rauschenberg, and other artists like John Cage. According to Downey, New York is "a city of outsiders, a sort of hospital with an open-door situation like nowhere else in the world," and it promotes nomadic art, about "leaving, going away, and taking off" (Stellweg 293–99). This nomadism is perhaps the best concept for defining the expatriate condition of many of the Hispanic artists who live in New York today, in part because the majority of them have never been very patriotic with respect to their countries of origin, and in part also because the sociocultural circumstances of the large metropolis means that cities like New York assimilate and internationalize every message of a nationalist character.

In 1964 José Guillermo Castillo, Luis Camnitzer, and Liliana Porter founded the New York Graphic Workshop, a collective that would serve as a platform for artistic activities of a social character. Porter has commented on the group that "[w]e gave a lot of consideration to the political and moral aspects of art-making, and through prints there was this idea we were working toward mass culture" (Stellweg 311). In 1970 the workshop disbanded and Castillo returned to Venezuela; however, both Porter and Camnitzer continued to be very active in the realm of political art, and Camnitzer is today leading a similar collective that is not located in New York. Together with other artists, including Julio Le Parc, Mathias Goeritz, José Luis Cuevas, Luis Felipe Noé, and Gordon Matta-Clark, they produced a book attacking the São Paulo Biennial entitled Counter Biennial. Within the group behind this book, known as the Museo para la Independencia Cultural Latinoamericana group, was also to be found a number of other Hispanic artists, including Rafael Ferrer from Puerto Rico, Leandro Katz, Eduardo Costa, and Nicolás Uriburu, all from Argentina, and the Brazilians Rubens Gerchman, Antonio Dias, Lygia Clark, and Helio Oiticica. The culmination of the Hispanic presence in the New York art scene was reached with the "Information" exhibit in 1970 at MoMA. Among those whose works appeared were twenty-one Latin Americans: "These artists made global communication and nomadic information the centerpieces of their work" (Stellweg 311).

Informational space as a global, transnational site, openly accessible to all, became definitively materialized in the 1990s thanks to the Internet. Today, a number of the Spanish and Latin American artists already mentioned are undertaking cybernetic projects on the World Wide Web, signaling that art is no longer necessarily localized in any particular geographic center. Of course this delocalization must be considered in the context of the fact that New York continues to be, if not the absolute center, one of the most important centers of the world art market.

Also in the 1970s a number of other studios were created whose leaders were the Puerto Rican artists who had resided temporarily or permanently in New York. The well-known organization the Friends of Puerto Rico included figures like Juan Maldonado, Victor Linares, Rafael Tufiño, Carlos Osorio, Domingo López, Domingo García, Rafael Colón-Morales, and Carlos Irizarry. This artists' group also mounted exhibitions in various galleries such as the Caravan House, the Galería Hoy, and the Galería Sudamericana. In 1969 another studio space was set up, the Taller Alma Boricua (known as the Puerto Rican Workshop), continuing the work begun by the Friends of Puerto Rico. A number of Puerto Rican artists established international profiles for themselves without membership in these groups: Olga Albizu, Ralph Ortiz, Rafael Ferrer, and José Morales; Morales emigrated to Europe (Spain, France, and then Sweden), where he no longer had to labor under the label of "Latino artist." Today, in fact, artists such as Pepón Osorio and the painter Juan Sánchez occupy important places in U.S. art for their own accomplishments, although the Latino label reappears whenever they are mentioned.

Photography has been a field of artistic endeavor whose historical trajectory has been similar to that of the other Hispanic visual arts in New York. Although space does not allow us to go into the detail its history merits, the "Photography in Latin America: A Spiritual Journey" show should be mentioned, one of the most important recent exhibitions sponsored by the Brooklyn Museum (September 1996 to January 1997). Also in 1997 (February to May) MoMA presented a retrospective exposition of the Mexican photographer Manuel Álvarez Bravo (1902–2002). Finally, two Latino photographers, both born in New York, have distinguished themselves recently: Andrés Serrano and Joseph Rodríguez.

The most recent mass arrival of Dominicans, in addition to the Dominicans already living in the city for some time, has meant that this community has assumed a tremendous importance in various domains of Hispanic culture and society in New York. The latest evidence of this cultural presence was the "Art in Transit. A Dominican Experience" show held in 1996 (September to October) at the INTAR gallery. Of the innumerable Hispanic artists living and working in New York today, all of them appear to be finding their proper place in the history of U.S. art and that of the national arts of their respective countries. Lucy R. Lippard's book, *Mixed Blessings: New Art in a Multicultural America*, seems to be the best point of reference for evaluating the importance of Latino artists. However, it remains to be seen whether this phenomenon is only a multicultural fashion or whether it marks in fact a new and definitive opening up of U.S. institutions and markets. Only the twenty-first century will give us the answer to this question.

Let us return to the Spanish presence in the New York art world. According to the critics Octavio Zaya and Carlos E. Pinto, "since the famous exhibition organized by Frank O'Hara at MoMA in 1960, the Spanish artists who appear to most enjoy critical attention and popular consideration are the well known and historically important figures of Tàpies and Chillida, artists worthy of the attention reserved for the great masters. Tàpies is represented in the most prestigious U.S. collections and museums of contemporary art and is exhibited regularly in New York in internationally renowned and critically recognized galleries. Chillida, together with de Kooning, received the Andrew W. Mellon Prize in 1979; was the subject of a retrospective at the Guggenheim Museum in 1981; and was the only Spanish artist included in the just closed Transformation in Sculpture (Four Decades of European and American Art) exhibition at the Guggenheim" (Zaya and Pinto 1985, 2). If we were to round out a panoramic and reasonably comprehensive picture of the Spanish artists of the 1950s whose work continues to have a presence in the New York art scene, we would have to add to the figures of Tàpies and Chillida the names of Manolo Millares, Antonio Saura, Antonio López García, Juan Genovés, Esteban Vicente, Martín Chirino, Senen Ubina, José Guerrero, and César Manrique. In addition, we should mention an exhibition held at the Guggenheim in 1991, "New Images from Spain," as well as many other more recent exhibits by Spanish artists, but to go into all of that would make this essay interminable. In the last three decades several generations of Spanish artists have passed through New York, and a number of these artists have stayed; Antonio Muntadas, Francesco Torres, Juan Uslé, and Francisco Leiro are already distinguished figures in the world art scene. Once again, to be comprehensive we would have to add an extensive list of Spanish artists resident or formerly resident in the city, artists who have, some more than others, made a name for themselves in the international art market or simply returned to Spain to continue their work. As evidence of the vital presence of Spanish artists in the New York scene we might mention Juan Muñoz's installation at the Dia Center for the Arts in 1997 (September–December). As a final point of reference for the new phenomena of decentralization and decolonization in the relations between the New York art world and Spain, we should also note the opening of the monumental Museo Guggenheim, in Bilbao, Spain, in October 1997.

In the 1990s a number of books focusing special attention on Latino art in the United States were published. These books have been preceded by various exhibitions and their respective catalogues. The following exhibition-related publications have stood out from the crowd: *Bridge Between Islands: Retrospective Works by Six Puerto Rican Artists in New York* (Henry Street Settlement, Bronx Museum, and El Museo del Barrio 1979); *Exhibition: Hispanic Artists in New York* (Association of Hispanic Artists 1982); *Hispanic Artists in New York* (City Gallery 1981); *Ten Latin American Artists Working in New York* (International House 1984); *The Latin American Spirit: Art and Artists in the United States, 1920–1970* (Bronx Museum of the Arts 1988); *Taller Alma Boricua 1969–1989: Reflections on Twenty Years of the Puerto Rican Workshop* (El Museo del Barrio 1989); and outside New York, *Latin American Artists in New York Since 1970* (Austin, University of Texas 1987). With respect to critical studies, Lucy R. Lippard's *Mixed Blessings: New Art in a Multicultural America* (1990), was a pioneering work in that it took up the study of Latino artists established in New York in the context of U.S. multiculturalism. Shifra M. Goldman's *Dimensions of the Americas: Art and Social Change in Latin America and the United States* (1994) was also important in this context, particularly its chapter on Latin American art in the United States. The volume *Latin American Art in the Twentieth Century* (1996), edited by Edward J. Sullivan, is a less interesting one in this context in that, although it has a chapter on Chicano art, it has ignored New York City as a center of production for U.S. Latino art.

CONCLUSIONS

We have attempted here to trace the path of the word; which is to say, we have lingered over all those aspects of Latino culture in New York in which the Spanish language has been and is the principle tool and referent. Within these geographic limits, limits established not by political powers but rather by language, it can be stated that the cultural manifestations mentioned in this account form part of the general Hispanic domain, but at the same time are also part of the cultural history of the United States. In mapping the coordinates of Latino verbal culture in New York we have paid little attention to its elite manifestations, at the risk of presenting a tiresome or overwhelming crush of facts. However, this account does seek to reflect the cultural activities that have been informed by the Spanish language in general, and not only its most distinguished achievements. While the criterion of "quality" has not determined the selection of information offered, and while it is undeniable that what is presented here is not an index or an exhaustive catalogue, we do hope we have given a series of useful references for the orientation of those readers who seek to deepen their understanding in one or more of the cultural areas we have explored.

In the last week of March 1995 the "Primer Encuentro sobre la Cultura Latina en la frontera de un nuevo siglo" ["First Congress of Latino Culture on the Cusp of the New Century"] was held in Granada, Spain. In a speech before the delegates, Eduardo de Lourenço expressed his hope that "[a]t the very least we dream—and not only in order to amuse the erudite—of a bell tower whose peal reaches farther, a knell which is above all more ours than that one which resounds to the rap of Harlem and the Mc-Donald's hamburger" (Lourenço 19). This simplification of U.S. culture is not only crude, it is unfair.

In 1886, with the publication in New York of his *Bibliotheca Americana Vetustissima* [The Most Venerable American Library], the scholar Henry Harrise (1829–1910) established himself as the "Prince of the Americanists," opening up, thus, the way for the many other U.S. Hispanists who have contributed to the fortification of that culture. Later, in a text entitled "The Spanish Element in Our Nationality" written in the form of a letter dated 20 July 1883, Walt Whitman would declare:

> The seething materialistic and business vortices of the United States, in their present devouring relations, controlling and belittling everything else, are, in my opinion, but a vast and indispensable stage in the new world's development, and are certainly to be follow'd by something entirely different—at least by immense modifications. Character, literature, a society worthy of the name, are yet to be establish'd, through a nationality of noblest spiritual, heroic and democratic attributes—not one of which at present definitely exists—entirely different from the past, though unerringly founded upon it, and to justify it. To that composite American identity of the future, Spanish character will supply some of the most needed parts.
>
> (553)

T. S. Eliot, Ezra Pound, Ernest Hemingway, and Wallace Stevens would view Hispanic culture with a similar generosity. These examples, I believe, clearly demonstrate both the error of reducing U.S. culture to the image of a colossal "Big Mac" and that Latino culture forms an integral part of U.S. identity.

When in a poem Rubén Darío described New York City as composed of "fifty storey buildings," he succeeded, perhaps in all innocence, in defining the paradox of being Hispanic in the Big Apple: Hispanics feel themselves to be emotionally tied to the notions of hearth and home, and yet at the same time they live as if in a state of homelessness with respect to any national history, in a world of apartment blocks. It is, thus, hardly surprising that so many immigrants have gathered there, in the beginning, in associations whose names contain the word "casa": Casa de España, Casa de Galicia, Hispanic House, and the phenomenon of "Las Casitas" (small modern sheds) that New York's Puerto Ricans have created in their backyard gardens. In an autobiographical article Isaías Lerner, another nomad, has written: "la casa como fortaleza de la identidad era más que una metáfora" (61) ("the home as the castle of identity is more than a metaphor"); for the Hispanics of New York, including those who express themselves in English, it can be said that "language is the castle of identity." In fact, this essay may be said to work only this vein: the historical presence of the Spanish language as a site and reference point for defining the identity of the Hispanic population of New York. Although those who write in English hear, as it were, inside themselves only the echoes of the Spanish of the Americas in their parents, their grandparents, or their peers, they do not for all that become any less Hispanic than those who still use the maternal language as a means of expression. Let us conclude with the Caribbean words of Arcadio Díaz Quiñones, who with great lucidity has said:

In the midst of the inequalities that constitute the central nucleus of U.S. democracy, the Puerto Rican experience—just like that of the Haitians, Mexicans, Dominicans, or Cubans—has throughout the twentieth century been a paradigmatic case of displacement and diaspora. It is the question of a culture in transit, transformed in diverse places, whose compass is incommensurable.

(10)

—Luisa García Conde assisted with the preliminary research on the African
American contribution to Hispanic culture in New York

WORKS CITED

Antush, John, ed. 1994. Introduction. *Nuestro New York: An Anthology of Puerto Rican Plays*. New York: Penguin Books. ix–xxxii.

Ashton, Dore. 1979. *The New York School: A Cultural Reckoning*. New York: Penguin Books.

Binder, Frederick M. and David M. Reimers. 1995. *All the Nations Under Heaven: An Ethnic and Racial History of New York City*. New York: Columbia University Press.

Brod, Richard, and Elizabeth B. Welles. 2000. "Foreign Language Enrollments in United States Institutions of Higher Education, Fall 1998." *ADFL Bulletin*. 31.2: 22–29.

Bueno, Gustavo. 1997. *El mito de la cultura: ensayo de una filosofía materialista de la cultura*. 4th ed. Barcelona: Prensa Ibérica.

Burma, John H. 1954. *Spanish-Speaking Groups in the United States*. Cambridge: Durham: Duke University Press.

Cañas, Dionisio. 1994. *El poeta y la ciudad. Nueva York y los escritores hispanos*. Madrid: Cátedra.

—— 1995. "Latinos o hispanos?: los escritores hispanos en Nueva York." *Latinos: la cultura latina en la frontera de un nuevo siglo*. Ed. Mariano Maresca and Horacio Rébora. Granada: Comares. 217–227.

Carpentier, Alejo. 1972. *La música en Cuba*. Colección Popular, 109. Mexico City: Fondo de Cultura Económica.

Cooper, Martha, and Joseph Sciorra. 1992. *R.I.P.: Memorial Wall Art*. New York: Henry Holt and Company.

—— and Henry Chalfant. 1984. *Subway Art*. New York: Henry Holt and Company.

Darío, Rubén. 1918. *Los raros. Obras completas*. Vol. 6. Madrid: Mundo Latino.

—— 1919a. *El viaje a Nicaragua*. Obras completas. Vol. 17. Madrid: Mundo Latino.

—— 1919b *Lira póstuma. Obras completas*. Vol. 21. Madrid: Mundo Latino.

Davis, Thomas J. 1985. *A Rumor of Revolt: the "Great Negro Plot" in Colonial New York*. New York: Free Press.

Díaz Quiñones, Arcadio. 1997. "La literatura y la metanación puertorriqueña." *El Nuevo Día*. San Juan. 7 Dec: 10.

Ellis, Edward Robb. 1966. *The Epic of New York City*. New York: Old Town Books.

Ernst, Robert. 1949. *Immigrant Life in New York City*. New York: King's Crown Press, Columbia University Press.

Esquenazi-Mayo, Roberto, ed. 1993. *A Survey of Cuban Revistas, 1902–1958*. Washington: Library of Congress.

Fernández Olmos, Margarite. 1989. *Sobre la literatura puertorriqueña de aquí y de allí: aproximaciones feministas*. Santo Domingo: Alfa & Omega.

Figueroa, Pablo. 1977. *Teatro: Hispanic Theater in New York City, 1920–1976*. New York: Off Off Broadway Alliance, Inc. and El Museo del Barrio.

Flores, Juan. 1996. "Puerto Rican and Latino Culture at the Crossroads." *Latinos in New York: Communities in Transition*. Ed. Gabriel Haslip-Viera and Sherrie L. Baver. Notre Dame, IN: University of Notre Dame Press. pp. 331–338.

Fox, Geoffrey. 1996. *Hispanic Nation: Culture, Politics, and the Constructing of Identity*. Secaucus, NJ: Birch Lane Press, Carol Publishing Group.

García, Ofelia. 1997. "New York's Multilingualism: World Languages and Their Role in a U.S. City." *The Multilingual Apple: Languages in New York City*. Ed. Ofelia García and Joshua A. Fishman. Berlin: Mouton de Gruyter. 3–50.

García Lorca, Federico. 1940. *Poeta en Nueva York*. Mexico City: Séneca.

Giordano, Jaime. 1989–90. "La poesía de los hispanos en el área de Nueva York: una somera introducción." *Extremos*. (New York) 4–5.6: 81–89.

González, José Luis. 1990. *El país de cuatro pisos*. Maplewood: Waterfront Press.

Goodfriend, Joyce D. 1992. *Before the Melting Pot: Society and Culture in Colonial New York City.* Princeton: Princeton University Press.

Goris, Anneris and José Hernández, eds. 1996. *Latin Communities in New York City.* New York: Department of Black and Puerto Rican Studies, Hunter College, City University of New York.

Hendricks, Glenn. 1974. The Dominican Diaspora: From the Dominican Republic to New York City–Villagers in Transition. New York: Teachers College, Columbia.

Hernández, Ramona, and Silvio Torres-Saillant. 1996. "Dominicans in New York: Men, Women, and Prospects." *Latinos in New York: Communities in Transition.* Ed. Gabriel Haslip-Viera and Sherrie L. Baver. Notre Dame, IN: University of Notre Dame Press. 30–56.

Jiménez, Juan Ramón. 1917. *Diario de un poeta recién casado.* Madrid: Calleja.

Kammen, Michael. 1975. *Colonial New York: A History.* Oxford: Oxford University Press.

Kanellos, Nicolás. 1990. *A History of Hispanic Theater in the United States: Origins to 1940.* Austin: University of Texas Press.

—— 1993. "Brief History of Hispanic Theater in the United States." *Handbook of Hispanic Cultures in the US: Literature and Art.* Ed. Francisco Lomelí. Houston: Arte Público Press. 248–67.

—— 1997. *Hispanic Firsts: 500 Years of Extraordinary Achievement.* Detroit: Gale.

Katz, William Loren. 1997. *Black Legacy: A History of New York's African Americans.* New York: Ethrac Publications.

Kirking, Clayton. 2000. *A Vital Dialogue: Mexican Artist in New York.* New York: Mexican Cultural Institute of New York.

Leeds, Mark. 1996. *Ethnic New York: A Complete Guide to the Many Faces and Cultures of New York.* 2nd ed. Chicago: Passport Books.

Lerner, Isaías. 1998. "La experiencia judía en la Argentina de hace medio siglo." *Claves de razón práctica* (Madrid) 79: 60–64.

Lippard, Lucy R. 1990. *Mixed Blessings: New Art in a Multicultural America.* New York: Pantheon Books.

Lourenço, Eduardo de. 1995. "Digresión sobre la latinidad." *Latinos: la cultura latina en la frontera de un nuevo siglo.* Mariano Maresca y Horacio Rébora eds. Granada: Comares. 17–23.

Manuel, Peter, Kenneth Bilby and Michael Largy. 1995. *Caribbean Currents: Caribbean Music from Rumba to Reggae.* Philadelphia: Temple University Press.

Márceles Daconte, Eduardo. 1993. *Narradores colombianos en U.S.A.* Bogota: Instituto Colombiano de Cultura.

Martín, Manuel. 1997. "The Development of the Hispanic-American Theater in New York City: from 1960 to the Present." *Ollantay: Theater Magazine* 1.2 (Summer/ Autumm): 11–37.

Miller, John C. 1984. "Contemporary Hispanic Theater in New York." *Hispanic Theater in the United States*. ed. Nicolás Kanellos. Houston: Arte Público Press. 24–33.

Monge-Rafuls, Pedro R. ed. 1993. *Visual Arts: A Different Approach/Desde otro punto de vista: Dialogue from the First Latin American Visual Arts Conference in New York on May 26, 1990*. New York: Ollantay Press.

Museum of Modern Art. 1940. *Twenty Centuries of Mexican Art*. New York: The Museum of Modern Art.

O'Neill, John P., ed. 1990. *Mexico: Splendors of Thirty Centuries*. New York: Bullfinch Press and the Metropolitan Museum of Art.

Orjuela, Héctor H. 1975. *La obra poética de Rafael Pombo*. Bogota: Institute Caro y Cuervo.

Paz, Octavio. 1987. "Estela de José Juan Tablada." In *Mexico en la obra de Octavia Paz* Vol 2. eds. Octavio Paz and Luis Mario Schneider. Mexico: Fondo de Cultura Económico.

Pereda, Prudencio de. 1960. *Windmills in Brooklyn*. New York: Atheneum.

Pottlitzer, Joanne. 1988. *Hispanic Theater in the United States and Puerto Rico*. New York: Ford Foundation.

Prieto, Guillermo. 1994. *Obras completas*. Ed. Boris Rosen Jélomer. Vol. 8. Mexico City: Consejo Nacional para la Cultura y las Artes.

Ripoll, Carlos. 1971. *Patria. El periódico de José Martí*. New York: Eliseo Torres.

Roberts, John Storm. 1979. *The Latin Tinge: The Impact of Latin American Music on the United States*. New York: Oxford University Press.

Rodríguez Juliá, Edgardo. 1985. *El entierro de Cortijo*. Rio Piedras: Ediciones Huracán.

Rodríguez de León, Francisco. 1998. *El furioso merengue del norte: una historia de la comunidad dominicana en los Estados Unidos*. New York: Editorial Sitel.

Rueda, Germán. 1993. *La emigración contemporánea de españoles a Estados Unidos, 1820–1950*. Madrid: Editorial MAPFRE.

Shearer, James F. 1954. "Periódicos españoles en los Estados Unidos." *Revista Hispánica Moderna* 20: 45–57.

Sims, Lowery. 1988. "New York Dada and New World Surrealism." *The Latin American Spirit: Art and Artists in the United States, 1920–1970*. New York: Bronx Museum of the Arts. 152–183

Sobejano, Gonzalo. 1988. "Revista Hispánica Moderna." *Romanische Forschungen* 100: 1–3, 222–30.

Sotelo Vázquez, Adolfo. 1994. Introduction. "Los artículos de Leopoldo Alas *Clarín* publicados en *Las Novedades*, Nueva York, 1894–1897." *Cuadernos Hispanoamericanos* (Los complementarios) 13–14: 5–23.

Stellweg, Carla. 1988. "*Magnet-New York*: Conceptual, Performance, Environmental, and Installation Art by Latin American Artists in New York." *The Latin American*

Spirit: Art and Artists in the United States, 1920–1970. New York: Bronx Museum of the Arts. 284–311.

Torres-Saillant, Silvio, and Ramona Hernández. 1998. *The Dominican Americans*. Westport: Greenwood Press.

Ugalde, Antonio, and Erick Larson. 1988. "Flujo migratorio del Caribe a los Estados Unidos: el caso de la República Dominicana." *EME-EME. Estudios Dominicanos* (Santo Domingo) 15.81: 97–113.

Veciana-Suarez, Ana. 1987. *Hispanic Media, USA: A Narrative Guide to the Print and Electronic Hispanic News Media in the United States*. Washington DC: Media Institute.

Vega, Bernardo. 1994. *Memorias de Bernardo Vega: contribución a la historia de la comunidad puertorriqueña en Nueva York*. Ed. César Andreu Iglesias. 5th ed. Río Piedras, Puerto Rico: Ediciones Huracán.

Whitman, Walt. 1964. *The Collected Writings of Walt Whitman*. Ed. Gay Wilson Allen and Sculley Bradley. Vol. 2. New York: New York University Press.

Zaya, Octavio y Carlos E. Pinto. 1985. "Artistas españoles en Nueva York (Una introducción provisional)." *Hartísimo* (Tenerife) 8–9: 1–8.

Zentella, Ana Celia. 1997. "Spanish in New York." *The Multilingual Apple: Languages in New York City*. Ed. Ofelia García and Joshua A. Fishman. Berlin-New York: Moyton de Gruyter, 1997. pp. 167–201.

NOTES

1. For an update of demographical data, see the introduction, this volume.—EDITOR

2. See editor's note to Zentella's essay, this volume.—EDITOR

3. As of March 2009 a very partial list of Spanish-language authors of fiction, nonfiction, poetry, and theater who live in or near to New York City or who spent long periods of residence here until recently includes Spaniards Francisco Álvarez Koki, José María Antolín, Dionisio Cañas, María del Mar Gómez, Eduardo Lago, Elvira Lindo, Marta López-Luaces, Antonio Muñoz Molina, Carlos Perellón, Gerardo Piña-Rosales, Emma Reverter, Gonzalo Sobejano, and Paquita Suárez-Coalla (editor of *Aquí me tocó escribir*, an anthology of New York-based Spanish-language writers); Mexicans Margarita Almada, Carmen Boullosa, Lorea Canales, Mónica de la Torre, Aura Estrada (dead at age 30 in 2007 in a beach accident), Maité Iracheta, Arcadio Leos, and Naief Yehya; Cubans Raquel Virginia Cabrera, Lourdes Casal, Enrique del Risco (coeditor of yet another recent anthology, published by Páginas de Espuma in Spain), José Kozer, Gustavo Pérez-Firmat, Dolores Prida, José Manuel Prieto, Sonia Rivera-Valdés, Alexis Romay, and Armando Suárez Cobián; Puerto Ricans Giannina Braschi, Orlando José Hernández, Ángel Lozada, Carlos Ocasio Díaz, Carmen Valle, Lourdes Vázquez, and Carlos Vázquez Cruz; Dominicans José Acosta,

Raquel Virginia Cabrera, Franklin Gutiérrez, Miriam Mejía, Keiselim A. Montás, and Joanne Rodriguez; Honduran Roberto Quesada; Nicaraguan Eva Gasteazoro; Colombians Carlos Eduardo Aguasaco, Gustavo Arango, Adriana Aristizábal, Joaquín Botero, Luis Javier Henao, Paloma Valencia Laserna, Juan Pablo Lombana, Silvio Martínez Palau, Eduardo Márceles, Juan Fernando Merino, and Ricardo León Peña-Villa (Colombian-born English-language novelist Jaime Manrique writes poetry in Spanish and Jorge Franco, who does not live in New York, has nevertheless set one of his latest novels, *Paradise Travel*, about Colombian immigrants in New York); Venezuelans Dina Piera di Donato, Alejandro Varderi, and Ely Rosa Zamora; Ecuadorean Alex Lima; Peruvians César Céspedes, Mariela Dreyfus, Renato Gómez, Isaac Goldemberg, Jorge Ninapayta, and Michelle Zumarán (fellow Peruvian Odi Gonzales writes poetry in Quechua, the dominant indigenous language of the Andes region); Bolivians Eduardo Mitre and Edmundo Paz Soldán; Chileans Pedro Lastra, Lina Meruane, Alejandro Moreno, Manuel Santelices, Cecilia Vicuña, María José Viera-Gallo, and, for a brief but active period, Rafael Gumucio; Argentines Sergio Chejfec, Hernán Iglesias Illa, Néstor Lacorén, Tomás Eloy Martínez, Sylvia Molloy, María Negroni, Ricardo Piglia, Rodolfo Quebleen, Mercedes Roffé, Mario Szichman, and Lila Zemborain. Among the active Latino narrators, essayists, poets and playwrights connected with New York and who are also part of the city's English-Spanish bilingual literary tradition, we must mention Miguel Algarín, Daniel Alarcón, Julia Álvarez, Annecy Báez, Angie Cruz, Nilo Cruz, Junot Diaz, Martín Espada, Sandra María Esteves, Cristina García, Francisco Goldman, Alma Guillermoprieto, Oscar Hijuelos, Caridad de la Luz, Jaime Manrique, Mirta Ojito, Felipe Ossa, Judith Ortiz Cofer, Ernesto Quiñonez, Louis Reyes Rivera, Abraham Rodríguez, Tato Laviera, Nelly Rosario, Esmeralda Santiago, Ilan Stavans, David Unger, and Edwin Torres, among many others. —EDITOR

PUERTO RICAN VOICES *in* ENGLISH

Carmen Dolores Hernández

ABSENCE DOES NOT MAKE THE HEART GROW FONDER

Like so many other islanders, I was only peripherally aware of the English-language literary production of my fellow Puerto Ricans living in the United States. I had received part of my education in the mainland, and some members of my extended family were among the several thousand who migrated after World War II, settling primarily in cities of the Northeast, especially New York.[1] Nevertheless, neither in my readings nor as an assiduous student of Puerto Rican literature had I followed the writing of a sector of our population that had been forgotten, for all practical purposes, on the island and that was mostly known in the States through negative attention. Puerto Ricans were frequently mentioned there in relation to crime, violence, inner-city strife, and drug use. The image projected by *West Side Story* seemed to have become a standard.

Some names, however, began to crop up sporadically in my readings: Pedro Pietri, Miguel Algarín, Piri Thomas. Some books claimed my attention as a regular reviewer for San Juan's *El Nuevo Día* newspaper, especially Nicholasa Mohr's *Rituals of Survival* and Judith Ortiz Cofer's *The Line of the Sun*. At first I ignored them, not knowing where I was to place a hybrid kind of writing that did not belong (according to the traditionally accepted canon) to Puerto Rican literature, because it was not in Spanish. Nor did literature written by Puerto Ricans in English seem to have found a place in American literary tradition, being intimately connected in themes to a displaced sector of the Caribbean population. This writing also made liberal use of Spanish forms of expression: words, idioms, and whole sentences. Indeed, it did not seem to fit anywhere.

The writer I first read with some attention was Pedro Pietri. I was struck by the strength of his irony and the dynamic quality of his poetic images. I went on to Miguel

Piñero's plays, their playful but savage bite, their strange perspectives. His and Miguel Algarín's anthology, *Nuyorican Poetry: An Anthology of Puerto Rican Words and Feelings* (New York: William Morrow, 1975), introduced me to the work of the poets, as did Efraín Barradas and Rafael Rodríguez's *Herejes y mitificadores: muestra de poesía puertorriqueña en los Estados Unidos* (San Juan: Huracán, 1980).

Soon afterward Ed Vega, a Puerto Rican novelist living in New York, called my attention to the quantity and quality of Puerto Rican writing in the United States. It was the beginning of a literary friendship that would encompass, with time, many more writers. In Vega's books I found fantasy and humor. His realism, in fact, became magic because of his works' incongruous settings and unexpected contrasts in cultural perceptions, as well as his depiction of the pathos of lives that were striving to become ordinary but were marked by an unrecognized, unresolved loss.

Those first readings were the thread that, when pulled, unraveled for me the fabric of U.S. Puerto Rican writing. With my curiosity piqued and my interest aroused by what I was reading, I kept on looking and found what could be described as a tradition: a notable body of work written by Puerto Ricans in the mainland. It helped document a migration that had gone from a trickle to a flood in the course of the century.[2] Names such as Arturo Alfonso Schomburg,[3] Jesús Colón,[4] Bernardo Vega,[5] and Clemente Soto Vélez,[6] among others, gave me a trail to follow up on the abundant production of the sixties, seventies, and beyond.

(BEST) SELLING A PUERTO RICAN STORY

In 1967 Knopf published a "shocking" book, full of four-letter words. It was narrated in the first person and was a novelized memoir depicting the life of a young black Puerto Rican delinquent who had grown up in the streets of Harlem, ending up in jail after attempting an armed robbery. Reviewed in many newspapers and periodicals, it was hailed as a major work and became a best-seller.

Piri Thomas's *Down These Mean Streets* was a narrative of fall and redemption. In a manner somewhat akin to Claude Brown's *Manchild in the Promised Land* (1965), which documents the lives of African Americans in an urban community, it revealed the feelings of a young boy besieged in the streets by prejudiced gangs, troubled at home because of poverty and racial distinctions (he was the blackest of five children), and displaced later within the white Long Island neighborhood where his parents had relocated, looking for a better life. Like *The Autobiography of Malcolm X as Told to Alex Haley* (1964) and Eldridge Cleaver's *Soul on Ice* (1968), in both of which rage against society is turned into a life of commitment to a cause after a stint in prison, Piri Thomas's book tells about the time served in Sing Sing and Comstock prisons. There he turned to both religion and a writing career. His story, told with both anger and grace, in a strangely poetic gutter English interspersed with Spanish, was compelling[7]: "The daytime pain fades alongside the feeling of belonging and just being in swing with all the humming kicks going on around. I'd stand on a corner and close my eyes and look at everything through my nose. I'd sniff deep and see the *cuchifritos* and hot dogs, stale sweat and dried urine. I'd smell the worn-out mothers with six or seven kids, and the nonpatient fathers beating the hell out of them. My nose would go a high-pitch tingling from the gritty wailing and bouncing red light of a squad car passing the scene like a bat out of Harlem, going to cool some trouble, or maybe cause some."[8]

His book established the parameters for a genre of novels set in the New York ghettos (Spanish Harlem, the Lower East Side) where most Puerto Ricans lived, spawning a tradition whose latest offshoot is Abraham Rodríguez, Jr.'s *Spidertown*. These novels document, narrate, and dramatize the life conditions of a marginalized sector of society that has had serious problems adjusting to an English-speaking white majority of Anglo-Saxon background. This sector has not only remained in relative poverty, but has also had to deal on a daily basis (having remained in great numbers in the inner cities), with crime, violence, and temptation in the streets. Its young people tend to suffer from a confusion between two conflicting codes of behavior: a Puerto Rican ethos that puts loyalty to the family before everything else and that also encompasses a male code of "machismo,"[9] versus American individualism and energetic enterprise (often subverted in the ghetto into criminal enterprise).

CROSSOVER GENRES

Within this genre of adventure and violence in the ghetto, certain variations have appeared, such as the ones contained in Judge Edwin Torres's novels, especially *Carlito's Way*. This writer, who is a judge of the Supreme Court of the State of New York and who has also written *Q & A* and *After Hours*, combines the Puerto Rican cum gangster novel formula with another kind of street delinquency from a far different time and place: sixteenth-century Spain. It was there and then that the picaresque novel developed. It is a curious type of narrative told directly, under an autobiographical guise, by a small-time delinquent whose aimless life (within a society of dramatic contrasts between rich and poor, whose imperialist schemes contrasted with the decaying conditions of its cities) takes him from master to master and often from licentious freedom to prison.

Suggestive parallels could be made between two hegemonic nations whose politics shaped a certain age (Spain was the dominant country in Europe during the sixteenth and seventeenth centuries, with a huge overseas empire that brought it immense riches, while the United States has become the major world power during our century), but whose economic policies gave rise to a floating population of unemployed drifters. There are also certain similarities regarding the respective situations of marginalized sectors of each society. They can be seen in such apparently diverse works as *Carlito's Way* and *El Lazarillo de Tormes* (generally thought to be the first picaresque novel, published shortly before 1554; author unknown). Whereas *El Lazarillo* reflects a sort of philosophical resignation to a life eschewing accepted conventions, in other novels of the genre—*Guzmán de Alfarache*, by Mateo Alemán (1599), and *El Buscón* (written between 1603 and 1604 by Francisco de Quevedo but published in 1620)—the tone gets progressively more disenchanted and cynical. That same tone permeates *Carlito's Way*. The first-person narration in this novel underscores a likeness that is also emphasized in the way the protagonist moves from one patron to another (in the form of gangs with diverse ethnic bosses). Savagely realistic—even naturalistic—in its portrayal of atmosphere, the picaresque novel seems a mirror in which the urban Puerto Rican novel of America in the twentieth-century can recognize itself.

Much as Edwin Torres grafts a different literary tradition from the American one onto his gangster novels, the young writer Abraham Rodríguez creates in *Spidertown* a Dickensian atmosphere, especially close to that of *Oliver Twist*, with its vivid portrayal of Fagin's school for crime. By giving us the world of present-day Puerto Rican junkies and pushers in the South Bronx, this author describes a highly structured community in which the young are instructed by a master (a small-time drug lord nicknamed Spider for his building-climbing abilities and who, not so coincidentally, loves to read *Oliver Twist*) and live according to his rules. Their society is a mirror image of the legitimate one in terms of hierarchies, differentiated tasks, progress, and rewards. It is just as exacting, competitive, and stressful as that other one, prompting Miguel, the main character, to wish for a less pressured life.

The picaresque novel and the Victorian one are not the only genres that "cross over" into Puerto Rican literature written in English in the United States. Curiously enough, the *auto sacramental* has exerted a fascination for Jack Agüeros.[10] A poet and short-story writer, he is also a playwright who feels drawn to the moral implications of that medieval dramatic genre ultimately developed by Calderón de la Barca in the seventeenth century, although the meaning of morality and its scope is different for him from what it was in that century. Using allegorical allusions, he expresses moral and spiritual positions regarding tolerance, racial relations, and the interpretation of past historical events.

These "crossover genres" and others that may develop in the future may prove to be an enriching stimulus within American literature. There is a long tradition of such combinations within Spanish literature, where the first known literary works have turned out to be lyrical verses arranged in short stanzas tagged on at the end of Arabic or Hebrew poems called "moaxajas." Moreover, the famed Spanish mystical poets from that country's Golden Age of literature have been found to have more than a few points of contact with Islamic medieval mystics, whose works may have come to their attention through various channels, among them their transmission through the Arab minorities who remained in Spain after the conquest of Granada.[11]

POETS IN THE CITY

At about the time that Piri Thomas was publishing *Down These Mean Streets*, some New York Puerto Rican poets were expressing—in a different literary idiom—the incongruities between the myth of the American Dream and the harsh realities encountered by their families upon migrating. Drawing on a long, centuries-spanning oral tradition of poetry common in the rural parts of the island—where troubadours can still be counted on to improvise verses at a moment's notice in order to liven up a party, singing them to the strains of a cuatro (a guitar-like instrument) or a guitar—the poetic movement that was later to be called Nuyorican began as a performance. A poet like Jorge Brandon, who could be seen in the streets of the Lower East Side pushing along a shopping cart full of discarded odds and ends, made up verse—some very patriotic—as he walked through the streets. Another "foreign" tradition was thus made part of the New York City scene, which took to it with the fervor accorded to similar manifestations that originated from Southern black song and oral literature. The impromptu audiences responded enthusiastically, and the resonance of their poetry quickly expanded beyond specific neighborhoods as the poets—among them Miguel Algarín, Pedro Pietri, Miguel Piñero, Lucky Cienfuegos, Sandra María Esteves, Bimbo Rivas, and Jesús Papoleto Meléndez—wrote down and published their work.

These poets were in the right place at the right time. New York during the late sixties and the seventies was a hotbed of protest against the Vietnam War and of activism for civil, racial, and feminist rights.[12] It had also just been through the literary commotion occasioned by a group of writers who exhibited a contempt for conventions—including those in the sexual sphere—and a profound dissent in relation to established society—which they dubbed materialistic and conformist—and who denounced the dominance of the military-industrial complex which seemed to have driven the country into the Korean War. They also exhibited considerable enthusiasm for altered mind-states provoked by drugs.

They were the writers known as the Beat Generation (so-called because of the connotations of the word *beat* (down and out, beat up).[13] Among them were Allen Ginsberg, Jack Kerouac, William Burroughs, Gregory Corso, and John Clellon Holmes. They were committed to a "New Vision" in art, especially literature. They drew on their experiences of bohemian city life, writing about jazz musicians and Times Square junkies. In various genres, they projected a mood that could be described as one of cultural disaffection with the prevailing, central currents of thought and the presumed moral values of the United States. Many experiences that had until then been alien to American literature became part of this movement: homosexual sex, drugs, the low street life of a sector of society.[14]

In introducing these themes in literature, the Beats had set the stage in which the young Puerto Rican–New York poets would appear. The fact that they lived in New York was, then, central to their poetry, and they fittingly adopted the name *Nuyorican* that referred both to that city and the Puerto Rican origins that gave them their particular perspective.[15] The city had opened the way for them to develop their own expression: they could relate directly to the Beats' literary scene. But unlike Burroughs (who was a Harvard graduate), Ginsberg, or Kerouac (who attended Columbia), the Puerto Ricans were "the real thing." They were literally as well as figuratively "beat up" by their place in the city's lowest socioeconomic rungs as the children of poor, uneducated immigrants who knew no English. Their protests took a literary turn, but they referred to a concrete situation. They also found America's established values wanting, but not because of surfeit or exhaustion, but because of privation. It was a time of solidarity against the perceived "enemy." Of the group, Pietri was sent to the Vietnam War and Miguel Piñero landed in prison. Besides being a poet, Piñero was also a playwright who won an Obie and the New York Drama Critics Best American Play Award for the 1973–1974 theater season for his prison drama, *Short Eyes*.

Nuyorican poetry used the words of everyday speech among Puerto Ricans in New York, writing down what was popularly known as "Spanglish" but can be more aptly described as "code-switching." It is the back and forth shift between English and Spanish, using words and phrases of one and the other within a framework that is predominantly English. It also entails the juxtaposition of two distinct cultural sets of references implicit in the respective languages, both of them highly developed and of European origin. They used it to their poetic advantage, "playing" one language against the other in plentiful puns and metaphors. Their themes were also commonplace for Puerto Ricans: the frustrations of daily life, the sting of prejudice, the incomprehension of bureaucrats, the inadaptation to life in the city. Like the Beats, they also wrote highly erotic poetry, either heterosexual or homosexual, and dealt with the culture of drugs in their poems.

And just as Spanish Harlem—*El Barrio*—had become identified with the group of Puerto Rican novelists already mentioned, the Lower East Side (dubbed *Loisaida* by Puerto Ricans, loosely following the Spanish pronunciation of the name) became the place where *Nuyorican Poetry* was born. In 1972 the poets had begun to meet in Miguel Algarín's apartment on the Lower East Side to read their work. Soon that space was too small. The Nuyorican Poets Café opened in a small locale on East 6th Street. It quickly became a gathering place for the poets and their ever larger audiences. The popularity of the place was helped, of course, by the fact that writers like Allen

Ginsberg and William Burroughs were often to be seen at the Café, as was also the black playwright Amiri Baraka.

Plays began to be performed there on a regular basis besides poetry readings. In 1980 the Café moved to 3rd Street but closed three years later to reopen in 1989. Since then, it has become a cultural haven not only for Latino poets but for those from all ethnicities and persuasions. The well-attended weekly poetic competitions (called "poetry slams"), are broadcast on the last Saturday of every month to Tokyo, Chicago, and San Francisco. Miguel Algarín has widened both his aesthetics and his audiences, becoming ever more universal.[16]

Other poets who were not among the original Nuyorican group share some aspects of their aesthetics in terms of language and poetic rhythm. Most of them speak Spanish at home; it is the language of feelings and affection. In contrast, English has been learned at school and in the streets. Many of them claim, however, not to have sufficient command of literary Spanish to write in it. For some, to write in English seemed to signal a surrender of their cultural personality. Thus, *Spanglish* seemed the solution because it was the language of the Puerto Rican community, both in the Lower East Side and in El Barrio. They also strove to express through it a resistance to a norm or standard imposed by the two "uncontaminated" groups: the Spanish-speaking island writers, seen as an elite who defended that language as a symbol of the nation, and the English-speaking writers of mainstream United States literature. Neither of those languages by itself could transmit the experience of the Puerto Rican migrant in New York. Code-switching thus became a response to a sociocultural situation.[17] In the introduction to his first anthology, Miguel Algarín writes: "The poet is responsible for inventing the newness. The newness needs words, words never heard before or used before. The poet has to invent a new language, a new tradition of communication."[18]

STAYING ALIVE

Tato Laviera has emphasized the role of the poet as a recorder of a community's experience. In his book, *La Carreta Made a U-Turn*, he writes that as a poet, his purpose is to document the life of his people: *I am nothing but a historian....* His poetry is an affirmation of Puerto Ricans in the United States as neither wholly American nor Puerto Rican—nor even Nuyorican—but AmeRícan, as reads the title of another of his books.

Based on an intuition born out of a cultural substratum, this is a role assumed by Puerto Ricans who, like the narrator of the stories in the *Arabian Nights*, write "to forestall death."[19] Their writing is an affirmation of individual and collective survival. It is born of the pressure to keep on being distinct, to record the life of a forgotten community, marginalized within a host country that has refused to take into account its particular experience within its accepted repertory of images. It is a community that has also been forgotten in its society of origin, which has obliterated their memory in the context of daily life. In a way, this situation has literally driven them into writing. Paradoxically, their American experience, in effect—the *American Dream* gone awry—may have helped them become the important writers they have come to be, relevant both to the multicultural experience in the United States and to the exemplary expressions of distinctiveness within a Metropolis that has not swallowed them, as opposed to the isolated culture of the island itself.

It is fascinating here to posit a historical reverse parallel that may be found in the literature of the last Muslims in Spain, also called "moriscos." Rejected in the place where they had been born and raised and unable to adapt to the Arab world to which they did not fully belong because of their hybrid experiences, some also turned to writing as a way of surviving. Luce López Baralt has written: "precisely out of the crypto-muslim's troubled identity came an unexpected literary creativity. The underground moriscos took to the task of urgently trying to preserve from oblivion their rich cultural heritage, and, in the very process of rewriting their classical literature 'del arabi en aljamí'—from Arabic to Spanish in the Arabic script—they ended up re-inventing themselves as authors and readers."[20]

Their rapidly changing new environment was another important stimulus for Puerto Rican writers in the United States. "Nobody was writing down these experiences," says Judge Edwin Torres. Silence, in this case, could be equivalent to non-existence, oblivion, and forgetfulness because there would be no other record of the impact of their lives and feelings and of the identity that they were collectively forging. Their writing gives a widespread voice to a people at the fringes not only of U.S. but also of island society. Historically, in Puerto Rico writers as a rule had until then belonged to the bourgeoisie with access to the means of intellectual and artistic production (universities, libraries, learned societies, some amount of leisure, editorial possibilities). Most of the Puerto Ricans who began writing in the States during the sixties and seventies (and all those interviewed in this book) have a working-class background with little or no academic tradition in their families. The overwhelming majority have been the first generation to be college-educated. Some are self-taught.

Many of their experiences were unique. When Victor Hernández Cruz writes about a journey in time as well as in place, he is aptly describing what it must have been like to go from a backwater little town in the center of the island of Puerto Rico in the 1940s and 1950s to the center of New York, a city at the height of its power and influence. The shock of such a change could be devastating, especially when we consider that it was compounded by language difficulties and by enormous differences in climate, landscape, and social mores. The documentation that some of this writing provides about the encounter between two such different stages of development is invaluable, since the experience may never be repeated again in quite the same terms. No matter how many Puerto Ricans migrate now to the mainland and no matter where they come from, the island's industrial development during the last fifty years and its wealth of communications have turned it into a country aware of what is happening in the rest of the world, and particularly in the United States.

WOMEN, WOMEN EVERYWHERE

One aspect that was not amply "documented" at first in the New York–Puerto Ricans' creative literature of the sixties and seventies was the women's perspective. Whereas young males were constantly exposed to violence in the streets of the ghetto, women's lives were subject to another kind of oppression. They were doubly invisible, both because they came from a segment of society that had been marginalized by poverty and ignorance and also because their roles were circumscribed to the home by male dominance within their community. Even when they were heads of families and worked outside the home, their need to support and care for their children kept them from taking part in artistic and social projects. Therefore, their range of both experience and action has been different from that of men. Rather than being the direct subjects or objects of street violence (although they have been victims of the domestic variety), they have often suffered its after-effects.

Sandra María Esteves in her poetry and Nicholasa Mohr in her novels and short stories were among the first Puerto Rican women to become successful writers. Esteves was the most visible—if not the only—woman among the Nuyorican poets. Using the Nuyorican emphasis on colloquialism and its continuous references to a specific context, she explores the conflicting identities of a Latino woman within both the marginalized Puerto Rican community and North American society as a whole. Poems like her *María Christina* express that conflict (and its resolution: found wanting by another Puerto Rican woman poet, Luz María Umpierre, who replied to what she thought was the expression of a subservient role in another poem titled *My Name Is Not María Christina*). Other Esteves poems, such as *From the Commonwealth*, express a greater resistance to being subservient to the prevailing Latino concept of culture.

Today, however, a numerous group of women poets—the aforementioned Luz María Umpierre, Giannina Braschi, Gloria Vando, Magdalena Gómez, Rosario Morales, Aurora Levins Morales, and Judith Ortiz Cofer, among others—are creating a strong body of poetry in different styles, themes, and emphases. Their works mirror the complex issues involving race, gender, nationality, and migration.

Other women who write prose have striven to overcome their invisibility. Many seem to prefer the autobiographical novel, or *bildungsroman*, which places the feminine subject at the center of the action, thus overcoming its marginality.

Nicholasa Mohr was the first to document immigrant Puerto Rican women's lives in a semiautobiographical mode in *Nilda* (1973), a novel about a girl who grows up in the Barrio within a hard-working lower middle-class family. The gently developing story line follows Nilda's growing consciousness of family economic hardships and the disruption of traditional ties. A different street culture is seen encroaching within the atmosphere of the home. She becomes conscious of that difference while being kept somewhat shielded from the turbulence of the first line of confrontation taking place outside the apartment, the school, the summer camp.

Recent novelized memoirs or semiautobiographical novels by Puerto Rican women in the States have established a continuity of sorts with Mohr's *Nilda*. In *The Line of the Sun*, Judith Ortiz Cofer—who lives in Georgia—develops two parallel stories. On the one hand, there is a somewhat mythical Puerto Rico constructed out of family tales and folklore, with a family black sheep at its center. On the other, there is the young girl growing up between a Latino household and a typical American education in Paterson, New Jersey. The book reclaims the unusual past of the first part for an American girl who is in the process of being acculturated to a different way of life than that of her forebears.

Another narrative, avowedly autobiographical, also has a young feminine protagonist, this time in a rags-to-riches story. Negi, in Esmeralda Santiago's *When I Was Puerto Rican* starts out her life on the island in a rural community. The deteriorating relationship between her parents determines her mother's move, with all her brood, to the States. There they all have to come to grips with the wider social issue of discrimination before attaining one of the biggest rewards the United States has to offer: a college education at prestigious Harvard University.

All is not unconditionally well after that goal is reached, however, in a reversal of the usual trajectory of the American Dream narrative. Scholastic achievement and financial independence, American-style, may seem to pave the road to fame and fortune, or at least to full integration within American society, but they also exact a price. Negi's goal is only achieved, it seems, at the expense of a profound uprooting and an implied break from her origins as indicated by the past tense used in the title and the nostalgic tone of the prologue.

Esmeralda Santiago's latest novel, *América's Dream*, though not a memoir or an autobiography, recreates circumstances that often affect women's lives. América is isolated in her job as a maid with a Westchester County family, where she has gone after fleeing from an abusive lover. In a sense, the action mirrors the wider Puerto Rican experience. While seeking escape from an oppressive situation, a person or a group may find a life of isolation that may cripple them emotionally if they are unable to come to terms with it.

OF RACE AND RACISM

One important aspect of Puerto Rican writing in the States has to do with racial considerations. Present in Piri Thomas's and in Tato Laviera's works (they are both black men), race and its implications are also central in Louis Reyes Rivera's poetry. In his works he emphasizes the common historical, cultural, and literary roots of Antillean and American people, with African ascendancy as the source of similar experiences, rhythms, and aesthetic considerations. Rivera is also aware of the nuances of racism, from the Caribbean variety (which appears to be subtler and less aggressive, but is nevertheless present and limiting in the social and professional fields) to the North American one. If it is all part of the same situation of injustice and oppression, then "black" poetry comes from the same tradition, be it written in English or in Spanish. Louis Reyes Rivera points to similar word rhythms and themes in Caribbean and in North American black poetry. It was the Harlem Renaissance which first seemed to point along this way. Writers Claude McKay, whose book of poetry, *Harlem Shadows*, was one of the first literary successes of the Harlem Renaissance, and Wilfred Adolphus Domingo were born in Jamaica, as was also Marcus Garvey. During the early twenties, Garvey galvanized African-American political sentiment in the United States, thus setting the stage for an increased racial cultural consciousness that was simultaneous with a burst of literary production. Langston Hughes, on the other hand, went to Cuba in 1931 and became acquainted with Afro-Caribbean poetry. He translated many of Nicolás Guillén's writings into English.[21]

Both Louis Reyes Rivera's and Tato Laviera's poetry is indebted not only to Afro-Caribbean poetry and to the Négritude movement[22] but also to African-American poets like Ishmael Reed and Imamu Amiri Baraka (LeRoi Jones). Baraka used his writing as a political instrument and founded the Black Repertory Theater of Harlem, with which Sandra María Esteves was closely associated. In this way, Baraka brought together the *Nuyorican* and "black" aspects of Puerto Rican poetry in the States, both of which were entirely open to include different ethnic responses to the challenge posed by the New York type of North American experience.

Not all Puerto Rican writers in the United States focus on race or gender. The experience some of them mirror in their writings can also be seen as a variant of a wider North American experience by shifting the emphasis from the particular ethnic concerns of Puerto Ricans to the way this experience relates to those of other groups. Jack Agüeros' stories in *Dominoes* strive to portray the Puerto Ricans within the wider panorama of the city and its racial and ethnic multiplicity. His characters are not so much typical as common, in the sense of men and women who are well adjusted within an already established sector of society that may not be central but is nevertheless accepted. They sometimes shun—as Max Vázquez does in the wonderful story, *Horologist*—any protagonism that may single them out as spokespersons or representatives of their particular group, taking them out of their settled routine of work. Yet their difference is always there, lurking in the background and beneath the surface, waiting to erupt at a provocation (as in the title story) or a temptation (as in *Horologist*). Normality may not be as normal for Puerto Ricans in the States as for other, more established groups.

Many of those who appear in Ed Vega's short stories (especially in *Casualty Reports*) have also subdued their differences and appear to have fully adapted to the society in which they live and work. In this case, however, the differences do not so much erupt as implode inside of them in the form of a sudden consciousness of irreplaceable loss.

On an aesthetic plane the difference is played up in the stories of Vega's book, *Mendoza's Dreams*. In some of these stories, New York turns into a surreal city in the process of trying to deal with people who have another cultural frame of reference from that which is the organizing principle of a society. The space between stereotype and expectation becomes the characters' field of action. They are thus able to subvert and turn to their advantage the blind spot society has toward their distinctness. Mercury Gómez, in the story that bears his name, creates a flourishing messenger business by using to his advantage the physical stereotyping of his ethnic group. Vega's work examines prejudices and conventions on both sides of the cultural divide and plays each side against the other.

BETWEEN REALITY AND MYTH

Where did these writers find their models? What stimulated them to resort to the written word as a form of expression and communication?

The pervasive influence in their work is that of the oral tradition, which may have been received by direct means, such as the telling of family stories and traditional lore or through the influence of the radio, which many refer to as crucial in their artistic development.[23]

Music—popular Puerto Rican music, which was recorded to a significant extent in New York during the thirties and forties[24]—is also an influence (and not only Puerto Rican music, but all kinds of Latino and North American music).

Some of these writers are the sons and daughters of people uprooted in Puerto Rico's "Industrial Revolution," whose parents had strong country roots and were thus familiar with the troubadour tradition of improvised verse.[25]

This literature, therefore, was born from varying stimuli within the context of a Puerto Rican immigrant community that seemingly provided no models for the written word. When Abraham Rodríguez was young, a teacher told him: "There's no such thing as a Puerto Rican writer." Pedro Pietri thought that blacks and Hispanics didn't write books. (He discovered otherwise when he came across García Lorca while work-ing in the Columbia University library reshelving books.) Nevertheless, they did come into contact with books and learning in many ways which had to do with the educa-tional opportunities they found in the States. Moreover, a city such as New York, with its multiethnic, multiracial population, made differences in culture and in levels of technological advancement much more palpable than they had been on an island which, until the fifties, was mostly agrarian and had a fairly homogeneous population. Literature was a venue that seemed apt to express their contradictions and frustra-tions (especially, as we have seen, after the Beats turned to it in protest). Their situa-tion also suggested themes that seemed to be begging to be put into writing: the con-trasts between present reality and past memories (or myths).

For all of them, the island is a problem both in itself and in relation to the society in which they find themselves. Some (like Abraham Rodríguez) have a love-hate relation-ship with Puerto Rico and look back in anger and disappointment; others (Esmeralda Santiago, Judith Ortiz Cofer) look back with some degree of sadness; and still others (Ed Vega and Victor Hernández Cruz) mythologize the island as a lost paradise from which many were forcibly ejected.

Some coined the term *Nuyorican* to describe Puerto Ricans *in* and *of* New York. They embraced their present situation but kept alive the memory of where they had come from. Not all of them favor being called *Nuyoricans*, nor are they all now in and of New York. With increasing frequency, Puerto Ricans have moved out of that city and into others, settling in sizable communities.[26] They have thus constituted a kind of "floating island," a culture that does not depend so much on a geographic location as on a shared horizon of references. This culture deals not only with common origins but also with perceived differences that come to the fore only when they are far from the original "home" and put into direct contact with a reality perceived as alien. This phenomenon, of course, is not exclusively Puerto Rican or even Latino. Migratory groups worldwide are conforming geo-cultures that, more than geo-nations, define them.[27] North Africans in France; Indians and West Indians in Great Britain; Turks in Germany; even the Dominicans who flock illegally to Puerto Rico; and, of course, the Chinese in a great many places are coexisting without melting, and their artistic pro-ductions (literary or otherwise) are generally distinct from a main, internationalized, Westernized current of canonic art and literature.

Yet second-generation Puerto Ricans in the States (or even these of the first gen-eration), are already different from those who live on the island. Even the term *Puerto Rican* can have another meaning in the mainland. It may simply be an expression of a distinctness within the United States with no specific reference to the island, or a sociopolitical position, which in the past has been equated with radicalism (as exemplified, for instance, in the organization of the Young Lords, active during the seventies).

Writers become especially relevant in such a situation. They must help the nascent community to re-imagine itself through new perspectives. Having reclaimed a distinctive past through their texts, they must define, in imaginary terms, their present and project the future. Their position is two-edged. It often applies to the island of origin the critical stance to which those who have championed a cause through thick and thin are entitled. They may see more clearly than those who are immersed in Puerto Rican society the changes that have occurred and the transformations that are taking place. The close contact with other cultures has given them a breadth of experience difficult to attain within insular confines. They are able to take from many and to give back. This could be a step toward the *mestizaje*[28] which in nations with a Hispanic heritage has seen the fusion of races, cultures, and traditions (with plenty of problems, to be sure) or a broader comprehension of a hybrid kind of society where contact and conflict result in a dynamic culture. The United States' Puerto Ricans are at the cutting edge of a linguistic and cultural frontier between the island and the mainland, crossing over it continuously. Their experience may be immensely valuable for all involved. As Homi Bhabha has written:

> A range of contemporary critical theories suggest that it is from those who have suffered the sentence of history—subjugation, domination, Diaspora, displacement—that we learn our most enduring lessons for living and thinking. There is even a growing conviction that the affective experience of social marginality—as it emerges in non-canonical cultural forms—transforms our critical strategies. It forces us to confront the concept of culture outside *objets d'art* or beyond the canonization of the "idea" of aesthetics, to engage with culture as an uneven, incomplete production of meaning and value, often composed of incommensurable demands and practices, produced in the act of social survival."[29]

WHATEVER HAPPENED TO THE MELTING POT?

Some of the writers interviewed for this work were taken by their families as children to the States (e.g., Miguel Algarín, Pedro Pietri, Victor Hernández Cruz, Ed Vega, and Esmeralda Santiago). A fairly equal number (Piri Thomas, Edwin Torres, Abraham Rodríguez, Sandra María Esteves, Nicholasa Mohr, Jack Agüeros, and Louis Reyes Rivera) were born in New York, to one or both Puerto Rican parents. This circumstance entails a further interest. What makes that second generation retain a distinctive—an affirmative—Puerto Rican identification? Why the resistance to melting away in the famous pot?

Some writers, like Ed Vega, allude to race as the reason why the Puerto Ricans will not assimilate fully into the American mainstream. (They would have to identify themselves as black or white. Since many of them are not, in fact, white and since to be identified as black would entail a considerable amount of prejudice, they prefer to remain Puerto Rican.)

According to Esmeralda Santiago, since Puerto Ricans are already U.S. citizens, there is no need to make any further effort to blend in. The cake can be had and eaten at the same time.

A generalized view is that the frequency and ease with which Puerto Ricans go to and from the island to the mainland constantly renews their contacts with their "roots" and keeps alive the hope of returning. (Many do, in fact, return: among those interviewed, Victor Hernández Cruz has returned to his native town of Aguas Buenas.)[30]

There is yet another aspect of this situation. Far from "melting," Puerto Ricans—and, indeed, Latinos in general—have made of the United States a place of encounter, an equivalent of a nationally unaffiliated *locus* (amoenus?) where they can recognize each other as more equal among themselves than they are with their "hosts." Moreover, for Caribbean writers, the United States has become an equivalent of what Europe (especially Paris and Barcelona) was in the sixties for the Latin American ones who initiated the so-called "boom."[31]

THE ISLAND STRIKES BACK

How does Puerto Rico relate to these writers? It has, for the most part, ignored them. Save for a few scholars who have studied and anthologized their writings (mostly their poetry), a void has surrounded their texts, the immense majority of which are not even translated.

The main reason for this is that they write in English. Spanish is not only the language commonly used in Puerto Rico, but it has also become a symbol of the island's national identity, in conflict with what is traditionally considered—especially by an important intellectual and artistic elite—the United States' encroaching cultural imperialism. As Nancy Morris has written: "In the early twentieth century, as the United States overhauled Puerto Rican institutions by fiat, Puerto Ricans' sense of difference was reinforced, and so were their opposition to U.S. domination and their attachment to symbols felt to be under attack. Language is paramount here. . . . Throughout the century, language has both engendered opposition and provided an excuse for it."[32] Within this context, which directly affected the class from which most writers emerged, literature has traditionally been assigned the mission to preserve linguistic integrity and purity. Thus there is little room for English-speaking and -writing Puerto Ricans in the traditional cultural circles, no matter how passionately they also might resist assimilation into the North American reality.[33]

Their language represents a problem that not many people know how to face. The easiest way out is simply to ignore their existence, developing a blind spot toward this literary production. Although this attitude is changing, especially among the younger intellectuals, many of whom have been educated in the United States, the consensus is still against an English-language Puerto Rican literature. There is, however, a growing perception that although the preservation of an endangered language is important for a colonized people, there is also danger in "the fixity and fetishism of identities within the calcification of colonial cultures."[34] Stateside developments in politics and the arts are now being seen as crucial for Puerto Rico's future. Responses are required, not just the apparent indifference or passive resistance to colonial pressures.

The influence of stateside Puerto Ricans must be acknowledged on both island and mainland as part of the continuous transactions that culture must engage in if it is to endure as a living, dynamic force that inflames and inspires a society. To be closed to new experiences is a neoconservative stance "associated with a past that is no longer recoverable except by denying or somehow downgrading the lived experience of those who, in Aimé Césaire's great phrase, want a place at the rendezvous of victory."[35] This goes for both sides of the cultural frontier which the Puerto Ricans are straddling.

The literature written by Puerto Ricans in the United States may contribute strongly to the island's cultural atmosphere by defusing the kind of stifling oppositional discourse traditionally associated with island letters.[36] It may also prove to be innovative and refreshing within U.S. literary contexts in ways that the following interviews will reveal.

NOTES

1. Puerto Ricans have been migrating to the United States ever since the early 1800s, mostly in connection with the rum, molasses, and tobacco trade. A Puerto Rican and Cuban Benevolent Merchants Association was established in New York early in that century. In the 1890s the New York-based Puerto Rico Section of the Cuban Revolutionary party attracted many illustrious political refuges and émigrés.

2. It was not only the post–World War II expansion of industries in the States that favored this migratory trend, but also the establishment of a new political formula in Puerto Rico, called a Commonwealth. Inaugurated in 1952 according to Law 600, approved by Congress in 1950, the policies of the ruling popular Democratic party, which had devised the new political status, called for the industrialization of a traditionally agricultural economy, thus displacing a large number of farm workers from the lands they had either owned of helped to cultivate. They migrated from the countryside to San Juan (where many settled in slums) or directly to the States.

3. Arturo Alfonso Schomburg (1874–1938) was a black Puerto Rican who went to New York in 1891 and there became a member of the Cuban Revolutionary Part's Puerto Rican Section. He started to publish a steady stream of articles and essays on Caribbean and North American black culture. In 1911, together with John E. Bruce, David Fulton, W. Wesley Weeks, and William E. Braxton, he founded the Negro Society for Historical Research in order to further the study of black history and to collect books, photographs, letters, and works of art dealing with African-American culture. His collection of black literature and art, donated in 1926 to the New York Public Library, became the basis for the Schomburg Center for Research in Black Culture, now located in Harlem.

4. Colón (1901–1974), another black Puerto Rican, migrated to the States in 1918. His experiences in New York, where he encountered not only the diversity of stories, *A Puerto Rican in New York and Other Sketches* (published 1961), which appears to be the first full-fledged book by a Puerto Rican in the United States to have been written and published in English.

5. Bernardo Vega (1885–1965), Puerto Rican tobacco worker who migrated to New York in 1916. His memoir about his life within the Puerto Rican community in the States was published posthumously in Puerto Rico in 1977, as edited by César Andreu Iglesias.

6. Clemente Soto Vélez (1905–1993), who wrote vanguardist poetry in Puerto Rico during the twenties, was imprisoned in the States for taking part in Nationalist meetings and activities in Puerto Rico in 1935. After his release from prison in 1942, he stayed in New York returning for brief periods to Puerto Rico from the mid-eighties until his death.

7. Daniel Stern, in a review for *The New York Times Book Review*, wondered at "the pervasiveness of the Hispanic cultural and social legacy" in the street of Harlem (May 21, 1967), p. 44.

8. Piri Thomas, *Down These Mean Streets*, (New York: Vintage, 1991), p. 106.

9. The exaggerated esteem for what are considered overtly male traits, such as physical courage, dominance over the female, and sexual aggressiveness.

10. The *autos sacramentales* were medieval morality plays and others with ecclesiastical themes-especially the seven sacraments-further developed by playwright Calderón de la Barca in Spain in the seventeenth century.

11. See Luce López Baralt, *San Juan de la Cruz y el Islam* (Colegio de México 1985) and also her edition of Miguel Asín Palacios, *Sadilíes y alumbrados* (Madrid: Hiperión, 1990).

12. There were serious manifestations on campus in Columbia University in 1968, and in June 1969 the famous Stonewall Rebellion, which launched the gay rights movement, erupted in a bar in Greenwich Village. That decade was also marked in New York by racial disturbances such as those that took place in the UN building in 1961 and in Harlem in 1963. There were also riots in nearby Newark in 1967.

13. Ann Charters, ed., *The Portable Beat Reader* (New York: Penguin Books, 1992), p. xvii.

14. On November 16, 1952, an article by Holmes in the Sunday Magazine of *The New York Times* described the group as a culturally disaffiliated one that could not identify with the

moral values of a country entering the Cold War. In 1957 Allen Ginsberg's book *Howl and Other Poems* brought the writers to national attention through a censorship trial in San Francisco, while Jack Kerouac's novel, *On the Road*, attracted much attention and became, with *Howl*, the hallmark of the Beat Generation.

15. This was the way Miguel Algarín identified the group of poets and playwrights who were Puerto Rican in origin but who lived in New York and wrote either in English or in mixed English and Spanish. He used it in the title of the anthology he edited together with Miguel Piñero, *Nuyorican Poetry: An Anthology of Puerto Rican Words and Feelings* (New York: William Morrow, 1975).

16. For a history of the Nuyorican Poets Café, see Akira Nogami, "Fervent Wind from the Poets Café in Miguel Algarin's *Time's Now/Ya es tiempo*" (Tokyo, 1992).

17. Frances Aparicio explains this very clearly in her essay "La vida es un Spanglish disparatero: Bilingualism in Nuyorican Poetry," which appears in *European Perspectives on Hispanic Literature of the United States*, edited by Genvieve Fabre (Houston: Atre Público Press, 1988), pp. 147–160.

   Code-switching, the practice of going back and forth continuously between two or more languages—either in speech or writing—has also been used by other Latino groups and their writers, especially Chicanos (Mexican Americans). It was in the Southwest, in fact, that code-switching was first used in folksongs during the late nineteenth century. Alurista, a Chicano writer who took active part in the literary and political awakening of that ethnic group during the 1960s (in which poets undertook affirmative actions, reading their verses at meetings, strikes, and marches), is credited with being one of the first to use bilingualism with a literary intent in his poetry.

18. *Nuyorican Poetry: An Anthology of Puerto Rican Words and Feelings*, p. 9.

19. Michel Foucault, "What Is An Author?" in *The Foucault Reader*, ed. by Paul Rabinow (New York: Penguin, 1984), p. 102.

20. Luce López Baralt, "Al-Andalus," in *The Cambridge History of Arabic Literature*, to be published by Cambridge University Press.

21. Cuban poet Nicolás Guillén (1902–1989) may be the most widely known of the Afro-Antillean poets who flourished during the twenties and thirties. Others were the Cuban Emilio Bollagas, the Dominican Manuel del Cabral, and the Puerto Rican Luis Pales Matos.

22. *Négritude* was a term coined in France during the thirties by Martinican poet Aimé Césaire, then a student in Paris. He sought to signify a supranational black cultural and artistic identity and a pride in African heritage. It also became a springboard for political action. Among those writers who became identified with Négritude were Léopold Sedar Senghor of Senegal and Léon Damas of Guyana.

23. The presence of Spanish-speaking radio in the States dates back to the 1920s. Spanish-language programs and then stations began in California and Texas and later were established in New York.

24. See Ruth Glasser, *My Music Is My Flag: Puerto Rican Musicians and Their New York Communities 1917–1940* (Los Angeles: University of California Press, 1995).

25. These songs, composed in the poetic form of the decimal or ten-verse stanza, have only recently begun to be collected in written works. See Santiago Díaz Orlando, *Decimario Nacional* (Santo Domingo: Comité Amigos del Autor Puertorriqueño, 1994).

26. The states with the biggest Puerto Rican populations are, in that order, New York, New Jersey, Florida, Massachusetts, Pennsylvania, Connecticut, Illinois, California, Ohio, and Texas. See Francisco Rivera-Batiz and Carlos Santiago, *Puerto Ricans in the United States: A Changing Reality* (Washington, D.C. The National Puerto Rican Coalition, 1994).

27. A discussion of such relations can be found in Immanuel Wallerstein, *Geopolitics and Geoculture* (Cambridge: Cambridge University Press, 1991).

28. A condition that usually refers to the mixing of races through intermarriage but that can also be applied to cultural matters in the sense that different traditions can merge and develop into a "new" cultural product.

29. Homi K. Bhabha, *The Location of Culture* (New York: Routledge, 1994), p. 172.

30. During the 1970s there was a reversal of the migratory trend from the island to the States. See Juan Hernández Cruz, *Migratory Trends in Puerto Rico* (San Germán: Universidad Interamericana, 1994).

31. This was the name given to the sudden burst of Latin American narrative writing which took the Americans and Europe by surprise in the sixties and seventies.

32. Nancy Morris, *Puerto Rico: Culture, Politics, and Identity* (Westport, Conn.: Praeger, 1995), p. 153.

33. In 1991 the Commonwealth government, then ruled by the Popular Democratic party, passed a law making Spanish the only official language in Puerto Rico. The next year the island received a prestigious award, the Príncipe de Asturias Award, from Spain for this action. The law was later repealed by an administration dominated by the New Progressive party, which favors statehood.

34. Bhabha, *The Location of Culture*, p. 9.

35. Edward Said, *Representations of the Intellectual* (New York: Pantheon Books, 1994), p. 39.

36. A comprehensive view of this literature in relation to island literature can be found in Frances R. Aparicio's "From Ethnicity to Multiculturalism: An Historical Overview of Puerto Rican Literature in the United States," in *Handbook of Hispanic Cultures in the United States: Literature and Art*, ed. By Francisco Lomelí (Houston: Arte Público Press and Instituto de Cooperación Iberoamericana, 1993), pp. 19–39.

SPANISH in NEW YORK

Ana Celia Zentella

INTRODUCTION

I remember the signs in shop windows when I was growing up in the South Bronx in the 1950s: *Aquí se habla español* "Spanish spoken here." My mother and father made their purchases in English because they had been in New York City (NYC) for decades and spoke it with ease, but increasing numbers of Puerto Rican immigrants were aided by Spanish-speaking merchants, often Sephardic Jews. Their centuries-old Spanish, maintained in the diaspora since the expulsion of the Jews and Moors from Spain in 1492, was rekindled to serve the burgeoning Puerto Rican community. Puerto Ricans formed the earliest Spanish-speaking settlements in New York at the end of the nineteenth century, and they have constituted the majority of the city's Spanish speakers during the twentieth century, but as we approach the twenty-first century the varieties of Spanish heard in New York's stores and subways include those of all Latin America and Spain. Most of the signs that announced *Aquí se habla español* are gone because it is assumed that at least one clerk will be able to attend to customers' needs in Latino neighborhoods, although it is impossible to predict which variety of Spanish s/he will speak.[1]

The official Hispanic population of NYC grew from 16 percent in 1970 to 20 percent in 1980, and in 1990 the 1,783,511 Latinos in NYC comprised a quarter of the city's total population. It is projected that Latinos will outnumber African Americans by the year 2000 and outpace Anglos and African Americans by 2010, when they are expected to make up 35 percent of the city's population (Bouvier and Briggs 1988). References to "Latinos" or "Hispanics"—the Spanish term is preferred by most activists but the English term is favored by government officials—obscure significant differences in the historical, political, economic, and linguistic histories of nearly two dozen groups.

Because of those differences, and because their identification with the homeland remains strong, groups prefer to be identified by their national origin, e.g., Puerto Rican, Mexican, Cuban, instead of by a pan-ethnic label like *Latino* or *Hispano*, or as a hyphenated American. Significantly, a national survey conducted among Mexicans, Puerto Ricans and Cubans found that 80 percent or more "do not see themselves as very similar culturally or politically" (de la Garza et al. 1992: 8). The variety of Spanish that each group speaks is the most distinctive marker of its individuality, but the Spanish language also is their most powerful unifier, thanks to more than 300 years of Spanish colonization. Because the dialects of Latin American Spanish are more mutually intelligible than some dialects in Spain (Zamora Vicente 1979), speakers resent being asked "Do you speak Puerto Rican, Dominican, etc?" The unity of the Spanish language is due to the proximity of the nations, the normalizing efforts of the Royal Academy of the Spanish Language, and the fact that some countries in Latin America were still part of the Spanish empire less than 100 years ago. Still, there are notable distinctions in some of the words and sounds favored by each group, and in the attitudes and customs surrounding the use of language. Because some dialects of Spanish are considered more prestigious than others, certain groups of speakers suffer from linguistic insecurity which may affect their maintenance of Spanish negatively. This chapter provides a brief overview of the dialects of Spanish spoken by the major Spanish-speaking communities in NYC, and discusses the historical, socio-economic and political forces which shape their linguistic diversity and which will determine whether or not a pan-Latino NYC Spanish lies in NYC's future.

2. PUERTO RICANS AND THE INCREASING DIVERSITY

A pioneering Puerto Rican community existed in the Brooklyn Navy Yard area even before Puerto Rico became a United States colony in 1898, and migrants who came after the U.S. granted island residents citizenship in 1917 moved into other areas. When my mother and father arrived in NYC in the 1920s—Mami from Puerto Rico and Papi from Mexico—they met and married in the small community of Spanish-speakers from Spain and Latin America who had settled in Central and East Harlem in Manhattan. Mami knew more English than her fellow Spanish-speakers because the U.S. had imposed English-only in the schools and courts of Puerto Rico soon after the 1898 invasion and she was fortunate enough to have graduated from eighth grade, but the 50-year-long English-only policy resulted in more dropouts than English speakers. The arrival of approximately 50,000 Puerto Ricans a year during the post World War II decade (1945–1955) prompted the *Aquí se habla español* signs. Washington's "escape valve" policies—designed to defuse the nationalist powder keg that the widespread poverty and unemployment of Puerto Rico represented—included mass

TABLE 14.1

Puerto Rican neighborhoods[a] in NYC, 1987*

BRONX NEIGHBORHOODS	% Puerto Rican
MOTT HAVEN/HUNTS POINT	53.2%
UNIVERSITY HEIGHTS/FORDHAM	41.5
SOUNDVIEW/PARKCHESTER	39.1
HIGHBRIDGE/GRAND CONCOURSE	33.1
KINGSBRIDGE HEIGHTS/MOSHULU	28.2
MANHATTAN NEIGHBORHOODS	
EAST HARLEM (EL BARRIO)	36.3
LOWER EAST SIDE (LOISAIDA)/CHINATOWN	21.8
BROOKLYN NEIGHBORHOODS	
BUSHWICK	49.6
SUNSET PARK	32.1
WILLIAMSBURG (LOS SURES)/GREENPOINT	27.7
EAST NEW YORK/STARRETT CITY	21.0

[a] Neighborhoods with Puerto Rican concentrations of 20% or more.

* Source: Falcón et al 1989: 6.

emigration as their centerpiece. The establishment of direct San Juan–New York air-line service provided the garment industry with skilled machine operators and made NYC the center of Puerto Rican migration. By 1950, there were 245,880 Puerto Ricans in NYC, and so many were concentrated in Manhattan's East Harlem that it was known as *El Barrio* "the neighborhood." In the decades after Puerto Rico was declared a Commonwealth of the United States in 1952, city urban relocation policies helped make the South Bronx (Mott Haven, Hunts Point) the NYC area with the highest Puerto Rican concentration. Other significant *barrios* were created in Manhattan and Brooklyn, some of which were re-labeled with Spanish names, e.g., *Loisaida* (recalling both "Lower East Side" and *Loíza Aldea*, a town in Puerto Rico) and *Los Sures* ("the Southside"). Towards the end of the twentieth century, Puerto Ricans made up 20 percent or more of eleven areas in NYC.

Puerto Ricans were the first group to make the presence of Spanish felt in NYC and they still account for the majority of the city's Spanish speakers, but at a decreasing rate. In 1980 Puerto Ricans constituted 61 percent of New York's Latinos, but by 1990 that figure had dropped to 50 percent. The mix of Spanish-speakers intensified as im-migration from several Latin American countries began to out-pace the rate of Puerto

Rican arrivals in the 1980s. The Dominican community grew by 165 percent, and so many settled in the upper west side of Manhattan (11,392 Dominicans are registered in one Washington Heights zip code) that the area is referred to as *Quisqueya* (the Taíno name for the island of Hispaniola that the Dominican Republic shares with Haiti) *plátano* "plantain land," or *el platanal* "plantain grove." In other sections of the city, e.g., Manhattan's Lower East Side, Brooklyn's Sunset Park, and Tremont in the Bronx, Dominicans live in close contact with Puerto Ricans. More educated and prosperous Dominicans are concentrated in the Elmhurst-Corona section of Queens, an area which they share with newcomers from various Central and South American countries. In the 1990s, the Dominican Republic alone accounted for one out of five immigrants to the city (Dept. of City Planning, 1997).

The only other Latino group besides Puerto Ricans and Dominicans that has at least one identifiable ethnic neighborhood in NYC is the Colombian community. "Little Colombia" or "*Chapinero*" (a middle class suburb in Bogotá) in Queens traces its beginnings to the few hundred educated Colombians who emigrated to Jackson Heights at the end of World War I. It grew after WWII when the political unrest at home caused many to flee *la violencia* "the violence," and in the 1970s high rates of unemployment in Colombia contributed to its further expansion (Orlov and Ueda 1980). In 1990 Jackson Heights was home to almost half of all Colombians in NYC, and the area has attracted increasing numbers of newer arrivals, e.g., Ecuadorians, Argentineans (Hays 1993). The extent of Jackson Heights' Latino diversity is obvious in the proliferation of restaurants and groceries in close proximity, e.g., La Colombianita, Fiesta México, La Uruguaya, La Bonaerense, and Inti Raymi: Peruvian Cuisine/*Cocina Peruana*. War in Central America was responsible for making the number of Salvadorans in NYC grow the most dramatically—280 percent between 1980–1990—50 percent of whom live in Queens. Perhaps a "Little El Salvador" will be established in the future, as well as "Little Ecuadors" etc., and even a "Little Mexico" is possible.

The largest concentrations of Mexicans in the U.S. traditionally have been in the Southwest and California. When my father and his friends founded the *Centro Mexicano de Nueva York* circa 1930, its membership included many non-Mexicans because few immigrants left Mexico for NYC. As late as 1980, there were less than 13,000 Mexicans in NYC, but just before my father died in 1987, he welcomed many newcomers to the *Centro*. The amnesty provided by the 1986 Immigration Reform and Control Act contributed to a 173 percent increase in the number of Mexicans in NYC, and put New York State in tenth place in terms of the number of Mexican residents in the country (Valdés de Montano and Smith 1994). No definable Mexican neighborhood exists yet, but *taquerías* "taco stands" have replaced several of the *cuchifrito* restaurants that sold typical Puerto Rican food in El Barrio and parts of the Bronx.

The only Latino group to decline in NYC in the 1980s was the Cuban population, despite the arrival of 125,000 Mariel boatlift "entrants" in 1980. They formed the Third

TABLE 14.2

Percent distribution of Hispanics by descent, NYC 1990*

(Department of City Planning, 1993: Table A)

Hispanics	Total	% of all
TOTAL HISPANICS	1,783,511	100.0%
PUERTO RICAN	896,763	50.3
DOMINICAN	332,713	18.7
COLOMBIAN	84,454	4.7
ECUADORIAN	78,444	4.4
MEXICAN	61,722	3.5
CUBAN	56,041	3.1
SALVADORAN	23,926	1.3
PERUVIAN	23,257	1.3
PANAMANIAN	22,707	1.3
HONDURAN	22,167	1.2
SPANIARD	20,148	1.1
GUATEMALAN	15,765	0.9
ARGENTINEAN	13,934	0.8
NICARAGUAN	9,660	0.5
COSTARICAN	6,920	0.4
CHILEAN	6,721	0.4
VENEZUELAN	4,172	0.2
BOLIVIAN	3,465	0.2
URUGUAYAN	3,233	0.2

* Sources: 1990 Census Summary Tape File I and Summary Tape File 3. For populations under 20,000 the source is: 1990 Census Public Use Microdata Sample A.

Wave of Cubans to arrive, after the First Wave that fled the Cuban Revolution (1959–1965), and the Second Wave (1965–1973) that was characterized by family reunification (García and Otheguy 1988). The Cuban community in NYC, which had preceded Dominicans on the upper west side and in Elmhust-Corona, grew smaller while Cuban communities in Dade County and West New York-Union City grew larger: more than 70 percent of the Cubans in the U.S. are concentrated in Florida and New Jersey.

Nevertheless, Cubans were among the six groups that contributed more than 50,000 to NYC's total Latino population in 1990 (see table 14.2).

The reliability of the figures in table 14.2 has been questioned. Census Bureau officials admit that the Latino community was undercounted, e.g., the undercount for Mexicans alone was estimated at 6,000 in New York State (Valdés de Montano and Smith 1994). Leaders of the Dominican community believe that including undocumented immigrants more than doubles their numbers in NYC. Notwithstanding these limitations, table 14.2 establishes some important contrasts. The great majority of Spanish dialects have at least 3,000 speakers in NYC: the only Spanish-speaking country in the western hemisphere that is not represented is Paraguay. All groups trail far behind Puerto Ricans, who along with the second and sixth place Dominicans and Cubans, respectively, make Caribbean Spanish the dialect that is spoken by 72 percent of NYC's Latinos.

3. LATIN AMERICAN SPANISH

3.1. History and Lexicon

The Caribbean is one of the five geographic zones of Latin American Spanish first proposed by the Dominican linguist Pedro Henríquez Ureña in 1921 (Henríquez Ureña 1940). In it, he included much of Venezuela and the Atlantic coast of Colombia as well as Puerto Rico, Cuba, and the Dominican Republic. The other four regions are: Chile, the Andes (Peru, Ecuador, Bolivia, northwest Argentina, most of Colombia and part of Venezuela), the River Plate basin (Argentina, Uruguay, Paraguay), and Mexico (Mexico, Central America, Southwest U.S.). The linguistic features of these dialect areas and their major subdivisions are summarized in various overviews of Latin American Spanish, including Lope Blanch 1968, Rosario 1970, Canfield 1981, Cotton and Sharp 1988, and Moreno de Alba 1988. Henríquez Ureña based his divisions on the common geography, history, and substratum of indigenous languages that united each zone, and although scholars have questioned the validity and usefulness of such broad dialect areas and proposed other formulations (cf. Moreno de Alba 1988 for a review), his classification remains useful. This is particularly true for the Spanish Antilles: all three islands were explored during Columbus' first and second trips, and had established cities before Cortés arrived in Mexico. Columbus's landing on the north coast of the Dominican Republic in 1492 and the settlement of Santo Domingo in 1496 made Quisqueya the cradle of Spanish in the "New World."

San Juan in Puerto Rico (established by Ponce de León in 1508) and Havana in Cuba (1514) also provided important ports of entry and resupply for the Spanish galleons that dropped off new settlers and slaves on their way to the South American mainland. The early extermination of the Taínos makes it difficult to determine the extent of their linguistic influence beyond the lexicon. Nevertheless, most studies maintain that the Taíno contribution was greater than the African (Alvarez Nazario 1961, López Morales 1971, Megenney 1982, 1990), due to "*la rápida acomodación del negro a los patrones culturales del europeo dominador*" [the rapid accommodation of the black man to the cultural patterns of the European ruler] (Rosario 1969: 13). The extent of African influence on the Spanish of the area, particularly in the Dominican Republic, is being re-investigated (Green 1993). As for the regional origin of the peninsular Spanish brought to the Caribbean, immigration figures from southern Spain and characteristics of Andalusian Spanish favor Andalusia over Castile (Cotton and Sharp 1988). The Spanish that is spoken in NYC by the descendants of the Taíno-African-Spanish mix that took place five hundred years ago in the Caribbean reflects its original multicultural heritage, as it continues to integrate new linguistic contributions and to influence features of other dialects of Spanish.

Elsewhere I have described the lexical levelling that is occuring in NYC among Puerto Ricans, Dominicans, Cubans, and Colombians (Zentella 1990a). Each group maintains its ways of speaking, especially for in-group conversations, but almost everyone picks up features of another dialect, primarily the lexicon. I have talked with Mexican newcomers who abandoned their traditional *chile* in favor of the Caribbean word for hot sauce (*pique*), Ecuadorian taxi-drivers who referred to *chavos* "money" like Puerto Ricans, and speakers from many countries who have adopted *guagua*, the Caribbean term for "bus." Close contact in neighborhoods, schools, and the work place, and especially intermarriage, makes some dialect levelling inevitable. The prevalence of speakers of Caribbean Spanish suggests that the levelling should take on an overwhelmingly Caribbean flavor, but social and linguistic factors that stigmatize Caribbean Spanish militate against that tendency.

3.2. Linguistic Security and Insecurity

Negative attitudes towards Caribbean Spanish frequently are expressed by all Spanish speakers, including Dominicans, Cubans, and Puerto Ricans. Their linguistic security, expressed as evaluations of their dialect as positive or negative and as superior or inferior to others (Labov 1966), is in stark contrast to that of other Spanish speakers, especially Colombians. In response to the question, "Should the Spanish of your group be the one taught in NYC schools?," only Colombians (n=51) responded "yes" in the majority (64 percent). Most of the Puerto Rican (n=73), Cuban (n=20), and Dominican (n=50) subjects answered in the negative: 60 percent, 61 percent, and 80 percent respectively. The majority stressed the importance of teaching a general standard Spanish in their response, but the extent of linguistic insecurity among Dominicans was further underscored by the percent who believed their Spanish should not be the dialect of choice for classrooms because it was *incorrecto* "incorrect" or *malo* "bad." In stating their reasons, only 2 percent of the Colombians, 13 percent of the Puerto

Ricans, and 19 percent of the Cubans expressed negative opinions of their dialect, but 35 percent of the Dominicans expressed negative opinions about Dominican Spanish (Zentella 1990a).

Latino linguistic security/insecurity can be traced to social and linguistic factors that are interrelated. In the first place, the educational level of the subjects—which has important implications for their socio-economic status—is mirrored in the pattern. Fewer Colombians (16 percent) and Puerto Ricans (19 percent) had ended their education at the elementary level, and Cubans had the highest percent with some graduate schooling (25 percent). Dominicans had the largest percent who did not go on to secondary school (34 percent) and the smallest percent who went on to graduate school (8 percent). The fact that those who had completed fewer years of formal education expressed more condemnation of their Spanish is not surprising. Since Puerto Ricans and Dominicans in NYC have a much lower rate of college graduates (6 percent each) compared to Colombians (11 percent) and Cubans (18 percent) (Department of City Planning 1993), it seems logical that the latter groups would feel more linguistically secure than the former. But the correlation between education and linguistic security in my NYC study was not a stable one. Some Colombians who had studied only a few years were prouder of their groups' Spanish than some Dominicans who had studied many more years. Dominican linguistic insecurity reflected a more widespread rejection of Dominican Spanish by the other groups, explicity verbalized in the high level of dismay they said they would express if someone were to tell them that they sounded like a Dominican. Puerto Rican Spanish was rejected to a slightly lesser degree, and Colombian Spanish was praised the most.

The political, socio-economic, and racial factors that are at work in establishing the hierarchy of prestige among these dialects cannot be ignored. The negative impact of U.S. language policies in Puerto Rico (Zentella 1981) and of decades of dictatorial repression in the Dominican Republic, as well as the lower incomes and darker skins of Dominicans and Puerto Ricans in NYC, place them at the bottom of the language status ladder. In 1989, 39 percent of Dominican families and 36 percent of Puerto Rican families lived below poverty level, compared with 15 percent of the city's Colombian families (Department of City Planning 1993). The percent of Cuban families in poverty rose to 14 percent in 1992 (IPRP 1993) because of the immigrants from Mariel and the more recent *balseros* "raft people," but it remains significantly lower than that of most other Latino groups. The influx of black and unskilled Cubans since 1980 and the arrival of an increasing number of Puerto Rican professionals over the last decade have diversified the variety of class dialects from the Caribbean that are heard in New York, but unequal comparisons between working class Puerto Rican and Dominican speech on the one hand and middle class Cuban, Central and South American speech on the other continue to abound. Usually, negative attitudes are not expressed in racial or class terms. They are couched in criticisms of Caribbean Spanish, particularly how it is pronounced, while the dialectal differences of all other regions and classes are conveniently down-played or ignored.

3.3. Pronunciation

3.3.1. CARIBBEAN SPANISH PRONUNCIATION The phonology of the Caribbean was inherited from Andalusian Spanish, and some of its features may have been influenced by the African language mixtures during the extensive slave trade in the Caribbean. Most noteworthy is the instability of word/syllable final -s, particularly in informal speech. As in *Andalucía* to this day, it can be rendered as an aspirated /h/, as in "he," or be dropped altogether. In Puerto Rican, Dominican, and Cuban Spanish, e.g., *Nosotros gastamos* "We spend" can sound like *Nosotroh gahtamoh* or *Nosotro gatamo*. Deletion is more prominent among the less educated in every group, but quantitative research by Terrell (1982a, b) proved that Dominicans deleted more than Puerto Ricans and Cubans—in ascending order—no matter what the educational level. Dominicans who had attended university omitted syllable/word final -s 76 percent of the time, and deletion was almost categorical (94 percent) among those who had not gone beyond elementary school.

Cultural attitudes toward the retention of -s in the Caribbean explain the high deletion rates. Among Dominicans, those who stress -s are accused of *hablando fisno* "talking fine/high class" (with an intrusive -s in *fino*) or *comiendo espagueti* "eating spaghetti," and there is the added connotation of effeminacy when men do it. In NYC, therefore, social pressures on Caribbean speakers to aspirate or delete -s conflict with the insistence on its enunciation by higher status speakers from other regions. This conflict contributes to feelings of linguistic insecurity, particularly for those groups with the highest deletion rates. It is as if U.S. Americans were made to feel ashamed of their English because they pronounce words like "water" and "butter" with a flap sound that is like a Spanish r in the middle of the word instead of the British t, when adoption of the British pronunciations would earn them ridicule. My solution, and that of many others who are aware of the negative attitudes and are bidialectal, is to reserve my informal Caribbean Spanish for in-group members, and switch to a more conservative variety for formal communication with outsiders.

In addition to the features that distinguish Caribbean Spanish speakers as a group, each country is known for its intonation, i.e, the particular rise and fall voice pattern that identifies each group, and at least one distinctive phonological feature:

a. Puerto Rican Spanish The trilled r, written as single r at the beginning of words and as double rr in the middle of words, may be pronounced as a velar R which can be raspy like the German ch in *Achtung* or *Bach*. It is similar to the Spaniards' pronunciation of j or g before i/e, all of which are transcribed as /x/.

b. Dominican Spanish The most salient aspect of Dominican Spanish is the substitution of /i/ for -r in syllable final position, e.g., *doctor>doctoi* "doctor," *cuarto>cuaito* "room" or "money," characteristic of the northern Cibao region, the original home of many NYC Dominicans. Speakers from the south are distinguished by the -r that replaces syllable final l in their speech (*tal vez>tar ve* "perhaps"), and those from the capital are known for replacing syllable final r with l (*carne>calne* "meat").

c. **Cuban Spanish**   Traditionally, Cubans have been distinguished by the absence of syllable final -l and -r and the doubling of the following consonant, e.g., *Alberto>Abbetto*.

3.3.2. CENTRAL AND SOUTH AMERICAN SPANISH PRONUNCIATION   The varieties of Spanish that are spoken in the Caribbean are considered more "radical" (Guitart 1982) than Central and South American dialects because they drop or change several consonants, particularly syllable/word-final -s, even though some inland/highland varieties of Spanish delete vowels. Rosenblat (1970: 136) described the contrasting pattern of *"las tierras altas y las tierras bajas"* [highlands and lowlands] with a humorous analogy based on "dietary" habits:

> Yo las distingo, de manera caricaturesca, por el régimen alimenticio: las tierras altas se comen las vocales, las tierras bajas se comen las consonantes.

[I distinguish them, in caricature form, by their diet: the highlands eat their vowels and the lowlands eat their consonants.]

Inland Mexican, Central, and South American dialects were less exposed to Andalusian Spanish than the Caribbean ports, and some inland areas were off limits to Blacks, so inland dialects tend to conserve syllable final -s like the Castilian dialect of north central Spain. Speakers of conservative dialects tend to be highly critical of radical speakers from the coasts, and Guitart (1982) claims that radical speakers are more likely to imitate conservative pronunciation than vice versa. But illegal immigrants who try to "pass" as Puerto Rican citizens, and South/Central American activists who identify with the plight of Puerto Ricans and Dominicans have found it useful to blend in linguistically by adopting -s deletion. Additionally, contraction and deletion are normal processes present in every dialect, e.g., the replacement of syllable/word initial /s-/ by /h/ is not unknown in some varieties of Central and South American Spanish, so that *si pasamos* "if we pass by" can become */hi pahamos/.*

3.4. Variations in Grammar: Pronoun Placement, Frequency, and Forms

I have concentrated on pronunciation because it is the focal point of most criticisms, and because Spanish dialects vary less in grammar. Of the nine supposedly widespread differences in Caribbean Spanish listed by Rosario (1970), most are frequent in all Spanish, e.g., preference for the periphrastic future (*ir a* "to go to" + infinitive) instead of the future verb form. Only the placement of personal pronouns before the verb in questions clearly separates Caribbean Spanish from other varieties, e.g., *¿Cómo tú te llamas?* instead of *¿Cómo te llamas tú?* "What's your name"? One feature that Rosario does not mention is the redundant use of pronouns which Spanish does not require. The deletion of syllable final -s on second person verbs in Caribbean Spanish makes many first, second and third person verbs undistinguishable, e.g., *yo, tú, Ud., él, ella: hablaba*, and may trigger the expression of more personal pronouns to aid in subject identification. Furthermore, pronouns may be employed more frequently by English dominant bilinguals because English requires them, e.g., redundant first person pronouns were employed by a young *cubana*: "... *son los puertorriqueños que* **yo** he conocido aquí porque cuando **yo** fui a Puerto Rico ..." "those are the Puerto Ricans that **I** have met here because when **I** went to Puerto Rico ..."

The most distinctive use of pronouns in the Spanish-speaking world occurs in some parts of Central and South America. The second person singular pronoun for familiarity or informality is usually *tú*, but the archaic *vos* and its accompanying verb forms are preserved in a few regions, e.g., *vos sos* vs. *tú eres* for "you (familiar) are." Central American and Argentinean friends in NYC speak with *vos* among themselves, but like the Salvadorans and Hondurans surrounded by Mexicans in Houston (Lipski 1979), many are adopting *tú*, particularly when speaking with other Latinos informally. In general, the traditional distinction between the polite and familiar forms (*Usted [Ud.]* and *tú/vos*) is less pervasive in the Caribbean than in Central and South America, where formal *Ud.* sometimes is extended to parent-child communication.

Different and changing social norms are involved: what seems an appropriately respectful form of address to some groups is interpreted as cold and distancing by others, particularly when used within the family. A study of pronoun usage by Dominican and Puerto Rican immigrants in NYC in the early 1970s found an age-related pattern: speakers reported that they maintained the Caribbean habit of addressing others as *tú* and being addressed as *tú* (=reciprocal *tú*) in early childhood, moved to non-reciprocal *Ud.* at the onset of adolescence as a sign of growing maturity (adolescents addressed elders as *Ud.* but were addressed with *tú*), and increased reciprocal *tú* for solidarity in adulthood (Keller 1975). More recently, I have heard it argued that the use of *tú* (*tuteo*) has increased at the expense of *Ud.* because of a loss of crucial cultural values such as *respeto* "respect." A more positive interpretation is that the preference for *tú* is due to greater feelings of equality and comradeship among Latinos in the U.S. Additionally, there is the possibility that the omnibus "you" English pronoun, which makes no polite vs. familiar distinction, is contributing to the change.

3.5. The Influence of English

The tendency to blame English for every difference in U.S. Spanish has been criticized because it ignores similar changes that are occurring in Latin America among speakers who do not know English, and universal processes affecting language change (Silva-Corvalán 1986). But the influence of English is inevitable given the close but unequal contact—in power and status—between NY's English and Spanish speakers. Even purist Hispanists who chide the members of the second and third generations for speaking an English-influenced Spanish or "Spanglish" are not immune. After a few years in NYC, the impact of English is visible in almost everyone's Spanish (see below). As is traditionally the case in language contact situations all over the world (Weinreich 1968), the lexicon is most affected, as follows:

1. English words, often representing new or different cultural realities encountered in NYC, are borrowed and frequently transformed by Spanish pronunciation and grammar in the process, e.g., *biles* "bills," *la boila* "the boiler," *un jolope* "a hold-up." These words are known as "loans," or specifically "anglicisms" when they are borrowed from English.

2. Spanish words that are phonologically similar to English words but differ in meaning may take on the English meaning, e.g., *librería* ("bookstore" replaces *biblioteca* for "library," *papel* ("paper," i.e., stationery) replaces *periódico* for "newspaper." García and Otheguy (1988) label these "merged word calques" because of the overlap in form and semantic field.

3. English words or phrases may be translated literally into Spanish, e.g., "to lose weight"=*perder peso* instead of *rebajar*. The lack of phonological resemblance, e.g., between English "lose" and Spanish *perder*, distinguishes "independent word calques" from the merged word calques (see 2 above) in García and Otheguy's framework (1988). Finally, "phrasal calques" are composed of "a series of elements that belong to the Spanish language but are being used as they would be if they were English elements" (García and Otheguy 1988: 182), e.g., "Prescriptions filled here"=*Recetas* (or *prescripciones*) *llenadas aquí* instead of *Aquí se despachan recetas* (Varela 1992).

Loans and calques usually are part of what is included when people criticize "Spanglish," but the term also refers to speech that contains Spanish and English segments, as in the following:

I remember when he was born *que nació bien prietito, que* he was real black and my father said *que no era hijo de'l* because *era tan negro*.

[I remember when he was born "that he was born real dark, that" he was real black and my father said "that it wasn't his son" because "he was so black."]

This recollection by a seven year old boy of his baby brother's birth reveals crucial cultural knowledge about racial diversity in Puerto Rican families and excellent bilingual skills. His switching without hesitation at appropriate points before/after conjunctions, dependent and independent clauses—all of which he knew how to say in both languages—is characteristic of fluent adult bilinguals for whom code-switching is a significant discourse strategy.

Contrary to the belief that "Spanglish" is a chaotic hodge-podge used by people who are deficient in one or both languages—signaling the deterioration of both Spanish and English—the rule governed nature and important functions of Spanish-

English alternation beyond that of filling in for vocabulary gaps have been proven conclusively (see collections by Durán 1981; Amastae and Elías-Olivares 1982). Most of the research has been conducted among U.S. Mexicans and Puerto Ricans, but other bilingual Latinos report code-switching in the same way and for the same reasons, including—but not limited to—quotation, emphasis, translation, aggravation and mitigation of requests, and bonding with fellow bilinguals. Language alternation has passionate detractors and supporters: some view it with alarm as evidence of cultural confusion and others embrace it as evidence of adaptability and creativity. Those Latinos—often well educated members of the first generations—who insist that Spanish and English should never be mixed, repudiate the bilingual speech and poetry of their younger and/or less educated compatriots. Purists repudiate "Spanglish" as an epithet, along with identity labels like "Nuyorican" and "Dominican York" or "Chicano," because of their insistence on a idealized language and identity that is static and unrealistic. Instead of promoting Spanish maintenance, the net effect of Spanglish bashing is the promotion of language shift, with negative repercussions for the communities' academic and bilingual excellence. Latinos who end up convinced that their Spanish is bad or *mata'o* "killed," rush to adopt English and eventually do kill off their Spanish. After all, when they speak a Hispanized English most Latinos sound alike so it is easier to avoid being singled out for criticism. Some speakers of Caribbean Spanish, who report higher levels of language alternation than Central or South Americans, adopt code-switching as a step toward greater English proficiency in an attempt to escape being discriminated against because of their stigmatized Spanish, color, and socio-economic condition (García et al. 1988, Zentella 1990a).[2] In the end, the effort backfires because their code-switching becomes the symbol of their stigmatized racial, class, and linguistic status.

Other bilinguals, however, like the writers of *Nuyorican Poetry* (Algarín and Piñero 1975), are generating a process of semantic inversion of the sort experienced by African Americans with "black" and "African." From their perspective, the terms "Nuyorican," "Dominican York," "Chicano" and "Spanglish" do not constitute a repudiation or degeneration of the homeland's culture and language, but a graphic way of displaying membership in two worlds—a proud straddling of cultural borders. The linguistic cross-over that it encourages is reflected in the appearance of English lyrics in *salsa* dance music and the creation of Spanish "raps" by English dominant bilinguals who identify with both languages proudly, e.g., Latin Empire, Latin Alliance.

4. THE SPANISH MEDIA

New Yorkers who are used to hearing Spanish all around them remain incredulous when told that the language is being lost at a rapid rate, as Veltman (1988) has documented nationwide, and as I corroborate below. In addition to the many Latino faces they see, the proliferation of newspapers, signs, and advertisements in Spanish and the availability of all-day radio and television programming contribute to the impression that Spanish will never die out, and even that English is in danger of being displaced. While it is true that "the Hispanic media has rocketed to unprecented heights," there is some debate as to whether the Spanish media contribute "to preserve the traditions and values of the Hispanic immigrants and to facilitate their integration to the North American culture" (Paladin 1994: 3) or whether it is a big business that sells self-hate. The type of Spanish that is used in different formats varies in ways that shed light on the issue.

As Paladin 1994: 3 indicates, the expansion of the Spanish media has been formidable:

> In 1991 there were 32 television stations with dozens of affiliates, 11 newspapers, 160 weekly magazines and 54 scientific and literary magazines in the United States.... *Univisión* is the fifth largest network in the U.S. reaching 92 percent of the Hispanic households via 37 broadcast affiliates and more than 600 cable affiliates....On the other hand, the number of Hispanic radio stations has grown from 322 to 390 since 1990.

In New York City, the print media is clearly divided along regional, national, and local lines. At least 23 dailies in Spanish can be bought at newstands in Latino neighborhoods throughout the city, although some of them can be found only in certain areas.[3] Two of the dailies are produced locally, and they have the largest circulation: *El Diario/La Prensa*, New York's oldest Spanish daily sells 60,000 copies a day, with the greatest number of readers in the Bronx. *Noticias del Mundo*, 14 years old, has 28,000 readers. The next most widely read daily is *El Nacional*, a leading paper in the Dominican Republic which circulates 25,000 copies of a special New York edition every day. The remainder come from the countries and cities of Latin America which contribute the largest number of immigrants in New York City:

– In addition to *El Nacional*, five more dailies come from the Dominican Republic: *El Listín Diario, Hoy, El Siglo, Ultima Hora, El Jaya* (*El Jaya* is published in el Cibao and the rest are published in the capital). Most are available in Washington Heights and the Lower East Side (Manhattan), Jackson Heights/Corona (Queens), Bushwick (Brooklyn) and the South Bronx.
– 4 from Colombia, in the Jackson Heights area of Queens:
    2 from Bogotá, the capital: *El Espectador, El Tiempo*
    1 from Medellín: *El Colombiano*
    1 from Cali: *El País*

– 3 from Ecuador:

    1 from Guayaquil, *El Universo*, in Washington Heights

    1 from Quito, *El Comercio*, in Washington Heights

    1 from Cuenca, *El Mercurio*, in Jackson Heights/Corona

– 2 from Honduras, both in the South Bronx:

    1 from Tegucigalpa, the capital, *La Tribuna*

    1 from San Pedro Sula, *Tiempo*

– 2 from Guatemala City, both available in Jackson Hts/Corona:

    Gráfico and *Prensa Libre*

– 1 each from the following cities:

    San Juan, Puerto Rico's *El Vocero*, widely available

    Miami, Florida's *Diario Las Américas*, in Washington Heights

    San Salvador, El Salvador's *El Universo*, in Washington Heights

    San José, Costa Rica's *La Nación*, in Jackson Hts/Corona

Several important facts are gleaned from this summary of dailies: many first generation immigrants are literate in Spanish and they make an economic sacrifice to keep up with events in their homelands via the national newspapers, for which they pay an average of $1.25 per day.[4] Most surprising is the presence of newspapers from El Salvador and Ecuador in Washington Heights, communities that are not highly visible among the Dominican majority in that area. Following a time honored practice in New York, newer immigrants enter the poorest neighborhoods, contributing to the dialectal levelling discussed above.

At the local level, more than nine weeklies, several of them free, are designed to meet the needs of specific communities. *El Especial* and *Impacto* are sold most widely and address a broader range of Latinos than others which print more items of interest to the Cuban (*El Tiempo, El Continental*), Dominican (*Visión Hispana, Eco Latino*), Colombian (*Noticiero Colombiano e Hispano*), Mexican (*El Sol de México y Latinoamérica*), and South American (*Resumen*) communities. As neighborhoods become home to a greater diversity of Latinos, the newspapers adapt their contents to appeal to the newer residents. For example, *El Sol*, a free weekly published in Queens, was originally *El Sol de Colombia*. As its readership changed, the reference to Colombia was dropped, although the editor continues to favor a Colombian Spanish style.

Whereas the dailies from Latin America are written in the national variety of standard Spanish and are likely to include local words and expressions, the two that are published in New York try to reach out to a variety of nationalities and limit their regionalisms accordingly. As one editor explained it, the general practice is to write a Spanish that is *"accesible a todo el mundo"* [accessible to everybody], but when various lexical alternatives conflict, it is likely that the form most commonly heard in New York will be chosen, namely the Caribbean or specifically Puerto Rican term.

In a revealing comparison of the ethnic press in the U.S., García et al. (1985) found that the Spanish press expresses more negativity toward its ethnic mother tongue and its ethnicity than the French, German, or Yiddish presses. The NY Spanish press has expanded but it has not changed significantly in this regard. Each paper criticizes the others' Spanish in private, e.g., one *Noticias del Mundo* staffer said that subscribers often characterized their Spanish as more refined—*"con más cordura"* [with greater restraint]—than that of *El Diario/La Prensa*, which was *"muy común"* [very common], while the editor of another paper described the Spanish of *Noticias del Mundo* as *"un desastre"* [a disaster]. Spurred on by a regular "watch your p's and q's" column in the Cuban oriented *Diario Las Américas* from Miami, a columnist for *El Diario-La Prensa* recently announced the formation of *Proyecto MADE* (Por un Manejo Adecuado del Español) "Project MADE, For an Adequate Command of Spanish" (Chávez-Vásquez 1994a). Its avowed purpose is to combat the *"violentos cambios lingüísticos"* [violent linguistic changes] that are *"injustificables"* [unjustifiable] and *"ofensivos"* [offensive] (Chávez-Vásquez 1994b). Apparently, violation of the adjective-noun placement rule is not targeted because the article included three such violations, e.g., *graciosas anécdotas* "funny anecdotes" follows the English pattern (noun-adjective) instead of the Spanish norm, *anécdotas graciosas*. The organizers of many well intentioned prescriptivist efforts often get caught in the inevitable web of the linguistic changes they censure.[5]

In regard to anglicisms, a favorite pet peeve of the Spanish press, NY editors with extensive experience adopt a policy that nods to the purists but achieves their principal objective—communicating with the largest possible readership. They go to great lengths to avoid anglicisms, but recognize that some English words are so widespread that the Spanish version might prove incomprehensible. In those cases, they use the anglicism and sometimes follow it with a translation in parentheses, e.g., "welfare (*bienestar público*)."

In recognition of the importance of English to their readership, *El Diario/La Prensa* translates its editorial and *Noticias del Mundo* publishes a bilingual page for children. These efforts also serve those in the majority community who are trying to learn Spanish, the foreign language most studied in New York's high schools and universities. The Spanish press has long made overtures to English speakers, and the mainstream English press is beginning to pursue Spanish readership. None of the English dailies has a section in Spanish, but in November of 1994 the *Daily News* began to circulate 250,000 free copies of *Noticias de los Pueblos Latinoamericanos*. It had approximately twelve pages of text devoted to the most important events in Latin America and New York's Latino communities, and was supported completely by advertisers. *Noticias de los Pueblos Latinoamericanos* was discontinued in 1995.

Even when newspapers are free, their success is limited by the number of people literate in Spanish and the extent of their distribution network. Radio and TV transcend these limitations and are part of every Latino's daily life. Two of the four Spanish radio stations are at the top of the charts in NYC: La Mega (97.9FM) and Radio WADO (1280AM). The former plays the rhythms popular with youths and includes at least one bilingual program, while the latter has a long history of offering music and programs that appeal to a broader range of Latin American immigrants. Both stations provide news from many homelands. The news reporters and talk show hosts usually speak a more standard Caribbean Spanish than the disc jockeys, and the most informal and regionally linked Spanish is heard on the programs that are directed at specific nationalities. The music programs attract a multi-generational audience because the lyrics and patter are within everyone's reach. Overall, Spanish radio is much more reflective of life in New York than Spanish television in programming, advertisements, and in the type of Spanish that is spoken, because most radio programs are produced locally and many people call in.

Since "research shows that TV watching is the major form of entertainment for U.S. Latinos" (Fernández 1994: 14), it is important to take a close look at television programming. Two Spanish-language broadcast networks, *Univisión* and *Telemundo*, and one cable network, *Galavisión*, compete for markets all across the United States and in Latin America. In New York, *Univisión* (channel 41) is available approximately 19 hours a day for a total of 130 hours a week, *Telemundo* (channel 47) has 84 hours of programming, and *Galavisión* provides 192 hours to those who subscribe.[6] The great bulk of the shows come from Latin America, primarily Mexico, and except for daily newscasts and a few hours devoted to educational and religious programs and talk shows, most offer entertainment. Soap operas and movies made in Mexico and Venezuela are the most popular programs, although they often are criticized for their racist, sexist, and classist themes. Whatever the ideological effects, the lexical impact is clear. My students know how to say "male friend/buddy" in Mexican Spanish (*cuate*) and "maid" in Venezuelan Spanish (*cachifa*), as well as other regional vocabulary, although their pronunciation and grammar do not change. The only time they hear the variety of Spanish that is spoken in their homes is when reporters take to the streets in Latin America or during shows transmitted from their homeland. For example, five cable channels transmit about five erratic hours per week each from the Dominican Republic, and much of their comedy depends on knowing regional dialectal differences.

The supra-standard spoken by newscasters and by the spokespersons for the blue-chip advertisers, which is always difficult to locate nationally, is consonant with their looks, which also are bleached of Latino diversity—most are very light skinned and often blonde because "white sells":

There are proportionately less black faces on Spanish-language TV than on its Anglo counterpart, and the more important the show or the ad the fewer Indian features that will appear. Try to sell black faces, try to sell Indian faces, and you will no longer be in the

TV business. Spanish language TV reflects the racism endemic in the community. Except that it does more than reflect it: it streamlines it and makes a business of it (Fernández 1994: 81).

And big business it is, with the Latino market's current purchasing power at $206 billion. When some Latinos organized a protest against the lack of diverse racial/ethnic types on *Univisión*, the management candidly admitted that it was a business decision meant to achieve the highest ratings. The protesters did not target the Spanish of the anchors, probably because a Spanish expunged of local idiosyncracies is easier for a wider audience to understand. But those who subscribe to the translations available for English premium cable TV (192 hours weekly each on Disney, HBO, and Showtime) hear the Spanish of Spain. Thus it turns out that the electronic media is stratified linguistically and economically, i.e., the cheapest and most easily available format, radio, is the one that incorporates the most local Spanish. As the medium gets more expensive—Spanish broadcast television, Spanish cable and English cable—the variety of Spanish that is preferred is more and more distant. The net effect is that the young shy away from Spanish TV and even their elders prefer English TV as soon as they can understand it, because they get more choices and higher quality programming. Thus, Spanish TV offers little in the way of Spanish maintenance for the second generation while English TV helps pave the way for the first generation's shift to English.

5. LANGUAGE SHIFT

5.1. Generational Language Shift Among Puerto Ricans

The great majority of Latinos in NYC speak English, making recent immigrants most responsible for keeping Spanish alive. Those who arrive at a young age make the transition from Spanish monolinguals to English dominant bilinguals within a few years, precipitated by schooling and aided by their devotion to English TV, movies, radio. Birthplace is the most significant determinant of language loss or maintenance. Children born in the U.S. are more likely to become English monolinguals than those born in the homeland, especially those of the third generation. Beginning with the 1980 census and escalating in the 1990 census, less than half of all Puerto Ricans in NYC were born in Puerto Rico. This augurs greater language loss for Puerto Ricans than for all other Latinos, most of whom were born in their homeland.

I observed language shift in one lower working class East Harlem *bloque* "block" where, in 1979, 20 Puerto Rican families lived with 26 children between 3 and 20 years old—four of whom had been born in Puerto Rico but had come to NYC before they were eight years old—and eleven infants (Zentella 1997). Most of the children (61 percent) were more proficient in English than Spanish, but only one was an English

TABLE 14.3

Language proficiency spectrum of *El Bloque*'s children, 1980–1993

	SM	SD	SB	BB	EB	ED	EM	Eng?
1980	0%	8%	8%	23%	38%	19%	4%	0%
(N = 26)								
1993	0%	0%	0%	7%	22%	37%	17%	17%
(N = 62)								

SM = Monolingual in Spanish, limited English comprehension

SD = Spanish dominant, weak English [limited vocab, tenses]

SB = Spanish dominant bilingual, fluent English

BB = Balanced bilingual, near equal fluency in both languages

EB = English dominant bilingual, fluent Spanish

ED = English dominant, weak Spanish [limited vocab, tenses]

EM = English dominant, limited Spanish comprehension

Eng ? = either English dominant or English monolingual (based on the evaluation of others)

TABLE 14.3.1

I = born in PR, immigrated before 8 years of age 50% = Balanced Bilinguals, 50% = English dominant Bilinguals

II = born in US, has/had at least one caregiver born in PR who immigrated in post-teens 44% = BB & EB, 56% = ED,EM,E?

III = born in US, has/had Group I caregiver(s) 6% = BB & EB, 94% = ED, EM, E?

IV= born in US, has/had Group II caregiver(s) 100% = ED, EM, E?

monolingual. By 1993, the original 37 children and 25 more—including siblings and children of the first group—had moved conclusively toward the English end of the language proficiency spectrum (see table 14.3).

Citywide figures for Puerto Ricans corroborate *el bloque's* trend: "sixty-three percent of all Puerto Ricans aged five and over reported a "strong" command of English in 1990, up from 53 percent in 1980" (Department of City Planning 1993: 4). The increase in English proficiency extended to the island-born, whose strong English speakers went from 37 percent to 46 percent over the decade. Improved English proficiency need not be at the expense of Spanish, but that was the unfortunate outcome for almost all former members of *el bloque*. In 13 years, English monolinguals (EM) had risen 13 percent among those I interviewed, and those who had moved away were evaluated by their relatives as either English dominant (ED) or monolingual in English. At the other end of the scale, there was no longer anyone more proficient in Spanish than English, and the percent of bilinguals who were equally at ease in both languages (BB) had decreased three-fold. Four generational groups were identified, each one of which manifested a higher degree of language shift:

The three groups of speakers who were born in the U.S. (NYC) exhibited distinct levels of Spanish proficiency that were related to the birth-place of their parents and the age at which immigrant parents came to NYC. Parents who arrived after they had established a strong base in Spanish and had completed most or all of their schooling in Puerto Rico were most likely to speak Spanish to each other and to raise their children in Spanish. Those who came as young children or who were born in NYC became English dominant and usually spoke more English than Spanish to their partners and children. On Fishman's (1991) eight level measure of community language shift—at level eight only a few old speakers are left—the former members of *el bloque* were between stages five and six.

After studying language maintenance efforts all over the world, Fishman (1991: 91) concludes that nothing "can substitute for the re-establishment of young families of child-bearing age in which Xish is the normal medium or co-medium of communication and/or of other culturally appropriate home, family, neighborhood and community intergenerational activity." The young parents I observed were raising their children primarily in English, and their Spanish was limited to several tenses. Spanish was part of their children's lives because poverty kept them living with or near Spanish dominant grandparents in Spanish-speaking neighborhoods. Visits to Puerto Rico were rare, but visitors from the island brought the children in contact with relatives who were monolingual in Spanish, and local schools had increasing numbers of Mexican and Dominican children whose parents spoke to them in Spanish. Most of the third generation offspring of *el bloque* understood a little basic Spanish, but they would not be able to raise a fourth generation of bilinguals unless they went to school in Puerto Rico and/or married a newcomer.

Language shift in the NYPR community must be interpreted in the light of community-specific definitions of bilingualism and identity. The parents of *el bloque* considered children bilingual if they understood and obeyed Spanish requests; most did not insist that children respond in Spanish since almost all elders understood English. It was possible for children with only passive or receptive skills in Spanish to follow the community's frequent switching between Spanish and English, but a small and growing number had to rely on English translations. As a result, the relationship between Puerto Rican identity and Spanish has been transformed: the majority of the second generation and even some members of the first generation believe that it is possible to be a Puerto Rican without speaking Spanish (Attinasi 1979, Zentella 1990b). The idea of a non-Spanish speaking Puerto Rican, anathema to island residents, takes root in NYC to accommodate the growing number of young Puerto Ricans who identify with the culture but cannot speak the language. In order to include everyone in the larger pan-Puerto Rican family, Puerto Ricanness is re-defined in NYC without pre-requisites of birthplace and/or language: you are a Puerto Rican "if you have Puerto Rican blood in you."

5.2. Language shift and English language proficiency

Immigrants from other Latin American countries have not been subjected to the imposition of English on their native land the way Puerto Ricans have, and most still belong to the first generation, unlike Puerto Ricans, but there are many indications that their working classes are undergoing a similar process of generational language shift. As the ranking in table 14.4 indicates, communities that reported the smallest percent of people who spoke only English at home also had the smallest percent of members who spoke English very well of those who spoke only Spanish or both Spanish and English at home.

Table 14.4 refutes the common belief that Spanish speakers do not know or want to speak English. Not surprisingly, the newest immigrant groups have the lowest figures in both columns. We can assume that with time more Guatemalans, Salvadorans, Dominicans, Ecuadorians, Colombians, Peruvians, and Nicaraguans will speak English "very well," significantly beyond the 31–37 percent that already do. As that percent increases, so will the percent of those who speak only English at home, presently 7 percent or less. Since it is likely that most of those who speak only English at home would evaluate themselves as speaking it "very well" if asked, adding the two columns in table 14.4 provides a better idea of the extent of advanced English proficiency in each community. That rate exceeds one third in the first seven groups, which range from 35 percent–44 percent, and rises dramatically in the groups with a longer immigration history.

The relationship between newness of immigration and place in the scale holds for many groups, but not all. Puerto Ricans are not in last place, as might be expected given the length and strength of their immigration stream. Although 58 percent of those Puerto Ricans who spoke a language other than English at home reported they spoke English "very well," only 13 percent of all Puerto Ricans 5 years and older never

TABLE 14.4

Percent that speaks only English at home, compared with percent of others who speak English very well*

Hispanic Origin	Speak only English at home	Don't speak only English at home, but speak it *Very Well*[a]
1. GUATEMALA	3%	34%
2. EL SALVADOR	4%	31%
3. DOMINICAN REPUBLIC	4%	34%
4. ECUADOR	4%	37%
5. COLOMBIA	5%	35%
6. PERU	5%	37%
7. NICARAGUA	7%	37%
8. ARGENTINA	9%	52%
9. HONDURAS	10%	39%
10. CHILE	11%	45%
11. PUERTO RICO	13%	58%
12. CUBA	13%	47%
13. COSTA RICA	14%	62%
14. MEXICO	15%	31%
15. VENEZUELA	19%	55%
16. PANAMA	22%	69%

* Source: Percentages, based on persons 5 years and older, were calculated from numbers provided for New York City in the US Census, Table 192, Social Characteristics for Selected Hispanic Groups: 1990, CP-2–34.

TABLE 14.4.1

Colombians	Puerto Ricans	Cubans	Dominicans
100%	97%	95%	94%

spoke Spanish at home, a rate lower than that of three other groups with fewer highly proficient English speakers. Greater access to their island homeland via plane and telephone may account for this difference. The majority (69 percent) of the Mexicans who speak Spanish at home, in contrast, reported they did not speak English very well, yet another 15 percent reported speaking only English at home. The implications for communication in households where members do not speak the same language are unclear without ethnographic data to supplement census figures. Children who are monolingual in English may become estranged from Spanish monolingual elders, as Wong-Fillmore's research (1991) with early childhood programs maintains. Or, non-reciprocal bilingual conversations in which children speak in English and adults answer in Spanish may be the norm, as was the case in the families of *el bloque* whose parents were members of the first generation.

The self reports of some groups may have been influenced by different perceptions of what constitutes speaking English "very well." Perhaps some groups base their evaluation on their ability to get along in English and others base it on their literacy skills in the language. Still others may be attempting to provide evidence of assimilation by reporting that family members, especially young children, speak no Spanish. Notwithstanding these possibilities, the overall pattern in table 14.4 is consistent: the more English Latinos know, the more English is the only language they speak at home. Panamanians exemplify this pattern the best. They occupy the last place in both columns, which puts them in first place in terms of English ability. More than one fifth (22 percent) of the city's Panamanians speak only English at home, and in addition, 69 percent of those who speak Spanish or Spanish and English at home speak English "very well." In total then, 91 percent of NY's Panamanians reported high levels of English ability. These figures can be explained as a result of anglophone West Indian immigration to Panama, the U.S. presence in the Panama Canal, and residential patterns in NYC. Many Panamanian immigrants come knowing English, and in NYC they live near English speaking Caribbeans and African Americans, predominantly in Brooklyn. The percent of Panamanian families living in poverty in NYC (13 percent), however, is higher than that of groups with less English ability, e.g., Chilean (8 percent), Argentinean (10 percent), Peruvian (12 percent), and Venezuelan (12 percent). The idea that the more a group speaks English, the better off it will be economically, does not always hold true.

The Argentinean community represents an interesting exception in that 91 percent of Argentineans in NYC speak some Spanish at home, but the majority of that group (52 percent) reports speaking English very well. Argentinean bilingualism is no doubt related to their education (43 percent had "some college or higher") and occupations (28 percent were in "managerial and professional specialty occupations"), as well as their racial and class congruence with the dominant society. Advantages for the Latino elite in NYC include professional jobs, elevated incomes, and bilingualism. For too many others, high levels of English proficiency do not necessarily result in higher incomes or education, and progress in English is achieved at the expense of Spanish. Without the experience and the resources to counteract negative attitudes towards Spanish and the power of the English media, and without widespread availability of bilingual programs which maintain and develop Spanish and English skills, language shift by the third generation is inevitable. Children who are now speaking English at home will raise their children in English, barring marriage with a recent immigrant or an extraordinary commitment to do otherwise.

6. LATINO UNITY RE: BILINGUALISM

It is important to underscore the fact that despite major contrasts in education, occupations, and years in the U.S. that separate Latinos on the one hand, and the inexorable shift to English that all are experiencing on the other hand, all Latino groups shared high levels of Spanish use at home in 1990. Latino unity concerning loyalty to the home language and a desire to improve in English was a significant finding in a study that included Dominicans, Cubans, Puerto Ricans, and Central and South Americans in NYC (n=294) (García et al. 1988: 508):

> Communities with differences in social class and ethnic composition, as well as different Hispanic national origin groups, have great interest in speaking English well, great loyalty toward Spanish as the means of communication with others in the country of origin and the family in the United States and as a resource for the ethnic community, and great desire to have the schools teach Spanish to their children.

Similarly, the four groups reported on in Zentella 1990a overwhelmingly wanted bilingualism for their children:

The few Puerto Ricans, Cubans, and Dominicans who did not want their children to be bilingual believed that their children would be more successful in this country if they became English monolinguals; no one favored raising Spanish monolinguals. The differences were not statistically significant, but the unanimity of the Colombians in favor of bilingualism and the last place of the Dominicans mirrored each group's level of linguistic security/insecurity, discussed above. It is doubtful that any Latino group will achieve the level of bilingualism that it desires for its future generations, but that desire *is* achieving high levels of Latino unity—among groups that are otherwise divided—on language policy issues of local and national importance, e.g., against English-only laws and in favor of bilingual ballots and bilingual education (Rosario 1994).

7. GOVERNMENTAL AND EDUCATIONAL SERVICES IN SPANISH

Insecurity about spiraling budgets and intractable social problems have led to a rise in anti-Latino violence in NYC over the last decade.[7] Hispanophobia also is at the root of a national movement to make English the official language of the United States, couched in terms of fear of losing English as the *lingua franca* despite evidence to the contrary (Crawford 1992, Zentella 1994b). During the 1980's fifteen states passed constitutional amendments making English their official language. In New York State, Senator Marchi proposed such an amendment (# 2514) in 1989, but the opposition has kept the legislation in committee up to now. Many people on both sides of the issue are confused about the scope of the amendment. If it were to become law, most Spanish advertisements would not disappear because they are produced by private companies, e.g., the telephone company's Spanish Yellow Pages, and the government-funded public service announcements that qualify as "directions or other informational devices" (# 2514, line 11) would remain also. Targeted for elimination, however, are bilingual ballots and education that goes beyond providing "supplemental instructional programs for pupils of limited English proficiency" (NY State Amendment Proposal # 2514, line 10). At least one NYC candidate for the State Assembly in 1994 campaigned on an English-only platform.[8]

At present, government funds provide for bilingual 911 operators. There are 150 full time interpreters in the city's courts—all Spanish speaking. Districts where at least 10 percent of the population is limited to a language other than English must provide a ballot in that language: they are available in predominantly Spanish- and Chinese-speaking areas. In the interests of health, efficiency, and public safety, hospitals try to provide Spanish-speaking personnel and help in other languages.[9] Puerto Ricans and other Latinos in NYC are overwhelmingly in support of bilingual services and against English-only laws that would eliminate bilingual ballots and bilingual education (Zentella 1990c, Rosario 1994).[10]

In the wider community, bilingual education is hotly debated. The program was established in 1974 as a result of a consent decree between the Board of Education and Aspira, a Puerto Rican educational agency, "for students whose English language deficiency prevents them from effectively participating in the learning process and who can more effectively participate in Spanish" (Consent Decree cited in Facts and Figures 1993–94, Board of Education/ Division of Bilingual Education). In 1993–1994, 15 percent of the 1,015,756 students enrolled in NYC public schools were identified as Limited English Proficient (LEP), and 57 percent of them were enrolled in bilingual education (84,517).[11] Spanish-speakers made up 68 percent of the LEP students and 84 percent of the students in bilingual education, but children from eleven other language backgrounds were also served by bilingual programs.[12] Well-grounded national research found that NYC has some outstanding bilingual programs in which there is "a direct and consistent correlation between Spanish-language development and student gains" in English language, reading, and math (Crawford 1992: 230), but no newspaper mentioned this. In contrast, a report based on unsound methodology that compared the city's bilingual education to English as a Second Language unfavorably enjoyed extensive coverage (Dillon 1994, *Daily News* 1994, Leo 1994). One encouraging sign is that, despite unfair press, there is increasing interest in two-way bilingual programs, in which children from language minorities and English monolinguals learn each other's language as well as their own.

8. CONCLUSIONS

References to Latinos, Hispanics, Spanish, and Spanish speakers in NYC obscure many important differences in language form, use, and attitudes. These differences follow regional and national boundary lines above all, and each Latino group prefers to be recognized individually because it sees itself as distinct from the others. The specific history of each Spanish-speaking group, including the origin and dialects of its first settlers and subsequent invaders in the homeland, and the regional, racial and class origin of different waves of immigrants to the new land—as well as their reasons for emigrating and the welcome they receive—shape the present and future of Spanish in NYC as well as their educational and socio-economic progress. The most complete understanding of this complex language picture requires an anthro*political* linguistics (Zentella 1994a).

Latino unity is being simultaneously strengthened by support for the Spanish language in general and weakened by attacks on specific dialects in particular. Puerto Ricans, who constitute half of the Latinos in NYC, leave their homeland because of conditions created by direct U.S. economic and political control of the island; they arrive as U.S. citizens from a Caribbean island that is an unincorporated territory of the United States with an official bilingual policy for the government, after being subjected to a half century of English imposition in the schools and courts. For linguistic, racial, and socio-economic reasons, Caribbean Spanish—the variety spoken by the majority of Spanish speakers in NYC—does not enjoy the prestige of other dialects, and negative attitudes, coupled with the shift from more island-born to more U.S.-born Puerto Ricans in NYC, create a degree of linguistic insecurity that promotes language shift and a re-definition of Puerto Rican identity. Other groups with similar backgrounds, e.g., Dominicans, can be expected to follow suit while whiter, wealthier, better educated, and more linguistically secure Latinos may be more successful at achieving advanced levels of bilingualism in speaking and writing. All groups, however, are unlikely to pass Spanish on to the next generations, despite their fervent desire to do so, if they do not make special efforts to raise their children bilingually.

These include insisting on Spanish at home and demanding developmental—not transitional—bilingual education in the public schools, and Spanish for Native Speakers courses at the university level.

The replacement of Spanish by English may be encouraging news for advocates of English-only, but the loss of native ability in any language should be lamented for individual, group, and national reasons. NYC is home to one of the largest and most diverse concentrations of Spanish speakers, at a time in the history of this nation when multilingual and multicultural skills are necessary for the resolution of educational, economic, and political problems. Lack of concrete support for the bilingualism of its Latinos—and speakers of other languages—is tantamount to discarding a national treasure. Only a nation-wide commitment to making multiculturalism less of a slogan and more of a reality will avert language loss among Spanish speakers and others, and enable us to extend the benefits of bilingualism to all. More than 500 years of Caribbean experiences at integrating different races, cultures, and languages continue in *La Gran Manzana* "The Big Apple," as multiple dialects of Spanish come into contact with many varieties of English and other languages. Spanish-speaking communities that recognize and respect the differences among themselves but are united in their defense of bilingualism should be in the forefront of the opening of New York's linguistic and cultural frontiers.

NOTES

Since this article was published, New York's Spanish-language media underwent a radical transformation—largely as a result of the information technology revolution that occurred over the past decade, but also because of the demographic and business-cycle changes that occurred during the same period. *El Diario/La Prensa,* currently owned by the ImpreMedia group, continues to be the leading daily, while *Noticias del Mundo* folded in 2004. In 1999, the Tribune Company, owner of the Long Island-based paper *Newsday,* launched the Spanish-language *Hoy* to compete with *El Diario/La Prensa.* In 2006, after a tumultuous debate over inflated circulation figures that led to federal charges of fraud against its management, *Hoy* turned to free distribution, and a year later it was sold to the ImpreMedia group, which eventually transformed it into an online-only publication (*Hoy Nueva York*). Other free-circulation papers launched in the past few years include *Hora Hispana,* a spinoff of the *Daily News.* Still other publications, such as *El Correo de Queens,* of Schneps Publishers, which also produces *The Queens Courier,* have a restricted geographical circulation. Among these there are a number of daily, weekly, and monthly titles aimed at specific national groups, including newspapers from the original countries that are imported into New York, such as the Dominican Republic's *Listin Diario* and Ecuador's *El Diario.* National-oriented publications include *El Especial, El Especialito, El Caribe,* and *Primicias* (Dominicans); *Diario de México* (Mexicans); *Ecuador News* (Ecuadoreans); *El*

Espectador (Colombians), *Peruanísimo News* and the *Ayllu Times* (Peruvians); the monthly *La Prensa* (Hondurans, mostly in the South Bronx); and *De Norte a Sur* (Argentines and Uruguayans in the area of Queens), among many others.

The local radio waves have also experienced a surge of Spanish-language or bilingual programming. In 2008, according to the specialized publication *New York Radio Guide* (http://www.nyradioguide.com), the city had five major Spanish-language radio outlets: the FM stations La Mega (WSKQ, 97.9), whose sassy early-morning show *El Vacilón de la Mañana* became national news because of its huge audience success; Amor (WPAT, 93.1 FM), owned by the Miami-based Spanish Broadcasting System; La Kalle (WCAA, 96.3 FM), which plays mostly reggaetón; and La Qué Buena (WQBU, 92.7 FM), first New York station dedicated exclusively to Mexican popular music; and the news-and- sports-oriented WADO (1280 AM). As of January 2009, Emisora Nueva Granada, related to Colombian group RCN, had also started broadcasting from headquarters in Queens. There are also several stations featuring Spanish-language religious programming and noncommercial stations such as WBAI (99.5 FM) and Columbia University's WKCR (89.9 FM), which disseminate contemporary Latin jazz, Afro-Cuban music, and other genres that are largely overlooked by commercial radios. In TV broadcasting, the long-established networks Univisión (Channel 41, owned by Saban Capital Group) and Telemundo (Channel 47, NBC-Universal), now share the screen with other channels and cable networks such as Telefutura and Galavisión (both owned by Univisión); NY1 Noticias (Time Warner); HITN; and V-Me, a nationwide partnership between Channel Thirteen and the Baeza Group. At the same time, satellite television has expanded the choices of the U.S. Spanish-language audience to virtually any channel in Latin America and Spain. That offering is compounded by the Spanish-dubbed versions of originally English-language shows broadcast by Discovery en Español and similar franchises, and by the programming of Spanish-language movies by channels such as Sundance of IFC. Local public stations also include some shows in Spanish, such as *Nueva York*, the award-winning twice-monthly cultural magazine produced for CUNY TV by Jerry Carlson and hosted by Carmen Boullosa and Patricio Lerzundi. Last but not least, the continuously expanding possibilities of the Internet have allowed the existence a host of online publications such as the Latino cultural and lifestyle magazine NY*Remezcla* and scores of blogs, Web sites, and the so-called social network groups such as Latinos in Social Media (http://www.latism.org/) and Being Latino (http://www.facebook.com/Being.Latino), among many others. —EDITOR

—Maruxa Relaño Tennent contributed to this report

1.   Thanks to the editors, Ofelia García and Joshua Fishman, and to my colleagues John Holm and José Manuel Torres Santiago, for their comments and suggestions.

2.   The notion that darker skinned Latinos are more likely to maintain their Spanish in an effort to distinguish themselves from African Americans deserves to be investigated.

3.   I am grateful to Juan Lulio Blanchard, a student of Ofelia García, for collecting newspapers from throughout the city for me, and for gathering data about their publication.

Given the vast number of newstands in New York, the list provided here does not pretend to be exhaustive.

4. The more than two dozen magazines in Spanish, almost all of which are imported and some of which are translations of U.S. magazines, e.g., *Mecánica Popular [Popular Mechanics]* and *Selecciones de Reader's Digest*, are much more expensive. Although not mentioned in my analysis, the magazines seem similar in linguistic policy and objectives to the national TV networks.

5. In a personal response to my letter of inquiry about MADE, in which I pointed out the noun-adjective violations, Ms. Chávez-Vásquez correctly noted that adjective-noun placement in Spanish can serve to mark emphasis. She also acknowledged the inevitable influence of English on Spanish and adopted a realistic attitude toward cultural and linguistic change: *"Soy realista en que (sic) el sentido de que acepto las consecuencias del choque cultural y por ende idiomático."* [I am a realist in that I accept the consequences of cultural and consequently linguistic clash.] (Chávez-Vásquez, personal communication).

6. I am indebted to Celeste Fondeur, Ofelia García's student, for the information presented on the number of TV stations and programs.

7. The Latino Coalition for Racial Justice keeps track of bias incidents like the Sept. 1994 murder of Manuel Aucaquizhpi, an Ecuadorian immigrant who was beaten to death by a gang of Italian American youths who were "yelling obscene epithets about Mexicans" (Steinhauer 1994:39).

8. Frank Borzellieri, the Republican challenger in the 38th district, Queens, where "Hispanics are the largest minority with 26 percent of the population," campaigned for "eliminating foreign languages from government-issued documents and banning from public schools books he considered anti-American, like biographies of Martin Luther King, Jr." (Onishi 1994).

9. Clinic and hospital needs for Spanish, Chinese, Russian, and Haitian Creole speakers are partially met by programs like Hunter College's Community Interpreter course. An English-only law that was voted down in Suffolk county in 1989 was so repressive that it would have forbidden county health workers from communicating with patients in any language except English (Schmitt 1989).

10. The majority of all other ethnic groups also supported bilingual services, but many also were in favor of making English the official language, presumably because they did not understand the law's repercussions.

11. The LEP label has been critized because it conjures up leprous images. Casanova (1991) offers SOL, Speakers of Other Languages, as a substitute.

12. Bilingual education includes English as a Second Language (ESL) instruction, native language arts instruction, and social studies, science, and math using the native language and English as media of instruction. Programs are available in Spanish, Chinese, Haitian Creole, Russian, Korean, Arabic, Vietnamese, Polish, Bengali, French, Urdu, and Albanian. In 1993–1994 another 63,014 LEPs received ESL only, and 5 percent, or nearly 7,000 students, received neither bilingual education nor ESL.

REFERENCES

Algarín, Miguel, and Miguel Piñero, eds. 1975. *Nuyorican Poetry.* New York: William Morrow.

Alvarez Nazario, Manuel. 1961. *El elemento afro-negroide en el español de Puerto Rico.* Río Piedras, Puerto Rico: Editorial de la Universidad de Puerto Rico.

—— 1977. *El influjo indígena en el español de Puerto Rico.* Río Piedras, Puerto Rico: Editorial de la Universidad de Puerto Rico.

—— 1982. *Orígenes y desarrollo del español en Puerto Rico.* Río Piedras, Puerto Rico: Editorial de la Universidad de Puerto Rico.

Amastae, Jon, and Lucía Elías Olivares, eds. 1982. *Spanish in the United States: Sociolinguistic aspects.* Cambridge: Cambridge University Press.

Attinasi, John. 1979. "Language attitudes in a New York Puerto Rican community," in Raymond Padilla (ed.), *Bilingual education and public policy in the United States.* Ypsilanti, MI: Eastern Michigan University, 408–461.

Bean, Frank D., and Marta Tienda. 1987. *The Hispanic population of the United States.* New York: Russell Sage.

Bouvier, Leon and Vernon Briggs. 1988. *The Population and labor force of New York: 1990–2050.* Washington, D.C.: Population Reference Bureau.

Canfield, Lincoln. 1981. *Spanish Pronunciation in the Americas.* Chicago: University of Chicago Press.

Casanova, Ursula. 1991. "Bilingual education: Politics or pedagogy?," in Ofelia García (ed.), *Bilingual Education: Focusschrift in honor of Joshua A. Fishman on the occasion of his 65th birthday.* Amsterdam/Philadelphia: John Benjamins, 167–180.

Chávez-Vásquez, Gloria. 1994a. "La fuerza del idioma," *El Diario/La Prensa*, domingo, 11 septiembre, 21.

—— 1994b. Estimado(a) amigo(a), PROYECTO MADE subscription,' letter, Oct. 15.

Cotton, Eleanor Greet, and John Sharp. 1988. *Spanish in the Americas.* Washington, D.C.: Georgetown University Press.

Crawford, James. 1992. *Hold your tongue: Bilingualism and the politics of "English Only."* Reading, Mass.: Addison Wesley.

Daily News. 1994. "Talking turkey about English," Editorial, Oct. 21, 1994: 24.

de la Garza, Rodolfo, Angelo Falcón, Chris García, John García. 1992. *Latino national political survey: Summary of findings.* New York: Institute for Puerto Rican Policy.

Department of City Planning. 1993. Demographic and socioeconomic profiles, selected tabulations, selected Hispanic origin groups, NYC and Boroughs [Unpublished MS.]

—— 1997. *The Newest New Yorkers.* New York: City of New York.

Dillon, Sam. 1994. "Report faults bilingual education in New York," *New York Times*, Oct. 20: A1.

Durán, Richard (ed.) 1981. *Latino language and communicative behavior.* Norwood, N.J.: Ablex Press.

Falcón, Angelo, Minerva Delgado, Gerson Borrero (eds.) 1989. *Towards a Puerto Rican–Latino agenda for New York City.* New York: Institute for Puerto Rican Policy.

Fernández, Enrique. 1994. "Our mirror, ourselves: Latino-made Latino images in the media," *Culture-front* 3, no 2.

Fishman, Joshua. 1991. *Reversing language shift.* Clevedon, England: Multilingual Matters.

García, Ofelia, and Ricardo Otheguy. 1988. "The Language situation of Cuban Americans," in Sandra McKay and Sau-ling Cynthia Wong, (eds.), 166–192.

García, Ofelia, Joshua Fishman, Silvia Burunat, and Michael Gertner. 1985. "The Hispanic press in the United States: contents and prospects." In Joshua Fishman, *The Rise and fall of the ethnic revival.* Berlin: Mouton, 343–362.

García, Ofelia, Isabel Evangelista, Mabel Martínez, Carmen Disla, and Bonifacio Paulino. 1988. "Spanish language use and attitudes: A study of two New York city communities." *Language in Society* 17: 475–512.

Green, Kate. 1993. The genesis and development of Dominican vernacular Spanish: Evidence of creolization? [Unpublished Dissertation proposal, CUNY Graduate Center.]

Guitart, Jorge. 1982. "Conservative vs. radical dialects in Spanish: Implications for language instruction," in Joshua Fishman and Gary Keller (eds.), *Bilingual education for Hispanic students in the U.S.* New York: Teachers College Press, 167–190.

Hays, Constance. 1993. "To Markets! To Markets!" *New York Times*, section 13, November 28, 14–16.

Henríquez Ureña, Pedro. 1940. *El español en Santo Domingo.* Buenos Aires: La Universidad de Buenos Aires.

Institute for Puerto Rican Policy (IPRP). 1993. "Puerto Ricans and other Latinos in the United States: March 1992," *Data-note on the Puerto Rican Community* #14.

Keller, Gary. 1975. "Spanish *tú* and *Ud*: Patterns of interchange," in William Milán, John Staczek and Juan Zamora (eds.), *1974 Colloquium on Spanish and Portuguese Linguistics.* Washington, D.C.: Georgetown University Press, 84–96.

Labov, William. 1966. *The social stratification of English in New York City.* Washington, D.C.: Center for Applied Linguistics.

Leo, John. 1994. "Some straight talk on a bad bilingual plan," *Daily News*, Nov. 2 [Reprinted from *US NEWS and World Report*].

Lipski, John. 1979. Pronominal hybridization of Central American Spanish in the United States. [Unpublished MS.]

Lope Blanch, Juan. 1968. *El español de América.* Madrid: Ediciones Alcalá.

López Morales, Humberto. 1971. *Estudios sobre el español de Cuba.* Long Island City, N.Y.: Las Américas Publishing Co.

Mann, Evelyn, and Salvo, Joseph. 1984. *Characteristics of New Hispanic immigrants to New York City: A comparison of Puerto Rican and non-Puerto Rican Hispanics.* New York: Department of City Planning.

McKay, Sandra and Sau-ling Cynthia Wong (eds.) 1988. *Language Diversity: Problem or resource.* New York: Newbury House.

Megenney, William. 1982. "Elementos subsaháricos en el español dominicano," in Orlando Alba (ed.), *El español del Caribe.* Santiago, R. D.: Universidad Católica Madre y Maestra.

—— 1990. *Africa en Santo Domingo: Su herencia lingüística.* Santo Domingo: Editorial Tiempo.

Moreno de Alba, José. 1988. *El español en América.* México, D.F.: Fondo De Cultura Económica.

Navarro Tomás, Tomás. 1948. *El español de Puerto Rico.* Río Piedras, Puerto Rico: Editorial de la Universidad de Puerto Rico.

Onishi, Norimitsu. 1994. "An 'America-first' challenger is resonating in English Only," *NY Times,* Nov. 6, 1994.

Orlov, Ann, and Reed Ueda. 1980. "Central and South Americans," in Stephen Thernstrom (ed.), *Harvard encyclopedia of American ethnic groups.* Cambridge, Mass.: Harvard University Press.

Paladin, Karina. 1994. "The Hispanic media in the United States," *Mexican Notebook,* Vol. 3, No. 9, December, 3–5.

Rosario, Rubén del. 1970. *El español de América.* Sharon, Conn.: Troutman Press.

Rosario, Sandra. 1994. American identity and the language question: Should English be the official language of the United States? Paper presented at Hunter College Mellon Fellows annual luncheon, April 21. [Unpublished MS.]

Rosenblat, Angel. 1962. "La diversidad lingüística americana," in Rosario, 1970: 132–140.

Schmitt, E. 1989. "English-only bill ignited debate and fear on L. I.," *New York Times,* February 14, B3.

Silva-Corvalán, Carmen. 1986. "Bilingualism and language change: The extension of *estar* in Los Angeles Spanish," *Language* 62: 587–608.

Steinhauer, Jennifer. 1994. "Killing of immigrant stuns a Brooklyn area," *NY Times,* Oct. 1994.

Terrell, Tracy. 1982a. "Current trends in the investigation of Cuban and Puerto Rican phonology," in John Amastae and Lucía Elías-Olivares (eds.), 47–70.

—— 1982b. "Relexificación en el español dominicano: Implicaciones para la educación," in Orlando Alba (ed.), *El español del Caribe: Ponencias del VI simposio de dialectología.* Santiago, R.D.: Universidad Católica Madre y Maestra.

Valdés de Montano, Luz María, and Robert Smith. 1994. *Mexican migration to the New York City metropolitan area: An Analysis of selected socio-demographic* traits and the links being formed between a Mexican sending region and New York. New York: Tinker Foundation.

Varela, Beatriz. 1992. *El español cubano-americano*. New York: Senda Nueva de Ediciones.

Veltman, Carl. 1988. *The future of the Spanish language in the United States*. New York/Washington, DC: Hispanic Policy Development Project.

Weinrich, Uriel. 1968. *Languages in Contact*. The Hague: Mouton.

Wong Fillmore, Lily. 1991. "When learning a second language means losing the first." *Early Childhood Research Quarterly* 6(3): 323–46.

Zamora Munné, Juan. 1976. *Indigenismos en la lengua de los conquistadores*. Río Piedras, P.R.: Editorial Universitaria.

Zamora Vicente, Alonso. 1979. *Dialectología española*. 2ed. Madrid: Gredos.

Zentella, Ana Celia. 1981. "Language variety among Puerto Ricans," in Charles A. Ferguson and Shirley Brice Heath (eds.), *Language in the U.S.A.* Cambridge; Cambridge University Press, 218–238.

—— 1990a. "Lexical leveling in four New York City Spanish dialects: Linguistic and social factors," *Hispania* 73 (4): 1094–1105.

—— 1990b. "Returned migration, language, and identity: Puerto Rican bilinguals in dos worlds/two mundos," in Florian Coulmas (ed.), *Spanish in the U.S.A.: New quandries and prospects* [Special issue]. *International Journal of the Sociology of Language* 84: 81–100.

—— 1990c. "Who supports English-Only and why?: The Influence of social variables and questionnaire methodology," in Karen Adams and David Brink (eds.), *Perspectives on Official English: The campaign for English as the official language of the USA*. Berlin/New York: Mouton de Gruyter, 160–177.

—— 1994a. Towards an anthropolitical linguistic perspective on the Spanish competence of U.S. Latinos. Paper delivered at NWAV, New Ways of Analyzing Variation. Stanford University, Oct. 21. [Unpublished MS.]

—— 1994b. The Anti-Spanish thrust of the English-Only movement. Paper delivered at American Anthropological Association, Atlanta, Ga., Nov. 30. [Unpublished MS.]

—— 1997. *Growing up bilingual: Puerto Rican children in New York City*. Oxford: Basil Blackwell.

SPANISH *in* NEW YORK

A Moving Landscape

Antonio Muñoz Molina

On my street corner, at 107th and Broadway, there are almost daily get-togethers, except on the very coldest winter days, of Cuban seniors. They disappear during the harshest weeks of snow and ice. But as soon as the sun manages to stay out for a while and warms up the air, there they are once more, wearing caps and earmuffs and heavy jackets in winter and *guayaberas* with white socks in summer. You can tell by looking at them, even from afar, by the way they sit in their chairs on the edge of the sidewalk, by the way they gesture with their hands, that they're not from around here. And you need only draw near to hear their Cuban way of talking and with it, there comes that eternal tangle of diatribes about trivial issues, the memories of Havana back in the fifties, and of Fidel Castro, who just never dies, *chico*, and about that Cuban food place that shut down a few months back because of higher rents. It was called La Rosita and it was owned by a Spanish guy who had moved to Cuba after the war and later moved here, like so many others. A little further south is La Flor de Mayo, which sells Chinese and *criollo* food: The veteran waiters are from Peru and the delivery boys and kitchen help are from Mexico, as are the ones in charge of cutting and selling flowers at the Korean grocery stores. In the supermarket the chatty cash register girls, who all wear their shiny hair pulled back tight in the style of Jennifer Lopez, switch with complete ease between the Spanish of Santo Domingo and that of Puerto Rico and then into the expeditious English of New York: The customers may talk to them in English, but, among themselves, they keep up their racy cackling banter in Spanish, about their boyfriends and dates, about their weight-loss diets, and about the Mexican and Colombian TV soaps they watch on channels beamed in from Miami. They leap with elasticity from one language to another, but sometimes they mix them together: "You guys take a look at the *moreno chaparrito*."

Traveling north a few subway stations, I can immerse myself in the populous Dominican neighborhood of Washington Heights. Close by, on Amsterdam Avenue, there is a Mexican meat market, touchingly called Los dos Cuñados Meat Market. And if I cross the park, I come to Spanish Harlem, El Barrio, where what you hear is the language of Puerto Rico, with its Caribbean singsong and its PR L-sounds: *Puelto Rico, Puelco, Niuyol.*

In Miami, on a single afternoon, in the company of a Colombian publisher and bookseller who came from Bogotá fourteen years ago and is perfectly bilingual, I go to the massively Colombian Radio Caracol, to a television program directed by a Cuban called Ricardo Brown, and that same evening I find myself in the studio of Peruvian Jaime Bayly, who goes through his monologues looking into the camera with a serenity that falls somewhere between Liman and Buddhist and the subtle sarcasm that his accent so clearly facilitates. Miami, which, until not long ago, was a branch of Cuba, now harbors a multitude of newcomers from all over Latin America, so that one also hears the accents of the River Plate, of Venezuela, of Bolivia, of Chile. In New York you can even hear the rarest, the oldest of Spanish argots, the Judeo-Spanish that some of the children and grandchildren—especially the grandchildren—of immigrants from the old Ottoman Empire now nostalgically wish to recover. An acquaintance gives me the manuscript of a book to read, a work that compiles expressions that he heard his grandparents use, expressions that nobody in the family paid any attention to because they thought of them as vestiges of a discredited and anachronistic culture, Old World baggage of which the sons and daughters of émigrés wanted to rid themselves: "Al amigo que no es sierto, con un ojo cerrado y el otro avierto"; "Eskupe en su cara, piensa que está lloviendo"; "Para palabra y palabra su moko savrozo."

Nor can I forget the "super" at my place, David Jiménez, who came from Guatemala twenty-five years ago, fleeing the civil war, and who is now so proud of his daughter, who went "al College"; or Dr. Valentín Fuster, who speaks Spanish with the most extraordinary mix of accents—Catalan and English, English and Catalan; or Dr. Miguel Trujillo, who maintains his Seville accent intact after more than thirty years.

Paradoxically, the best observation point from which to understand the Spanish language right now is in the United States of America, in cities like New York, Miami, or Los Angeles, which serve as a confluence for all rivers of the language, for every accent. And where one's ear becomes attuned to distinguishing and appreciating its musical diversity, while the intellect is simultaneously astonished by its splendid unity. Each and every variation is immediately intelligible for anyone who speaks the language: Instead of limiting it, they enrich it, because they teach us ways of calling things that are different from our own and yet never deny us their meaning—as long as we are paying attention. When we were kids, many of us read the Superman comic strips translated in Mexico by the Navaro Publishing Company in which the bad guys (*malos*) were *pillos* (scoundrels) and the autos (*coches*) were *carros* (cars), and they had *cajuelas* (trunks) instead of *maleteros* (boots). Then, when we were teens, we got seriously into Latin American literature. We read *Mafalda* comic books, and their Argentine *porteño* language was never as much a problem as an inducement. Our children laughed themselves sick watching *El Chavo del Ocho y el Chapulín Colorado,* just as we had laughed at Cantinflas. And those who let themselves be seduced by the word fest of *Betty la Fea* (the original title of *Ugly Betty*) now have a chance to repeat their elation with yet another series I had heard much about in Bogotá, the complete collection of which I brought with me from Miami: namely, *Sin tetas no hay paraíso* (which translates literally as "Without tits there's no Paradise").

Let me just say that I'm not getting haughty about the language of Spain, seeing as how things are as they are in my country: Rather, I'm just trying to establish the existence of a reality that makes me breathe deeper and realize that I am a citizen of a much broader and more open world than any meager little national or regional or local space. I'm not getting haughty because, among other reasons, in that world Spain is not the capital, but rather a province, not only behind Mexico but also behind the United States, where there are now forty-four million people whose native language is Spanish. We have the good luck of sharing in that world of words, although, of course, this guarantees nothing: The Hispanic world has, from time immemorial, tended toward closing itself into its own territorial, physical, and mental interior, and the extension and universality of our language coexist, strikingly, with an acute cultural fragmentation. We tend to live in smaller, stuffier rooms with a lot less ventilation than a really big house. We even tend to shut ourselves up in closets and attics within each of our respective rooms. Books circulate little from one country to another, not only in Spain and America, but within the interior of the Americas themselves. No more than a handful of names maintain a sustained languagewide presence, no magazine is a truly borderless reference point. *Granta,* the *New York Review of Books,* the *Times Literary Supplement,* these are all accepted benchmarks in any English-language cultural sphere. The *Revista de Occidente y Sur,* in other times, and, later, *Vuelta* and now *Letras Libres* have pursued this purpose with rigorous merit, but perhaps what we are lacking is entrepreneurial drive and a broader viewpoint with which to achieve it, just as we are lacking a sufficiently broad public with which to maintain it.

Personally, the discovery of the practical and tangible universality of Spanish has been one of the greatest gifts of my life, as a literary enthusiast and as a citizen. I believe that it is an antidote against suffocating Spanish skirmishes, against verbal jingoism, in which they try to miseducate us from the time we are small, and against today's passion for balkanization. Spanish in not in danger because its future doesn't depend on the mediocre comings and goings of Spain's politics or on the idiocies of our education system. Spanish is the language of the colonizers and also of those who rebelled against them, the language of the first books printed on the American continent and that of some of the most beautiful novels being written right now. It is spoken by those who have emigrated escaping hunger and those who are fleeing political persecution, the language of dissidence and orthodoxy, and, even as we speak, it is the language of the immigrant newcomer who is washing dishes or delivering food on a bike and of the young physicist who has come to the States to get his master's degree and of the banker who attends some of his wealthy clients in Spanish and of the ER doctor who has learned the language in order to understand patients like the one who has just been brought to him. Spanish is a country that permits one to travel through an unlimited variety of landscapes, without being hindered at any border, a fluent and flexible identity that permits us to be from many places at the same time and from one alone.

Now, between one group and another, that they seem bent on leaving me without a country—with the ferocious energy and demented fervor of Groucho Marx, when he tore apart a train in order to feed the locomotive that was driving it at breakneck speed—at least I can have the peace of mind of knowing that they can't take away my language.

TRANSLATED BY DAN NEWLAND

MUSIC AND ART: LATINO, LATIN AMERICAN, AMERICAN

NEW YORK'S LATIN MUSIC LANDMARKS

Frank M. Figueroa

Soon after Hispanic musicians began to settle in New York at the end of World War I, the city became the capital of Latin music. Artists were drawn to the Big Apple by its recording and entertainment industries. Most of the new immigrants first lived near the port, in an area called Red Hook in Brooklyn. Later on, many of them moved to East Harlem, a section that eventually was called Spanish Harlem or "El Barrio."

LANDMARKS IN "EL BARRIO HISPANO"

As would be expected, the first Latin music landmarks in New York were to be found in Spanish Harlem. The earliest locations were small music and record stores, social clubs, movie theaters and musician hangouts such as pool halls and cafes. These were indeed humble landmarks, but quite significant in the history of Latin music in New York City.

Hispanic musicians first found employment in New York City, by providing music for small parties in private homes. It has been reported that, in 1920, Puerto Rican composer and musician Rafael Hernández was perhaps the first to play Latin music in New York when he entertained at an apartment party in Spanish Harlem. These apartment parties provided an escape from the boredom of factory work for the "barrio people." They were usually held on Saturday nights at the apartment of a family who provided room for dancing to the music of a small local group. There was a twenty-five cent admission charge. Since it was the time of Prohibition, the family sold distilled rum and home brewed beer illegally at twenty-five cents per drink. The income provided the family with funds to pay the rent.

As the community grew, social clubs were organized and dances were scheduled in rented reception halls. It has been generally acknowledged that the first bona fide Latin dance was held at the Golden Casino at 111th Street and 5th Avenue. The hall was rented for the night by a Puerto Rican civic association. Another such establishment was the Park Palace Caterer's Hall, located on the corner of 110th Street and 5th Avenue in an area next to Central Park and Frawley Circle. It was predominantly a Jewish catering hall where weddings and other special occasions were celebrated. Mrs. Anna Hersh, proprietress of the Palace Caterers, rented out her premises for Saturday night dances. Eventually, that spot would become the most important Latin music landmark in Spanish Harlem. There were actually two dance halls in that location. The larger one, known as the Park Plaza, was upstairs and below was the Park Palace, a smaller facility. Frequently, different Latin bands would be performing simultaneously in the two halls. In the following years, more dance halls in the neighborhood became available to the Latin community. Dances were regularly scheduled at such places as: the Club Cubanacán—114th Street and Lennox Avenue, (MOP) Mutualista Obrero Puertorriqueño—110th Street and Lexington Avenue, the San Juan Club—102nd Street and Madison Avenue, American Legion Hall—East 112th Street and the Oddfellows Temple—106th Street between Park and Lexington Avenues.

Some of the Latino community's music needs were met at first by variety stores owned by non-Hispanic businessmen. Some of them hired Hispanics as sales clerks in their record departments. A Spaniard named Daniel Castellanos claimed to be the first New York Hispanic merchant of Spanish-language records. His first music store, located in the South Ferry area of lower Manhattan, was established before 1922. Castellanos later opened two record shops in the Barrio section of East Harlem. Eventually, some Puerto Rican entrepreneurs bought record shops from their non-Hispanic owners. One of the first to do so was Victoria Hernández, who, in 1927, bought a shop from its Jewish owners.

Another pioneer in the Latin music business in New York was Puerto Rican Gabriel Oller. His Tatay's Spanish Music Center was located around the corner from the Park Palace, on 5th Avenue. He sold guitars, sheet music, 78 recordings and piano rolls. Oller's establishment was a gathering place for musicians who came to purchase instrument parts, to engage in small talk and once in a while to make recording masters. Gabriel was a sound engineer and provided a service for artists who wanted to make acetate-recording masters. The artists in turn sold them to big record companies. Oller named his test record service Dynasonic Records. Years later, he established the very successful independent recording labels Coda and SMC.

The music store founded in 1927 by Victoria Hernández was another Latin music landmark in El Barrio. It was the first Puerto Rican–owned record shop in the community. Victoria was Puerto Rican composer Rafael Hernández's sister, and she gave it the name "Almacenes Hernández." The store was located at 1635 Madison Avenue between 113th and 114th Streets. In 1930, the business was moved to 1724 Madison Avenue. In the room behind the store, Victoria kept a piano with which she gave private lessons and Rafael Hernández used to write some of his compositions. Allegedly, that is where he wrote his famous *Lamento Borincano*. Sister Victoria tells that Rafael would meet regularly with his fellow musicians and other expatriates in that room to alleviate their nostalgia by drinking rum and singing Puerto Rican songs. In 1927, Victoria Hernández founded Hispano Records in an attempt to provide recording opportunities for her brother's music. Her efforts failed when she could not beat the competition presented by the big recording companies.

Casa Seigel, one of the non-Hispanic variety stores in El Barrio, remained in business until the 1950s. Its owner, Sidney Seigel, founded Seeco Records. For many years, the label featured some of the most popular Latin artists. In the early 1940s, Victoria Hernández sold her record shop to Puerto Rican Luis Cuevas. He kept the name "Almacenes Hernández." Soon after, Cuevas founded Verne Records, a label that became a favorite in the Latin community. In the following years, other record shops such as the famous Casa Latina, owned by Vicente Barreiro opened in El Barrio.

Musical instruments and records were sold in a variety of stores. At 116th Street and Lennox Avenue, there was a combination bakery and musical instrument shop. The owner was a Cuban man known to everyone as Simón. In addition to delicious pastries, he sold bongó and conga drums as well as skins for drumheads. In those days, he would sell you a set of bongós for $8.00 and a conga drum for $15.00. The drums were heat-tunable with the drumheads tacked on.

El Barrio also had several musician hangouts such as "El Billar de los Músicos" (The Musician's Pool Hall) at 113th Street and Madison Avenue. The place also served as a hiring hall for unemployed musicians. There was a blackboard on which musicians could post their names if they were available for engagements. The owner, a Spaniard known as "El Gallego," also listed notices on the walls concerning available gigs. Another popular gathering point for Latin musicians was "Piquito Marcano's Photo Shop," located on the corner of 111th Street and 5th Avenue. The owner was Pedro "Piquito" Marcano, the singer who founded the famous Cuarteto Marcano. There was also a shoe repair shop that attracted musicians seeking to share news and to hear about job opportunities. "La Zapatera Collazo" was named after the proprietor. He was a very generous man, always willing to lend musicians a helping hand. Collazo offered them cash loans and even a place to sleep overnight. Singer Bobby Capó was one of those who slept in the back room of the shop when he had no place to stay.

The Latino community also found entertainment in the movie and show theaters that sprang up in El Barrio. During the silent film era, local musicians provided background music for the movies. Such was the case with the most famous Spanish theater in the area, "El Teatro Hispano," also known as "El Teatro Campoamor." Later on, some of the biggest names in Latin show business graced the stage of El Teatro Hispano.

Other barrio theaters were the Photoplay Theater (Teatro San Jose), El Teatro Municipal (El Meaíto), the Azteca theater and El Teatro Triboro.

LANDMARKS BEYOND THE BARRIO

Starting in the early 1940s, the Latin community from El Barrio began to move to other areas of New York. A large number of them settled in the areas of the East Bronx that began at East 138th Street and reached north as far as 177th Street. In 1943, Victoria Hernández opened a record shop on Prospect Avenue, one block east of Westchester Avenue. Composer Tite Amadeo and his son Mike established their music store known as Casa Amadeo. Years later, Al Santiago opened his Casa Alegre at 852 Westchester Avenue and La Casa Latina del Bronx began operations at 217 Brook Avenue, near 135th Street.

The Bronx had its good share of ballrooms. Perhaps the most important was the Tropicana Ballroom located on Westchester Avenue. Its bandstand featured such groups as Rafael Muñoz, Arsenio Rodríguez, Gilberto Valdés, Conjunto Casino, Vicentico Valdés and Charlie Palmieri. The Hunts Point Palace on Southern Boulevard and 163rd Street was the scene of many musical battles between the top Latin bands in the city. Other ballrooms worthy of mention are the Caravana Club (the home of the pachanga) located at 149th Street and Brook Avenue, and the Tropicoro, operated by boxer Carlos Ortiz on Longwood Avenue.

There were several movie theaters in the Bronx and some of them booked stage shows on special occasions. However, the Teatro Puerto Rico on Brook Avenue was the only one to offer a continuing series of live shows. Chucho Montalbán, who was movie star Ricardo Montalban's older brother, managed the theater. Chucho was able to entice international stars such as Libertad Lamarque, Pedro Vargas, Leo Marini and Bobby Capó to perform at the Teatro Puerto Rico.

As would be expected, the most important Latin music landmarks are to be found in midtown Manhattan. For example, one of the first nightclubs featuring Latin entertainment in New York City was El Chico. Spaniard Benito Collada and his Puerto Rican wife, singer Rosita Berrios, opened the club in 1927 in Greenwich Village, New York. For several decades, El Chico was one of New York's favorite nightspots. From then on, many other future Latin landmarks came into existence. In 1933, the Club Maison Royal in midtown Manhattan made its debut with Antobal's Cubans as the main attraction. Antobal Azpiazú led the band. He had taken over the group originally organized by his brother Don Azpiazú. Cuban pianist and composer Eliseo Grenet in partnership with Roche and Richards opened the cabaret El Yumurí on 52nd Street and Broadway in 1935. One year later, Cubans impresarios Roche and Roldán opened the nightclub La Conga on Broadway between 52nd and 53rd Streets. In 1940, the same Mr. Roche established the Club Cuba in mid-Manhattan and gave the house band job to Machito and his orchestra. In subsequent years, the Havana-Madrid, the China Doll and other similar nightspots emerged.

In addition to the clubs where only Latin music was played, there were many cabarets featuring two bands, one playing American music and the other a rumba band. That was the policy in such places as the Stork Club, El Morocco, Copacabana, Rio-Bamba, Versailles and many others. The Arcadia and Roseland Ballrooms on Broadway also drew more than their share of Latin dancers. Those who preferred more typical music favored weekend dances at the Hotel Diplomat on West 53rd Street, one block from Times Square, the Audobon Ballroom on the upper West Side, the Manhattan Center on West 34th Street and the old Lincoln Square Center on West 66th Street. Also worthy of mention as landmarks are the Casa Galicia, originally on West 14th Street, the Club Caborrojeño on Broadway and 145th Street, and the Broadway Casino in the area of Washington Heights.

The most important Latin music landmark in New York City, however, has to be the Palladium Ballroom on 53rd Street and Broadway. In an article I wrote a few years ago, I stated: "On the corner of Broadway and 53rd Street, in New York City, for twenty years there existed a magic place called the Palladium Ballroom. Access to the Hall of the Mambo Kings was gained by climbing a rather steep staircase. At the foot of these steps there was a ticket booth where one could purchase the right to participate in a unique musical experience. The moment your foot touched this hallowed ground you were captivated by the throbbing Latin rhythms and transported to Mamboland. There you remained in an animated state until you descended back into the reality of Broadway."

The Palladium Ballroom was the Mecca of all good Latin dancers in the Metropolitan Area and remained as such until its closing on May 1, 1966.

Not too far from the Palladium Ballroom on 53rd Street and 7th Avenue was another music landmark that will forever be remembered by Latin musicians—the Lasalle Cafeteria. It was nothing more than a cafeteria with many tables where musicians and other lovers of Latin music met. The Lasalle Cafeteria was open 24 hours a day and one could count on meeting Latin musicians there at any time. It was ideally located next to the China Doll Club and the Palladium Ballroom. It was convenient for musicians from those and other nearby clubs to spend their rest periods at the cafeteria. While sitting at a table sipping a cup of coffee, one could eavesdrop on a conversation among well-known artists, get the latest information about job openings, critiques about the performance of popular orchestras, and gossip about Latin artists.

Once the Palladium Ballroom closed its doors in 1966, other clubs moved in to take its place. One favorite spot was The Chez José, located at the Hotel Park Plaza, 50 West 77th Street between 8th and Columbus Avenues. Although it opened for business in mid-1965, it did not attract big crowds until 1966. The Chez José closed in 1970.

In the Yorkville section of Manhattan, two dance halls had been trying to lure the Latin dancers for quite some time. They were the Gloria Palace and the Corso Ballroom, located at 205 East 86th Street, off the corner of 3rd Avenue. Ironically, in the early 1930s, Desi Arnaz had introduced the Cuban conga to the predominantly German-American dancers at the Gloria Palace. It was El Corso, however, that became the legitimate heir to the Palladium's Wednesday night dancing devotees. The crowds were so large on Wednesday night that by 1968, El Corso was open to Latin dancers five nights a week.

Monday night has traditionally been a popular night for jazz jam sessions and Latin music *descargas* (jam sessions). Most musicians are off on that night and are ready to relax, listening to and playing with their peers. In New York City, many of these sessions have been held in small clubs in Greenwich Village. One famous Monday night Latin jazz descarga took place for almost 30 years at the Village Gate, a club located near the corner of Bleecker and Thompson Streets in Manhattan. In 1966, DJ Symphony Sid hosted the first of the "Salsa Meets Jazz" concerts at the Village Gate. Some of the biggest names in Latin music performed there to the delight of thousands of their fans. Sadly, on February 22, 1993, the Village Gate had to close its doors due to financial reasons. Another Latin music venue that must be mentioned is The Cheetah, located on 52nd Street and 8th Avenue. It was the scene of many memorable happenings, including a historic concert by the Fania All-Stars. On the night of August 26, 1971, Fania Records put together an all-star aggregation (including 14 musicians and 7 singers) led by Johnny Pacheco. The concert produced a total of four records, *All-Stars Live at the Cheetah*, a double album, and *Our Latin Thing*, also in two volumes. The concert was filmed by Leon Gast and a movie "Our Latin Thing" was released. The nightclub remained a favorite dancing spot for a few years, but eventually fell into hard times and had to close in 1974.

In the ensuing years, new clubs emerged. Two of the best known are La Maganette at 825 Third Avenue on the corner of 50th Street, and the Copacabana Club on 57th Street between 11th and 12th Avenues, which closed and recently reopened at 560 West 34th Street. We apologize for any names we may have missed, for surely there has never been a shortage of places to listen and dance to good Latin music in the Big Apple. The old landmarks may have disappeared from the New York scene, but they will live forever in our memory. We shall never forget such places as the Park Plaza, the Club Caborrojeño, the Tropicana Club and the Palladium Ballroom. On their dance floors, our parents and grandparents and in some cases even we danced away many an evening. The new generations have seen new landmarks rise. In due time, they shall become as venerable as the ones mentioned above. We can be certain that all those landmarks that we have remembered over the years shall help us to unlock the precious musical memories we keep in our hearts.

THE STORY *of* NUYORICAN SALSA

Ed Morales

In some ways it's obvious what we mean by salsa. Salsa is a style of music that dominates dance floor tastes in Latin music clubs throughout the United States and Latin America, with extravagant, clave-driven, Afro-Cuban-derived songs anchored by piano, horns, and rhythm section and sung by a velvety voiced crooner in a sharkskin suit. On the other hand the definition of salsa is the subject of endless dispute in Latin music circles. If mambo was a constellation of rhythmic tendencies, then, as leading salsa sonero (lead singer) Rubén Blades once said, salsa is a concept, not a particular rhythm. But although salsa is nothing more than a new spin on the traditional rhythms of Cuban music—son, cha-cha, mambo, guaracha, guaguancó, and danzón—it is also at once a modern marketing concept and the cultural voice of a new generation. Though the quicker, almost synthetic-feeling tempo salsa is played at gives the music a new feeling, it is still based on the traditional Cuban son structure—a basic melody is introduced, followed by a coro section in which both the singer and the band are allowed to improvise.

Salsa is different from its forebears because it represents the crystallization of a Latino identity in New York in the early 1960s. By the time people became conscious of it, the crystallization was complete. The man who first used the term salsa to publicize New York-based Latin music, a magazine editor and graphic designer named Izzy Sanabria, pointed out that many musicians who are now associated with the genre worked hard to innovate new styles without knowing that they were playing what would become known as salsa. Many musicians actively rejected the term. Mambo bandleader Machito said salsa was nothing but a new version of what he had been playing for forty years. When Tito Puente was asked about salsa, he commented sourly, "I'm a musician, not a cook." But salsa as sauce is an excellent metaphor for cultural mixing, and a reference to a special kind of spiciness. And as Sanabria said, if he had been completely honest and said that salsa was nothing but the same old music that bandleaders like Machito and Puente were playing, would the world have paid attention to New York Latin music?

Several urban legends surrounding the creation or coining of the term salsa are worth reflecting on, if only because they locate the energy that informs the genre. In the most simplistic sense, salsa refers to a mixture of ingredients that "spices up" the proceedings. Most food eaten in Latin American countries would be unthinkable without local sauces, or salsas. So when in 1932 Ignacio Piñeiro, the pioneering Cuban bassist and orchestra leader, shouted out "salsa" on *Échale salsita*, he was saying "Put some salsa on it," telling his band to shift the tempo and put the dancers into high gear. Later in that decade, renowned vocalist Beny Moré would merely shouted "salsa!" to acknowledge a musical moment's heat, as well as perhaps to express a kind of cultural nationalist sloganeering, celebrating the "hotness" or "spiciness" of Latin American cultures. (Celia Cruz continued this tradition in a similar vein with her own, perhaps more feminine slogan, *Azucar* [Sugar]!) Finally, "salsa" was legendarily invoked by Izzy Sanabria as a way to categorize the modern version of Afro-Cuban music being made in New York in the late 1960s and early 1970s. The ingredients brought from Cuba to New York were given a different flavor by a multinational group of Latino, African-American, and sometimes Anglo-American musicians who were essential to the creation of salsa.

The mambo era of the '40s and '50s was critical to Latin music in the United States because it popularized the basic Afro-Cuban sound, while introducing an array of international contributors operating within the context of the New York and Los Angeles jazz scenes. Mambo was a significant force in keeping the jazz big band alive, albeit in a different context, during a period when the smaller configurations of the bebop era took jazz in a different direction. But as the 1950s wound down, two important shifts occurred: The Latin big bands began to shrink in members, going the way of the old jazz big band; and the 1959 Cuban revolution greatly reduced contact between the island and New York musicians. The domination of the New York Latino community by Puerto Ricans, which had begun in the post–World War II era, now entered a new dimension. Afro-Cuban music being played in New York began to evolve into something different.

The post-mambo-era Latin music that prevailed in New York in the 1960s, played by bands led by percussionist Ray Barretto and pianist Eddie Palmieri, for example, had two major influences. The first was music fads like charanga and pachanga from Cuba, which continued to provide the latest in styles and arrangements for New York–area players until the political economic and cultural blockade that set in after the Cuban Missile Crisis of 1962. The second was the growing interaction between New York Latinos and African-Americans in the working-class neighborhoods of Manhattan, Brooklyn, and the Bronx. The result of that interaction, the so-called Nuyorican or New York Latino identity, would be a hybrid culture, basically Puerto-Rican in-spired, but incorporating influences from many of the existing U.S. Latino groups, mostly from Cuba and from Caribbean cities like Panama City, Cartagena and Bar-ranquilla, Colombia, Caracas, Venezuela, and Santo Domingo, Dominican Republic.

The big fad from Havana in the late 1950s and early 1960s was the reborn charanga style, a throwback to the early part of the century that was a kind of reaction to the slick mambo ballroom style. Led by the extremely precise and swing-strong Orquesta Aragón, the charanga bands helped popularize cha-cha and several variations of mambo, guaracha, and guaguancó. Charanga's main features were the use of flute and violins in the role that the horn section would otherwise play. The charangas that were imported to New York by Cuban migrants like bandleader Gilberto Valdés were super-fast versions of the stately, traditional danzón. Their speed allowed for a flippant deliv-ery by the vocalists, and the high-range flutes embellished the jams like up-the-neck electric guitar solos.

Charanga orchestras maintained a strong influence over the New York Latin music scene through the mid-1970s. But in their early years, they trained musicians who would play a major role in what became known as salsa. After Gilberto Valdés's first percussionist, Mongo Santamaría, left in 1957 to become involved in the Latin-fusion experiments on the West Coast spearheaded by vibist Cal Tjader, Valdés took on Johnny Pacheco, a young Dominican congero who would galvanize the core players of salsa in the years to come.

In 1959 Pacheco, who had arrived in the city ten years before, left the Valdés group with the New York-born Puerto Rican pianist Charlie Palmieri to form Charanga Duboney, a charanga orchestra dominated by flutes and violins. It only lasted eight months, but its album, called *Viva Palmieri*, set the stage for the new harmonic and arranging trends that would eventually become the standard for salsa orchestras. The band was smaller; the harmonies used by backup singers became tighter, sharpening the call and response. Pacheco would move on to form his own band, releasing *Johnny Pacheco y su Charanga Vol. 1* on Alegre Records in 1962. In an attempt to distinguish himself from Charlie Palmieri's Charanga Duboney, he began to call his music *pachanga*, despite the fact that it didn't vary from the charanga style. (Duboney re-leased a charanga album in 1962 called *Salsa Na' Ma*, meaning, "it just needs a little salsa, or spice," which also anticipated the use of the word salsa.)

Pacheco was taking advantage of a dance fad called the pachanga, which lasted for a few years in the early to mid-1960s and involved a hopping and sliding turn that re-called the North American Charleston. Eschewing trips downtown to the trendy Pal-ladium, the dancers who flocked to see Pacheco's and Palmieri's bands were remaining in their local Bronx and East Harlem neighborhoods and going to clubs like Teatro Puerto Rico and the Park Plaza. Smaller and more flexible than the Latin big bands of the mambo era, the charanga orchestra created a new style, but also set musicians off in a search for ever-more different fusions in what had been a static post–Tito Puente–Machito world. The Pacheco-Palmieri era, as well as the move away from Midtown to the barrios, ushered in a sensibility called típico, a rustic, simpler, funkier feel that coincided with nostalgia for the Caribbean lands left behind.

Conga-playing bandleader Ray Barretto was also a significant contributor to the charanga craze, especially on albums like *Charanga Moderna*. Barretto, a Brooklyn native of Puerto Rican descent, took up playing the conga while stationed with the U.S. Army in Germany. On *Charanga Moderna*, the flute-playing characteristic of the genre seems to fly wildly off the rhythm section and urgent bursts of Alfredo de la Fe's violin. The simple cha-cha rhythms of *El Watusi*, however, presaged the soul-psychedelic path that Barretto would follow in the mid to late-1960s. His version of psychedelia had more to do with extended recording time than with actual rock-influenced sonic tendencies, but it still expressed a preoccupation with spiritual inner growth.

La Perfecta, an eight-piece band led by pianist Eddie Palmieri, Charlie Palmieri's brother, continued the trend toward consolidation and a return to the típico. The band at its peak in the early 1960s featured the invigorating tenor of Puerto Rican-born Ismael Quintana and an unusually emphasized trombone section of Barry Rogers and the Brazilian-born Joao Donato. The basic Cuban son piano riffs that ran through both charanga and bugaloo were the backbone of La Perfecta's dance sound. Another key member of La Perfecta was percussionist Manny Oquendo, who went on in the 1970s to form Libre, an orchestra that would carry the essence of the golden age salsa sound well into the 1990s.

Eddie Palmieri's hard-driving and classical- and jazz-influenced piano style personified the cutting edge of salsa and Latin jazz. He and Charlie, who died at sixty-two in 1988, were gifted and innovative pianists, giants in the genre. In his early teens Eddie was already developing a highly original soloing technique that opened the door to improvisation. Eddie's first major gig came in 1958, when he joined Tito Rodríguez's band. Two years later he left to go solo, and in 1961 formed La Perfecta. La Perfecta's frontlining of the trombone section was a precursor to the signature sound of the 1970s Golden Age of Salsa.

In his 1980 book *El Libro de la Salsa* (The Salsa Book) Venezuelan scholar César Miguel Rondón observed that Palmieri arranged the trombones "in a way that they always sounded sour, with a peculiarly aggressive harshness." The combination of this attitudinal shift from the Afro-Cuban style and the institution of the trombone as a constant counterpoint to the lead vocalist is one of the key staples of the New York salsa sound. Palmieri's own style of frantic, bluesy piano runs worked to a climax with the sassy-sounding brass section, giving a hard New York edge to the Cuban sound.

Palmieri also played with Johnny Pacheco's longest-lasting group, Johnny Pacheco y su Nuevo Tumbao. Pacheco's band returned to the Afro-Cuban style conjunto format, which goes back to the days of Arsenio Rodríguez, but featured two trumpets in the lead instead of Rodríguez's tres. About the same time that Pacheco formed the group, he befriended the man who would become salsa's main impresario, Jerry Masucci, an Italian-American lawyer. The two formed a record label, Fania, which would become synonymous with the best salsa players. Johnny Pacheco y su Nuevo Tumbao's debut album, *Cañonazo* (coincidentally the name of a nightly ritual still held in Havana involving the setting off of several cannon blasts in the tradition of the Spanish regime), was the first of fourteen to be released between 1964 and 1973.

Palmieri released eight albums with La Perfecta, including two in collaboration with Cal Tjader, until Palmieri disbanded it in 1968. In his subsequent solo career, he collaborated with legends like trumpeter Chocolate Armenteros, Cachao López, and the vocalist Cheo Feliciano. In the early 1970s Palmieri flirted with R&B fusion and also cut a classic record with the African-American players Benard Purdie and Ronnie Cuber in 1971 called *Harlem River Drive*.

Although Eddie Palmieri was not as accomplished an arranger and orchestral innovator as his brother, his unusually experimental improvisatory style was a major force in the creation of salsa as a New York-based movement. Palmieri was influenced by European classical music, especially Debussy, and he was also mentored by McCoy Tyner, a jazz-fusion experimentalist. He had a kind of Thelonius Monk-esque style of stressing weak beats, as if he were playing between notes and spaces in the rhythm, as well as a European impressionist shading that was bordering on, and perhaps anticipatory of, the psychedelia that swept the Latin, jazz, and rock worlds in the 1960s.

SALSA'S AFRO–NEW YORK ESSENCE

In Piri Thomas's novel *Down These Mean Streets* and Richard Brooks's film *Blackboard Jungle*, we can see evidence of New York Puerto Ricans forming part of the core constituency of a black-oriented urban culture, which would ultimately explode as hiphop culture in the late 1970s. The antecedents to black-Latin fusion were in the doo-wop era (two of Frankie Lymon's Teenager backups were Latino) and R&B. In the mid-1960s, a new sensibility crystallized in Nuyorican barrios—house parties began playing James Brown funk as well as traditional Latin music. Nuyoricans had the ability to retain the traditional roots of their music while simultaneously incorporating and modernizing African-American influences, which in turn had the effect of influencing soul and R&B.

Bugaloo, its name derived from the same African-style scat onomatopoeia as cha-cha, was the first Latin music to regularly use English lyrics, epitomizing the changing sensibility of a Latino population that was beginning to use English as its dominant language. The creator of the first million-selling Latin music hit, Joe Cuba (Gilberto

Miguel Calderón) was one of the primary practitioners of bugaloo. One of the first generation of New York Puerto Rican musicians, Cuba grew up in East Harlem and learned to play music with peers like Cuban percussionists Patato Valdez, Changuito (who would return to Cuba and become a central piece of the Cuban band Los Van Van), and future West Coast jazz figure Willie Bobo. Cuba began his career in the 1950s by taking over leadership in the Joe Panama Quintet, renaming it the Joe Cuba Sextet. Members of the old Panama crew, who had been playing stripped-down variations of mambo and conjunto music, had been experimenting with the use of English lyrics, and the Cuba edition continued this tendency, expanding its audience by playing at Jewish and Italian dances.

Despite the mix-it-up nature of Cuba's approach, the songs on classics like *Wanted Dead or Alive* are mostly in Spanish, with tunes like *Mujer Divina*, and *La Malanga Brava* capturing the raw feeling of the early Havana-style rumbas. With its lilting vocals and improvisational break, *Así Soy* is a prototypical salsa song. *Triste* is a pretty, unassuming ballad that functions like an R&B slow jam. The sextet's first big success, released in 1965, was a hit single, *El Pito* (I'll Never Go Back To Georgia), from their fourth release for the Tico label, *Estamos Haciendo Algo Bien/We Must Be Doing Something Right*. But the real breakthrough came from the group's main vocalist, Jimmy Sabater, who co-wrote *Bang! Bang!*, an easygoing, vibes-dominated party song that appeared on the 1966 hit album *Wanted: Dead or Alive*, and became one of the most significant top forty Latin hits since rock and roller Ritchie Valens's 1959 hit *La Bamba*. Sabater's *Oh Yeah* also placed on the U.S. charts; he later recorded three solo albums. Cuba went on to record four more albums, the last in 1979, but he was never able to recapture the success of bugaloo's crowning moment in the early 1960s.

Joe Cuba also used slowed-down cha-cha and son rhythms, as well as some catchy English-language choruses, and played up electric keyboards and particularly the vibraphone. His Spanglish classics like *Bang! Bang!* have the feeling of being recorded live at a party, with many background voices like much of the early work of 1970s R&B group Kool and the Gang. With its irresistible yet simple beats, *Bang! Bang!* might be the easiest Latin song to dance to ever recorded. *Oh Yeah* has the feel of a Ramsey Lewis Trio song, with its easy groove, call and response, and cool, vibes-driven melody. *Push, Push, Push* is pretty much more of the same, but its welcome, relentless invitation to groove captures the essence of bugaloo's short but happy life.

Joe Cuba's work is at the core of the Spanglish bugaloo sound, but others made their mark. Johnny Colón, a bandleader and Latin music educator based in East Harlem, released two albums in 1967, *Bugaloo Blues* and *Bugaloo '67*, that are nothing short of state of the art. Other bugaloo classics include *I Like It Like That*, by Cuban vocalist Jimmy Sabater, and *El Watusi*, by rapidly ascending congero-bandleader Ray Barretto. *I Like it Like That* opens a conversation between Afro-Cuban son and Ray Charles-style stride piano. It paved the way for much of the Latin-tinged American pop music by instrumental groups in the mid-1960s. Rock classics like *Tequila*, *Wipe-out*, and the garage classic *96 Tears* sprang from bugaloo's attitude.

THE GOLDEN AGE OF SALSA—THE FANIA YEARS

The closing of the Palladium in 1966 signaled the official end of the mambo era, and the energy and direction of Latin musicians in New York was clearly changing. Promoters like Jerry Masucci became central players, booking groups in a new, Manhattan-oriented club circuit that included places below Ninety-Sixth Street like the original Cheetah Club, Casino 14, the Corso, and the Village Gate. A new magazine, *Latin New York*, appeared, with Izzy Sanabria at the helm.

Musically, Eddie Palmieri's La Perfecta and other groups were moving closer to salsa, as elements of bugaloo and charanga battled with elements of rock and rhythm and blues, all in an environment suddenly bereft of Cuban influence. As a marketing term and social phenomenon, salsa is inextricably linked to Fania Records. Fania's debut album, *Cañonazo*, recorded in 1964 by Pacheco's Nuevo Tumbao group (featuring Pete "El Conde" Rodríguez, who became a Fania All Star, on vocals), is often referred to as the formal beginning of the salsa era, if for nothing else than its decided break from charanga. But with the exception of releases by Bobby Valentín (a Pacheco bassist and trumpeter) and Larry Harlow (a pianist known as *El Judio Maravilloso* (the Marvelous Jew), perhaps because of his fondness for the work of "El Ciego Maravilloso," Arsenio Rodríguez), Fania's output did not gather momentum with the listening public. In 1967, Fania embarked on an aggressive and phenomenally successful program of recording and promotion to push the new music and corner the market for itself, signing many new bands and booking them for appearances on the New York club circuit.

Fania also put together all-star shows containing members of its best groups. Live recordings of two of Fania All-Stars' early shows, at the Red Garter and the Cheetah Club, became enormously popular releases in 1968 and 1971, respectively. Fania All-Star concerts were not quite a promotional appearance for a hot group, nor an overwrought "concert" of earnest rock poetry—they were tribal jams perhaps influenced by the 1960s counterculture and explosions of improvisational creativity. Overwhelming percussion sections that included Ray Barretto and Johnny Pacheco fed off trombone-dominated horn sections. A four-to-five member choral section, often teaming up vocalists Hector Lavoe, Ismael Miranda, Santos Colón, and Adalberto Santiago, took turns improvising the coro section with the rest of the band.

The formula for the Fania sound was not different from the Afro-Cuban mambo promulgated by Cachao and Orestes López or Arsenio Rodríguez. What was new was the personality and style of the vocalists, and what they were singing about. The text for these songs was often ancestral memories and nostalgia for Puerto Rico. On *Ana-canoa*, from *Live at the Cheetah, Vol. 1* (1971) the All Stars invoked Puerto Rico's oral tradition—they riffed barrio memories and salutes to Taino goddess Anacanoa in the declamatory style of décima poets. The concerts became a dazzling display of the energy and style of salsa in its golden age (usually dated from 1971–1978). In various incarnations, the Fania All Stars also recorded ten other studio albums. Some, like *Crossover* and *Delicate and Jumpy*, were attempts to commercialize the band through collaborations with jazz fusion and rock musicians.

At the center of the Fania movement was trombonist and salsa innovator Willie Colón. Born in 1950 and raised in the Bronx's hardscrabble Latino barrios, Colón was influenced by American pop music and the inner-city toughness of his youth, as well as the pop and folkloric music of his parents' native Puerto Rico. He was not content with simply reproducing the music that was coming out of the Caribbean. Colón combined two previous innovations, making them characteristic of his brand of salsa. First, like Palmieri, he used the trombone as a lead instrument—like Puente, he even moved his instrument to the front and center of the stage. Second, he went outside the traditional clave to incorporate several South American beats, most notably Panama's murga, a cumbia-like dance rhythm, into his music.

Colón's recording career began in the late 1960s when he was still a teenager. He formed his first band at age fourteen, as a trumpeter, but soon discarded his trumpet for a trombone, heavily influenced by the powerful sound of this instrument and the dynamic style of Barry Rogers and José Rodrígues, trombonists in Eddie Palmieri's La Perfecta. By comparison, Colón's style was grittier and less mannered. In 1968, he recorded *El Malo* (The Bad Guy) for Fania, the first in what became a series of albums that epitomized the Fania style at its best, capturing the restless energy and aggressive dynamism of early salsa. Colón's band always had the most impressive singer, or sonero, on the scene, beginning with their first, Hector Lavoe. Lavoe had emigrated to New York from the city of Ponce, Puerto Rico, in the early 1960s, at age seventeen. He brought with him the traditional styles of island singers like Bobby Capó and Ismael Rivera.

When they finally teamed up, an encounter immortalized on records like *El Malo*, *The Hustler* (1969), and *Cosa Nuestra* (1971), Colón and Lavoe were electric, especially on tunes like *El Malo*, *Que Lio*, and *Che Che Cole*. Lavoe brought a rural soul feel and Colón the cutting edge of the street intellectual, ambitious to make his music American and international. *Che Che Cole*, like *La Murga de Panama*, was one of Colón's "world-salsa" experiments, and a highly successful one. Combining jazz, samba, and elements of Puerto Rican bomba and plena, as well as a chorus that hinted at Central African language (*Che che cole/che che cofisa/cofisa langa*), it was an internationalizing song that broke salsa out of previous New York Afro-Cuban models.

Because of his lifelong battle with drug and alcohol addiction, Hector Lavoe was salsa's ultimate tragic figure, acquiring a martyr-like aura in his embodiment of the new dynamism of the Nuyorican identity. It was as if the sudden rush to modernity had burned out the self-styled country *jíbaro*. When Lavoe sang *Mi Gente* (My People) at Yankee Stadium as a member of the Fania All Stars in the Massucci-produced *Salsa* documentary in August 1973, it was a cathartic moment, one that marked the birth of this new identity—Nuyoricans had found a way to reconcile their island and New York points of view. When Lavoe, fighting through a drug-induced haze and a fantasy of returning to his native Puerto Rico, sang the line, *Yo soy un jíbaro de Puerto Rico* (I'm a country guy from Puerto Rico), the effect on Nuyoricans was not unlike the effect on Cuban exiles when they hear *Yo soy un hombre sincero* (I'm a sincere man), which begins the classic *Guantanamera*. The strong identification with Caribbean culture by newly established populations in North America began a new kind of identity, one in which nostalgia became a permanent state of mind for a transplanted individual.

By declaring himself a jíbaro, Lavoe allowed thousands of transplanted Puerto Ricans to connect to their island roots while at the same time feeling a new sense of homeland in the middle of the South Bronx, which at the time was being ravaged by the phenomenon known as white flight, which was hastened by the deterioration of New York's industrial economy. The psychological devaluation of Nuyoricans and African-Americans was accompanied by a rash of arson, used by landlords to collect money for buildings they didn't want to rent to blacks and Latinos. The music of the Fania era, and particularly the collaboration between Lavoe and Colón, helped restore pride to the community through an era of struggle that culminated in the riots following the 1976 New York blackout and the fiscal crisis.

In 1976, Hector Lavoe's problems with drugs and health came to a head, and he had to leave Colón's band. His spot was taken by Panamanian sonero/songwriter Rubén Blades, who soon became a central figure in his own right. Blades was a fascinating figure in that he passed for a Nuyorican even though he was from a relatively middle-class family in Panama and did graduate studies in law at Harvard. He had a passion for the great soneros of Puerto Rico (such as Cheo Feliciano and Ismael Miranda), and Panama has a similar colonial relationship with the United States. But Blades got deep into the city's heartbeat, starting out as a stock boy with Fania Records and prowling New York clubs like the Corso, the Village Gate, and Casino 14.

As Lavoe's replacement, Blades had enormous shoes to fill, but his collaboration with Colón continued Colón's status as the strongest of the Fania Records lineup in the mid-1970s, during which he produced classics like *Siembra*, an album that became a staple for a generation of socially conscious Latin New Yorkers. Although Blades wrote most of the songs for their collaboration, the two shared a creative bond that made them the Lennon and McCartney of salsa, an unprecedented team that produced groundbreaking tunes. *Siembra* included *Pedro Navaja*, a barrio reworking of *Mack the Knife*, from the *Three-Penny Opera*, and *Plástico*, a song that warned against the evils of the materialist culture of the North. *Pedro Navaja* became the *Stairway to Heaven* of salsa, the most requested song of the genre.

Siembra is one of those albums that defines a crowning moment in a genre—it contained several classic songs that functioned like mini-documentaries of the New York Latino experience. While the basic subject matter of salsa (and most of Latin music), dancing, and romance, was represented here, through songs like *Ojos* (Eyes) and *Dime* (Tell Me), both laments of a lost love, the album also included a strong political statement in *Plástico*, and island nostalgia in *Buscando Guayaba*. Colón's maturing, swing-filled arrangements and steady trombone act both as a rhythmic accompaniment and a second melody.

Siembra's extraordinary ability to symbolize a time comes from tunes like *Plástico*, which begins with a funk-disco bassline and evolves into a politicized critique of consumer materialism. But its crowning moment is a roll call of Latin American nations at the end of a long jam. *Pedro Navaja*, perhaps the most famous salsa song ever, is a poetic narrative flashback about the downfall of a small-time gangster on a barrio street corner. The hooks and edgy chemistry between the horn section, the piano, and the rhythm sections are flawless Fania. Sentimental nationalism has never been such partying fun as on this record, and *Plástico's* chanting of Latin American country names is a fixture in salsa concerts to this day.

Salsa continued to enjoy a great popularity after *Siembra*, but it began to go on the wane in the next decade. Blades and Colón continued their reign, recording several albums like 1981's excellent *Canciones del Solar de los Aburridos* (Songs From the Neighborhood of the Bored), but they went their separate ways after making the Latino-exploitation movie *The Last Fight* in 1982. Blades became highly successful as a world-music artist, performing and acting in over fifteen films alongside the likes of Jack Nicholson and Harrison Ford. In the film *Crossover Dreams*, directed by a New York-based Cuban, León Ichaso, Blades played a less successful singer. *Crossover Dreams* is one of the most significant U.S. Latino films of the 1980s, because it portrays the pain of assimilation and the increasing marginalization of New York salsa culture.

In the 1980s, Blade was able to extricate himself from his contract with Fania records, and he signed with Sony. His superior voice, now liberated from earlier criticisms that it was a carbon copy of Cheo Feliciano, a former singer for Eddie Palmieri and the Fania All Stars, and his ability to market himself to an Anglo audience, intensified tension between Blades and Colón, who seemed to lose luster without his star vocalist. Blades's career continued into the 1990s, when he released strong efforts like 1991's *Caminando* and 1992's *Amor y Control*. After an unsuccessful bid for the presidency of Panama in 1994, he reemerged at the turn of the twenty-first century with two superior albums, 1999's *Tiempos* and 2002's *Mundo*. These two releases, recorded with Costa Rican jazz fusion group Editus, evidenced Blades's maturity as a poet and a master of a variety of world musics.

Colón was less successful than Blades at keeping himself in the limelight, but he put out some extremely important work in the 1980s, such as *Doble Energía* with Ismael Miranda and *Vigilante* (1983), his last album with Hector Lavoe. His best albums of the late 1980s to the early 1990s, *Altos Secretos* and *Color Americano*, continued the social commentary that began during his collaboration with Blades. A song from *Altos Secretos*, titled *El Gran Varón*, was a huge success because it confronted for the first time in a salsa tune the issue of homosexuality and AIDS in the Latin community. While it's hard to argue that Colón ever faded away, these early 1990s albums constituted something of a comeback. Colón also appeared in commercials and television and in 1993 ran, unsuccessfully, as a Democrat for state representative in Westchester County, New York. In 1995, Colón and Blades, realizing that their fans made it lucrative for them to renew their collaboration, recorded *Tras la Tormenta*—in separate studios. They finally staged a tumultuous reunion in a concert at the Hollywood Bowl in 1997. As the century drew to a close, Colón continued to perform sporadically, starred in *Demasiado Corazón*, a Mexico City-based soap opera in 1998, and ran for public advocate of New York in 2001, where he finished second in the Democratic primary with 17 percent of the vote. His next CD, *Contrabanda*, issued on the independent Sonographica label, demonstrated that he was still a stirring force in Latin music.

TÍPICA '73

With the crystallization of the Fania sound in the late 1960s and early 1970s, there was a rush to a new conformity in Latin music. Salsa's upfront horns and percussion section had wiped out the violins and flutes of the charanga era. It was more soulful and funky and left more room for extended improvisation by percussion and chorus. But it also lost some of the discipline of the traditional Cuban dance orchestra. In the early 1970s a change got under way that would restore some of that discipline, break apart one of salsa's most successful bands, and reunite the New York tradition with Havana for the first time since the Cuban revolution.

A series of jam sessions held in Manhattan in 1972 by a young session percussionist named Johnny Rodríguez Jr., the pianist Sonny Bravo, and trombonist Leopoldo Pineda began to attract influential onlookers and musicians. The band, which would eventually be called Típica '73, recruited several members of the Ray Barretto Band, which in 1972 had scored a solid Fania hit called *Message*. Trumpeter René López, percussionist Orestes Vilato, bassist Dave Pérez, and vocalist Adalberto Santiago defected from Barretto's band, much to that bandleader's dismay. Típica '73's sound focused more on traditional Cuban son and gradually incorporated more Cuban instrumentation. On the band's second album, *Típica '73* (its first two albums are both named *Típica '73*), it brought in a tres player, Nelson González, and on 1975's *La Candela*, the band began a series of musical exchanges with musicians living in revolutionary Cuba, such as Los Van Van's Juan Formell. Synthesizers and distortion pedals (used by tres player González) mirrored the experimentation going on in Cuba and made Típica '73 a remarkable fusion between old-style and new-style Cuban music, all the while grounded in Fania-style funkiness.

In the mid-1970s vocalist Adalberto Santiago, percussionist Vilato, and guitarist González all left Típica '73 to start new bands. A group of new players would take their places, most notably violinist Alfredo de la Fe, who grounded the group in the charanga sound. *The Two Sides of Típica '73*, released in 1977, showed the band flexing its varied musical directions, flowing seamlessly through Cuban son, Latin jazz, Fania salsa, and the latest electric-oriented sound from Cuba, the songo. Later that year, José "El Canario" Alberto became the band's lead singer, and the band embarked on its most controversial period. In 1979 it would participate in the first informal residency of a New York salsa band in Cuba. Fleshed out by conga master Angel "Cachete" Maldonado and saxophonist Mario Rivera, the band recorded *Típica '73 in Cuba, Intercambio Cultural*. Cuban guest artists included the conga player Tata Güines, the tres player Niño Rivera, and trumpeter Felix Chappotín, among the best contemporary Cuban musicians at the time.

But by the time the group recorded *Charangueando con la Típica '73* in 1980, a backlash, caused by anti-Castro sentiments, began to set in. New York club owners with ties to the Cuban-American community began to blackball the group, refusing to book them. By 1982 Sonny Bravo and Johnny Rodríguez dissolved the band, but many of its players continued to be influential on the New York scene. Típica '73 reunited for some live shows in 1994 and 1999, and Sony released *Live Concert Series* in 2003, culled from some of those dates.

During a time when salsa was beginning to move toward a stage where the singer's star appeal became more important than musicianship, Típica '73 remained dedicated to the high standards of an Afro-Cuban dance orchestra. But the band was never trapped in the mold of being a nostalgia group—it continued to evolve and seek inspiration from Cuba when interaction between New York and Havana was at a nadir.

CELIA CRUZ

Celia Cruz is the most recognizable and most powerful voice in contemporary Latin music. Though she has been recording and performing from a New York base since the early 1960s, she represents the last gasp of Cuban influence on what would informally become known as the New York school. Born in Havana in 1924, she performed in various talent shows, finally enrolling in Cuba's Conservatory of Music in 1947.

Cruz was a devotee of Paulina Álvarez, a vocalist with Orquesta Antonio María Romeu, but in 1950 latched on to the extremely important band Sonora Matancera, which took its name from the town of Matanzas, Cuba. Formed in 1924, the band was led by guitarist/singer Regelio Martínez. Matancera was an institution in Cuba and over the years featured close to one hundred vocalists from the Caribbean and Mexico, including Puerto Rican legend Daniel Santos. Cruz replaced Puerto Rican singer Myrta Silva, who began her career in New York in the 1930s with Rafael Hernández's Cuarteto Victoria. This was the start of Cruz's classic period from about 1950–1960, when she was cementing her reputation as the most popular female singer in Cuba.

Cruz appeared in several clubs and hotels and on the radio and sang typical fare like *Ritmo Pilón* and the more esoteric, Santería-related *Mata Siguaraya*. She also played with several other groups (Sonora Cubana, Armando Romeu, and Sonora Caracas, to name a few). During her tenure with Sonora Matancera, Cruz and the band left Cuba for a tour that never made it back to their homeland, applying for residency in the United States, where they were able to secure a long-term gig at the Hollywood Palladium. In 1962, Cruz moved to New York and married Pedro Knight, the trumpeter of Sonora Matancera, who eventually became her manager, and the couple made it clear they were political exiles from Cuba.

In 1965 Cruz left Sonora Matancera—which continued on until at least 2003, making it one of the longest-lasting groups in Latin music history—and began to record with Tito Puente. With Puente she recorded *Cuba y Puerto Rico Son*, *Quimbo Quimbumbia*, and *Etc., Etc., Etc.*, between 1965 and 1970, but she also released albums with Orquesta de Memo Salamanca (with which she had earlier recorded *Cuando Salí de Cuba*, the exile anthem), and the Alegre All-Stars, a South Bronx band lead by Al Santiago and featuring both Palmieris on keyboards.

Cruz had the visual impact of a Hotel Tropicana show dancer but her inimitable voice had such power that, like the great jazz divas, she held even the most difficult audiences in the palm of her hand with her biting alto. She brought the funky Cuban essence when she appeared, often dressed in fire-engine red, snapped her fingers and shouted *¿Azucar!* (sugar) in the manner of Beny Moré or countless Cuban vocalists. Her flight from the Cuban revolution was a major contradiction of the notion that Castro's plan liberated Cubans of African ancestry; her decision to become an exile placed her alongside the predominantly white bourgeoisie who left the island in the first exodus.

Cruz's effect on New York salsa as an Afro-Cuban woman, in a field dominated by light-skinned Puerto Rican men, was considerable. Her ability to epitomize the Afro-Cuban experience allowed her to forge ties with Tito Puente, a devotee of Cuban music despite his Nuyorican innovations. Together, they were Latin music's one-two punch before and after the 1970s Fania Records era. In 1966 alone Cruz and Puente recorded eight albums, many of which are now out of print. Her collaborations with

Larry Harlow, who wrote one of her signature tunes, *Gracia Divina*, and Willie Colón, with whom she performed the electric *Usted Abusó*, are among the best records of the peak Fania years. Harlow, a veteran of the Palladium days, and Colón, linchpin of the Fania sound, provided her with exhilarating arrangements and excellent session players.

Cruz's ability to translate the culmination of the Afro-Cuban style into the harder, edgier rhythms of New York salsa made for music that was authentic to both tastes. In the 1980s and 1990s, she exploited her position as one of the few female salsa vocalists of note. Her appearance in the movie *The Mambo Kings*, based on the Oscar Hijuelos book, gave her an Ella Fitzgerald-like appeal to the mainstream. In fact, her singing style is very much centered on her ability to unite virtuoso scat techniques in the manner of Fitzgerald with the improvisational style of salsa singing. At the turn of the century, Cruz remained enormously successful as a recording artist and performer, first with Sony and then for Ralph Mercado's RMM label, which was bought out by Universal in 2001. The most interesting of these were *Azucar Negra*, released in 1993 and featuring input from Miami singers Gloria Estefan and Jon Secada, and 1997's *Duets*, which ventured outside of salsa through duets with Brazilian singer Caetano Veloso and Argentine rockers Los Fabulosos Cadillacs, as well as two members of RMM's stable, José Alberto and La India. In 2002, Cruz won a Grammy for *La Negra Tiene Tumbao*, which featured state-of-the-art arrangements, an indefatigable sense of swing, and nods to club music like house and hip-hop—it's a rare late-career album that demonstrated growth and a feeling that Cruz was still peaking as an artist.

Enshrined in the Smithsonian and having received an honorary doctorate from Yale, Cruz is a symbolic cornerstone of salsa music, primarily because of her technically and aesthetically superior voice. Her career as a lead singer with Sonora Matancera and as a collaborator with salsa's key artists (Colón, Pacheco, Puente, and Harlow) put her at the center of the genre's history, at once an innovative performer and an extremely talented perfectionist.

EDDIE PALMIERI

After the breakup of La Perfecta in 1968, pianist Eddie Palmieri began playing with the Fania All Stars, a lesser-known label group called the Tico All-Stars, and with singers like Justo Betancourt. While Palmieri was disappointed with the end of the Palladium era and the battle-of-the-bands atmosphere surrounding it, he continued to perform in what was known as the *cuchifrito* circuit, an analog of the African-American chitlin' circuit. During this relentless period of touring he made *The Sun of Latin Music*, an album that contained high-concept salsa highlighting Palmieri's virtuosity, and won the first Latin Grammy award in 1974. *The Sun of Latin Music* featured an all-star lineup along with classic compositions and virtuoso performances by Palmieri. The playing was crisp and loose while maintaining a discipline even during the improvisational sequences. Palmieri lead the band with his eccentric pummeling of the piano, using an extraordinarily rhythmic and harmonically textured technique. The idiosyncratic plucking of legendary charanga violinist Alfredo de la Fe only hinted at the driving ecstasy of Palmieri's improvisation in *Nunca Contigo*. The percussion section of Tommy López Jr. on bongó, Eladio Pérez on conga, and Nicky Marrero on timbales fueled the album's many dance-friendly moments. And Palmieri's nine-minute Debussy-ish passage introducing into *Un Dia Bonito* was a journey into a new salsa universe only he could navigate.

Sun of Latin Music also features the stunningly impressive debut of sonero Lalo Rodríguez, who also appeared on 1974's *Unfinished Masterpiece*. Palmieri had originally wanted to use Andy Montañez, then the lead singer of the influential Puerto Rican salsa group El Gran Combo, but the band only agreed to release the singer to do one or two tracks, and Palmieri wanted one vocalist for the whole album. Contacts in Puerto Rico led him to the sixteen-year-old Rodríguez. Strongly influenced by Hector Lavoe, Rodríguez's tenor is stridently nasal, meshing perfectly with the disciplined drumming, the howling horns of Ronnie Cuber and Mario Rivera, the soulful backup vocals of bugaloo king Jimmy Sabater, and Palmieri's provocative piano. *Mi Cumbia* was perhaps the most avant-garde evocation of authentic Colombian cumbia recorded at that time. And there may never have been as elegant a Spanish re-make of a Beatles' song as *Una Rosa Española*, which re-imagines *You Never Give Me Your Number* from *Abbey Road* as a danzón in Havana's Hotel Tropicana.

Palmieri's 1978 release *Lucumí, Macumba, Voodoo* placed the various African syncretic religions of the Caribbean in the forefront and featured Palmieri's typically eccentric big band salsa flourishes, while also containing some less interesting jazz-fusion vocal experiments. *La Verdad/The Truth*, released nine years later, was his fifth Grammy-award winner, with a more fulfilled repertoire of jazz-fusion and African-inflected salsa (*Congo Yambumba* is a standout jam). Of his uneven mid-1980s releases, 1982's *Sueño*, produced by Kip Hanrahan, an avant-garde jazz-Latin bandleader, is the most memorable, particularly for its revised version of the Palmieri classic *Azucar*. As of 2003, Palmieri still toured occasionally and played a major part in New York's Latin music scene—his collaboration with salsa vocalist La India helped bring a legion of younger Latinos into the salsa fold and played a big part in the music's late-1990s revival. Surviving members of La Perfecta were reunited in 2002 and were joined by younger players like trumpeter Brian Lynch, flutist Dave Valentín, and percussionist Richie Flores for *La Perfecta II* (Concord Jazz).

The Fania label's fortunes began to decline in the mid-1980s, partially because of the ascension of a new, slicker style of salsa that focused on the star potential of the lead singer, and partially because of owner Jerry Masucci's failing health. In 1995

Masucci shut down the label after more than fifteen years of success, in which it was compared to labels such as Blue Note and Motown in terms of sustained excellence. The shutdown of Fania, which was revived shortly before Masucci's death in 1997, signaled the end of the golden age of salsa.

MEANWHILE, BACK IN PUERTO RICO

In the period between the 1960s and 1980s, at the same time that, in New York, salsa was reaching its peak, significant musical developments were occurring in Puerto Rico that eventually influenced what was going on in New York. On its own terms, the music being played in Puerto Rico could stake a claim as being as modern as New York salsa. There was continual exchange of musical knowledge and influences facilitated by the migration of musicians from the island to New York, as well as the relatively easy flow of information between Puerto Rico, the Caribbean, and the rest of Latin America.

During the mambo explosion of the post–World War II era, many Cuban bands played in Puerto Rico, and local orchestras playing mambo, bolero, and various Afro-Cuban fusions influenced by local music and what was going on in New York made for a lively scene. Standouts included bands led by trumpeter César Concepción (playing orchestra-arranged plenas), Lito Peña (Orquesta Panamericana, which featured a young Ismael Rivera on vocals), and trumpeter Miguelito Miranda. They all began to play at a San Juan beachside club called El Escambrón, which was located at the Caribe Hilton Hotel. Puerto Rico's hotel scene was on a smaller scale than Havana's, but it provided a platform for bands like that of pianist Noro Morales into the 1960s.

A reaction to the bourgeois hotel scene came from newer acts, which called for a return to funky nativism. At the forefront of modernizing the street-derived sounds of Puerto Rican bomba and plena, two musical traditions roughly analogous to Cuban rumba, was congero Rafael Cortijo's combo. From the early '60s to the '80s, Cortijo fulfilled the theory of Luís Rafael Sánchez, a Puerto Rican novelist, that the people's music should be traditional, avant garde, and popular at the same time. Cortijo, who began his musical career in 1954, traveled to New York in 1961 and had a strong influence on that city's Latin music throughout the decade. Cortijo's songs reflected a black perspective that was less filtered by European influences such as the danzón-like underpinnings of the Cuban orchestra repertoire.

His bands, often fronted by one of the all-time great soneros, Ismael Rivera, were innovative by modernizing the bomba and to a lesser extent the plena, homegrown Puerto Rican rhythms, giving them an almost urban feel. Songs like *María Teresa* and *Micaela*, both from the 1960 release *Cortijo y su Combo*, epitomize the fusion of storytelling lyrics typical of bomba with the dance's swirling, bouncy rhythms. The bomba is less restricted than Afro-Cuban dance music, with perhaps more in common with

Colombia's cumbia and Brazil's samba. Cortijo was also very inspired by Brazilian samba and by the Colombian hybrid rhythm, the mere-cumbé, invented by Colombian bandleader Pacho Galán as a fusion of merengue and cumbia. The infusion of Cortijo's bomba and plena innovations into the salsa sound is one of the important characteristics that distinguish salsa from Cuban popular music.

In a self-conscious attempt to bring the music closer to its African origin, Cortijo stripped down the Afro-Cuban orchestra format to the "combo" or conjunto, a move that paralleled the innovations of Cuban tres player Arsenio Rodríguez, by lessening the number of horn and string players in his band. His music reflected the tight, aggressive feel that an emphasis on the rhythm section and more popular themes bring about. Cortijo had a major influence on the developments in merengue in the Dominican Republic, during the emergence of that country from the reign of dictator Rafael Trujillo in the early 1960s.

One of the most significant spinoffs from Cortijo's bands was El Gran Combo, formed in 1962 by ex-Cortijo pianist Rafael Ithier. Ithier didn't create a stripped down bomba and plena unit but returned to the orchestra format, retaining a strong percussion focus. El Gran Combo became Puerto Rico's house band in the way that the Grateful Dead became the house band for the San Francisco counterculture in the late 1960s. For Ithier and his band, more is more—he used two pianists, two saxophonists, two trumpeters, and three lead vocalists, amounting to a thirteen-piece dance orchestra. Perhaps by staying on the island and not becoming part of the Nuyorican scene, El Gran Combo escaped the phasing out of the big bands in New York. Ithier used a massive number of instruments to keep the rhythms traditional, with little room for lengthy improvisation. Sticking to less improvisational call and response, El Gran Combo kept out the edgier, jazz-and-rock influenced arrangements of the Fania posse, who, through local pianist Papo Lucca, were well-known on the island. The most notable vocalist to emerge from El Gran Combo was Andy Montañez, but his partners Elliot Romero and Charlie Aponte formed a harmonic barrage that cut through vast concert rooms as well as intimate dance floors.

Founded in 1954 by pianist Enrique Lucca, La Sonora Ponceña was, with El Gran Combo, one of Puerto Rico's two most important continually performing bands over almost forty years. Hailing from Puerto Rico's second largest city, Ponce, La Sonora Ponceña featured a two-piano attack (Lucca's son Papo, one of the most talented salsa pianists of his generation, and Rafael Ithier); a barrage of lead trumpets; and the well-balanced harmonies of a trio of singers, at one time including a woman, Yolande Rivera—besides Myrta Silva and Celia Cruz, a rarity. Papo Lucca eventually became the group's leader in 1968 at the age of twenty-two, and his father, Enrique, became more of an arranger/musical director.

After their label, Inca, was purchased by Fania in the late 1960s, La Sonora Ponceña began to get far more international exposure. The band recorded Arsenio Rodríguez classics, *Hachero Pa' Un Palo* and *Fuego En El 23*, which became immensely popular. Larry Harlow produced albums like 1972's *Desde Puerto Rico a Nueva York*, 1974's *Sabor Sureño*, and 1975's *Tiene Pimienta*. The lead vocalists were Luís "Luigi" Texidor and Tito Gómez, who provided a grittier, more nasal style that was opposed to the smooth, often bolero-fixated vocalists of the hotel circuit.

With La Sonora Ponceña, Papo Lucca recorded over thirty albums, of which the recognized standout is 1988's *On the Right Track*. One of the greatest straight-ahead salsa records ever made, *On the Right Track* is a relentless assault on the senses. Although it sometimes sounds as if it were recorded in an echo chamber, the extremely high level of playing—especially the keyboard improvisation by Papo Lucca and Rafael Ithier—and the inventive arrangements make this a salsa classic. The often-overlooked trio of vocalists who worked with the band in the 1980s—Hector "Pichy" Pérez, Manuel "Manix" Roldan, and Daniel "Danny" Davila—are at their peak here.

In addition to original material written by Lucca, Ponceña drew from an astute variety of sources for its songs, from Cuban nueva trova composer Pablo Milanés (*Pensando en Tí*) to fusion jazz pianist Chick Corea (*Capuccino*). Milanés's song was given a lilting swing-salsa treatment, replete with singalong chorus, while the version of *Capuccino* drew out the Latin piano elements in Corea's original version in an eminently danceable way.

Like Eddie Palmieri, Lucca demonstrated a profound affection for Colombia's musical traditions, dedicating *A Cali* to Cali, the Colombian city where salsa is most popular (albeit while dabbling in a little cumbia). But perhaps the most powerful track on this album is Danny Rivera's *Jíbaro en Nueva York*, the classic narrative, written in décima form, of the Puerto Rican immigrant experience. The lyrics are declaimed in the traditional décima style, setting off a frenzy of improvisation by the monster band. If that weren't enough, *On the Right Track* concludes with another burst of raw energy, with the band giving the full orchestral treatment to a quintessential Cuban son, Adalberto Alvarez's *La Rumba Soy Yo*.

In 1978, Lucca replaced Larry Harlow as pianist of the Fania All Stars, playing on *Rhythm Machine*, *California Jam*, *Tribute to Tito Rodríguez*, and *Guasasa*, while continuing to perform with La Sonora Ponceña. In 1993 he recorded a cult favorite, *Latin Jazz*, in which, like Tito Rodríguez before him, he demonstrated his considerable abilities as a jazz composer and arranger. Influenced by Harlow's hard-edged style (sometimes known as *salsa dura* or "hard salsa") Lucca added a rich body of work to salsa's electronic keyboard repertoire. His technique was also extraordinarily rhythmic—Lucca's tumbaos were staccato bursts of energy, and he was free to improvise, exploiting the keyboard's percussive potential. As a soloist and arranger he appeared on Albita's *Mujer Como Yo* (1997), Willie Colón's *Hecho en Puerto Rico* (1993), and Celia Cruz's *La Ceiba* (1992). Although La Sonora Ponceña continued to tour Europe, and occasionally the United States on the strength of its authentic salsero status, its last major release was 1998's *On Target*. Lucca remains a legend and was frequently invited to guest in all-star lineups in concerts in New York and Puerto Rico.

Another important and overlooked figure of Puerto Rican salsa is percussionist Willie Rosario, born in 1930 in Coamo, Puerto Rico. As a teenager in 1948 he visited New York and took in all the energy of the mambo era, particularly inspired by Tito Puente. After his solo recording career began in the 1960s, Rosario crafted a music based on the innovations in New York rather than the traditional Afro-Cuban orchestras. In her essay "Is Salsa Music a Genre?" author Marisol Berríos-Miranda made a case that Rosario's orchestras epitomized the genre of salsa because the rhythms played by both the percussion and melodic instruments were "locked" together (sometimes known by the term *afinque*). By opposing this characteristic to the Afro-Cuban orchestra's ability to play with less constraint, Berríos-Miranda distinguished salsa from its precursor. Rosario, who released close to fifty albums, put out one of the genre's most electric releases of 2002, *The Master of Rhythm and Swing: Live in Puerto Rico*, which more than amply demonstrates the timbál player's ability to re-create the jazz/salsa excitement of Tito Puente.

SALSA ROMÁNTICA AND THE HEGEMONY OF THE SONERO

The period of conservative retrenchment throughout North America in the 1980s, largely inspired by the installation of a conservative presidential administration in the United States, created a strong ripple effect throughout Latin America. The increased role of the United States in political conflicts in Central America during the 1980s may have inspired Rubén Blades in 1981 to write the song *Tiburón*, which has lyrics that are a thinly veiled reference to U.S. intervention in Honduras, El Salvador, and Nicaragua. Blades's collaborative effort with Willie Colón turned out to be one of the last gasps of politically conscious salsa. Just as American cinema turned away from the rough-featured antiheroes of the 1970s toward the teen idols of John Hughes movies, mainstream salsa began to promote baby-faced soneros. Though this phenomenon would be criticized for its deleterious effect on salsa's aesthetic, it gave salsa expanded sales and influence unprecedented in the history of Latin music.

According to Christopher Washburne's essay "Salsa Romantica: An Analysis of Style," salsa romantica emerged as the Fania empire collapsed (at one point it owned several smaller labels like Tico, Alegre, and Inca, and controlled most live performance venues) and Dominican merengue began to make inroads on New York Latin music listeners and dancers. Two records released in 1982 and 1983 on K-Tel, called *Noche Caliente 1 & 2*, produced by Louie Rivera, and featuring young singers José Alberto, Tito Allen, Johnny Rivera, and Ray de la Paz, were credited with inaugurating the genre of salsa romantica. "Tempos were slower . . . vocals were sung in a smooth, crooning style," Washburne suggested, and of course, the lyrics were about love, not struggle. In addition, standard pop and lite-jazz chords were substituted for "hard" salsa's "harmonic tension." A young assistant producer, Sergio George, who first appears on *Noche Caliente 2*, is also credited with introducing North American pop music conventions to the new style.

Puerto Rican studio recordings followed suit. Oddly enough, probably the first star of what became known as "salsa romantica" or "salsa sensual" was Lalo Rodríguez, a vocalist who made his debut on two of Eddie Palmieri's peak golden age recordings in the 1970s, *The Sun of Latin Music* and *Unfinished Masterpiece*. Palmieri, who liked to maintain the high standards of Palladium-era bands, became one of salsa romantica's leading critics. Rodríguez had slipped into relative obscurity after leaving Palmieri after 1974, performing with the Puerto Rico All-Stars and avoiding the end-of-Fania malaise. His breezy tenor was lighter than the prototypical Fania singers, but meshed well with Palmieri's classically influenced, painterly improvisations.

The remarkable success of Julio Iglesias during the Reagan years, which helped establish Latin pop as a genre, also had an effect on the marketing of salsa. Iglesias, a Spaniard, used a simple format—he compiled many of Latin America's favorite traditional ballads and created a kind of pan Latino format that had a broad appeal. While salsa romantica didn't follow Iglesias's methodology, the Latin music industry couldn't help but notice the way he brought back the pretty-boy central figure to the music world, and the resulting spike in sales, especially from women listeners.

In 1986, Lalo Rodríguez resurfaced with a song that has become *the* standard of salsa romantica, *Ven, Devórame Otra Vez*, which appeared on the album *Un Nuevo Despertar*. The song establishes the basic narrative strategy of the salsa romantica sonero: I am incapable of resisting a beautiful woman, and I hope that she will give herself to me, because otherwise I just might die right here and now. Though Rodríguez never produced another song that equaled the enormous international popularity of *Ven, Devórame Otra Vez*, he inspired a string of vocalists who held sway on the salsa scene for more than fifteen years, including Pupy Santiago, Tommy Olivencia, Frankie Ruiz, Jerry Rivera, Frankie Negrón, and Eddie Santiago. The songs followed a strict formula of introductory verses, instrumental break, and a coro section with limited improvisation on the vocalist's part. While increased production values made salsa romantica recordings burst from the speakers, eliminating any trace of tinniness or imperfection from the golden age, and the arrangements allowed for some improvisation, the overall effect of this style was to diminish the intensity of salsa.

Salsa romantica also signaled a vast change in the center of production of salsa music, from New York to San Juan and Miami. Most of the bright lights of salsa romantica were from Puerto Rico, although Miami's Cuban exile community were big players in making the careers of singers Willy Chirino, Pupy Santiago, and a Nicaraguan transplant, Luís Enrique. Perhaps because he was from a country where salsa orchestras are rare, Enrique's orchestra was less processed, creating a kind of 1950s Cuban feel in appearance (their suits) and instrumentation (horns and percussion upfront). Although he scored with romantica hits like *San Juan Sin Tí*, from 1989's *Mi Mundo* and *Desesperado*, from the 1990 follow-up *Amor y Alegría*, Enrique managed to fit more vocal improvisation into the formula, as if to prove that a Central American could throw down with the best that the Caribbean had to offer. Enrique's position on the charts slipped after his initial success. But he did put out the innovative *Timbaleye* in 1999, which featured pop songs and attempts to mine folkloric Afro-Caribbean rhythms, and in 2002, *Evolución*, a mannered collection of salsa and ballads that still didn't recapture the excitement of his impressive beginnings.

THE RALPH MERCADO PERIOD

The conservative 1980s slowly took hold in New York, where allegiance to salsa's Golden Age reluctantly eroded. Stepping into the vacuum created by the demise of the Fania empire, another promoter, Ralph Mercado, worked to stockpile the remaining big names in salsa music in New York, forming a parallel empire that controlled the city's Latin scene from the mid-1980s on.

A native of the Dominican Republic, Mercado had been promoting concerts on the cuchifrito circuit beginning in the 1970s. By the late 1980s it was almost impossible to get a quality club date without Mercado's involvement. His enormous influence seemed to hold sway at every major venue for Latin music in the city. At one point in the early 1990s, Mercado had in his stable Tito Puente, Celia Cruz, Eddie Palmieri, Venezuelan sonero Oscar D'León, Cruz's heir apparent La India, the surprisingly competent Japanese band Orchesta de la Luz, Hector Lavoe, Johnny Pacheco, former Típica '73 vocalist José Alberto, bugaloo-salsa revivalist Tito Nieves, and most of the surviving Fania All-Stars. Of the major salsa figures only Rubén Blades, who had diversified his career, Ray Barretto, who had restructured his career as a Latin jazz artist, and Willie Colón could operate independently. The Mercado hegemony was at its peak when the producers of the *Mambo Kings* movie featured his stable of musicians in the film. The appearances by Tito Puente and Celia Cruz—whose version of "Guantanamera" was epic—signaled a new momentum for Latin music in the '90s.

Mercado clearly played a key role in steering New York salsa towards its renaissance in the 1990s. He tirelessly promoted his acts in venues like the Palladium (not the one from the '50s, but a post-Studio 54 "Downtown/New Wave" lair on East Fourteenth Street), the Copacabana, and the Latin Quarter. With Jack Hooke, a former associate of famous DJ Symphony Sid (who emceed radio broadcasts and stage introductions of everything from the bebop era on Fifty-Second Street to the Fania All-Stars' stand at the Cheetah Club), Mercado was a partner in the long-running Salsa

Meets Jazz series at the Village Gate. The series teamed up quality salsa orchestras with guest soloists from the jazz world and kept salsa music's reputation as "serious" music intact.

The shows at the Palladium were crucial in keeping a younger crowd of Latinos involved with salsa. They also provided the impetus for the newest generation of salseros, by creating space for old and new elements to mix in a club context. Two groups, one usually a salsa romantica group, would play a show, but between sets, the DJ would mix in mostly house and R&B dance music to keep the kids interested. It was during this Palladium period that Hector Lavoe made one of his last appearances onstage. Troubled by continuing problems with drugs, which had prompted a suicide attempt from a hotel balcony in 1988, Lavoe tried to keep performing in the early 1990s, even if it meant being escorted to the microphone in a wheelchair. On a Valentine's Day showcase, Lavoe appeared with a Puerto Rican flag draped over his legs and sang *Mi Gente* one last time.

The establishment of Tito Puente as the living legend of Latin music was largely Mercado's doing. After the end of the old mambo/Palladium era, Puente had been relegated to a long string of Latin jazz releases on the California-based Concord Jazz label. In the late 1980s, he began to play more shows to a new crowd of adoring fans—his new alliance with Ralph Mercado made him the grandfather of salsa in way similar to Neil Young's mid-career resurrection as an antecedent to punk rock. In an attempt to build on this new generation of fans, Mercado enlisted house DJ Little Louie Vega, who was married to an up-and-coming salsa singer, La India, to produce a new version of Puente's *Ran Kan Kan*. A little-known young sonero, Marc Anthony, contributed vocals. Anthony, like La India, had cut a few records as a Latin hiphop/freestyle singer, but neither had had much success. Eager to expand his fan base and take advantage of an opportunity to return to his musical roots, Anthony used the Puente collaboration to launch a new career as a sonero, while Puente used it to stay relevant to young people. Mercado expanded his power and influence with this revival, adding Marc Anthony and La India to his roster, and also capitalized on a revival of Celia Cruz's popularity.

SALSA'S NEW WAVE

Marc Anthony is at the forefront of the new generation of Latin musicians who want to celebrate their roots even as they flaunt their savvy American-ness. Born in 1969 in Manhattan and named after Marco Antonio Muñiz, a famous Mexican singer who became popular as a balladeer in Puerto Rico, Anthony was raised in East Harlem. He had a typical Nuyorican upbringing, speaking both English and Spanish and listening to both salsa and soul music. He began his career in the mid-1980s singing house music in local New York clubs, often accompanied only by a DAT rhythm track. Anthony was singing backup vocals for a Backstreet Boys-like group called the Latin Rascals when Little Louie Vega, acting as the band's producer, decided to feature him on some of his dance tracks, including the widely heard *Rebel*. When Tito Puente had the Vega-Anthony act open for him at Madison Square Garden in 1992, Anthony was so impressed by the crowd and its reaction that he decided it might be time to return to his roots and sing salsa music in Spanish. As Anthony tells it, one day while he was driving around he heard Mexican crooner Juan Gabriel's version of the ballad *Hasta Que te Conocí* on the radio, something clicked in his mind, and he decided to record in Spanish. Anthony shot to the top of the new wave of salsa in the late 1990s, recording six albums for Sony, *Otra Nota, Todo a Su Tiempo, Contra la Corriente, Libre*, and two fairly successful English-language albums, *Marc Anthony* and *Mended*. The keys to his success were a spectacular, wide-ranging tenor; a key collaboration with Sergio George, a new wave salsa keyboardist and producer whose dynamic keyboard style and electrified percussion arrangements helped create a new salsa sound; and Anthony's ability to bring some of the techniques he acquired singing soul and R&B into the salsa vocabulary, enabling city kids who felt a strong connection with African-American culture to return to their salsa roots.

With its remarkably clean, brilliant sound, expert arrangements, and powerful, melodic tunes, 1995's *Todo a su Tiempo* is one of the best examples of the new wave of salsa. George anchored the album with premium salsa sessionists including bassist Rubén Rodríguez, percussionists Marc Quiñones and Bobby Allende, trombonist William Cepeda, and trumpeter Angel Fernández—Anthony's voice was pushed to its astonishing limits. Songs like *Te Conozco Bien, Te Amaré*, and *Y Sigues Siendo* have become show-stoppers in Anthony's ecstatic live appearances. While these songs echo the post-Fania salsa romantica style in their concern with lost loves and frustrating lonely nights, the conviction of Anthony's singing and the powerful, sharply percussive, R&B-influenced arrangements make his music revelatory. Instead of the rapid-fire syllable-straining vocal improvisation that marked Fania-era salsa, Anthony riffed on his powerful voice, to create Whitney Houstonesque moments of splendor.

Marc Anthony's 1999 eponymous album, with most of the songs in English, was the culmination of several steps calculated to promote him as a major entertainment figure transcending his salsa niche. Also part of that campaign were his acting career in movies and on Broadway, starring opposite Rubén Blades in *The Capeman*; publicity campaigns that painted him in the same light as Frank Sinatra; and his duet with Jennifer Lopez on her debut solo album, *On the 6*. The arrangements and style of the songs on *Marc Anthony* were not at all like salsa—they were conceived as the kind of lite Latin pop that Ricky Martin and Enrique Iglesias pioneered. Although Anthony's record had a bit more funk and creativity than his Latin-pop contemporaries, it was clear that the salsa romantica style had come full circle. After almost a decade of salsa's attempt to slowly return to its roots, Marc Anthony had made a record that brought the Latin sensibility fully into the contemporary world.

While *Marc Anthony* got fairly good critical notices, and its single, *I Need to Know*, became almost as much a part of the zeitgeist as Ricky Martin's *Livin' La Vida Loca*, 2002's follow-up, *Mended* was roundly panned as flaccid and unimaginative. Anthony, who delighted in working with mainstream producers and, like many Latinos of his generation, was very influenced by North American pop, did not see his English work as a novelty, but needed to work harder to stay in that arena. The resounding success of 2001's Spanish-language *Libre*, in which his salsa became increasingly sophisticated, incorporating influences like Colombian vallenato and Peruvian charango, indicated that his strength and fan base was largest in the world of the Latin beat.

GILBERTO SANTA ROSA

Too young to be part of the older generation of Fania classic soneros and too accomplished to be compared with salsa romántica contemporaries like Eddie Santiago and Tony Vega, Gilberto Santa Rosa quietly took the salsa spotlight from New York City and brought it to Puerto Rico. Although his lyrics and arrangements were farmed out to guest collaborators, and the songs were all about *cositas de amor*, Santa Rosa maintained a dignity over his twelve years of recording that helped save the genre from pop tackiness.

Santa Rosa began his career in 1979 as a member of the Puerto Rico All-Stars (a collective of emerging singers and veteran players that goes back to the 1970s). He had a two-year stint with the Tommy Olivencia Orchestra, then went solo in 1986 on the Combo label. But he really made his mark with his second album for Sony, 1991's *Perspectiva*, which featured arrangements and guest trombone appearances by Luís "Perico" Ortiz, who made albums that were island equivalents to the Fania scene in the '70s. *Perspectiva*'s songwriting was unusually good for its time, one of increasing vapidity. "My love is like a time bomb," he insisted on *Bomba de Tiempo*. The song has a double entendre in that the rhythm it traffics is a variation of the Puerto Rican bomba, but it features salsa-like baritone sax riffs engaging in call and response with a barrage of high-register trumpets.

Santa Rosa's excellent tenor compared favorably with that of the Venezuelan salsa singer Oscar D'León (another member of Ralph Mercado's stable in the '80s and '90s). This helped bring back a focus on Puerto Rican salsa when South American bands like D'León's, Joe Arroyo's and Grupo Niche began to revive Golden Age salsa values in the late '80s. Santa Rosa often chose brooding, self-reflective songs, like *A quien? A Mi?* (Who, Me?), in which he narrates a character "disoriented, trying to find myself." On *Perspectiva*'s *Concienca*, he wrestles with the ambiguity of loving someone he probably shouldn't, and on *Se Supone*, where he laments impending rejection, he engages in an affecting, artful conversation with the listener.

Through the 1990s, Santa Rosa was the most important sonero in salsa, regardless of point of origin. Though he stuck to the same formulas on albums like *Escencia* (1996), *De Corazón* (1997), *Intenso* (2001), and *Viceversa* (2002), his voice continued to mature. Santa Rosa's side projects, working with string orchestras and staging major theatrical revues in Puerto Rico, made him a kind of renaissance salsero. He was also a mentor to rising talents like Domingo Quiñones, who starred in the successful stage play *Quien Mató a Hector Lavoe?* (Who Killed Hector Lavoe?), and like Victor Manuelle, one of the best new singers of the early 2000s.

VICTOR MANUELLE

While Puerto Rican vocalist Victor Manuelle is yet another pretty face emerging from contemporary salsa's hit factory, he possesses a formidable tenor. At times sounding like progenitors Rubén Blades and Gilberto Santa Rosa, his music trades on the anguished love-lost laments that pushed Marc Anthony to the top. His band draws from some of Puerto Rico's best sessionists, New York school cohorts like producer Sergio George on keyboards and drummer Marc Quiñones, and is anchored by the ubiquitous bassist Ruben Rodríguez. They do a stellar job setting up Manuelle for the mid-song improvisational scatting that makes or breaks top soneros.

The thirtyish Manuelle, who was born in New York but grew up in Puerto Rico, began his career in storybook fashion when he spontaneously leapt onto the stage while Gilberto Santa Rosa was singing in Puerto Rico in 1986. Santa Rosa was so impressed with Manuelle that he signed him to sing background choruses in his band, and he has mentored him ever since. Manuelle has since released eight CDs as a soloist on Sony Discos, and he is the standout figure among the current crop of young singers promoted in the salsa romantica star system.

On his 1999 release, *Ironias*, Manuelle waded through a litany of heartbreak with a confident swing, not stretching beyond the capabilities of his range. He frequently returned to a signature yelp that sounds like a cowboy kicking his horse into high gear. His second album, *Inconfundible*, released in 1999, retained the throbbing sensuality of the kiss-and-tell style while going back to the harder and heavier Fania years for inspiration. For sheer dance-floor appeal, *Pero Dile*'s manic momentum makes the heart race and *Como Duele* edgily delivers on the promise of jazz-influenced salsa. In *Si por ti Fuera*, Manuelle rode the rolling cumbia beat into a standard salsa format, delivering one of his simplest and most satisfying flights of romantic fantasy. With *Le Preguntaba a la Luna*, released in 2002, Manuelle made the transition between emerging talent and star. On his most polished releases, he evoked the power of a maturing

Rubén Blades. His status as salsa's ultimate ladies' man was solidified with tunes like *Devuélveme*, and *El Tonto que No te Olvidó*, and the sheer swing in the horn section in a song like *Tengo* does bring back memories of the 1970s Fania era.

What's most impressive about Manuelle (besides his good looks and charismatic presence) is his ability to improvise. After Puerto Rico's forty-year history of interplay between hotel-style bolero singers and rustic-roots innovators like Rafael Cortijo, Manuelle, and to a degree his contemporary Domingo Quiñones, fused the smooth melodic lines demanded by commercial salsa with the edgy, scat shouts of a more primal source.

As of 2003, salsa music is still immensely popular despite a number of controversies and contradictions. In 2002, old guard musicians like Larry Harlow and Eddie Palmieri made public pronouncements over what they called *salsa monga* (lazy salsa), their term for salsa romantica, even as younger musicians like Sergio George continued to innovate by bringing in more R&B and hip-hop influence to recordings from Marc Anthony to Celia Cruz. In the late 1990s to the early part of the new century, there was renewed interest in "serious" salsa. Trombonist Jimmy Bosch and percussionist Ralph Irizarry developed followings in New York for playing music that was truer to the Afro-Cuban and jazz roots of the Cuban dance orchestra, and in 2002, Oscar Hernández, a long-time Rubén Blades collaborator, released the debut of the Spanish Harlem Orchestra, *Un Gran Día en el Barrio*, reviving classic 1970s salsa tunes.

Statistics from the Recording Industry Association of America showed that sales of "tropical" music, which includes merengue, were down in the United States, and sales of Mexican regional music was up, but salsa radio stations on the East Coast continued their dominance in Nielsen ratings, and salsa dance classes continued to expand. Latin pop and rock continued to gain in popularity, but these genres' vitality often seemed to increase as a function of their ability to include Afro-Caribbean rhythms.

Salsa began as, and will always be, a hybrid, urban music. As new hybrids of Latin music appear, salsa may continue to evolve, but like jazz, it always evokes a special time and place. In the end salsa belongs to a moment when Latin American identity in the United States crystallized, and it created a ripple effect felt everywhere in the world.

MARIACHI REVERIE

Paul Berman

I.

Up the street from Macy's in downtown Brooklyn is a modest little shop called Fast & Fresh Deli, which, at a glance, appears to be a down-at-the-heels grocery-and-sandwich shop like thousands of others in New York, but turns out to be, at second glance, a bit of Mexico City transplanted into the distant north. I stop at that place a few times a month and order beef tacos, and I sit on a stool at the counter and listen to the boom box above the stove. And, like everyone else at Fast & Fresh, sometimes I find that one song or another has thrown me into unexpected moods and reveries, and little stabs of savory emotion compete for my attention with the equally savory stabs of cilantro and raw onion in my mouth. More than once the boom box has played a mariachi classic called "Volver, Volver"—"To Return, to Return"—in the version belted out by Vicente Fernández, the Mexican mariachi king. A reedy organ proclaims a few opening notes, two trumpets blare a melodious fanfare, the greasy beef dissolves into the grainy corn tortilla, and—surely I'm not the only one to have had this experience, seated on a stool at Fast & Fresh—my heart swells.

How many times I have heard "Volver, Volver"! I walk through the New York streets, and phrases from that song seep from the back doors of restaurants, where the dishwashers are toiling. I hear the song in the Mexican groceries that have popped up everywhere in New York during these last few years. I hear it on the sidewalks of an East Harlem that long ago ceased to be Italian (except for a few lingerers), and is scarcely even Puerto Rican anymore, though it pretends to be, but has managed to become, in its tastes and storefronts and in the look of the passing crowds, an outpost of Puebla, Mexico. Or I listen as one of New York's innumerable mariachi bands strikes up the song in a restaurant. Or someone drives past in a beat-up old car, and the song comes vibrating out the windows—"Vol-vair, volll . . . VAIR!" And each new time the song recurs, I am somehow reminded of the previous times, until the merest phrase from that song sends me hurtling downward into caverns of fathomless nostalgia.

The most sensational rendition I have ever heard was in San José, Costa Rica, many years ago. It was Christmas Eve. Costa Rica is an agrarian place, and every year horsemen come into the capital from the farms and go cantering past the cathedral and the main plaza and through the streets in an equestrian parade called "el Tope," showing off their most spectacular horses and waving at cheerful crowds. I was late in getting to the parade and had to make my way into one of what are called the "popular" barrios—which is to say, the poor people's districts—to catch the tail end. The parade had gotten a little bedraggled by then. Even so, horsemen came trotting by dressed in the finery that you see in the old-fashioned Westerns, the ancient Spanish costumes from centuries ago—the embroidered short jackets and bolero hats and the magnificent tooled boots. Sometimes, as the horsemen cantered by, they pulled on the reins and their horses reared and pranced—"el Tope," the prance—and girls in the crowd laughed and waved and ran into the street, and now and then a horseman scooped up a girl with one arm and with a single swoop seated her on the back of his saddle and trotted off, the horse swaggering its silky flanks and the crowd cheering at the merry scenes of rapture.

The crowd had grown a little beery by the time I arrived, and the aluminum cans spilled across the sidewalk and onto the street. And yet, just as the beer seemed to have won a final victory over the tropical afternoon, the most magnificent horseman of all came lazying along on a stolid white horse. This grandest of horsemen was a mariachi singer, dressed in a short, white embroidered jacket and studded tight pants, with a gun holstered to his thigh. The horseman held the reins with one hand and a microphone with the other, and behind him rolled a big sound truck with the horseman's broad white charro hat atop the cabin, next to the loudspeaker. The horseman braced himself on his stirrups to firm up his diaphragm, and, with the loud-speaker blaring the background music, he held up his mike and belted out his own version of "Volver, Volver":

> Este amor apasionado
> Anda todo alborotado
> Por volver!
> Voy camino a la locura
> Y aunque todo me tortura,
> Sé querer!

This impassioned love
Keeps me all stirred up
To return!
I'm going straight into madness
And though everything tortures me,
I know how to love!

That singer was magnificent. His voice was as big as his horse.

Nos dejamos hace tiempo
Pero me llegó el momento
De perder.
Tu tenías mucha razón.
Le hago caso al corazón
Y me muero por volver.

We left each other long ago,
But the moment of heartbreak
Has come.
You were very right.
I listen to my heart.
And I'm dying to return.

He rose still higher on the stirrups and gestured to the crowd. And everywhere along the sidewalks, the tipsy and uproarious people took up where he had left off, bellowing out the chorus in a burst of beer fumes—a raucous crowd, thousands of people, bawling the words in unison, every single person at the top of his lungs, in a roar:

Y volver, volver, volll-VERRR!
And to return, return, ree-TURRRN!
The horseman answered:
A tus brazos otra vez!
Llegaré donde estés.
Yo sé perder, yo sé perder.
Quiero volver, volver, volver.
To your arms once again!
I will come where you are.
I know how to lose, how to lose,
I want to return, return, return!

And he went once more through the song, until the crowd, swaying to the music and waving their cans, roared once again, "Volver, volver, volll-VERRR!"

II.

I worry that, describing the song in this way, and in recalling the mariachi horseman of Costa Rica and the tipsy crowd, I am giving the wrong impression of this song. Or I may be feeding an ignorant prejudice—a notion of mariachi as music for drunkards and louts, something crude, artless, a music for roughnecks and the uneducated, and not for anyone more refined. But no, no—there are jewels in this music. Besides, I don't want to sneer at the crowd. Even feelings that are roared in the street may have their justification. And there are traditions to consider, which suggest refinements and emotions of their own, unto the most fantastic complications.

Those costumes, to begin with, the studded pants and the beholstered uniform—there is something to say about that. I have a CD of what is supposed to be the earliest and most classic of the mariachi orchestras, the Mariachi Vargas de Tecalitlán, which was founded in 1897 in Jalisco, Mexico, on the West Coast. A photo in the album brochure shows the Mariachi Vargas in its early days, when the instrumentation consisted of two violins, a wooden-box harp, and a more-or-less standard guitar called a *guitarra mariachera*. Everyone dressed in white linens, short neckties, and straw sombreros—the traditional *campesino* clothes of long ago. But that was then.

By the 1930s, mariachi orchestras had come to include several violins, the wooden-box folk harp (sometimes replaced by an accordion or even an electric organ), a couple of trumpets, and three kinds of guitars—a standard guitar; a tiny round-backed *vihuela*, which I suppose might be considered a lute; and an acoustic bass guitar called a *guitarrón*, as big as a cello. The costumes likewise evolved, until they had arrived at what is standard today—the tight, studded pants opening onto cowboy boots, the broad silk neckties or scarves, the short brocaded jackets, and, for the singer and sometimes for the entire orchestra, an enormous, broad-brimmed charro hat of the sort that Mexican restaurants hang on the wall. Plus the singer's gun and holster, strapped to his hip. These costumes have something in common with a matador's uniform—flamboyant costumes of an armed aristocracy. Here is homage to the Spanish Empire and its medieval virtues, and yet homage as well to the rustic spirit of Western Mexico—a mix of European martial arrogance and humble farm life. You don't see anything like this in the conventional folk culture of the United States, except maybe in a few corners of the magnolia-and-moonlight Confederacy, where people have gone on dreaming of Sir Walter Scott, or in the Western rodeos, where the gringo cowboys were always doing their best to imitate the Mexicans, anyway.

From a strictly musical standpoint, mariachi has a few idiosyncrasies that someone accustomed to the conventions of American pop and folk music might fail to notice, and the first of those peculiar musical traits is surely this same mixture of the elegant and the rustic. Violins in a mariachi orchestra are not country fiddles. They are classical instruments, and vibrato is everything. Mariachi violins do tend to get a little wavery and screechy now and then, even on some of the best recordings (which adds a touching note of frailty to the music—the pathos of the out-of-tune). But the violins are not supposed to be frail and feeble, and in better orchestras the violins do produce, at least sometimes, a pure and rich sound, tasty and sweet—the delicacy of a zarzuela orchestra from the musical theatre of Madrid, or a light opera from the Paris music halls. (According to one of the theories about mariachi and its origins, the music owes something to the occupying French Army of the Emperor Maximilian, during France's 1860s adventure in Mexico.)

But there are trumpets, too, and the trumpets tend to be played with the ferocity of a bullfight band—sometimes bleating noisily, often a little sharp (though some of the trumpeters do know what they're doing, needless to say, and are perfectly capable of performing with the greatest delicacy, sometimes with a sweetening mute, like the trumpets that accompany Caribbean trios). And so, in a mariachi orchestra, the violins rustle like flowers and the trumpets roar like farm animals. The orchestra might end up sounding in one passage like a slightly peculiar opera orchestra, and, a moment later, like a jaunty country band, inebriated and aggressive. And, in that fashion, mariachi orchestras go teetering forward—refined and rustic, sweet and braying, orchestras of the high and the low—like nothing else I have ever heard.

The rhythms, too, play with ideas and customs that depart pretty radically from the customary rhythms of American folk music and pop music. A traditional mariachi song might lurch from one pattern to another within a song—sometimes varying the tempo, sometimes the syncopation, tripping from one Mexican hat-dance complexity to the next, or settling for a moment into a rhumba or a two-beat gait. Variation is the thing, not monotony and groove—a variation that descends from Spain and not from Africa (except when the orchestra strikes up a rhumba). The rhythms are meant for dancing, but, at least in some of the more traditional mariachi songs, the dancing is supposed to be elaborate and formal, a "shoeing" or *zapateando* that requires certain specific steps and a lot of well-defined heel-tapping and skirt-swishing. And yet the most striking aspect of all has got to be the singing, and this, once again, because of the range of variation.

A first-rate mariachi singer commands several vocal techniques and might very well put every one of those techniques to use in a single song—a syrupy crooning, an open-throated singing in the broad style of Italian opera, an occasional sob, and a series of yelps, which come in regional variations. A yelp from Jalisco, where mariachi got its start (and all mariachi seems to have remained, in some respect, Jalisciense, no matter where the orchestra makes its home), is a high-pitched, extended *ay-ay-yi-iiii* that can sound genuinely weird. This is not the cheerful *yippee-yi-yo* of a singing cowboy—this is a cry of anguish, unto insanity, something hair-raising, a wild tone. And, having done all that, a singer might conclude his phrase by sliding down a fourth, as if slipping alcoholically from his chair to the floor, from F to C. And these vocal maneuvers and techniques, in their marvelous variety, their idiosyncrasy, humor, intensity, and virtuosity, make for a lyrical exposition that is, in the end, theatrical in the extreme—passionate, tender, raucous, violent, operatic, lunatic, demagogic, and hammy beyond all hamminess. All of which is performed above the courtly-and-rustic instruments and the varying syncopations—a music that has very little in common with the main impulses of American folk and pop, and everything to do with the folk and theatre traditions of Spain and probably France, too, long ago.

But now I worry that, having pointed out a few mariachi oddities, I may have made the music seem excessively exotic or foreign from American life, as if this kind of music were nothing but an immigrant import. That would be a big mistake—even if, nowadays, there do seem to be a lot of immigrants, and some of them have formed orchestras, and entire neighborhoods seem to feel a civic obligation to turn up their boom boxes in order to augment the public joy. No, mariachi ought to count as, in its fashion, an authentically American music. Or so I want to argue, and I will cite highest authority.

For what does it mean, really, to be American—what are the distinctly American qualities? The qualities of the United States, I mean, and not of the Americas as a whole. An unanswerable question, you may say. But there is a way to answer, and that is to glance at the first group of people to pose this question in a recognizably modern version.

III.

Those people were the poets and intellectuals of the generation that came of age forty or fifty years after the American Revolution—writers like Longfellow in Massachusetts and Whitman in New York, who wanted to know what it meant to be American, and what America's purpose ought to be. The Revolutionary generation, the Founding Fathers, had answered those questions with legal and political principles. The writers who came along a few decades later wanted to speak, instead, about culture and history. They wanted to dig up folk traditions from the past, the unique qualities of American life, and to discover in those qualities a sap and vigor capable of shooting upward and blossoming in the future. They knew very well that American culture was rooted in the English past, but they also wanted to show that American culture drew on other roots, far, far from the British Isles—and the farther, the better.

Longfellow mooned over the shores of Gitchie Gumee precisely because the Indians offered an indigenous tradition that was not England's—because the Indians helped define what was distinctively American, just as the last of the great Eastern Woodlands tribes were being pushed across the Mississippi. That was a big theme for the writers of Longfellow's time—for Thoreau, Parkman, Cooper, and so many others, each one of them fascinated by the Indian past. And, on that same logic, Longfellow and William H. Prescott and Washington Irving and more than a few other writers insisted on taking seriously the Spanish origins of the United States—the origins that could be found in the Southwest mostly, though also in Florida, New Orleans, the Northwest, and other places from the days of Spanish greatness: "When the flag of Spain unfurled / Its folds o'er this western world," in Longfellow's phrase.

Spain had spent several hundred years as England's hated enemy, on grounds of imperial rivalry as well as religion, and the American writers knew they were being slightly insolent in claiming a Spanish heritage for themselves. But insolence was itself an American trait. Whitman loved the Spanish on that count. He pointed to what he called, in the title of one of his essays, "The Spanish Element in Our Nationality," and he even set about incorporating a bit of fake Spanish into *Leaves of Grass*—"As I lay with my head in your lap camerado," and that sort of thing (though the correct Spanish word would be *camarada*). "Comrade Americanos!" Whitman cried out. His was the original Spanglish in literature. He loved the word *libertad*. Saying "liberty" in Spanish gave those syllables an extra dignity. Or maybe the Spanish word signified a bit of American solidarity with the freedom fighters of monarchical Spain and Latin America. *Libertad* was the key to Whitman's "A Broadway Pageant"—which is to say, he plunked down his Spanish word in the center of Manhattan.

But the "Spanish element" attracted these writers for another reason, too. These people, every one of them, were Romantics, and the Romantic writers in every country went looking for medieval roots and eternal national characteristics and historical destinies, and they tended to find these many things in a dream landscape that everyone described as Spain. The Romantics were a little nauseated by the ravages of liberal civilization and by the bleached-out Protestantism and rationalism of the Northern countries, and Spain was, for them, the great alternative. It was a pure land of medieval tradition and high passion, a land of the pre-bourgeois and of Catholic nostalgias, of impetuous emotion, a land of the gut and the heart and not the brain. Even the cruelty of the Spanish Inquisition had its perverse allure. The French Romantics were especially excited by these Iberian qualities, and they threw themselves into composing even more fake Spanish than Whitman ever did. Victor Hugo was always salting his plays, poems, and novels with passages of fake-Spanish dialogue, and sometimes even a bit of correct Spanish. It made him feel he was saying something rougher and more violent than could possibly be said in French.

These writers wanted to resurrect the literary and song traditions of the Middle Ages, if only they could figure out where to find those lost traditions; and here Spain was truly useful, not just in the zones of fantasy. People in Spain were already nostalgic for the distant past—more keenly nostalgic, I think, than anyone else in Western Europe. The Spanish enthusiasm had long ago turned into a tradition of its own. In whole regions of the Spanish countryside, people did remember the medieval lyrics. The Spanish were in this respect Romantics before Romanticism. They had long ago set the old lyrics into print in the *Romancero*, the medieval songbook. And these authentic traits of Spanish life drove the poets in other countries into ecstasies of artistic inspiration.

Hugo found in the *Romancero* a way of writing immense stories in a fragmentary lyric fashion, as if composing ballads to be sung to guitar accompaniment, in the Spanish fashion. Whitman never even tried to do anything similar. Yet he, too, went out of his way to sing the virtues of Spanish tradition. He did this in an essay called "British Literature," where he recommended Cervantes and the tales of *el Cid*, meaning the *Romancero*, in preference even to Shakespeare. This was carrying the anti-British insolence a little far. Whitman couldn't help himself. The multicultural was one of his tropes, and the more multiculti he was, the more democratic and even nationalist he felt. But I can imagine that, in nodding to Spain, Whitman meant to express something more than openness to a polyglot world. He felt the same inspiration that Hugo felt. It was a feeling for the grand sweep of human affairs—a feeling for whatever is overarching in world history—the universal and not the parochial or the particular.

In its many ballads, the *Romancero* told stories of kings and knights and lovers, but the nineteenth-century writers glimpsed in those separate tales a larger, vaguer story. This was the immense epic of the *Reconquista*—the Christian crusade to retake Spain from the Moors, a seven-hundred-year affair. This was not a narrow theme—this was the very struggle that, at its end, sent the conquistadors, as if propelled by giant catapults, across the Atlantic to continue the same crusade against ever-new populations of Moors, and to convert the Western Hemisphere to the Christian cross. This was the story of all mankind (if you could get yourself for a moment to picture Catholicism's progress, and mankind's, as the same). Something in the notion of composing a fragmentary verse epic of universal history did seem to appeal to the author of *Leaves of Grass*. You can see another version of the same influence still more clearly in Longfellow and his "Tales of the Wayside Inn" and other ballads. Longfellow wanted to compose a national epic in lyric fragments—the national epic that, for him, too, was going to speak of universal progress, from servitude to freedom. Longfellow's ear was tuned to English tradition. Yet, he, too, went out of his way to acknowledge the Spanish heritage, and not just in his translations of Lope de Vega and other writers. He wrote "The Bells of San Blas" on a Mexican theme—which is to say, Longfellow made a point of acknowledging the Spanish heritage not just in faraway Spain, but in places where the Spanish flag unfurled across the Western world.

The heritage of the Spanish *Romancero* was, in any case, a living thing in the United States of Longfellow's day. In New England, Spanish legacies (yes, even in New England) had mostly died out by the nineteenth century, but maybe not entirely. Longfellow remembered them in his poem about the Newport Jews—legacies courtesy of the Sephardic. But in other places, farther south, the Spanish heritage had never ceased to flourish. The conquistadors brought the *Romancero* to the Western world just as much as they brought the cross and the sword. And the *Romancero* and the culture that surrounded it—the nostalgia for the Middle Ages, the tradition of heroic ballads—took root. New variations of the old "romances" or ballads sprang up in all of the Spanish regions of the New World, and those regions included the zones eventually incorporated into the United States.

The Mexican scholar Mercedes Díaz Roig compiled a fascinating volume a few years ago called the *Romancero tradicional de América*, and, in her catalogue of the Romances of the Western Hemisphere and its several regions, she included a section on the Latin American zone known as Estados Unidos, which had generated some highly traditional "Romances," unknown in other places. None of this ever withered away. For what are the *corridos* of the American Southwest today, and of northern Mexico—what are those two-beat and three-beat polka-rhythm ballads about wetbacks, bandits, and the like, the "narco-*corridos*" with their drug-smuggler heroes? Those are living fruits of a very old tree. The "Spanish element" that Whitman and Longfellow wanted to claim for the American nationality, the *Romancero* and its New World legacies, the Catholic memories, the peculiar Spanish nostalgias—these are things of the present, not just of the forgotten and exotic past.

v.

In drawing a few connections between the mariachi orchestras and these older Spanish traditions, I don't want to turn the mariachis into conquistadors, and I don't want to attribute the typical lyrics of mariachi repertory to the old *Romancero* and its heritage. The *corridos* tell elaborate stories and are visibly in the grand tradition, and this is not true of the more typical mariachi lyrics (though mariachi orchestras do perform *corridos*, sometimes). Still, there are many ways to tell a story, and the mariachi orchestras do tell a story. The costumes by themselves conjure the past. And that gun on the singer's hip, the mandatory gun—what is that, if not a sign that the singer is a warrior, and these are warrior songs, ballads that a wandering knight might pluck on his guitar? The *Romancero* expresses one kind of medieval nostalgia, and here is another. Jorge Negrete, the mariachi film star of some sixty years ago, sang a hit called "El Charro Mexicano" on this theme—on the glories of his own brocaded sombrero, silk tie, pistol, guitar, and spurs. And Negrete concluded, like a knight warbling his creed:

Soy la noble tradición!
Soy el charro mexicano,
Noble, valiente, y leal!

I am the noble tradition!
I am the flashy Mexican dude,
Noble, valiant, and loyal!

Then again, the mariachi orchestras have a history of their own, something modern, and I think that, at least in Mexico, audiences understand this, too, if only by intuition. The Mexican Revolution broke out in 1910 and proved to be vast and traumatic—the largest and most violent single event to occur anywhere in the Western Hemisphere in the twentieth century. The revolutionary generals warred with one another, which was a disaster that lasted twenty years. Eventually, though, the generals had the good sense to join together in the massive national organization that became known, in time, as the Party of the Institutional Revolution, the PRI. And the PRI turned out to be wonderfully successful at creating a sense of order and unity in Mexico, in the name of nationalism and revolutionary ideals.

The greatest of those early PRI leaders was Lázaro Cárdenas, who became president in 1934—a kind of Franklin Roosevelt, except more radical. And Cárdenas, with his cunning and his vision of a Mexican future, set out to construct not just order and peace but something more, a national culture. Mariachi music had gotten started, as I say, in Jalisco in the late nineteenth century. Cárdenas came up with the inspired idea of bringing the best of the Jalisciense orchestras, the Mariachi Vargas de Tecatitlán, to Mexico City to play at his inauguration. Then he put the orchestra on the payroll of the Mexico City police department and took the musicians on tour with him around the country, and in this way set about creating a revolutionary popular culture for Mexico as a whole. Mexican radio and film arose in those same years, and the people who built these new industries likewise turned to mariachi in search of a national culture, something with commercial appeal, which they increased by adding trumpets to the original set of instruments (or, at least, that is one version of how trumpets came to play a part in the mariachi orchestras) and by making the uniforms standard for everyone. Mariachi orchestras appear in some 200 movies from the Golden Age of Mexican filmmaking, which is pretty astounding, if you try to picture the experience of sitting in a Mexican movie theatre during these last many decades.

Mariachi offered a revolutionary answer to a fearfully difficult question for Mexicans—namely, how to compete with the commercial music and film products from the United States, and how to do so without turning to Spain, the oppressor from the past. The PRI's achievement was to bring together impossible contradictions into a single, disciplined, national organization. Mariachi did something similar in the alternative universe of music. Mariachi gathered together medieval memories, revolutionary populism, knightly arrogance, rustic humility, *campesino* rebelliousness, and the modernizing drive of the national state and the radio and film industries, not to mention a cult of Mexican regionalism—and somehow, by pickling these things in a spirit of tragedy and pathos and nationalism, ended up with a marvelous and moving mythology, musical and theatrical at the same time.

Does that seem impossible? You must see the movies of Pedro Infante. There is a scene in *Las Mujeres de mi general* (Ismael Rodríguez, 1950) where the great star leads an army in the revolution, scandalizes high society by proposing to marry his low-class camp-follower, and serenades the young lady by organizing what appears to be the entire revolutionary armed forces in the middle of the night to put down their rifles and pick up guitars and sing to her in the stony streets, with the radiant young lady replying with lyrics of her own from her balcony—a glorious noir-filmed scene that expresses the eternal values of ardent love, military valor, Mexican nationalism, revolutionary commitment, disdain for the prejudices of the past, and reverence for the virtues of the past, not excluding the crucifix on the wall. Now, that's movie-making!— Not to mention choral harmonizing! Not to mention guitar-playing! Not to mention those fabulous hats!—the hats that grandly perpetuate the image of the gigantic sombreros worn by Emiliano Zapata, the most radical of the rural leaders from the most radical period of the revolution, when the *campesino* millennium seemed plausibly at hand and the age of oppression and injustice seemed to have disappeared into the past. (Not to mention, in addition, that Manuel M. Ponce, one of Latin America's finest classical-music composers, arranged the serenade.)

And so, in those years of the mariachi boom, from the 1930s to the 1950s, a story hovered behind the mariachi orchestras that audiences could instinctively recognize. It was the story of the Mexican Revolution in its many impossible complexities—the revolution that was forward-looking and backward-looking at the same time, feudal and populist and sometimes even socialist. This story underwent a few twists and turns of its own in the next few years, and the new twists added still more echoes and themes to the music. The 1930s to 1950s were glory years for the PRI. But the whole structure of Mexican life began to sag after a while, and, by 1968, a new generation of sophisticated young people had come of age, filled with impatience at the Institutional Revolution and its byzantine and heavy-handed customs, and fed up with the commercial arts of the official culture. The new cultural radicals saw in the old mariachi orchestras the music of an authoritarian culture of the older times—the culture of the one-party state and the feudal past. Mariachi began to appear, in the eyes of the cultural radicals, as a music of a slightly loony male domination, in an antique style that no one in his right mind could tolerate anymore. Now, this last complaint was not always fair. Lola Beltrán was one of the greatest of the mariachi singers, and her throaty and fiery singing expressed the same kind of hot-blooded ferocity as that of her male colleagues, or maybe even hotter, if that were possible, which it is.

But the hot-blooded style, whether male or female, was itself a sign of a macho universe—a lover's universe in which the amorous and the murderous were erotically entwined, and the holster on the singer's hip symbolized a lover's tyranny, and violent jealousy seemed the highest expression of ardor. The radical sophisticates of 1968 couldn't abide that stuff any longer. Plus there was the rigidity of the music itself. The 1968 student uprisings were genuinely massive in Mexico, especially in Mexico City; and, as everywhere that year, those uprisings were about music as much as anything else. They were uprisings against the old state-sanctioned music, in favor of different kinds of music, which seemed liberating and exciting to the students. And what kinds of music were those? Cuban-influenced protest music—but also a few styles and performers from the English-speaking world. The radical students took to listening to the Beatles and Joan Baez—the anti-machistas, singers of the gentle instead of the violent (except sometimes), singers who were positively cute and wistful, singers who did not wear guns on their hips. The older, revolutionary generation in Mexico found this hard to take. The revolutionary elders accused the young people of being Soviet agents, and this accusation tended to mean, in regard to music, that young people had forsaken the national patrimony not just for Fidel Castro's cultural productions but for crappy music from the historic enemy across the border, and from the historic enemy's linguistic forebears and allies—musical treason, in a word. But then, for the younger people, English-language music was not really the point.

Up-to-dateness was the point. The same kind of people in Mexico who grooved to gringo musicians in 1968 went on, in later years, to become the fans of the new Cuban dance bands, not because of any association with Fidel but simply on grounds of musical hipness and love of artistry—this, together with a continued revulsion for the patriarchal and feudal memories that seemed to cry out from the old mariachi orchestras. I have watched people respond in very similar ways to mariachi in Nicaragua, where the music established itself long ago, thanks to the influence of Mexican recordings and movies. During the violent struggles between the left and right in Nicaragua in the 1980s and 1990s, the sophisticated leftists of Managua and the universities tended to be fans of American folk and pop music in the 1980s (as well as of the Cuban-influenced protest music) and then went on, in later years, to become the lovers of Afro-Caribbean dance music. But the rural enemies of the Managua leftists were solidly the fans of mariachi. The Sandinistas answered to one set of musical tastes, the contras to another. Wall posters in the Sandinista towns might feature José

José or some other Mexican or Spanish pop star, but wall posters in the contra zones of the faraway rural districts were likely to feature Vicente Fernández, grinning from under his charro hat.

Or maybe the controversies over mariachi in the last few decades have had to do with a relatively simple sense of past and present—a feeling that mariachi comes out of a long-ago time that, in some people's eyes, seems, in its antiquity, a little repulsive. There is in Mexico a genuinely large class of people who are mendicant musicians, people who roam the streets begging for coins or hoping for a commission to go perform at someone's party or to go stand under some woman's window and serenade her. It's hard to believe, but these people, some of them, have been organized into the PRI, where they make up the rank-and-file of the street-accordionists' union and other sturdy structures of what used to be the giant party-state. But the street musicians express nothing of what once used to be the PRI's commitment to the modern and the efficient. Those musicians are the failed, the ancient, the impoverished. There is something appalling about them, in their studded, tight-fitting uniforms that long ago decayed into rags, carrying their dented instruments and radiating an air of hopeless poverty and even of crime.

Mariachi orchestras wander around Plaza Garibaldi in Mexico City looking for work, and those musicians can be a pretty fearful sight, as if at any moment they might turn into Pedro Infante's guitar-playing serenaders in reverse, and might put down their guitars and violins, and pull out guns, and finish you off, quick. There's a bit of a homosexual desperado underground in some of this, too, at Plaza Garibaldi (a natural component of a music that so insistently exaggerates the masculine), which makes, all in all, a frightening scene: run-down, pathetic, ragged, and impoverished, a vista of every wretchedness of ages past. Yet those same musicians, for the equivalent of five or ten dollars, can still break your heart with a well-performed rendition of this or that classic of the repertory, depending on your command. And everyone knows it. In Mexico and in Central America, too, people on the left as well as on the right, the sophisticates and the anti-sophisticates, the sexual Neanderthals and the sexual progressives, all of them, so far as I can judge, with a few curmudgeonly exceptions, do seem to have a soft spot for mariachi. And who could not?

v.

"Volver, Volver," then. On second thought, I once heard a rendition that was even more astonishing than the horseback performance at the Tope parade in San José. This was at Radio City Music Hall, in New York, in the mid-1990s. Vicente Fernández was performing. Radio City is an enormous auditorium with seats for several thousand people, and tickets for that performance cost sixty dollars, which was expensive; even so, those thousands of seats were sold out, and crowds were clamoring at the entrance. And who were those fans, demanding their seats? Mexicans and Central Americans almost entirely, most of them young, and more men than women.

This was not the new, young, prosperous Mexican-American middle class, except for some. This was an audience of immigrant proletarians who had spent a huge portion of their week's pay to get into that concert hall. A sizable percentage of New York's restaurant dishwashers must have been in attendance, together with any number of construction laborers and random workers, throwing away their money in an extravagant gesture. And why were they doing so? It was easy to imagine. The Mexican Revolution was the single largest social or political event of the twentieth century in the Western Hemisphere, and the Mexican emigration to the United States may well end up as the single largest such event in our new century.

Already there are said to be twenty million Mexicans in the United States, an astounding figure. These people have been wrenched out of traditional settings and thrown into modern American life, at its bottommost rung, without families or wives or girlfriends, living a kind of half-existence in which they toil in the United States, send most of their earnings back home to Mexico, and dream of their own return, someday—immigrant existences in which their wallets are in the United States and their hearts are in Mexico. And so, those young men may have lost their women and their hometowns and everything they used to know and love, but for sixty dollars, they could have Vicente Fernández and his Aztec mariachis—"Chente" Fernández, the mariachi king. They could count on Chente to re-create for them, on the Radio City Music Hall stage, everything they did not have. And Chente proved reliable.

His orchestra was in full uniform, with short jackets and studded pants, deployed across the enormous stage—guitar, *vihuela, guitarrón*, several violins, two trumpets, folk harp, and electric organ. The great man himself bounded onto the stage with his charro hat in his hand, which he immediately set down. He launched into one beloved hit after another. There have been a lot of these hits, for thirty years now. He began with current songs, in the knowledge that present-day music always carries less emotional weight. This was a man who knew how to send his concerts aloft on a proper orbit, starting at a level of mere excitement and then arching slowly upward into the heavens of sheerest hysteria, where the oldest hits, like shiny stars, are forever twinkling. The audience enjoyed those current hits, the ones he played at the start. The cheers were already loud and boisterous.

Chente's performing style was peculiar. The music required vast extremes of emotion and hammy theatricality, and not least a genuinely athletic vocal skill, opera-style in full vibrato. All the while he strutted dramatically up and down the stage, sometimes leaning on one of the stage wings, then racing to the other side, the image of energy and stamina, in his brocaded jacket. Yet, as he sang, a constant stream of audience members, one or two at a time, made their way up the auditorium aisle, past the bodyguards, to the foot of the stage, where they held up concert programs for Chente to autograph. He idled to the front of the stage, knelt on one knee to reach down, and regally affixed his signature, even as he went on singing. It was pretty strange to see him do this, given the exuberant nature of his songs and his own singing—an odd kind of distancing, to use the theatre term. The singer on his knee signing concert programs made you reflect that his many outlandish emotions and his thrilling vibrato and his athletic strutting were merely an act that he had repeated ten thousand times, and he could perfectly well sign autographs while he sang, and maybe he was contemplating his post-concert dinner, too, and perhaps he was reminding himself to hire an auditor to keep an eye on his accountant. And he never missed a beat or dropped a lyric.

A woman came to the foot of the stage and handed up a little girl of about four or five for Chente to kiss. He did kiss her, then stood her upright on the stage while he knelt at her side. I wondered if this wasn't a setup—if the little girl wasn't actually the guitarist's daughter, who had spent her entire life being dandled on don Vicente's knee and standing next to him on the stage to be cheered by enthusiastic crowds. Every single person at Radio City must have expected the girl to burst into tears or to leap from the stage into her mother's arms. The little tyke did nothing of the sort. Chente wooed her tenderly with his giant tenor voice, the violins and guitars serenaded from the rear of the stage, and the girl suddenly smiled and accepted her homage and even kissed his cheek—a coup de théatre (which, by the way, reprised a scene from Pedro Infante's *Las Mujeres de mi general*). Then another few people straggled to the foot of the stage to have their concert programs signed, and Chente went back on his knee, autographing still more programs. And still the hits came, one after another, sung at full throttle, and the guitars plucked and strummed, and the violinists sawed away, and the trumpets played fanfares and countermelodies.

I was never bored—that would have been impossible at such a performance. But I did wonder, after a while, at what moment the intermission was going to arrive. Chente's performance was a high-energy extravaganza, and I noticed that the sturdy *guitarronista* at the rear supported his heavy instrument from a cord around his neck without any sort of stand or prop to share the weight, which must have put quite a strain on the man's back. The other musicians, too, must have been pretty tired, standing upright in their natty uniforms without a single chance to sit or even stretch their legs. The concert had begun at 8, and by 10:30 it was reasonable to wonder how much longer these guys could go on.

But there was no question of an intermission. Nor did anyone ever leave the stage, except Chente himself for a moment, only to return at full volume. The audience had been enjoying their beers, and, after a couple of hours, people were fairly drunk, streaming up and down the aisles on their way to the bathrooms. Someone dropped a paper cup of beer on me from an upstairs balcony. After a while, a straggle of people began to make their way to the foot of the stage to pass along to Chente flasks containing something or other, and the great man took swigs from the flasks and smiled and passed the flasks back down, and went on singing. I did think he had begun to stagger a little, and after a while I concluded that Vicente Fernández had become drunk on stage. At least, he seemed to be.

A good many mariachi songs are about liquor and drunkenness—songs of alcoholism, really, though the alcohol mostly figures in a larger theme, which is the topic of masculinity and its tragedies. This is, finally, the single most insistent theme in the mariachi songbook, at least on its *ranchera* side—songs of one hero after another who has had to embrace failure, the tragedy of the defeated, the rage and self-pity and the alcoholic hiccups of heroes who have struggled in life and in love and have gotten knocked down at every turn, and who hold their heads high even so, and have learned how to lose, and how to maintain their masculine dignity by singing at top volume with a bravura rebellious spirit, no matter what. Some of these songs tell the story of farm laborers who never make any money and never get their girl and live a migrant life, and keep going, nonetheless—songs of labor and suffering.

Chente launched into "De un rancho a otro"—"From One Ranch to Another"—one of his greatest hits. The crowd roared. The size and depth of that roar made me realize that, at Radio City, the audience consisted very largely of people like the wandering farmworker in that song—people who had made their way through God-knows-what miseries from Mexico to New York, and had taken jobs at the lowest of low pays, and had shown an insuperably tough spirit, and had kept at their labors, and damn well deserved the recognition they were getting from a song like that. On the other hand, I found myself reflecting that Vicente Fernández himself was hardly such a person. His listeners were the oppressed and the exploited of New York, and he himself was a wealthy pop star who was probably staying at the fanciest of hotels, swathed in satin. Such were my thoughts as I sat in the center of the orchestra section, wiping the beer suds off my shoulder.

But then Chente himself must have worried, from his place on the stage, that somewhere in the gigantic hall an audience-member like me might be harboring just such thoughts, perhaps even questioning his bona fides in regard to toughness and grit—the principal topic of his own songs. Or, who's to say what he was thinking? He did seem to notice, after a while, that he was singing into a microphone, which was not an unusual thing to do, especially in a hall as cavernous as Radio City. And yet, he seemed to ask himself, does a man, a real and authentic man, a man with indomitable spirit—a *man*, in short—need the aid of something as petty and artificial as a mike? He stared at his mike, astonished. In a disdainful gesture, he put it down—the ugly, electronic thing. And, as if naked, he went on singing, unamplified, unprotected, unaided, his voice suddenly reduced to mere human scale—a shocking change, the real voice suddenly audible, the kind of voice that you never get to hear in pop concerts, the actual vibrations. Yet he sang with genuine technique, up from the belly and chest, his voice warbling with a giant vibrato, and, by God, those powerful throbs filled the hall—the voice of a slightly dented and battle-hardened opera singer who knows how to make enormous buildings resonate to his own implacable will. The audience could barely believe its eyes and ears.

It was not just that Chente was visibly drunk and that it was 11 P.M. and there had not been an intermission, and the man had been singing for three hours at the top of his lungs. By throwing away his mike, that man had just managed to drink his audience under the table. The mere mortals in the audience went on dragging themselves up and down the aisles to the bathrooms, reeling in their drunkenness and exhaustion. Chente was reeling a bit himself, from one side of the gigantic stage to the other. Yet he was visibly stronger than before, stronger than the microphone, stronger than the giant auditorium. He was Samson. He was saying, in effect, to hell with technology. To hell with the modern age and its electric cords and props! To hell with anything but the lonely hero! And behind him, imperturbable, inexhaustible, the guitarists went on plucking and strumming, the violinists bowed, the trumpeters blared, the harpist plucked—one rhythm piling onto the next, from one ranch to another, hit after hit. And, as the evening wore on, the hits wended ever farther into the past.

VI.

"Volver, Volver" is one of the songs that made Vicente Fernández's career—one of his oldest hits. It is a song with the simplicity of a folk tune, but it is, in fact, carefully confected, the composition of one of Chente's earliest arrangers and conductors, Fernando Z. Maldonado, a mainstay of mariachi sophistication. Maldonado arranged and did some of the conducting for the album ¿Arriba Huentitán! from the early 1970s. The mere sound of the opening notes—a throb from an organ—is bound to drive fans into frenzies of recognition and expectation. I once heard Chente perform this song years ago at Madison Square Garden, where he sang with his son, Alejandro Fernández. Alejandro dresses in mariachi costume, but he is really an ordinary pop singer—a good enough singer, with a respectable ear and a syrupy voice that is pleasant to listen to, within its limited range. Alejandro has become a big star in Latin America in the last few years, thanks to his pretty face and tousled hair—or rather, thanks to his very skillful arrangers and composers. The tours Alejandro used to make with his dad back in the 1990s must have done him a world of good, introducing him to a popular audience. The comparison with Chente was never in Alejandro's favor, except from the point of view of youth. Still, father and son made a moving duo, when I saw them. The two of them brought mom on stage to take a bow, which sent the audience into ecstasies of family values.

And then father and son, on the stage of the Garden, lit into "Volver, Volver," with gusto, and hammed it up, too, stretching out the syllables, "VOL-VAIR, VOLLLLLL-VAIRRRRRR!" in a contest to see which set of Fernández lungs could hold out longest. It was a tie. The audience was thrilled. Hamming it up killed the song, to be sure. Alejandro was a little too young and sweet for the grainy edge the song requires, and he seemed to drain all the scariness out of his dad. All in all, the old man was better off performing this song by himself at Radio City, even if he was drunk and his audience was drunker.

So, then, back to Radio City. The reedy electric organ began to throb. The audience erupted in excited recognition that Chente was about to sing his greatest hit from *¿Arriba Huentitán!* The trumpets announced their opening fanfare, and, holding the mike once again, Chente broke into the wildest yelp I have ever heard, a painful *ay-yi-iiiiii-yi!* at an impossibly high pitch—a yelp of sheer anguish, of tragedy, of rebellion, the yelp of a man who cannot be held down, a hyena's gulping laughter.

Fernando Maldonado's composition and arrangement are deceptively simple, such that, in the opening trumpet fanfare, you are already getting a melody, which you don't yet recognize as melody but which turns out to be the countermelody to the one that Chente will soon enough begin to sing:

> This passionate love
> Keeps me all stirred up
> To return!

The trumpets answered with a commentary of their own, and the *guitarrón* went loping forward at a packhorse gait, as if there was all the time in the world. This is a true *ranchera* song, reeking of farm life, a song where you can almost smell the horse and the saddle. But the key to the song rests on a single point, which is the range of Chente's vocal technique. You hear it on the album. He sings at first with a soft crooning—the sweet, echo-chamber sound of a pop star cradling the mike. It is strange to hear this saccharine singing so immediately after the hair-raising hyena scream. The crooning almost makes you put the yelp out of your mind, in the expectation that "Volver, Volver" will be a sentimental song of yearning and the bittersweet.

But when he turns to the chorus, "Volver, volver, volll-verr!" a couple of the guitarists join him in singing, and they belt out the words in vibrato harmony, with Chente barking his words with operatic violence. Then he sobs, and he yelps again like a laughing hyena, and he's back to crooning, and again to belting out "volll-verr!" operatically with his guitarists. Nearly every line is sung with a vocal technique different from the last, as if he were conducting a conversation among four different voices, every one of them his own: the sweet crooning, the operatic lyrical, the operatic violent, and the hysterical yelping. This is Chente's gift, his ability to raise his voice a notch in intensity, and then up a thousand notches, the ability to erupt, to go from soothing to sulfurous in no time at all, as if, all along, the man had been set to explode. And then, seething lava, he lapses back again. He is not everyone's favorite mariachi singer, and I think this is because some of the other all-time greats can outdo the sweetness of his voice. Pedro Infante, to return to him, commanded a singularly tender voice. Javier Solís, to cite another of the classic stars of the past (whose great hit "Payaso" was likewise composed by Fernando Z. Maldonado), always seems more touching than Chente Fernández—Solís, with his air of pugilistic toughness that manages to be ostentatiously vulnerable, too.

But I have never heard anyone outdo the violence of Vicente Fernández's eruptions. He sings correctly, without any sort of idiosyncratic warp, but when he goes rocketing upward from his crooning to his big-throated opera acrobatics, the abrasive edge in his voice is undeniable, and you get the feeling that Chente possesses in his own throat and chest the full range of tonality that is commanded by his warbling violins on one hand and his fanfare trumpets on the other, and maybe even a wider range, and he could out-sing them all, if he chose to do so. It is thrilling to watch him shift from one of those registers to the other. You catch your breath at the impetuosity of it all. And the hyena laughter puts an exclamation mark on his range—the animal cry of a man whose emotions seem to be veering unsteadily from one phrase to the next, as if he were tottering between the merely emotional and the utterly distraught.

There are wilder songs than "Volver, Volver." He sings "Amor de la Calle," which is still another of Fernando Z. Maldonado's compositions—a song that carries Chente deep into the realms of the heartbreaking, the hysterical, the ridiculous, the histrionic, and beyond. Nothing so extreme crops up in his rendition of "Volver, Volver," though you do feel the potential for it. But "Volver, Volver" has the surpassing virtue of offering, in its chorus, a chance for audiences to sing along. And so, at Radio City, the great Chente, staggering from those many swigs from flasks passed up to him on the stage, having already proved his ability to fill the hall with his own, unamplified operatic voice, joined with his singing guitarists to belt out the chorus, "Vol-ver! vol-ver! VOLLL-VERRR!" And thousands, literally thousands, of voices joined in. The massed dishwashers of New York, the construction laborers, the people who had made their way northward through routes unknown to anyone but God, the people who must have been living in terror of the immigration authorities, the young men who had left wives and children and parents at home, far away in Mexico—these people, who had splurged extravagantly on their concert tickets, roared out the words unprompted.

And with the exquisite poignancy of the heartfelt and the true, they sang, en masse, "To return! return! REEE-TURRRRN!"

They were singing to the accompaniment of an orchestra that, by its uniforms alone, evoked feudal memories of the Spanish Empire and the nostalgia of a perfect village life that had never existed. There was a touch of the Mexican Revolution in their singing—the Revolution that Lázaro Cárdenas had set to music more than half a century earlier by instituting the Mariachi Vargas as the orchestra of the Institutional Revolution. But that audience was singing, finally, an anthem of their own experience—an anthem of the immigrant tidal wave, of the people who had fled the beaten-down villages and the tired old city of Puebla or the provinces of El Salvador or some other place for a worse life, but a better paycheck, in the faraway United States. These were the people who had made their way from one ranch to another until they had arrived at whatever toilsome lot may have been theirs in New York. And they were singing their plain desire—"To return, return, return!"

You may ask, was this really a ballad? This was a ballad. These lyrics expressed something more than a sentiment or an affirmation. The lyrics and the loping rhythms and even the costumes told a story, which was the story of many millions of people undergoing the hugest of historical experiences, the uprooting of the Mexican rural world that had already made a revolution early in the twentieth century and was now making another revolution, if only by fleeing to other climes.

"To return!" To return to what? you might ask. To Mexico, or maybe to the distant tropics of Central America. To the feudal world of the Catholic Middle Ages, maybe. To the Mexican Revolution and its grand promise. To the lovely celluloid plaza where Pedro Infante led his soldiers in song and wooed his girl. But, most of all:

> To your arms once again!
> I will come where you are.
> I know how to lose, how to lose,
> I want to return, return, return!

—a few thousand balladeers, drunk on their own emotions, heartbroken and inconsolable, except by song.

But I don't mean to reduce "Volver, Volver" to a sociological phenomenon. For who am I, plunked down on my stool at Fast & Fresh, with nary a worry about the Federal immigration laws, and no far-away rural village where I imagine someday returning? Mine is a non-*campesino* heart. And yet it swells. Vicente Fernández's rendition comes to an end on the boom box, some other song starts to play, I pay six bucks for my tacos to the dueño behind the counter, and he and I exchange a few wisecracks in Spanglish, our common language. And then, having passed all of fifteen minutes at his excellent deli, I am out on the street again in this modern day of ours, where some people, less astute than Longfellow and Whitman, may think the Spanish Middle Ages have nothing to do with us, and the Mexican Revolution was not our revolution, and we have no reason to pore over the intricate pleats and folds of the American nationality—this modern street where, in spite of the Brooklyn appearance of things, my ears go on ringing with Spanish fanfares and Mexican rhythms and vibrato choruses and lunatic Jalisciense shrieks.

THE ART OF BABEL IN THE AMERICAS

Luis Pérez-Oramas

I.

Consider the following statements:

- The Museum of Modern Art began to acquire work by European artists right from the time of its founding, in 1929.
- The Museum of Modern Art began to acquire work by North American artists right from the time of its founding, in 1929.
- The Museum of Modern Art began to acquire work by artists from Latin America and the Caribbean in the early 1930s, virtually from the time of its founding.

These statements seem banal. However, since we could not insert Asian, African, or Oceanic artists into the last sentence, this one, indeed, becomes quite striking.

In April 2001, in a report on the Museum's "Non-Western Holdings" submitted to the Museum's Curatorial Forum (a periodic gathering of staff from every curatorial department), Fereshteh Daftari, Assistant Curator in the Department of Painting and Sculpture, argued that the case of Latin American artists should be considered in the context of art produced in the Western Hemisphere. Despite this acknowledgment, the problem the report addresses is still relevant. "We all know that today universalism has been replaced with a sensitivity toward difference. The question is, how can we incorporate this new sensibility into our operations here at The Museum of Modern Art?"[1]

Through the scope of its holdings, the ambition of its aspiration to the "modern," and its international reputation, The Museum of Modern Art is a museum with a universal vocation. It must inscribe itself, in other words, in the history of the "universal museum," of which it is one avatar, and as such must draw on "enlightened" or "humanistic" roots, and on a utopian aspiration to contain—as in a *ficción* by Borges—a fragment of every fragment that makes up the world of art.[2]

Yet given that the object of the collection is modern art at a time when the concept of modernity is fading into the past, the Museum confronts a paradoxical challenge in attempting to continue to be a universal museum. It cannot help but integrate into the parameters of its future operations a certain notion of the modern and of modernity in general, with its myriad international styles and local schools—whether the School of Paris or the New York School—that through the contingencies of artistic reception have become global models of aesthetic legitimization. According to that notion, the modern was perhaps the final period of a utopia of universality that emerged in the West with the French Encyclopedists and the Enlightenment: namely, the aspiration to identify a cultural lingua franca in which, like the image that takes shape in a kaleidoscope, the differences, striations, boundaries, and breaks in time and space that make up the world in its entirety would have no effect as such.

The Museum of Modern Art, then, cannot help but try to continue to be a universal museum. At the same time, as a bearer of the legacy of modernity, it cannot help but try to subject the very idea of universality that modernity demands to a thorough critique. In Gianni Vattimo's words, "Even should a perfecting of the tools of conservation and information transmission allow a 'world history' to be recorded, the very idea of a 'world history' is impossible."[3]

Consequently, to state that The Museum of Modern Art has collected Latin American art does not seem so trivial. In a museum whose collections are clearly identified by their formal mediums—painting, sculpture, drawings, film, video, architecture, design, photography, prints—and by these mediums' ability to express a "generic universality," the mention of a Latin American collection appears to relegate it to a remote geographical outpost, a territory apart. The nomenclature acts like a symptom of these works' resistance to the universality of a modern lingua franca—precisely when the Museum seeks to represent the modern in its totality. This may have great significance in the self-critique in which the Museum is constantly engaged. Many works in the Museum's holdings do not fit easily into the reading of modernity that the institution has proposed through its displays of its collection and its exhibitions: some appear "modern despite modernism," to borrow the title of Robert Storr's well-known book;[4] others, while overlooked and unknown to most curators and historians, are assimilated surprisingly easily; some works simply defy integration.

This trait is not of course unique to twentieth-century Latin American art. The Museum of Modern Art holds many works by artists of different nationalities and origins that are unlikely to fit into the canonical idea of modernity. The Museum's power to legitimize and popularize notwithstanding, and regardless how basic it may seem, we must state an obvious truth: no one can legitimately use the idea of these works as "outposts of resistance against the modern canon" as a critical matrix for dismissing their quality. Nor, by the same token, can anyone use the works as a pretext for stigmatizing the idea of a modern artistic canon—relative though that idea is—that over time The Museum of Modern Art has come to embody.

The problem is different. It is, first, a problem of the policies of The Museum of Modern Art, and of the Museum as a political entity: to what point has the Museum's interest in South American art been regulated by logics outside its strict collecting strategy? Second, it is a problem in philosophy, and specifically in epistemology: is it perhaps possible to establish a precept for the modern? Is it legitimate to turn the features of major European and North American modernist works into signifiers of "distinction,"[5] aesthetic criteria with universal meaning? Then the problem is also academic: if historians, and to a certain degree curators, are necessarily the interpreters of a particular community, how can they then resonate with what a community outside their area of expertise has produced? What are the means by which works produced outside the United States enter the academic arenas where Museum of Modern Art curators are trained? Finally, the problem is also anthropological, and banal: on the broad boulevards of the First World, who cares what is happening in La Paz or Caracas?

II.

"MoMA at El Museo" demonstrates the history of a geographically oriented collection within a museum marked by a formal tradition, a museum that divides and differentiates its collection by a taxonomy of art form or genre. It is the history, or one chapter of the history, of a generous interest. It is also, at times, an account of a strategy to be faulted for omissions and exclusions. It is a history of a utopian image: that of a "torpedo" advancing through the art world, carrying in its "tail" the oldest works of art and in its "nose" the avant-garde art of "the United States and Mexico," as Alfred H. Barr, Jr., the Museum's first director, imagined in 1933.[6] The show is a history of several shared shining moments in art both north and south of the "border," whose proper names—Diego Rivera, David Alfaro Siqueiros, Matta, Wifredo Lam—form part of the world heritage of the modern. It is a history of the belated recognition of a few artists—Joaquín Torres-García, Frida Kahlo, Hélio Oiticica, Gego (Gertrude Goldschmidt); and it is a history of many omissions and vast misunderstandings.

"MoMA at El Museo" is not an exhibition of The Museum of Modern Art's entire Latin American collection, nor is it an exhibition about the art of Latin America, like exhibitions previously organized by the Museum. It is an exhibition that reflects on and historicizes the Museum's Latin American and Caribbean collection by taking a series of cross-sections of it, and then by arranging those works so that they engage each other in dialogue, illuminate each other, and even contradict each other, thereby redefining themselves.

The works are displayed chronologically, partly for reasons of clarity, partly because the history of Latin American acquisitions at the Museum begins at a specific point and continues to this day. The curatorial premise of the exhibition calls for two kinds of grouping: the first comprises four sections of emblematic, interrelated works belonging to key acquisition periods; the second contains works chosen independently of their dates of acquisition to form currents of meaning, like small archipelagos or "transformation groups"[7] in which stylistic or thematic similarities and differences function as drivers of meaning.

The four central, emblematic groupings are defined chronologically by decade: the 1930s, '40s, '60s, and the '90s to the present. These are periods in which the Museum's collecting of Latin American and Caribbean art had a special intensity. It was in the 1930s that the Museum received its first gifts of Latin American art—primarily works by the three great Mexicans, Rivera, Siqueiros, and José Clemente Orozco. Then, in the early 1940s, the U.S. government's participation in World War II unquestionably helped strengthen ties with Latin American countries. In fact the Museum began a deliberate program of seeking out art from South America and Cuba, as evidenced by Lincoln Kirstein's travels in Argentina, Brazil, Chile, Colombia, Ecuador, and Uruguay. Barr himself journeyed to Cuba and Mexico; he was interested in acquiring work to complete the representation of Latin American art in the collection. What had been an exclusively Mexican perspective rapidly broadened to include artists from Argentina, Bolivia, Brazil, Chile, Cuba, Peru, and Uruguay. But the 1940s were more complex than this cursory overview of their geopolitical traits suggests: these years would establish not only the political and military axes that would govern the global balance of power until the end of the twentieth century, but also the critical and aesthetic alignments that, after 1945, would divide the future visual arts of the American continents into north and south.

On the one hand, different parts of the South American continent produced a powerful reaction against the figurative and social modes of the Mexican muralist tradition, leading to the formation of groups and schools of abstract and nonobjective art, principally in Argentina, Brazil, Uruguay, and Venezuela. Yet since the major polemics over Latin American abstraction did not take place until after 1945 and the end of World War II, when the interest in acquiring South American art waned, the fruits of this development were not assimilated into the Museum's collection.

The crystallization of a powerful critical theory to accompany the emergence of new tendencies in abstract painting in New York after 1940—principally under the influence of Clement Greenberg—would make it impossible to fit much Latin American art, including its abstract modes, into the formalist criteria. These same criteria would lead to the prevalence of self-reflective art forms whose ambition lay in being identified with the purity of their medium.[8] The emergence of this basic formalist thought in the mid-1940s was certainly a factor in the epistemological rift within the visual arts of the Americas. At that point, artists who had communicated with one another in three languages—English, Spanish, and Portuguese—and had shared a single expressive universe began to "speak" numerous, often mutually untranslatable "languages" in their work.

It was only in the mid-1950s and in the 1960s, another period of geopolitical convergence between North and South America, that the Museum began to acquire artistic styles produced in Latin America since the 1940s. During the era of the Kennedy administration's Alliance for Progress, and with renewed purchases through the Inter-American Fund, works that had not been made a part of the Museum collections, such as some lyrical and geometric abstractions, were acquired. Between 1954 and 1956, for example, the Museum purchased the first Latin American abstract geometric works since it acquired Torres-García's 1932 *Composition*, in 1942. These were works by the Colombians Edgar Negret and Eduardo Ramírez Villamizar and the Cuban Luis Martínez-Pedro, and they mark a renewed aesthetic dynamic for Latin American acquisitions that would continue throughout the 1960s.[9]

During the 1960s, Pop art emerged as an international style, even while it was often stigmatized as a veiled mode of academicism or a kitsch form of artistic expression.[10] Although not reflected in the Museum collection, artistic consonances among the arts in the Americas existed during this period as they had not since the 1940s: between the Argentine Jorge de la Vega and Andy Warhol, for example, or the Venezuelan Marisol Escobar and the Argentines León Ferrari and Antonio Berni. It seemed that the arts on these continents began to suture the stylistic and aesthetic fissures that had followed the imposition of the New York canon in the late 1940s and the 1950s. Artists were once again "speaking" in a similar language: sarcastic, ironic, often cynical, always political. Once again, however, the principal beneficiary was North American, as the dynamic, consuming force of U.S. Pop imposed a hegemonic model that left many questions unanswered. Not only did many Latin American works remain out of circulation or without viewers outside their respective countries, but also, and above all, a noticeable ideological difference between Latin American and North American styles of Pop art—one that would also be a characteristic of Conceptual art on both sides of the border—was suspended.

III.

At the beginning of the 1990s, and perhaps for the first time in the Museum's history, a series of institutional, historical, and strategic developments contributed to an awareness within the Museum of the existence of a specific history of Latin American art—and of the difference inherent in that history.[11] Among those developments were the renewal of democratic forms of government in a number of Latin nations; a perceptible shift in U.S. foreign policy in the region; the growing internationalization of the art world; the emergence of collections of Latin American art with international profiles both within and beyond the Americas; and, finally, the resurgence of efforts by Museum curators and trustees to support the collecting and exhibiting of works by artists from Latin America.

For the first time since the Museum began to collect Latin American art, its acquisitions were dictated by the necessity of filling in certain lacunae, making up certain deficits. Major figures in twentieth-century art had gone unrepresented in the collection. A series of external factors helped to nurture this change in strategy: the growth in North American and European academic programs for the study of Latin American art, for example. The inclusion of work by Latin American artists—until recently ignored by hegemonic curatorial practices—in global exhibitions organized by curators with high international profiles was another factor. Decisive initiatives from benefactors and patrons played a major role. Finally, public debate—often skewed by resentment and politics—on the Museum's historical role in shaping the international visibility of twentieth-century Latin American art played its part as well.

The Museum's Latin American collection contains many major works, works that are legendary for their iconic value and plastic force. Some of these are already enshrined in the collective Western imaginary. But alongside them are many artworks that are rarely if ever shown to museum-goers and are accordingly little-known, yet that evidence seminal moments in the researches of major artists and shed light on others who are rarely studied or discussed. We have tried to establish ensembles of meaning among these works and to ensure they are seen in proximity to the acknowledged masterworks, because we believe that modern art is not solely a history of prominent figures and individual names, a sum of geniuses. On the contrary, if anything distinguishes the modern interpretation of meaning, it is the formation of structural synchronies: the idea that signs, icons, symbols, styles, texts, visual forms, and works of art are dynamic elements subject to constant transformation and only make sense through comparison, analogy, repetition, and differentiation among themselves.

From the iconographic point of view, it is interesting to note that the crucial works in the Latin American collection include visual testimonies of the first political revolutions of the twentieth century: the Mexican Revolution and the Russian Revolution. The former, which began in 1910, had as its "official" artists the three great muralists Rivera, Orozco, and Siqueiros. Rivera also traveled to Russia and brought back startling images of the 1928 May Day procession in Moscow. That date, incidentally, coincides with the institutionalization of both revolutions within a repressive state apparatus identified with a single party. By 1931, the year Orozco painted his emblematic *Zapatistas*, the end of *Carrancismo*[12] and the dawn of the autocratic governments of Alvaro Obregón and Plutarco Elías Calles had dashed the Zapatista dream and thwarted its assimilation into the fledgling apparatus of the Mexican state. Similarly, the consolidation of Joseph Stalin's regime in 1920s Russia would bring with it the death of both the revolutionary dream and, with the implementation of a Socialist Realist orthodoxy, the hopes of the avant-garde for a social and aesthetic role.

The entire body of figurative Latin American art from the first half of the twentieth century has been judged erroneously by the criteria of this realist canon, which disparages the fantastic creative motifs and enduring interest in the surreal that many Latin American figurative artists share. It also prevents an accurate understanding of the complex constellation of figurative work that, to a greater or lesser extent, shared twentieth-century creativity with vanguard modes. In Latin America or anywhere else, one cannot speak of a "return" to figuration in the 1920s unless one deems that at some point progress was made toward another mode.[13] The nonobjective modes of avant-garde art—even the most radical of them, such as Suprematism—never ceased to be inscribed within the logic of representation. Similarly, in the Americas, Asia, and Africa, relatively mimetic forms of visual representation were always practiced without this quality being a detriment to the artworks' historical relevance for the communities in which they were produced.

It is my concern here to argue for the diversity of figuration in the modern period without falling into anachronistic stigmatizations or historicist exclusions. The breadth of this art's role in modernity remains to be fully explored. Rivera and Orozco's "political" images, which bear witness to the institutionalization of the Mexican and Russian revolutions, may be set against the "tragic" images of Siqueiros, which manifest the iconographic weight of art history—in the guise of a pre-Columbian mask in *Echo of a Scream* (1937), for example, or in the more complex legacy of classical images, as in the reiteration of Uccello's fifteenth-century battle scenes in *Collective Suicide* (1936). Similarly, in the single brief decade between 1932 and 1942, the involuntary, sarcastic modernity of Pedro Figari shared space with narrative and representational practices as diverse as those of the Mexicans Roberto Montenegro, Juan O'Gorman, and Antonio Ruiz; the Brazilian Alberto da Veiga Guignard; and the Peruvians José Sabogal and Mario Urteaga. The iconographic and symbolic abstraction of the Uruguayan Torres-García and the caustic, metaphysical monumentality of Berni coexisted with some of the most significant visual manifestations of international Surrealism, such as the works of Kahlo, Lam, and Matta.

The earliest examples of Latin American nonobjective abstraction appeared between 1945 and 1948. Some were related to the Constructivist and Russian Suprematist experiments, others were aligned with De Stijl or the Bauhaus. In all cases these manifestations sparked reactions and debates that established contrasts not only between the basic concepts of abstraction and figuration but between national and global trends, political and aesthetic utopias, the optical and the narrative in visual art, and the ideas of "plastic objectivity" and "subjectivity" within abstraction. This was evident in Argentina and Uruguay in the polemics between the adherents of Torres-García and the Madí, Arte Concreto-Invención, and Revista Arturo groups; in Brazil, among the various groups tied to Concrete and Neo-Concrete art; in Venezuela, between the Taller Libre de Arte group, the Disidentes group, and, more generally, the Kinetic art movement; in Colombia, the presence of artists such as Eduardo Ramirez Villamizar and Edgard Negret; and in Mexico with outstanding, though isolated, figures such as Mathias Goeritz. However, with the exception of that of Torres-García, no major work affiliated with these movements and debates became part of The Museum of Modern Art's collections until the late 1960s.

Recent acquisitions have begun to fill in the gaps in the Museum's picture of modern Western art, and "MoMA at El Museo" brings together a more complete representation of abstract tendencies in Latin America. Along with constructivist, optical propositions—addressing effects of dematerialization considerably more complex than the simplistic label "Op art," and the condensation of that work in the Museum's exhibition "The Responsive Eye," organized by William Seitz in 1965, might lead one to expect—we see various forms of *informel*, as well as the Fluxus-like "destructivist" experiments of the Puerto Rican artist Rafael Montañez Ortiz. Goeritz's *Message 7B, Ecclesiastes VII* (1959), its biblical references charging it with prophetic intent, is utterly unique, yet we might link its Baroque materiality to that of Jesús Rafael Soto's *Vibraciones* (Vibrations) and *Leños* (Logs) of the late 1950s, this Venezuelan artist's moment of greatest experiment, and to Gego's diagrams and sketches of the 1960s. The inclusion of Lygia Pape's *Book of Creation* (1959–60), a major work of Brazilian Neo-Concretism, testifies to the survival of a symbolic form of visual narrative within nonobjective geometric abstraction, and adds an engagingly complex nuance to the strictly perceptual styles represented by the Venezuelan artist Carlos Cruz-Diez's *Physichromie, 114* (1964), or by the Argentine Julio Le Parc's *Instability Through Movement of the Spectator* (1962).

In 1956, through the Inter-American Fund, the Museum acquired a beautiful drawing by Ramirez Villamizar, *Black and White* (1956), a precursor to the three-dimensional forms that the artist would develop later. But for a work by Negret acquired in 1954, this was the first abstract geometric work by a Latin American artist in the Museum's collection. *Black and White* testifies not only to an important moment in 1950s Latin American abstraction but also to what Roberto Pontual has called a "sensitive geometry," that is, a subjective geometry open to the organic.[14] Nevertheless, to convey Latin American geometric abstraction of the 1950s and '60s in a more representative way, as it does for the first time in this exhibition, the Museum must rely on recent acquisitions. In "MoMA at El Museo" one can compare the early work of

Ramírez Villamizar, influenced by Victor Vasarely and Auguste Herbin, with the more concrete inquiries of the young Oiticica, whose "*Metaesquemas*" (Meta-schemes, 1957–58), diagrammatic representations of frozen movement and variations on unstable forms, are early drafts, outlines, of what the artist called "adversity"[15]—in this case volatile matter, movement rendered schematically. These concepts would later become more literal in Oiticica's "*Nucleos*" (Nuclei, 1960) and "*Penetraveis*" (Penetrables, 1960–1969), in which "adversity" materializes in space. That is also the case of the fragile "*Bólides*" (Flaming meteors, 1963–1967) and "*Parangolés*" (Fabric capes, 1964–1979), where forms are fleshed out by the bodies that wear them.

In Latin America, and particularly in Brazil, the 1950s were actually among the most significant periods in the production of geometric abstraction. Alongside abstract and nonobjective forms of geometry, they are broadly characterized by aesthetic devices, expressive solutions, and modes of operation, including viewer participation, that focus on the subjectivity of perception, revealing the artists' awareness of the fact that even the most objective artistic forms are destined to be personalized in the experience of the viewer.

The subjectivization of abstraction was not limited to its most explicit historical manifestation, Brazilian Neo-Concretism; it also appears in the kinetic experiments of Cruz-Diez, Le Parc, Almir Mavignier, Manuel Ocampo, and Soto, artists who demonstrate the unreliability of perception through optical and chromatic illusions of dematerialization, or through seriality and tonal contrast. More singular artists should be mentioned as well, some of them working independently, without knowing each other: Mira Schendel in Brazil, Goeritz in Mexico, and Gego in Venezuela.

Although their biographies differ in many ways, these three artists of German origin all arrived in Latin America as a result of the Holocaust. Both Goeritz and Schendel, who had already begun working as artists when they emigrated, created work informed by Christian humanism, as well as by the scars of war and genocide. Gego arrived in Venezuela in 1938 with a degree in architecture, then discovered the energy of the country's art scene. All three artists made key contributions to modern art in Latin America and deserve further study and discovery by the museum-going public. Here the gaze of outsiders burdened by the tragedies of Europe enriched the "expanded field" that was the Latin American art scene in the mid-twentieth century.[16] These three artists evoke Aby Warburg's description of the art of the Florentine Renaissance in relation to antiquity: for Warburg, the artists of the Quattrocento did not seek to rebuild the classical period so much as to inscribe the motifs of antiquity in the reality of Florence.[17] In much the same way, Goeritz in Mexico, Schendel in Brazil, and Gego in Venezuela diverted modern motifs to inscribe them deeply into the reality of Latin America.[18]

One cannot, then, conceive of Latin American modernity exclusively in terms of a displacement of models from one continent to another, nor can it simply be compared to "non-Western" forms of modernity, or be engaged simply in terms of anachronism, or of modern art "against the grain."[19] If this exhibition demonstrates anything, it is the irreducible complexity of the different processes and manifestations of modern Latin American art. Goeritz, Schendel, and Gego particularly exemplify the survival in abstract form of an interrogation of the organic and the temporal: of originary memory, in Goeritz's metaphysical references; of concepts of writing and existential trace, in the work of Schendel; and in Gego's work, of the intuition of a dense, striated, centerless field that evolves from the margins without a master plan, particularizing space with its irregularities.

It is important to understand that to either side of the rift that came about in the art of the Americas in the 1940s lie different models of the modern, informing the transition from modernity to the contemporary scene differently on both continents. Perhaps the obsession with the concept of "presence" that arose in North American art after Abstract Expressionism explains the triumph of theatrical Minimalism[20] and post-Conceptual art, broadly informed by the Pop legacy. In Latin America, meanwhile, the concern with articulating a modern expressive grammar of existential concepts such as "writing," "symbolic narrative," and "time" informed another modernity and thus another contemporary scene. Here Conceptual art did not do battle with materiality but held fast, with paradoxical richness, to the idea of the object.[21] Moreover, the idea of that object's ideological circulation, particularly exemplified in the work of Cildo Meireles, prevailed over the perceptual and tautological experiments that marked North American conceptualism.

The two scenes, North and South America, are not distinguished, as in an all-too-common simplification, by figuration south of the border and abstraction north of it. A complex interrogation of the human organism—the body—as a metaphor for the world informs practically all the Latin American political art that might be associated with Pop, such as the work of de la Vega, Marisol, Antonio Dias, and Ferrari. The contributions of these artists to "MoMA at El Museo" suggest interrogations that go beyond a purely stylistic historiography. It is not surprising, then, that one possible explanation for the recent growth of interest in contemporary Latin American art is the exhaustion of the formalist criteria that for so long held sway in the model of hegemonic modernity. Perhaps a world recognized as ever more complex politically and socially is rediscovering the virtues of allegory and narrative in locating the fragmented possibilities of representation. The often scorned idea of an art linked to real communities then comes to seem like an attainable goal.

It is too soon to determine whether the aesthetic borders between the two continents have been permanently transformed—whether love and death (Ana Mendieta, Felix Gonzalez-Torres, Doris Salcedo), space and place (Guillermo Kuitca, Fernando Bryce), body and fame (Leonilson, Gabriel Orozco, Enrique Chagoya), representation, reproduction, and anamorphosis (Jean-Michel Basquiat, Beatriz Milhazes, Vik Muniz,

Arturo Herrera, Kcho), and opacity and transparency (Meireles, Waltércio Caldas) can once again meet in a common language in the arts of the Americas. Perhaps it is naive to seek to elude the fate of Babel. In any event, the curatorial premise of "MoMA at El Museo" demonstrates that for the past seventy years a major art institution in the "north" has embraced the arts of the "south," proving that borders may have always been fictions—as elusive as are, for us, the four cardinal points.

NOTES

1. Fereshteh Daftari, "Report on the Non-Western Holdings at MoMA," April 18, 2001.

2. For the "encyclopedic" foundation of the "Universal Museum," and the early polemics to which it gave rise, see Antoine de Quatremère de Quincy, *Lettres à Miranda sur les déplacements des monuments de l'art de l'Italie* (n.p., 1796). See also Jean-Louis Déotte, *Le Musée, l'origine de l'esthétique* (Paris: L'Harmattan, 1993), and Douglas Crimp, *On the Museum's Ruins* (Cambridge, Mass.: The MIT Press, 1993).

3. Gianni Vattimo, "La Fin de la modernité," *Nihilisme et herménéutique dans la culture post-moderne* (Paris: Editions du Seuil, 1987), p. 15. The bibliography on the critique of modernity is overwhelmingly vast. For a brief history of the concept see Hans Robert Jauss, *Pour une esthétique de la reception* (Paris: Editions Gallimard, 1978). Other works include those of Michel Foucault, Jean-François Lyotard, Giorgio Agamben, Antoine Compagnon, Niklas Luhmann, T. J. Clark, and Edward Said. More recently, on modernity as an ideological aesthetic acting in the schools of the Western intellectual marketplace, see Fredric Jameson, *A Singular Modernity: Essay on the Ontology of the Present* (London: Verso, 2002). For a recent critique of the concept of universality, see Alain Badiou, *Saint Paul: La Fondation de l'universalisme* (Paris: Presses Universitaires de France, 1997).

4. Robert Storr, *Modern Art Despite Modernism*, exh. cat. (New York: The Museum of Modern Art, 2000).

5. See Pierre Bourdieu, *La Distinction: Critique sociale du jugement* (Paris: Minuit, 1979), Eng. trans. as *Distinction: A Social Critique of the Judgement of Taste*, trans. Richard Nice (Cambridge, Mass.: Harvard University Press, 1984).

6. In this early comparison of the structure of the Museum's collection to the shape of a torpedo, Alfred H. Barr, Jr., included a selection of ancient works ("a Fayum portrait, a Byzantine panel, Romanesque miniatures, Gothic woodcuts, a Giotto school piece, . . . Coptic textiles, . . . African and pre-Columbian objects") in the torpedo's tail while modern works by Europeans, Americans, and Mexicans were grouped in its nose. See Kirk Varnedoe, "The Evolving Torpedo: Changing Ideas of the Collection of Painting and Sculpture of The Museum of Modern Art," in *The Museum of Modern Art at Mid-Century: Continuity and Change*, Studies in Modern Art no. 5 (New York: The Museum of Modern Art, 1995), pp. 20–21. Barr's torpedo metaphor has been widely quoted but still deserves

more reflection in terms of the fundamental economy of the Museum and its relationship to an image of conquest: "The Permanent Collection may be thought of graphically as a torpedo moving through time, its nose the ever advancing present, its tail the ever receding past of fifty to a hundred years ago." See Barr, *Painting and Sculpture in the Museum of Modern Art 1929–1967* (New York: The Museum of Modern Art, 1977), p. 622.

7.   Taking his cue from Claude Lévi-Strausss, Hubert Damisch has developed the idea that a work of art, like a symbol, has no intrinsic, invariable meaning. Instead, its meaning varies with its position in relation to other works. Following the vocabulary of structural anthropology, the group of works being compared is called a "transformation group." See Damisch, *L'Origine de la perspective* (Paris: Flammarion, 1987), pp. 256–62, and Lévi-Strauss, *Mythologiques I: Le Cru et le cuit* (Paris: Plon, 1964), pp. 59–64.

8.   "The arts, then, have been hunted back to their mediums, and there they have been isolated, concentrated and defined. It is by virtue of its medium that each art is unique and strictly itself. To restore the identity of an art the opacity of its medium must be emphasized. For the visual arts the medium is discovered to be physical; hence pure painting and pure sculpture seek above all else to affect the spectator physically." Clement Greenberg, "Toward a Newer Laocoön," *Partisan Review 7*, no. 4 (July–August 1940): 307. Also: "It follows that a modernist work of art must try, in principle, to avoid dependence upon any order of experience not given in the most essentially construed nature of its medium." Greenberg, "The New Sculpture," in *Art and Culture: Critical Essays* (Boston: Beacon Press, 1961), p. 139. For a brilliant, conclusive critique of Greenberg's modernism, see Storr, "No Joy in Mudville: Greenberg's Modernism Then and Now," in *Modern Art and Popular Culture: Readings in High & Low* (New York: The Museum of Modern Art, 1990), pp. 161–90.

9.   In understanding this moment one cannot underestimate the weight of another geopolitical coordinate: the triumph of the Cuban Revolution and the attempt to export it to Latin America, as well as the United States' attempt to oppose that effort by establishing some kind of cultural strategy promoting ideas of democratic freedom and an open society.

10.   See, e.g., Greenberg, *Clement Greenberg, Late Writings*, ed. Robert C. Morgan (Minneapolis: University of Minnesota Press, 2003), pp. 10–11.

11.   This assertion was made, virtually verbatim, at the first preparatory curatorial meetings for "MoMA at El Museo" by Paulo Herkenhoff, Adjunct Curator in the Department of Painting and Sculpture from 1999 to 2002, and the first curator of Latin American origin invited to join the Museum's staff.

12.   *Carrancismo* refers to the unstable government of Venustiano Carranza (1859–1920), which lasted from 1915 to 1920, a period that saw the assassination of Emiliano Zapata (1883–1919).

13.   "The concept of the historical progress of mankind cannot be sundered from the concept of its progression through a homogeneous, empty time. A critique of the concept of such a progression must be the basis of any criticism of the concept of progress itself." Walter Benjamin, "Theses on the Philosophy of History," *Illuminations: Essays and Reflections*,

edited and with an introduction by Hannah Arendt, trans. Harry Zohn (New York: Schocken Books, 1969), p. 261. No one can deny the avant-garde's contribution in the renewal of the arts in the West, but whether or not this contribution can legitimately be considered in terms of "progress" is open to debate. See Benjamin H. D. Buchloch, "Figures of Authority, Ciphers of Regression," in *October* 16 (Spring 1981), pp. 39–68. Reprinted in Brian Wallis, ed., *Art after Modernism* (New York: New Museum of Contemporary Art, 1984) and Jean Clair, *Malinconia, Motifs Saturniens dans l'art de l'entre deux guerres* (Paris: Gallimard, 1996).

14. See Roberto Pontual, *Geometria sensível* (Rio de Janeiro: Museu de Arte Moderno, 1978).

15. "De adversidade vivimos" (We live on adversity), a paraphrase of a line by Maurice Merleau-Ponty, was an artistic slogan of Hélio Oiticica's. See Oiticica, "Esquerna geral da nova objetividade," 1967, reprinted in *Hélio Oiticica* (Rio de Janeiro: Centro de Arte Hélio Oiticica, 1992), and Maurice Merleau-Ponty, "Man and Adversity," in *Signs*, trans. Richard C. McCleary (Evanston, Ill.: Northwestern University Press, 1990).

16. For the notion of the "expanded field," see Rosalind E. Krauss, "Sculpture in the Expanded Field," in *The Originality of Avant-Garde and Other Modernist Myths* (Cambridge: The MIT Press, 1986).

17. See Philippe-Alain Michaud, *Aby Warburg et l'image en mouvement* (Paris: Macula, 1998), p. 78. Adolf Goldschmidt, one of the great German medievalists of the first half of the twentieth century and a contemporary of Aby Warburg's, was Gego's uncle. Gego trained in Warburg's intellectual circle in Hamburg, and throughout her life she would preserve the memory of her illustrious uncle in books and photograph albums.

18. See Luis Pérez-Oramas, "Gego, Residual Reticuláreas and Involuntary Modernism: Shadow, Traces and Site," in *Questioning the Line: Gego in Context*, ed. Mari Carmen Ramírez (Houston: International Center for the Arts of the Americas and Museum of Fine Arts Houston, 2003).

19. For the notion of "history brushed against the grain," see Benjamin, *Illuminations*, pp. 256–57, and Georges Didi-Huberman, *Devant le temps. Histoire de l'art et anachronisme des images* (Paris: Minuit, 2000), pp. 85–155.

20. See Michael Fried, *Absorption and Theatricality: Painting and Beholder in the Age of Diderot*, 1980 (reprint ed. Chicago: University of Chicago Press, 1988), and *Art and Objecthood: Essays and Reviews* (Chicago: University of Chicago Press, 1998).

21. See Mari Carmen Ramírez, "Blueprints Circuits: Conceptual Art and Politics in Latin America," in Alexander Alberro and Blake Stimson, eds., *Conceptual Art: A Critical Anthology* (Cambridge: The MIT Press, 1999).

THE WRITING ON THE WALL

The Life and Passion of Jean-Michel Basquiat

Frances Negrón-Muntaner

> Es más difícil ser rey sin corona. (It's harder to be king without a crown.)[1]
> —*Shakira*

In New York City, the 1970–1980 decade gave way to a multi-ethnic, queer-inflected urban culture that spurred new forms in music, the visual arts, and dance. In the words of curator Jeffrey Deitch, it "was an era of greater sexual openness to different cultures, and interchange between races."[2] Though fueled to a great extent by blacks and Latinos, it was white artists like Keith Haring and Madonna who mostly injected this fusion into the main cultural bloodstream. Yet few figures from this—or indeed any other time—most fully embody the torment and triumph of the commodification of New York's emergent cultures than the Brooklyn-born son of a Haitian accountant and a Puerto Rican art lover: the painter Jean-Michel Basquiat.

As with hip-hop culture in general (to which he had an ambivalent relationship), Basquiat has been studied primarily as an African American artist. Called the integrator of "African-American culture,"[3] and "the most financially successful Black visual artist in history,"[4] the majority of critics who have to date written on Basquiat generally ignore the potential significance of his Caribbean roots to his production and construction of his star persona. Equally perplexing, Puerto Rican and other Latino critics also tend to exclude Basquiat from their reflections on U.S. Hispanic cultures. This last oversight underscores how black artists—with the notable exception of musicians—are often construed as outside the pale of Latin/o American artistic production.

But as Robert Farris Thompson, one of the few critics to engage with Basquiat in all his cultural complexity, observed, "Wherever Iberian and Anglo-Saxon came together ... [Basquiat] was ready. When Spanish was the move, everything turned Afro-Caribbean, accent, diction, pacing, intonation."[5] Placed at the crossroads of multiple traditions and conflicting definitions of what is artistically valuable, Basquiat—painter, performer, and urban legend—is of great significance to thinking about hemispheric American cultures. Through his life and work, it is possible to both delve into the complex negotiations needed to "make it" as an Afro-Caribbean artist in the late twentieth century, and to consider how artistic practices are part of what anthropologist Fernando Ortiz once called "transculturation," the process by which different cultural formations clash and produce new possibilities.[6]

LABOR REPRESSIVE: ART, BASQUIAT, AND CAPITAL

Born in 1960 into a middle class household, Basquiat began his rise to fame as the graffiti provocateur SAMO. As SAMO, a collaboration with school friend Al Diaz, Basquiat wrote public poetry and aphorisms on walls throughout the power corridors of Manhattan during the late 1970s. In at least two ways, the SAMO period anticipated the central paradoxes of Basquiat's artistic career. On the one hand, the tags alluded to the "same old shit" and often entailed a critique of greed and white privilege, encapsulated in writings like "SAMO@AN ALTERNATIVE TO JOE NORMAL AND THE BOURGEOISIE FANTASY."[7] On the other hand, SAMO's writings were strategically placed outside art galleries, and aimed at influential patrons and art power brokers. In this sense, if as writer Rene Ricard suggests, becoming an artist "is an honest way to rise out of the slum . . . the money earned is rather a proof pure and simple of the value of that individual, The Artist,"[8] Basquiat emerged not so much from the ghetto as from the faith that white recognition would free him of a devalued racial identity and secure him a safer place in the world.

SAMO's objectives were, however, easier to write down than to execute. For Basquiat aspired to become recognized beyond the tag of the "big Black artist" in one of the most hostile cultural environments for racialized people: high art. In critic's Greg Tate's unequivocal words, "To this day [the visual arts] remains a bastion of white supremacy, a sconce of the wealthy whose high-walled barricades are matched only by Wall Street and the White House and whose exclusionary practices are enforced 24-7-365."[9] Despite the odds, it was Basquiat's fate to receive considerable recognition as an artist, and to succeed at a time when artists could attain major celebrity status in ways that before were mostly available to Hollywood actors and rock stars.

Being brand "Basquiat," however, came at a high cost. Facing a sharply racialized cultural context that simultaneously valued his work as a commodity yet humiliated him as a "colored" artist, Basquiat coped though various modes of accommodation and defiance that came to define his artistic persona and substantially inform his work. While art critics have often decried the fact that attention to Basquiat's biography—including his public "acting outs"—have to date overshadowed his art, both can be understood as performances that used different media toward the same aim: incorporation into the Big White Way of high art.

Consistent with alternative definitions of what is worthy and how to measure value, Basquiat rejected regulated forms of labor and was often disrespectful when interacting with corporate employers. As Haring recalls, "He [SAMO] bought a canvas at Utrecht's and paint and put all this paint on the canvas and let cars run over it and got the paint all over himself and then got on the subway and went to an appointment at Fiorucci and got paint on EVERYTHING on the way and at Fiorucci he got paint on the rug and couch and rich ladies' furs. He was asked to leave before his appointment."[10] Although from the start of his career, Basquiat "maintained that all he wanted was to be famous. He could learn how to draw later,"[11] fame and money were not ends in themselves. Rather, they were means through which Basquiat hoped to enjoy the "real luxury goods" denied to many African descended people in the Americas: respect, celebrity, and freedom from want—and shame.[12]

Complementarily, Basquiat lived as a drifter for most of his life. Basquiat's nomadism was evident in his long history of running away from home as a teenager, dropping out of school, and subsisting on the streets (including a time when he slept in a cardboard box) until he was twenty years old. His legendary forays into the club scene were also initially motivated to "see what my prospects were"[13] in terms of finding a place to crash. Basquiat's practices of flight have been often perceived as symptomatic of his inability to, in the words of biographer Phoebe Hoban, "maintain a single emotional bond—whether it was to friends, lovers, or art dealers."[14] Yet, these may be more compellingly understood as desires to be free from subjecting structures, be they school, family or capital.

Not surprisingly, Basquiat's first relationship with a professional art dealer, Annina Nosei, was deeply conflicted. Since Basquiat lacked a suitable place to paint, Nosei provided him the gallery's basement as a studio where she also ushered prospective (white) buyers through to watch him at work. Though Basquiat was extraordinarily productive, creating up to three paintings a day, the quasi-circus atmosphere prompted collector Doug Cramer to say that, "He looked like a slave, or very close to it."[15] Significantly, this was the first time that Basquiat had ample space to work but the fact that he was on display as a sideshow curiosity transformed painting into "hard labor," immediately changing the artist's relationship to his work. In Basquiat's words, "They set it up for me so I'd have to make eight paintings in a week, for the show the next week. . . . I made them in this big warehouse there, Annina, Mazzoli, and Bruno were there. . . . It was like a factory, a sick factory. . . . I hated it."[16]

Basquiat responded to the fact that fame and a high market value did not protect him from racism in several ways, most of them implicating his body into ritual performances of capital exorcism. To address Nosei's pressure to supply new works, for instance, Basquiat created large, unfinished paintings for the collectors, so that he could concentrate on small, layered paintings for himself. Companion Suzanne Mallouk further comments that Basquiat refused to sell some of his paintings, writing "'NOT

FOR SALE' on them."[17] Later, when the Swiss dealer Bruno Bischofberger began to represent him, Basquiat insisted on being told who each buyer was, refusing to sell to speculators and stashing his unsold paintings in a warehouse in Washington Heights.[18]

Similarly, Basquiat's inability to fully control the conditions under which he painted often erupted in violence toward his own work, with the goal of subverting its value and preventing its acquisition by the "wrong" (greedy) people. "Sometimes he would complete up to eight paintings a week," wrote journalist Patricia Bosworth. "But he would fly into rages about being pressured to paint; sometimes he slashed his canvases to bits."[19] After Basquiat decided to sever his ties to Nosei, he also made sure to spoil the stock of paintings that had caused him such injury. In a move perhaps unintentionally symbolic, Basquiat poured "a bucket of white paint over the shredded paintings,"[20] destroying not only the goods but also part of himself in the process.

While Basquiat's behavior was often noted as a symptom of mental instability, his tense relationship with his body as an instrument of labor is common among Afro-diasporic peoples, as these groups have experienced different forms of labor coercion, including slavery, colonial subjection, undesirable work, and even the inability to obtain work. Basquiat's attitude in relation to work also bears great resemblance to what perplexed American anthropologists have often written about the Puerto Rican laborers' resistance to capital's demands, "their sense of personal dignity seemed to clash often with the requirements of the work discipline."[21] The following anecdote narrated by writer Jennifer Clement is emblematic, "Suzanne and Jean-Michel have terrible fights because only Suzanne is making money. One day, Jean-Michel says 'Fine, I'll get a job.' He goes to work as an electrician's assistant at the apartment of a rich, white woman. . . . When Jean-Michel gets back he is furious, clapping his hands together. 'That white bitch looked at me as if I was a worker!' he says."[22]

Basquiat's conflicts with capitalist logic should then not be confused with lacking a work ethic or understanding exchange value. A hard-working artist, Basquiat wanted his paintings to sell. At the same time, he insisted in being in control of his creative process, even when he had assistants, and took enormous pride in the fact that the product was his own. Unlike his idol Andy Warhol, who dreamed of becoming a machine, or his contemporary Keith Haring, who according to friends actually did become one,[23] Basquiat saw art as "expressive" of a unique individuality and as part of a competition to be the "best," and hence worthy in excess of the product's exchange value. In Hoban's terms: "It was . . . to his despair, that for dealers, collectors, and even his friends, money was the first priority; that the art world was primarily a marketplace that functioned according to the laws of supply and demand."[24] For Basquiat, art was strictly business, but of a different kind: an "achievement" produced by exceptional labor and a "gift" or means to offset the shame of his racialized identity.[25]

In addition to the larger context of Afro-diasporic relationships to labor, Basquiat's acute sense of his status as a racialized commodity cannot be separated from the specific juncture of the 80s, in which art acquired the fluidity of money, collapsing the distinctions between dealer and collector, art and stocks, trading commodities and acquiring unique objects. This novel context made Basquiat a star; he was commodified based upon a significant if sometimes too rapidly produced body of work, almost instantaneously, to feed the frenzy of art speculation. Or in critic Rene Ricard's words, "We are no longer collecting art, we are buying individuals. This is no piece by Samo. This is a piece of Samo."[26] The implications were great for Basquiat. Not only was he reduced to the status of a "thing" (a commodity), his high productivity also entailed a process of dismemberment, painfully chronicled in most of his paintings.

The awareness of being a "thing" was reinforced through a second conflictual site of pleasure and shame: sexuality. As is well known, one of the ways that Basquiat sought to challenge his subaltern status was by almost exclusively seeking relationships with white women. As his commodification, however, Basquiat's fetishized sexuality was double edged. According to Jennifer Clement, "a very famous gallery owner in SoHo" chased Basquiat's lover Suzanne around his home, asking her how "big Jean's penis was and if it was true that Jean had herpes."[27] Ricard's alleged first words to Basquiat upon seeing him naked are equally illustrative: "Not only are you the greatest artist that I have ever seen, you have the most beautiful penis I have ever seen."[28] The persistence of representing Basquiat through his genitals recalls Fanon's classic observation that "the Negro is eclipsed. He is turned into a penis. He *is* a penis."[29]

Furthermore, even if key art-scene players treated Basquiat as a star, everyday experiences underscored his precarious social position as a black man. "I go on the street," the artist once commented to an interviewer, "wave my hand and they just drive past me. Normally I have to wait for three or four cabs."[30] That this treatment was not confined to the United States was also not lost on Basquiat A typical experience took place when, upon returning from his second show in Modena, the Italian authorities detained Basquiat and his entourage for carrying substantial amounts of money. "They wanted to know where we got the money. We told them Jean-Michel earned it. And it was like, sure, this black guy made a hundred thousand dollars for eight paintings. They didn't believe it for a minute."[31]

These multiple contexts of devalorization greatly explain why, under most circumstances, Basquiat preferred to literally throw his money "out the window" than show restraint or respect toward it. Sometimes, this financial waste took the form of purchasing what Basquiat perceived to be the "best" (and most expensive) available commodities to show off his wealth in the face of those who would doubt that a black man could be rich. "He always appreciated expensive things," wrote Jennifer Clement, "as if consuming them would make him valuable."[32] Basquiat was also prone to excessive displays of generosity such as leaving extravagant tips at restaurants, which, according to Clement, was akin to "punching someone" who may have looked down on him.[33] He particularly enjoyed giving dollar bills to homeless people or people doing menial jobs like washing windshield wipers [rather] than pay taxes or direct the accumulation of his wealth. Always living for the moment, Basquiat spent much of his earnings on perishable goods—like himself.

WHITE AT THE TOP

Basquiat's reluctance to view his own production as merely a commodity greatly contrasts with the careers of other (white) artists, who amassed fortunes by keeping an eye on their money, getting the right counsel, and wisely investing it. Although they may all have been aware of the contradictions of exchange, being a high priced commodity did not seem as disturbing, in part because it was commensurate with their social value as white subjects. Key figures of this period like Madonna may have also sought to challenge the subalterity of race, but only Basquiat was continuously re-racialized in his attempts to become culturally valued.

The specific challenges faced by Basquiat can be appreciated through a comparison with fellow traveler Keith Haring, a queer artist with links to hip hop and a ravenous appetite for black Puerto Rican men and culture. Since both were generally perceived as "the most original artists of the new decade"[34] and they initially were influenced by similar cultural practices, the Haring-Basquiat counterpoint enables an analysis of what roles race, sexuality, and ethnicity can play in the making of artists and the valorization of art. Haring's close relationship to Puerto Rican cultures and communities also allows us to further consider the comparative "load" of (white) homosexuality and race in the commodification of black-Latino practices.

As Basquiat, Haring began his career as a wall writer in 1980 by tagging two images, "dog" and "The Baby." Writing graffiti, however, had dramatically different repercussions for Basquiat and Haring on several levels. Unhampered by racism, Haring was able to engage in relatively dangerous feats such as drawing on black paper on the subway, "I made these drawings where I saw other people's tags, and I did them so that they would be acknowledged by other graffiti artists."[35] Yet, although Haring broke the law and often risked being caught, once he was arrested, the artist received lenient treatment: "all the cops are wondering what this nerdy white boy could possibly have done."[36]

While Basquiat himself was never arrested for his activities, Haring's experience with wall writing greatly contrasts with the fate of other men of color such as the African-American wall writer Michael Stewart. Detained in 1983 for writing graffiti in a Manhattan subway station, Stewart apparently died of cardiac arrest after suffering strangulation while in police custody. Significantly, though Haring was distraught over Stewart's death, Basquiat became paranoid that he would be "next"[37] since both men shared the "dreadlocks" look.[38] According to friends, Basquiat became so afraid that he even refused to cooperate with his girlfriend Suzanne Mallouk's legal efforts to learn more about what happened to Stewart. Perhaps to both ward off the fear and pay his respects, in 1983 Basquiat painted a haunting tribute work, *The Death of Michael Stewart*, in which two blue-clad policemen beat a suspended black figure crowned with a halo.

Like Haring, Basquiat was not oblivious to the bravado of graffiti in affirming masculine iconicity. But while Basquiat knew that being caught writing graffiti could cost him more than a fun arrest or awkward photo opportunity, Haring's identification with African American and Puerto Rican male culture provided him with a surrogate ("real") masculinity, particularly in the context of the hypermacho art establishment that had considered Andy Warhol too "swish" to be one of the boys. As Farris Thompson observed, in incorporating "black bodies in motion" into his work, Haring "conquers" his "macho" painter predecessors—Jackson Pollock, Jules Olitski, and Frank Stella.[39] If as a queer man Haring had to contend with the shame of gay identity and homophobia, his privileged racial identity allowed for the appropriation of graffiti practices in ways that graffiti writers themselves were unable or afraid to do so. Or in Jennifer Clement's succint words, "Keith was gay and white and could glamorize graffiti in a way that Jean could not."[40]

Equally important, although graffiti offered Haring the rewards of masculinity, street respect, and a distinctive edge with the art establishment, Basquiat's links to it rendered him naturally "primitive," rather than purposefully "primitivist" like European painters like Pablo Picasso or Paul Gauguin. Marc Miller, the curator for the Queens Museum, had no qualms in broaching the subject with Basquiat in the following terms, "so you're seen as some sort of primal expressionist . . ."[41] Basquiat was also called the "'wild child' of contemporary art, who . . . embodies the raw primal energy of the urban jungle."[42] It should not then be surprising that Basquiat fought the graffiti association for most of his career, as it became a stain that brought his value down as a "serious" painter. In Basquiat's words, "I don't really consider myself a graffiti artist, you know? And then they have this image of me [as a] wild man, a wild, monkey man, whatever the fuck they thought."[43]

The gesture of tagging Basquiat as a graffiti artist was not the only way that critics used racial assumptions to detract from his artistic achievements. A second instance arose at the moment where he reached the snow-covered mountaintop of art legitimacy: Andy Warhol. After years of approaching Warhol, Basquiat was finally able to collaborate with him in a joint show at the Tony Shafrazi gallery. The 1985 show proved to be life altering, although not in the salutary ways that Basquiat expected.

According to Warhol, the collaboration process was fraught with difficulties from the beginning. Basquiat, for instance, reportedly had frequent paranoid outbursts in which he would accuse Warhol of "using" him while they were working.[44] Furthermore—and more devastating—the show was panned by critics, who assumed that only Warhol had the ability to artistically influence Basquiat, and that, more generally, people attributed the younger artist's success "to the fact that [you] knew how to gain Andy Warhol's attention."[45] This opinion prevailed among most critics, even when influential artists like Haring, who was close to Warhol and Basquiat, asserted that both artists greatly energized each other's work.[46]

To address these claims, Basquiat angrily responded to interviewers who queried him with the statement that, "I was the one who helped Andy Warhol paint!"[47] But this defense was to little avail. Although Basquiat deeply valued Warhol and, in retrospect, he felt that this period corresponded to the "best times" of his life, [48] getting too close to Warhol had, as usual, side effects. When Warhol could (or would) not protect Basquiat from racist remarks, Basquiat decided to break up the friendship, losing some of his larger-than-life celebrity status in the process. Despite the cost, Basquiat saw the severing of ties as essential to his personal and artistic survival: "I wanted to be a star," stated Basquiat to whoever would listen, "not a gallery mascot."[49]

OFF THE WALL: BASQUIAT'S TRANSCULTURAL WORK

Despite the assessment of many of his contemporary critics, Basquiat's work remains an extraordinary site to think about the production of artistic value and the making of American cultures.[50] On the one hand, Basquiat visualized Afro-diasporic practices not as exotic or marginal to Euro-American cultures, but as mobile resources to critique the legacies of capital, enslavement, and racism. On the other, his work is both a symptom and a way to understand hemispheric American culture as a product of continuous and relentless transculturations involving Native, African, and European practices over hundreds of years.

The transcultural in Basquiat can be appreciated at various levels. Immediately recognizable features include the deployment of various languages (primarily English and Spanish, but also Italian, French, and Latin), high art traditions (Leonardo da Vinci, Pablo Picasso, Cy Twombly), and mass mediated culture (comic books, popular music). Moreover, it is significant that some of the most influential musical forms in Basquiat's work—hip hop, Afro-Cuban, and jazz—are all characterized by multiple cultural fusions and improvisation.[51] Basquiat's method itself, assembling his paintings from disparate physical and symbolic materials, also evokes transculturation as he combines multiple textures, media, and found materials on one plane.

Understandably, the majority of commentary on Basquiat's transcultural production has focused on the influence of African American practices and the Euro-American canon. Yet, in exploring the full scope of Basquiat's art, it is important to include an unstudied source that textures his visual work in key ways: Latin American history and culture. In his paintings, Basquiat included a wide range of scenes (cook-

ing "arroz con pollo"), figures (Spanish conquistadors, island politicians like Luis Muñoz Rivera, his own grandmother or "abuelita") that spoke to both Puerto Rican affec-
tive universe and historical processes such as slavery and colonialism as they were
specifically constituted in Latin America. If blackness persisted in Basquiat's work as
an easily communicable sign of alterity to a white audience, Latin American references produced a "hidden transcript" which could address Puerto Rican and other
Latinos in different terms than other (American) subjects.

The extensive use of Spanish as asides—often in parentheses—or as seeming throw-
aways and puns further makes Basquiat's paintings a significant canvas for bilingual
written expression and the production of Afro-Caribbean diasporic cultural competence. In this regard, Basquiat's Spanish is a way to both encode his outsider status in
relation to U.S. culture and inscribe Puerto Rican structures of feeling regarding dignity and freedom. His use of the word "Negro," for instance, can be understood to refer
both to a pre-civil rights context in the U.S., when the devaluation of enslaved Africans
and their descendants was sanctioned by law, and to the ambivalent way—as a term of
endearment and depreciation—that it is used in Puerto Rico. Basquiat's strategic employment of words such as "gringo" and "colonization" also point to a different way of
framing American history, as one of the few groups to use these terms are Puerto Ricans, given the island's enduring colonial relationship to the United States.

Similarly, in *Natives Carrying Some Guns, Bible, Amorites on Safari*, Basquiat considers the toxic relationship between capital, colonialism and enslavement by refer-
encing both Anglo and Latin American experiences. While at the center and right side
of the canvas, Basquiat refers to poaching, missionaries and corporate expeditions,
the canvas's lower right, points to the three forces of Spanish conquest in Latin
America—the search for gold, the ambition of the church, and the scramble for power
of the courts—by writing the last name of the Spanish colonizer of Mexico, (Hernán)
"Cortez" [sic] three times. The first time, Basquiat writes the name in full, then as
"Corte" (court) with a line crossing out the word, and later simply as Corte (cut). Below
the three "cortes," a bilingual phrase provides the ultimate logic to the colonial enterprise, "I WON'T EVEN MENTION GOLD (ORO)."

Moreover, Basquiat's constant allusion to Latin American history and the Spanish
language raises the question of gender politics. For the most part, as critic bell hooks
has argued, Basquiat focused his attention on examining male subjectivity and privileged masculine arenas such as boxing and jazz as sites of Afro-diasporic valorization.
At the same time, it is the culture of the mother and her mother tongue—if not her
particular name—that is indispensable to the artist's understanding of himself and
the world that he lives in. As Basquiat once put it, "I'd say my mother gave me all the
primary things. The art came from her."[52] Not coincidentally, it was Mrs. Basquiat who
handed her son one of his most enduring artistic reference points to visualize himself—
the book *Gray's Anatomy*—after a car hit him at age eight.

The juxtaposition of languages and maternal memories further converges on a general faith in art as a practice of alchemy or "voodoo science," a performance that references Caribbean syncretic religious practices and upward mobility. Basquiat attributes his magical qualities to his mother who he called a "bruja" (witch), an ambivalent term that nevertheless acknowledges the power of creativity and transformation. In a painting titled *K* (1982), for instance, Basquiat painted a gold crown, and inside the crown, he wrote "oro" (gold). Later, Basquiat would reflect on this work, "I was writing gold on all that stuff and I made all this money right afterwards."[53]

Language is not the only sign to encode African diasporic valorization strategies. Although Basquiat himself has stated that the inspiration for the "crown" in his work originated in *The Little Rascals* logo, Basquiat's interest in—if not obsession with—royalty is shared by Afro-diasporic communities and has common roots: offsetting the shame of racialization and the pain of incommensurable definitions of value by affirming the self in alternative terms. Through his paintings on wood, glass, canvas, and wall surfaces, Basquiat memorialized past kings and offered crowns to ordinary men and outlaws, affording them the dignity denied by racism, regardless of their location, station in life and relationship to money or the law. The simultaneous impulses to be "king," to invent royalty, to honor the dead kings and queens of raced history, and to crown new kings and queens are also a feature of the carnival aesthetic, a key cultural practice in the Caribbean.

Despite Basquiat's rich cultural context and insights, however, he was deeply aware of the peril inherent in being valorized as a black king by white art consumers. The historical relationship between low-paid work and devaluation, not only as an individual, but as part of a racialized group, was noted in many of Basquiat's visual works, including a collaborative painting with Warhol titled *Arm and Hammer* (1984), in which "black" labor is portrayed as the other side of the coin, the unacknowledged foundation of the American economy. A second painting, *Untitled (History of Black People*, 1983), portrays slave labor not only as degrading because it exploits the work of people treated as things but also due to how black subjectivity in itself is often transformed into a humiliating "spectacle"—"el gran espectáculo."

The ways that becoming a commodified spectacle defaces the black subject is also evident in how Basquiat visualized black figures in his work: as skulls, deformed, or colorfully transparent, with their internal organs exposed. As Basquiat well knew, the process that makes you a black king inevitably defaces you; the white gaze that valorizes may also kill you. A clear example is a 1984 painting titled *Zydeco*, where Basquiat writes, "don't look into the camera." This insight arguably accounts for the dystopia of Basquiat's visual work and star persona: he painted his pained insides for all to see while defacing his bodily self; both were masks in the sense not only of disguise but as "a necessary sign of the actual situation of disunion."[54] In this sense, a productive vernacular methodology for this inquiry can be summed as "the writing on the wall," for not only does the story start there, the social forces that offered Basquiat what he desired also tore him apart, prefiguring the artist's short but intense life.

In the end, Basquiat's demise as an artist had little to do with the assessment that his "talent had not kept pace with his fame," as his biographer Hoban suggests. Rather, what was evident in Basquiat's life and passion is that once he realized that even if the work was deemed valuable, the commodity's worth would never fully extend to the artist who created it, there was little motivation to continue to paint—or live. If Basquiat's enterprise was, in part, an epistemology of valorization, what killed him as an artist was the knowledge that commodification would never liberate him from racial devalorization, even when it could produce handsome profits for himself and others.

This is why on the 1988 painting *TV Star*, Basquiat boldly declares, "NOTHING TO BE GAINED HERE," thus setting himself up for failure in his final attempt to get his "soul" back: participating in a cleansing ceremony performed by shamans in the Ivory Coast.[55] The possibly life-saving performance never took place; perhaps Basquiat realized that there was no longer a "soul" to save. As Warhol put it, "when all these dealers heard there was a really talented black artist who would probably die off soon from drugs, then they hurried to buy his things and now I guess they're frustrated because he's staying alive."[56] Not disappointing, Basquiat died that same year from a drug overdose. His last artistic work, *Riding with Death*, at last brings physical and symbolic death together on one moving plane.

After Basquiat's death, his value surged as his work became rare and his place as the "big black painter" was vacated. The legal rush and commercial bustle that followed was a snapshot of Basquiat's realization of what he had become: a rare, exotic, commodified object to be continuously exchanged and appreciated, perhaps ending on someone's wall like the head of a hunted lion. At this point, Basquiat took his place in a long line up of dead kings like Jesus and John the Baptist (patron saint of derelicts), who have worn the crown of thorns in life, to only be fully appreciated after death. Yet, although Basquiat commands the highest prices of any 1980s painter, critics do not concede defeat, underscoring how the art world still is hesitant to fully own (up) to Basquiat. The dealer Richard Polsky, for instance, has written that, "it's not clear whether his work will survive the test of time. Many museums own Basquiat paintings, but it's odd how one rarely sees his work on display when their permanent collections are exhibiting. It's as if the museums are hedging their bets." But if Basquiat's transcultural work continues to appreciate, it is in part because his experience has become more recognizable, valued, and indispensable for Latinos, African Americans, and everyone living in conflicted cultural contexts.

The King is dead, long live the King!

NOTES

1. "Octavo día." Single by Shakira from the album "¡Dónde Están los Ladrones?" (1998).

2. John Gruen, *Keith Haring: The Authorized Biography* (New York: Fireside, 1991), 86.

3. Louis Armand, "Jean-Michel Basquiat©: Identity and the Art of Dis(empowerment)," www.geocities.com/louis_armand/basquiat.html.

4. Greg Tate, "Nobody Loves a Genius Child: Jean Michel Basquiat, Flyboy in the Buttermilk," in *Flyboy in the Buttermilk* (New York: Fireside, Simon and Schuster, 1992): 231–44, 233.

5. Robert Farris Thompson, "Royalty, Heroism, and the Streets," in Marshall, *Jean-Michel Basquiat*, 28–42, 30.

6. Fernando Ortiz, *Cuban Counterpoint: Tobacco and Sugar* (Durham: Duke University Press, 1995), 95–96.

7. Robert Knafo, The Basquiat File," www.spikemagazine.com/0397basq.htm; Armand, "Jean-Michel Basquiat©: Identity and the Art of Dis(empowerment)," www.geocities.com/ louis_armand/basquiat.html.

8. Rene Ricard, "The Radiant Child," *Artforum*, December 20, 1981, pp. 35–45, 38.

9. Greg Tate, "Nobody Loves a Genius Child: Jean Michel Basquiat, Flyboy in the Buttermilk," *Flyboy in the Buttermilk* (New York: Fireside, 1992), pp. 231–244, 234.

10. Keith Haring, *Journals* (New York: Penguin Books, 1996), pp. 64–65.

11. Patricia Bosworth, "Hyped to Death," *New York Times Review*, August 9, 1998, p. 4.

12. Karl Marx, *Grundrisse: The Foundations of Political Economy* (New York: Vintage, 1973).

13. Interview with Henry Geldhazhler," *Basquiat* (Milano: Edizione Charta, 1999), lvii–lix, lix.

14. Phoebe Hoban, *Basquiat* (New York: Penguin Books, 1998), p. 56.

15. Ibid., p. 83.

16. Kathleen McGuigan, "New Art, New Money," *New York Times Magazine*, February 10, 1985, p. 32.

17. Clement, *Widow Basquiat* (Edinburgh: Payback Press, 2001), p. 80.

18. Hoban, *Basquiat*, p. 140.

19. Bosworth, "Hyped to Death," p. 4.

20. Hoban, *Basquiat*, 131.

21. López, "Post-Work Selves and Entitlement 'Attitudes' in Peripheral Post-Industrial Puerto Rico," 38.

22. Clement, *Widow Basquiat*, 32.

23. George Condo, quoted in Gruen, *Keith Haring: The Authorized Biography*, 126.

24. Hoban, *Basquiat*, 268.

25. Carl D. Schneider, *Shame, Exposure, and Privacy* (Boston: Beacon, 1977), 10.

26. Ricard, "The Radiant Child," 38.

27. Ibid., 84.

28. Clement, *Widow Basquiat*, 49.

29. Frantz Fanon, *Black Skin, White Masks* (New York: Grove Weidenfeld, 1967), 170.

30. "Interview with Isabelle Graw," in *Basquiat* (Charta), lxvii.

31. Hogan, *Basquiat*, 115.

32. Clement, *Widow Basquiat*, 108.

33. Ibid., 44.

34. Elisabeth Sussman, Whitney Museum, 1997: 14.

35. Gruen, *Keith Haring: The Authorized Biography*, 65.

36. Ibid., 84.

37. Clement, *Widow Basquiat*, 132.

38. Warhol, *The Andy Warhol Diarie*s, 533.

39. Robert Farris Thompson, Introduction to Haring, xxxi.

40. Clement, *Widow Basquiat*, 136.

41. Hoban, *Basquiat*, 168.

42. Ibid., p. 265.

43. Ibid., 41.

44. Warhol, *The Andy Warhol Diaries*, 605.

45. "Interview with Demosthenes Davvetas," in *Basquiat* (Charta), lxiii.

46. Keith Haring, "Painting the Mind," in *Basquiat* (Charta), xlvi–xlvii, xlvi.

47. "Interview with Demosthenes Davvetas," lxiii.

48. Hoban, *Basquiat*, 300.

49. *Basquiat* (Charta), 136.

50. bell hooks, "Altars of Sacrifice: Re-membering Basquiat," *Art in America* (June 1993, 68–74), 74.

51. Hoban, *Basquiat*, 17.

52. *Basquiat* (Charta), 24.

53. Schneider, *Shame, Exposure and Privacy*, 7.

54. Ibid., 308.

55. Warhol, *The Andy Warhol Diaries*, 627.

56. Richard Polsky, "Jean-Michel Basquiat," www.auctionwatch.com/awdaily/collctors/bsh/basquiat/.

A SPLENDID OUTSIDER

Archer Milton Huntington and the Hispanic Heritage in the United States

Claudio Iván Remeseira

I

When the 2000 census confirmed that Hispanics outnumbered African Americans as the second largest ethnic group in the United States, the country was already spellbound by the Latino craze. A self-consciously pluralistic America, ready to celebrate its ethnic and racial diversity, sings and dances to the pace of the Caribbean *salsa*, eats Mexican burritos or Spanish *tapas,* and embraces the cult of tango. The very word *Latino* has become a badge of honor for the Spanish-speaking population in the U.S. American citizens of Hispanic descent proudly claim a dual identity in which the traits of their cultural ancestry blend with those of American civilization. At the same time, more and more non-Latino Americans are showing a keen interest in learning Spanish. Apparently, the United States has come to terms with its Hispanic side.

A closer look, however, reveals how limited that trend is. The interest in Hispanic-American culture scarcely goes beyond showbiz celebrities like pop singers Ricky Martin or Shakira (who, of course, shift to English while performing for American audiences) or actors like John Leguizamo, Antonio Banderas, and Penélope Cruz (the rumors that she was the reason why Tom Cruise divorced Nicole Kidman adding just one more spicy touch to the sex-predator Latina image). That restrictive view only goes to enhance the stereotype of Latinos as a sensual and festive people, a sort of Hispanic Jim Crow, if you will.

While it is true that politicians increasingly address their growing Hispanic constituencies in the language of Cervantes, the culture embodied in that language—literature, art, worldview—remains, for the most part, unknown, if not overtly disparaged. As the increasing concerns over the impact Latin American immigration may have on the fabric of American society will testify, many Americans still regard the Hispanic influence in their country with a certain uneasiness.

That was not Archer Milton Huntington's case. At the turn of the twentieth century, this member of the WASP elite devoted his life to the study and promotion of Hispanic culture in the United States. His legacy, embodied in the Hispanic Society of America in New York City and the Hispanic Foundation at the Library of Congress in Washington, D.C., represents one of the most conscientious efforts ever undertaken in this country to bridge the differences between the Anglo-Saxon and Hispanic cultures. Exploring his legacy may help us understand the complex relationship between the United States and Hispanic America and even to reach a surprising insight into the United States' own Hispanic background.

The only child of Collis Porter Huntington, mastermind behind the Central Pacific and Southern Pacific Railroad, Archer Milton Huntington (1870–1955) was an outstanding representative of the genteel humanism of the late nineteenth century. The scope and depth of his achievements as an art collector and philanthropist, let alone his academic deeds, put him into the highest ranks of that tradition. But his commitment to the diffusion of Hispanic civilization in America was clearly at odds with his contemporaries' prejudices.

When the twenty-year-old Huntington shared with some friends the idea of creating a Spanish museum, they laughed at him. (One of his most derisive critics was his cousin Henry Huntington, who was to play an important role in Archer's future.) On another occasion, Morris K. Jessup, director of the American Museum of Natural History, dismissed his project by saying that it was pointless to study a "dead civilization."

Jessup's viewpoint was more representative of nineteenth-century American public opinion than Huntington's was—he wasn't even in the right place at the right time: The outbreak of the Spanish-American war found him at the ruins of Italica, near Seville, conducting an archeological expedition.

The oddity of his self-assigned mission was reinforced by his family origins. There is a strange sense of divine retribution in the fact that the son of one of the robber barons spent a large part of his father's fortune erecting libraries and museums, amassing impressive art collections, and creating natural parks (another of Archer's passions) for public use. Huntington senior's involuntary generosity was, after all, in line with the philanthropist movement represented by the Morgans, Carnegies, Mellons, Rockefellers, and other captains of industry and finance who established the network of America's public cultural institutions. What is ironic is that it was a Protestant New Englander's money that paid for providing Catholic Spain with a greater measure of respect in the United States.

Despite his lack of academic credentials (since he was educated by private tutors, his application to Columbia University was rejected as not fulfilling the formal requirements for a Ph.D. candidate), Archer Milton Huntington was a remarkable scholar. In 1892, he made the first of his many trips to Spain in the company of his tutor, Yale professor William Ireland Knapp. The two men spent several months on the peninsula following Don Quixote's route. At the age of twenty-seven he published his own translation and annotated edition of the *Poem of Mio Cid*, the first literary landmark of the Spanish language. "Until recently, it remained the standard English version of the poem," says Theodore S. Beardsley Jr., former director of the Hispanic Society of America.

In order to address this task within the full scope of multicultural eleventh-century Spain, he undertook the study of Arabic, Catalan, and Portuguese. His three-volume edition of the epic poem was highly praised by one of the patrons of modern Spanish literary studies, Ramón Menéndez Pidal, who added that it was an invaluable aid to his own edition. During his lifetime, Huntington also published an account of his Spanish travels (*A Note-Book in Northern Spain*, 1898), a monograph on Spanish medieval miniatures, forty editions of classic works of Spanish and Portuguese literature, and thirty volumes of his own poetry, replete with Spanish and Moorish themes.

He thought of himself primarily as a poet. At any rate, it is in his poems (conventionally skillful and irredeemably old-fashioned for today's taste) that we can catch a glimpse of his inner motivations. In a letter to his mother, he described his conception of a Hispanic museum as a poem capable of capturing Spain's essence: "I wish to know Spain as it is, and reflect it all in one singular place." That concept finally materialized in 1904, when he founded the Hispanic Society of America and commissioned the construction of a neoclassic building at Audubon Terrace, 155th Street and Broadway, to house it.

Huntington donated his own collection of works of art, archeological objects, maps, and manuscripts as the starting point for the society. The range and quality of that collection, acquired over a twenty-year period, is overwhelming: paintings and drawings from the Middle Ages to the twentieth century; fifteen thousand books printed before 1701, among them first editions of classics like *La Celestina* (donated by J. P. Morgan), *Tirant Lo Blanc* and *Don Quixote*; the most extensive manuscript collection of Spanish medieval charters and illustrated Bibles in the United States; hundreds of catechisms and dictionaries of the Amerindian languages, printed for use by Spanish missionaries; literary manuscripts from the eleventh to the twentieth centuries; and one of the finest American collections of Hispano-Moorish lusterware. What makes this collection worthier still was Huntington's early decision to purchase only objects that were auctioned or sold outside of Spain.

A site devoted to Hispanic civilization wouldn't have been complete without a Catholic church. In 1912 Huntington funded the erection of Our Lady of Hope on 156th Street and Broadway. He personally regretted the excessive power of the Spanish

Catholic Church and was furious about the destruction of the Roman and Moorish records by the Inquisition. As for religious beliefs, he seemed to have been a skeptic.

In 1922 the society temporarily hosted the activities of the newly created Columbia University Department of Spanish, today known as Casa Hispánica. At the suggestion of his friend, then president of Columbia, Nicholas Murray Butler, Huntington recruited the first director for that department. He chose Federico de Onís, a disciple of the great Spanish writer Miguel de Unamuno and a direct descendant of the diplomat who signed the Florida treaty in 1819 as a representative of the Spain crown. For some time, Huntington even paid Onís's salary. In Spain he also contributed financially to the installation of the Cervantes Museum in Valladolid and the restoration of the El Greco house in Toledo.

Spanish and Latin American contemporary writers such as the aforementioned Menéndez Pidal, Rubén Darío, Vicente Blasco Ibáñez, María de Maetzu, and Ramón Pérez de Ayala lectured at the society and other New York City cultural institutions, usually under Huntington's personal patronage. He became directly involved in the promotion of artists like the Spanish painters Ignacio de Zuloaga and Joaquín Sorolla (from whom he commissioned the massive Regions of Spain canvases, one of the society's most splendid exhibits) or the Argentine rural-style painter Bernardo de Quirós. He also commissioned the translation and publication of the first volume of poetry ever published in the United States by Spanish Nobel laureate Juan Ramón Jiménez.

Particularly remarkable was his relationship with Darío, the most influential poet in the Hispanic world at the turn of the twentieth century. On Huntington's suggestion, the Nicaraguan writer was invited to lecture at Columbia University. On February 4, 1915, Darío read his poem "Pax" to a small audience at Havemeyer Hall. Huntington provided for Darío's honorarium and invited him to join the society as a full member. According to the correspondence exchanged between the two men at that time, an already seriously ill, morally battered, and financially pressed Darío was profoundly grateful for his host's generosity and even dedicated a poem to him. Shortly after Darío's death in Nicaragua, in 1916, Huntington commissioned the translation and publication of an anthology of his work.

In 1927 Huntington endowed the Library of Congress with a $105,000 fund in Central Pacific gold bonds for the purchase of books relating to Spanish, Portuguese, and South American arts, crafts, literature, and history. Twelve years later, the library inaugurated the site for the collection, a 130-foot-long room decorated in Spanish and Portuguese Renaissance style. This collection—officially the Hispanic Foundation in the Library of Congress—is perhaps the most important archive of Latin America's historical memory.

Huntington was probably the first English-speaking scholar to use the term *Hispanic* to embrace both the Spanish and the Portuguese cultures and their offspring in Latin America. That fact alone could have represented someone else's lifelong contribution to scholarship. In Huntington's case, it was just a brief footnote in an astonishingly productive career. As for his academic merits, they were eventually to be acknowledged by Columbia, Harvard, and Yale in the form of honorary degrees.

I I

High-pitched Spanish voices fill the air on the sidewalk alongside Audubon Terrace. In an unexpected twist of history, the society and the cluster of cultural institutions surrounding it are now engulfed in a densely knit *barrio*, the most populous Dominican enclave in New York City.

At the turn of the twentieth century, Audubon Park—so named after ornithologist John James Audubon, who owned that land in the mid 1840s—was a residential area dotted with gardens and lawns. Huntington wished to turn the place into a thriving hive of learning. His vision became a reality in the mid-1920s with the construction of a massive group of classic revival edifices designed by his cousin Charles Pratt Huntington: the American Numismatic Society (to which he donated his own collection of thirty-five thousand coins), the American Geographic Society (today the site of the Boricua College, an institution mostly attended by the Hispanic and African American communities), the Museum of the American Indian and the Heye Foundation (both recently moved to a new site downtown), and the American Academy of Arts and Letters.

After passing through an austere portico guarded by two limestone lions—a symbol for Spanish grandeur—the visitor enters a small hall presided over by two bronze bas-reliefs depicting Archer Milton Huntington and his father. Opposite the entrance, a door opens on the main court of the museum, an ample room designed in Spanish Renaissance style. The terra-cotta walls accentuate the warm gravity of the ambience; one feels that one is treading into an ancient world hovered over by serene spirits.

Hanging at the center of the room, Francisco de Goya's *Portrait of the Duchess of Alba* immediately catches the eye with its smooth colors. A few steps away, three portraits by Diego Velázquez provide a remarkable example of seventeenth-century Spanish painting. And among the sixteenth-century paintings, a small *Pietá* executed in jewel-like colors by Domenikos Theotokopoulos, El Greco, reminds us of the Byzantine influences on Hispanic civilization. Pottery, church plate, textiles, and archeological objects ranging from the pre-Roman period to the nineteenth century are displayed in glass cases. The collection of sculptures includes a couple of extraordinarily well-preserved Gothic alabaster tombs.

The court is enclosed by a lavishly ornamented arcade, which in turn supports an elevated gallery. The gallery walls are lined with paintings by the masters of the Golden Age (sixteenth to seventeenth centuries) and a sample of medieval decorative and minor arts: polychrome wood carvings, ivory, *retablos* (ornamental panels to be placed at the fore of the altar), gold and silverwork, and ceramics. The steps of the staircase that communicates between the gallery and the first floor are decorated with Moorish lusterware.

A long, narrow corridor links the main court to a room that used to serve as a library. Its octagonal walls are now occupied by Joaquín Sorolla's huge Regions of Spain canvasses. Sorolla, one of the masters of Spanish postimpressionistic painting, performed here what some critics consider his artistic testament. After the dim-lit atmosphere of the main court, the bright colors of his palette strike our eyes as fireworks in the broad light. All the human types and landscapes of the peninsula are depicted with powerful touches. The overall effect, however, is rather that of an ethereal melody, an embracing wave of luminous images lifting our spirit into thin air.

As most foreigners do, I discovered the Hispanic Society in the tourist guides to New York City. But what really lured me to the place was the equestrian sculpture of El Cid erected at the heart of Audubon Terrace. A replica of that sculpture has been standing for decades at one of the most important crossroads of my home city, Buenos Aires. Fascinated by this artistic coincidence, I wished to see what I thought was the original work. So it was I found that it is also a replica of the statue made in the mid-1920s by Huntington's second wife, Anna Hyatt, and donated by the couple to the city of Seville. A third replica was lost in a shipwreck while on its way to Japan. Thanks to Huntington, then, it may be claimed that El Cid and the culture he represents ride even at the bottom of the sea.

At Audubon Terrace Hyatt transformed the statue in the center of a monumental group. A double flight of stairs leads down from the street level to the inner plaza. At the foot of the stairs, bronze sculptures of a red stag and a red doe face each other. Four bronze warriors are seated at each corner of the granite base on which the sculpture of El Cid is mounted. Carved into the rear walls that enclose the plaza, huge limestone reliefs of Boabdil, the last Moorish king of Granada, and Don Quixote, astride his mythical Rocinante, enhance the visual effect of El Cid's triumphant gesture. Two massive flagpoles, decorated with struggling human and animal figures, complete the scene. "Here, in short, is a truly unified design," wrote Huntington, "in which a rich conception is expressed with unfaltering energy, sustained fire."

III

Archer Milton Huntington: The name has the ring of a Henry James character. His life was in fact a novelistic one. And, as in a Jamesian plot, nothing in it was exactly the way it was presented in the first place.

A 1937 *Fortune* profile described him in this fashion: "Mr. Huntington is six feet five inches tall, weighs 240 pounds, break chairs when he sits on them, and sometimes puts down the telephone so hard that it etches a semicircle on the mahogany table top." He was frequently described as a blend of a modern philanthropist and an ancient Maecenas. "Last of Titans," the title of a biographical sketch written by Arthur Upham Pope, seems a very appropriate description for him. Despite this contented appearance, Pope tells us, Huntington was also "impatient, biased, imperious, with a strong distaste for mediocrity or indolence."

He exerted total control over the society. It is said that not even a lightbulb could be changed without his approval. He also was something of a feminist, albeit a very peculiar one. Huntington thought that women were more fit than men for academic research, and he personally interviewed applicants for a job at the society. The odd thing was that he apparently preferred to hire *deaf* women. "He insisted on a noiseless library," says one of his biographers.

Overall, he was a reclusive person. He frequently resented having to waste his time attending dinners and fulfilling social obligations and used to quarrel with his first wife, his cousin Helen Gates Criss, about the seats they would take at the theater: While she pushed for the pit stalls, he preferred the less conspicuous seats at the back of the boxes. His inner circle did include some high-ranking New York personalities like Columbia president Butler, but he basically found himself more at ease in the company of scholars and artists. When his wife left him for the British producer Harley Granville Barker, Huntington plunged into a deep depression. He was pulled out of it by the sculptor Anna Hyatt, whom he met while looking for an artist to design an honorary medal for his admired William Dean Howells. They married in 1923 on the date of their common birthday, March 10, and spent their honeymoon cruising the Caribbean in Huntington's yacht *Rocinante*.

The main sources of information about his life are the correspondence he exchanged with his mother for more than thirty years and the minute account of their relationship he wrote at her request in 1920, four years before she died. Most of this material rests in the society's archives, not available to the public. The reason, says Mitchell A. Codding, current director of the institution and one of the few people who has read through these papers, is that they remain unclassified. But it seems to have been Huntington's will that his private life remain private, as if he wished to vanish behind his own work.

Huntington himself hedged in his own privacy with a firewall of silence. From the early age of twelve he kept a diary, but he destroyed it around 1900. His scarce biographies (most of them written by society staffers) do not explain much of his personality. The one notable exception is the account written in 1980 by A. Hyatt Mayor, Huntington's nephew by his second marriage, in the introduction to a book on Brookgreen Gardens. Mayor disclosed the uncomfortable truth that explains why he retreated from social circles and was so reluctant about his own private life. "The reticence imposed by his illegitimacy," the author says, "scarred him with a compulsion for secrecy that kept him from confiding the whole of any major project to any one person."

Collis P. Huntington, indeed, had adopted him at the age of fourteen, when he married Archer's mother Arbella after his first wife's death. According to James T. Maher in *The Twilight of Splendor: Chronicles of the Age of American Palaces* (1975), the railroad mogul never completed the legal procedure of adoption. Since at that point Collis and Arbella had been lovers for fifteen years, there is a good reason to conclude that he was Archer's father. Some people, however, disagreed. "There is no question that the unresolved mystery of his paternity profoundly affected his life and philanthropies," wrote David Whitesell in the obituary published by the Grolier Club after Huntington's death in 1955.

The key to this story is not Collis P. Huntington but his young mistress. She was the primary influence in Archer's life. He left abundant evidence of that, especially in his poetry. His *Collected Verses* bears the inscription "To my mother," which is also the title of the first poem of the collection, published one year after Arbella's death. (Significantly enough, that same piece is entitled "Madre," in Spanish, in the 1953 edition.) The intensity of Archer's feelings for his mother is evident: "Deep in the secret night new meanings thronging, / Softly still my senses know your spirit breathes my name." The poem "The Garment" bears an epigraph in Spanish: "Pero mi más tierna / memoria eres tú / madre idolatrada / De mis ojos luz." Another poem goes: "Into the waste a butterfly came broken / Hailing death upon the lips of Sphinx, wheron it sought / An answer unto pleading, some word to anguish spoken."

Secret. A butterfly came broken into the waste. Sphinx. These are accurate metaphors for Arbella's life. "Few women in American history have managed to conceal their past as successfully as her," says Stephen Birmingham in *The Grandes Dames* (1982) The chapter dedicated to Arbella in Birmingham's book is titled "A Woman of Mystery." That mystery is so thick that even her real name remains unclear. Some documents refer to her alternatively as Arbella or Arabella Yarrington Worsham, Arabella Duval Worsham or, more simply, Belle D. Worsham or B. D. Worsham. Not even her birthdate and birthplace are indisputable. The inscription at her mausoleum, ordered by her beloved son, reads: "Born 1850, Union Spring, Alabama." In his extensive research, however, Maher found no city, county, state, or church record in Alabama to confirm that statement. It seemed that she had no past.

Cerinda Evans, a biographer of Collis P. Huntington and librarian emeritus of the Mariner's Museum at Newport News, Virginia, tries to sketch that past. "Arabella Duval Yarrington was the daughter of Richard Milton Yarrington and Catherine J. Yarrington. . . . The Yarringtons were natives of Alabama and Texas, but members of the family had resided in Virginia since 1850. There was a R. M. Yarrington— presumably her father—listed in the *Richmond Directory* from 1850 to 1856," the year of his death.

It was in Richmond that Arbella met Johnny Archer Worsham, the owner of a faro parlor in that city during the Civil War. "He was the king of the faro bankers of the Confederacy, and, quite incidentally, a taste maker whose *décor* was remarked, and remembered," says Maher. Johnny's kingdom came to ashes when the Union army entered the city and set it on fire. He then moved to New York and got into a partnership at a gambling house off Fifth Avenue on West 24th Street, opposite Madison Square, the heart of Manhattan's high life. Arbella was with him, and so were her mother and siblings. The extended family lived in a rented house on 35 Bleecker Street and by the end of 1869 moved to 5 Bond Street.

It was around that time that Arbella became pregnant. Her son was born on March 10, 1870, and was baptized with the names Archer (Johnny's middle name) Milton (Arbella's father's middle name) Worsham. Maher found no birth certificate in New York County records, but Worsham, Arbella, and little Archer were listed in the 1870 census as living at Bond Street under the names John De Worsion, Bell De Wersion, and their three-month-old child John De Wersion. The record adds that the baby was born in Virginia. "Sloppy census methods might be blamed for these errors," Maher says. "But a census is an official record, and both John Worsham and Arbella may have had good reason to cloud it." That reason may have been that Wosham was already married to another woman, Annete Worsham, with whom, according to the same 1870 census, he was living in Richmond. In any case, Worhsam/De Worsion was soon off the scene. After Johnny's exit, Arbella and her mother moved to 109 Lexington Avenue, between E. 27th and 28th Streets. Her new neighbors were the Morgans, the Astors, and the Vanderbilts. And her landlord was Collis P. Huntington.

It is plausible that Huntington and Arbella met for the first time at Worsham's parlor in Richmond. By 1869 he had already taken over the Chesapeake-Ohio Railroad and was then making frequent business trips to Virginia. This may shed some light on Archer's origin or muddle it even more. Birmingham speculates that Arbella may have been sleeping with the two men at the same time; in that case there would be no way of knowing who the child's father really was.

What is beyond any doubt is Arbella's stunning beauty. The photographs of that period show her, in Birmingham words, as "dramatically tall, slender, full bosomed, with dark hair, enormous and luminous dark eyes and a beautifully formed, if somewhat determined, mouth and chin." By the time she met Huntington, he was close to his fiftieth birthday. Little wonder that the ruthless businessman was smitten by this Southern belle almost half his age.

Birmingham bluntly describes Arbella as the "successful courtesan." She certainly rose from obscure origins to the peak of wealth and power in a peculiar but not at all unusual version of the American Dream. Actually, it quite matched Collis P. Huntington's version: a tinker's sixth son, he was reared in a house next to a swamp known as Poverty Hollow in Harwinton Township, Connecticut.

In 1877 Arbella arrived in Austin, Texas with her little son. A local paper described her as Mrs. B. D. Worsham, Collis P. Huntington's niece. That same year she bought a new property at 4 W. 54th Street, New York and personally oversaw the mansion's decoration. Her success may be witnessed at the Museum of the City of New York and the Brooklyn Museum, where original furnishing of some of its rooms are on exhibit.

How did Arbella get her savvy taste? We know that Joseph Duveen, one of the most influential art dealers of those days, was one of her tutors. Worsham, a tastemaker of his own, might have been another. In any event, Arbella became a true connoisseur and even made her husband interested in art collecting. (For the sake of the Spanish trivia of our story, it is worth mentioning that Huntington senior used the code name Carlos to make his bids at auction.)

The most impressive room of 4 W. 54th Street was the Moorish salon, a parlor located at the rear of the 1,000-square-foot main living room. A romantic vogue started by the success of Washington Irving's *Tales of the Alhambra,* the "Spanish touch" was then a must in every high-society household. "The *diwan* and its decoration had passed from the tents—the mirage like desert palaces—of the great Muslim princes to Moorish Spain to Fifth Avenue," says Maher. It was in this environment, permeated by the spirit of *The Arabic Nights,* that Archer Milton Huntington grew up.

Collis P. Huntington passed away in 1900, making Arbella one of the richest widows in America. He also left Archer out of his will. Instead, one third of his estate—roughly estimated as worth $150,000,000—went to his nephew Henry Edwards Huntington, the son of that brother with whom Collis had got his start-up sixty years earlier.

If Archer Huntington's retreat from social life was determined by his family story, one particular scandal must have strengthened his scruples: the William D'Alton Mann trial. "Colonel" Mann was the publisher of *Town Topics,* a sort of *National Enquirer* of the time. Whenever he discovered some sexual scandal involving prominent people, he would go and tell them what he knew and suggest that the story need not be printed, on condition of a generous purchase of advertising space in his paper. The scheme paid off, and Mann became rich.

Mann's nemesis was Emily Post, America's future arbiter of elegance. Mann discovered, in 1905, that Post's husband was having an affair and tried to blackmail him. Ashamed, the unfaithful spouse confessed to his wife, who went immediately to the police and got Mann arrested. As the trial progressed, it became known that one of the people bribed by the colonel over the years was none other than Mrs. Collis P. Huntington. She was to be subpoenaed to testify but sailed instead to Europe, where she spent the next five years.

In 1913 Arbella married her son's cousin Henry. "That marriage was a purely business issue," says Beardsley. "It was meant for reuniting the two main parts of Collis P. Huntington's fortune." The news, however, was shocking. To add another weird twist to the story, Henry had previously been married to Collis's foster child Clara, who in reality was Collis's first wife's sister. After such a confusion of family roles, it is not surprising that Archer decided not to have children.

San Marino, a 550-acre ranch at the foothills of the San Gabriel Mountains, was the main repository of the couple's collections. After Arbella and Henry died, the estate went into the public domain as the Huntington Art Museum and the Huntington Library. "She was the American equivalent of Madame de Pompadour and Isabella d'Este," says Maher. This is quite an epitaph for someone who had started her career half a century before at a dubious gambling parlor in Richmond.

Arbella died in her Fifth Avenue palace on September 14, 1924. The web of misleading statements and mystery spun by her during her lifetime raises another intriguing question: is it possible that she might have been of Spanish descent? The citrine complexion, the black hair, the dark bright eyes, the obscure origin may very well suggest so. Beardsley dismisses that possibility. "She had a strong distaste for the Hispanic culture and loved the French culture," he said. True. But is should be remembered that a reaction like that is not uncommon among Spaniards and Spanish Americans. In any event, it's something we'll never know for sure.

IV

What we do know is that Arbella transmitted to her son a love for art and museums. In 1882 he made his first trip to Europe in her company. She steered the twelve-year-old boy through the National Gallery and the Louvre (due to her disdain for Spain, El Prado was not on the itinerary). That marked Archer for the rest of his life. It was in London that he read *The Spanish Gypsies* by George Borrow. "That book," says Codding, director of the Hispanic Society, "sparked his lifelong passion for Hispanic culture."

But it was not in Europe but in America that he first got in touch with that culture. Huntington heard Spanish for the first time in Texas, during the visit Arbella paid to her "uncle" Collis in 1877. That must have been an indelible experience for a seven-year-old child. At the age of fourteen he seriously undertook the study of Spanish with a private teacher from Valladolid, Spain. Alejandro Quijano, a Mexican journalist who interviewed him in 1918, said that Huntington spoke Spanish with "the purity of a Toledo nobleman."

Archer returned to Texas several times as a teenager to spend summers at his father's ranch in San Marcos. "It was necessary to speak Spanish if one wished to communicate to the people," says Beardsley. In fact, one of the provisions of the Treaty of Guadalupe Hidalgo, by which Mexico ceded in 1848 the northern part of its territory to the United States, was that the local population would be allowed by the U.S. government to keep their own language.

His early familiarity with the Southwest may have been the psychological undercurrent that led Archer to define his Hispanic mission. He left no explicit testimony of that, however. In any event, it is more plausible than the idea of an affluent New York teenager conceiving the full-fledged idea of committing his life to the study of an alien culture out of the blue.

In assessing Huntington's career, one is tempted to think that he was quite conscious of the intertwining paths of the Hispanic and the Anglo-Saxon civilizations in the United States. "We often forget that the earliest European settlers in what is now the continental United States were not English but Spanish," says Beardsley, "and that as late as 1762 two thirds of today's United States territory was part of Spain." The influence of Spanish on American English, for example, would not have passed unnoticed to an amateur philologist like Huntington. The list of Spanish loanwords is really impressive: *Alligator, bit* (the Spanish *real*; the expression "two bits" is a translation of the Spanish *dos reales*), *cargo, cowboy, garbage, gusto, manta ray, mulatto, Negro, palisade, renegade, sack, sambo, sherry, spinach, talisman*, and *torpedo* are just a few examples. And, even fifty years after the Declaration of Independence, Spanish coinage was legal currency in the country (the dollar was then called *hard dollar*, probably a borrowing from the Spanish *peso duro*).

Huntington never forgot the Southwest. In 1927 he endowed the University of Texas with the rents of a rural property in Galveston County to fund a museum of fine arts, today's Blanton Museum of Art. His links to Mexico, where his father was the main railroad contractor, were strong too. At the age of nineteen he met President Porfirio Díaz. At that time Collis still hoped that his son would some day take control of the business and asked Archer to join him for dinner at the presidential palace. Twenty-five years later, Archer Huntington designated president Díaz as one of the members of the Hispanic Society's board. In 1910, the same year of the revolution that ousted Díaz from power, Huntington sponsored the founding of the International School for American Archeology and Ethnography in Mexico City. The influence of this institution on the development of Mexican archeology—and, indirectly, on the development of the governmental-led establishment of Mexico's national identity over the next decades—cannot be underestimated.

One year later he sponsored the Yale Peruvian expedition, led by Hiram Bingham, that rediscovered the Incan citadel Machu Picchu. The finding of this high-mountain fortress (hidden by a dense jungle from Western eyes for more than three centuries) was a momentous step in the unveiling of Latin America's history. Throughout the twentieth-century rise of nationalism, Machu Picchu became entrenched as a symbol of Latin American identity, a pilgrimage destination for people seeking to fathom the indigenous Latin American soul.

Bingham's successful expedition certainly kindled Huntington's interest in Latin America. One can surmise just how deep that interest ran by looking at the number of publications supported by the society after that date: the edition of the *Crónicas de Nueva España*'s manuscript, a key source for studying the history of the Mexican Conquest, written in the sixteenth century by Cervantes de Salazar (1914); *El folklore de Oaxaca* (*Oaxaca's Folklore*), by Paul Rodin (1917); *The Odes of Bello, Olmedo and Heredia*, three classics of nineteenth-century Latin American poetry, edited by E. C. Hills (1920); a monograph on El Inca Garcilaso de la Vega, a sixteenth-century Peruvian *mestizo* author, by Julia Fitzmaurice-Kelly (1921); *Spanish Colonial Literature in South America*, by Bernard Moses (1922); Joseph Auslander's translation of a fragment of José Hernández's *Martin Fierro*, Argentina's national poem, and *Calandria*, a groundbreaking theatrical play by Argentine author Martiniano Leguizamon (1923); and *The Intellectual Background of the Revolution in South America*, also by Moses (1926).

This feverish activity mirrored the pan-American movement that swept the continent during Huntington's youth. However, in spite of his close relationship with Díaz and other Latin American leaders, he was not engaged in the political side of that movement. His friendship with former Argentine president Bartolomé Mitre, for example, was established more on the basis of their personal affinities as literary men and art collectors (Mitre, a historian and modest poet himself, translated Dante's *Commedia* into Spanish and was the founder of the Argentine Numismatic Society as well as of the *La Nación* daily, the same newspaper that counted José Martí among its foreign correspondents) than on any political considerations.

Huntington's reserve shouldn't be taken as a lack of interest on his part. Quijano recalled that during their meeting the American queried him extensively about Mexican politics. It is deeply regrettable then that Huntington never made public his reflections on the combative relationship between the United States and the Hispanic world during his lifetime, a period that included the Spanish-American War, President Theodore Roosevelt's Big Stick policy, the Mexican revolution, the American invasions of Mexico and Central America, and the Good Neighbor policy instituted by the second Roosevelt.

Notwithstanding his silence, he played a significant role in reconstructing diplomatic relations with Spain after the 1898 war—not only as the key promoter of Hispanic culture in the States but also as the negotiator of a trade agreement between the two countries, commissioned to that effect in 1918 by President Wilson. His mission was acknowledged by King Alfonse XIII with the Order of Isabel the Catholic, one of the highest decorations granted at that time in Spain to a foreign citizen.

According to Codding, the only slightly political reference in Huntington's papers is a comment on World War I and its tragic outcome. To that period belongs one peculiar incident. Huntington and his wife were in Germany when the war broke out. One hotel employee noted that his suitcase was full of maps and called the authorities on the suspicion that they might be spies. They were arrested and confined to their room and were released only after the intervention of the U.S. ambassador to Switzerland.

The heyday of Archer Milton Huntington's career coincided with the golden years preceding the outbreak of World War I. He belonged in the cosmopolitan world that ended with the slaughter on the European battlefields, the world of genteel ideals, aesthetic sophistication, and unlimited economic optimism. He was a member of an American upper class that sprang from the corrupt and thriving business world of the nineteenth century to transform the United States into the most powerful industrial country in the world. At the same time, with their donations and endowments, they left an impressive cultural legacy to their new nation.

As those people filled the country with universities, libraries, and art galleries, they sought in the timelessness of classical art the models after which they wanted to be depicted for posterity. That is what we can see in Huntington's portrait by the Spanish painter José María López Mezquita, today at the Hispanic Society: a tall man in his late fifties, supremely elegant and confident, clad in a black suit, one hand loosely hidden in the pocket of his jacket and the other holding a little book against his waist. The aristocratic allure of this pose is the same that we can find in the portrait of a sixteenth-century Spanish *gentilhombre*, the only difference between them being obviously their garments.

"When I created the Hispanic Society, Americans did not know what Spain was," he recalled a few years before his death. "I had to work for fifty years to awaken my countrymen. Now it seems they are beginning to realize that the Spanish people, more than any other in Europe, has known how to preserve the true essence of Western Civilization."

CARLOS GARDEL IN NEW YORK

The Birth of a Hispanic-American Myth

Claudio Iván Remeseira

I.

Carlos Gardel arrived in New York on December 28, 1933, from Cherbourg, France, aboard the *Champlain*. He was in the company of his musical director, Alberto Castellano, and guitarist Horacio Pettorosi. Waiting for him at pier 57 was Uruguay's Hugo Mariani—then conductor of the NBC orchestra—and a member of that musical group, Argentine violinist Terig Tucci. The main sources of material available with which to reconstruct the tango singer's days in the city are Gardel's personal correspondence and a book that Tucci published in 1969 called *Gardel en Nueva York* (Gardel in New York). Tucci recalls that the first exclamation out of Gardel's mouth when he disembarked was "Man, is it ever cold!" And then, with typically ironic *porteño* wit, he added: "Let's get outa here, there's still time!"

But his joshing actually sought to mask a genuine concern. The frigid weather (the next day was the coldest in fourteen years) wasn't the only cold reception Gardel got in New York. The city's main Spanish-language newspaper, *La Prensa* (whose editor was José Camprubí, a brother-in-law to Juan Ramón Jiménez), announced the singer's arrival on the front page. But, despite his already big name, the English-language papers ignored Gardel's arrival completely. That would all change a few months later, but, for the time being, New York was unknown and inhospitable terrain, a major question mark in a career that, up to then, had been an ever rising line of successes. Four years earlier Paris laid itself at his feet. And the River Plate region and Spain were unconditionally his market. By setting up shop in New York, Gardel was taking the biggest risk of his star-studded career, and the outcome was still immersed in uncertainty.

Gardel arrived in New York with a contract from RCA Victor—then owner of the NBC network—to cut some records and sing on the radio. His radio recitals included some historic transmissions direct to Argentina. It was during one of these, on August 17, 1934, that the famed Gardelian tango "Mi Buenos Aires querido" was heard in Argentina for the very first time.

But Gardel's real goal was to conquer the silver screen. Talkies were less than a decade old, and the success he attained with the filming of *Luces de Buenos Aires* (The lights of Buenos Aires), put out by Joinville Studios of Paris in 1931, convinced him that this was the way to go if he was ever to have real international projection..

He immediately got into touch with Paramount, which owned Joinville. As a result, between May 1934 and February 1935, he filmed four pictures (*Cuesta Abajo, El Tango en Broadway, El día que me quieras,* and *Tango Bar*) and also took part in the company's promotional film production entitled *The Big Broadcast* (1936). The films were shot at the Paramount Astoria Studios, in the area of Queens that faces Harlem on the opposite bank of the East River. (Today the installations are a museum, the Kaufman Astoria Studios).

These movies required songs for their soundtracks, and it was thus in New York that Gardel reactivated his career as a composer. The tangos that he wrote in the city (all with lyrics by Alfredo Le Pera, who also wrote the screenplays for the pictures), were destined to become some of his greatest classics: "Mi Buenos Aires querido," "Cuesta abajo," "Golondrinas," "Soledad," "El día que me quieras," "Sus ojos se cerraron," "Volver," "Por una cabeza," and "Arrabal amargo," among others

II.

Gardel's first home away from home in New York couldn't have been more aristocratic: namely, the Waldorf-Astoria. Later, he moved to the Beaux Arts complex at 307 East 44th Street. After a brief vacation in Europe in the summer of 1934, he moved into the Hotel Middletowne, at 148 East 48th Street. All of these places are within a few minutes walking distance from NBC's studios in the main tower of Rockefeller Center. Not a single one of the buildings bears a plaque to recall this international star's stay in the city.

His inner circle of friends was indeed a small one: Le Pera, who arrived from France a few weeks after Gardel, Tucci, who became, literally, Gardel's right-hand man and scribe (since the singer-composer couldn't read music), his guitarists, and a handful of other acquaintances. The youngest member of this tight little clique was twelve-year-old boy musician Astor Piazzolla, whose family had emigrated to New York years earlier. In his outstanding biography of Gardel, historian Simon Collier says, "Astor was one of his bilingual guides and often accompanied him when he went shopping for clothes and shoes." The singer became very attached to the boy and even arranged for the young Astor to play the small part of a newsboy in *El día que me quieras*. The star even invited the boy to go along as his assistant on a Caribbean tour, but Astor's father objected, saying that his son was still too young. (This probably saved Piazzolla from dying in the same air accident that killed Gardel).

Gardel's daily routine was simple: long days of intensive work, broken by sessions of physical exercise, long lunches, and get-togethers with friends at night. His concern about keeping in shape is explained by his unquestionable weakness for good food. His favorite restaurant was Santa Lucía, on West 54th and Seventh Avenue. Regarding his love life, if indeed he had one, nothing is known. He is rumored to have had a romance with Mona Maris, his costar in *Cuesta Abajo*, and it is known that it was while in New York that he decided to end a long-standing relationship with Isabel Del Valle. Tucci writes that, in this sense, Gardel was "a very discreet gentleman" and never bragged about his affairs.

And, he listened to a lot of music: Italian operas at the Metropolitan Opera House, concerts at Carnegie Hall, and musical comedies on Broadway. On at least one occasion he visited the Cotton Club in Harlem. He was also a regular at El Chico, a deluxe cabaret at Sheridan Square, and a nightclub called Don Julio, both of which were top spots for Latino nightlife.

At one point Gardel decided that he wanted to write an American-style tune. His two inspirations for this were probably "Smoke Gets in Your Eyes," one of the Jerome Kern hits from the musical comedy *Roberta*, and "Flying Down to Rio," title song from the film that launched Fred Astaire to stardom. What Gardel finally came up with was a foxtrot called "Rubias de New York" (New York blondes).

But experimenting with different musical styles wasn't something new for Gardel. In fact, the first time he did it was with tango itself. In 1917, when his duo with José Razzano was one of the most popular acts in Argentine folk music, Gardel sang as a soloist and recorded "Mi Noche Triste," with lyrics penned by Pascual Contursi for a Samuel Castriota melody called "Lita," considered to have been the very first tango with lyrics. But even after he became the number one idol in this new trend of vocal tango, Gardel maintained his repertory of folk music and also explored other styles and even other languages such as French and Italian. By the 1930s, Gardel understood that, in order to reach a wider public, the tango itself had to attain a broader spectrum. In the songs he wrote in New York, for example, the lyrics became much less local in nature (terms in *lunfardo*—the underground argot of tango and the *porteño* streets— practically disappeared), while the melodies took on a more international flavor. Even the staccato typical of traditional tango gave way to a more fluid melodic line, as in "El día que me quieras," one of Gardel's greatest hits.

III.

Cuesta Abajo premiered at the height of Gardel's stay in New York, showing for the first time at the Campoamor Theater on August 10, 1934, a date that can be considered to mark the beginning of Gardelmania, the popular craze that is associated with his name throughout Latin America even seventy years after his death.

That night, the crowd totally surpassed the capacity of the theater located at 116 Street and Fifth Avenue, in the heart of Spanish Harlem (a building now occupied by the Church of the Lord Jesus Christ of the Apostolic Faith). Gardel had to have a police escort to leave the building after the show, so that he wouldn't be crushed by the excited throngs that clamored outside the door to see him. Gardel was genuinely surprised by people's extraordinary reaction. But this was to become the patent treatment he would receive at every stop on the Caribbean tour on which he was to embark a few months later. The legend had been born.

Another multitude turned out to wave goodbye at Pier 15 on the East River when Gardel boarded the *Coamo* headed for Puerto Rico. That was the first stop on a tour that would take him to Venezuela, Curaçao, Aruba, Colombia, Panama, Cuba, and Mexico, which was destined to end tragically in the city of Medellín on June 24, 1935.

Gardel's body would return once more to New York. His friend and executor Armando Defino brought it back from Colombia, and the coffin containing the singer's remains lay in state at the Hernández Funeral Parlor from January 7 to 14, 1936. The funeral home was located at 114 Street and Fifth Avenue, just two blocks from the theater where Gardel got a fleeting glimpse of his lasting stardom. Today the site is occupied by an enormous complex of concrete living units. From there the coffin was transported to Pier 48, where it was loaded and shipped aboard the freighter *Pan America* to Buenos Aires.

And the rest is all part of the legend.

TRANSLATED BY DAN NEWLAND

FURTHER READING

GENERAL REFERENCE

Augenbraum, Harold, ed. *Latinos in English: A Selected Bibliography of Latino Fiction Writers of the United States*. New York: Mercantile Library of New York, 1992.

Augenbraum, Harold, and Margarite Fernández Olmos, eds. *The Latino Reader*. New York: Houghton Mifflin, 1993.

——*U.S. Latino Literature: A Critical Guide for Students and Teachers*. Westport, CT: Greenwood, 2000.

Augenbraum, Harold, and Ilan Stavans, eds. *Growing Up Latino: Memoirs and Stories*. New York: Houghton Mifflin, 1993.

Burrows, Edwin G., and Mike Wallace. *Gotham: A History of New York City to 1898*. New York: Oxford University Press, 1999

Cancel, Luis et al. *The Latin Amerian Spirit: Art and Artists in the United States, 1920–1970*. New York: Bronx Museum of the Arts, with Abrams, 1988.

Darder, Antonia, and Rodolfo D. Torres, eds. *The Latino Studies Reader: Culture, Economy, and Society*. Oxford: Blackwell, 1998.

Figueredo, D. H. *Latino Chronology: Chronologies of the American Mosaic*. Westport, CT: Greenwood, 2007.

Figueroa, Frank M. *Encyclopedia of Latin American Music in New York*. St. Petersburg, FL: Pillar, 1994.

García, María Cristina. "Cuban Women in the United States." In, ed. Félix Padilla, *Handbook of Hispanic Cultures in the United States; Sociology*, pp. 203–17. Houston: Arte Público, 1994.

González, Carolina, and Seth Kugel. *Nueva York: The Complete Guide to Latino Life in the Five Boroughs*. New York: St. Martin's, 2006.

González, Juan. *Harvest of Empire: A History of Latinos in America*. New York: Viking, 2000.

Gutiérrez, David, ed. *The Columbia History of Latinos in the United States Since 1960*. New York: Columbia University Press, 2004.

Halperín Donghi, Tulio. *The Contemporary History of Latin America*. Trans. John Charles Chasteen. Durham. Duke University Press, 1993.

Hanson-Sanchez, Christopher. *New York City Latino Neighborhoods Databook*. New York: Institute for Puerto Rican Policy, 1996.

Jackson, Kenneth T., ed. *The Encyclopedia of New York City*. New Haven: Yale University Press, 1995.

Kanellos, Nicolás. *Hispanic Literature of the United States: A Comprehensive Reference*. Westport, CT: Greenwood, 2003.

——*Hispanic Periodicals in the United States, Origins to 1960: A Brief History and Comprehensive Bibliography*. Houston: Arte Público, 2000.

Kanellos, Nicolás, ed. *Biographical Dictionary of Hispanic Literature in the United States: The Literature of Puerto Ricans, Cuban Americans, and Other Hispanic Writers*. Westport, CT: Greenwood, 1989.

—— *En otra voz: Antología de la literatura hispana de los Estados Unidos*. Houston: Arte Público, 2002.

—— *The Greenwood Encyclopedia of Latino Literature*. 3 vols. Westport, CT: Greenwood, 2008.

Kanellos, Nicolás, and Claudio Esteva-Fabregat, eds. *Handbook of Hispanic Cultures in the United States*. 4 vols. Houston: Arte Público; Madrid: Instituto de Cooperación Iberoamericana, 1993–1994.

Kanellos, Nicolás et al., eds. *Herencia: The Anthology of Hispanic Literature of the United States*. New York: Oxford University Press, 2002.

Lankevich, George J. *American Metropolis: A History of New York City*. New York: New York University Press, 1998.

Montero-Sieburth, Martha, and Edwin Meléndez, eds. *Latinos in a Changing Society*.Westport, CT: Praeger, 2007.

Oboler, Suzanne, and Deena J. González, eds. *The Oxford Encyclopedia of Latinos and Latinas in the United States*. 4 vol. New York: Oxford University Press, 2005.

Riggs, Thomas, ed. *St. James Guide to Hispanic Artists: Profiles of Latino and Latin American Artists*. Detroit: St. James, 2002.

Sánchez Korrol, Virginia, and Vicky L. Ruiz. *Latinas in the United States: A Historical Encyclopedia*. 3 vols. Bloomington: Indiana University Press, 2006.

——*Latinas in History: An Interactive Project*. Department of Puerto Rican and Latino Studies, Brooklyn College, City University of New York, March 1, 2009, http://depthome.brooklyn.cuny.edu/latinashistory/lessonplanslatino.html.

Shorris, Earl. *Latinos: A Biography of the People*. New York: Norton, 1992.

Silveira Cardozo, Manoel da. *The Portuguese in America, 590 B.C.–1974: A Chronology and Fact Book*. Dobbs Ferry, NY: Oceana, 1976.

Suárez-Orozco, Marcelo, and Mariela M. Páez, eds. *Latinos: Remaking America*. Berkeley: University of California Press, 2002.

Stavans, Ilan, and Harold Augenbraum, eds. *Encyclopedia Latina: History, Culture, and Society in the United States*. Danbury, CT: Grolier Academic Reference, 2005.

Zimmerman, Marc. *U.S. Latino Literature: An Essay and Annotated Bibliography.* Chicago: MARCH/Abrazo, 1992.

INTRODUCTION: HISPANIC NEW YORK AND THE EMERGENCE OF A NEW HEMISPHERIC IDENTITY

Acosta-Belén, Edna. "The Building of a Community: Puerto Rican Writers and Activists in New York City." In Ramón A. Gutiérrez and Genaro M. Padilla, eds., *Recovering the U.S. Hispanic Literary Heritage*, pp. 179–95. Houston: Arte Público, 1993.

Acosta-Belén, Edna, and Carlos E. Santiago. "Merging Borders: The Remapping of America." In Antonia Darder and Rodolfo D. Torres, eds., *The Latino Studies Reader: Culture, Economy, and Society*, pp. 29–42. Oxford: Blackwell, 1998.

Adams, Rachel. "The Worlding of American Studies." Review of *Literary Culture and U.S. Imperialism: From the Revolution to World War II* by John Carlos Rowe, *Post-nationalist American Studies* by John Carlos Rowe, ed., and *Postcolonial Theory and the United States: Race, Ethnicity, and Literature* by Amritjit Singh and Peter Schmidt, eds. *American Quarterly* 53, no. 4 (2001): 720–32.

Alba, Richard, and Victor Nee. *Remaking the American Mainstream: Assimilation and Contemporary Immigration.* Cambridge: Harvard University Press, 2005.

Anderson, Benedict. *Imagined Communities: Reflections on the Origin and Spread of Nationalism.* London, New York: Verso, 1983.

Anzaldúa, Gloria. *Borderlands/La Frontera: The New Mestiza.* San Francisco: Aunt Lute, 1987.

Arias, Claudia M. Milian. "Playing with the Dark: Africana and Latino Literary Imaginations." In Lewis R. Gordon and Jane Anna Gordon, eds., *A Companion to African-American Studies.* Malden, MA: Blackwell, 2005.

Bakhtin, Mikhail M. *Problems of Dostoevsky's Poetics.* University of Minnesota Press, 1984.

Belnap, Jeffrey, and Raúl Fernández, eds. *Jose Marti's "Our America": From National to Hemispheric Cultural Studies.* Durham: Duke University Press, 1998.

Benítez-Rojo, Antonio. *The Repeating Island: The Caribbean and the Postmodern Perspective.* Durham: Duke University Press, 1996.

Bhabha, Homi K. *The Location of Culture.* New York: Routledge, 2004.

Bolton, Herbert Eugene. *Bolton and the Spanish Borderlands.* Ed., with an introduction, John Francis Bannon, S.J. Norman, OK: University of Oklahoma Press, 1964.

——*History of the Americas: A Syllabus with Maps.* Boston, New York: Ginn, c. 1935.

Brickhouse, Anna. *Transamerican Literary Relations and the Nineteenth-Century Public Sphere.* Cambridge: Cambridge University Press, 2004.

Calderón, José. "'Hispanic' and 'Latino': The Viability of Categories for Panethnic Unity." *Latin American Perspectives* 19, no. 4 (Fall 1992): 137–44.

Cervantes-Rodriguez, Margarita, Ramón Grosfoguel, and Eric H. Mielants. *Caribbean Migration to Western Europe and the United States: Essays on Incorporation, Identity, and Citizenship*. Philadelphia: Temple University Press, 2009.

Chambers, Iain. *Migrancy, Culture, Identity*. New York: Routledge, 1994.

Chang-Rodríguez, Eugenio. "Nueva York, ciudad cosmopolita." In *Entre dos fuegos. Reminiscencias de las Américas y Asia,* pp. 224–53. Lima: Fondo Editorial del Congreso del Perú, 2005.

Charvat, William. *Literary Publishing in America, 1790–1850*. Philadelphia: University of Pennsylvania Press, 1959.

Choldin, Harvey. "Statistics and Politics: The 'Hispanic' Issue in the 1980 Census." *Demography* 23, no. 3 (August 1986): 403–18.

Dávila, Arlene. *Latinos, Inc.: The Marketing and Making of a People*. Berkeley: University of California Press, 2001.

Davis, Mike. *Magical Urbanism: Latinos Reinvent the U.S. Big City*. New York: Verso, 2000.

de la Campa, Román. *Latin Americanism*. Minneapolis: University of Minnesota Press, 1999.

——"Latinas/os and Latin America: Topics, Destinies, Disciplines." In Juan Flores and Renato Rosaldo, eds., *A Companion to Latina/o Studies*, pp. 461–68. Malden, MA: Blackwell, 2007.

——"Latin, Latino, American: Split States and Global Imaginaries." *Comparative Literature* 53, no. 4 (Autumn, 2001): 373–88; rpt. in David Leiwei Li, ed., *Globalization and the Humanities*, pp. 101–17. Hong Kong: Hong Kong University Press; London: Eurospan, 2004.

——"Latin Lessons: Do Latinos Share a World . . . or a Word?" *Transition* 63 (1994): 68–76.

DeGuzmán, María. *Spain's Long Shadow: The Black Legend, Off-Whiteness, and Anglo-American Empire*. Minneapolis: University of Minnesota Press, 2005.

DeSipio, Louis. "More Than the Sum of Its Parts: The Building Blocks of a Pan-Ethnic Latino Identity." In Wilbur C. Rich, ed., *The Politics of Minority Coalitions: Race, Ethnicity, and Shared Uncertainties*. Westport, CT: Praeger, 1996.

Duany, Jorge. "Puerto Rican, Hispanic or Latino? Recent Debates on National and Pan-ethnic Identities." *Centro Journal* 15:256–67.

Duncan, T. Bentley. *Atlantic Islands: Madeira, the Azores and the Cape Verdes in Seventeenth-Century Commerce and Navigation*. Chicago: University of Chicago Press, 1972.

Fernández-Armesto, Felipe. *The Americas: A Hemispheric History*. New York: Modern Library, 2005.

Flores, Juan. *From Bomba to Hip Hop: Puerto Rican Culture and Latino Identity*. New York: Columbia University Press, 2000.

——"Nueva York, Diaspora City: Latinos Between and Beyond." In Doris Sommer, ed., *Bilingual Games: Some Literary Investigations*, pp. 70–86. New York: Palgrave Macmillan, 2003.

——*The Diaspora Strikes Back: Caribbean Latino Tales of Learning and Turning*. New York: Routledge, 2007.

Flores, Juan, and George Yúdice. "Living Borders/ Buscando América: Languages of Latino Self-Formation." *Social Text* 24 (Fall 1990): 57–84.

Fox, Claire. "The Transnational Turn and the Hemispheric Return." *American Literary Review* 18, no. 3 (2006): 638–47.

Fusco, Coco. *English Is Broken Here: Notes on Cultural Fusion in the Americas.* New York: New Press, 1995.

García Canclini, Néstor. *Hybrid Cultures: Strategies for Entering and Leaving Modernity.* Minneapolis: University of Minnesota Press, 2005.

Gerstle, Gary. *American Crucible: Race and Nation in the Twentieth Century.* Princeton: Princeton University Press, 2001.

Gilroy, Paul. *The Black Atlantic: Modernity and Double Consciousness.* Cambridge: Harvard University Press, 1993.

Glissant, Edouard. *Caribbean Discourse.* University Press of Virginia, 1999.

Golash-Boza, Tanya. "Dropping the Hyphen? Becoming Latino(a)-American Through Racialized Assimilation." *Social Forces* 85, no. 1 (2006): 29–60.

Gracia, Jorge J. E. *Hispanic/Latino Identity: A Philosophical Perspective.* Malden, MA: Blackwell, 2000.

——*Latinos in America: Philosophy and Social Identity.* Malden, MA: Blackwell, 2008.

Gracia, Jorge J. E., and Pablo De Greiff, eds. *Hispanics/Latinos in the United States: Ethnicity, Race, and Rights.* New York: Routledge, 2000.

Gruesz, Kirsten Silva. *Ambassadors of Culture: The Transamerican Origins of Latino Writing.* Princeton: Princeton University Press, 2002.

——"The Gulf of Mexico System and the 'Latinness' of New Orleans." *American Literary History* 18, no. 3 (2006): 468–95.

——"The Mercurial Space of 'Central' America: New Orleans, Honduras, and the Writing of the Banana Republic." In Caroline F. Levander and Robert S. Levine, eds., *Hemispheric American Studies*, pp. 140–65. New Brunswick, NJ: Rutgers University Press, 2008.

Hayes-Bautista, David E., and Jorge Chapa, "Latino Terminology: Conceptual Basis for Standarized Terminology." *American Journal of Public Health* 77, no. 1 (1987): 61–68.

Henríquez Ureña, Pedro. *A Concise History of Latin American Culture.* Trans. Gilbert Chase. New York: Praeger, 1966. Translation of *Historia de la Cultura en la América Hispánica*, México, D.F.: Fondo de Cultura económica, 1947.

Hornsby, Alton, Jr., ed. *A Companion to African American History.* Malden, MA: Blackwell, 2004.

Kapchan, Deborah A., and Pauline Turner Strong. "Theorizing the Hybrid." *Journal of American Folklore* 112, no. 445 (1999): 239–53.

Klein, Herbert S. *African Slavery in Latin America and the Caribbean.* Oxford: Oxford University Press, 1986.

Knox, Paul L. and Peter L. Taylor, eds. *World Cities in a World-System.* Cambridge: Cambridge University Press, 1995.

Kotkin, Joel. *The City: A Global History*. New York: Modern Library, 2005.

Laó-Montes, Agustín. "Decolonial Moves: Translocating African-Diaspora Spaces." *Cultural Studies* 21, nos. 2–3 (March-May 2007): 309–38.

——"Mambo Montage: The Latinization of New York City." In Agustín Laó-Montes and Arlene Dávila, eds., *Mambo Montage: The Latinization of New York*, pp. 1–53. New York: Columbia University Press, 2001.

Lazo, Rodrigo "La Famosa Filadelfia: The Hemispheric American City and Constitutional Debates." In Caroline F. Levander and Robert S. Levine, eds., *Hemispheric American Studies*, pp. 57–74. New Brunswick, NJ: Rutgers University Press, 2008.

——*Writing to Cuba: Filibustering and Cuban Exiles in the United States*. Chapel Hill: University of North Carolina Press, 2005.

Levander, Caroline F., and Robert S. Levine, eds. *Hemispheric American Studies*. New Brunswick, NJ: Rutgers University Press, 2008.

Levander, Caroline F., and Robert S. Levine. "Introduction: Hemispheric American Studies." *American Literary History* 18, no. 3 (2006): 397–405.

Levitt, Peggy. *The Transnational Villagers*. Berkeley: University of California Press, 2001.

Lewis, Oscar. *La Vida: A Puerto Rican Family in the Culture of Poverty. San Juan and New York*. New York: Vintage, 1966.

Lipsitz, George. "Their America and Ours: Intercultural Communication in the Context of *Our America*." In Jeffrey Belnap and Raúl Fernández, eds., *Jose Marti's "Our America": From National to Hemispheric Cultural Studies*, pp. 293–313. Durham: Duke University Press, 1998.

Lomas, Laura. *Translating Empire: José Martí, Migrant Latino Subjects, and American Modernities*. Durham: Duke University Press, 2008.

López, David, and Yen Espíritu, "Panethnicity in the United States: A Theoretical Framework." *Ethnic and Racial Studies* 13 (1990): 198–224.

Lotman, Juri. *Universe of the Mind: A Semiotic Theory of Culture*. Introduction by Umberto Eco. Indiana University Press, 2001.

Mignolo, Walter D. *The Idea of Latin America*. Malden, MA: Blackwell, 2005.

Milian Arias, Claudia. "Playing with the Dark: Africana and Latino Literary Imaginations." In Lewis R. Gordon and Jane Anna Gordon, eds., *A Companion to African-American Studies*, pp. 543–67. Malden, MA: Blackwell, 2006.

Miller, Marilyn Grace. *Rise and Fall of the Cosmic Race: The Cult of Mestizaje in Latin America*. Austin: University of Texas Press, 2004.

Miyares, Ines M. "Changing Latinization of New York City." In Daniel D. Arreola, ed., *Hispanic Spaces, Latino Places: Community and Cultural Diversity in Contemporary America*, pp. 145–66. Austin: University of Texas Press, 1994.

Morales, Ed. *Living in Spanglish: The Search for Latino Identity in America*. New York: St. Martin's, 2002.

Murguia, Edward. "On Latino/Hispanic Ethnic Identity." *Latino Studies Journal* 2, no.3 (September 1991): 8–18.

Murphy, Gretchen. *Hemispheric Imaginings: The Monroe Doctrine and Narratives of U.S. Empire.* Durham: Duke University Press, 2005.

Negrón-Muntaner, Frances. *Boricua Pop: Puerto Ricans and the Latinization of American Culture.* New York: New York University Press, 2004.

—— "Bridging Islands: Gloria Anzaldúa and the Caribbean." *PMLA* 121, no. 1 (January 2006): 272–78.

New York City Department of City Planning. http://home2.nyc.gov/html/dcp/html/census/popcur.shtml.

—— *The Newest New Yorkers, 2000: Immigrant New York in the New Millenium.* New York: Department of City Planning, 2004.

Nostrand, Richard Lee. "Mexican Americans Circa 1850." *Annals of the Association of American Geographers* 65, no. 3 (September 1975): 378–90.

Oboler, Suzanne. *Ethnic Labels, Latino Lives: Identity and the Politics of Representation in the United States.* Minneapolis: University of Minnesota Press, 1995.

O'Gorman, Edmundo. *The Invention of America: An Inquiry into the Historical Nature of the New World and the Meaning of Its History.* Bloomington: Indiana University Press, 1961.

Padilla, Félix. *Latino Ethnic Consciousness: The Case of Mexican Americans and Puerto Ricans in Chicago.* Notre Dame, IN: University of Notre Dame Press, 1985.

Paz Soldán, Edmundo. "Latino, Latin American, Spanish American, North American, or All at the Same Time?" In Nelsy Echávez-Solano and K. C. Dworkin y Méndez, eds., *Spanish and Empire*, pp. 139–52. Nashville: Vanderbilt University Press, 2007.

Pew Hispanic Center. "U.S. Population Projections: 2005–2050." http://pewhispanic.org/reports/report.php?ReportID=85.

Porter, Carolyn. "What We Know that We Don't Know: Remapping American Literary Studies." *American Literary History* 6, no. 3 (1994): 467–526.

Quijano, Aníbal and Immanuel Wallerstein. "Americanity as a Concept, or the Americas in the Modern World-System." *International Social Science Journal* 44, no.4 (1992): 549–57.

Remeseira, Claudio Iván. "Is New York the New Center of Latin American Literary Culture?" *Salmagundi* 161/162 (2009): 182–91.

—— "Nueva narrativa de la identidad americana: *El esposo divino*, de Francisco Goldman." *Primera Revista Latinoamericana de Libros* 1, no. 5 (2008): 20.

—— "Nueva York, América Latina" *La Nación*, September 26, 2004. http://www.lanacion.com.ar/nota.asp?nota_id=639512&high=Remeseira.

Rodriguez, Richard. *Brown: The Last Discovery of America.* New York: Penguin, 2002.

Rosario, Nelly. "On Becoming." In Juan Flores and Renato Rosaldo, eds., *A Companion to Latina/o Studies*, pp. 151–56. Malden, MA: Blackwell, 2007.

Ruiz, Vicki L. "Nuestra América: Latino History as United States History." *Journal of American History* 93, no.3 (2006): 655–72.

Sadowski-Smith, Claudia, ed. *Globalization on the Line: Culture, Capital, and Citizenship at U.S. Borders.* New York: Palgrave, 2002.

Sadowski-Smith, Claudia, and Claire Fox. "Theorizing the Hemisphere: Inter-Americas Work at the Intersection of American, Canadian, and Latin American Studies." *Comparative American Studies* 2, no. 1 (2004): 5–27.

Saldívar, José David. *Border Matters: Remapping American Cultural Studies.* Berkeley: University of California Press, 1997.

—— *The Dialectis of Our America: Genealogy, Cultural Critique and Literary History.* Berkeley: University of California Press, 1991.

Sánchez, Luis Rafael. "Nueva York es el gran sueño de Bolívar." Interview with Norberto Bogard. *El Diario/La Prensa,* November 11, 1994, pp. 6–7.

Sánchez Korrol, Virginia. "The Star in My Compass." In Juan Flores and Renato Rosaldo, eds., *A Companion to Latina/o Studies,* pp. 194–201. Malden, MA: Blackwell, 2007.

Santí, Enrique Mario. "'Our America,' the Gilded Age, and the Crisis of Latinoamericanism." In Jeffrey Belnap and Raúl Fernández, eds., *Jose Marti's "Our America": From National to Hemispheric Cultural Studies,* pp. 180–90. Durham: Duke University Press, 1998.

Santiago, Silviano. *The Space In-Between: Essays on Latin American Culture.* Durham: Duke University Press, 2001.

Sassen, Saskia. *The Global City: New York, London, Tokyo.* Princeton: Princeton University Press, 2001

Sassen, Saskia, ed., *Global Networks, Linked Cities.* New York: Routledge, 2002.

Schiller, Nina Glick, and Ayse Çalar. "Towards a Comparative Theory of Locality in Migration Studies: Migrant Incorporation and City Scale." *Journal of Ethnic and Migration Studies* 35, no. 2 (2009): 177–202.

Stavans, Ilan. *The Hispanic Condition: Reflections on Culture and Identity in America.* New York: Harper Collins, 1995.

"The 2008 Global Cities Index." *Foreign Policy,* November/December 2008. http://www.foreignpolicy.com/story/cms.php?story_id=4509&page=0; accessed March 1, 2009.

Thornton, John. *Africa and Africans in the Making of the Atlantic World, 1400–1800.* New York: Cambridge University Press, 1998.

Torres-Saillant, Silvio. *An Intellectual History of the Caribbean.* New York: Palgrave Macmillan, 2005.

—— "New Ways of Imagining the Caribbean" in *Review: Literature and Arts of the Americas 74* 40, no.1 (2007): 6.

Totti, Xavier F. "The Making of a Latino Ethnic Identity." *Dissent, In Search of New York,* special issue (Fall 1987): 537–43.

Treviño, Fernando M. "Standarized Terminology for Standarized Populations." *American Journal of Public Health,* vol. 77.

U.S. Bureau of the Census. *Coming from the Americas: A Profile of the Nation's Foreign-Born Population from Latin America.* Washington, DC: U.S. Department of Commerce, January 2002.

—— *Guidance on the Presentation and Comparison of Race and Hispanic Origin.* Washington, DC: Department of Commerce, June 2003.

——"Methodology for the United States Resident Population Estimates by Age, Sex, Race, and Hispanic Origin." April 1, 2000 to July 1, 2008. http://www.census.gov/popest/topics/methodology/2008-nat-meth.html.

—— *Overview of Race and Hispanic Origin*. Washington, DC: Department of Commerce, 2000.

—— *The Hispanic Population*. Washington, DC: U.S. Department of Commerce, 2000.

—— *2005–2007 American Community Survey*. Washington, DC: U.S. Department of Commerce.

Wallerstein, Immanuel *World-Systems Analysis: An Introduction*. Durham: Duke University Press, 2004.

Whitaker, Arthur Preston. *The United States and the Independence of Latin America, 1800– 1830*. Baltimore: Johns Hopkins Press, 1941.

—— *The Western Hemisphere Idea: Its Rise and Decline*. Ithaca: Cornell University Press, 1954.

Whitman, Walt. *Complete Poetry and Collected Prose*. Ed. Justin Kaplan. 3 vols. New York: Library of America, 1982.

Wilson, Chris. *The Myth of Santa Fé: Creating a Modern Regional Tradition*. Albuquerque: University of New Mexico Press, 1997.

Young, Robert J. C. *Colonial Desire: Hybridity in Theory, Culture and Race*. New York: Routledge, 2003.

PART 1: PEOPLE AND COMMUNITIES

Acosta-Belén, Edna, and Carlos E. Santiago. *Puerto Ricans in the United States: A Contemporary Portrait*. Boulder: Lynne Rienner, 2006.

Acosta-Belén, Edna, Marquarita Benitez, Jose E. Cruz, Yvonne Gonzalez-Rodriguez, Clara E. Rodriguez, Carlos E. Santiago, Azara Santiago-Rivera, and Barbara K. Sjostrom. *Adiós Borinquen querida: The Puerto Rican Diaspora, Its History, and Contributions*. Albany: CELAC, 2000.

Aponte, Sarah. *Dominican Migration to the United States, 1970–1997: An Annotated Bibliography*. New York: CUNY Dominican Studies Institute, 1999.

Ashley, Wayne. "The Stations of the Cross: Christ, Politics, and Processions on New York City's Lower East Side." In *Gods of the City: Religion and the American Urban Landscape*, ed. Robert A. Orsi, 341–66. Bloomington: Indiana University Press, 1999.

Balick, Michael J. et al. "Medicinal Plants Used by Latino Healers for Women's Health Conditions in New York City." *Economic Botany* 54, no. 3 (2000): 344–57.

Beardsley, Theodore S., Jr. "Instituciones norteamericanas dedicadas al hispanismo." *Arbor* 451– 54 (1983): 195–206.

Bernadete, Maír José. *Hispanic Culture and Character of the Sephardic Jew*. New York: Foundation for the Advancement of Sephardic Studies and Culture and Sephardic House, 1982.

Beserra, Bernadete. *Brazilian Immigrants in the United States: Cultural Imperialism and Social Class*. El Paso: LFB Scholarly Publishing, 2006

Capdevila, Carles. *Nova York a la catalana*. Barcelona: La Campana, 1996.

Carroll, Peter N., and James D. Fernández, eds. *Facing Fascism: New York and the Spanish Civil War*. New York: New York University Press, 2007.

Castaño, Javier. *New York Colombiano*. Queens, NY: Latin American Cultural Center of Queens, 2004.

Chin, Margaret M. "When Coethnic Assets Become Liabilities: Mexican, Ecuadorian, and Chinese Garment Workers in New York City." In Héctor R. Cordero-Guzmán, Robert C. Smith, and Ramón Grosfoguel, eds., *Migration, Transnationalization, and Race in a Changing New York*, pp. 280–99. Philadelphia: Temple University Press, 2001.

Cordero-Guzmán, Héctor R., Robert C. Smith and Ramón Grosfoguel, eds. *Migration, Transnationalization, and Race in a Changing New York*. Philadelphia: Temple University Press, 2001.

Cruz, Domingo A. de la. *Comunidad dominicana en Nueva York. Una historia cultural*. Nueva York: Cruvision, 2004.

Cruz, Nelly V., and Ana Suárez Díaz. "Notas preliminaries sobre los vínculos entre las comunidades puertorriqueñas y cubanas en Nueva York en la década de 1930, basados en documentos de las colecciones de Jesús Colónn y Juan Marinello." *Centro Journal* 5:117–18.

Dávila, Arlene. *Barrio Dreams: Puerto Ricans, Latinos, and the Neoliberal City*. Berkeley: University of California Press, 2004.

——*Latino Spin: Public Image and the Whitewashing of Race*. New York: New York University Press, 2008.

Delgado, Linda C. "Jesús Colón and the Making of a New York City Community, 1917 to 1974." In Carmen Teresa Whalen and Víctor Vázquez Hernández, eds., *The Puerto Rican Diaspora: Historical Perspectives*, pp. 68–77. Philadelphia: Temple University Press, 2005.

Díaz-Stevens, Ana María. "Aspects of Puerto Rican Religious Experience: A Sociohistorical Overview." In Gabriel Haslip-Viera and Sherrie L. Baver, eds., *Latinos in New York: Communities in Transition*, pp. 147–86. Notre Dame, IN: University of Notre Dame Press, 1996.

Douglas, Ann. *Terrible Honesty: Mongrel Manhattan in the 1920s*. New York: Farrar, Straus, and Giroux, 1995.

Duany, Jorge. *Quisqueya on the Hudson: The Transnational Identity of Dominicans in Washington Heights*. New York: City University of New York, Dominican Studies Institute, 1994.

——*The Puerto Rican Nation on the Move: Identities on the Island and in the United States*. Chapel Hill: University of North Carolina Press, 2002.

——"The Rough Edges of Puerto Rican Identities: Race, Gender, and Transnationalism" *Latin American Research Review* 40, no. 3 (2005): 177–90.

Dworkin y Méndez, Kenya C. "Caught Between the Cross and the Crescent and Star: Orientalist Co-Ethnic Recognition Failure and New York's Sephardic Jews." In Ignacio López-Calvo, ed.,

Alternative Orientalisms in Latin America and Beyond, pp. 325–35. Newcastle: Cambridge Scholars, 2007.

England, Sarah. *Afro Central Americans in New York City: Garifuna Tales of Transnational Movements in Racialized Space*. Gainesville: University Press of Florida, 2006.

Estrade, Paul. "Los clubes femeninos en el Partido Revolucionario Cubano (1892–1898)." *Anuario del Centro de Estudios Martianos* 10 (1987): 175–201.

Falcón, Angelo. "A History of Puerto Rican Politics in New York City: 1860s to 1945." In James Jennings and Monte Rivera, eds., *Puerto Rican Politics in Urban America*, pp. 15–42. Westport, CT: Greenwood, 1984.

Falconi, José Luis, and José Antonio Mazzotti, eds. *The Other Latinos: Central and South Americans in the United States*. Cambridge: Harvard University Press, 2007.

Fischer, Sybille. *Modernities Disavowed: Haiti and the Cultures of Slavery in the Age of Revolution*. Durham: Duke University Press, 2004.

Flores, Juan. "Creolité in the Hood: Diaspora as Source and Challenge." In Franklin W. Knight and Teresita Martínez-Vergne, eds., *Contemporary Caribbean Cultures and Societies in a Global Context*, pp. 117–29. Chapel Hill: University of North Carolina Press, 2005.

—— "Islands and Enclaves." In Marcelo Suárez-Orozco and Mariela M. Páez, eds., *Latinos: Remaking America*, pp. 59–74. Berkeley: University of California Press, 2002.

Foner, Nancy, ed. *New Immigrants in New York*. New York: Columbia University Press, 2001.

Franconi, Rodolfo A. "Being Brazilian in the States: Between Fiction and Reality." *Hispania* 88, no. 4 (2005): 726–32.

Fuentes, Norma. "The Immigrant Experiences of Dominican and Mexican Women in the 1990s: Crossing Boundaries or Temporary Work Spaces?" In Caroline Brettell, ed., *Constructing Borders/Crossing Boundaries: Race, Ethnicity, and Immigration*, pp. 94–119. Lanham, MD: Lexington, 2007.

Gandy, Matthew. "Between Borinquen and the *Barrio*: Environmental Justice and New York City's Puerto Rican Community, 1969–1972." *Antipode* 34, no. 4 (2002): 730–61.

Garcia, Bobbito. "Las Leyendas de Aquí y de Allá: The Nuyorican Playground Legends. *Bounce* 19 (2009): 34–51.

—— *Where'd You Get Those? New York City's Sneaker Culture, 1960–1987*. New York: Testify, 2003.

García Márquez, Gabriel. "Nueva York 1961: El drama de los dos Cubas." *Areito* 6, no. 21 (1979): 31–33.

Glazer, Nathan, and Daniel Patrick Moynihan. *Beyond the Melting Pot: The Negroes, Puerto Ricans, Jews, Italians, and Irish of New York City*. Cambridge: MIT Press, 1963.

Gonzalez, Evelyn. *The Bronx*. New York: Columbia University Press, 2004.

Grasmuck, Sherri, and Patricia R. Pessar. *Between Two Islands: Dominican International Migration*. Berkeley: University of California Press, 1991.

Gregory, Steven. *Santería in New York City: A Study in Cultural Resistance*. New York: Garland, 1999.

Grosfoguel, Ramón, and Chloé S. Georas. "Latino Caribbean Diasporas in New York." In Augustín Laó-Montes and Arlene Dávila, eds., *Mambo Montage: The Latinization of New York*, pp. 99–118. New York: Columbia University Press, 2001.

Guarnizo, Luis Eduardo, Arturo Ignacio Sánchez, and Elizabeth M. Roach. "Mistrust, Fragmented Solidarity, and Transnational Migration: Colombians in New York City and Los Angeles." *Ethnic and Racial Studies* 22, no. 2 (March 1999): 367–96.

Guarnizo, Luis Eduardo. "Los Dominicanyorks: The Making of a Binational Society." In Mary Romero, Pierrette Hondagneu-Sotelo, and Vilma Ortiz, eds., *Challenging Fronteras: Structuring Latina and Latino Lives in the U.S.*, pp. 161–74. New York: Routledge, 1997.

Hacker, Louis M. "The Communal Life of the Sephardic Jews in New York City." *Jewish Social Service Quarterly* 3, no. 2 (December 1926): 32–40.

Hanson-Sánchez, Christopher. *New York City Latino Neighborhoods Databook*. New York: Institute for Puerto Rican Policy, 1998.

Haslip-Viera, Gabriel, and Sherrie L. Baver, eds. *Latinos in New York: Communities in Transition*. Notre Dame, IN: University of Notre Dame Press, 1996.

Haslip-Viera, Gabriel, Angelo Falcón, and Félix Matos Rodríguez, eds. *Boricuas in Gotham: Puerto Ricans in the Making of Modern New York City*. Princeton: Wiener, 2004.

Hernández, Orlando José. "Hostos in New York." *Hostos Connection* (Spring 2008): 6.

Hernández, Ramona. "Living on the Margins of Society: Dominicans in the United States." In Martha Montero-Sieburth and Edwin Meléndez, eds., *Latinos in a Changing Society*, pp. 34–57. Westport, CT: Praeger, 2007.

Hernández, Ramona, and Silvio Torres-Saillant. *The Dominican Americans*. Westport, CT: Greenwood, 1998.

Hernández-Delgado, Julio L. "Pura Teresa Belpré, Storyteller and Pioneer Librarian." *Library Quarterly* 62, no. 4 (1992): 425–40.

Hoffnung-Garskof, Jesse. *A Tale of Two Cities: Santo Domingo and New York After 1950*. Princeton: Princeton University Press, 2007.

——"The Migrations of Arturo Schomburg: On Being Antillano, Negro, and Puerto Rican in New York, 1891–1938." *Journal of American Ethnic History* 21, no. 1 (2001): 3–49.

Itzigsohn, José, and Carlos Dore-Cabral. "The Manifold Character of Panethnicity: Latino Identities and Practices Among Dominicans in New York City." In Agustín Laó-Montes and Arlene Dávila, eds., *Mambo Montage: The Latinization of New York*, pp. 319–35. New York: Columbia University Press, 2001.

James, Winston. "The Peculiarities of Afro-Hispanic Radicalism in the United States: The Political Trajectories of Arturo Schomburg and Jesús Colón." In *Holding Aloft the Banner of Ethiopia: Caribbean Radicalism in Early Twentieth-Century America*, 195–231. London and New York: Verso, 1998.

Jones-Correa, Michael. *Between Two Nations: The Political Predicament of Latinos in New York City*. Ithaca: Cornell University Press, 1998.

Julca, Alex. "Peruvian Networks for Migration in New York City's Labor Market, 1970–1996." In Héctor R. Cordero Guzmán, Robert C. Smith, and Ramón Grosfoguel, eds., *Migration, Transnationalization, and Race in a Changing New York*, pp. 239–57. Philadelphia: Temple University Press, 2001.

Kasinitz, Philip, John H. Mollenkopf, Mary C. Waters, and Jennifer Holdaway. *Inheriting the City: The Children of Immigrants Come of Age*. Cambridge: Harvard University Press, 2008.

Laó-Montes, Agustin, and Arlene Dávila, eds. *Mambo Montage: The Latinization of New York*. New York: Columbia University Press, 2001.

LeBlanc, Adrian Nicole. *Random Family: Love, Drugs, Trouble and Coming of Age in the Bronx*. New York: Scribner, 2003.

Lopez, Nancy. "Unraveling the Race-Gender Gap in Education: Second-Generation Dominican Men's High School Experiences." In Philip Kasinitz, John Mollenkopf, and Mary Waters, eds., *Becoming New Yorkers: Ethnographies of the New Second Generation*, pp. 28–56. New York: Russell Sage Foundation, 2004.

——"Transnational Changing Gender Roles: Second-Generation Dominicans in New York City." In Ernesto Sagas and Sintia E. Molina, eds., *Transnational Perspectives on Dominican Migration*, pp. 175–99. Gainesville: University of Florida Press, 2003.

López Mesa, Enrique. *Algunos aspectos culturales de la comunidad cubana de New York durante el siglo XIX*. Havana: Centro de Estudios Marianos, 2002.

Mahler, Sarah. "Suburban Transnational Migrants: Long Island's Salvadorans." In Héctor R. Cordero-Guzmán, Robert C. Smith, and Ramón Grosfoguel, eds., *Migration, Transnationalization, and Race in a Changing New York*, pp. 109–30. Philadelphia: Temple University Press, 2001.

Margolis, Maxine L. *An Invisible Minority: Brazilians in New York City*. Boston: Allyn and Bacon, 1998.

——"Becoming *Brazucas*: Brazilian Identity in the United States." In José Luis Falconi and José Antonio Mazzotti, eds., *The Other Latinos: Central and South Americans in the United States*, pp. 213–30. Cambridge: Harvard University Press, 2007.

——*Little Brazil: An Ethnography of Brazilian Immigrants in New York City*. Princeton: Princeton University Press, 1994.

—— "We Are *Not* Immigrants! A Contested Category Among Brazilians in New York City and Rio de Janeiro." In Carole A. Mortland, ed., *Diasporic Identity: Selected Papers on Refugees and Immigrants VI*, pp. 30–50. Arlington, VA: American Anthropoligcal Association, 1998.

Marks, Morton. *Brooklyn's Hispanic Communities*. Brooklyn, NY: Brooklyn Historical Society, 1989.

Martes, Ana Cristina Braga. "Nos EUA, o que somos nós? Latinos, Hispanics, Brancos ou 'Others'" In Sylvia Dantas DeBiaggi and Geraldo José de Paiva, eds., *Psicologia, E/Imigração e Cultura*, pp. 97–110. São Paulo: Casa de Psicólogo, 2004.

Martín-Alcoff, Linda. "Latino/as, Asian Americans, and the Black-White Binary." *Journal of Ethics* 7, no. 1 (2003): 5–27.

Martín-Rodríguez, Manuel. "Mapping the Trans/Hispanic Atlantic: Nuyol, Miami, Tenerife, Tangier." In Ana Ma. Manzanas, ed., *Border Transits: Literature and Culture Across the Line*, pp. 205–22. New York: Rodopi, 2007.

Martínez-San Miguel, Yolanda. "'Caribe Two Ways': Nueva York o el otro enclave caribeño." In *Caribe two ways: Cultura de la migración en el Caribe insular hispánico*, pp. 323–96. San Juan: Callejón, 2003.

Marwell, Nicole P. *Bargaining for Brooklyn: Community Organizations in the Entrepreneurial City*. Chicago: University of Chicago Press, 2007.

Marzán, Gilbert, Andrés Torres, and Andrew Luecke. *Puerto Rican Outmigration from New York City: 1995–2000*. New York: Centro de Estudios Puertorriqueños, Hunter College (CUNY). *Policy Report* 2, no. 2 (Fall 2008).

Matos Rodríguez, Félix V., and Pedro Juan Hernández. *Pioneros: Puerto Ricans in New York City, 1896–1948*. Charleston: Arcadia, 2001.

Meihy, José Carlos Sebe Bom. *Brasil fora de sí. Experiências de brasileiros em Nova York*. São Paulo: Parábola, 2004.

Mele, Christopher. "Neighborhood 'Burn-Out': Puerto Ricans at the End of the Queue." In Janet L. Abu-Lughod et al., *From Urban Village to East Village: The Battle for New York's Lower East Side*, pp. 124–40. Cambridge: Blackwell, 1994.

Melendez, Miguel. *We Took the Streets: Fighting for Latino Rights with the Young Lords*. New Brunswick, NJ: Rutgers University Press, 2005.

Mirabal, Nancy Raquel. "No Country But the One We Must Fight For: The Emergence of an Antillean Nation and Community in New York City, 1860–1901." In Augustín Laó-Montes and Arlene Dávila, eds., *Mambo Montage: The Latinization of New York*, pp. 57–72. New York: Columbia University Press, 2001.

Moreno Vega, Marta. *The Altar of My Soul: The Living Traditions of Santería*. New York: Ballantine, 2000.

Navarro, Mireya. "Falling Back: A Special Report, Puerto Rican Presence Wanes in New York." *New York Times*, February 28, 2000.

Negrón-Muntaner, Frances, ed. *None of the Above: Puerto Ricans in the Global Era*. New York: Palgrave Macmillan, 2007.

Negrón-Muntaner, Frances and Ramón Grosfoguel, eds. *Puerto Rican Jam: Essays on Culture and Politics*. Minneápolis: University of Minnesota Press, 1997.

New York City Department of City Planning. *The Newest New Yorkers, 2000: Immigrant New York in the New Millenium*. New York: Department of City Planning, 2004.

Ojeda, Félix. "Early Puerto Rican Communities in New York." In *Extended Roots: From Hawaii to New York: Migraciones puetorriqueñas a los Estados Unidos*, pp. 41–51. New York: Centro de Estudios Puertorriqueños, Hunter College, 1986.

Ortiz, Altagracia. "Historical Vignettes of Puerto Rican Women Workers in New York City, 1895–1990." In Felix Padilla, ed., *Handbook of Hispanic Cultures in the United States: Sociology*, pp. 219–38. Houston: Arte Público, 1994.

Pantoja, Antonia. *Memoir of a Visionary: Antonia Pantoja*. Houston: Arte Público, 2002.

Pantoja, Segundo. *Religion and Education Among Latinos in New York City*. Boston: Brill, 2005.

Pérez, Lisandro. "De Nueva York a Miami." *Encuentro* 15 (1999/2000): 25–32.

Pessar, Patricia R. "Dominicans: Forging an Ethnic Community in New York." In Maxine Seller and Lois Weiss, eds., *Beyond Black and White: New Faces and Voices in U.S. Schools*, pp. 131–49. Albany: State University of New York Press, 1997.

Pessar, Patricia R., and Pamela Graham. "Dominicans: Transnational Identities and Local Politics." In Nancy Foner, ed., *New Immigrants in New York*, pp. 251–73. New York: Columbia University Press, 2001.

Pribilsky, Jason. *La Chulla Vida: Gender, Migration, and the Family in Andean Ecuador and New York City*. Syracuse: Syracuse University Press, 2007.

"Rabbi Isaac Aboab de Fonseca (1605–1693)." Jewish Virtual Library: A Division of the American-Israeli Cooperative Entrerprise. http://www.jewishvirtuallibrary.org/jsource/biography/Fonseca.html; accessed March 1, 2009.

Ricourt, Milagros. *Hispanas de Queens: Latino Panethnicity in a New York City Neighborhood*. Ithaca: Cornell University Press, 2003.

——*Power from the Margins: The Incorporation of Dominicans in New York*. New York: Routledge, 2002.

Rivera-Batiz, Francisco L. "Newyorktitlan: A Socioeconomic Profile of Mexican New Yorkers." *Regional Labor Review* 6, no. 2 (2004): 32–43.

Rivera Sánchez, Liliana. "Expressions of Identity and Belonging: Mexican Immigrants in New York." In Jonathan Fox and Gaspar Rivera-Salgado, eds., *Indigenous Mexican Migrants in the United States*, pp. 417–46. San Diego: Center of U.S.-Mexican Studies and the Center for Comparative Immigration Studies, University of California, 2004.

——"La formación y dinámica del circuito migratorio Mixteca-Nueva York-Mixteca: Los trayectos internos e internacionales." *NORTEAMÉRICA* 2, no. 1 (2007): 171–203.

Rodríguez, Clara E. *Changing Race: Latinos, the Census and the History of Ethnicity in the United States*. New York: New York University Press, 2000.

Rogler, Lloyd H., and Rosemary Santana Cooney. "From Puerto Rico to New York City." In Carlos Antonio Torre, Hugo Rodríguez Vecchini, and William Burgos, eds., *The Commuter Nation: Perspectives on Puerto Rican Migration*, pp. 187–220. Rio Piedras: Editorial de la Universidad de Puerto Rico, 1994.

Sánchez, José Ramon. *Boricua Power: A Political History of Puerto Ricans in the United States*. New York: New York University Press, 2007

Sánchez-González, Lisa. "Luisa Capetillo: An Anarcho-Feminist Pionera in the Mainland/Puerto Rican Narrative/Political Transition." In *Recovering the U.S. Hispanic Literary Heritage, Volume II*, ed. Erlinda Gonzales-Berry and Chuck Tatum, 148–67. Houston: Arte Público, 1996.

Sánchez Korrol, Virginia. "Building the New York Puerto Rican Community, 1945–1965: An Historical Interpretation." In Gabriel Haslip-Viera, Angelo Falcón, and Félix Matos Rodríguez, eds.,

Boricuas in Gotham: Puerto Ricans in the Making of Modern New York City, pp. 1–18. Princeton: Wiener, 2004.

——*From Colonia to Community: The History of Puerto Ricans in New York City, 1917–1948*. Westport, CT: Greenwood, 1983.

——"Latinismo Among Early Puerto Rican Migrants in New York City: A Sociohistoric Interpretation." In Edna Acosta-Belén and Barbara R. Sjostrom, eds., *The Hispanic Experience in the United States: Contemporary Issues and Perspectives*, pp. 150–61. New York: Prager, 1988.

——"Mujeres Rebeldes: Women and Antillean Independence, 1868–1898." In *Latinas in History: An Interactive Project*. Department of Puerto Rican and Latino Studies, Brooklyn College, City University of New York. http://depthome.brooklyn.cuny.edu/latinashistory/mujeresrebeldes.pdf; accessed March 1, 2009.

Schomburg, Arthur A. "Questions by a Porto-Rican." *New York Times*, August 9, 1902, p. 8.

Sciorra, Joseph. "Return to the Future: Puerto Rican Vernacular Architecture in New York City." In Anthony D. King, ed., *Re-Presenting the City: Ethnicity, Capital, and Culture in the Twenty-First-Century Metropolis*, pp. 60–92. New York: New York University Press, 1996.

Singer, Audrey, and Greta Gilbertson. "Naturalization in the Wake of Anti-Immigration Legislation: Dominicans in New York City." International Migration Policy Program, Working Papers no. 10. Washington, DC: Carnegie Endowment for International Peace, 2007.

——"The Blue Passport: Gender and the Social Process of Naturalization Among Dominican Immigrants in New York City." In Pierrette Hondagneu-Sotelo, ed., *Gender and U.S. Immigration: Contemporary Trends*, pp. 359–78. Berkeley, CA: University of California Press, 2003.

Siu, Lok Chun Debra. "In Search of Chino Latinos in Diaspora: Cuban Chinese in New York City." In Andrea O'Reilly Herrera, ed., *Cuba: Idea of a Nation Displaced*, pp. 123–31. Albany: State University of New York Press, 2007.

Smith, Robert C. *Mexican New York: Transnational Lives of New Immigrants*. Berkeley: University of California Press, 2006.

——"Mexicans: Social, Educational, Economic, and Political Problems and Prospects in New York." In Nancy Foner, ed., *New Immigrants in New York*, pp. 275–300. New York: Columbia University Press, 2001.

——"Racialization and Mexicans in New York City." In Víctor Zúñiga and Rubén Hernández-León, eds., *New Destinations: Mexican Immigration in the United States*, pp. 220–43. New York: Russell Sage Foundation, 2005.

Smith, Robert C., Hector R. Cordero-Gozmán, and Ramón Grosfoguel. "Introduction: Migration, Transnationalization, and Ethnic and Racial Dynamics in a Changing New York." In Héctor R. Cordero-Guzmán, Robert C. Smith, and Ramón Grosfoguel, eds., *Migration, Transnationalization, and Race in a Changing New York*, pp. 1–32. Philadelphia: Temple University Press, 2001.

Solís, Jocelyn. "Immigration Status and Identity: Undocumented Mexicans in New York." In Augustín Laó-Montes and Arlene Dávila, eds., *Mambo Montage: The Latinization of New York*, pp. 337–61. New York: Columbia University Press, 2001.

Solis, Jocelyn, and Liliana Rivera Sánchez. "Recovering the Forgotten: The Effect of September 11th on Undocumented Latin American Victims and Families." *Journal of Latin American and Caribbean Studies* 29, no. 57–58 (2004): 93–115.

Suro, Roberto *Strangers Among Us: Latino Lives in a Changing America*. New York: Random House, 2002.

Thompson, Gabriel. *There's No José Here: Following the Hidden Lives of Mexican Immigrants*. New York: Nation, 2007.

Tinajero, Araceli. *El lector de tabaquería: historia de una tradición cubana*, Madrid: Verbum, 2007.

——*El Lector: A History of the Cigar Factory Reader*. Trans. Judith E. Grasberg. Austin: University of Texas Press, 2010.

Torres, Andrés. *Between Melting Pot and Mosaic: African Americans and Puerto Ricans in the New York Political Economy*. Philadelphia: Temple University Press, 1995.

Torres-Saillant, Silvio. "Dominican Americans." In John D. Buenker and Lorman A. Ratner, eds., *Multiculturalism in the United States: A Comparative Guide to Acculturation and Ethnicity*, pp. 99–115. Rev. ed. Westport, CT: Greenwood, 2005.

——"Pitfalls of Latino Chronologies: South and Central Americans." *Latino Studies* 5 (2007): 489–502.

——"Problematic Paradigms. Racial Diversity and Corporate Identity in the Latino Community." In Marcelo Suárez-Orozco and Mariela M. Páez, eds., *Latinos: Remaking America*, pp. 435–55. Berkeley: University of California Press, 2002.

—— "The Unlikely Latina/os: Brazilians in the United States." *Latino Studies* 6 (2008): 466–77.

Totoricaguena, Gloria P., with Emilia Sarriugarte Doyaga and Anna M. Renteria Aguirre. *The Basques of New York: A Cosmopolitan Experience*. Reno: University of Nevada, 2004.

Vieira, Else R. P. "The Formative Years of the Brazilian Communities of New York and San Francisco Through the Print Media: *The Brazilians/The Brasilians* and *Brazil Today*." In Clémence Jouët and Leticia J. Braga, eds., *Becoming Brazuca: Brazilian Immigration to the United States*. Cambridge: Harvard University Press, 2008.

PART 2: CULTURAL HYBRIDIZATIONS

Language and Literature: A Bilingual Tradition

Linguistic Issues

Ben-Ur, Aviva. "'We Speak and Write This Language Against Our Will': Jews, Hispanics, and the Dilemma of Ladino-Speaking Sephardim in Early Twentieth-Century New York." *American Jewish Archives* 50, no. 12 (1998): 131–42.

Betti, Silvia. *El Spanglish, ¿medio eficaz de comunicación?* Bologna: Pitagora, 2008.

Castillo, Debra. "Los 'nuevos' latinos y la globalización de los estudios literarios" In Boris Muñoz and Silvia Spitta, eds., *Más allá de la ciudad letrada: Crónicas y espacios urbanos*, pp. 439–59. Pittsburgh: Instituto Internacional de Literatura Iberoamericana, 2003.

——*Redreaming America: Toward a Bilingual American Culture*. Albany: State University of New York Press, 2005.

Del Valle, José, ed. *La lengua, ¿patria común? Ideas e ideologías del español*. Madrid: Iberoamericana; Frankfurt: Vervuert, 2007.

Del Valle, José, and Luis Gabriel-Stheeman, eds. *The Battle Over Spanish Between 1800 and 2000: Language Ideologies and Hispanic Intellectuals*. New York: Routledge, 2002.

Dicker, Susan J. "Dominican Americans in Washington Heights, New York: Language and Culture in a Transnational Community." *International Journal of Bilingual Education and Bilingualism* 9, no. 6 (2006): 713–27.

Echávez-Solano, Nelsy, and Kenya C. Dworkin y Méndez, eds. *Spanish and Empire*. Nashville: Vanderbilt University Press, 2007.

Fairclough, Marta. "El (denominado) Spanglish en Estados Unidos: polémicas y realidades." *Revista Internacional Lingüística Iberoamericana* 2 (2003): 185–204.

Lago, Eduardo. "Seis tesis sobre el español en Estados Unidos." *El País* (Spain), November 28, 2008. http://www.elpais.com/articulo/opinion/tesis/espanol/Estados/Unidos/elpepiopi/20081128elpepiopi_12/Tes.

Lipski, John M. "Spanish, English or Spanglish? Truth and Consequences of U.S. Latino Bilingualism." In Nelsy Echávez-Solano and Kenya C. Dworkin y Méndez, eds., *Spanish and Empire*, 197–218. Nashville: Vanderbilt University Press, 2007.

——*Varieties of Spanish in the United States*. Washington, DC: Georgetown University Press, 2008.

Lodares, Juan: "Language, Catholicism, and Power in the Spanish Empire." In Nelsy Echávez-Solano and Kenya C. Dworkin y Méndez, eds., *Spanish and Empire*, pp. 3–31. Nashville: Vanderbilt University Press, 2007.

López Morales, Humberto, ed. *Enciclopedia del español en los Estados Unidos. Anuario del Instituto Cervantes*. Madrid: Instituto Cervantes y Santillana, 2009.

Marzán, Julio. "Found in Translation: Reflections of a Bilingual American." In Doris Sommer, ed., *Bilingual Games: Some Literary Investigations*, pp. 221–34. New York: Palgrave Macmillan, 2003.

Stavans, Ilan. *Spanglish: The Making of a New American Language*. New York: HarperCollins, 2003.

Valdés Bernal, Sergio, and Nuria Gregori Torada. *La lengua española en los Estados Unidos*. La Habana: Academia, 1997.

Valenzuela, Luisa. *La travesía*. Buenos Aires: Norma, 2001.

Zentella, Ana Celia. "Commentary. A Nuyorican's View of Our History and Language(s) in New York, 1945–1965." In Gabriel Haslip-Viera, Angelo Falcón, and Félix Matos Rodríguez, eds., *Boricuas in Gotham: Puerto Ricans in the Making of Modern New York City*, pp. 21–34. Princeton: Wiener, 2004.

—— *Growing Up Bilingual: Puerto Rican Children in New York.* Malden, MA: Blackwell, 1997.

——"Latin@ Langauages and Identities." In Marcelo Suárez-Orozco and Mariela M. Páez, eds., *Latinos: Remaking America*, pp. 321–39. Berkeley: University of California Press, 2002.

——"Recuerdos de una Nuyorican." *Insula* 679–680 (2003): 37–40.

Primary Sources
POETRY

Aguasaco, Carlos, José Jesús Osorio, Rafael Hernández Saavedra, eds. *Encuentro: Diez poetas latinoamericanos en USA.* Cali/New York: Fundación Literaria Botella y Luna/Sin Frontera, 2003.

Agüeros, Jack. *Correspondence Between the Stonehaulers.* New York: Hanging Loose, 1991.

Alfau, Felipe. *Sentimental Songs/La poesía cursi.* Trans., with introduction, Ilan Stavans. Elmwood Park, IL: Dalkey Archive, 1992.

Algarín, Miguel. *Love Is Hard Work: Memorias de Loisaida.* New York: Scribner, 1997.

Algarín, Miguel, and Bob Holman, eds. *Aloud: Voices from the Nuyorican Poets Café.* Introduction by M. Algarín. New York: Holt, 1994.

Algarín, Miguel, and Miguel Piñero, eds. *Nuyorican Poetry: An Anthology of Puerto Rican Words and Feelings.* New York: William Morrow, 1975

Álvarez Koki, Francisco, ed. *Piel-palabra. Muestra de la poesía española en Nueva York.* New York: Consulado General de España, 2003.

Álvarez Koki, Francisco, and Pedro R. Monge Rafuls, eds. Introduction by Ana María Hernández. *Al fin del siglo (Veinte poetas).* Nueva York: Ollantay, 1999.

Armistead, Samuel G. *Judeo-Spanish Ballads from New York*, Berkeley: University of California Press, 1981.

Artel, Jorge. "Palabras a la ciudad de Nueva York." In *Tambores en la noche, 1931–1934.* Cartagena: Bolívar, 1940.

Báez, Josefina. *Dominicanish: A Performance Text.* New York: I Ombe, 2000.

Barradas, Efraín, and Rafael Rodríguez, ed. *Herejes y mitificadores: Muestra de poesía puertorriqueña en los Estados Unidos.* Río Piedras: Huracán, 1980.

Bezzubikoff Díaz, Evgueni. *Cartas de Nueva York.* Lima: Hipocampo, 2007.

Blanco, Yolanda. *De lo urbano y lo sagrado.* Managua: Asociación Nicaragüense de Escritoras, 2005.

Borges, Jorge Luis. "The Cloisters." Trans. W. S. Merwin. In Stephen Wolf, ed., *I Speak of the City: Poems of New York*, pp. 84–85. New York: Columbia University Press, 2007.

Braschi, Giannina. *Empire of Dreams.* Trans. Tess O'Dwyer. New Haven: Yale University Press, 1994.

Burgos, Julia de. "Adiós en Welfare Island/Farewell in Welfare Island." In Jack Agüeros, ed. and trans., *Song of the Simple Truth: The Complete Poems of Julia de Burgos*, pp. 356–57. Willimantic, CT: Curbstone, 1997.

Burgos, Julia de. *Song of the Simple Truth: The Complete Poems of Julia de Burgos*. Ed. and trans. Jack Agüeros. Willimantic, CT: Curbstone, 1997.

Cardenal, Ernesto. "Viaje a Nueva York" In *Nueva antología poética*, pp. 241–63. Mexico: Siglo Veintiuno, 1988.

Casal, Lourdes. *Palabras juntan revolución*. La Habana: Casa de Las Américas, 1981.

Conget, José María. *Cincuenta y tres y Octava*. Zaragoza: Xordica, 1997.

Coronel Urtecho, José. "Con Salomón de la Selva en Nueva York." In *Prosa reunida*, pp. 189–206. Managua: Nueva Nicaragua, 1985.

—— "Memorama de Gotham." In *Rapido Transito (Al ritmo de Norteamérica)*, pp. 101–28. Managua: Nueva Nicaragua, 1985.

Darío, Rubén. *Selected Writings*. Ed., with an introduction, Ilan Stavans. Trans. Andrew Hurley, Greg Simon, and Steven F. White. New York: Penguin, 2005.

Echavarren, Roberto, José Kozer, and Jacobo Sefami, eds. *Medusario: Muestra de poesía latinoamericana*. México, D.F.: Fondo de Cultura Económica, 1996.

Espada, Martín, ed. *El Coro: A Chorus of Latino and Latina Poetry*. Amherst: University of Massachusetts Press, 1997.

Esteves, Sandra Maria. *Bluestown Mockingbird Mambo*. Houston: Arte Público, 1990.

Florit, Eugenio. *Obras completas*. Ed. Luis González-del-Valle and Roberto Esquenazi-Mayo. Lincoln, NE: Society of Spanish and Spanish-American Studies, 1982–1991.

García Lorca, Federico. *Poeta en Nueva York y otras hojas y poemas: Manuscritos nuyorkinos*. Ed. Mario Hernández. Madrid: Taba, 1990.

Gazarian, Marie-Lise, ed. *Entre rascacielos: Nueva York en nueve poetas*. Riobamba: Casa de la Cultura, 1999.

—— *Entre rascacielos /Amidst Skyscrapers: Doce poetas hispanos en Nueva York/Twelve Hispanic Poets in New York*. Riobamba: Casa de la Cultura, 2000.

Gómez Rosa, Alexis. *New York City en tránsito de pie quebrado*. 2d ed. Santo Domingo: Buho, 1997.

Guillén, Nicolás. "A las Ruinas de Nueva York" In Luis Iñigo Madrigal, ed., *Summa poética*, pp. 231–32. Madrid: Cátedra, 1976.

Gutiérrez, Franklin, ed. *Niveles del imán: Recopilación de los jóvenes poetas dominicanos en Nueva York*. New York: Alcance, 1983.

—— *Voces del exilio. Poetas dominicanos en la ciudad de New York*. New York: Alcance, 1986.

Henríquez Ureña, Pedro. "Frente a las 'palisades' del Hudson." In Juan Jacobo de Lara, ed., *Obras completas: Tomo I, 1899–1909*, p. 32. Santo Domingo: Universidad Nacional Pedro Henríquez Ureña, 1976.

Heredia, José María. "Niágara." In Harold Augenbraum and Margarite Fernández Olmos, eds., *The Latino Reader*, pp. 66–70. New York: Houghton Mifflin, 1993.

Hierro, José. *Cuaderno de Nueva York*. Madrid: Hiperión, 1998.

Kozer, José. *Stet*. Trans. Mark Weiss. New York: Junction, 2006.

Laviera, Tato. *AmeRícan.* Houston: Arte Público, 1985.

—— *Enclave.* Houston: Arte Público, 1985.

—— *La Carreta Made a U-Turn.* Houston: Arte Público, 1992.

Lázaro, Felipe. *Poetas cubanas en Nueva York: Antología breve/Cuban Women Poets in New York: A Brief Anthology.* Madrid: Betania, 1991.

——*Poetas cubanos en Nueva York.* Madrid: Betania, 1988.

Lihn, Enrique. *A partir de Manhattan.* Valparaiso: Ganymedes, 1979.

López Adorno, Pedro, ed. *La ciudad prestada: Poesía latinoamericana posmoderna en Nueva York.* Dominican Republic: Colección de Poesía Luna Cabeza Caliente no. 9, 2002.

López-Adorno, Pedro, ed. *Papiros de Babel: Antología de la poesía puertorriqueña en Nueva York.* Río Piedras: Editorial de la Universidad de Puerto Rico, 1991.

Martí, José. "Amor de ciudad grande/Love in the City." Trans. Kelly Washbourne. In Kelly Washbourne, ed., *An Anthology of Spanish American Modernismo,* pp. 23–27. New York: Modern Language Association of America, 2007.

——*Versos Sencillos (Simple Verses).* Trans. Manuel A. Tellechea. Houston: Arte Público, 1997.

Marzán, Julio, ed. *Inventing a Word: An Anthology of Twentieth-Century Puerto Rican Poetry.* New York: Columbia University Press, 1980.

Matilla, Alfredo, and Iván Silén, eds. *The Puerto Rican Poets.* New York: Bantam, 1972.

Miranda Archilla, Graciany, and Orlando José Hernández, ed. and trans. *Hungry Dust/Polvo Hambriento.* Lima: Santo Oficio/Latino Press, Latin American Writers Institute, Hostos Community College, CUNY, 2005.

Mistral, Gabriela. *Desolación.* Nueva York: Instituto de las Españas, 1922.

Moreno Villa, José. *Jacinta la pelirroja.* Madrid: Castalia, 2000.

——*Pruebas de Nueva York.* Valencia: Pre-textos, 1989.

Negroni, María. *Islandia: A Poem.* Trans. Anne Twitty. Barrytown, NY: Barrytown, 2001.

Ortiz-Vargas, Alfredo. *The Towers of Manhattan: A Spanish-American Poet Looks at New York.* Trans. Quincy Guy Burris. Albuquerque: University of New Mexico Press, 1944.

Paz, Octavio. "Central Park." In *Árbol adentro,* pp. 119–20. Barcelona: Seix Barral, 1987.

Perdomo, Willie. *Postcards of el barrio.* San Juan, P.R.: Isla Negra, 2002.

—— *Where a Nickel Costs a Dime.* New York: Norton, 1996.

Pietri, Pedro. *Puerto Rican Obituary.* New York: Monthly Review Press, 1974.

Piñero, Miguel. "A Lower East Side Poem." In Nicolás Kanellos et al., eds., *Herencia: The Anthology of Hispanic Literature of the United States,* pp. 239–41. New York: Oxford University Press, 2002.

Poetas en Nueva York. Granada: Caja General de Ahorros de Granada, 1998.

Risso, Santiago. *Prosa de Nueva York.* Lima: Alejo, 2003.

Rivera, Héctor. *Los emigrantes del siglo. Obra poética.* Santo Domingo: Nacional, 2006.

Roffé, Mercedes. *Like the Rains Come: Selected Poems, 1987–2006.* Trans. Janet Greenberg. Exeter: Shearsman, 2008.

Selva, Salomón de la. *Tropical Town and Other Poems*. Ed., with an introduction, Silvio Sirias. Houston: Arte Público, 1999.

Silén, Iván, ed. *Los paraguas amarillos: Los poetas latinos en New York*. Hanover, NH: Ediciones del Norte; Binghampton, NY: Bilingual Press, 1983.

Sousândrade. "The Wall Street Inferno." Trans. Robert E. Brown. *Latin American Literary Review* 14, no. 27 (1986): 92–98.

Tapia, Juan Luis, ed. *Miaradas de Nueva York (Mapa Poético)*. Granada: Cuadernos del Vigia, 2000.

Valdez, Pedro Antonio. *Naturaleza muerta*. Santo Domingo: Universidad Central del Este, 2001.

Valle, Carmen. *Haiku de Nueva York*. Córdoba: Alción, 2008.

Vázquez, Lourdes. *Bestiary: Selected Poems, 1986–1997*. Trans. Rosa Alcalá. Tempe, AZ: Bilingual/Bilingüe, 2004.

——*La estatuilla*. San Juan: Cultural, 2004

——*May the Transvestites of My Island Who Tap Their Heels Exquisitely*. Brooklyn: Belladona, 2004.

——*Park Slope*. Provincetown, MA: Duration, 2003.

Vicuña, Cecilia. *The Precarious: The Art and Poetry of Cecilia Vicuña*. Ed. M. Catherine de Zegher. Hanover, NH: University Press of New England, 1997.

Zemborain, Lila. *Malvas Orquídeas del Mar (Mauve Sea Orchids)*. Trans. Rosa Alcalá and Mónica de la Torre. Brooklyn, NY: Belladonna, 2007.

——*Rasgado*. Buenos Aires: Tsé-Tsé, 2006.

Zemborain, Lila et al., eds. *Mujeres mirando al Sur: An Anthology of Contemporary Poetry in the U.S.* Madrid: Torremozas, 2004.

PROSE

Acosta, José. *El efecto dominó: Cuentos*. Santo Domingo: Universidad Central del Este, 2001.

——*Perdidos en Babilonia*. Santo Domingo: Nacional, 2005.

Acosta, José, ed. *Voces de ultramar: Literatura dominicana de la diáspora*. Santo Domingo: Ferilibro, 2005.

Agostini de del Río, Amelia. *Puertorriqueños en Nueva York: Cuentos*. New York: Mensaje, 1970.

Agüeros, Jack. *Dominoes and Other Stories*. Willimantic, CT: Curbstone, 1993.

Alarcón, Daniel. *War by Candlelight: A Collection of Short Stories*. New York: Harper Perennial, 2006.

Albues, Tereza. *O berro do cordeiro em Nova York: Romance*. Rio de Janeiro: Civilização Brasileira, 1995.

Alemán Bolaños, Gustavo. *La factoría: Novela de un americo-hispano en Nueva York*. Ciudad de Guatemala: Tipografía Sánchez y De Guise, 1925.

Alfau, Felipe. *Chromos*. Elmwood Park, IL: Dalkey Archive, 1990.

——*Cuentos españoles de antaño*. Trans. to Spanish, with an introduction, Carmen Martín-Gaite. Madrid: Siruela, 1991.

——*Locos: A Comedy of Gestures*. Afterword by Mary McCarthy. Elmwood Park, IL: Dalkey Archive, 1988.

——*Old Tales from Spain*. Garden City, NY: Doubleday, Doran, 1929.

Álvarez Koki, Francisco. *Ratas en Manhattan*. Santiago de Compostela: Sotelo Blanco, 2007.

Alvarez, Julia. *How the García Girls Lost Their Accents*. New York: Plume, 1991.

Arenas, Reinaldo. *Adiós a mamá: De La Habana a Nueva York*. Miami: Universal, 1996.

——*Before Night Falls*. Trans. Dolores M. Koch. New York: Viking, 1993.

——*Mona and Other Tales*. Ed. and trans. Dolores M. Koch. New York: Vintage, 2001.

——*The Doorman*. Trans. Dolores M. Koch. New York: Grove Weidenfeld, 1991.

Arrabal, Fernando. *Levitación*. Barcelona: Seix Barral, 2000.

Athayde, Roberto. *Brasileiros em Manhattan*. Rio de Janeiro: Topbooks, 1996.

Barnet, Miguel. *La vida real*. La Habana: Letras Cubanas, 1986.

Beldá, Joaquín. *En el país del bluff: Veinte días en Nueva York*. Madrid: Hispania, 1926.

Betances de Pujadas, Estrella. *Perico Grillo se va a Nueva York y otros relatos*. Madrid: Asociación Literaria Calíope, 1999.

Boullosa, Carmen. *El fantasma y el poeta*. México, D.F.: Sexto Piso, 2007.

——*La Novela perfecta*. México, D.F.: Alfaguara, 2006.

Burgos, Julia de. *Julia de Burgos: Periodista en Nueva York*. Ed. Juan Antonio Rodríguez Pagán. San Juan: Ateneo Puertorriqueño, 1992.

——"Ser o no ser es la divisa." *Semanario hispano*, 1945.

Camba, Julio. *La ciudad automática*. Buenos Aires: Espasa Calpe, 1944.

Capetillo, Luisa. *Mi opinión*. San Juan: Biblioteca Roja 1913 [1911]. Ybor City: Mascuñana.

Cardoza y Aragón, Luis. "Nueva York." In *El río: Novelas de caballería*, pp. 354–64. México: FCE, 1986.

Carvajal, José. *Por nada del mundo*. New York: Mambrú, 1992.

Chamberlin, Vernon A., and Ivan A. Schulman. *La Revista ilustrada de Nueva York: History, Anthology, and Index of Literary Selections*. Columbia: University of Missouri Press, 1976.

Cocco De Filippis, Daisy. *Documents of Dissidence, Selected Writings by Dominican Women*. New York: CUNY Dominican Studies Institute, 2000.

Cocco De Filippis, Daisy, ed. *Tertuliando/Hanging out. Dominicanas y amiga(o)s/Dominican Women and Friends: Bilingual text(o)s bilinguales, 1994–1996*. New York: Ediciones Alcance, 1997.

Cocco De Filippis, Daisy, and Franklin Gutiérrez, eds. *Historias de Washington Heights y otros rincones del mundo: Cuentos escritos por dominicanos en los Estados Unidos/Stories from Washington Heights and Other Corners of the World: Short Stories Written by Dominicans in the United States*. New York: Latino, 1994.

——*Literatura dominicana en los Estados Unidos: Presencia temprana, 1900–1950*. Santo Domingo: Buho, 2001.

Colón, Jesús. *A Puerto Rican in New York and Other Sketches*. New York: International, 1982.

——*Lo que el pueblo me dice: Crónicas de la colonia puertorriqueña en Nueva York.* Ed. Edwin Karli Padilla. Houston: Arte Público, 2002.

—— *The Way It Was, and Other Writings: Historical Vignettes about the New York Puerto Rican Community.* Ed., with an introductory essay, Edna Acosta-Belén and Virginia Sánchez Korrol. Houston: Arte Público, 1993.

Colón, Joaquín. *Pioneros Puertorriqueños en Nueva York.* Houston: Arte Público, 2002.

Cotto-Thorner, Guillermo. *Trópico en Manhattan: Novela.* Introduction by Mariano Picón-Salas. San Juan: Cordillera, 1969.

Coutinho, Domicio. *Duke, the Dog Priest.* Trans. Clifford E. Landers. Los Angeles: Green Integer, 2008.

Cruz, Angie. *Let It Rain Coffee: A Novel.* New York: Simon and Schuster, 2005.

——*Soledad.* New York: Simon and Schuster, 2001.

Díaz, Junot. "Language, Violence, and Resistance." In Daniel Balderston and Marcy Schwartz, eds., *Voice-Overs: Translation and Latin American Literature*, pp. 42–44. Albany: State University of New York Press, 2002.

——*Drown.* New York: Riverhead, 1997.

—— *The Brief Wonderous Life of Oscar Wao.* New York: Riverhead, 2007.

Díaz Guerra, Alirio. *Lucas Guevara.* Introduction by Nicolás Kanellos and Liz Hernández. Houston: Arte Público, 2001.

Díaz Valcárcel, Emilio. *Harlem todos los días.* San Juan: Huracán, 1978.

Dorfman, Ariel. *Death and the Maiden.* New York: Penguin, 1992. *El laúd del desterrado.* Ed. Matías Montes-Huidobro. Houston: Arte Público, 1995.

——*Heading South, Looking North. A Bilingual Journey.* New York: Farrar, Straus, and Giroux, 1998.

Ferreira, Sonia Nolasco. *Moreno como vocês: A Culpa Não é do Rio Nem de Nova York: A Culpa é Nossa.* Rio de Janeiro: Record, 1984.

Flores, Juan, ed. *Divided Arrival: Narratives of the Puerto Rican Migration, 1920–1950.* Princeton: Wiener, 2003.

Fonollosa, J. M. *Ciudad del hombre: New York.* Introduction by Pere Gimferrer. Barcelona: El Acantilado, 2000.

Galán, Tomás Modesto. *Los niños del Monte Edén (Cuentos).* Santo Domingo: Cocolo, 1998.

García, Cristina. *Dreaming in Cuban.* New York: Ballantine, 1992.

García Martín, José Luis, ed. *Líneas urbanas: Lectura de Nueva York.* Gijón: Libros del Pexe, 2002.

Glantz, Margo. "Nueva York es el barroco." In *Erosiones*, 33–35. México: UAEM, 1984.

Goldman, Francisco. *The Divine Husband.* New York: Atlantic Monthly, 2004.

González, José Luis. *En Nueva York y otras desgracias.* 3d ed. Río Piedras: Huracán, 1981.

—— "The Night We Became People Again." Trans. Kal Wagenheim. In Kal Wagenheim, ed., *Cuentos: An Anthology of Short Stories from Puerto Rico*, pp. 117–41. New York: Schocken, 1978.

Guzmán, Martín Luis. *A orillas del Hudson*. México: Botas, 1920.

Hecho(s) en Nueva York. Cuentos latinoamericanos. New York: Latino, 1994.

Hijuelos, Oscar. *The Fourteen Sisters of Emilio Montez O'Brien*. New York: Farrar Straus Giroux, 1993.

——*The Mambo Kings Play Songs of Love*. New York: Farrar Straus Giroux 1989

Hostos, Eugenio María de. *En barco de papel/In a Paper Boat*. Trans. Elizabeth Macklin and Orlando José Hernandez. New York: Moria, 1989.

——*Obras completas*. Tomo 2: Diario, vol. I y II. Facsimilar de la edición conmemorativa del Gobierno de Puerto Rico. San Juan: Coquí 1969 [1939].

I [love] NY. Diez autores en busca de una ciudad. Madrid: Planeta, 2002.

Krauze, Ethel. *Mujeres en Nueva York*. México, D.F.: Grijalbo, 1993.

Labarthe, Pedro Juan. *The Son of Two Nations: The Private Life of a Columbia Student*. New York: Carranza, 1931.

Lago, Eduardo, *Llámame Brooklyn*. Barcelona: Destino, 2006

Laguerre, Enrique A. *The Labyrinth*. Trans. William Rose. Maplewood, NJ: Waterfront, 1984.

Loriga, Ray. *El hombre que inventó Manhattan*. Barcelona: El Aleph, 2004.

——*Trífero*. Barcelona: Ediciones Destino, 2000.

Madrid, Juan. *Restos de Carmín*. Madrid: Espasa, 1999.

Manrique, Manuel. *Island in Harlem*. New York: John Day, 1966.

——*Una isla en Harlem*. Madrid: Alfaguara, 1965.

Marín, Francisco Gonzalo "Pachín." "New York from Within: One Aspect of Its Bohemian Life." Trans. Lizabeth Paravisini-Gebert. In Harold Augenbraum and Margarite Fernández Olmos, eds., *The Latino Reader*, pp. 108–11. New York: Houghton Mifflin, 1993.

Martí, José. *José Martí: En los Estados Unidos: Periodismo de 1881 a 1892*. Ed. Roberto Fernández Retamar and Pedro Pablo Rodríguez. Paris: Colección Archivos, 2003.

——*Selected Writings*. Ed. and trans. Esther Allen. Introduction by Roberto González Echevarría. New York: Penguin, 2002.

Martín Gaite, Carmen. *Caperucita en Manhattan*. Madrid: Siruela, 1990.

——*Visión de Nueva York*. With texts by Ignacio Álvarez Vara and A. B. Márquez. Madrid: Siruela; Barcelona: Círculo de Lectores, 2005.

Martínez Palau, Silvio. *Made in USA: Estudio en naturalezas muertas*. Hanover, NH: Ediciones del Norte, 1986.

Menai, Tania. *Nova York do Oiapoque ao Chuí: Relatos de brasileiros na cidade que nunca dorme*. Rio de Janeiro: Casa da Palavra, 2007.

Mendes, Lucas. *Conexão Manhattan: Crônicas da Big Apple*. Rio de Janeiro: Campus, 1997.

——*Manhattan re-conexões*. São Paulo: Harbra, 2004.

Mendoza, Eduardo. *Nueva York*. Barcelona: Destino, 1986.

Menéndez, Ronaldo, Ignacio Padilla, and Enrique del Risco, eds. *Pequeñas Resistencias/4. Antología del nuevo cuento norteamericano y caribeño*. Foreword by Andrés Neuman. Madrid: Páginas de Espuma, 2005.

Merejo, Andrés. *Cuentos en New York*. Santo Domingo: Búho, 2002.

Mistral, Gabriela. 1. "Cómo edifican." *La Nueva Democracia* (Nueva York) 12, no 1 (1931): 12–14.

—— "La Estátua de la Libertad." *Puerto Rico Ilustrado*, April 5, 1931.

Modesto, Tomás. *Los cuentos de Mount Hope*. Santo Domingo: Buho, 1995.

Mohr, Nicholasa. *El Bronx Remembered: A Novella and Stories*. New York: Harper, 1993

—— *In Nueva York*. Houston: Arte Público, 1988.

—— *Nilda: A Novel*. Houston: Arte Público, 1986.

Molloy, Sylvia. *El común olvido*. Buenos Aires: Norma, 2002.

Moreno Villa, José. *Vida en claro. Autobiografía*. México: El Colegio de México, 1944.

Moya, José. *Al este de Broadway*. Riverdale, NY: MC, 1999.

Muñoz Molina, Antonio. *Sepharad*. Trans. Margaret Sayers Peden. Orlando, FL: Harcourt, 2003

—— *Ventanas de Manhattan*. Barcelona: Seix Barral, 2004.

O'Neill, Gonzalo. *La Indiana Borinqueña*. New York, 1922.

Ortíz Cofer, Judith. *The Latin Deli*. Athens: University of Georgia Press, 1993.

Paz Soldán, Edmundo, and Alberto Fuguet, eds. *Se habla español: Voces latinas en USA*. Miami: Alfaguara, 2000.

Pérez, Loida Maritza. *Geographies of Home: A Novel*. New York: Viking, 1999.

Pineda Botero, Alvaro. *Trasplante a Nueva York*. Bogotá: Oveja Negra, 1983.

Polzonoff, Paulo, Jr. *A face oculta de Nova York*. São Paulo: Globo, 2007.

Prieto, Guillermo. *Viaje a los Estados Unidos por "Fidel."* 3 vols. México, D.F.: Dublan y Chávez, 1877–78.

Puig, Manuel. *Estertores de una década, Nueva York '78; seguido de Bye-bye, Babilonia: crónicas de Nueva York, Londres y París, publicadas en Siete días ilustrados, 1969–1970*. Buenos Aires: Seix Barral, 1993.

—— *Eternal Curse on the Reader of These Pages*. New York: Random House, 1982.

—— *Kiss of the Spider Woman and Two Other Plays*. New York: Norton, 1994.

Quesada, Roberto. *The Big Banana*. Trans. Walter Krochmal. Houston: Arte Público, 1999.

Quiñonez, Ernesto. *Bodega Dreams*. New York: Vintage, 2000.

—— *Chango's Fire: A Novel*. New York: Rayo, 2004.

Ramírez, Sergio. "Charles Atlas también muere." In *Cuentos Completos*, 123–36. México, Alfaguara, 1997.

Rey Rosa, Rodrigo. *Ningún lugar sagrado*. Barcelona: Seix Barral, 1998.

Rivera, Edward. *Family Installments: Memories of Growing Up Hispanic*. New York: Penguin, 1983.

Rivero, Juan. *Nueva York 2014. 40 Vidas en la historia de un barrio*. Brooklyn, NY: Punto 7, 1999.

Rodriguez, Abraham, Jr. *Spidertown*. New York: Penguin, 1994.

—— *The Boy Without a Flag: Tales of the South Bronx*. Minneapolis: Milkweed, 1999.

—— *The Buddha Book: A Novel*. New York: Picador, 2001.

Rodríguez, Antonio Orlando. *Chiquita*. Madrid: Alfaguara, 2008.

Sabino, Fernando. *Mêdo em Nova Iorque: A cidade vazia*. Rio de Janeiro: Sabiá, 1969.

Salazar, Boris. *La otra selva*. Bogotá: Tercer Mundo, 1991.

Sánchez, Luis Rafael. "The Flying Bus." Trans. Elpidio Laguna-Díaz. In Nicolás Kanellos, ed., *Herencia: The Anthology of Hispanic Literature of the United States*, pp. 631–38. New York: Oxford University Press, 2002.

Sánchez Féliz, Rubén, ed. *Viajeros del rocío: 25 narradores dominicanos de la diáspora*. Santo Domingo: Nacional, 2008.

Santiago, Esmeralda. *The Turkish Lover: A Memoir*. New York: Da Capo, 2005

——— *When I Was Puerto Rican*. New York: Vintage, 1994.

Santiago, Silviano. *Stella Manhattan*. Trans. George Yúdice. Durham: Duke University Press, 1994.

Sarmiento, Domingo Faustino. *Diario de un viaje de Nueva York a Buenos Aires, de 23 de julio al 20 de agosto de 1868*. Santiago: Cruz del Sur, 1944.

——— *Obras completas XXIX: Ambas Américas*. Buenos Aires: Universidad Nacional de La Matanza, 2001.

——— *Travels in the United Status in 1847*. Trans. Michael Aaron Rockland. Princeton: Princeton University Press, 1971.

Scotto, Luiz Alberto. *46th Street: O caminho americano*. São Paulo: Brasiliense, 1993.

Seis narradores españoles en Nueva York. Granada: Dauro, 2006.

Skármeta, Antonio. "The Cartwheel." In Janet Brof and Hortense Carpentier, eds., *Doors and Mirrors: Fiction and Poetry from Spanish America, 1920–1970*. New York: Grossman, 1992.

——— *Watch Where the Wolf Is Going: Stories*. Trans. Donald L. Schmidt and Federico Cordovez. Columbia, LA: Readers International, 1991.

Soto, Pedro Juan. *Spiks: Stories*. Trans., with an introduction, Victoria Ortiz. New York: Monthly Review, 1973.

Stavans, Ilan. "Autobiographical Essay." In *The Essential Ilan Stavans*, 75–86. New York: Routledge, 2000.

Suárez Coalla, Paquita. *Para que no se me olvide*. New York: Campana, 2007.

Suárez Coalla, Paquita, and Sonia Rivera-Valdés. *Aqui Me Tocó Escribir: Antologia de Escritor@s Latin@s de Nueva York*. Uviéu: Trabe, 2005.

Tablada, José Juan. *La babilonia de hierro: Crónicas neoyorkinas de José Juan Tablada*. Ed. Esther Hernández Palacios. Veracruz: UV/UNAM, 2000.

Tato Cumming, Gaspar. *Nueva York: Un español entre rascacielos*. Madrid: Febo, 1945.

Thomas, Piri. *Down These Mean Streets*. New York: Vintage, 1967.

Tobón, Orlando. *Las crónicas de Jackson Heights*. New York: Atria, 2006.

Torres, Omar. *Apenas un bolero*. Miami: Universal, 1981.

——— *Fallen Angels Sing*. Houston: Arte Público, 1991.

Valenzuela, Luisa. *Black Novel with Argentines*. Trans. Toby Talbot. New York: Simon and Schuster, 1992.

——*El gato eficaz*. Buenos Aires: de la Flor, 1991.

——*Los deseos oscuros y los otros. Cuadernos de New York*. Buenos Aires: Norma, 2002.

Valle, Carmen. *Tu versión de las cosas*. Buenos Aires: de la Flor, 2007.

Vanasco, Alberto. *Nueva York, Nueva York*. Buenos Aires: Sudamericana, 1967.

Varela, Félix. *Jicoténcal*. Ed. Luis Leal and Rodolfo J. Cortina. Houston: Arte Público, 1995.

——*Letters to Elpidio*. Transl. Felipe J. Estévez. New York: Pauslist Press, 1989.

Vázquez, Lourdes. *Sin ti no soy yo*. San Juan: Puerto, 2005.

Vega, Ed. *Mendoza's Dreams*. Houston: Arte Público, 1987.

——*The Lamentable Journey of Omaha Bigelow Into the Impenetrable Loisaida Jungle*. Woodstock, NY: Overlook, 2004.

Veríssimo, Erico. *Gato prêto em campo de neve*. Rio de Janeiro: Globo, 1961.

Vilas Boas, Sergio. *Os estrangeiros do trem N*. Rio de Janeiro: Rocco, 1997.

Vivas Maldonado, José Luis. *A vellón las esperanzas o Melania (Cuentos de un puertorriqueño en Nueva York)*. New York: Las Américas, 1971.

Yglesias, José. *The Goodbye Land: The Memorable Account of an American's Journey to Uncover the Truth About His Past*. New York: Pantheon, 1967.

Zapata Olivella, Manuel. *He visto la noche: Las raíces de la furia negra*. Medellín: Bedout, 1969.

THEATER

Algarín, Miguel, and Lois Griffith, eds. *Action: The Nuyorican Poets Cafe Theater Festival*. New York: Simon and Schuster, 1997.

Antush, John V., ed. *Nuestro New York: An Anthology of Puerto Rican Plays*. New York: Mentor, 1994.

——*Recent Puerto Rican Theater: Five Plays from New York*. Houston: Arte Público, 1991.

Boulet, Rosa Ileana. "Encuentros La Habana–New York en el siglo pasado." *Revista Teatro/CELCIT* 32 (2007): 148–57.

Cammarata, Joan F. "Nuyorican." In Eladio Cortés and Mirta Barrea-Marlys, eds., *Encyclopedia of Latin American Theater*, pp. 343–56. Westport, CT: Greenwood, 2003.

Cruz, Nilo. *Ana in the Tropics*. New York: Theatre Communications Group, 2003.

Dávila López, Grace. "Construction of New Cultural identities: Puerto Rican Theater in New York." In Mario J. Valdés and Djelal Kadir, eds., *Literary Cultures of Latin America: A Comparative History*, 3:442–47. New York: Oxford University Press, 1994.

De la Roche, Elisa. *Teatro hispano! Three Major New York Companies*. New York: Garland, 1995.

Feliano, Wilma. "'I Am a Hyphenated American': Interview with Dolores Prida." *Latin American Theater Review* 29, no. 1 (1995): 113–18.

——"Language and Identity in Three Plays by Dolores Prida," *Latin American Theater Review* 28, no. 1 (1994): 125–38.

Figueroa, Pablo. *Teatro: Hispanic Theater in New York City, 1920–1976*. New York: Museo del Barrio and Off-Off Broadway Alliance, 1977.

Irizarry, Roberto. "The House of Pretension: Space and Performance in Miguel Piñero's Theater." *Latin American Theater Review* 37, no. 2 (2004): 77–94.

Martín, Manuel, Jr. "The Development of the Hispanic-American Theater in New York City: From 1960 to the Present." *Ollantay Theater Magazine* 5, no.2 (1997): 11–37.

Miller, John C. "Contemporary Hispanic Theater in New York." In Nicolás Kanellos, ed., *Hispanic Theatre in the United States*, pp. 24–33. Houston: Arte Público, 1984.

—— "Hispanic Theater in New York, 1965–1977." *Revista Chicano-Riqueña* 6, no. 1 (1978): 40–59.

Morton, Carlos. "The Nuyoricans." *Latin American Theater Review* 10, no. 1 (1976): 80–89.

Piñero, Miguel. *Outrageous: One Act Plays*. Houston: Arte Público, 1986.

——*Short Eyes*. Introduction by Marvin Felix Camillo. New York: Hill and Wang, 1975.

—— *The Sun Always Shines for the Cool; A Midnight Moon at the Greasy Spoon; Eulogy for a Small Time Thief*. Houston: Arte Público, 1984.

Prida, Dolores. "The Show Does Go On." In Asunción Horno-Delgado et al., eds., *Breaking Boundaries: Latina Writing and Critical Readings*, pp. 181–88. Amherst: University of Massachusetts Press, 1989.

Puleo, Gus. "Living and Working in the Border Town: An Interview with Miriam Colón Valle." *Review: Latin American Literature and Arts* 54 (1997): 11–18.

Rizk, Beatriz J. "Cuatro dramaturgos latinos: María Irene Fornés, Miguel Piñero, Tato Laviera y Piedro Pietri." In Miguel Falquez-Certain, ed., *New Voices in Latin American Literature/ Nuevas voces en la literatura latinoamericana*, pp. 141–56. Jackson Heights, NY: Ollantay Center for the Arts, 1993.

——"El teatro hispano en Nueva York." In Moisés Pérez Coterillo, ed., *Escenario de dos mundos: Inventario teatral de Iberoamérica*, 2:307–23. Madrid: Centro de Documentación Teatral/Ministerio de Cultura, 1988.

Roepke, Gabriela. "Tres dramaturgos en Nueva York." In Pedro R. Monge Rafuls, ed., *Lo que no se ha dicho*, pp. 73–96. Jackson Heights, NY: Ollantay Center for the Arts, 1994.

Román, David and Alberto Sandoval. "Caught in the Web: Latinidad, AIDS, and Allegory in *Kiss of the Spider Woman, the Musical*." *American Literature* 67, no. 3 (1995): 553–85.

Rubin, Rachel, and Jeffrey Melnick. "Broadway, 1957: *West Side Story* and the Nuyorican Blues." In *Immigration and American Popular Culture: An Introduction*, pp. 88–128. New York: New York University Press, 2007.

Sandoval-Sánchez, Alberto. *José, Can You See? Latinos On and Off Broadway*. Madison: University of Wisconsin Press, 1999.

——"*West Side Story*: A Puerto Rican Reading of 'America.'" In Clara E. Rodríguez, ed., *Latin Looks: Images of Latinas and Latinos in the U.S. Media*, pp. 164–79. Boulder: Westview, 1997.

Se vende, se alquila o se regala: Antología de dramaturgia latina en Nueva York. New York: Campana, 2008.

Smith, Paul Julian. "Black Wedding: García Lorca, Langston Hughes, and the Translation of Introjection." In *The Theatre of García Lorca: Text, Performance, Psychoanalysis*, pp. 44–70. New York: Cambridge University Press, 1998.

Sturman, Janet L. *Zarzuela: Spanish Operetta, American Stage*. Urbana: University of Illinois Press, 2000.

Vásquez, Eva C. *Pregones Theatre: A Theatre for Social Change in the South Bronx*. New York: Routledge, 2003.

Secondary Bibliography on Poetry and Prose

Alvarez-Borland, Isabel. *Cuban-American Literature of Exile: From Person to Persona*. Charlottesville: University Press of Virginia, 1998.

Amarante, Héctor. *La novela dominicana en Nueva York*. New York: Circe de la Maga, 1998.

——"La novelistic dominicana en New York." In R. A. Ramírez-Báez, ed., *Primer Foro de Cultura y Literatura Dominicana en Nueva York*, pp. 57–69. Queens, NY: Sitel, 2003.

Aparicio, Frances. "La vida es un Spanglish disparatero: Bilingualism in Nuyorican Poetry." In Genvieve Fabre, ed., *European Perspectives on Hispanic Literature of the United States*, pp. 147–60. Houston: Arte Público, 1988.

Arango, Alfredo. "Apuntes sobre la literatura latina de los Estados Unidos." In Miguel Falquez-Certain, ed., *New Voices in Latin American Literature/Nuevas voces en la literatura latinoamericana*, pp. 225–32. Jackson Heights, NY: Ollantay Center for the Arts, 1993.

Balestra, Alejandra. "Alberto O'Farrill y Jesús Colón: Dos cronistas en Nueva York." In José F. Aranda Jr. and Silvio Torres-Saillant, eds., *Recovering the U.S. Hispanic Literary Heritage*, 4:133–44. Houston: Arte Público, 2002.

Barradas, Efraín. *Partes de un todo. Ensayos y notas sobre literatura puertorriqueña en los Estados Unidos*. San Juan: Editoral de le Universidad de Puerto Rico, 1998.

Beardsley, Theodore S., Jr. "Rubén Darío and the Hispanic Society: The Holograph Manuscript of *¡Pax!*" *Hispanic Review* 35, no. 1 (1967): 1–42.

Bonilla, Janira. "Transnational Consciousness: Negotiating Identity in the Works of Julia Alvarez and Junot Díaz." In Ernesto Sagas and Sintia E. Molina, eds., *Transnational Perspectives on Dominican Migration*. Gainesville: University of Florida Press, 2003.

Bramen, Carrie Tirado. "Dominican-American Literature." In Alpana Sharma Knippling, ed., *New Immigrant Literatures in the United States: A Sourcebook to Our Multicultural Literary Heritage*, pp. 207–19. Westport, CT: Greenwood, 1996.

——"Puerto Rican-American Literature." In Alpana Sharma Knippling, ed., *New Immigrant Literatures in the United States: A Sourcebook to Our Multicultural Literary Heritage*, pp. 221–39. Westport, CT: Greenwood, 1996.

Brickhouse, Anna. "'A Story of the Island of Cuba': William Cullen Bryant and the Hispanophone Americas." *Nineteenth-Century Literature* 56, no. 1 (2001): 1–22.

Browitt, Jeff. "'En híbrida mezcolanza': Exile and Anxiety in Alirio Díaz Guerra's *Lucas Guevara*." In Paul Allatson and Jo McCormack, eds., *Exile Cultures, Misplaced Identities*, pp. 225–44. New York: Rodopi, 2008.

——"Sexual Anxiety in Alirio Díaz Guerra's *Lucas Guevara*." *Hispania* 88, no. 4 (2005): 677–86.

Burgos, William. "Puerto Rican Literature in a New Clave: Notes on the Emergence of Dia-spoRican." In José L. Torres-Padilla and Carmen Haydée Rivera, eds., *Writing off the Hyphen: New Critical Perspectives on the Literature of the Puerto Rican Diaspora*, pp. 125–42. Seattle: University of Washington Press, 2008.

Cabanillas, Francisco. "Both Ways: Entrevista a Yolanda Martínez-San Miguel, Autora de *Caribe Two Ways* (2003)." *Centro Journal* 20:218–29.

Campbell, Susan M. "Nuyorican Poetry, Tactics for Local Resistance." In Nelsy Echávez-Solano and Kenya C. Dworkin y Méndez, eds., *Spanish and Empire*, pp. 117–38. Nashville: Vanderbilt University Press, 2007.

Cañas, Dionisio. *El poeta en la ciudad: Nueva York y los escritores hispanos.* Madrid: Cátedra, 1994.

Cánepa, Mario A. *Con tres poetas hispanoamericanas en Nueva York: Yolanda Blanco, María Negroni, Carmen Valle.* Madrid: Ollero and Ramos, 2003.

Caro, Gabriel Jaime. "Las estancias logradas de algunos escritores colombianos en Nueva York." In Miguel Falquez-Certain, ed., *New Voices in Latin American Literature/Nuevas voces en la literatura latinoamericana*, pp. 17–21. Jackson Heights, NY: Ollantay Center for the Arts, 1993.

Caulfield, Carlota and Darién J. Davis, eds. *A Companion to U.S. Latino Literatures.* Rochester, NY: Boydell and Brewer, 2007.

Cevallos, Petronio Rafael. *Un lugar bajo el sol, o EcuaYork.* Riobamba: Casa de la Cultura Ecuatoriana "Benjamín Carrión," 2005.

Cocco de Filippis, Daisy. *Desde la diáspora: Selección bilingüe de ensayos/A Diaspora Position: A Bilingual Selection of Essays.* New York: Alcance, 2003.

——"Una flor en la sombra: A Critical Edition of the Complete Works of Virginia de Peña de Bordas." In José F. Aranda, Jr. and Silvio Torres-Saillant, eds., *Recovering the U.S. Hispanic Literary Heritage,* 4:50–58. Houston: Arte Público, 2002.

Cocco de Filippis, Daisy, ed. La *literatura dominicana al final del siglo: Diálogo entre la tierra natal y la diáspora.* New York: CUNY Dominican Studies Institute, 1999.

Coronado, Carmen Dinorah. "Apuntes para una literatura infantil dominicana en New York." In R. A. Ramírez-Báez, ed., *Primer Foro de Cultura y Literatura Dominicana en Nueva York,* pp. 177–82. Jackson Heights, NY: Sitel, 2003.

Cortina, Rodolfo J. "Cuban Literature of the United States, 1824–1959." In Ramón A. Gutiérrez and Genaro M. Padilla, eds., *Recovering the U.S. Hispanic Literary Heritage*, pp. 69–88. Houston: Arte Público, 1993.

——"Varela's *Jicoténcal* and the Historical Novel" In María Herrera-Sobek and Virginia Sánchez Korrol, eds., *Recovering the U.S. Hispanic Literary Heritage,* 3:450–455. Houston: Arte Público, 2002.

Covarrubias, Jorge Ignacio. "Siguiendo las huellas de Gabriela Mistral en Nueva York." In *Homenaje a Gabriela Mistral.* New York: Academia Norteamericana de la Lengua Española, 2010.

Cruz-Malavé, Arnaldo. "Colonial Figures in Motion: Globalization and Translocality in Contemporary Puerto Rican Literature in the United States." *Centro Journal* 14:4–25.

Dalleo, Raphael, and Elena Machado Sáez. *The Latino/a Canon and the Emergence of Post-Sixties Literature*. New York: Palgrave Macmillan, 2007.

de Onís, José. *The United States as Seen by Spanish American Writers, 1776–1890*. New York: Hispanic Institute in the United States, 1952.

del Río, Angel. *El mundo hispánico y el mundo anglo-sajón en América: Choque y atracción de dos culturas*. Introduction by Germán Arciniegas. Buenos Aires: Asociación Argentina por la Libertad de la Cultura, 1960.

Domínguez Miguela, Antonia. "Literary Tropicalizations of the Barrio in Ernesto Quiñonez's *Bodega Dreams* and Ed Vega's *Mendoza's Dreams*." In José L. Torres-Padilla and Carmen Haydée Rivera, eds., *Writing Off the Hyphen: New Critical Perspectives on the Literature of the Puerto Rican Diaspora*, pp. 165–83. Seattle: University of Washington Press, 2008.

Falcón, Rafael. *La emigración puertorriqueña a Nueva York en los cuentos de José Luis González, Pedro Juan Soto y José Luis Vivas Maldonado*. New York: Senda Nueva de Ediciones, 1984.

Falquez-Certain, Miguel. "Habitación de la palabra." In Miguel Falquez-Certain, ed., *New Voices in Latin American Literature/Nuevas voces en la literatura latinoamericana*, pp. 44–54. Jackson Heights, NY: Ollantay Center for the Arts, 1993.

Fay, Eliot G. "Rubén Darío in New York." *Modern Language Notes* 57 (1942): 641–48.

Flores, Juan. "Life Off the Hyphen. Latino Literature and Nuyorican Traditions." In Augustín Laó-Montes and Arlene Dávila, eds., *Mambo Montage: The Latinization of New York*, pp. 185–206. New York: Columbia University Press, 2001.

Font, Mauricio A., and Alfonso W. Quiroz, eds. *The Cuban Republic and José Martí: Reception and Use of a National Symbol*. Lanham, MD: Lexington, 2006.

Galasso, Regina. "Latin from Manhattan: Transatlantic and Inter-American Cultural Production in New York (1913–63)." Ph.D. diss., John Hopkins University, 2008.

——"Más que un poeta en Nueva York: La ciudad y José Moreno Villa" *Hybrido: Arte y Literatura* 10, no. 11 (2008): 10–13.

——"Una tradición literaria americaniard: Felipe Alfau y Eduardo Lago." *Galerna: Revista Internacional de Literatura* 8 (2009).

García-Calderón, Myrna. "Current Approaches to Hispanic Caribbean Writing: An Overview." *Review: Literature and Arts of the Americas 74*, 40, no. 1 (2007) 61–72.

Garland, Marissa L. "Deism and the Authorship of *Jicoténcal*" In Antonia I. Castañeda and A. Gabriel Meléndez, eds., *Recovering the U.S. Hispanic Literary Heritage*, 4:199–212. Houston: Arte Público, 2002.

Gelpí, Juan G. "The Nomadic Subject in the Poetry of Julia de Burgos." In Conrad James and John Perivolaris, eds., *The Cultures of the Hispanic Caribbean*, pp. 37–49. London: Macmillan, 2000.

Glickman, Nora. "La New York de Luisa Valenzuela, contrastada." In Gwendolyn Díaz, ed., *Luisa Valenzuela sin máscara*, pp. 141–53. Buenos Aires: Feminaria, 2002.

Gracia, Jorge J. E., Lynette M. F. Bosch, and Isabel Alvarez Borland, eds. *Identity, Memory, and Diaspora: Voices of Cuban-American Artists, Writers, and Philosophers.* Albany, NY: State University of New York Press, 2008.

Gutiérrez, Franklin. *Literatura dominicana en los Estados Unidos: Historia y trayectoria de la diáspora intelectual.* Santo Domingo: Fundación Global Democracia y Desarrollo, 2004.

——*Palabras de ida y vuelta.* New York: Calíope, 2002.

Henríquez Ureña, Pedro. "Carta de Pedro Henríquez Ureña a Alfonso Reyes sobre Rubén Darío (Nueva York, 9 de mayo de 1916)." In Ernesto Mejía Sánchez, *Cuestiones rubendarianas,* pp. 53–59. Madrid: Ediciones de la Revista de Occidente, 1970.

—— *Literary Currents in Hispanic America: The Charles Eliot Norton Lectures, 1940–1941.* Cambridge: Harvard University Press, 1945.

Islas, Maya. "Reflexiones sobre los arquetipos femenistas en la poesía cubana de Nueva York." In Pedro R. Monge Rafuls, ed., *Lo que no se ha dicho,* pp. 239–52. Jackson Heights, NY: Ollantay Center for the Arts, 1994.

Kanellos, Nicolás. "A Socio-Historic Study of Hispanic Newspapers in the United States." In Ramón A. Gutiérrez and Genaro M. Padilla, eds., *Recovering the U.S. Hispanic Literary Heritage,* pp. 107–28. Houston: Arte Publico, 1993.

Labarthe, Pedro Juan. *Gabriela Mistral: Cómo la conocí yo, y cinco poemas.* San Juan: Campos, 1963.

Lazo, Rodrigo. "'A Man of Action': Cirilo Villaverde as Trans-American Revolutionary Writer." In María Herrera-Sobek and Virginia Sánchez Korrol, eds., *Recovering the U.S. Hispanic Literary Heritage,* 3:315–331. Houston: Arte Público, 2002.

Llopesa, Ricardo. *Rubén Darío en Nueva York.* Valencia: Instituto de Estudios Modernistas, 1997.

Lolo, Eduardo. "Martí en Nueva York, Nueva York en Martí." In *Después del rayo y del fuego. Acerca de José Martí,* pp. 51–61. Madrid: Betania, 2002.

López, Antonio. "Chronicling Empire: José Martí on the Avenue of the Americas." In Mauricio A. Font and Alfonso W. Quiroz, eds., *The Cuban Republic and José Martí: Reception and Use of a National Symbol,* pp. 128–34. Lanham, MD: Lexington, 2006.

López, Edrik. "Nuyorican Spaces: Mapping Identity in a Poetic Geography." *Centro Journal* 17:202–19.

López-Coño, Dagoberto. "La diáspora poética en Nueva York." In R.A. Ramírez-Báez, ed., *Primer Foro de Cultura y Literatura Dominicana en Nueva York,* pp. 135–54. Queens, NY: Sitel, 2003.

Loustau, Laura Rosa. *Cuerpos errantes: Literatura latina y latinoamericana en Estados Unidos.* Rosario: Beatriz Viterbo, 2002.

Lozano Herrera, Rubén. *José Juan Tablada en Nueva York: Búsqueda y hallazgos en la crónica.* México, D.F.: Universidad Iberoamericana, 2000.

Luis, William. *Dance Between Two Cultures: Latino Caribbean Literature Written in the United States.* Nashville: Vanderbilt University Press, 1997.

McCarl, Clayton. "La ciudad a la deriva: Nueva York en las obras de Walt Whitman y José Martí." *LLJournal* 1, no. 1 (2006): 98–107.

Manrique, Jaime. *Eminent Maricones: Arenas, Lorca, Puig, and Me*. Madison: University of Wisconsin Press, 1999.

Marzán, Julio. *The Spanish-American Roots of William Carlos Williams*. Foreword by David Ignatow. Austin: University of Texas Press, 1994.

Molina, Sintia E. "Writing New York City: A Study on Transnational Dominican-American Literature." In Ernesto Sagás and Sintia E. Molina, eds., *Dominican Migration: Transnational Perspectives*, pp. 230–43. Gainesville: University Press of Florida, 2004.

Molloy, Sylvia. "His America, Our America. José Martí Reads Walt Whitman." In Betsy Erkkyla and Jay Grossman, eds., *Breaking Bounds: Whitman and American Cultural Studies*, pp. 83–91. New York: Oxford University Press, 1996.

Montero, Oscar. *José Martí: An Introduction*. New York: Palgrave Macmillan, 2003.

Negroni, María. "Cultura latinoamaricana en Nueva York: Un castigo del cielo." In *Ciudad gótica*, 27–32. Rosario: Bajo la Luna Nueva, 1994.

Negrón-Muntaner, Frances, and Yolanda Martínez-San Miguel. "In Search of Lourdes Casal's 'Ana Veldford.'" *Social Text 92* 25, no. 3 (Fall 2007).

Noel, Urayoán. "In the Decimated City: City, Translation, and the Performance of a New York Jíbaro from Ladí to Luciano to Lavoe." *Centro Journal* 19:120–39.

Ortíz, Ricardo L. "Cuban-American Literature." In Alpana Sharma Knippling, ed., *New Immigrant Literatures in the United States: A Sourcebook to our Multicultural Literary Heritage*, pp. 187–206. Westport, CT: Greenwood, 1996.

Padilla, Edwin. "Jesús Colón: Relación entre crónica periodística, lenguaje y publico." In Maria Herrera-Sobek and Virginia Sánchez Korrol, eds., *Recovering the U.S. Hispanic Literary Heritage*, 3:371–83. Houston: Arte Público, 2000.

Padilla Aponte, Edwin Karli. "La prensa puertorriqueña en Nueva York ante el discurso colonial: Reescritura de un imaginario nacional." In Kenya Dworkin y Méndez and Agnes Lugo-Ortiz, eds., *Recovering the U.S. Hispanic Literary Heritage*, pp. 81–91. Houston: Arte Público, 2006.

Pérez-Firmat, Gustavo. *Life on the Hyphen: The Cuban-American Way*. Austin: University of Texas Press, 1994.

—— *Tongue Ties: Logo-Eroticism in Anglo-Hispanic Literature*. New York: Palgrave Macmillan, 2003.

Podestá, Guido A. "Cultural Liasons in *American* Literatures." In Anthony L. Geist and José B. Monleón, eds., *Modernism and Its Margins: Reinscribing Cultural Modernity from Spain and Latin America*, pp. 168–85. New York: Garland, 1999.

Pratt, Heather. "New York, New York: Lorca and Cendrars." *Modern Language Review* 82, no. 3 (1987): 625–37.

Ramírez Báez, R.A., ed. *Primer Foro de Cultura y Literatura Dominicana en Nueva York*. Jackson Heights, NY: Sitel, 2003.

Ramos, Julio. "Pasajes de ida y vuelta: El Dr. William Carlos Williams bajo el sol de Puerto Rico." *Cupey* 17–18:188.

Remeseira, Claudio Iván. "Nueva York y la literatura hispanoamericana." *El País*, May 17, 2007, http://www.elpais.com/articulo/opinion/Nueva/York/literatura/hispanoamericana/el pepiopi/20070517elpepiopi_5/Tes/.

—— "The Case for a U.S. National Spanish-Language Literature." *Review: Literature and Arts of the Americas* 78 (2009).

Reyes, Israel. " Modernization and Migration in Manuel Ramos Otero's *El Cuento de la Mujer del Mar.*" *Journal of the Midwest Modern Language Association* 29, no. 1 (1996): 63–75.

Ríos Ávila, Ruben, "Caribbean Dislocations: Arenas and Ramos Otero in New York." In Silvia Molloy and Robert McKee Irwin, eds., *Hispanisms and Homosexualities*, pp. 101–19. Durham: Duke University Press, 1998.

Rivero, Juan. "La diáspora y la literatura Dominicana (USA): Apuntes para la historia." In R. A. Ramírez-Báez, eds., *Primer Foro de Cultura y Literatura Dominicana en Nueva York*, pp. 115–20. Jackson Heights, NY: Sitel, 2003.

Rodríguez Pagán, Juan Antonio. *Julia de Burgos. Tres rostros de Nueva York . . . y un largo silencio de piedra.* Humacao: Oriente, 1987.

Romero, Mario Germán. *Pombo en Nueva York.* Bogotá: Kelly, 1983.

Rotker, Susana. *The American Chronicles of José Martí: Journalism and Modernity in Latin America.* Hannover, NH: University Press of New England, 2000.

Sánchez-González, Lisa. *Boricua Literature: A Literary History of the Puerto Rican Diaspora.* New York: New York University Press, 2001.

Sandín, Lyn Di Iorio.*Killing Spanish: Literary Essays on Ambivalent U.S. Latino/a Identity.* New York: Palgrave Macmillan, 2004.

Sandin, Lyn Di Iorio, and Richard Perez, eds. *Contemporary U.S. Latino/a Literary Criticism.* New York: Palgrave Macmillan, 2007.

Sandlin, Betsy A. "Manuel Ramos Otero's Queer Metafictional Resurrection of Julia de Burgos." In José L. Torres-Padilla and Carmen Haydée Rivera, eds., *Writing off the Hyphen: New Critical Perspectives on the Literature of the Puerto Rican Diaspora*, pp. 313–31. Seattle: University of Washington Press, 2008.

Schulman, Ivan A. "Construyendo la imagen literaria de Martí en los Estados Unidos." In Mauricio A. Font and Alfonso W. Quiroz, eds., *The Cuban Republic and José Martí: Reception and Use of a National Symbol*, pp. 135–45. Lanham, MD: Lexington, 2006.

Shell, Marc, ed. *American Babel: Literature of the United States from Abnaki to Zuni.* Cambridge: Harvard University Press, 2002.

Sirias, Silvio. "The Recovery of Salomón de la Selva's *Tropical Town*: Challenges and Outcomes." In Maria Herrera-Sobek and Virginia Sánchez Korrol, eds., *Recovering the U.S. Hispanic Literary Heritage*, pp. 268–314. Houston: Arte Público, 2000.

Sommer, Doris. *Bilingual Aesthetics: A New Sentimental Education.* Durham: Duke University Press, 2004.

Soto, Francisco. "Tres poetas hispanoamericanos de Nueva York: Manuel Marshall, Miguel Falquez-Certain y Pedro López-Adorno." In Miguel Falquez-Certain, ed., *New Voices in Latin American Literature/Nuevas voces en la literatura latinoamericana*, pp. 108–29. Jackson Heights, NY: Ollantay Center for the Arts, 1993.

Stavans, Ilan. *The Hispanic Condition: The Power of a People.* New York: HarperCollins, 2001.

Suarée, Octavio de la. "Silencio, memoria, sueños: tres temas de la poesía cubana de Nueva York." In Pedro R. Monge Rafuls, ed., *Lo que no se ha dicho*, pp. 253–62. Jackson Heights, NY: Ollantay Center for the Arts, 1994.

Tillis, Antonio D. "Afro-Hispanic Literature in the US: Remembering the Past, Celebrating the Present, and Forging a Future." *Ipotesi: Revista de Estudos Literários* 12, no. 1 (2008): 21–29.

Torres-Padilla, José L., and Carmen Haydée Rivera, eds. *Writing off the Hyphen: New Critical Perspectives on the Literature of the Puerto Rican Diaspora.* Seattle: University of Washington Press, 2008.

Torres-Saillant, Silvio. "Before the Diaspora: Early Dominican Literature in the United States." In Maria Herrera Sobek and Virginia Sánchez-Korrol, eds., *Recovering the U.S. Hispanic Literary Heritage*, 3:250–67. Houston: Arte Público, 2000.

Williams, Frederick G. "Sousândrade em Nova Iorque: Visão da Mulher Americana." *Hispania* 74, no. 3 (1991): 548–55.

—— "Sousândrade's 'Wall Street Inferno.'" *Latin American Literary Review* 1, no. 2 (1973): 143–48.

Music

Alava, Silvio H. *Spanish Harlem's Musical Legacy, 1930–1980.* Charleston: Arcadia, 2007.

Allen, Ray, and Lois Wilcken, eds. *Island Sounds in the Global City: Caribbean Popular Music and Identity in New York.* New York Folklore Society and the Institute for Studies in American Music, Brooklyn College, City University of New York, 1998.

Amigo, Christian. "Etnografía musical en New York/Nueva York: Localizando EL Taller Latinoamericano." Anais do V Congresso latinoamericano da Associação Internacional para o Estudo da Música Popular, Rio de Janeiro, 21 a 25 de junho de 2004. http://www.hist.puc .cl/iaspm/rio/Anais2004%20(PDF)/CristianAmigo.pdf; accessed April 2, 2009.

Aparicio, Frances R., and Wilson A. Valentín-Escobar. "Memorializing La Lupe and Lavoe: Singing Vulgarity, Transnationalism, and Gender." *Centro Journal* 16:78–101.

Arévalo Mateus, Jorge. "Everything You've Ever Heard, and Nothing You've Ever Heard: Ricanstruction, New-Nuyorican Punk Activists." *Centro Journal* 16:248–71.

Austerlitz, Paul. "From Transplant to Transnational Circuit: Merengue in New York." In Ray Allen and Lois Wilcken, eds., *Island Sounds in the Global City: Caribbean Music and Culture in New York*, pp. 44–60. New York: Institute for Studies in American Music, Brooklyn College, 1998.

———"The Jazz Tinge in Dominican Music: A Black Atlantic Perspective." *Black Music Research Journal* 18, nos. 1/2 (1998): 1–19.

Azzi, María Susana, and Simon Collier. *Le Grand Tango: The Life and Music of Astor Piazzolla.* Foreword by Yo-Yo Ma. New York: Oxford University Press, 2000.

Banes, Sally. "La Onda Próxima: Nueva Latina Dance." In *Writing Dancing in the Age of Postmodernism*, pp. 327–33. Hanover, NH: Wesleyan University Press, 1994.

Beardsley. Theodore S., Jr. *Ernesto Lecuona: Discografía.* New York: Hispanic Society of American, 2008.

———"Hispanic Music in the United States." In Ray B. Browne and Pat Browne, eds., *The Guide to United States Popular Culture*, pp. 388–89. Bowling Green, OH: Bowling Green State University Popular Press, 2001.

Boggs, Vernon W. *Salsiology: Afro-Cuban Music and the Evolution of Salsa in New York City.* New York: Excelsior Music, 1992.

Brown, Charles T. "A Latin American in New York: Alejandro Monestel." *Latin American Music Review* 3, no. 1 (1982): 124–27.

Cabanillas, Francisco. "Entre la poesía y la música: Victor Hernández Cruz y el mapa musical nuyorican." *Centro Journal* 16:14–33.

———"The Musical Poet: A Session with Victor Hernández Cruz." *Centro Journal* 16:34–41.

Calvo Ospina, Hernando. *Salsa! Havana Heat, Bronx Beat.* Trans. Nick Castor. New York: Monthly Review, 1995.

Cannata, David Butler. "Making It There: Piazzolla's New York Concerts." *Latin American Music Review* 26, no. 1 (2005): 57–87.

Cepeda, Raquel. "Riddims by the Reggaetón: Puerto Rico's Hip-Hop Hybrid Takes Over New York." In Mary Gaitskill, ed., *Da Capo Best Music Writing 2006*, pp. 253–59. Cambridge: Da Capo, 2006.

Collier, Simon. *The Life, Music and Times of Carlos Gardel.* Pittsburgh: University of Pittsburgh Press, 1986.

Del Barco, Mandalit. "Rap's Latino Sabor." In William Eric Perkins, ed., *Droppin' Science: Critical Essays on Rap Music and Hip Hop Culture*, pp. 63–84. Philadelphia: Temple University Press, 1996.

D'Rivera, Paquito. *My Sax Life.* Trans. Luis Tamargo. Evanston, IL: Northwestern University Press, 2005.

——— "De Nueva York a la loma: Paquito D'Rivera entrevisto por Armando López." *Encuentro de la cultura cubana* 50 (2008): 15–26.

Fernandez, Raul A. *From Afro-Cuban Rhythms to Latin Jazz.* Berkeley: University of California Press, 2006.

Figueroa, Frank M. "Hispanic RadioActivity in the New York Area." *Latin Beat Magazine* 18, no. 2 (2008): 30–33, 44.

García, David F. *Arsenio Rodríguez and the Transnational Flows of Latin Popular Music.* Philadelphia: Temple University Press, 2006.

——"Embodying Music/Disciplining Dance: The Mambo Body in Havana and New York City." In Julie Malnig, ed., *Ballroom Boogie, Shimmy Sham, Shake: A Social and Popular Dance Reader*, pp. 165–81. Urbana: University of Illinois Press, 2009.

Gerard, Charley. *Music from Cuba: Mongo Santamaría, Chocolate Armenteros, and Cuban Musicians in the United States*. Westport, CT: Praeger, 2001.

Glasser, Ruth. *My Music Is My Flag: Puerto Rican Musicians and Their New York Communities, 1917–1940*. Los Angeles: University of California Press, 1995.

Knights, Vanessa. "Los placeres de la nostalgia en el bolero borincano de Nueva York." Actas del IV Congreso Latinoamericano IASPM, México, 2002. http://www.hist.puc.cl/historia/iaspm/mexico/articulos/Knights.pdf; accessed April 3, 2009.

Knights, Vanessa. "Nostalgia and the Negotiation of Dislocated Identities: Puerto Rican Boleros in New York and Nuyorican Poetry." In Ignacio Corona and Alejandro L. Madrid, eds., *Postnational Musical Identities: Cultural Production, Distribution, and Consumption in a Globalized Scenario*, pp. 81–96. Lanham, MD: Lexington, 2008.

Koegel, John. "Compositores mexicanos y cubanos en Nueva York, c. 1880–1920." *Historia Mexicana* 56, no. 2 (2006): 533–612.

Lipsitz, George. "Salsa: The Hidden History of Colonialism." In *Footsteps in the Dark: The Hidden Histories of Popular Music*, pp. 211–37. Minneapolis: University of Minnesota Press, 2007.

Loza, Steven. *Tito Puente and the Making of Latin Music*. Urbana, IL: University of Illinois Press, 1999.

Manuel, Peter, ed. *Creolizing Contradance in the Caribbean*. Philadelphia: Temple University Press, 2009.

—— "Representations of New York City in Latin Music." In Ray Allen and Lois Wilcken, eds., *Island Sounds in the Global City: Caribbean Music and Culture in New York*, pp. 23–43. New York: Institute for Studies in American Music, Brooklyn College, 1998.

Martínez-San Miguel, Yolanda. "'Con mi música pa' otra parte': Desplazamientos simbólicos dominicanos." In *Caribe Two Ways. Cultura de la migración en el Caribe insular hispánico*, pp. 263–320. San Juan: Callejón, 2003.

Miranda, Lin-Manuel (music and lyrics), and Quiara Alegría Hudes (book). *In the Heights: Piano-Vocal Selections*. New York: Hal Leonard, 2008.

Monette, Pierre. "Tango rápido en Nueva York." In Ramón Pelinski, ed., *El tango nómade: Ensayos sobre la diáspora del tango*, pp. 387–94. Buenos Aires: Corregidor, 2000.

Morales, Ed. "The Story of Nuyorican Salsa." In *The Latin Beat: The Rhythms and Roots of Latin Music from Bossa Nova to Salsa and Beyond*, pp. 55–93. Cambridge: Da Capo, 2003.

Otero Garabís, Juan. *Nación y ritmo. "Descargas" desde el Caribe*. San Juan: Callejón, 2000.

Pacini Hernández, Deborah. "A Tale of Two Cities: A Comparative Analysis of Los Angeles Chicano and Nuyorican Engagement with Rock and Roll." *Centro Journal* 11:70–93.

——"The Name Game: Locating Latinas/os, Latins and Latin Americans in the U.S. Popular Music Landscape." In Juan Flores and Renato Rosaldo, eds., *A Companion to Latina/o Studies*, pp. 49–59. Malden, MA: Blackwell, 2007.

Pérez Firmat, Gustavo. "Latunes: An Introduction." *Latin American Research Review* 43, no. 2 (2008): 180–203.

Rivera-Servera, Ramón H. "A Dominican-York in Andhra." In Susanna Sloat, ed., *Caribbean Dance from Abakuá to Zouk,* pp. 152–62. Gainesville: University Press of Florida, 2002.

Quintero Rivera, Ángel G. "Migration and Worldview in Salsa Music." Trans. Roberto Marquez. *Latin American Music Review* 24, no. 2 (2003): 210–32.

——— *Salsa, sabor y control! Sociología de la música "tropical."* México, D.F.: Siglo Veintiuno, 1999.

Ragland, Cathy. "Mexican Deejays and the Transnational Space of Youth Dances in New York and New Jersey." *Ethnomusicology* 47, no. 3 (2003): 338–54.

Rivera, Raquel Z. "Between Blackness and *Latinidad* in the Hip Hop Zone." In Juan Flores and Renato Rosaldo, eds., *A Companion to Latina/o Studies,* pp. 351–62. Malden, MA: Blackwell, 2007.

——— *New York Ricans from the Hip Hope Zone.* New York: Palgrave Macmillan, 2003.

Rivera, Raquel Z., Deborah Pacini Hernandez, and Wayne Marshall, eds. *Reggaeton.* Durham: Duke University Press, 2009.

Roberts, John Storm. *The Latin Tinge: The Impact of Latin American Music on the United States.* New York: Oxford University Press, 1979.

Rondón, César Miguel. *The Book of Salsa. A Chronicle of Caribbean Music from the Caribbean to New York City.* University of North Carolina Press, 2008.

Salazar, Max. *Mambo Kingdom: Latin Music in New York.* New York: Schirmer, 2002.

Sanchez, Ivan, and Luis "DJ Disco Wiz" Cedeño. *It's Just Begun: The Epic Journey of DJ Disco Wiz, Hip Hop's First Latino DJ.* Brooklyn, NY: PowerHouse, 2009.

Santos Febres, Mayra. "Salsa as Translocation." In Celeste Fraser Delgado and José Esteban Muñoz, eds., *Everynight Life: Culture and Dance in Latin/o America,* pp. 179–88. Durham: Duke University Press, 1997.

Serrano, Basilio. "Puerto Rican Musicians of the Harlem Renaissance." *Centro Journal* 19:94–119.

Singer, Roberta L. "Tradition and Innovation in Contemporary Latin Popular Music in New York City." *Latin American Music Review* 4, no. 2 (1983): 183–202.

Singer, Roberta L. and Elena Martínez. "A South Bronx Latin Music Tale." *Centro Journal* 16:176–200.

Tallaj, Angelina. "'A Country That Ain't Really Belong to Me': Dominicanyorks, Identity, and Popular Music." *Phoebe: Gender and Cultural Critiques* 18, no. 2 (2006): 17–30.

Tucci, Terig. *Gardel en Nueva York.* New York: Webb, 1969.

Van Buren, Thomas and Leonardo Ivan Dominguez. "Transnational Music and Dance in Dominican New York." In Ernesto Sagas and Sintia E. Molina, eds., *Dominican Migration: Transnational Perspectives,* pp. 244–70. Gainesville: University Press of Florida, 2004.

Wakefield, Dan. *Island in the City: Puerto Ricans in New York.* New York: Corinth, 1959.

Washburne, Christopher. *Sounding Salsa: Perfoming Latin Music in New York City.* Temple University Press, 2008.

Waxer, Lise. "Of Mambo Kings and Songs of Love: Dance Music in Havana and New York from the 1930s to the 1950s." *Latin American Music Review* 15, no. 2 (1994): 139–76.

Art, Performance, and Film

Amaral, Aracy A. "Intercâmbio Brasil-EUA: os parcos exemplos." In *Textos do Trópico de Capricórnio (Artigos e ensaios, 1998–2005)*, Vol. 2: *Circuitos de arte na América Latina e no Brasil*, pp. 49–54. São Paulo: Editora 34, 2006.

Anreus, Alejandro. *Orozco in Gringoland: The Years in New York*. Albuquerque: University of New Mexico Press, 2001.

Barnitz, Jacqueline. *Latin American Artists in New York Since 1970*. Austin: A.M. Huntington Art Gallery, College of Fine Arts, University of Texas at Austin, 1987.

Blocker, Jane. *Where Is Ana Mendieta? Identity, Performativity and Exile*. Durham: Duke University Press, 2005.

Caragol-Barreto Taína B. "Aesthetics of Exile: The Construction of Nuyorican Identity in the Art of El Taller Boricua." *Centro Journal* 17:6–21.

Center for Inter-American Relations Art Gallery. *Six Cuban Painters Working in New York*. New York: The Center, 1975.

Cockcroft, Eva. "The United States and Socially Concerned Latin American Art: 1920–1970" in *The Latin Amerian Spirit: Art and Artists in the United States, 1920–1970*, pp. 184–221. New York: Bronx Museum of the Arts, with Abrams, 1988.

Coelho, Frederico Oliveira. *Livro ou Livrome: Os Escritos Babilônicos de Hélio Oiticica (1971–1978)*. Rio de Janeiro: Tese de Doutorado, Departamento de Letras, Pontifícia Universidade Católica do Rio de Janeiro, 2008.

Colombian Artists in New York: A Selection of Paintings and Photographs/Artistas colombianos en Nueva York: Una selección de pinturas y fotografías. Bogotá: Flota Mercante Grancolombiana, 1985.

Contreras, Gloria. *What I Learned from Balanchine: Diary of a Choreographer*. Ed. Daniel Shapiro. Trans. K. Mitchell Snow, Lucinda Gutiérrez, and Roberto Mata. New York: Jorge Pinto, 2008.

Covarrubias, Miguel. *Blues: An Anthology*. New York: Boni, 1926.

Cruz-Malavé, Arnaldo. *Queer Latino Testimonio, Keith Haring, and Juanito Xtravaganza: Hard Tails*. New York: Palgrave Macmillan, 2007.

Cullen, Deborah, ed. *Nexus New York: Latin/American Artists in the Modern Metropolis*. New York: El Museo del Barrio, with Yale University Press, 2009.

Dávila, Arlene. "Culture in the Battlefront: From Nationalist to Pan-Latino Projects." In Augustín Laó-Montes and Arlene Dávila, eds., *Mambo Montage: The Latinization of New York*, pp. 159–81. New York: Columbia University Press, 2001.

Dávila, Arturo V., ed. *José Campeche y el taller familiar: Pinturas en la colección del Museo de Historia, Antropología y Arte, Facultad de Humanidades, Universidad de Puerto Rico, Recinto Río Piedras*. Río Piedras: La Universidad, 1999.

de La Vega, James. *De la Vega: Become Your Dream*. New York: HarperCollins, 2008.

de Zayas, Marius. *Crónicas y ensayos: Nueva York y París, 1909–1911*. Ed., with an introduction, Antonio Saborit. México, D.F.: Universidad Autónoma de México/Pértiga, 2008.

Díaz Quiñones, Arcadio. "Imágenes de Lorenzo Homar: Entre San Juan y Nueva York." In *El arte de bregar: Ensayos*, pp. 124–81. San Juan, P.R.: Callejón, 2000.

Flores Olea, Víctor. *Nueva York sobre Nueva York*. México, D.F.: Universidad Autónoma de México, Centro de Investigaciones Interdisciplinarias en Ciencias y Humanidades, 2003.

Fuentes-Rivera, Ada G. "Barrio, ciudad y 'performance': Cruce de fronteras en el proyecto mural de James de la Vega." *Centro Journal* 14:64–97.

Fusco, Coco. *The Bodies That Were Not Ours and Other Writings*. New York: Routledge, 2001.

Genocchio, Benjamin. "Brazil, with the Clichés Erased." Review of "Evolving Identities: Brazilian Artists in New York" Rockland Center for the Arts. *New York Times*, April 16, 2006.

Goldberg, Rachel, and Matt Doyle. *Discovering New York Artist De La Vega*. Charleston: Book-Surge, 2009.

Goldman, Shifra F. *Dimensions of the Americas: Art and Social Change in Latin America and the United States*. Chicago: University of Chicago Press, 1994.

—— "Living on the Fifth floor of the Four-floor Country." In *Juan Sánchez: Rican/Structed Convictions*, pp. 18–22. New York: Exit Art, 1989.

Hernández, Yasmín. "Painting Liberation: 1998 and Its Pivotal Role in the Formation of a New Boricua Political Art Movement." *Centro Journal* 17:112–33.

Herner de Larrea, Irene, et al. *Diego Rivera: Paradise Lost at Rockefeller Center*. Mexico, D.F.: Edirupes, 1987.

Herrera Navarro, Javier. "The Decisive Moments of Buñuel's Time in the United States, 1938–40: An Analysis of Previously Unpublished Letters." In Peter William Evans and Isabel Santaolalla, ed., *Luis Buñuel: New Readings*, pp. 43–61. London: BFI, 2004.

Jiménez, Lillian. "From the Margin to the Center: Puerto Rican Cinema in New York." In Clara E. Rodríguez, ed., *Latin Looks: Images of Latinas and Latinos in the U.S. Media*, pp. 188–99. Boulder: Westview, 1997.

Jiménez-Blanco, María Dolores, and Cindy Mack. *Spanish Art in New York: Guide*. Madrid: Asociación de Amigos de la Hispanic Society of America, 2004.

Latin American Prints from the Museum of Modern Art. New York: Center for Inter-American Relations, 1974.

Limón, José E. "Greater Mexico, Modernism, and New York: Miguel Covarrubias and José Limón." In Kurt Heinzelman, ed., *The Covarrubias Circle: Nickolas Muray's Collection of Twentieth-Century Mexican Art*. Austin: University of Texas Press, 2004.

Maldonado, Adal. *Out of Focus Nuyoricans*. Cambridge: David Rockefeller Center for Latin American Studies, Harvard University, 2004.

Merkin, Richard. *The Jazz Age as Seen Through the Eyes of Ralph Barton, Miguel Covarrubias, and John Held, Jr.* Providence: Museum of Art, Rhode Island School of Design, 1968.

Orozco, José Clemente. *The Artist in New York. Letters to Jean Charlot and Unpublished Writtings, 1925–1929*. Austin: University of Texas Press, 1974.

Paquette, Catha. "Critical Consequences: Mexican Art at New York's Museum of Modern Art During World War II." In Alberto Dallal, ed., *El proceso creativo. XXVI Coloquio Internacional de Historia del Arte*, pp. 529–59. México: UNAM, Instituto de Investigaciones Estéticas, 2006.

Ramírez, Yasmin. "Nuyorican Visionary: Jorge Soto and the Evolution of an Afro-Taíno Aesthetic at Taller Boricua." *Centro Journal* 17:22–41.

Roulet, Laura. *Contemporary Puerto Rican Installation Art: The Guagua Aérea, the Trojan Horse, and the Termite*. San Juan: Editorial de la Universidad de Puerto Rico, 2000.

Schomburg, Arturo A. "José Campeche, 1752–1809: A Puerto Rican Negro Painter." In Harold Augenbraum and Margarite Fernández Olmos, eds., *The Latino Reader: An American Literary Tradition from 1542 to the Present*, pp. 160–64. Boston: Houghton Mifflin, 1997.

Sims, Lowery. "New York Dada and New World Surrealism." In *The Latin Amerian Spirit: Art and Artists in the United States, 1920–1970*, pp. 152–83. New York: Bronx Museum of the Arts, with Abrams, 1988.

Sloat, Susanna. "Islands Refracted: Recent Dance on Caribbean Themes in New York. In Susanna Sloat, ed., *Caribbean Dance from Abakuá to Zouk*, pp. 320–35. Gainesville: University Press of Florida, 2002.

Smith, Roberta. "New School Unveils Its Restored Orozco Murals." *New York Times*, October 11, 1998, C15.

Stellweg, Carla. "'Magnet-New York': Conceptual, Performance, Environmental, and Installation Art." In *The Latin Amerian Spirit: Art and Artists in the United States, 1920–1970*, pp. 284–311. New York: Bronx Museum of the Arts, with Abrams, 1988.

Torres-García, Joaquin. *Historia de mi vida*. Barcelona: Paidós, 1990.

Torruella Leval, Susana. "Coming of Age with the Muses: Change in the Age of Multiculturalism." In Andy Warhol Foundation, *Paper* series, 1995. http://www.warholfoundation.org/grant/paper5/paper.html.

Williams, Adriana. *Covarrubias*. Ed. Doris Ober. Austin: University of Texas Press, 1994.

Wood, Yolanda. *Artistas del Caribe hispano en New York*. La Habana: Letras Cubanas, 1997.

CONTRIBUTORS

Jack Agüeros is a poet, playwright, fiction writer, TV scriptwriter, translator, and community activist. From 1976 to 1986, he was director of El Museo del Barrio. His publications include the collection of short stories *Dominoes and Other Stories*, the book of poems *Correspondence Between the Stonehaulers*, and a translation of Julia de Burgos's complete poetry.

Theodore S. Beardsley Jr. was director of the Hispanic Society of America from 1965 to 1995 and member of the North American Academy of the Spanish Language. He has published numerous articles on the Hispanic cultural heritage of the United States, literary criticism, linguistics and music. His most recent publication is a complete discography of Cuban composer and pianist Ernesto Lecuona, published by the Hispanic Society of America.

Paul Berman is a writer on politics and literature whose articles and reviews have appeared in the *New York Times*, the *New Republic* (where he is a contributing editor), the *New Yorker*, *Slate*, the *Village Voice*, *Dissent*, *Letras Libres*, and various other publications. Distinguished Writer in Residence at NYU's Arthur L. Carter Journalism Institute, his books include *Power and the Idealists: Or, The Passion of Joschka Fischer, and its Aftermath*.

Dionisio Cañas is a Spanish poet who lived in New York City from 1972 to 2005 and taught Hispanic Literature and Modern Spanish Poetry at Baruch College, City University of New York. He is the author of *The Poet and the City: New York and The Hispanic Writers* and of several books of poetry, among them *And he began not to speak*, and *The ballad of the man-woman*. He currently resides in his natal town of Tomelloso in La Mancha, Spain.

Ruby Danta has served as coordinator of the Translation Service Program at Queens College and Director of the Latin American Cultural Center of Queens. She is the co-author of *Hispanas de Queens: Latino Panethnicity in a New York City Neighborhood*.

Margarite Fernández Olmos is Matthew J. Fantaci Professor of Modern Languages and Literatures at Brooklyn College of the City University of New York. She is the author, editor, or co-editor of several books, among them *Contemporary Women Authors of Latin America: Introductory Essays and New Translations* (with Doris Meyer, 1983); *Rudolfo A. Anaya: A Critical Companion* (1999), *Remaking a Lost Harmony: Short Stories from the Hispanic Caribbean* (1995), *Pleasure in the Word: Erotic Writings by Latin American Women* (1993, originally *El placer de la palabra: literatura erótica femenina de América Latina,* 1991), *Sacred Possessions: Vodou, Santería, Obeah and the Caribbean* (1997), *Healing Cultures: Art and Religion as Curative Practices in the Caribbean and Its Diaspora* (2001), *Creole Religions of the Caribbean* (with Lizabeth Paravisini-Gebert, 2003) and the anthologies *The Latino Reader: An American Literary Tradition from 1542 to the Present* (1997) and *U.S. Latino Literature: A Critical Guide for Students and Teachers* (2000) with Harold Augenbraum.

Frank M. Figueroa was a disc-jockey at several New York City radio stations during the late 1940s and early 1950s and led a twelve-piece Latin band that played in some of New York's most famous ballrooms, including the Manhattan Center, Palladium Ballroom, and Lincoln Square Center. He then earned a Ph.D at Columbia University and worked for more than thirty years as a college professor of Spanish and television. Upon retiring from teaching, he began writing articles and books on Latin music, among them the *Encyclopedia of Latin American Music in New York*; *Cancionero de Agustín Lara*; *Doña Pepa: My Puerto Rican Grandmother*; *Glossary of Afro-Caribbean Terms*; *Latin American Music Almanac*; *Machito and His Afro-Cubans*; *Noro Morales: Latin Piano Man*; and *The Unforgettable Tito Rodríguez*. He lives in Miami and contributes regularly to *Latin Beat* magazine.

Gabriel Haslip-Viera is Chair of the Department of Sociology, City College, City University of New York. He was director of the Center for Puerto Rican Studies at Hunter College (1997–2000) and Chair of the former Department of Latin American and Hispanic Caribbean Studies at City College (1993–1995 and 1985–1991). Editor of *The Taíno Revival: Critical Perspectives on Puerto Rican Identity and Cultural Politics* and co-editor of *Boricuas in Gotham: Puerto Ricans in the Making of Modern New York City* and *Latinos in New York: Communities in Transition*, among other books and articles.

Carmen Dolores Hernández is the author of several books, including a biography of anthropologist Ricardo Alegría and two in which she interviews Puerto Rican writers, both those who live in the United States, *Puerto Rican Voices in English: Interviews with Writers*, and those from the island, *A viva voz: entrevistas a escritores puertorriqueños*. Since 1981 she writes weekly book reviews and articles on culture for *El Nuevo Día,* Puerto Rico's largest newspaper. She has also been the editor of the cultural magazines *Foro* and *Letras*.

Orlando José Hernández is a poet, translator, and critic who teaches at Hostos Community College, City University of New York. He is currently working on the recovery, compilation and publication of texts written in New York City by nineteenth-century Puerto Rican philosopher and educator Eugenio María de Hostos.

José Martí (1853–1895) was a poet, journalist, and leader in the movement for Cuban independence. He is a central figure in Latin American literary and political history. His writings in New York City, where he lived for fifteen years, offer profound insight into the Gilded Age in U.S. history.

Ed Morales is a Brooklyn-based journalist and poet whose work has been featured in numerous national newspapers and magazines. His writings include the books *Living in Spanglish:*

The Search for Latino Identity in America and *The Latin Beat: The Rhythms and Roots of Latin Music from Bossa Nova to Salsa and Beyond.*

Antonio Muñoz Molina is a prominent Spanish novelist and essayist, former director of of the New York branch of Instituto Cervantes, and a member of the Royal Academy of the Spanish Language. Margaret Sayers Peden's English-language translation of Muñoz Molina's novel *Sepharad* won PEN Book-of-the-Month Club Translation Prize in 2004. He divides his time between Madrid and New York.

Frances Negrón-Muntaner is an award-winning filmmaker, writer, and scholar. She is the author of *Boricua Pop: Puerto Ricans and the Latinization of American Culture* (named 2004 Choice Outstanding Book), the editor of four academic books, including *None of the Above: Puerto Ricans in the Global Era*, and director of the films *Brincando el charco: Portrait of a Puerto Rican* and *For the Record: Guam and World War II*. She is also a founding board member and past chair of NALIP, the National Association of Latino Independent Producers. She currently teaches Latino and Caribbean literatures and cultures at Columbia University. In 2005 she was named one of Hispanic Business's "100 Most Influential Latinos".

Lizabeth Paravisini-Gebert is a professor of Caribbean culture and literature in the Department of Hispanic Studies and the Program in Africana Studies at Vassar College, where she holds the Randolph Distinguished Professor Chair. She is the author of *Literatures of the Caribbean* (2009), *Creole Religions of the Caribbean* (2003, with Margarite Fernández Olmos) and *Jamaica Kincaid: A Critical Companion* (1999), and co-editor of a number of collections of essays, most notably *Sacred Possessions: Vodou, Santería, Obeah, and the Caribbean* (1997) and *Women at Sea: Travel Writing and the Margins of Caribbean Discourse* (2001). She is currently working on a biography of José Martí.

Luis Pérez-Oramas is The Estrellita Brodsky Curator of Latin American Art at the Museum of Modern Art (MoMA), where he has has organized, curated, and consulted on many exhibitions, including *New Perspectives of Latin American Art: Selections from a Decade of Acquisitions* (2007–2008); *Armando Reverón* (2007) with John Elderfield; and *Transforming Chronologies: An Atlas of Drawings* (2006). Outside exhibitions include *Latin American and Caribbean Art: Selected Highlights from the Collection of The Museum of Modern Art* (New York State Museum, 2008); and *MoMA at El Museo: Latin American & Caribbean Art from the Collection of The Museum of Modern Art* (El Museo del Barrio, 2004), co-organized with Gary Garrels and Deborah Cullen. In addition to teaching and writing several books of art history and criticism, Pérez-Oramas he has been a member of the board of directors at Venezuela's National Art Gallery and curator of the Patricia Phelps de Cisneros Collection.

Milagros Ricourt is Chair of Latin American and Puerto Rican Studies at Lehman College, City University of New York. She is the author of *Dominicans in New York City: Power From the Margins* and is co-author of *Hispanas de Queens: Latino Panethnicity in a New York City Neighborhood.*

Clara Rodríguez is a Professor of Sociology at Fordham University's College at Lincoln Center. She is the author of ten books, including *Heroes, Lovers and Others: The Story of Latinos in Hollywood* (2004) and *Changing Race: Latinos, The Census and the History of Ethnicity in the United States* (2000). She has written over fifty articles on Latinos in the United States and most recently co-authored of The *Culture and Commerce of Publishing in the 21st Century* (2007). She has also been a consultant to "Dora the Explorer" and "Sesame Street."

Virginia Sánchez Korrol is Puerto Rican and Latino Studies Professor Emerita at Brooklyn College, City University of New York. In 2007 she received the New York Public Library Award for Best of Reference for *Latinas in the United States: A Historical Encyclopedia*, co-edited with Vicki L. Ruiz, professor at the University of California, Irvine. Professor Sánchez Korrol is currently working on a book on Puerto Rican and Cuban women in New York during the movement for Antillean independence.

Roberto Suro is a journalist who wrote for *The New York Times*, *The Washington Post*, *Time* magazine *and The Chicago Tribune*, among other newspapers and magazines. He is the former director of the Pew Hispanic Center, a research organization in Washington D.C. which he founded in 2001 as a project of the Annenberg School for Communication. Currently he is a professor of journalism at the University of Southern California.

Bernardo Vega (1885–1965) was a trade-union leader and political activist in New York's Puerto Rican community during the first half of the twentieth century. His memoirs are a key source for the study of that period.

Walt Whitman (1819–1892) is arguably the greatest poet ever born in the United States. His *Leaves of Grass* cast its influence beyond languages and national boundaries.

Ana Celia Zentella, a professor in the Department of Ethnic Studies at UC San Diego, is an anthropologist and linguist and an authority U.S. Latino varieties of Spanish and English and bilingualism. Her book *Growing up Bilingual: Puerto Rican children in New York* won the 1998 Book Prize of the British Association of Applied Linguistics, and the 1999 Book Award of the Association of Latina and Latino Anthropologists of the American Anthropology Association.

TRANSLATORS

Esther Allen is the co-director of PEN American Center's World Voices Festival. Her translations include *The Selected Writings* of José Martí, *Lands of Memory* by Felisberto Hernández, *Dark Back of Time* by Javier Marías, *The Tale of Rose*, by Consuelo de Saint Exupèry, *In her absence*, by Antonio Muñoz Molina, and Alma Guillermoprieto's *Dancing with Cuba: A Memoir of the Revolution*.

Juan Flores is Professor in the Department of Black and Puerto Rican Studies at Hunter College (CUNY) and in the Sociology Program at the CUNY Graduate Center. One of the leading Latino intellectuals of the United States, Flores is the author of the seminal

From Bomba to Hip-Hop: Puerto Rican Culture and Latino Identity and of *The Diaspora Strikes Back: Caribbean Latino Tales of Learning and Turning*, among many other books and publications.

Colman Hogan has a background on theater and translation, and is a lecturer in English at Ryerson University, Toronto. He has recently co-edited (with Marta Marín-Dòmine) *The Camp: Narratives of Internment and Exclusion.*

Dan Newland is an Ohio-born writer and translator who has lived in South America since 1973. Besides freelancing for U.S. and British publications, he worked for thirteen years at the internationally award-winning *Buenos Aires Herald*, where, upon leaving, he was managing editor.

Claudio Iván Remeseira is an award-winning journalist, writer and critic. His literary and journalistic work has appeared in *Review: Literature and Arts of the Americas, Salmagundi, Primera Revista Latinoamericana de Libros, Hora Hispana (Daily News), El Nuevo Día* (Puerto Rico), *El País* (Spain), *La Nación, Página/12* (Argentina), among other publications in the United States, Latin America and Europe. Founder and director of the Hispanic New York Project, he teaches a seminar on the cultural history of Hispanic New York at Columbia University American Studies Program. He is also member of the Advisory Board of the Library & Archives of El Centro de Estudios Puertorriqueños at Hunter College, City University of New York, and was co-curator of the Hispanic New York film festival, co-sponsored by Columbia University and Instituto Cervantes, in collaboration with The Film Society of Lincoln Center.

SOURCE CREDITS

"The evolution of the Latino Community in New York City: Early Nineteenth Century to the Present," by Gabriel Haslip-Viera, from *Latinos in New York: Communities in Transition,* Haslip-Viera, G. and Sherrie L. Baver, editors. Notre Dame, Indiana: University of Notre Dame Press, copyright © 1996 by University of Notre Dame Press. Reprinted by permission of University of Notre Dame Press via the Copyright Clearance Center.

"Our America." "A Vindication of Cuba." from JOSÉ MARTÍ: SELECTED WRITINGS by José Martí, introduction by Roberto González Echevarría, edited by Esther Allen, translated by Esther Allen, copyright © 2002 by Esther Allen. Used by permission of Viking Penguin, a division of Penguin Group (USA) Inc.

Memoirs of Bernardo Vega: A Contribution to the History of the Puerto Rican Community in New York (excerpts), by Bernardo Vega, edited by César Andréu Iglesias, translated by Juan Flores. New York: Monthly Review Press, copyright © 1983 by Monthly Review Foundation. Reprinted by permission of Monthly Review Foundation via the Copyright Clearance Center.

"Halfway to Dick and Jane" by Jack Agüeros, copyright © 1971 by Doubleday, a division of Bantam Doubleday Dell Publishing Group, Inc., from THE IMMIGRANT EXPERERIENCE by Thomas C. Wheeler. Used by permission of Doubleday, a division of Random House, Inc.

"New York: Teetering on the Heights." from *Strangers Among Us* by Roberto Suro, copyright © 1998 by Roberto Suro. Used by permission of Alfred A. Knopf, a division of Random House, Inc.

"The Hispanic Impact upon the United States," by Theodore S. Beardsley. The Hispanic Society of America, 1976; reprinted 1990, copyright © 1976 by The Hispanic Society of America. Reprinted by permission of The Hispanic Society of America via the Copyright Clearance Center.

"In Search of Latinas in the U.S.," by Virginia Sánchez Korrol, copyright © 2009 by Virginia Sánchez Korrol. Used by permission of the author.

"The Spanish Element in Our Nationality," in *Collected Writings of Walt Whitman*, by Walt Whitman, copyright © 1965–1980 by New York University Press. Reprinted by permission of New York University Press via the Copyright Clearance Center.

"Racial Themes in the Literature: Puerto Ricans and Other Latinos," by Clara E. Rodríguez, from *Latinos in New York: Communities in Transition,* Haslip-Viera, Gabriel and Sherrie L. Baver, editors. Notre Dame, Indiana: University of Notre Dame Press, copyright © 1996 by University of Notre Dame Press. Reprinted by permission of University of Notre Dame Press via the Copyright Clearance Center.

"The Emergence of Latino Panethnicity," from *Hispanas de Queens: Latino Panethnicity in New York City*, by Milagros Ricourt and Ruby Danta, copyright © 2003 by Cornell University. Used by permission of the publisher, Cornell University Press.

Introduction and Chapter One ("Historical Background") from *Creole Religions of the Caribbean: An Introduction from Vodou and Santeria, to Obeah and Espiritism*, by Margarite Fernández Olmos and Lizabeth Paravisini-Gebert. New York: NYU Press, copyright © 2003 by New York Univesity Press. Reprinted by permission of New York University Press via the Copyright Clearance Center.

"New York City, Center and Transit Point for Hispanic Cultural Nomadism" by Dionisio Cañas, from *Literary Cultures of Latin America: A Comparative History* (2004), Valdés, Mario J. and Djelal Kadir, editors. Copyright © 2004 by Oxford University Press. Reprinted by Permission of Oxford University Press, Inc.

Puerto Rican Voices in English (Introduction) by Carmen Dolores Hernández. Copyright © 1997 by Carmen Dolores Hernández. Reproduced with permission of Greenwood Publishing Group, Inc., Westport, CT.

"Spanish in New York," by Ana Celia Zentella, from *The Multilingual Apple: Languages in New York City*, edited by García, Ofelia and Joshua A. Fishman. Berlin – New York, Mouton de Gruyter, 1997, copyright © 1997 by Walter de Gruyter. Reprinted by permission of Walter de Gruyter via the Copyright Clearance Center.

"Spanish in New York: A Moving Landscape," by Antonio Muñoz Molina, published in *El País* (Spain), March 24, 2007, copyright © 2007 by Antonio Muñoz Molina. Reprinted by permission of the author.

"New York's Latin Music Landmarks" Frank M. Figueroa, published in *Latin Beat* magazine 12/1/2002, copyright © 2007 by Frank M. Figueroa. Reprinted by permission of the author.

"The Story of Nuyorican Salsa," from *The Latin Beat: The Rhythms and Roots of Latin Music From Bossa Nova to Salsa and Beyond*, by Ed Morales. Copyright © 2003 by Ed Morales. Reprinted by permission of Da Capo Press, a member of Perseus Books Group.

"Mariachi Reverie," by Paul Berman, from *The Rose and the Briar: Death, Love and Liberty in the American Ballad*, Sean Wilentz and Greil Marcus, editors (New York: W.W. Norton, 2005) Copyright © 2005 by Paul Berman. Reprinted by permission of the author.

"The Art of Babel in the Americas," by Luis Pérez-Oramas, from *Latin American and Caribbean Art: MoMA at El Museo*, catalogue of the exhibition. New York City: El Museo del Barrio and the Museum of Modern Art, 2004. Copyright © 2008 by The Museum of Modern Art and El Museo del Barrio. Reproduced by permission of The Museum of Modern Art and El Museo del Barrio.

"The Life and Passion of Jean-Michel Basquiat," by Frances Negrón-Muntaner, from *Boricua Pop: Puerto Ricans and American Culture*, New York City: New York University Press, 2004.

Copyright © 2004 by New York University. Reprinted by permission of New York Univesity Press via the Copyright Clearance Center.

"A Splendid Outsider: Archer Milton Huntington and the Hispanic Society of America," by Claudio Iván Remeseira. Copyright © 2002 by Claudio Iván Remeseira.

"Carlos Gardel in New York: The Birth of a Hispanic-American Myth," by Claudio Iván Remeseira. Originally published in Spanish as "Gardel en Nueva York: Donde nació el mito." in *La Nación,* Argentina, June 19, 2005. Copyright *La Nación* © 2005. Reprinted by permission of *La Nación.*

INDEX OF NAMES

INDEX OF SUBJECTS

F128.9
S75H57
2010

6234148

hie